VIOLENCE
and NONVIOLENCE

Other Books by Gregg Barak

In Defense of Whom? A Critique of Criminal Justice Reform
Crimes by the Capitalist State: An Introduction to State Criminality (Editor)
Gimme Shelter: A Social History of Homelessness in Contemporary America
Varieties of Criminology: Readings from a Dynamic Discipline (Editor)
Media, Process, and the Social Construction of Crime: Studies in Newsmaking Criminology (Editor)
Representing O.J.: Murder, Criminal Justice and Mass Culture (Editor)
Integrating Criminologies
Integrative Criminology (Editor)
Crime and Crime Control: A Global View (Editor)
Class, Race, Gender, and Crime: Social Realities of Justice in America
(Coauthored with J. Flavin and P. Leighton)

VIOLENCE
and
NONVIOLENCE
Pathways to Understanding

GREGG BARAK
Eastern Michigan University

SAGE Publications
International Educational and Professional Publisher
Thousand Oaks ▪ London ▪ New Delhi

For information:

 Sage Publications, Inc.
2455 Teller Road
Thousand Oaks, California 91320
E-mail: order@sagepub.com

Sage Publications Ltd.
6 Bonhill Street
London EC2A 4PU
United Kingdom

Sage Publications India Pvt. Ltd.
B-42, Panchsheel Enclave
Post Box 4109
New Delhi 110 017 India

Printed in the United States of America

Library of Congress Cataloging-in-Publication Data

Barak, Gregg.
Violence and nonviolence: Pathways to understanding / Gregg Barak.
    p. cm.
Includes bibliographical references and index.
ISBN 0-7619-2695-X (Cloth)
ISBN 0-7619-2696-8 (Paper)
  1. Violence—United States. 2. Nonviolence—United States. I. Title.
HN90.V5B37 2003
303.6—dc21

                                        2002155653

This book is printed on acid-free paper.

03   04   05   06   10   9   8   7   6   5   4   3   2   1

Acquisitions Editor:	Jerry Westby
Editorial Assistant:	Vonessa Vondera
Copy Editor:	Catherine Chilton
Production Editor:	Denise Santoyo
Typesetter:	C&M Digitals (P) Ltd.
Cover Designer:	Janet Foulger

Table of Contents

List of Illustrations

Preface

Violence and Nonviolence: Pathways to Understanding is a unique book in that it tries to grapple with both violence and nonviolence. There are, of course, numerous books written about violence, mostly on one specific form or type of violence, such as homicide, terrorism, domestic violence, child abuse, sexual assault, or war. There are also a number of books that have addressed the subject matter of "criminal" violence in total, and fewer that have attempted to address violence, criminal and noncriminal, more generally. With a few notable exceptions, these books have addressed violence in particular or violence in general as individual or interpersonal occurrences and not as institutional or structural occurrences. By contrast, this book addresses virtually all forms of violence, from verbal abuse to genocide, and treats all of these expressions of violence as interpersonal, institutional, and structural phenomena.

Comparatively, there are not nearly as many books written about nonviolence as there are about violence. Those books that tackle the subject matter of nonviolence have generally focused their examinations on peace and conflict studies, legal rights, and social justice, or some combination of these. Books on nonviolence, in comparison to those on violence, have been more or less evenly concerned about institutional and structural relationships as well as interpersonal relationships. These books have also tended to present general histories of various nonviolent movements and struggles for peace and justice, or they have been discipline specific, such as those works based in peace studies or peacemaking criminology.

One of the overriding themes in the current book is that to study violence without studying nonviolence, or to study nonviolence without studying violence, is to study, in effect, only one side of the two-sided phenomenon of violence-nonviolence. Unfortunately, one cannot fully understand either violence or nonviolence without understanding the reciprocal relations between them. Hence, it is in the spirit of fostering a "joint" discussion of violence *and* nonviolence and bringing together the study of these two separate but inseparable phenomena that *Violence and Nonviolence* was written.

Following the Introduction, this text is divided into three parts: *Types of Violence, Pathways to Violence*, and *Pathways to Nonviolence*. Part I consists of four chapters. The first of these places violence into perspective. Chapters 2 through 4 address violent behavioral types and violence from, respectively, interpersonal, institutional, and structural perspectives. Part II consists of three chapters. Each of these addresses theoretical and practical questions on the production and reproduction of violence and nonviolence. Chapter 5 reviews the contemporary perspective on violence and violent behavior and introduces its own "reciprocal theory of violence." Chapters 6 and 7 examine the real and imaginary relations between media and violence, between sexuality and violence, and between all three. Part III also consists of three chapters. Each of these addresses nonviolence in terms of violence production, recovery from violence, and nonviolence production. In the first of these chapters, recovery from interpersonal, institutional, and structural violence is examined. In Chapter 9, models of nonviolence such as "mutuality," "altruistic humanism," "positive peacemaking," and "resilience" are described in the contexts of the *paradigms of adversarialism and mutualism*. The final chapter summarizes the findings and arguments of the book and presents policies of nonviolence and transformative justice as alternatives to policies of violence and repression.

Pedagogically, to make the material as "user friendly" as possible, case studies and boxed information have been generously sprinkled throughout most of the chapters. In those chapters without the boxed inserts or scenarios on violence or nonviolence, there are a number of tables and figures, as well as a few illustrations depicting the models presented in the discussions. Each of the main chapters, 1 through 10, for the purposes of generating both reflection and classroom discussions, have five review questions at the end. Adequately responding to these 50 questions translates into more than adequately demonstrating an understanding of the ideas presented in *Violence and Nonviolence*.

Acknowledgments

My debts and gratitude are to a number of people that have unknowingly influenced this work on violence and nonviolence. A nonexhaustive list includes Bruce Arrigo, David Barash, Birgit Brock-Utne, Robert Brown, Henry Brownstein, Susan Caulfield, Lynn Chancer, Stanley Cohen, Francis Cullen, Walter DeKeseredy, Rebecca and Russell Dobash, Jeanne Flavin, David Friedrichs, John Fuller, Riane Eisler, Robert Elias, James Gilligan, Nicholas Groth, Suzanne Hatty, Stuart Hall, Stuart Henry, Stuart Hills, Peter Iadicola, Ronald Kramer, Paul Leighton, Lyn Markham, Neil Malamuth, Karl Menninger, Alice Miller, Dragan Milovanovic, Ruth Morris, Charlotte Pagni, Harold Pepinsky, Anthony Platt, Richard Quinney, Jeffrey Reiman, Claire Renzetti, Diana Russell, Katheryn Russell, Herman and Julia Schwendinger, Elizabeth Stanko, Dennis Sullivan, Paul Takagi, Hans Toch, Larry Tiff, Mark Totten, Allison Young, Jock Young, and Howard Zinn.

There are also a few other people who were more directly involved in this project: First, I would like to thank Donna Killingbeck, my former graduate assistant, who provided yeoman's service in conducting literature searches and tracking down materials for me. Second, I would like to thank both undergraduate and graduate students who have listened to parts of this book and who have provided me with valuable feedback on "what works and doesn't work" in trying to communicate complex ideas about violence and nonviolence. Third, I would like to thank Robert Holkeboer and the Graduate School at Eastern Michigan University for a research fellowship during the fall 2000 semester and for a spring-summer research fellowship in 2001. These two releases from teaching allowed me to pursue full-time work on the book. Fourth, I would like to acknowledge the Sage reviewers for doing a wonderful job on the "rough draft" of the manuscript, including Marino Bruce, Walter DeKeseredy, Matthew T. Lee, Charis Kubrin, and Heather Melton. The criticisms and suggestions by all of these persons were very constructive, but I would especially like to thank Matthew T. Lee, whose rationale and critique persuaded me to reorganize the entire manuscript. Fifth, I would like to thank copyeditor Kate Chilton, not only for her meticulousness and skilled editing abilities, but for her sense of humor and keen intellectual sensibilities that helped me in fine-tuning the final version. Sixth and last, I would like to thank Sage Publications and Jerry Westby for acquiring this manuscript, for allowing me the necessary creative freedom and flexibility to pull this book off, and for being so easy to work with despite hectic schedules and busy agendas!

—Gregg Barak
Ann Arbor, Michigan

INTRODUCTION

Secrets of Violence and Nonviolence

In the wake of the World Trade Center and Pentagon attacks by Middle Eastern terrorists on September 11, 2001, President Bush and other political leaders were busy preparing the nation for a long and forthcoming war on international terrorism: A war expected to last some 5 to 10 years, well after the hoped for "dead or alive" capture of Saudi extremist Osama bin Laden. By the weekend following the terrorist destruction, the president had made it a point to visit the mosque at the Islamic Center of Washington to condemn the increased violence aimed at innocent American Arabs and Muslims. At that time, as reported by CNN's *Headline News* (2001), the U.S. attorney general had already stated that the FBI had initiated some 40 hate crimes investigations involving reported attacks on Arab American citizens and institutions, including the murder of a Pakistani Muslim store owner in Dallas, Texas, and a Sikh gas station owner in Mesa, Arizona, most likely an immigrant from India.

In addition, the Council on American-Islamic Relations said that it had received reports of more than 350 attacks across the country, ranging from verbal harassment to physical assaults (Milbank & Wax, 2001). In Palos Hills, Illinois, for example, two Muslim girls were beaten at Moraine Valley College. The council had also received reports that dozens of mosques had been fire-bombed or vandalized, including a mosque in Evansville, Indiana, that had been damaged by a man who had driven his car into it at 80 mph. In each of these cases, police had quickly arrested suspects.

At the Washington mosque, escorted by Islamic clerics and quoting from the Koran's prohibitions against evil, Bush made such statements as: "The face of terror is not the true faith of Islam" and "Islam is peace." He further stated that women who cover their heads should not fear leaving their homes and going out into the community. Speaking from a lectern in front of the *qibla*, the altar worshipers face when praying in the direction of Mecca, Bush stressed the importance of treating Muslim doctors, lawyers, soldiers, and parents respectfully: "Those who feel like they can intimidate our fellow citizens to take out their anger don't represent the best of America, they represent the worst of humankind, and they should be ashamed of that kind of behavior" (Milbanks & Wax, 2001, p. 5).

Bush's actions and remarks were both rational and poignant, as they expressed some of the common denominators in the pathways to violence and nonviolence. For example, these pathways are often established individually and collectively in the name of justice. In other words, not only are the violent efforts by terrorists like bin Laden and his associates, as well as those of counterterrorists like the CIA and its allies, committed in the name of freedom and liberty, but so too are the nonviolent efforts of steadfast, peacemaking pacifists. No matter what neutral parties may think, terrorists, counterterrorists, and peacemakers can each make their own internal, existential, and relative cases for the "moral justice" they seek. Morality aside, however, two of these groups share a belief in legitimate and illegitimate forms of violence. In terms of actions, both terrorists and counterterrorists engage in parallel practices that can acceptably include the infliction of "collateral damage." Pacifists, by contrast, delegitimate any form of violence and actively prefer peacekeeping to warmaking.

Although their forms of violence may or may not be one and the same, both terrorists and counterterrorists make their cases for self-sacrifice and the need for use of force, if not carnage, to achieve their ends. Regarding the September 11th terrorist attacks, those responsible threatened a "holy war" and counterterrorists from the United States launched "operation infinite justice." By contrast, pacifists (if not necessarily peacemakers), who view virtually all forms of violence as illegitimate because "violence begets violence" and because there are better ways to interact and socially organize people, called for political and economic rather than military responses to September 11th. Of course, the pathways to violence and nonviolence are more complex than the emotionality of either anger or calm might reveal. To understand these dynamic sets of behavior, one must grasp in time and space the interaction of psychic and social relationships.

For example, some of the pathways to violence taken by bin Laden and other terrorists of the organization al Qaeda ("the base") were also shared by those who had struck out at innocent Arabs and Muslims in this country in the aftermath of the terrorist destruction. In other words, what were (are) the psychic conditions shared in common— for example, between those suicide-homicide commandos aboard the Boeing 767s and the high-speed driver who crashed his car into the Indiana mosque, or even the several hundred other American citizens who engaged in abusive acts of ethnic profiling? What are the similarities of social context between those Middle Eastern terrorists and those Americans who have expressed

themselves in "blind" vengeance and retribution? What are the parallels or resemblances in the social psychologies shared by these two groups of people? What are the continuities and differences between these groups of violent perpetrators and other violent groups, such as batterers, rapists, and toxic polluters? Are there any common denominators ("ingredients") that constitute the continuums of violent and nonviolent behaviors? These are merely a representative sample of the types of questions that will be grappled with in this investigation of the multiple pathways to violence and nonviolence.

DECREASING VIOLENCE AND INCREASING NONVIOLENCE

If we are to significantly decrease violence and increase nonviolence at home and abroad, we will have to change the way we think about violence, nonviolence, and the relationship between the two. Usually when we think about violence, we think about interpersonal forms of violence, such as attempted murder or homicide, assault and battery, rape and sexual assault, robbery, kidnapping, and torture. Rarely do we think of suicide, anorexia, and self-flagellation, or of verbal abuse, threats, and intimidation as forms of interpersonal violence. More significantly, we usually ignore, deny, or accept other forms of institutional and structural violence that provide context for most of the personal violence that occurs. While "bureaucratic" and "environmental" forms of violence, for example, are perhaps more invisible than the more personal forms, they are nonetheless more systemic, widespread, and destructive than the "individualized" forms of violence one typically thinks about.

Other institutional or institutionalized forms of violence may include child and elder abuse; workplace abuse; military, police, and penal abuse; environmental devastation; and fundamental human rights violations. Related to prevailing political and economic arrangements are the structural forms of violence. These structurally organized forms of violence refer essentially to two distinct types. The first type of structural violence is pursued allegedly for the purposes of establishing, defending, and/or extending hierarchy and inequality. This can be accomplished by harassing, exploiting, beating, torturing, or killing people based on their age, class, ethnicity, gender, and/or sexual orientation. Some acts of terrorism, such as church or abortion clinic bombings, lynchings past or present, and other hate crimes come immediately to mind; the killing of more than half a million children from various sanctions against Iraq (Welch, 2002) and the subjection of two million young children daily to impoverished living conditions in America (Roark, 1996) do not.

The second type of structural violence is pursued allegedly for the purposes of decreasing privilege and/or increasing liberty by the resisting, protesting, and attacking of those persons, symbols, or things that represent the "Establishment" or the "powers that be." Acts of rebellion, protests, and assassinations come to mind; acts of whistleblowing or resisting illegal arrest do not. In the political and economic worlds of institutional and structural violence, discourse is a relative commodity: One man's eco-terrorist is another man's eco-hero; one man's rugged individualist is another man's harsh monopolist. Oftentimes, the only difference between the two (unfortunately) is a matter of winning and losing on or off the battlefield or in or out of a court of law.

However one defines or categorizes violence and nonviolence, it is my contention that to increase the latter and decrease the former in and between societies, the pathways to both will have to be increasingly liberated from the dominant paradigm of competition and "adversarialism," with its worldview of extreme individualism and its egocentric stance of winner-takes-all, zero-sum games of consumption. By contrast, the subordinate and yet evolving paradigm of cooperation and "mutualism," grounded in a worldview of international peace and the collective well-being of all people, provides an alternative way of organizing societies that engenders more pathways to nonviolence and fewer pathways to violence. Understanding violence and nonviolence in the context of both adversarial and mutualistic approaches to human behavior and social organization becomes the key pedagogical framework that holds my analysis together.

Let me point out at the beginning that the local, national, and global pathways to inspiring war or peace and violence or nonviolence may be related in both obvious and not-so-obvious ways. In terms of the less obvious ways (for example), James D. Wolfensohn (2002), president of the World Bank Group, remarked in an address he delivered on peacemaking, development, and terrorism: "We must recognize that while there is social injustice on a global scale—both between states and within them; while the fight against poverty is barely begun in too many parts of the world; while the link between progress in development and progress toward peace is not recognized—we may win a battle against terror but we will not conclude a war that will yield enduring peace" (p. 1).

Accordingly, if we are ever to evolve a holistic framework for decreasing violence and increasing nonviolence at home and abroad, it is imperative that when we think of these we do not limit ourselves to thoughts of personal forms of violence and nonviolence. We must remember to consider forms of institutional and structural violence and nonviolence. It is these impersonal expressions of violence and nonviolence that are often at the roots of interpersonal forms of violence and nonviolence. The point is that the interpersonal, institutional, and structural spheres of violence or nonviolence are overlapping and interconnected. Each of the spheres of violence or nonviolence reflects, interacts, and has some kind of accumulative relationship with the others. Hence, a complete picture of violence and nonviolence, such as the one presented herein, requires that each of these spheres be studied alone as well as together.

FEELINGS AND STRUCTURES

Many young people who have resorted to the killing of another person before their 18th birthday are among those children who have grown up in the inner cities of America. Pervasive throughout these locales are poverty, unemployment, poor schools, low educational attainment, fractured families, abuse of alcohol and drugs, and more than enough fear, mayhem, and violence to go around. Yet the overwhelming majority of youths residing in these urban ghettos—abused and/or neglected or not abused or neglected—do not resort to physically assaulting, let alone killing, another person because of their adverse conditions or experiences. This is also true for those youths who, although they have lived in environments and come from families that were not labeled socially as disorganized or dysfunctional, were nevertheless harmed as children.

In either scenario, just a tiny minority of these youths, most between the ages of 14 and 17, ever made free decisions, constrained only by their abilities (biological, physiological, and psychological) and their social circumstances, to kill another human being. In terms of specific social science research, a couple of ethnographers have identified three popular routes or pathways to homicide that adolescent killers have taken. Regardless of their routes—"ordinary," "risk," or "fantasy"—what all of these offenders

shared in common was that they "had suffered so much emotional damage during their lives that they were essentially functioning as *children* when they killed" (Kelly & Totten, 2002, p. xi, emphasis in original). James Gilligan (1997), former director of both the Bridgewater State Hospital for the criminally insane and the Center for the Study of Violence at Harvard Medical School, has similarly argued that essentially all of the most dangerous adult killers that he has personally known and treated were also childlike victims of violence who had never self-actualized out of their childhood states of victimization and violence into adulthood states of recovery and nonviolence.

By exposing some of the connections or linkages between the pathways to violence and nonviolence in this introduction, I hope to reveal a few of the ways in which these paths are related or interact. For example, when most people think about violence, they may think about anger, aggression, and bloodshed—acknowledging certain aspects of hate and vengeance—but rarely does anyone think about dependency, vulnerability, and insecurity or trust, respect, and shame. Moreover, violent interactions are not considered in the context of an absence or lack of a nonviolent love, in the context of disassociation from the self and alienation from the other, or in the context of humiliation and revenge as these are related to personal and social experiences of mood elevation and depression.

Part of the problem of these "secrets of violence" stems from the way Americans and most other people view violent perpetrators and victims: as separate and unrelated phenomena, rather than as integrative or interacting pieces of some kind of larger set of social, political, and economic relations. Part of the problem also stems from the dichotomization of violence and nonviolence into separate spheres or worlds and from the related failure to see the dynamic relations between the two. In short, the roots of violent and nonviolent behavior should not be viewed and consumed as though they inhabit different worlds.

It makes better sense to see violence and nonviolence as two sides of a domestic and international coin. For example, the social realities of both violence and nonviolence share a foundation in the need to resist shame and humiliation and the need for love and acceptance by self and others. In many instances, violence trails a need to defend one's self or family or nation from a loss of esteem, honor, or pride. Of course, the "choice" to resort to violence may have seemed like the only choice; there simply was no other choice. If this were so, then violent acts such as homicide or sexual assault may have been the result of people thinking that they had no alternatives that were less violent or nonviolent than the course of action they took (assuming that it was deliberate and not the product of negligence).

Defensive needs may include acts of violent revenge in response to perceived injustices, real or imagined. The all powerful emotion of shame, for example, includes the associated feelings of humiliation, mortification, rejection, marginality, isolation, and so on and so forth. As anthropologists have informed us, shame is a universal emotion found in all cultures. Interestingly, shame is responsible for both individual and collective accomplishments. In other words, shame can be the source of both destructive pandemonium and constructive civilization.

Feelings of embarrassment and the desire not to feel ashamed, for example, serve as great motivators and stimulators for every day as well as for lifetime achievement awards. Shame and lack of respect are also responsible for our individual as well as our collective acts of abuse and violence. When an individual feels disrespected for even the most trivial of slights, this may result in a "righteous" maiming, slaughter, or killing in

the form of a homicide or suicide. Similarly, when a nation-state feels humiliated by another nation-state or group of nation-states, collective violence of the most atrocious kinds may result, including mass murder and genocide. Putting aside the question of whether or not youths or adults who have killed felt compelled, out of control, or in control when their murdering occurred, it is instructive to examine the multiple pathways toward and away from both violence and nonviolence.

Although shame is fundamental to the human condition and to each and every one of us (excepting sociopaths for sake of argument), abuse and violence are also distinct possibilities in all of our lives. It is within these contexts that there are varying degrees of abuse and violence in most family histories. In reality, very few family trees reveal many generations free of serious violence. Hence, we have all been victims and/or perpetrators of violence directly—as children, as siblings, as parents, as lovers, as spouses, and/or as soldiers—and indirectly—as voyeurs and mass consumers of violent images, texts, and fantasies. At the same time, most of us, mostly through denial, downplay or dismiss selectively the violence in our own relationships, as we tend to think of or prefer the violence in the relationships of others. In a different and related way, most of us also fail to come to grips with the pathways that families, communities, and nations alike have engaged in to recover from and/or to move beyond the domains of violence to the domains of nonviolence.

Thus, when we think about violence and nonviolence, we need to think about these events in terms of our own lives as victims, perpetrators, healers, and recovering subjects. This type of multithinking and reflection helps us to identify more fully with the so-called others engaged in violence or nonviolence whom we generally tend to think about at a "safe distance" away from our own emotional psyches and pathways. Thinking of our own experiences with violence and nonviolence in simultaneously less detached and more objective ways also allows us to put the tragedies of all violence and the triumphs of all nonviolence into focus, whether experienced by victims or perpetrators. Reflecting on various episodes of violence in our own lives or in the lives of others who have been familiarly close further allows us to contemplate the ways in which people have dealt or coped with violence, the ways in which they recover from or struggle with violence, or the ways in which they use violence or abuse as a source of strength and character development.

PRIVATE AND PUBLIC SHAME

In a few words, differences in violence and nonviolence are related not only to our personal experiences with shame, honor, dignity, and identity formation or self-actualization but to our larger social and cultural experiences of trust, inequality, and hope as these are shaped by our relative participation or marginality in society. Whether we are talking about youths at risk or adults in crisis, by combining experiences of personal or private shame with experiences of social or public shame, and by recognizing the overlapping spheres of interpersonal, institutional, and structural forms of violence and nonviolence, we are able to take a holistic approach to violence reduction and nonviolence production.

As will be revealed in this book, pathways to violence and nonviolence are not merely interpersonal life courses. These pathways also involve institutional and structural life courses of violence and nonviolence. The dynamic sources and expressions of both violence and nonviolence, in other words, can be located within or across the personal, institutional, and structural relations of social, political, and economic organization. Thus, the secrets of violence and nonviolence refer not only to the human emotions of love, shame, and mutuality, but to other socially related and silent or as yet unconstructed cultural discourses about such activities. With respect to violence, for example, these secrets include

a. Violent activity and the punishment of violent offenders are both grounded in the common emotion of revenge.
b. Violence and violent acts are often social and political diseases before they are psychological malaises.
c. Multimedia and other public representations underplay most forms of violence and nonviolence but overplay other forms.

More inclusively, however, the pathways to violence and nonviolence are both adjusting to or engaging in balancing acts that revolve around emotions of revenge and forgiveness, feelings of malaise and optimism, and physical attraction and repulsion to the varied realities of violence and nonviolence.

As already suggested, perpetrators of violence may be thought of as engaging in a "defensive" reaction to some kind of real or imagined assault, injury, or harm perpetrated on or against the self, family, group, or nation. In a similar vein, state-executed pain or violence is about punishing offenders to avenge their wrongdoing and/or their victimization of others. It is also considered a defensive reaction by the community or nation-state against those violations of the "social contract" that allegedly threaten the well-being of the group. From this perspective, there is often no real difference between crime and punishment. In other words, private homicides and state-sanctioned capital punishment are reciprocal systems for the symbolic exchange of shame and honor.

In either case, when people commit violent acts on others or when others commit violent acts on violent or nonviolent perpetrators "in kind," both expressions of violence are trying to accomplish the same end. Namely, both types of violence are trying to bring about shame and humiliation or dishonor and disrespect to the objects of their respective harms or injuries. Victims of both forms of shame and humiliation, regardless of the associated rationales attached to those forms, may often respond with an escalation of their own violence, especially when there is an intensification of an already existing condition of shame, humiliation, frustration, anger, and so on. Despite the obvious psychic and symbolic similarities, violent crime and criminal punishment are generally represented in mass society as vastly different phenomena.

Typically, the two types of behavior are portrayed as if they were moral opposites. At their extremes, the violent criminals represent or symbolize a kind of evil people who are either "mad" or "bad," and the criminal punishments represent or symbolize a kind of ethical justification (e.g., "retributive," "reformative," or "restorative") for the administration of justice. Legal significances and fictions aside, the social realities of crime and punishment are often quite similar. Stories of the estrangement of the two are also exaggerated; the proverbial "violence begets violence" often runs smack into the philosophy of the "turn the other cheek" nonviolence approach to hate or abuse. Moreover, some victims of violence become perpetrators, some become survivors, and others withdraw or sink further into depression, paranoia, and/or quiet desperation.

To interpret both violence and punishment as acts of protection and preservation as well as reciprocal systems of shame and honor is to appreciate how "the attempt to achieve justice and maintain justice, or to undo or prevent injustice, is the one and only universal cause of violence" (Gilligan, 1997, p. 12). To appreciate these and other social relations of violence and nonviolence is essential for grasping the complex origins of violence and nonviolence as well as for developing strategies that might be helpful in decreasing violence and increasing nonviolence.

A GERM THEORY OF VIOLENCE AND NONVIOLENCE

Given all the talk, all the public discussion, and all the mediated concern over violence, there is relatively little attention paid to the sources, origins, or causes of violence, and even less agitation about the etiology of nonviolence. Instead, there is a lot of finger-pointing and some very derogatory name-calling of those guilty of perpetrating certain forms of violence. Similarly, there is an abundance of moralizing about violence and a relative absence of study or moralizing about nonviolence in relation to violence. Either way, moralizing about violent or nonviolent behavior should not be confused with providing explanations about violence or nonviolence. For example, pertaining to violent and nonviolent offenders alike and to their victims are the judgments of "bad," "evil," "guilty," and "insane." These are primarily value statements that shed little, if any, light on the production of either violence or nonviolence.

By contrast, theories or explanations of violence and nonviolence are more important than value judgments about these behaviors. This is because explanations frame the problem of social violence in an appreciation of its genesis or roots rather than in a condemnation or repudiation of the behavior. Explanations also provide insight into courses of action for decreasing violence and increasing nonviolence. In the marketplace of public ideas, unfortunately, there are relatively few theories of violence and nonviolence. As for the social and political claims that these explanations may have, most have been drowned out by the "moral" shouts for vengeance and retribution against all perpetrators of wicked deeds, culpable or nonculpable. Hence, as one alternative to this adversarial approach, a mutualistic explanation tries to capture the reciprocal social relations of violence and nonviolence.

For anybody who is interested in developing a holistic explanation of violence and nonviolence, Gilligan's (1997) "germ theory" of violence is a very useful place to begin. Grounded in a model of public health and preventive community medicine, the germ theory of violence is both literal and metaphoric, but not as one might expect. In his articulation and analysis of violence, Gilligan argues that violence is neither biological nor universal, nor is it to be found in our genetic material or evolutionary development. He further argues that there are "pathogens" that cause morally lethal forms of violence pathology; however, these pathogens are not microorganisms but human emotions. These emotional pathogens, shame in particular, are located in what Gilligan refers to as society's sewer systems, only he is not talking about physical sewers but social sewers, places like prisons and mental hospitals that act like "receptacles and conduits into which we as a society dump the human beings whom we treat like garbage and waste products" (p. 104). As incarcerated others, belonging to the internal worlds of the "society of captives," these violent and nonviolent persons become victims of the institutional and structural relations of violence that accumulate and intensify behind prison walls.

Gilligan's germ theory of violence also examines the "water supply" as a whole or in relation to the larger social and economic systems as these exist outside of the sewer system per se. According to this model, the dangerously violent are viewed as persons who carry the pathogenic emotions of violence. The model also demonstrates that it is relatively easy to identify where the violent pathogens are concentrated in society, whom they infect, and how they are grown and distributed. At the same time, it is easy to show how our social and economic arrangements are permeated with violent pathogens and how they spread the contagious disease in identifiable ways. This kind of epidemiology of violence includes such systematic and deadly forms of structural neglect and abuse as, for example, poverty, racism, sexism, and exploitation, not to mention other appearances of institutionalized privilege and inequality.

The germ theory of violence, in a nutshell, views shame and its private and public sources as the ultimate source of all violence. However, although shame is necessary for violence to occur, it is not a sufficient cause of violence in and of itself, "just as the tubercle bacillus is necessary but not sufficient for the development of tuberculosis" (Gilligan, 1997, p. 111). In explaining his derivative model of violence, Gilligan argues that there are a minimum of three preconditions that must be present before shame can lead to a full pathogenesis of violent behavior. These preconditions include (a) feeling too ashamed to admit that one feels shame, which only makes one feel further ashamed; (b) feeling that there is no other nonviolent means available for warding off or diminishing one's feelings of shame or low self-esteem; and (c) feeling an overwhelming sense of shame in the absence of feelings of either love or guilt. If these three feelings are all present, then the shame and a sense of rejection are more likely to stimulate rage as well as violent impulses toward the person or persons in whose eyes one feels ashamed than if one or more of these feelings were missing.

Despite the fact that most people experience some forms of shame throughout their life cycles, few of these aggrieved persons end up committing any significant acts of violence over the course of their entire lives.

Most people, in other words, have built up enough violence "antigens" and "antibodies" to this social disease, or they possess enough nonviolent means to protect or restore their wounded self-esteem. In addition, people who are at risk for violence, whether they are youths or adults, are those who have been and are subject to an accumulation of structural, institutional, and interpersonal forms of violence. Their shame is both public and private, both personal and social. They may become depressed and suicidal, or they may become angry and homicidal. At the same time, with proper intervention, they may suppress, struggle with, or neutralize their feelings of shame. They may, in fact, become stronger as a result of their adversities; some may even become overachievers, as has been the case in many of today's scenarios of recovery.

Part of the reason that society falsely views violence as something other than a social disease has to do with the overwhelming influence and consumption of mass media. Organizationally and managerially, mass media overemphasizes interpersonal violence and nonviolence while it ignores or downplays institutional and structural violence and nonviolence. In particular, news media consistently reproduce distorted and unrepresentative images of the trends in violence. The mediated message is that things are "getting out of control" and that violence is "getting worse." Two recent studies underscore this point. The first, by the Center on Media and Public Affairs (Hinds, 2000), found "that coverage of youth and adult homicide on three network news programs increased by 721 percent between 1992 and 1996, a period when the rate of homicide actually fell by 20 percent" (p. 3). The second, by the Berkeley Media Studies Group (Hinds, 2000), reported that most TV news about teenagers in 1998 was crime news, even though less than ½ of 1% of juveniles were arrested for violent crime that year. The consumption of mass-mediated violence and nonviolence is only part of the story, however, a part that is more often than not confusing and misrepresentative of the realities that it creates.

VIOLENT AND NONVIOLENT RHETORIC, YOUTH AT RISK, AND IMPLICATIONS FOR PEACEMAKING

The best kept "secrets" in the United States at the turn of the 21st century were that, like most forms of legally proscribed violence in general, youth and school violence in particular had declined throughout the 1990s. In light of the myth of an epidemic of violence inflicting the youth of America, it is necessary to present at least some data that can provide a kind of "objective" instruction on the social reality of teenage violence as we move squarely into the new millennium. So, when considering the state of violence in youthful America, ponder these representative bits of evidence.

- Juvenile violent crime is at its lowest level since 1987, and it fell 30% between 1994 and 1998.
- In 1999, law enforcement officers arrested some 104,000 juveniles for violent crimes, accounting for only 16% of all violent crime arrests.
- Six percent of all murders in 1999 were committed by juveniles.
- Comparatively, in the same year, 148 juveniles were murdered by other juveniles, 596 juveniles were murdered by adults, and 310 adults were murdered by juveniles.
- From 1997 to 2000, 47 kids were murdered at or around school; 3,000 kids were murdered at home during the same period.
- In 1998, the number of gun fatalities was 30,407; the number involving persons under 20 years old was 3,752.
- The annual murder rate among grade-school children (per 1 million, 6 to 12 years old) was 2.0 in the 1960s, 2.6 in the 1970s, 1.6 in the 1980s, 1.7 in the 1990s, and .6 in

1999. (Males, 2001; PBS Online, 2001; Thompkins, 2000)

By these measures and others, youthful violence may be rated the lowest that it has been in some 15 years. Nevertheless, sensational, distorted, and unrepresentative news stories in the late 1990s focused unwarranted attention on a relatively few isolated killings committed by rural and suburban students on school property. The national reaction to the "crisis" in, for example, U.S. public schools, endorsed by both Republicans and Democrats, has been a highly reactive security response, involving policies of zero tolerance, conflict resolution, and expensive technology. For the most part, these are overzealous reactions to relatively nonexistent problems. As Douglas Thompkins (2000) writes,

> The presence of security officers, metal detectors, and security cameras may deter some students from committing acts of violence, but this presence also serves to heighten fear among students and teachers, while increasing the power of some gangs and the perceived need some students have for joining gangs. (p. 54)

Even in some inner-city schools, where serious gang violence may exist and where such measures may be appropriate (as contrasted with the vast majority of suburban and rural schools), such high-tech security efforts to stem violence may at best keep out those gangbangers who have been already kicked out; they provide virtually no security against those students who have a legitimate right to be there. At the same time, schools embracing these security measures have begun to seem more like detention centers and prisons than educational places of learning. These and other so-called safe-school plans, often mandated by state governments, typically underanalyze the social problem as they overemphasize physical security.

For example, in the paper "School Violence: Identifying Factors and Characteristics of Students at Risk for Violent Behavior," which was presented at the American Society of Criminology's annual meeting in 2000, a team of five researchers conclude that "violent impulses and acts are more likely among a small group of students identified as the 'quietly armed' who may be more at risk of violence than the more visible 'hard core' acting-out students" (Lawrence, McLeod, McLeod, Birbilis, & Hines, 2000, p. 1). The researchers went so far as to offer some speculative psychological interpretations for the group they labeled "quietly armed students":

> A student in this group may be characteristic of the passive-aggressive pre-adolescent, unable to express anger directly. He puts on a well-adjusted face and acts as if everything is just fine. He may have weak ego strength, and may be overly sensitive to insults or perceived verbal attacks. He will become increasingly frustrated but take his anger out passively or symbolically, perhaps by taking an interest in violent entertainment, by writing morbid poetry, or obsessing about death-related themes. He rebels against authority, but passively rather than aggressively or boldly. He may vandalize school property as a means of "getting even." The tendency to stifle his anger and frustration may result in depression, and he may be on medication. There may be signs of self-hatred or perfectionism. This individual may lash out in isolated but unusual instances. Animal cruelty is not an uncommon outlet for anger in this individual.

> This individual may ask an authority for help when he believes a wrong has been committed against him. He may not persist in asking for help again, and may feel intensely disappointed and let down when he does not get an immediate response. Though his expectations may not be realistic, he will not ask for help again. This

individual may then feel that he cannot rely on or trust authorities, and may then feel justified to take personal actions to protect himself. (Lawrence et al., 2000, p. 15)

The quietly armed in the Woodbury, Minnesota, school study comprised only 2% of the researchers' sample. By contrast, 83.9% of the students in the sample were characterized as "good kids." Of the remaining 14%, two groups were identified as "scufflers" and "hard core." The larger of the two groups, the scufflers, tended to get into fights, threaten other students, use alcohol, and get into trouble occasionally. The hard core, readily identified by most school staff as the troublemakers, typically came from broken homes, received poor grades, skipped classes frequently, threatened and hurt other students, abused alcohol, and saw themselves as discipline problems. I could draw many points from this classification or breakdown of 1,500 junior high school students from Minnesota, but suffice it to say that when it comes to violence reduction, neither one size nor one prescription fits all. Responding to all youths as if they were dangerous, with high-tech security and draconian rules and regulations, when in actuality most students are "good kids," is overreacting at best and counterproductive at worst. It makes far more sense, of course, to design strategies of violence reduction that take into account a variety of populations and subgroups, each with different yet related sets of needs. It also makes more sense to employ strategies of conflict resolution, peacemaking, and nonviolence production, as these operate according to the principles of mutuality, human rights, and need-based justice.

In any event, the findings from this study and others suggest that the majority of school systems may be far off the beaten path where anger and violence walk. In other words, these schools and communities need to rethink their policies about violence and nonviolence in general. For example, they should "consider the impact of heightened fear, invasion of privacy, and the undermining of the educational mission that result from having hidden cameras, drug-sniffing dogs, metal detectors, and identity tags" on campus (Thompkins, 2000, p. 66). More pragmatically, schools and communities alike, especially those in the inner-city areas and other areas where gangs represent a potential draw for student resources and participation, need to provide students with alternative venues or opportunities to enjoy life, ones that can compete with the activities, kudos, excitement, community, and sense of challenge that gangs bring to their memberships.

VIOLENCE AGAINST YOUTH IS MORE IMPORTANT THAN VIOLENCE BY YOUTH

The last secret to be shared about violence and nonviolence in this introduction is more accurately a secret of social policy. That is to say, students and scholars of violence and nonviolence already know what needs to be done to decrease the vulnerability rates of those populations most likely to experience violence and victimization. Therefore, how to curb the levels of violence that plague American society and elsewhere or how to enhance the levels of nonviolence are not the problems. The problems are actually with our social and political policies, both domestically and internationally, which neither avail themselves of nor apply the necessary knowledge bases. For example, if one were to toss out a net to catch all the youths at risk of becoming violent, it would surely catch other youths besides those labeled quietly armed, scufflers, and hard core by the Minnesota researchers.

Probably the largest subgroup of potentially violent youths includes the millions of children who are directly and indirectly exposed to violence each year, whether in the home, at school, or in the street. National estimates based on a 1995 survey indicated that of this nation's 22.3 million children between the ages of 12 and 17, almost 9 million have witnessed serious violence, 3.9 million have been victims of a serious physical assault, and approximately 1.8 million have been victims of a serious sexual assault (Wilson, 2000). In addition, it should be stressed that especially at risk are

- Young children—for example, those younger than 4 years old, who account for 76% of child abuse and neglect fatalities;
- Children from families where violence against women occurs, who experience a 30% to 60% overlap in child maltreatment, involving an estimated 500,000 children encountered by police on domestic violence calls annually;
- Children from families where domestic violence occurs more generally, who also suffer emotional and developmental consequences from exposure to violence, direct and indirect. In fact, the 1995 survey found that approximately 2 million adolescents between the ages of 12 and 17 appeared to have suffered from posttraumatic stress disorder;
- Abused or neglected child victims, for whom the likelihood of arrest is increased by 53% percent and that of arrest for a violent crime as an adult by 38%. (Wilson, 2000, pp. xii-xiii)

Recognizing that the United States has been facing the consequences of previously inadequate investments in the protection of its children, the U.S. Departments of Justice (DOJ) and Health and Human Services (DHHS) convened a summit of 150 law enforcement and health and human service practitioners and policy makers in June 1999 to contemplate the problem of children's exposure to violence and to create a national blueprint for action. There was vast agreement among the participants that legislators and policy makers had to increase resources for prevention programs and other services at the front end of the system of human service delivery, such as programs and services for battered women and their children. For the criminal justice system, there was agreement that its professionals had to become more sensitive to the serious impact of domestic violence and victimization on children. However, the final plan called for the same old and tired, but admittedly necessary, steps for dealing with the problem. The plan was essentially a three-pronged approach to violence reduction. In a nutshell, it called for the usual continuum of "prevention," "intervention," and "accountability," emphasizing comprehensive responses that would incorporate professionals from multiple disciplines, who would work together, begin earlier, and think cognitively and developmentally.

The summit's goal—primary prevention—was to stop children's exposure to violence before it happened. Prevention meant (a) reaching at-risk families early; (b) investing in a full range of early childhood care and respite services; (c) teaching conflict-resolution skills; (d) challenging norms that allow men and boys to use power, control, and violence to dominate women and girls; (e) intensifying efforts to reduce domestic violence; and (f) providing community and educational resources to prevent violence. The problem with this national response to youth violence was that the summit's plan was not, as it claimed, engaging in primary prevention.

Instead, it was engaging in secondary prevention, reflecting the sad reality that a representative group of the "best and brightest" either didn't know the difference or didn't have the political willpower to debate or change public policy discourse and practice away from dealing only with the symptoms and not with the underlying causes of violence and nonviolence. To engage in the latter kinds of dialogues or courses of action, people have to be able to go beyond the nuclear family and the systems of human services and criminal justice. Policy makers and others have to be able to identify the social and cultural practices of socialization as well as the institutional and structural relations of inequality and power that reproduce the conditions of violence or nonviolence in the first place.

The summit's next goal of intervention was very vague and less well-defined than its goal of prevention. It referred simply to "improving the current system of services for children or creating new approaches so that the service system is responsive to the complexity of children's lives and rooted in and defined by communities" (Wilson, 2000, p. xiii). This rather vacuous and empty bromide for the most part has little appreciation or understanding of the interconnections between the systems of services for children on the one hand and the larger systems of health care, employment, and criminal punishment on the other. The way these systems interact with each other and in relation to the problems of violence and nonviolence can influence the informal workings of the relationships between the aforementioned systems of violence and nonviolence.

Moreover, the summit's very broad and undefined panaceas of intervention assume a highly individualistic response to violence, focusing exclusively on the interpersonal relations of violence while ignoring altogether the institutional and structural relations of violence. Keeping in mind, as we noted earlier, that shame, self-esteem, and violence are functions of both personal isolation and social marginality, to focus attention only on personal relations while disregarding the larger, cultural forces responsible for feelings of inadequacy, incompetence, and inferiority is tantamount, as a colleague of mine is fond of saying, "to mopping up the bathroom floor as the tub continues to overflow." Unfortunately, turning off the running faucet or changing the direction of the flow in our response to the reproduction of violence challenges at its very foundation the precarious balance of privilege and inequality characteristic of and basic to a *laissez-faire* or free-enterprise system of capitalist production.

Lastly, the summit's notion of accountability was limited to essentially "holding perpetrators of violence—against children and against the children's mothers and caretakers—accountable for their actions" (Wilson, 2000, p. xiii). This translates to bringing the full force of the criminal and legal justice systems to bear on the perpetrators of domestic and family violence, which usually means punishment without individual rehabilitation or social reform, in most jurisdictions. In other words, emphases on "retributive" rather than "restorative" justice seem to be the preferred order of the day. Punitive justice, either alone or combined with other types of justice such as "therapy," is not only painful to the perpetrator and harmful to the mission of decreasing violence, but it is actually counterproductive, as it often escalates the behavioral violence of many of its recipients. If "cycles of violence" are to be broken, we will have to engage in more restorative, nonviolent, community-based, or peacemaking forms of justice. These kinds of domestic policies, to alleviate violence and to motivate nonviolence, should be made operational both inside and outside family and neighborhood circles.

Similarly, making juveniles responsible for their behavior as youths or adults does not mean treating children as adults. This kind of harsher treatment moves the United States retrogressively in the wrong direction, a direction that our elders rejected more than a century ago. In a parallel fashion, the death penalty should also be abolished in America, and our nation should take its place beside all the democratic nations of the world that long ago abandoned the barbaric practice of state-sanctioned killing.

As for the far too many "abandoned" children and youth in America, who have been victims of both abuse and neglect and who find themselves living in the "social sewers" of our society along with the pathogens of everyday violence, there should be a national urgency to attend to their needs. I put this no simpler than to say that there is nothing as violent as absolute poverty—except relative poverty among affluence and wealth. The former may kill the body; the latter more likely kills the spirit. The results are that there are many more "dead" boys and "dead" girls without spirit or soul walking around than the actual numbers of physical and lethal violence would indicate. There are entire social ecologies or neighborhoods of children and impoverished communities, people living well below the poverty levels, without a basic health care plan or provider and with virtually no other social services. Today we spend more money in our society to punish, lock up, and warehouse than we do to educate, counsel, and treat the law-abiding or law-violating citizens of our nation.

In short, if we are to rescue those most vulnerable of persons to violence, abuse, and neglect, the young and deprived children of our society, who disproportionately experience their victimization in the first 10 to 15 years of life, some radical social policies are called for that reflect a more enlightened approach to social problems than the United States has adopted so far in its history of domestic policy reform. What is necessary is a set of policies that is grounded in such basic human rights as the right to housing, to food, to self-actualization, and more. These new social policies would include such minimal safeguards as "cost-of-living" wages and "guaranteed" health care for all residents. Whether or not it's called welfare, workfare, or whateverfare, these programs should not

be about punishment but about development, both individual and community. Investments in human and social capital should be considered and, ultimately, integrated with or incorporated into more traditional for-profit investments. Addressing the pathogenesis of violence and nonviolence at the structural and institutional as well as the interpersonal levels allows for social policies that grapple with both "targeted" and "non-targeted" at-risk groups, young or old, who need assistance and nurturing.

From this holistic and humanistic approach, it now makes sense to talk about raising responsible and resourceful youth, about strengthening families and empowering parents, and about creating safer neighborhoods and schools. By using this kind of integrative perspective, we are capable of addressing both the causes and the symptoms of violence. However, we can't confine ourselves to thinking only in terms of primary and secondary prevention. We must also develop plans and strategies for those who have already surrendered to lives involving varying degrees and kinds of violence. The recovery of violent perpetrators and victims requires that each empathizes with and acknowledges the needs of the other. Violence reduction will also require, as a matter of policy, the development of restorative justice programs and the expansion of professional counseling or treatment deemed appropriate by staff, abusive perpetrators, and abused victims acting in some kind of mutually established plan for violence reduction and nonviolence production.

ORGANIZATION OF THE BOOK

At its simplest, *Violence and Nonviolence: Pathways to Understanding* says that

"violence begets violence" and "nonviolence begets nonviolence." Unfortunately, the pathways to violence and nonviolence are more complex than these simple aphorisms imply. To begin with, the pathways to violence or nonviolence function at the interpersonal, institutional, and structural levels of society. What's more, the social relations between these spheres or domains of violence and nonviolence mutually reinforce each other. At the same time, pathways to violence and nonviolence involve states of action and nonaction or states of commission and noncommission. Making matters more difficult, these pathways also involve states of denial, states of responsibility, and states of reaction, repression, suppression, and accommodation. Finally, the pathways to violence and nonviolence are self-perpetuating: the psychic, social, and cultural forces of each engages the abilities or inabilities of individuals and collectivities alike to empathize with (or not) the abundance of persons victimized by violence worldwide.

The key to understanding the simplicity and complexity of these relations lies in the proper identification of violence and nonviolence in all their constituent manifestations—emotional, physical, and cultural. Understanding also involves the appreciation of the ways in which these manifestations of violence and nonviolence express themselves in behavioral terms. By viewing the reciprocal relationships of violence and nonviolence and by examining both sides of the violence/nonviolence "coin," as it were, I have tried to develop a comprehensive and integrative approach to the study of violence and nonviolence. In the process, I have employed an interdisciplinary framework that strives to incorporate the inclusion of the personal, social, cultural, and structural forces involved in the expressions of violence and nonviolence as these are exhibited locally, nationally, and globally. So that the reader may obtain the perquisite knowledge for minimizing violent relations and maximizing nonviolent relations, the rest of this book is divided into three parts: *Types of Violence, Pathways to Violence,* and *Pathways to Nonviolence.*

Part I: Types of Violence consists of four chapters. In Chapter 1, "Violence in Perspective," the nature and seriousness of American violence are portrayed from historical, contemporary, and comparative vantage points. At the end of the chapter, the case is presented for a reciprocal approach to the study of violence and nonviolence. In Chapters 2, 3, and 4, "Interpersonal Violence," "Institutional Violence," and "Structural Violence," demographic profiles are provided of the typical victims and victimizers for each of these types of violence. In each of these chapters, representative expressions of the various forms of violence are described, and case studies are used to depict both "life" and "death" and those points in between. The fullness of these illustrations allows readers to revisit the cases as in-depth examples of the concepts developed, elaborated upon, and articulated throughout the book.

Part II: Pathways to Violence consists of three chapters. In Chapter 5, "Explanations of Violence," an overview of the various explanations for violence and violent behavior is presented, beginning with the one-dimensional "ad-hoc" theories of violence, turning next to the "life-course" and "integrative-developmental" theories of violence, and finishing with a new "reciprocal" theory of violence. In Chapters 6 and 7, "Media and Violence" and "Sexuality and Violence," all types of relations are explored and examined, including mass-mediated violence and sexually explicit violence, in an effort to expose and move beyond the myth that mediated aggression causes adverse effects, into a world of commodification, full of its social meanings and representations about success, gender, and power that serve as cultural backdrops for both violence and nonviolence.

Part III: Pathways to Nonviolence consists of three chapters. In Chapter 8, "Recovering from Violence," voices of recovery are "discovered," and the stage is set in the last third of the book for an examination of the connections between violence, violence recovery, and nonviolence. In establishing the overlapping and intersecting pathways to recovery, this chapter provides a description and a discussion of representative cases of recovery from interpersonal, institutional, and structural forms of violence. In Chapter 9, "Models of Nonviolence," there are, first, discussions of the underlying assumptions of mutualism and the principles of cooperation, empathy, love, reciprocity, peacemaking, and resilience. Discussions follow on the struggle between mutualism and adversarialism, setting the stage for the final chapter on nonviolence and the transformation of justice. In Chapter 10, "Policies of Nonviolence," a summary of the major findings on violence is presented, followed by a critique of the limitations of traditionally based, interpersonal approaches to violence reduction, and ending with an introduction to the local and global emergence of alternatively based institutional and structural approaches to the production and reproduction of nonviolence.

REFERENCES

CNN Headline News [Television broadcast]. (2001, September 16). Atlanta, GA: Cable News Network.

Gilligan, J. (1997). *Violence: Reflections on a national epidemic.* New York: Vintage.

Hinds, M. deC. (2000). *Violent kids: Can we change the trend?* New York: National Issues Forums Institute and Public Agenda.

Kelly, K. D., & Totten, M. (2002). *When children kill: A social-psychological study of youth homicide.* Petersborough, Ontario, Canada: Broadview.

Lawrence, R., McLeod, J., McLeod, R., Birbilis, J., & Hines, D. (2000, November 17). *School violence: Identifying factors and characteristics of students at risk of violent behavior.* Paper presented at the annual meetings of the American Society of Criminology, San Francisco.

Males, M. A. (2001). *"Harper's index" of teenage myths.* Retrieved September 12, 2002, from http://home.earthlink.net/~mmales/Harpers.txt

Milbank, D., & Wax, E. (2001, September 18). Bush visits mosque to forestall hate crimes [Electronic version]. *Washington Post*, p. A01.

PBS Online. (2001). *Frontline: Juvenile justice: Basic statistics.* Retrieved September 12, 2002, from http://www.pbs.org/wgbh/pages/frontline/shows/juvenile/stats/basic.html

Roark, R. (1996, October). *The faces of poverty.* Retrieved October 12, 2002, from http://www.selfempowermentacademy.com.au/pdf/L3_LIVING_on_LIGHT/Glob_Journ/7-fop.PDF

Thompkins, D. (2000, January). School violence: Gangs and a culture of fear. *Annals of the American Academy of Political & Social Science, 567,* 54–72.

Welch, M. (2002, March). The politics of dead children: Have sanctions against Iraq murdered millions? *Reason-online.* Retrieved October 6, 2002, from http://www.reason.com/0203/fe.mw.the.shtml

Wilson, J. J. (2000). *Safe from the start: Taking action on children exposed to violence.* Washington, DC: Office of Juvenile Justice and Delinquency Prevention.

Wolfensohn, J. D. (2002, March 6). A partnership for development and peace. Remarks delivered to the Bretton Woods Committee and the U.S. State Department, Washington, DC.

Part I

TYPES OF VIOLENCE

CHAPTER 1

Violence in Perspective

It is most difficult, if not impossible, to fully grasp or actually locate violence "in perspective" because much of it remains hidden from or invisible to public eyes. On the other hand, much of it is overplayed, distorted, or sensationalized. Media commentators, for example, in the United States, Great Britain, and elsewhere depict their societies as engulfed in ever-rising tides of violence, chaos, and destruction. Anxieties of the modern and postmodern age are often contrasted with romantic notions of the good old days of "law and order." Historians, however, are quick to point out the relative continuities both in patterns of violent behavior and in society's responses to violence over time, acknowledging that the Middle Ages were more violent than our own contemporary period. At the same time, attitudes about violence may remain the same or change with the ages: stranger violence (violence perpetrated by strangers) has always been portrayed as a menace to society; while domestic and sexual violence, especially between intimates and acquaintances, has been viewed ambivalently to say the least.

As a substitute for knowing the factual extent and seriousness of violence in America or elsewhere, most scholars and other students rely on criminally classified violent behavior and on officially counted numbers from those designated categories reported to their governments. Although such data is woefully incomplete, it can nevertheless provide a useful calibration of some of the most obvious forms of violent behavior, especially when evaluated in combination with victimization and self-report surveys. Accordingly, with an eye focused on bringing forth the missing material of violence, this chapter begins by presenting a general idea of some of the recent trends in officially reported violent crime in the United States. It then moves to expand the discussion of "violence in perspective" through an overview of various historical and comparative sources of information.

Violent crimes as recorded by the police dropped in 2000 for the ninth consecutive year, representing the longest-running decline in violent crime since the Federal Bureau of Investigation began keeping records in 1960. In 1999, for example, homicides, rapes, robberies, and aggravated assaults fell a combined 7%, with slightly steeper declines in homicides and robberies than in rapes and assaults ("Serious crimes," 2000). In virtually every demographic category considered from 1993 to 1998, when almost half of all violent victimizations were reported to the police, violent victimization decreased (Rennison, 1999). During this period, for example, male violent victimization rates fell 39%, and black violent victimization rates fell 38%. In 1998, about half of the violent crime victims knew their offenders, more than 70% of rape or sexual assault victims knew their aggressors, and 50% of aggravated assault victims knew their perpetrators. In the same year, weapons were used in about a quarter of all violent victimizations, including about 2 out of 5 robberies and fewer than 1 in 10 rape or sexual assaults.

Variations in rates of violent crime are more generally influenced by the size of the community (e.g., big cities, rural areas, suburbs); the region of the country (e.g., West, Midwest, Northeast, South); and class, ethnicity, gender, and age compositions. For example, the F.B.I. reported that in 1999, homicide rates were down across the nation: 2% in cities over 500,000, 7% to 14% in smaller cities, 12% in the suburbs, and 17% in rural areas. In the same year, serious crime (which includes both property and violent crime) dropped 10% in the West, 8% in the Midwest, 7% in the Northeast, and 4% in the South ("Serious crimes," 2000). Perhaps more important, the nation's murder rate had, by 1998, reached its lowest level in three decades (6.3 per 100,000 people, compared to 4.5 per 100,000 in 1963), having peaked at just over 10 murders per 100,000 people in 1980 and again in the early 1990s, when gun homicides by teenagers and young adults were also peaking. Since 1993, teen homicides have fallen, as have the overall rates for murder. In cities with populations of more than 1 million, for example, the overall homicide rate fell from 35.5 per 100,000 inhabitants in 1991 to 16.1 per 100,000 in 1998 (Fox & Zawitz, 2000).

In a 1-year period, 1997 to 1998, the number of violent crimes per 1,000 persons age 12 or older declined demographically as follows: from 45.8 to 43.1 for males and from 33.0 to 30.4 for females; from 38.3 to 36.3 for whites, from 43.1 to 32.8 for Hispanics, and from 49.0 to 41.7 for blacks (Rennison, 1999). On average, between 1992 and 1997, for every 1,000 persons, those age 65 or older experienced about 5 violent crimes, those between 64 and 50 experienced about 18, those between 49 and 25 experienced about 48, and those younger than age 25 experienced over 100 (Klaus, 2000).

The tide in lowered homicide rates, however, had started to turn by the late 1990s. From 1997 to 1999, for example, the decrease in homicides was already slowing in the nation's largest cities—which is precisely where trends usually begin to rise and fall. These slowing trends in murder suggested to a number of experts that it would not be long before the rates leveled off and then reversed, going up. In fact, in New York City, the number of reported homicides had actually risen slightly by 1999, up to 671 from 633 the previous year ("Serious crimes," 2000). As of fall, 2001, trends in violent homicide overall had not reversed direction.

Unfortunately, these rates of officially reported violent crimes, as well as the actual numbers of recorded homicides, do not provide a perspective for grasping the relative seriousness either of violence in general or of any particular associated problem, such as family violence and child neglect. Nor do homicide rates and numbers by themselves provide any contexts necessary for making sense out of the reproduction of or reduction in violence, or for drawing any inferences about the reciprocal relationships between the pathways to violence and nonviolence. The biannual reports made available by the F.B.I. to the public on the "state" of crime and violence in America exclude a whole panoply of related and unrelated behaviors of interconnected expressions of violence.

Sanctioned and unsanctioned acts of violence are carried out by an assortment of individuals, groups, collectivities, institutions, and nation-states. Furthermore, the existing classification schemes for measuring some forms of violence ignore altogether the structural forms of violence that are part and parcel of the way in which societies, past and present, have been organized and stratified both locally and globally. When mediated attention is focused almost exclusively on the violence of the relatively powerless and away from the violence of the relatively powerful, a picture of violence emerges that is, at best, incomplete, and at worst, distorted and misguided.

Even if all the different measures and statistics on violence were in place, they would not begin to touch the human tragedy that violence is for both its victims and victimizers alike. To reemphasize, violence classification schemes do not provide much insight into the causes of violence and the ways it can be prevented, nor do they shed any light on the connections between the visible and invisible forms of violence—interpersonal, familial, institutional, and global. In short, a full-fledged study of violence calls for an alternative model of violence that includes both its sanctioned and unsanctioned forms.

SANCTIONED AND UNSANCTIONED VIOLENCE: AN ALTERNATIVE PERSPECTIVE

In *Violence, Inequality, and Human Freedom,* Iadicola and Shupe (1998) provide a conceptualization of violence that affords a comprehensive examination and dissection of violence in any society. These authors have divided the world of violence into three interacting spheres, domains, or contexts: (a) *interpersonal violence*—what happens between people acting in their private lives, without regard to occupational roles or formal institutions; (b) *institutional violence*—what happens within an institutional context vis-à-vis the action of institutional agents and others; and (c) *structural violence*—what happens within the context of establishing, maintaining, extending, and/or resisting hierarchy, privilege, and inequality (see Figure 1.1).

What follows is a nonexhaustive listing of examples of violence from each of the three fields.

INTERPERSONAL VIOLENCE

- Assault and battery
- Corporal punishment
- Homicide and murder
- Kidnapping
- Rape and sexual assault
- Robbery
- Suicide
- Verbal abuse, threat, and intimidation

INSTITUTIONAL VIOLENCE

- Family: child and elder abuse (i.e., physical, sexual, neglect), spousal abuse (i.e., battering, emotional taunting, marital rape)
- Economic: corporate and workplace abuse (i.e., distributing defective products, subjecting workers to unsafe or unhealthy conditions)
- Military: ranging from petty hazing of recruits to war crimes (i.e., torture and murder of civilian or noncivilian enemy populations)
- Religious: abuse in the name of religious organizations, sects, or beliefs (i.e., cultism, witch hunts, heresy persecutions, religion-based terrorism)
- State: abuse by authority (including criminal justice) of fundamental human rights (i.e., assassinations, discrimination, enslavement, genocide, state-supported terrorism)

STRUCTURAL VIOLENCE

The term *structural violence* refers to at least two kinds of group violence that are

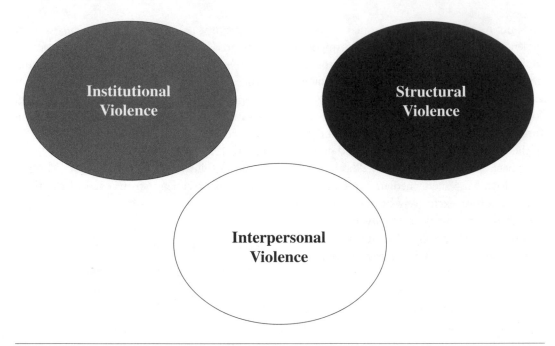

Figure 1.1 Three Contexts or Interactional Spheres of Violence

socially stirred in relation to the political and economic status quo.

1. One is allegedly for the purposes of establishing, defending, and/or extending hierarchy and inequality by the beating, exploiting, harassing, killing, and torturing of persons based on their age, class, ethnicity, gender, and/or sexual orientation (i.e., lynching, hate crime, terrorism).

2. The other is allegedly for the purposes of decreasing privilege and increasing liberty by resisting, protesting, and attacking those persons, symbols, or things that represent the established order, or "Establishment" (i.e., demonstrations, riots, terrorism).

At the same time, the domains of institutional and structural violence, in addition to the interpersonal forms of violence, overlap with and extend the boundaries of illegally or officially defined violence. Many definitions of and most inquiries into the study of

violence, unfortunately, are limited to legalistically narrow definitions that focus almost exclusively on the intent of the actions of individuals, ignoring altogether the latent consequences of institutionalized activities and policies that may or may not have reproduced the conditions of structural violence. For example, domestic violence, in its totality, is constituted by the interactions of (a) emotional, physical, and/or sexual abuse inflicted on at least one person by another person with whom he or she cohabitates, (b) the actions or nonactions of human service organizations (i.e., criminal justice and social welfare systems) responding to at least two parties in the cultural context of "private" and "public" relations, and (c) the structural arrangements of inequality and privilege as these shape or influence the familial experiences of children and adults.

Some definitions of violence even consciously exclude references to specific forms of violence. For example, "violence refers to

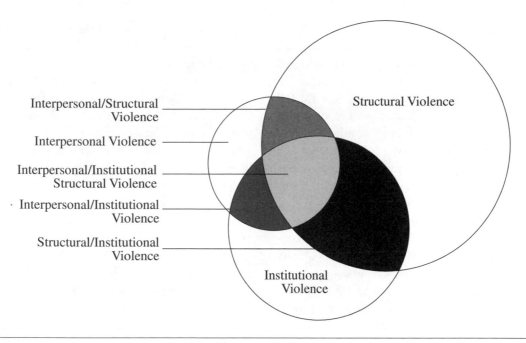

Figure 1.2   Intersections of the Three Spheres of Violence

the actual or threatened, knowing or intentional application of statutorily impermissible physical force by one person directly against one or more other persons outside the contexts both of formal institutional or organizational structures and of civil or otherwise collective disorders and movements for the purpose of securing some end against the will or without the consent of the other person or persons" (Weiner, 1989, pp. 37-38). Such definitions, of course, provide license, permission, or sanction for justifying and engaging in certain forms of "acceptable" violence.

These kinds of restrictive definitions of violence exclude not only the institutional and structural spheres of violence and violence-generating behavior, but even some of the interpersonal forms of violence, such as those inflicted by intimidation and emotional abuse. Similarly, there are other quasilegalistic formulations of violence that suggest a broader and more inclusive definition: "the threat, attempt, or use of physical force by one or more persons that results in physical or nonphysical harm to one or more persons" (Weiner, Zahn, & Sagi, 1990, p. xiii). Although this definition is an improvement on the one in the previous paragraph and expands the examination of interpersonal violence to include activities of groups and collectivities, there still remains the tendency to disregard structural forms of violence.

In most analyses of violence, only "deviant" or illegally defined forms of violence are considered violent. Violent perpetrators are too often represented as individuals who act alone or act as part of a marginal group, not as organizational functionaries, public or private, that act according to the accepted customs of various regimes of political and economic order. In short, "violence" typically refers to actions of individuals assaulting other individuals and the state; not to assaults of (our) government or of (our) corporations on citizens, consumers, or workers, and not to the overlapping realities of interpersonal, institutional, and structural forms of violence (see Figure 1.2).

In an attempt to be conceptually inclusive and to not exclude any of the forms and expressions of violence, I have adopted Iadicola and Shupe's (1998) simple definition of violence, which takes into account the full range of harms associated with a variety of interpersonal, institutional, and structural relationships and behaviors: "Violence is any action or structural arrangement that results in physical or nonphysical harm to one or more persons" (p. 26). In sum, the discourse of violence used here can refer to individual acts, institutional policies, and structural conditions. The various violent forms may or may not be against the law, criminal or civil. In either case, the injuries from these multifarious harms are no less (and often are more) painful and tragic to their victims (and victimizers) than those acts that have been defined as "illegally violent." Many differences between legitimate and illegitimate forms of violence are ideologically or morally constructed. They have more to do with variations in the extent of social outrage and in political denial or awareness of these and other forms of violence, harm, and victimization.

The rest of this chapter accomplishes three things: First, it characterizes violence in historical and contemporary America. Second, it situates the violence of the United States within a cross-cultural and global perspective. Third, it provides a rationale for a reciprocal approach to the study of violence and society.

VIOLENCE AS AN INTEGRAL PART OF AMERICAN LIFE

H. "Rap" Brown has been repeatedly quoted for having said in 1966, "Violence is necessary; it is as American as cherry pie." This statement reflects the violent realities and myths associated with this nation's birth and development. Born from two violent revolutions—the American War of Independence to overthrow colonialism and the Civil War to overthrow slavery—the early history of the United States is ripe with affirmative episodes of violence. In conjunction with an ideology of Manifest Destiny and a westward expansion achieved through force and frontier warfare and vigilantism, there is also a large amount of folklore populated with the celebrated outlaws of the Old West. Historically, violence has not been a matter of negativity alone. In fact, violence has been an American norm and a behavioral theme with positive as well as negative meanings.

On a daily basis, citizens of this country are exposed to violence in many forms, from contact sports to mass killings. Whether reading newspapers or magazines, listening to the radio or watching television, or going out to the movies, consumers find in violence a staple of both information and entertainment. Even globally, popular culture, East and West, certainly seems of late to cater to America's fascination with violence. This is not a new or recent development, however. Historically, most nations' art, media, and literature have been preoccupied with images and narratives of violence. Depictions of a violent United States in particular have always had an important presence in the American psyche. Similarly, it is relatively safe to claim that around the world violence has always been central to most peoples' psyches, especially when consciousness contemplates, fantasizes, and/or acts out certain forms of aggression and sexuality.

Today, however, because of the rapid fire of news coverage and instant telecommunication, lethal violence in particular seems to be pervading all settings all of the time. Despite America's declining rates in weapon assaults and homicides, mediated gunfire and bloodshed is simultaneously exploding everywhere, from inner city ghettos to rural school yards, from fast-food restaurants to postal office corridors. It is not a coincidence or a surprise that most people have a distorted, if not superficial, view of American violence. For the most part, this is because the average person lacks both historical and contemporary perspective. It is also the case because the average person lacks a comparative perspective.

AMERICAN VIOLENCE IN HISTORICAL PERSPECTIVE

For the purposes of this brief historical overview of violence in America, broad brush strokes are used to characterize the very loose patterns and trends in interpersonal violence, group violence, and institutionalized violence. Over the past two centuries, the trends have been toward lower levels of violence. As Ted Gurr (1990) has argued, to the extent that North America, from settlement to industrialization, was an extension of British culture and society, the underlying movement in violence has been downward. However, in culturally heterogeneous societies like the United States, "trends and cycles of interpersonal violence are instructive only about how disorderly society is, not about the social behavior of its constituent groups" (Gurr, 1990, p. 20).

The sparse availability of evidence shows for the most part that the Old West, or frontier America, was devoid of most forms of interpersonal violence, contrary to the many myths and images of television and motion pictures (McGrath, 1984). For example, bank robberies, rape, racial violence, and juvenile violence were virtually nonexistent. Armed robberies, burglaries, and thefts were infrequent and typically fewer in the frontier than in Eastern urban areas during the 19th century. On the other hand, homicides, especially shootings and shoot-outs among gamblers, bad men, and miners were fairly common events. Warfare between Native Americans and whites saw cruelty and savagery on both sides, and suicide rates among women were extraordinarily high. As McGrath (1984) concludes in his study of the mining towns around the Sierra Nevada, the lawlessness and violence took special forms and did not directly affect all activities or all people: "The old, the young, the unwilling, the weak, and the female—with the notable exception of the prostitute—were, for the most part, safe from harm" (p. 247).

The long downslope of interpersonal violence in the United States with respect to robberies, assaults, and homicides is irregular, and some of the irregularities have formed three sharp and sustained periods of increasing violence. These upsurges, or peaks, of violent crime have paralleled three distinct periods of American warfare: during the Civil War, the decade following World War I, and at the onset of the Vietnam War (Gurr, 1990). The most recent rise in interpersonal violence, experienced during the late 1980s and early 1990s, was not associated with any kind of sustained period of American warfare. After all, the Gulf War lasted only a few weeks. At the same time, one consequence of that conflict abroad and certain conflicts at home involving federal law enforcement agents, not the least of which were the incidents at Ruby Ridge, Idaho, and Waco, Texas, was the spawning of the likes of Timothy McVeigh and his infamous bombing of the federal building in Oklahoma City.

Over the past couple of decades, the historical record of group or collective violence in the United States has been fairly calm, with a few notable exceptions such as racially inspired protests and riots in reaction to the police use of deadly force in Los Angeles, Miami, New York, and Cincinnati. Until the recent period, political violence had been a staple of American society—from the Revolutionary War period to the rebellious days of the 1960s and 1970s. For example, New York City between 1788 and 1834 was disrupted by more than 70 political, ethnic, and labor clashes. Most of these mob attacks were relatively minor affairs. However, there were more than a dozen major riots over political and communal issues during that period that involved many hundreds of participants; some of those riots persisted for days at a time (Gurr, 1989).

With the exception of the Northeast, from the 1760s through the first decade of the 19th century, there were as many as 500 vigilante movements organized by local citizens in newly settled areas across the United States. These vigilantes dispensed a violent justice to renegades, horse thieves, claim jumpers, gunmen, and other rule breakers. In the South, during the decade after the abolishment of slavery, there were some 80 riots by whites against freed slaves and their Northern supporters. The establishment of white supremacy was also reinforced by the lynching of blacks in the South and elsewhere. The peak years of lynching, 1891 to 1901, saw more than 100 victims killed each year. In terms of the United States' bloody and violent labor history, hundreds of clashes between workers and employers occurred each decade from the 1870s to the 1930s.

One staple of interpersonal, institutional, and structural violence in American history, although marginally so, has been the constant presence of "hate crimes," whether directed at religious and ethnic minorities, political radicals, gays and lesbians, wife beaters, or others. From the postbellum period up to the 1960s, there were vigilante-like movements of social regulation, involving such groups as the Ku Klux Klan, the White Cappers, and the Black Legion, who performed whippings, arsons, bombings, and murders to instill fear and terror into the hearts and minds of their victims. This violent extremism of the "right" is still marginally alive in terms of its anti-Semitic and racist posturing and behavior today. Contemporary neo-Nazi groups include, for example, the Posse Comitatus and the Aryan

Nation. The goals of these and other like-minded groups have been to protect the way of life threatened by marginal Others.

On the other hand, most of the violent extremism from the "left" as well as from ethnically motivated activists was essentially confined to the protests of the 1960s and 1970s that were associated with issues of free speech, the Vietnam war, and racial and gender equality. For example, there were more than 500 race riots or rebellions that occurred in inner cities across the nation in the decade of the 1960s. At the same time, hundreds of antiwar demonstrations erupted on and off American university campuses. In the decade of the 1970s, acts of political terrorism by black militants, antiwar radicals, Puerto Rican nationalists, and a multitude of other groups peaked at more than 100 per year (Gurr, 1989). The goals of these and other groups were primarily about political empowerment and the expansion of rights to people traditionally denied them.

Other forms of interpersonal, institutional, and structural violence related to questions of inequality and privilege have also been part and parcel of the American experience. Although there are no actual lists, those populations which have been the most oppressed and dominated in this nation have always endured higher levels of violence than their "nonoppressed" middle-class constituent counterparts. In the past, there were the enslaved and indentured persons of colonial and early American history, as well as the victims of oppression throughout the antebellum period and later periods of "separate but equal" in the South and elsewhere. In the contemporary era, there is the higher rate of infant mortality among black and brown Americans—more than twice the rate for whites. There are also the significantly higher rates of disease, hunger, homelessness, murder, and incarceration for marginal peoples, accompanied by lower rates of longevity and development of physical, spiritual, and intellectual potential (Barak, 1991b; Barak, Flavin, & Leighton, 2001).

AMERICAN VIOLENCE IN CONTEMPORARY PERSPECTIVE

The following depictions are meant to be representative and not exhaustive of the various forms of violence in contemporary America. For example, interpersonal descriptions include suicide and homicide; institutional descriptions include domestic and workplace violence; and structural descriptions include corporate, hate, and state violence.

Suicide

Suicide, a growing social problem in the United States, is one of those hidden and rarely talked about forms of violence. It has been argued that today's high annual rates of suicide represent a public health crisis about which the public is in a state of conspicuous denial. In fact, suicide ranks second in causes of death for college students (after accidents), and it is the third leading cause of death (after homicides and accidents) for young people generally. In 1997, more young people died from suicide than from AIDS, cancer, stroke, pneumonia, influenza, birth defects, and heart disease combined; including 4,186 deaths among those 15 to 24 years old and 5,075 among those 25 to 34 years old (Centers for Disease Control and Prevention, 1997).

Half a million Americans are taken to hospitals every year because of suicide attempts, and the rate of suicide is climbing steadily. One study found that the likelihood in the 1990s of a young man committing suicide was 260% higher than in the 1950s. Another study found that half of those who have been diagnosed with manic-depressive illness will make a suicide attempt, and that 1 out of 5

people with major depression will do the same (Jamison, 1999). It has also been shown that the most successful method for killing oneself, especially among teenagers, is with a handgun (Putnam, 2000). Related to the self-inflicted violence of suicide is "self-mutilation" (i.e., cutting, burning), practiced by an estimated 1.5 to 2.0 million people, especially adolescent middle-class white girls, as a way of expressing their anguish and anger ("Hidden addictions," 2000).

Class, Ethnicity, and Gender Violence

Contemporary interpersonal violence involving two or many persons more generally expresses itself in a variety of forms not limited to street, domestic, youth, gender, or racial violence. It is often difficult to separate the overlapping relations of these forms of violence (see Box 3.1). Overall, as already noted, violent crime rates, inclusive of rape, robbery, aggravated and simple assault, and homicide declined generally in the 1990s. However, when differentiated by gender, race, or class, official rates of these forms of violence have varied from a little to a lot. For example, the approximate 31% decrease in serious, violent crime between 1994 and 1998 affected men much more than women. Not only was the decline in the victimization rate for women less than 15% during this period, it remained slightly higher than the levels of the 1970s.

When it came to intimate homicide (see Box 2.6), men continued to kill their partners at about the same rate as they did a quarter of a century ago, although it did appear that a downward trend for women as victims began around 1994. On the other hand, the long-term downward shift in the number of men killed by their intimate partners was much steeper (Chaiken, 2000). In sum, U.S. homicides of intimates by gender for the years 1976 through 1997 revealed that the number of men killed declined from a little over 1,400 to below 500 per year, while the number of women killed declined from about 1,600 to around 1,250 (Fox & Zawitz, 1999).

Kandel Englander (1997) reports that there were 1,848,520 cases of assault recorded by the National Crime Survey for 1992 and 24,526 murders reported in the 1993 Uniform Crime Report. About 15% of those murders involved people who did not know each other: The vast majority of the victims were killed by family members rather than by strangers. The National Crime Survey data on behavioral assault, however, confound the beliefs of most criminologists and other students of violence.

Two thirds of the assault victims canvassed during the 1992 National Crime Survey reported that they did not know their perpetrator. About half of these victims were women. This contradicts most of the research on victimization, which discloses that most assaults occur between people who know each other and that most of the victims are men. The National Crime Survey numbers would thus seem to suggest that many victims of domestic assault were either unable or unwilling to report the assault to the interviewers from the National Institute of Justice. If not that, then these women did not consider or conceptualize their domestic abuses or victimizations to have been cases of criminal assault. Whatever the reality, the number of officially reported cases of stranger assault extrapolated for 1992 was ½ of 1% of the U.S. population. Further, most of these occurrences were considered to be simple rather than aggravated assault (Kandel Englander, 1997).

The images of violence associated with weapons and great physical harm portrayed in contemporary media also appear to be exaggerated, as a small percentage of people are actually injured, let alone seriously injured, through typical incidents of assault.

According to a 1993 publication of the Bureau of Justice Statistics (BJS), of all the violent crimes reported in one study, less than a third involved a weapon of any kind. Similarly, relatively few violent victimizations resulted in serious injury (4%) and fewer than 25% of the victims received injuries of any kind. In short, "less than about 3 out of every 1,000 violent crime victims [were] shot, about 12 [were] wounded by a knife, and about 20 or so [had] broken bones or teeth knocked out. . . . only 9 percent of all victims of violent crime lost any time from work, and only 10 percent incurred medical expenses" of any kind (Kappeler, Blumberg, & Potter, 1996, p. 46).

Turning to interpersonal cases of sexual, gender, and domestic violence, it is most difficult to arrive at more than rudimentary figures for these acts. Few would disagree that acts of harassment, battering, and rape continue to be among the types of assaults least likely to be reported, especially among women in their teens or early 20s. For example, when the BJS compared the results of the National Crime Victimization Survey (NCVS) with the more sophisticated methods used in surveys conducted by the National Institute of Justice, the Centers for Disease Control and Prevention, and other BJS research, it became clear that many crimes of harassment, battering, and rape remained uncounted by the NCVS (Chaiken, 2000). Moreover, it is highly unlikely that any of these surveys include those thousands of young people, especially runaway girls, who are subject to verbal abuses, physical beatings, and rapes annually by "pimps, players, and johns" (Hodgson, 1997).

Nevertheless, according to the more sophisticated surveys, rape rates in the United States from 1973 to 1998, for an adjusted victimization rate per 1,000 people 12 years old and older, officially declined from 2.5 to .08. Such figures, however, unless they are broken down by subpopulations of women, can be highly misleading. As Chaiken (2000) has underscored,

> When we examine particular population subgroups, we find some categories of women who are more likely than men to be victims of crime. Women college students, for example, are at greater risk of victimization than women who are not in college. On the whole, the victimization of college women by crimes other than sexual assault is approximately the same as that for men, but women are in addition the primary victims of sexual assault. (p. 13)

Similarly, poor women and women of color are more likely than middle or upper class white women to become victims of violence.

For example, a 1999 study by the U.S. Department of Justice found that rates of sexual abuse against Native American women were the highest in the nation (Greenfeld & Smith, 1999). Seven Native American women out of 1,000 had been victims of rape or sexual assaults annually, compared with 3 blacks and 2 whites per 1,000. One of the most interesting findings from this study was that 9 out of 10 of the incidents of rape or sexual assault against Native American women were committed by non-Indians. Comparatively, this finding differs radically with the sexual attacks of white women, who were victimized 70% of the time by white men, and for black women, who were victimized 81% of the time by black men.

Domestic Violence

What does the picture look like when we focus more specifically on the institutionalized forms of domestic or gendered violence? In these domains, violence usually occurs within the family and/or dating relationships. These forms of violence typically include child abuse, date abuse, and marital (spouse)

abuse. Each of these forms of abuse is neither separate nor isolated from the others. Within, between, and over generations, these forms of violent behavior blend, overlap, and develop in relation to one another. At the same time, these forms of interpersonal and institutional violence cannot be disconnected from their cultural and structural roots of privilege and inequality, expressed through the social arrangements of private property and patriarchy both inside and outside the United States.

Child abuse generally refers to four kinds of abuse: physical, sexual, emotional (including verbal and psychological), and neglect. As with other forms of intimate or private abuse such as spousal rape, adequate estimates are difficult to come by, as many, if not a majority, of these acts of violence never come to the attention of authorities or researchers. Furthermore, with the exception of sexual abuse, there is often a lack of consensus and disagreement over the meaning of child abuse. For example, most people exclude corporal punishment from child physical abuse, removing "discipline" from abuse, by (usually) distinguishing among the objects (e.g., an open hand, a belt) used for inflicting pain and the type of physical injuries (e.g., broken arms versus minor bruises or cuts) incurred.

Probably what ties these forms of abuse together most is the emotional maltreatment and trauma, stemming from both the relative powerlessness and the associated degradation and humiliation of these victim experiences. Estimates for neglect (which appear to parallel poverty) and for emotional abuse are pretty much nonexistent. Estimates for the physical abuse of children in the 1980s and 1990s, depending on how physical violence was defined, ranged from 1.5 to 6.9 million per annum (Kandel Englander, 1997; Straus & Gelles, 1990). With respect to child sexual abuse, 25% to 33% of women and approximately 10% of men have recalled being sexually molested as children (Finkelhor, 1988; Russell, 1983). In general, compared to the victimization of adults, that of juveniles is underreported, with the exception of sexual victimization. Although there are more than a few reasons for this underreporting of physical violence, Finkelhor and Ormrod (1999) have concluded that "there is a cultural predisposition, shared by parents, youth, and the police, to view nonsexual assaults against juveniles" as something other than acts or crimes of violence; less offensive language is preferred, such as "fights, scuffles, or child maltreatment" (p. 5).

Youth Violence

This normalization of violence for youth, along with the presence of corporal punishment in the socialization experiences of many American children, suggests that there may be a connection here to the higher rates of antisocial behavior for these children. Five longitudinal studies (Straus, 1994; Straus, Sugarman, & Giles-Sims, 1997) have found that when parents used corporal punishment to reduce antisocial behavior, the long-term effects tended to be the opposite. Conversely, it was also found that avoiding corporal punishment resulted in enhanced cognitive development, less disruptive behavior, and less violence perpetrated against dating partners by teenagers. In general, despite the rapid decline of the use of corporal punishment by parents on their children after the age of 5 years, from a peak of 94% at 3 and 4 years to just over half by the time the children are 12 years old, a third at 14 years, and 13% at 17 years, it was found that parents who hit teenage children did so on an average of about six times per year. Moreover, severity, as measured by hitting the child with a belt or a paddle, was greatest for children 5 to 12 years old (at a rate of 28%). It was also found that corporal punishment was more prevalent among African American parents and parents of low socioeconomic status, in the South, for boys, and by mothers (Straus & Stewart, 1999).

With respect to gendered violence and youth, one study using longitudinal data from more than 4,500 high school seniors and dropouts from California and Oregon revealed a commonness of violence among youth generally: More than half the sample had engaged in some kind of violence, and 1 in 4 had committed predatory violence. Although boys were more likely to engage in all types of violence and in violence outside the home, both boys and girls were equally prone to violence within the family. Violent teenagers, especially boys, were generally more likely than nonviolent youths to have experienced additional emotional and behavioral problems, such as poor mental health, use of drugs, school dropout, and commission of other nonviolent felonies (Ellickson, Saner, & McGuigan, 1997).

Placing juvenile violence into some kind of general or contemporary perspective is not easy. For example, between 1984 and 1992, the number of juveniles arrested for homicide who were under 15 years old increased by 50%, and youths 10 to 17 years old, who accounted for 11% of the U.S. population during this time, were responsible for 16% of violent felonies (Greenwood, 1995). Consistent with these figures, the 1998 National Youth Gang Survey reported that in randomly selected samples from large, small, medium, urban, rural, and suburban police and sheriff departments, 48% of the respondents reported active youth gangs in their jurisdiction, compared with 51% in 1997 and 53% in 1996 (Moore & Cook, 1999). On the other hand, in 1994, when officially recorded juvenile crimes were at their highest and when 3 to 4 out of every 10 boys growing up in urban America were being arrested (Greenwood, 1995), "94 percent of the approximately 69 million youth under the age of 18 had never been arrested" (p. 92).

Additionally, "less than 10 percent of delinquents commit violent crime," and "five out of six youth referred to juvenile court for violent crime do not commit a subsequent violent offense" ("An evolving," 1999, pp. 7-8).

The seriousness of school violence is also difficult to evaluate (see Boxes 2.11 and 2.12). During the 1990s, there was a wave of gun violence in junior and senior high schools across the nation that included the killings of students, teachers, and parents: Peal, Mississippi (October 1, 1997); West Paducah, Kentucky (December 1, 1997); Jonesboro, Arkansas (March 24, 1998); Edinboro, Pennsylvania (April 24, 1998); Springfield, Oregon (May 21, 1998); and Littleton, Colorado (April 21, 1999). All totaled, there were 25 dead in 1997, 42 dead in 1998, and 24 in 1999 as a result of these incidents (Hinkle & Henry, 2000). Preliminary results of a study reported by the National School-Associated Violent Death Study Group indicated that between 1994 and 1998, approximately 200 school-associated violent deaths were identified, broken down as follows: 83% were homicides, 13% were suicides, and 4% were combination homicides/suicides (Hammond, 1999).

As it turned out, the number of school-associated violent deaths in the 1990s had reached an all-time high. A national victimization survey conducted by the U.S. Department of Justice (Bureau of Justice Statistics, 1998) reported a 25% increase in violent victimization of high school students between 1989 and 1995; however, a national self-report survey of high school students between 1991 and 1997 found a 20% decrease in the number of students injured in fights, as well as decreased involvement in fighting and weapon-carrying behavior (Brener, Simon, Krug, & Lowry, 1999). So although lethal violence was up during this period, it appears that nonlethal violence was down.

Gun Violence

Opponents of gun control are quick to point out that "guns don't kill, people do." Criminologists are not so quick to speak. However, upon reflection, most would say that "people don't kill, events do." In other words, when it comes to gun violence, criminologists will point out that this type of violence, like many other forms, is usually part of some kind of event or interactional transition involving specific contexts (e.g., "hot spots" such as liquor clubs or bars), attempted crimes gone wrong (e.g., drug deals or robberies), and objects (e.g., cheating spouses caught in the act; drug or alcohol abuse) frequently associated or correlated with situations of violence. Guns, too, are actually objects; they are not types of violence per se. At the same time, in a recently published study, Wells and Horney (2002) found "evidence of weapons effects that exist[ed] regardless of individual differences among assailants and regardless of a person's situation-specific intent to do harm" (p. 292).

Guns are also about expressive or instrumental violence. Surveys from incarcerated felons disclose that their primary purpose for carrying a weapon was to expedite the offense, to escape, or both. The most frequent reasons given for using a gun were to scare the victims (54%), for protection (30%), to kill the victim (14%), and to get away (12%) (Reidel & Welsh, 2002). Most of these felons had acquired their guns from nonretail sources, such as from their families, illegal markets, or thefts (Wright & Rossi, 1985).

For some sort of perspective on gun violence, one needs at a minimum to have a sense of the size of the problem. According to the NCVS, some 670,500 victims of serious violent crimes faced an offender with a firearm in 1998 (Bureau of Justice Statistics, 2000a). Of the 2.9 million violent crimes of rape and sexual assault, robbery, and aggravated assault for that year, 23% of the victimizations occurred with a firearm. Yet, the U.S. Department of Justice (Bureau of Justice Statistics, 2000b) found that the number of crimes committed with firearms declined dramatically from 1993 to 1998, falling to levels last experienced in the mid-1980s. At the same time, Uniform Crime Report data from 1997 revealed that two thirds (68%) of the 18,209 murders that occurred that year were committed with a firearm. Likewise, in 1998, "about 65 percent of all murders, 32 percent of all robberies, and 19 percent of all aggravated assaults reported to the police were committed with a firearm" (Reidel & Welsh, 2002, p. 297).

In repeated surveys, juveniles report having easy access to guns. Weapons arrest rates back them up. Per 100,000 population, the highest arrest rates are for teens, males, and blacks (Bureau of Justice Statistics, 2000a). Juvenile arrests for weapons-law violations doubled between 1987 and 1993. During the same period, gun homicides by juveniles in the United States tripled, although homicides involving other weapons declined. "From 1983 through 1995, the proportion of homicides in which a juvenile used a gun increased from 55 percent to 80 percent" (Reidel & Welsh, 2002, p. 300).

Sexual Violence

Dating, cohabitating, and marital violence typically refer to both physical and sexual abuse. In terms of violence in dating relationships, for example, about 20% of college students surveyed admitted to some kind of physical victimization (Kandel Englander, 1997); approximately 20% to 28% of college women surveyed admitted to having been forced into some sort of sexual encounter against their will, but only 5% to 15% of college males admitted to such behavior (Koss, Gidycz, & Wisniewski, 1987).

As for wife-to-husband abuse and husband-to-wife abuse, the 1985 National Family Victimization Survey revealed that 3.4% of couples could be characterized as "wife beating" and that 4.8% of couples could be characterized as "husband beating," meaning that at least 1.8 million women and 2.6 million men were assaulted by their intimates in 1985. This does not address the severity of beatings or types of injuries inflicted.

Men's assaults tended to be more offensive than defensive; women's tended to be more defensive than offensive. Injuries sustained by women were also greater than those sustained by men (Kander Englander, 1997). It is difficult to obtain reliable figures for marital rape. Nevertheless, using extrapolated data from Russell's (1983) study on the percentages of women experiencing a completed or attempted rape (ranging from 25% to 35%) with Kilpatrick's (1993) data, which suggested that some 40% of all rapes were perpetrated by husbands or other male live-in companions, Kandel Englander (1997) estimated that some 14.4 million women were victims of marital rape each year out of an overall, estimated total figure of 36 million rapes. These figures were significantly higher than the average number of sexual assaults, 840,000, reported to official law enforcement agencies during those same years.

Violence Against the Elderly

Data on violent acts committed against the elderly by non–family members is both easier to come by and more accurate than data regarding violence perpetrated by family members. U.S. rates of nonfatal violence against persons 65 years old or older declined from 1973 to 1997, as did rates of murder after 1976. These declines paralleled similar declines for all age groups, except for that group between 12 and 24 years old, for which the rates of murder fluctuated. In general, the elderly were much less susceptible to violence than were people younger than 65 years old. For example, from 1992 to 1997, violent crime rates for the elderly were about a 10th (5.3 acts per 1,000) the rate for persons younger than 65 years old. Among elderly victims during this period, men experienced lethal and nonlethal violence at rates that were about twice the level for women; blacks experienced higher rates than whites; and Hispanics experienced higher rates than non-Hispanics. In terms of homicide, about 3 per 100,000 persons 65 years old or older were murdered, making them one fifth and one third as likely, respectively, to be murdered as persons 12 to 24 and 25 to 49 years old. With respect to violence in the family, there were annually about 500 deaths and 36,000 injuries inflicted on elderly persons either by a relative, an intimate, or a close acquaintance (Klaus, 2000). An earlier survey of older Americans conducted in the late 1980s yielded a much higher estimate of around 1 million cases of elder abuse per year (Pillemer & Finkelhor, 1988).

Workplace Violence

If getting a handle on some of the already reviewed forms of violence is difficult, the situation regarding workplace violence is even more so. The relations and interactions involving daily life and workplace violence are complex. To begin with, there are several kinds of social activities that constitute violence in the workplace. Fundamentally, there are three definitions of workplace violence that correspond with the interpersonal, institutional, and structural fields of violence. As Brownstein (2000) points out:

> Workplace violence could be the product of what workers do, as in the case of workers who physically assault coworkers or consumers. Or workplace violence could be

what happens to workers at their workplace, such as accidents that are the result of intentional negligence by management. Or workplace violence could be viewed in terms of the impact on workers, consumers, or the public generally as a result of corporate decisions and actions, such as death or disease related to the intentional dumping of toxic waste. (p. 157)

The problem with measuring workplace violence is that most discussions ignore the institutional and structural meanings of worker violence, focusing mostly, if not exclusively, on the interpersonal meanings, which may or may not have anything to do with the workplace. For example, the Bureau of Labor Statistics conducts an annual Census of Fatal Occupational Injuries that is used to arrive at the number of workplace homicides committed each year in the United States. In 1995, 1,024 workplace homicides were reported. Seventy-one percent of those involved a robbery or other crime, and only 11% (113 persons killed) involved a conflictive relationship between work associates. Of the total number of homicides reported by the Bureau of Labor Statistics, 80% involved wage and salary workers, 76% involved males, 65% involved whites, and 74% involved shootings (Brownstein, 2000).

In terms of a mass psychology of workplace violence as interpersonal, the *Los Angeles Times* reported in November 1999 that "more than half of American companies have experienced at least one incident of workplace violence in the past three years" ("Survey: Companies," 1999). According to the Society for Human Resource Management, which surveyed 651 companies, shootings and stabbings accounted for 2% of all incidents of workplace violence in these companies, pushing and shoving 19%, and verbal threats 41%. Of all reported incidents in these companies, 55% involved "personality conflicts," and only 8% were directed by an employee against a supervisor.

The findings also revealed that 76% of the aggressors were men and 45% of the victims were women. Finally, firings had occurred in 18% of the cases, and 24% were attributed to work-related stress.

In his analysis of homicide in the American workplace from 1980 to 1989, Kellecher (1996) concluded that of all fatalities in the workplace, homicide accounted for only 12%; automobile accidents accounted for 24%. In terms of the numbers of workers who have experienced nonlethal violence in the workplace, the BJS, using data from the NCVS, concluded that for the period 1992 to 1996 there were about 1.5 million simple assaults and 396,000 aggravated assaults (Warchol, 1998). In combining rates of lethal and nonlethal violence in the workplace, the BJS also concluded that these assaults represented only about 15% of all violent victimization reports that it receives annually (Bachman, 1994).

By comparison, the number of victims of interpersonal, intentional workplace violence is small in relation to the number of institutional and "ostensibly unintentional deaths and injuries involving people simply doing their jobs in the workplace" (Brownstein, 2000, p. 159). According to the National Safety Council (1997), more than 126 million workers in all industries suffered unintentional injuries at work in 1996, including 4,800 who died and 3.9 million who suffered a disabling injury. In sum, there were 1,024 intentional (interpersonal) and 4,800 unintentional (institutional) deaths and 1.5 million interpersonal (intentional) and 126 million institutional (unintentional) injuries in the workplace in 1996.

Corporate, Hate, and State Violence

The social activities that constitute corporate violence represent a structural form of violence because they are organizationally based and intended to benefit the corporation at the physical expense of the employees, consumers, and general public. The result of deliberate decision making by corporate executives, these harms accrue from the production of "unreasonable risks" and from negligent and willful violations of health, safety, and environmental laws in the quest for profits at any cost (Hills, 1987; Kramer, 1983). Estimates of actual and potential harms and injuries from the "faulty" engineering and/or testing associated with the Ford Pinto gas tank, Three-Mile Island, the Challenger disaster, or the Bhopal incident suggest that the risk and dangers from corporate-structural violence may, in fact, be greater than those from other forms of workplace violence.

I will briefly review two other forms of structural violence, hate violence and state violence, before trying to place violence in the United States in a cross-cultural, comparative perspective.

True to the nature of structural violence, the injuries and harms that result from both hate and state violence are primarily the product of efforts to maintain order, privilege, and inequality. During the 1980s and 1990s, bias-motivated violent acts became legally recognized as "hate crimes," transforming previous injuries perpetrated by select private groups into public issues of justice, punishment, and compensation. Specifically selected for "bias crimes" victim status were people who had been consistently subjected to violence and bigotry based on their race, ethnicity, religion, gender, or sexual orientation: people of color, Jews, immigrants, women, gays and lesbians, and people with disabilities (Jenness & Broad, 1997).

Based on data from the Uniform Crime Report, preliminary figures for 1995 revealed 7,947 hate crime incidents, 10,469 victims, and 8,433 known offenders. Of the known offenders, 59% were white and 27% were black; the remaining 14% of offenders were of "other" or multiracial groups. Sixty-one percent of the incidents were motivated by racial bias, 16% by religious bias, 13% by bias against sexual orientation, and 10% by bias against ethnicity or national origin. Crimes against persons accounted for 72% of hate crimes reported, almost half of which were for the crime of intimidation. Eighteen percent were for simple assaults, and 13% were for aggravated assaults. For the year, there were 20 murders and 12 forcible rapes attributable to hate violence (U.S. Department of Justice, Federal Bureau of Investigation, Criminal Justice Information Services Division, 1995).

State violence refers generally to the abuse of power by the government or by its authorized or unauthorized agents against domestic citizens or citizens of other countries. State violence usually assumes the forms of assaults, intimidations, kidnappings, tortures, and assassinations (Barak, 1991a). Typically, such actions are carried out in violation of the democratic rule of law by the police, the courts, or institutions of penal sanction and reform. In the United States, although there have been several high-profile police beatings and killings, as well as numerous complaints against the abuse of force by various law enforcement agencies, the actual frequency of these episodes is rare (Kappeler et al., 1996). With respect to wrongful prosecutions, convictions, and state executions, the estimated numbers have also been quite small. Since 1973, when the death penalty was reinstated by the U.S. Supreme Court, 87 death-row inmates have been freed or exonerated (Johnson, 2000). The victimization and violence experienced by inmates may be of more significance.

Prisoners, in addition to the usual "pains of imprisonment" (Sykes, 1958), have been commonly subjected to psychological victimization in the forms of intimidation, sexual extortion, robbery, and blackmail, mostly at the hands of other inmates, but also at the hands, directly and indirectly, of some guards and staff members. Data in these areas have been extremely unreliable, as researchers have found, for example, that only 3% of prison sexual assaults are ever officially reported. Consequently, some criminologists have concluded that there are very few acts of sexual coercion in prison (Kappeler et al., 1996). However, there are a number of penologists who have been a bit closer to prison environments, and they have maintained that there are very few male inmates who have not been involved in some kind of involuntary sexual behavior behind bars, either as perpetrators or as victims (Cotton & Groth, 1984; Dumond, 1992; Rideau & Wikberg, 1992). Either way, the high levels of violence in American penal institutions may be attributed—aside from the obvious presence of a high percentage of dangerous persons—to heterosexual deprivation, inadequate supervision by correctional staff, and systems of control that promote rather than inhibit inmate exploitation.

In a similar vein, inmates have experienced social victimization, especially in the form of physical assaults, for belonging to various ethnic, racial, religious, and gang-related groups. Although statistics are not kept on this kind of prison violence, some researchers have estimated that inmates are 20 times more likely to be assaulted annually than are those persons living outside of prisons (Klofas, 1992). In addition, over the last couple of decades, the majority of states have experienced severe overcrowding in their institutions, a situation widely considered to contribute to the high levels of prison violence.

AMERICAN VIOLENCE IN COMPARATIVE PERSPECTIVE

Cross-cultural and comparative analyses reveal similarities as well as dissimilarities within and between developing and developed nation-states. For example, the incidents and trends of violence in the United States are not the same as those in seemingly comparable developed states, such as Germany, Japan, or Italy (Barak, 2000). Because the histories of these countries and their peoples are not one and the same, there are differences in the dynamics of their social and political relations that are linked to the varying levels of violence within and across societies. Making reference to these relations of social and cultural difference in violence does not simplify matters, however.

Cultures are, after all, far more elusive than anthropological concepts would suggest. First, because of the tendency to generalize when talking about cultures, observed descriptions rarely capture the accuracy and depth of intricacy that is required to get at the nuances of individuals and subgroups. Second, because the boundaries between cultural, cross-cultural, and other social influences on individual and collective behavior are frequently imprecise and overlapping, it is often difficult to disentangle the personal from the communal (Cottrol, 1998). The details of such influences, as well as the associated issues raised by questions of nature and nurture, for example, on mediated and real violence or on sexuality and aggression, will be examined in Chapters 6 and 7. In this section, the objective is restricted to situating homicide and the American experience with this form of lethal violence within the limited cross-national and global context of interpersonal violence.

It is now regularly assumed by most scholars that interpersonal violence in the Western world has essentially declined over the past 500 years. As the editors of *The Civilization of Crime: Violence in Town and Country since the Middle Ages* (Johnson & Monkkonen, 1996) concluded:

(1) Violent crime has decreased over the last five centuries; (2) violence was a common and often tolerated, if not fully accepted, form of dispute settlement in the rural areas and villages that dominated premodern society; (3) a major drop in violent crime in most countries took place in the seventeenth and eighteenth centuries; (4) this drop was associated with a "civilizing process" whereby dispute settlement was gradually worked out in court more often than in potentially deadly brawls in taverns and street corners—the growth of the state's power and monopoly over violence helped to retard interpersonal violence [even if it did contribute to an expansion of state violence]; (5) throughout the centuries as today, women have been far less prone to violence than men, but urban women have been more often involved in violence than have rural women, suggesting that their behavior has been quite different from that of men, whose violent acts were a more common feature of the countryside than of the town; (6) cities have not usually had exceptionally high crime rates in most societies in the past. (p. 13)

Of course, the United States came of age as a nation-state in the 19th century, well after the "civilizing process" was thought to have occurred in Europe. In terms of support for the general thesis of declining violence, the homicide rates in this country were already comparatively smaller (i.e., 4.0 and 2.2 per 100,000 in Philadelphia in the 1850s and 1890s, respectively) than what they had been in Europe only a century before. In New York City, the relatively high homicide rates dropped from 14 per 100,000 in 1860 to 4 in 1960 (Butterfield, 1994). However, these official homicide rates "naturally" ignore or exclude the unofficial rates of institutional and structural lethal violence of the period. These "homicides," in the forms of genocide, slavery, and lynching, were perpetrated against Native Americans, African Americans, Chinese Americans, and others.

Moreover, the rates (20 per 100,000) of homicide in late Medieval England and

France were about 2.5 times higher than the average rates of 8 per 100,000 in the United States during the 1990s. This was at a time when America's homicide rates were from 2.5 to more than 7 times higher than those of most developed democracies worldwide (Messner & Rosenfeld, 1993). In Mexico in 1992 and in Russia in 1993, the homicide rates were 16.2 and 19.5 per 100,000, respectively (Cottrol, 1998). At the beginning of the 21st century, the homicide rates in Western Europe hovered around 2.0 per 100,000. In some Eastern European countries, by contrast, rates were often in the teens (Barak, 2000). U.S. homicide rates, by comparison, were about 6 per 100,000 population.

These national comparisons, however, do not take into account the ethnic, racial, regional, or microcultural variations that exist despite the same set of dominant values or codes of behavior. For example, during most of the second half of the 20th century, homicide rates for blacks were from six to seven times higher than those of whites; although it was not until around 1910 that black homicide rates exceeded white homicide rates. In the mid-1990s, there was also great variability in homicide rates by geographic region and within microcultural groups (e.g., black females, Asian males, Hispanic boys). Even within similar groupings, wide variations in the levels of homicide can exist. In 1995, for instance, the white male homicide rate in Minnesota was 2.8, in Mississippi it was 15.5, and nationwide it was at 8.5 (Cottrol, 1998).

When one comparatively examines rates for other officially recorded forms of violence (e.g., assault, rape), one finds that by the turn of this century the U.S. rates for nonlethal violence were not any higher than they were in most other postindustrial developed nations, and they were certainly lower than in developing nations (Barak, 2000). And although national rates of lethal violence (e.g., homicide, suicide) were higher in America than they were in other advanced democratic states, this does not mean that men and women, people of color, old and young, gay and straight, and so on and so forth, experience the same rates or odds of violence. For Americans in general, the risks of most forms of violence, including homicide, are no greater than in any other part of the world. The overall rates of violence in America are still too high and undesirable, especially because of the ways in which these illegal and legal forms of violence differentially affect neighborhoods and communities.

From a comparative perspective, then, the history of American violence, domestic and international, is a relative phenomenon, subject both to the definitions of violence and to the personal situations, social experiences, and power relations of status interaction. Individually and collectively, these historical sites of violent interaction break down the national experience into microcultural occurrences, reflective of such factors as age, class, race and ethnicity, gender, and religion. Located in these differential contexts are the links to various types of interpersonal, institutional, and structural forms of violence.

A RECIPROCAL APPROACH TO STUDYING VIOLENCE

Since violence takes many forms—individual, interpersonal, family, group, mass, collective, organizational, bureaucratic, institutional, regional, national, international, and structural—it makes sense to study the interrelations and interactions between these. Most analyses of violence, however, tend to focus on one particular form of violence without much, if any, reflection on the other forms. In turn, these fragmented and isolated analyses seek to explain the workings of a given form of violence without trying to understand the common threads or roots that may link various forms of violence together. Furthermore, many of these "unreflexive" analyses of violence have also adopted a commonsense view, shared in the United States and in virtually all contemporary advanced societies, that makes ethical distinctions between "positive" and "negative" violence, "acceptable" and "unacceptable" violence, and "legitimate and illegitimate" violence.

These dichotomies, for example between "legal" and "illegal" violence or between "private" and "public" violence, are based on systems of morality and politics rather than on systems of science and knowledge (Gilligan, 1997). What are required are studies of violence and nonviolence that are not only inclusive but appreciative of the reciprocal influences between the various spheres, domains, or contexts of violence. As used in this book, *reciprocal influences* refers to (a) determinants that move alternately forward and backward between nonviolence and violence, (b) mutually responsive and inversely corresponding pathways of violence and nonviolence, and (c) crossroads that are equivalent for both violence and nonviolence. In different words, integrative and reciprocal kinds of analyses of violence and nonviolence recognize the interactive, accumulative, and synergistic natures of these levels of social engagement. These analyses also seek out the mutual, parallel, and interdependent connections between the varieties of violence and the types of political economy as a way to minimize violence and maximize nonviolence in the future.

For example, there are interconnections between unorganized, direct, microlevel violence involving nuclear families and the organized, indirect, macrolevel violence involving poverty and economic inequality (Brock-Utne, 1997). Similarly, there are links between battering women and battering nations (McWilliams, 1998; Tifft & Markham, 1991). In each of these illustrations of violence, there are relations between force-backed domination in the "public" sphere (e.g., the state) and force-backed domination in the "private" sphere (e.g., the home). In her examination of violence against women in societies under stress, such as Bosnia, Rwanda, and Northern Ireland, McWilliams (1998) concluded that distinctions between the different forms of violence did not make a whole lot of sense: "In situations of conflict, categorization of violent acts in the context of the family, the community, and the state may be even less appropriate, because the locus for the abuse is not tied to any single category but instead becomes a pervasive and interactive system for legitimizing violence" (p. 113).

Likewise, in her discussion of the links between force-backed domination in the state and force-backed domination in gender and parent-child relations, Eisler (1997) has remarked that "throughout history regimes noted for their human rights violations, such as Hitler's Germany, Khomeini's Iran, Stalin's Soviet Union, and Zia's Pakistan, have made the return of women to their traditional (or subservient) place in a male-headed family a priority" (p. 165). She continues that this connection

> between rigid male domination in the family and despotism in the state also helps explain the Muslim fundamentalist custom found in chronically violent areas—where terrorism continues to be seen as legitimate and honorable—of not bringing men to trial for the "honor" killings of their wives, sisters, and daughters for any suspected sexual independence. For it is through the rule of terror in the family that both women and men learn to accept rule by terror as normal, be it in their own societies or against other tribes or nations. (p. 165)

Despite the early and recent efforts of some social thinkers to develop broad theories of violence and nonviolence capable of connecting the links between the spheres of violence and nonviolence and the causes and ways of preventing violence and nonviolence (Adorno, Frenkel-Brunswick, Levinson, & Sanford, 1950; Arendt, 1969; Aron, 1975; Galtung, 1997; Gandhi, 1940; Gilligan, 1997; Iadicola & Shupe, 1998), most analysts have focused their attention on specialized forms of violence or nonviolence. As a consequence, the studies of both violence and nonviolence have become overly fragmented. Rarely are there any scholars or students studying both violence and nonviolence.

In addition, when it comes to the etiology of violence, the conceptual approaches taken by the behavioral and social sciences tend to divide up between (a) biological theories that argue that humans behave violently because of instincts, genes, or physiological abnormalities; (b) physical anthropology theories that argue that evolution produced naturally aggressive human beings; (c) psychological theories, which are more diverse, ranging from psychoanalytical explanations that argue on behalf of the "return of the repressed" or the effects of humiliation and shame on autonomy and identity to social-psychological theories that argue on behalf of learning and attachment, to psychiatric theories that argue on behalf of antisocial personality disorders; and (d) sociological and cultural anthropology theories that argue that hostility and aggression are a result of the influences of culture and social structure interaction, inclusive of institutional and stratified relations as these intersect with individuals, groups, and/or the nation-state.

From a holistic and reciprocal perspective on violence and nonviolence causation and prevention, there are sound reasons for putting the social and behavioral science of "Humpty-Dumpty" back together again. Integrative analyses, such as the one presented here, are necessary because "violence is caused not simply by individual psychological factors, biological impulses, or social-structural factors alone but by a web of causal connections between personal-level and global-level structures, processes, and behaviors" (Kurtz & Turpin, 1997, p. 207). The same, of course, is true of nonviolence. Today, however, the few "web" analyses of violence and nonviolence are overshadowed by the disconnected and disjointed analyses of violence and nonviolence that predominate in academe.

SUMMARY

The domestic policy arena in the United States is, in 2003, still dominated by individualistically oriented solutions to violence that primarily ignore the larger institutional and structural relations of violence and nonviolence. As a result, American policy for responding to violence has consisted of essentially three related "mock-ups" or representations. The first, "peace through strength," or law and order models, emphasize the differences between "good" and "bad" people. The second, "peace through therapy," or pathological models, emphasize the differences between "sick" and "well" people. The third, "peace through restoration," or conflict resolution models, emphasize the similarities between victimizers and victims. The limitation of these models, alone or together, is that they have helped to reproduce in the United States a culture of violent solutions rather than what could be called, in contrast, a culture of nonviolent solutions. As one alternative to the conventional wisdom of reducing violence with violence, Robert Elias (1997) and others have called for the establishment of nonviolence and for peace through cooperation rather than peace through war and conflict.

Finally, by addressing the interdependent relations of the various forms of violence and nonviolence, reciprocal models emphasize both the adversarial forces of individual, national, and global violence and the mutualistic needs of the earth's peoples for security, peace, and justice. These common security or peace models of nonviolence emphasize the building of institutions that mitigate the causes or sources of violence and strive to facilitate mutual cooperation and altruism among all people. These latter themes will be fully developed in the last part of this book.

REFERENCES

Adorno, T. W., Frenkel-Brunswick, E., Levinson, D. J., & Sanford, R. N. (1950). *The authoritarian personality*. New York: Harper and Row.

An evolving Juvenile Court: On the front lines with Judge J. Dean Lewis. (1999). *Journal of the Office of Juvenile Justice and Delinquency Prevention, 6*(2), 3-11.

Arendt, H. (1969). *On violence*. New York: Harcourt, Brace, and World.

Aron, R. (1975). *History and the dialectic of violence* (B. Cooper, Trans.). Oxford, England: Blackwell.

Bachman, R. (1994). *Violence and theft in the workplace*. Washington, DC: Bureau of Justice Statistics.

Barak, G. (Ed.). (1991a). *Crimes by the capitalist state: An introduction to state criminality*. Albany, NY: State University of New York Press.

Barak, G. (1991b). *Gimme shelter: A social history of homelessness in contemporary America*. New York: Praeger.

Barak, G. (Ed.). (2000). *Crime and crime control: A global view*. Westport, CT: Greenwood Press.

Barak, G., Flavin, J., & Leighton, P. (2001). *Class, race, gender, and crime: Social realities of justice in America*. Los Angeles: Roxbury.

Brener, N. D., Simon, T. R., Krug, E. G., & Lowry, R. (1999). Recent trends in violence-related behaviors among high school students in the United States. *Journal of the American Medical Association, 282*, 440-446.

Brock-Utne, B. (1997). Linking the micro and the macro in peace and development studies. In J. Turpin & L. R. Kurtz (Eds.), *The web of violence: Interpersonal to global* (pp. 149-160). Chicago: University of Illinois.

Brownstein, H. H. (2000). *The social reality of violence and violent crime*. Boston: Allyn and Bacon.

Bureau of Justice Statistics. (1998). *School crime supplement to the National Crime Victimization Survey, 1989 and 1995*. Washington, DC: Office of Justice Programs.

Bureau of Justice Statistics. (2000a). *Firearms and crime statistics*. Retrieved September 17, 2002, from http://www.ojp.usdoj.gov/bjs/guns.htm

Bureau of Justice Statistics. (2000b). *By 2000, the number of crimes committed with firearms had stabilized to levels last experienced in the mid-1980s*. Retrieved October 6, 2002.

Butterfield, F. (1994, January 4). A history of homicide surprises the experts: Decline in U.S. before recent increase. *The New York Times*, p. A8.

Centers for Disease Control and Prevention. (1997). *Risk of death by age: 10 leading causes of death, United States: 1997, all races, both sexes*. Hyattsville, MD: National Center for Health Statistics. Retrieved October 6, 2002, from http://liferisk.netfirms.com/Death_by_age.htm.

Chaikan, J. M. (2000, January). Crunching numbers: crime and incarceration at the end of the millennium. *National Institute of Justice Journal, 246*, 10-17.

Cotton, D., & Groth, N. (1984). Inmate rape: Prevention and intervention. *Journal of Prison and Jail Health, 2*(1), 47-57.

Cottrol, R. J. (1998, fall). Submission is not the answer: Lethal violence, microcultures of criminal violence and the right to self-defense. *University of Colorado Law Review, 69*(4), 1029-1080.

Dumond, R. W. (1992). The sexual assault of male inmates in incarcerated settings. *International Journal of the Sociology of Law, 20*, 135-157.

Eisler, R. (1997). Human rights and violence:

Integrating the private and public spheres. In J. Turpin & L. R. Kurtz (Eds.), *The web of violence: From interpersonal to global* (pp. 161-186). Chicago: University of Illinois.

Elias, R. (1997). A culture of violent solutions. In J. Turpin & L. R. Kurtz (Eds.), *The web of violence: From interpersonal to global* (pp. 117-148). Chicago: University of Illinois.

Ellickson, P., Saner, H., & McGuigan, K. A. (1997). Profiles of violent youth: Substance use and other concurrent problems. *American Journal of Public Health, 87*(6), 985-991.

Finkelhor, D. (1988). An epidemiologic approach to the study of child molestation. In R. Prenty & V. Quinsey (Eds.), *Human sexual aggression: Current perspectives* (pp. 136-142). New York: Annals of the New York Academy of Sciences.

Finkelhor, D., & Ormrod, R. (1999, November). *Reporting crimes against juveniles* (Juvenile Justice Bulletin NCJ 178887). Retrieved September 17, 2002, from http://www.ucjrs.org/pdf-files1/ojjdp/178887.pdf

Fox, J. A., & Zawitz, M. W. (1999, January). *Homicide trends in the United States*. Retrieved September 17, 2002, from http://www.ojp.usdoj.gov/bjs/pub/pdf/htius.pdf

Fox, J. A., & Zawitz, M. W. (2000, March). *Homicide trends in the United States: 1998 update* (Crime Data Brief NCJ 179767). Retrieved September 17, 2002, from http://www.ojp.usdoj.gov/bjs/pub/pdf/htius98.pdf

Galtung, J. (1997). Is there a therapy for pathological cosmologies? In J. Turpin & L. R. Kurtz (Eds.), *The web of violence: From personal to global* (pp. 187-206). Chicago: University of Illinois.

Gandhi, M. (1940). *An autobiography: The story of my experiments with truth*. Ahmedabad, India: Navajivan.

Gilligan, J. (1997). *Violence: Reflections on a national epidemic*. New York: Vintage.

Greenfeld, L. A., & Smith, S. K. (1999). *American Indians and crime* (Bureau of Justice Statistics NCJ 173386). Retrieved September 17, 2002, from http://www.ojp.usdoj.gov/bjs/pub/pdf/aic.pdf

Greenwood, P. (1995). Juvenile crime and juvenile justice. In J. Q. Wilson & J. Petersilia (Eds.), *Crime* (pp. 91-117). San Francisco: Institute for Contemporary Studies.

Gurr, T. R. (Ed.). (1989). *Violence in America: Protest, rebellion, reform* (Vol. 2). Newbury Park, CA: Sage.

Gurr, T. R. (1990). Historical trends in violent crime: A critical review of the evidence. In N. A. Weiner, M. A. Zahn, & R. J. Sagi (Eds.), *Violence: Patterns, causes, public policy* (pp. 15-23). Fort Worth, TX: Harcourt Brace.

Hammond, R. W. (1999, November). *School-associated violent deaths, United States, 1994-1998*. Paper presented at the annual meetings of the American Society of Criminology, Toronto, Ontario, Canada.

Hidden addictions [Television special report]. (2000, May 30). New York: USA Network.

Hills, S. L. (Ed.). (1987). *Corporate violence—Injury for death and profit*. Totowa, NJ: Rowan and Littlefield.

Hinkle, W. G., & Henry, S. (Eds.). (2000). *School violence*. Annals of the American Academy of Political and Social Science. Thousand Oaks, CA: Sage.

Hodgson, J. F. (1997). *Games pimps play: Pimps, players and wives-in-law*. Toronto, Ontario, Canada: Canadian Scholars Press.

Iadicola, P., & Shupe, A. (1998). *Violence, inequality, and human freedom*. Dix Hills, NY: General Hall.

Jamison, K. R. (1999). *Night falls fast: Understanding suicide*. New York: Alfred A. Knopf.

Jenness, V., & Broad, K. (1997). *Hate crimes: New social movements and the politics of violence*. New York: Aldine de Gruyter.

Johnson, D. (2000, May 21). No executions in Illinois until system is repaired. *The New York Times*, p. Y13.

Johnson, E. A., & Monkkonen, E. H. (1996). Introduction. In E. A. Johnson and E. H. Monkkonen (Eds.), *The civilization of crime: Violence in town and country since the Middle Ages* (pp. 1-13). Chicago: University of Illinois.

Kandel Englander, E. (1997). *Understanding violence*. Mahwah, NJ: Lawrence Erlbaum.

Kappeler, V. E., Blumberg, M., & Potter, G. W. (1996). *The mythology of crime and criminal justice* (2nd ed.). Prospect Heights, IL: Waveland.

Kellecher, M. D. (1996). *New arenas for violence—Homicide in the American workplace.* Westport, CT: Praeger.

Kilpatrick, D. G. (1993). Rape and other forms of sexual assault. *Journal of Interpersonal Violence, 8*(2), 193-197.

Klaus, P. A. (2000, January). *Crimes against persons age 65 or older, 1992-97* (Bureau of Justice Statistics NCJ 176352). Retrieved September 17, 2002, from http://www.ojp.usdoj.gov/bjs/abstract/cpa6597.htm

Klofas, J. (1992). The effects of incarceration. In S. Stojkovic & R. Lovell (Eds.), *Corrections: An introduction* (pp. 295-327). Cincinnati, OH: Anderson.

Koss, M., Gidycz, K. A., & Wisniewski, N. (1987). The scope of rape: Incidence and prevalence of sexual aggression and victimization in a national sample of higher education students. *Journal of Consulting and Clinical Psychology, 55,* 162-170.

Kramer, R. C. (1983). A prolegomena to the study of corporate violence. *Humanity and Society, 7,* 149-178.

Kurtz, L. R., & Turpin, J. (1997). Conclusion: Untangling the web of violence. In J. Turpin & L. R. Kurtz (Eds.), *The Web of violence: From interpersonal to global* (pp. 207-232). Chicago: University of Illinois.

McGrath, R. D. (1984). *Gunfighters, highwaymen and vigilantes: Violence on the frontier.* Berkeley: University of California.

McWilliams, M. (1998). Violence against women in societies under stress. In R. E. Dobash & R. P. Dobash (Eds.), *Rethinking violence against women* (pp. 111-140). Thousand Oaks, CA: Sage.

Messner, S. F., & Rosenfeld, R. (1993). *Crime and the American dream.* Belmont, CA: Wadsworth.

Moore, J. P., & Cook, I. L. (1999, December). *Highlights of the 1998 national youth gang survey* (Office of Juvenile Justice and Delinquency Prevention Fact Sheet 123). Retrieved September 17, 2002, from http://www.ncjrs.org/pdf-files1/ojjdp/fs99123.pdf

National Safety Council. (1997). *Accident facts, 1997 edition.* Itasca, IL: Author.

Pillemer, K., & Finkelhor, D. (1988). The prevalence of elder abuse: A random sample survey. *The Gerontologist, 28*(2), 51-57.

Putman, J. (2000, May 21). Teen suicides linked to handguns in homes. *Ann Arbor News,* pp. A1.

Reidel, M., & Welsh, W. (2002). *Criminal violence: patterns, causes, and prevention.* Los Angeles: Roxbury.

Rennison, C. M. (1999, July). Criminal victimization 1998: Changes 1997-98 with trends 1993-98 (Bureau of Justice Statistics NCJ 176353). Retrieved September 17, 2002, from http://www.ojp.usdoj.gov/bjs/abstract/cv98.htm

Rideau, W., & Wikberg, R. (Eds.). (1992). *Life sentences: Rage and survival behind bars.* New York: Times Books.

Russell, D. (1983). *Rape in marriage.* New York: Collier.

Serious crimes fall for 8th consecutive year [Electronic version]. (2000, May 8). *The New York Times,* p. A21.

Straus, M. A. (1994). *Beating the devil out of them: Corporal punishment in American families.* San Francisco: Jossey-Bass/Lexington Books.

Straus, M. A., & Gelles, R. J. (1990). *Physical violence in American families.* New Brunswick, CT: Transaction.

Straus, M. A., Sugarman, D. B., & Giles-Sims, J. (1997). Spanking by parents and subsequent antisocial behavior of children. *Archive of Pediatric Adolescent Medicine, 151,* 761-767.

Straus, M. A., & Stewart, J. H. (1999). Corporal punishment by American parents: National data on prevalence, chronicity, severity, and duration, in relation to child and family characteristics. *Clinical Child and Family Psychology Review, 2*(2), 55-70.

Survey: Companies reporting violence. (1999, November 3). *Ann Arbor News,* p. A1.

Sykes, G. M. (1958). *The society of captives.* Princeton, NJ: Princeton University Press.

Tifft, L. L., & Markham, L. (1991). Battering women and battering Central Americans: A peacemaking synthesis. In H. E. Pepinsky & R. Quinney (Eds.),

Criminology as peacemaking. Bloomington: Indiana University Press.

U.S. Department of Justice, Federal Bureau of Investigation, Criminal Justice Information Services Division. 1995. Uniform crime *reports: Hate crimes— 1995.* Washington, DC: Author. Retrieved October 6, 2002, from http://www. fbi.gov/ ucr/hatecm.htm

Warchol, G. (1998). *Workplace violence, 1992–1996* (Bureau of Justice Statistics Special Report NCJ 168634). Retrieved September 17, 2002, from http://www. ojp. usdoj. gov/ bjs/abstract/ wv96.htm

Weiner, N. A. (1989). Violent criminal careers and "violent career criminals": An overview of the research literature. In N. A. Weiner & M. E. Wolfgang (Eds.), *Violent crime, violent criminals.* Newbury Park, CA: Sage.

Wells, W., & Horney, J. (2002, May). Weapon effects and individual intent to do harm: Influences on the escalation of violence. *Criminology, 40*(2), 265-296.

Wright, J., D., & Rossi, P. H. (1985, July). *The armed criminal in America: A survey of incarcerated felons* [Research report]. Washington, DC: National Institute of Justice.

REVIEW QUESTIONS

1. What is the difference between sanctioned and unsanctioned forms of violence, and why is it important to study both?

2. Define interpersonal, institutional, and structural violence. Provide at least two examples of each of these three fundamental forms of violence.

3. Compare and contrast violence in 19th- and 20th-century America.

4. From a cross-cultural perspective, how would you characterize American violence in relation both to other developed nations and to developing nations?

5. What are some of the advantages of a reciprocal over a nonreciprocal approach to the study of violence and nonviolence?

CHAPTER 2

Interpersonal Violence

The primary objectives of Chapters 2 through 4 are to provide demographic profiles for typical victims and victimizers of interpersonal, institutional, and structural violence. Distinguishing between the three spheres of violence is very useful and important for thinking about violence generally. Anyone performing such an examination, however, should not lose sight of the fact that these three worlds are typically not isolated from or unrelated to one another (refer to Figure 1.2). In everyday reality, the three worlds are interactive and reciprocal in the social formation and production of violence. In the case of sexual harassment or sexual assault, for example, it is often most difficult, if not impossible, to separate the interpersonal from the institutional (see Box 2.1). Thus, it makes sense not only to think of the spheres of violence as being connected and interdependent, but to view the different forms of violence as representing overlapping and accumulating relations of violence.

As a way of grasping the complexity of violence, the nature, context, motives, interests, and conditions of five representative types or expressions of the occurrences of interpersonal, institutional, and structural violence are presented. Sprinkled unevenly throughout the three chapters are case studies of violence, derived almost exclusively from online news stories. These stories are meant to provide richer descriptions and fuller characterizations of the various experiences of violence than abstract or generic portrayals do. In these examples, whether the subject is verbal abuse, sexual assault, suicidal terrorism, or mass genocide, attempts are made to expose the common elements and dynamics found within and between the different domains of violence.

Regarding interpersonal violence in particular, acts such as assault, rape, homicide, and kidnapping come immediately to mind. These acts, involving two or more people, are usually associated with overt acts of physical harm or injury: someone is pushed around, roughed up, hit, stabbed, invaded, shot, or restrained. "Acts of interpersonal violence," however, also refers to violations of personhood, or to pain and injury that need not be physical (Brown, 1987). These "covert" and emotional harms infringe upon, disregard, abuse, and/or deny another person's right to selfhood. In addition, these emotional violations recognize that individuals can be victimized as both objects and subjects. In other words, any act that depersonalizes, dehumanizes, or transforms human beings into "things" would qualify as interpersonal violence.

Box 2.1   Harassment and Silence

The sexual harassment case of 2000 that found that Lt. General Claudia J. Kennedy, the Army's highest ranking woman, had been the victim of inappropriate sexual advances, revived "the question of how pervasive sexual harassment remains in the military and how such cases should be handled." In the article prepared for the *New York Times,* 16 senior women officers were interviewed. All of these women officers wished to keep their identities anonymous. All but three of the women stated that to protect their careers, they never reported a one-time case of sexual harassment. In point of fact, military guidelines advise that victims of a one-time incident handle the matter privately unless it involves a flagrant assault. Second-time incidents are to be reported, and they are generally handled with counseling and/or letters of reprimand. In more serious cases, the charges are likely to become maltreatment of a subordinate or assault and battery rather than sexual harassment.

The interviewed officers all "marveled that General Kennedy, so close to retirement, would have subjected herself to the backlash and tarnished reputation that would inevitably come from making a sexual harassment charge," even in the improving military environment. They also took Kennedy at face value, when she stated that she brought the complaint against Maj. Gen. Larry G. Smith 4 years after the incident had occurred because she had learned "that he had been appointed inspector general of the Army, a position that included investigating sexual harassment." All agreed, too, that overt occurrences of sexual harassment were fewer today than they had been a couple of decades ago. However, as the military began cracking down on inappropriate behavior, harassment had become more subtle, or "stealth-like," in the words of some women officers.

In general, women are reluctant to file complaints, the officers noted, because they fear opening their personal lives to examination and being blamed for inviting a sexual advance. Lt. Col. Elspeth Cameron Ritchie, a forensic psychiatrist who works with women who have brought charges of sexual assault or harassment, said that the typical reaction of these victims is one of shame, humiliation, and wanting to get out of the service quickly: "What is most likely to happen [in these cases] is a negative effect on your career. . . . The women who bring charges . . . against a man that leads to a trial generally resign from the Army within a year whether the man was found guilty or innocent."

One woman, who was a high-ranking officer at the time of this interview, related a personal story of when she was still a lieutenant colonel. At the time, some 5 years earlier, she sought out her boss for advice about advanced training schools. Her commanding officer's response was that he could get her into any program that she wanted to go to. All she had to do to make it happen was to give him a "blow job." The lieutenant colonel turned around without saying a word and walked out of the office. She spent the next 3 days asking herself what she had done wrong and seriously considered retiring from the military. She finished her story by saying that the experience had changed her life: "I was personally and professionally cut to the core. I feel it just as deeply today as I did then."

Source: Becker, E. (2000, May 12). Women in military say silence on harassment protects careers. *New York Times,* p. A1.

Strictly speaking, "acts of interpersonal violence," as previously noted, refers to abuse or injury that happens between people acting in their private lives without regard to occupational roles and formal institutions. These acts generally reflect situations or events wherein both the victims and the victimizers are similar, to the extent that in the context of their present or past circumstances, each has experienced some kind of harm or pain. In the rest of this chapter, attention is focused on the following five forms of interpersonal violence:

- Homicide
- Juvenile victimization
- Physical and sexual child abuse
- Rape (sexual assault)
- Stalking

HOMICIDE

Box 2.2   Serial Killer

One of the nation's most prolific serial killers, Tommy Lynn Sells, was arrested on January 1, 2000. Sells had been identified by 11-year-old Krystal Surles, who had survived a slashed throat administered by Sells at her house in Del Rio, Texas. Also attacked by Sells was Surles' friend, Kaylene Harris, 13, who died. Sells, 35, a drifter and eighth-grade dropout who often made money as a "carnie" (carnival worker), told police when questioned by them that he had committed dozens of murders over the past 20 years as he crossed the country, the first occurring during a street fight in Hollywood, California.

In fact, he may be responsible for more than 70 killings involving men, women, and children. By February 2001, police had confirmed 13 killings committed by Sells, including a multiple murder in Illinois in 1987. In destroying an Illinois family, Sells bludgeoned to death Elaine Dardeen, 7 months pregnant at the time, and her 3-year-old son, Peter. Police believe that the shock of the attack caused Elaine to give birth, that her newborn girl was alive, and that Sells clubbed her to death. In a nearby field, Dardeen's husband, Keith, was found dead. He had been shot in the head.

According to Sells, he had a rough upbringing. When he was 18 months old, his mother abandoned him. He then was raised by a "crooked family." Sells further claims that he was sexually abused by a man in the neighborhood. At age 13, Sells began roaming the country. He served time in a variety of prisons throughout the United States for many offenses, including assault and auto theft. When asked why he killed people, Sells explained that he did so when they angered him: "I lose it. I lose control of my thoughts, I lose control of my emotions. When you are not in control, bad things happen."

Source: Dead men tell no tales [Television series episode]. In S. Zirinsky (Executive Producer), *48 hours*. New York: CBS News.

According to law, homicide is the killing of one human being by another. Legally, homicide can be criminal or noncriminal. Criminal homicides are usually divided into four kinds: (1) first-degree murder is when one person causes the death of another with premeditation and intent, (2) second-degree murder is when a death results from malice and intent but not from premeditation, (3) voluntary manslaughter is when a death occurs involving intent to inflict bodily injury without the intent to kill, and (4) involuntary manslaughter is when a death results from negligence or recklessness without intent to harm. By contrast, non-criminal homicide refers to two forms of (legally) excusable homicide: *self-defense* and *justifiable*. The former involves the taking of a life in the course of the lawful defense of habitation, property, or person. The latter involves the killing of a person under the authority of law, as when a police officer kills a felon or when a convicted offender is executed by the state (Gifis, 1975; Wolfgang & Zahn, 1990).

From a behavioral perspective, homicide is more complicated and complex. For example, in the *Pocket Guide to the Crime Classification Manual: A Standard System for Investigating and Classifying Violent Crimes,* 43 homicide categories were identified (Douglas, Burgess, Burgess, & Ressler, 1992). In each of these categories, such as criminal enterprise homicide, personal cause homicide, argument/conflict murder, sexual homicide, group cause homicide, or extremist murder (see Box 2.3), there are varying motivations, defining characteristics, and other considerations, especially as these may be related to the crime scene and its investigation.

Box 2.3   Retaliatory Bombing

Organized mass murderer Timothy McVeigh, who killed 160 people in the Oklahoma City bombing of a federal building in 1995, was executed in June 2001. This mass killing, in the words of McVeigh, involved "collateral damage." The persons murdered were not his targeted "offenders" per se. Those persons would have been high-ranking government officials, such as former attorney general Janet Reno, former director of the Federal Bureau of Investigation Louis J. Freeh, or other federal agents that McVeigh regarded as responsible for the killing, on February 28, 1993, of some 80 people, including 17 children, who belonged to an obscure sect, the Branch Davidians, in Waco, Texas. In short, McVeigh viewed his response to the Waco massacre as a retaliatory assault on the U.S. government.

McVeigh knew, for example, at the time he planted the truck bomb, that there were children present, but he rationalized that the timing of the bombing was too important to deviate from. Ultimately, McVeigh did acknowledge that he regretted killing the 19 children. However, his deepest regret was that he "didn't knock the building down." (One can only speculate about what McVeigh would have thought about the overly "successful" efforts of the suicidal terrorists who toppled two buildings at the World Trade Center on September 11, 2001, when their goal had only been to wipe out the top floors, according to Osama bin Laden in his first video-released message after the historic attack.)

Was Tim McVeigh mentally ill? Was he a sociopath, a borderline schizophrenic, or someone suffering from posttraumatic stress disorder? Was he simply an evil person? Or, none of the above? According to those lawyers, psychologists, and journalists who interacted with McVeigh following his arrest, he was a surprisingly "normal" mass murderer with above-average intelligence and good social skills, someone who was found by most to be a pleasant and likable human being. In his own mind, McVeigh's self-image was allegedly that of a "just warrior." As he wrote in his letter from death row, the bombing of a federal building in Oklahoma was "morally and strategically equivalent to the US hitting a government building in Serbia, Iraq, or other nations" (Sky News, 2001).

(Continued)

Box 2.3 (Continued)

The online article "Inside McVeigh's Mind," by the BBC's Robin Aitken (2001), was based on an interview with John R. Smith, an Oklahoma psychiatrist. Dr. Smith, who has interviewed many murder suspects for the courts, spent more than 20 hours talking to McVeigh after his arrest in 1995. One of the most notable things Smith had to say about McVeigh was that the bomber saw himself as someone who had struck a blow for freedom. At the time of the bombing, McVeigh could very well have been experiencing a form of posttraumatic stress disorder. Smith was also quoted as saying,

> He's a real human being. He feels love. He feels anger. He's a young man capable of feeling great anger particularly at people or institutions that he considers to be bullies. (Aitken, 2001)

According to Smith, McVeigh's hatred of bullies stemmed from his unhappy childhood. At school, he was often the object of bullying. At home, his parents often argued violently, which frightened him as a young boy. Smith says that McVeigh took refuge in a fantasy world where he was a hero vanquishing the bullies, a common fantasy that is no doubt shared by countless youth every day. However, at the age of 20, McVeigh joined the Army, where he would eventually live part of that fantasy. In retrospect, it now appears that what might have been "dreams of redemption" may have actually turned into "nightmares of revenge."

As many readers will know, McVeigh was a successful recruit, an expert marksman, and he was rapidly promoted to sergeant. During the Gulf War in the early 1990s, he saw action and in one incident killed some Iraqi soldiers manning a machine gun. Dr. Smith related the impact of this combat episode on McVeigh: "They later went over and of course he saw the Iraqis he had killed and it was very moving to him" (Aitken, 2001). At the same time, there were other Iraqis who were coming out, giving up their guns, and surrendering. Immediately afterwards, McVeigh returned to his armored vehicle, sat alone, and began crying. Nothing more was said about this while McVeigh was in the Gulf.

Back in the United States in 1992, McVeigh, still in the Army, applied for candidacy to a special forces unit, only to be rejected. Shortly thereafter, his period of enlistment was up and he chose not to reenlist in the military. Unable to find meaningful employment in and around his home in upstate New York, he became a drifter of sorts. During this period, McVeigh even sought help from an Army veterans' mental health clinic. He was turned down because he wanted to be counseled under an assumed name. It was also during this time that McVeigh, who had deep concerns about the federal government's abuses of ordinary citizens and its attempts to restrict gun ownership, began to strongly identify with the victims at Waco.

Dr. Smith believes that this was a turning point for McVeigh. He associated the federal government with "the ultimate bully," upon whom he would take revenge 2 years to the day after the incidents at Waco with the bombing in Oklahoma City. In the end, McVeigh may have gotten some of the things that he wanted, but he was denied some things as well. For example, he wanted to die and become a martyr on behalf of the "people versus the government." He accomplished the former, but not the latter.

Sources: Sky News. (2001, April 28). *The McVeigh letter in full*. Retrieved September 19, 2002, from http://www.sky.com/skynews
Aitken, R. (2001, June 1). *Inside McVeigh's mind*. Retrieved September 18, 2002, from http://news.bbc.co.uk/1/hi/world/americas/1382540.stm

Three types of homicidal events—*situational felony murders, gang-related murders,* and *erotomania-motivated killings*—are illustrative of the varying "states of mind" that can be associated with the same generic behavior. In other words, these types of killings are really quite different in nature. Their modus operandi are also very different.

Situational felony murder involves the unplanned killing of a person during the commission of a felony. These murders are typically the result of panic, confusion, or impulse. The offenders have, rightly or wrongly, perceived the victim as a threat or an impediment. The victims in these scenarios are ones of opportunity, or cases of being in the wrong place at the wrong time. Gang-related murder involves the death of people resulting from issues of status or respect and from criminal acts perpetrated by street-affiliated members for economic and territorial gain. The victims in these scenarios are generally one of three kinds. They are either members or associates of a rival gang, innocent bystanders, or local businesspersons being extorted. Erotomania-motivated killing usually involves the murder of a well-known person preceded by the perpetrator's fantasized relationship with the victim. These victims are always viewed as having higher status than the perpetrators. The victims may have high media visibility or simply be superiors in the perpetrator's workplace.

Even within the same categories of homicidal killers, there are divergent expressions of the same kinds of violence. Consider some of the characteristics of sexual homicide. In general, all sexual homicides involve elements or acts of sexuality that accompany murder. Real or symbolic, the sexual dimensions vary with the offender in terms of both meaning and performance. For example, sexual homicides "may range from actual rape involving penetration (either before death or postmortem) to symbolic sexual assault, such as insertion of foreign objects into [the] victim's bodily orifices" (Douglas et al., 1992, p. 42). Sexual homicides can also be subdivided further into *organized* and *disorganized* killings, based on the presence or absence of various factors and on the examination or evaluation of the act itself, an analysis of the victim, the scene or staging of the killing, and other forensic reports. Organized sexual homicide typically refers to sexual killers who have carefully planned their murders in advance. In contrast, disorganized sexual homicide typically refers to those killings that were unplanned or appear to have been spontaneous in nature, such as a classic case of homosexual panic escalating into homicide and attempted murder (see Box 2.4). Less extreme forms of homosexual panic might include such hate crimes as assault and battery directed at gay persons or groups.

Box 2.4   Homosexual Panic Leading to Murder

The case of Ronald K. Crumpley, who shot and killed two people and wounded six others outside a Greenwich Village gay bar in 1980, is a classic illustration of homosexual panic leading to murder. Crumpley, 59, and a resident for more than 16 years at the Kirby Forensic Psychiatric Center on Wards Island, was found not to be responsible for his crimes by reason of insanity. In the 2001 hearings to determine whether or not Crumpley was no longer insane and a danger to the community, he claimed that some Kirby staff members and other state officials were taking his words out of context to assert that he had a "psychotic hatred of gay men."

  Mr. Crumpley, a former transit police officer, began committing crimes in the 1970s to support his drug and alcohol dependencies. In 1973, he resigned from the police force after being convicted of using stolen credit cards. Two days before the 1980 shootings, "he called his father and said that he was being pursued by hundreds of gay men." The next day he stole his father's car and drove to Virginia, where he robbed a gun store. From there, Crumpley drove back to New York City and to Greenwich Village, where he "shot two men on the corner of Washington and 10th Streets" and then "opened fire at a gay bar on West Street."

Source: Saulny, S. (2001, June 14). Man who killed 2 outside gay bar remains mentally ill, a jury finds. *New York Times*, p. B8.

Some sexual homicides, for a variety of reasons, may reflect aspects of both organized and disorganized sexual homicide (see Box 2.5). For example, the primary motive for an attack may be rape, but the offender's emotional state and/or the victim's resistance leads to escalation, especially common with hostile or retaliatory rapists. A very different kind of sexual homicide involves sadistic murder, in which the offender, prior to the killing, tortures the victim physically and/or psychologically. Some of these serial sexual killers may be nondiscriminating in selecting their victims; others violently attack strangers "who possess triggering physical characteristics or who are socially or physically vulnerable, such as prostitutes, hitchhikers, or children" (Weiner, Zahn, & Sagi, 1990, p. 44).

Box 2.5   Rape and Homicide

Accused killer-rapist Arohn Kee, a 26-year-old computer whiz, over the objections of his lawyers, insisted on being the first defense witness at his own trial. During nearly 2 days of testimony, Kee laughed, cried, and railed at cops and medical examiners, who he accused of framing him in an elaborate conspiracy. Charged in the slayings of three Harlem girls and the rapes of four others between 1991 and 1998, Kee maintained that "three 'corrupt cops' and an employee in the city medical examiner's office" rigged "DNA and other evidence against him" (Ross & Standora, 2000). DNA evidence in the form of hair and semen recovered from all but one of the victims matched Kee's. The one victim without any DNA evidence had been doused with an accelerant and burned beyond recognition.

In what amounted to a mostly uninterrupted monologue, Kee rambled on about drug dealers, rap performers, his previous arrests, and even details of his jailhouse meals. During his second day on the stand, Kee was granted permission to remove the t-shirt he was wearing because it contained notes that "he took shortly after viewing a computer disk detailing a supposed scheme by the city medical examiner's office to sell human organs" (Ross & Hutchinson, 2000). At one point in his testimony, he stated: "I'm looking at the faces in here and realize that some people think I'm full of [expletive], but that's what I saw" (Ross & Hutchinson, 2000). After a jury found him guilty of all 22 counts in what had been a vicious 8-year rape, robbery, and murder spree involving young women and teenage girls, Kee could only curse his victims' relatives. As he was led out of a courtroom packed with kin of three of the women he killed in his East Harlem neighborhood, Kee spat "F— all of you" (Ross, Peterson, & Goldiner, 2000).

Testimony revealed that Kee stalked his victims in dark stairways and desolate rooftops. In terms of his detached relationship with reality, his rape victims testified that he taunted them. For example, he told one that she was "lucky" to be raped by someone as handsome as him. He told his youngest victim, a 13-year-old girl, to "take it like a woman" (Ross et al., 2000).

Sources: Ross, B., & Hutchinson, B. (2000, December 15). Slay trial's t-shirt twist. *New York Daily News*, p. 22. Retrieved September 18, 2002, from http://nydailynews.com

Ross, B., Peterson, H., & Goldiner, D. (2000, December 21). Kee guilty in rape-slay spree, faces life term. *New York Daily News*, p. 4. Retrieved September 18, 2002, from http://nydailynews.com

Ross, B., & Standora, L. (2000, December 14). Rape-slay defendant denies guilt on stand. *New York Daily News*, p. 17. Retrieved September 18, 2002, from http://nydailynews.com

Most homicides, however, do not involve strangers. Typically, homicides involve people who know one another, including acquaintances, friends, or intimates. Most murders occur in the evening or early morning hours, on the weekends, and involve informal, nonwork, and leisure social settings (e.g., home, car, tavern). These criminal homicides are regarded as "situated transactions" in that they are the end product of a chain of interaction between two or more persons that lasts during the time they are in each other's physical presence (see Box 2.6). As Luckenbill (1990) has concluded on the basis of his examination of all criminal homicide cases over a 10-year period (1963-1972) in one medium-sized (350,000) California county,

> Criminal homicide does not appear as a one-sided event with an unwitting victim assuming a passive, non-contributory role. Rather, murder is the outcome of a dynamic interchange between an offender, victim, and, in many cases, bystanders. The offender and victim develop lines of action shaped in part by the actions of the other and focused toward saving or maintaining face and reputation and demonstrating character. Participants develop a working agreement, sometimes implicit, often explicit, that violence is a useful tool for resolving questions of face and character. (pp. 64-65)

Box 2.6   Situated Transactions

In a classic case of intimate rejection and humiliation resulting in lethal violence, the jury convicted Julius C. Walker, 37, of the first-degree premeditated murder of his 29-year-old wife, Veronica Walker, in Ypsilanti, Michigan. The prosecutor's case was a circumstantial one, as no evidence was found by the police to link Walker to his wife's murder. Similarly, the knife used in the killing was never found.

Washtenaw County Assistant Prosecutors Anthony Kendrick and Lela Rashid argued that "Walker planned to kill his wife because she was divorcing him and ha[d] found someone else" (Cobbs, 2000, p. C1). Testimony from family and friends during the trial showed that the couple had marital problems and that Veronica had been physically and verbally abused by Julius. In fact, she had left her husband several times and had taken their four daughters with her. At the time of the murder, the girls, 8 years old and younger, were living with Veronica's parents. The day before the killing, Veronica had served Julius with divorce papers, and witnesses testified that in response he had threatened to kill her and the man she had been dating.

On the day of the murder, Veronica, who worked as a contract analyst for Washtenaw County Mental Health, dropped off her kids at day care and was to meet with her supervisor later that morning. Again, witness testimony indicated that Veronica had agreed to meet her estranged husband that morning in person to tell him that the marriage was over. She never showed up for the meeting with her supervisor, and was found in the early afternoon by a Washtenaw County sheriff's deputy, stabbed to death in her Chevrolet Venture minivan. According to medical testimony, Veronica Walker had been the victim of a very personal crime. She had "been stabbed numerous times, her throat had been cut, her wrists slashed," and the "autopsy showed she died of a stab wound to the upper torso" (p. C4).

As Julius Walker was about to be sentenced to life in prison for killing their mother, he turned to his four daughters and told them: "I love you, I want you to remember that . . . I would not take the person you love away from you. I would not hurt your mother" (p. C1) (echoes of O. J. Simpson's postcriminal and civil protestations). After the sentencing, Walker turned to his mother-in-law and told her that he "sensed her hatred toward him but asked her not to make his children hate him. He also said that he loved Veronica and asked [her mother] to take care of his children" (p. C4).

Source: Cobbs, L. (2000, August 4). Convicted murderer gets life in prison. *Ann Arbor News,* pp. C1, C4.

Other types of homicide, such as infanticides, for example, are situational transactions of another kind because infants are not free to come and go as they choose (see Boxes 2.7 and 2.8). Hence, their contributions to violence are minimal, if any. As a result, their murders are typically very one-sided events. This was certainly true for Bob Rowe, a loving and supportive father, and Andrea Yates, a loving and supporting mother. These parents methodically killed their young children. Both parents believed that they loved their victims very much at the time of the murders. Although there are similarities in the psychologies of these tragedies of lethal violence, there are also unique differences, some related to gender and patriarchy and some to the sources of their adjustment reactions to adult life. In cases of infanticide like these, mothers are less likely than fathers to take the life of their spouse following the murder of the children.

Box 2.7   Altruistic Killings

On the morning and afternoon of February 21, 1978, a Mill Basin, New York, lawyer killed his three children and wife. Subsequently he was found not guilty by reason of insanity. In *Facing the Wind*, Julie Salamon captured the severe depression, exculpatory delusion, and altruistic killings of Bob Rowe. Her book is also a case study of lives experiencing human tragedy, of the inner depths of violence, and of emotional recovery.

On the day of the killings, while Bob Jr., Rowe's teenage son, was still sound asleep, the father took a baseball bat and smashed his son's head with one deliberate and forceful blow. A few hours later, when his adopted daughter, Jennifer, age 8, worrying that Bobby was sleeping too late, came to her father, Rowe tucked her into bed with her 12-year-old brother, Christopher. He then told the two children that they were going to play a game and to close their eyes. Using the bat, he killed them both with swift blows to their heads. Late in the afternoon, he called his wife at work and urged her to hurry home. Upon her arrival, Rowe instructed her to stand in the middle of the living room with her eyes closed, as the children had a surprise for her. One more swift blow to the head, and his wife Mary lay dead on the floor. The next day, he turned himself over to the authorities, admitting that he had killed his family.

Mary and Bob Rowe's second son, Christopher, had been born blind, deaf, and brain damaged. Consequently, Mary and Bob had become active during the 1960s in organizing parental support groups for others with severely handicapped children. Both were considered ideal role models: "The Rowes were devoted, selfless parents, dealing with extreme adversity with an awe-inspiring combination of optimism, determination and sense of humor" (Stewart, 2001, p. 10). Indeed, many of the mothers had wished that their husbands were as involved with their special kids as Bob was. Needless to say, Bob's killing of his children and Mary came as a total shock to their friends, families, and other associates. Preceding the killings, Bob Rowe had been extremely depressed and down on his luck, unable to find work as a lawyer in his chosen profession. Prior to that, and for more than a decade, he had been a fairly successful attorney in the insurance industry.

His explanation for the four murders was simply that he thought his family would be better off dead than living with a loser, a failure, an unemployed lawyer—like him. Rowe also told the various doctors who worked up psychological examinations on him to determine whether, according to New York criminal law, he was an "incapacitated defendant" not capable of mentally standing trial, that he had been depressed, and that the pressures of raising a handicapped child had been getting to him.

Rowe's case history was coauthored by Kings County Hospital forensic psychiatrists Daniel W. Schwartz and Richard L. Weidenbacher. The two psychiatrists concluded that Rowe was insane at the time of the murders. Whether or not one agrees with their findings, excerpted quotations from their diagnoses provide much insight into Rowe's behavior.

Schwartz's diagnosis was (1) adjustment reaction to adult life, with psychotic features and (2) personality disorder, with obsessive features. More specifically, his findings said,

(Continued)

Box 2.7 (Continued)

[Rowe] is a rather bright man, with a verbal I.Q. of 120. His performance I.Q. (108) has been affected by the fact that he is considerably depressed. Dynamically, he appears to be vulnerable to emotional pressures and troubled by extremely forceful unconscious homo-sexual wishes, feelings of inadequacy as a man and feelings of insatiable needs for emotional support, things that his mother had never provided.

He somehow attributed the killing of his wife and children to his mother, but in a very con-fusing, unclear way. The test suggests that unconsciously he may have viewed his wife as his mother when he killed her, and his children as himself. There is a tendency to dissociate, to put off anxiety-arousing thoughts and feelings and therefore his inability to deal with emo-tional problems in a rational way. He says that he had "a compulsion to kill." (Salamon, 2001, pp. 133-134).

Weidenbacher's diagnosis was adjustment reaction to adult life, with depressive and psychotic features. His findings also said,

It appears that the essential problem may be seen as one of pathological reaction to the death of mother, some years ago. Fairly clearly, the relationship between mother and son had been a difficult one, the son feeling frustrated by his mother and harboring strong and mixed feel-ings towards her. She, in turn, left her estate entirely to his younger brother, disinheriting the defendant, in effect. It seems clear that within a few years of her death the defendant was affected by a psychotic disorder, entailing visual and auditory hallucination of his mother, during which she commanded him to destroy his family. She had disapproved of his mar-riage and his wife; his wife had borne him one normal child, and one grossly defective child.

He may well also have been affected by delusion, with regard to his conduct. Although the hallucination and the likely delusion with regard to conduct resolved during the course of psychiatric treatment, including medication, there is reason to believe that he was subse-quently, and around the time of the reported offense, exercised by delusion regarding poverty. . . . the defendant appears incapable at this time of adequate participation in his defense. He still "hasn't sorted out his thoughts"; he has not as yet grasped what has tran-spired, so that he still rather expects his family to reappear. It would appear proper and wise to arrange for further psychiatric hospitalization, probably over a period of months, with an eye to greater emotional and mental stability and further perspective on the part of the defendant. (Salamon, 2001, pp. 135-136)

After his acquittal, Rowe was assigned to the Creedmoor Psychiatric Center in Queens. Some 2 years later, using lawyerly acumen, he was discharged (this is record time). In December 1980, his new life began as he went to work outside the confines of law. In fact, Rowe had unsuccessfully pursued his rights to be reinstated to practice before the bar of New York, employing every creative legal argument that he and his attorneys could muster.

A few years later, through a mutual acquaintance, Bob met a woman some 20 years his junior. Colleen was a deeply religious and shy woman who had been sexually molested as a girl. Along her way to adulthood, she would abandon her quest to become a nun. Immediately, she and Bob formed an unexplainable emotional bond. Her feelings for Bob only became stronger once she learned of his former life. The seemingly unmatched pair evidently found solace in each other as they were able to exchange their feelings of shame, humiliation, and mortification for love and redemption. Nine years after Bob's release, he and Colleen married, and shortly thereafter, Colleen gave birth to their one and only child, a daughter.

Sources: Salamon, J. (2001). *Facing the wind: The true story of tragedy and reconciliation.* New York: Random House.
Stewart, J. (2001, April 10). A case of insanity: A review of *Facing the wind.* *New York Times Review of Books*, p. 10.

Box 2.8   Motherhood and Mental Illness

Texas mother Andrea Yates was formally indicted for drowning Luke, 2; Paul, 3; John, 5; Noah, 7; and Mary, 6 months, on June 20, 2001, and her attorneys began preparing for an insanity defense. Nine months after her conviction for capital murder and her sentencing to life in prison, her husband and the natural father of the five deceased children, Rusty, remained supportive of his wife by reason of her mental illness. However, the question under Texas law was whether or not Andrea Yates knew the difference between right and wrong, not whether or not she was insane.

Accordingly, the prosecutor made the case one about motherhood, and the defense tried to make it about mental illness (Fleming, 2002). Unfortunately for Yates, "motherhood trumped mental illness"; although she was far from sane, it could be shown from her behavior that this mother did know the difference, if not the consequences, of her actions. Immediately following the five killings, she had called the police for assistance. She had also called her husband at work, suggesting that he come home, as she had done something bad to the kids.

After the 37-year-old mother had systematically drowned her five children, she laid them out on a bed, wrapped in sheets like some kind of little martyrs. Her oldest son was the lone exception; he was found lying face down in the bathtub.

According to police testimony, Yates was discovered by the oldest boy, Noah, when she had just finished drowning the baby and fourth child. She ordered Noah into the tub, but he ran, and she caught him and brought him back to the tub for drowning.

Apparently, Yates, once before and at the time of the murders, suffered from postpartum psychosis. Many women experience "the blues" after giving birth, perhaps 1 in 10 becomes depressed, and 1 in 1,000 becomes severely depressed. Clinically speaking, Yates was psychotic and subject to delusions. Even in a postconviction interview from her prison cell, shown on an evening prime-time news magazine program, Yates "explained" that she murdered her children to protect them from her and to bring them safely to heaven and the arms of God.

Historically the perfect child, valedictorian of her high school graduating class, winner of numerous swimming trophies, and diligent nurse at a Texas cancer clinic, Andrea married Russell (Rusty) Yates, a computer expert at NASA's Johnson Space Center in

(Continued)

Box 2.8 (Continued)

Houston, and a former football star and class standout at Dupont High near Nashville. Following the 1993 marriage, the two immediately started a family and decided that Andrea should give up her job and stay at home to raise the kids. Education and faith alike were both centered at their home rather than at school or church. For example, Andrea taught the four boys phonics and math with workbooks from a home-schooling service. As the pregnancies and babies kept coming, the always compassionate Andrea also took on the daily care of her father, who was suffering from Alzheimer's disease. Between the feeding, bathing, and disciplining of her four rambunctious boys and caring for her sick father, Andrea had no time for herself—to say the least.

After the birth of the fourth boy, serious psychological problems began surfacing in Andrea's life. She was treated not only with antidepressants, Effexor and Wellbutrin, but with Haldol, a very strong antipsychotic medication. In June 1999, she tried to kill herself by overdosing on a handful of pills prescribed for her ailing father. Subsequently, it appeared that Andrea had snapped back to "normal." Despite the knowledge that another baby could trigger another recurrence of severe postpartum depression, Andrea became pregnant with Mary. The degree to which Andrea felt willing to voluntarily raise another child versus the degree to which she felt guilty for not wishing to do so is certainly open to speculation, especially in light of some comments made by Rusty in reply to a reporter's questions about the danger and risks associated with having children: "I talked to Andrea when she was feeling a little better. We had a good talk about that. And, you know both of us really went into the marriage saying we'll just have as many kids as come along. And that's what we wanted" (Thomas, 2001, p. 24).

After the birth of the fifth child, Yates' depression returned with a vengeance, perhaps exacerbated by the death of her father. In any event, her condition spiraled downward, and she became "robotic" or "zombie"-like. The house had become a mess, dirty and unkempt, dishes and clothes everywhere. After killing her children, Yates told the police during her confession that she had been a bad mother and that she was damaging her children. At the scene of the crime, as Andrea sat on the couch watching officer Frank Stumpo trying to find a clean glass in which to give Rusty some water to calm him (he was being kept outside, away from Andrea and the crime scene), she quietly pointed him in the direction of the china cabinet.

Sources: Fleming, A. T. (2002, March 17). Ideas and trends: Crime and motherhood; maternal madness. *New York Times*, §4, p. 3.
Thomas, E. (2001, July 2). Motherhood and murder. *Newsweek*, pp. 20-25.

When it comes to discussions on the taking of human life, it has been suggested by those social and behavioral scientists with and without a psychoanalytic bent that homicide and suicide and, to a lesser extent, aggravated assault and attempted suicide are closely related behaviors in the repertoire of human violence (Gilligan, 1997; Menninger, 1938; Miller, 1990). That is to say, these behaviors share similar underlying motivations. For example, regarding the homicide-suicide connection, it is often held that the two are related and that they spring from the same soil: Some theorists regard suicide and homicide as sharing similarly based unconscious desires to kill (Pokorny, 1990).

What's more, there is plenty of sociological evidence to support the thesis of some kind of inverted relationship between these two rather divergent ways of taking lives. In nations such as Scandinavia and Japan, there have been relatively high suicide rates, accompanied by low homicide rates. Conversely, in countries with traditionally higher rates of homicide, there have been lower rates of suicide, such as in Spain, Ireland, and Italy. Similarly, wars and political crises tend to decrease suicides and increase homicides, urban areas tend to have higher rates of suicide and lower rates of homicide compared to rural areas, and Catholic countries tend to have higher rates of homicide and lower rates of suicide than protestant countries (Wolfgang, 1958). As was pointed out in the previous chapter, U.S. suicide rates in the 1990s were rising and homicide rates were dropping.

In a not too different sense, there are also many social scientists who discuss aggravated assault and criminal homicide as belonging to basically the same category of behavior. Whether an offense remains an aggravated assault or becomes a homicide (with the exception of "cold-blooded," premeditated, first-degree murder) depends on a matter of degree or chance, subject to whether or not the murders were preceded by instances of highly charged, emotional arguments and/or fights. In one comparative study, Pokorny (1990) examined homicide, aggravated assault, suicide, and attempted suicide. The data revealed that homicide and aggravated assault are most similar in their place and time of occurrence and in victim and offender characteristics. These violent behaviors typically occurred away from home; in public places such as bars, streets, and sidewalks; and between the hours of 5:00 P.M. and 2:00 A.M. They both usually occurred on weekends, with a peak on Saturdays. By contrast, suicides and attempted suicides typically occurred at home, or in private, secluded places; the former during the week and usually in the early morning hours, the latter usually on the weekends and mostly later in the day or evening.

Some breakdowns by racial and ethnic groupings reveal that African Americans have had the highest rates of aggravated assaults and homicides and medium rates of suicides and attempted suicides, Latin Americans have had the lowest rates of suicide and attempted suicide and medium rates of aggravated assaults and homicides, and whites have had medium rates of suicides and attempted suicides and the lowest rates of aggravated assaults and homicides. Regarding sex, men accounted for about three fourths of the perpetrators and victims of suicide, aggravated assault, and homicide. Women accounted for three fourths of the perpetrators and victims of attempted suicide.

JUVENILE VICTIMIZATION

Box 2.9   Homosexual Juvenile Homicide

Twenty-three-year-old Joshua Brown was convicted of the rape and first-degree murder of a 13-year-old boy, Jesse Dirkhising, in Bentonville, Arkansas. "Jesse was allegedly

(Continued)

Box 2.9   (Continued)

---

drugged, bound, gagged, raped and sodomized in 1999 [September 26th] at the apartment that Brown shared with his gay lover, Davis Don Carpenter, 39." Carpenter was to face trial later in the year for rape and capital murder charges, as the state prosecutor maintained that the older man had mapped out the assault and watched a portion of it. Brown, who was found competent to stand trial, admitted that he had bound and gagged the boy and raped him with a variety of objects that caused the victim to bleed. Moreover, he "characterized the assault on Jesse as 'horseplay' and claimed that Jesse was a willing participant." The prosecutors argued that Jesse suffocated to death during the sexual assault because of a combination of the drugs and the way he was trussed up and strapped down to Brown's bed, which included the use of duct tape to bind him as well as the stuffing of Jesse's underwear into his mouth.

Source: Skoloff, B. (2001, March 22). *Jury split on rape, murder sentence.* Retrieved September 18, 2002, from http://www.cbsnews.com

---

The risks of juveniles (12 to 17 years old) becoming victims of either fatal or nonfatal violent crime increased between 1987 and 1991. Specifically, the homicide victimization rate for juveniles 14 to 17 years old had nearly doubled since the mid-1980s, although the rates for younger juveniles had remained relatively constant. The homicide victimization rate for this birth cohort (children born between 1976 and 1990) rose from fewer than 5 to more than 10 per 100,000. From 1985 through 1992, there were nearly 17,000 persons under 18 years old who were murdered in the United States (see Boxes 2.9 and 2.10). In 1992, 2,595 juveniles were killed, an average of 7 per day. Generally, homicide victimization rates are higher for children 5 years old and younger than for those between 6 and 11 years old. From 12 years through adolescence the rate increases, especially for boys. Before then, there is no appreciable difference between boys and girls. Approximately 3 out of 4 children killed are older that 11 years (Snyder & Sickmund, 1995).

Box 2.10   College Murder

In the case involving two sophomore friends in Hempstead, New York, Shaun Alexander, 23, a banking and finance major from an affluent suburb of Atlanta, had used a kitchen knife to stab and partly dismember Max Kolb, 20, an honors student from Kingston, Massachusetts. The killing occurred when Kolb had rejected the sexual advances of Alexander in a Hicksville motel. Alexander had lured Kolb to the motel under false pretenses, telling him that he needed to discuss some personal problems with him privately. After his advances were spurned, Alexander told authorities that he became very angry with Kolb and did the deed.

In videotaped statements to the police, Alexander told them where the body was buried. It could be found "behind a brick backyard barbecue at 539 West Park Avenue in Long Beach, where he had recently rented an apartment facing the Atlantic Ocean with money from his father, an investment banker. There, in a shallow grave, wrapped in plastic bags and a tarp, was Mr. Kolb's partly dismembered body" (Baker, 2001, p. B2). Police questioned Alexander about the possibilities of having committed other, similar acts, but he denied it. However, the police looked into it anyway, as they thought that this murderer "was very methodical and violent for a first-time offender" (p. B2).

Source: Baker, A. (2001, May 17). The search for a Hofstra sophomore becomes a college murder case. *New York Times,* pp. B1-B4.

The growth in juvenile homicide during this period was most pronounced in larger cities, those larger than a quarter million in population. Older boys were three times more likely to be killed than older girls, and black males 14 to 17 years old were significantly more likely than other juveniles to be homicide victims. Most juvenile victims knew their attackers quite well; young children were often killed by parents, older juveniles by their peers or by young adults. Most juvenile homicides involved victims and offenders of the same race (i.e., 92% for blacks and 93% for whites). "Forty percent of juvenile homicide victims were killed by family members, most of them by parents. Of these parent-killing-child cases, slightly more than half of the boys (53%) were killed by their fathers, and slightly more than half of the girls (51%) were killed by their mothers" (Snyder & Sickmund, 1995, p. 25).

In 1991, more than half of juvenile victims were killed with a firearm, followed in number by beatings, and then by use of a cutting or stabbing instrument. Characteristics of juvenile homicide also differed by sex and age. In one study (Loper & Cornell, 1996) of a national sample of 38,749 homicide arrestees identified in the Federal Bureau of Investigation's *Supplemental Homicide Reports* for 1984 and 1993, it was found that although little had changed about the circumstances of homicides committed by adolescent girls, there were consistent offense differences between boys and girls and between girls and women. For example, homicides involving adolescent girls tended to involve more interpersonal conflicts; homicides involving adolescent boys tended to involve an economic motive such as robbery. School killings in the mid- to late 1990s, however, seemed to be more about interpersonal conflicts in the context of extreme feelings of inadequacy and inferiority, as well as a lack of self-esteem and respect from the other (see Boxes 2.11 and 2.12). Moreover, girls were more likely than boys to use a knife rather than a firearm, and their victims were more likely than boys to be under the age of 13 years. Finally, compared to women (18 years old or older), adolescent girls were more likely to act with an accomplice, and their victims were more likely to be female and a peer between 13 and 20 years old (Loper & Cornell, 1996).

Box 2.11 High School Homicide

Kip Kinkel, a junior at Thurston High School, shot and killed his parents at their Oregon home one spring evening in May 1998. The next morning, he sprayed the high school cafeteria, which was full of students, with 50 rounds from a semiautomatic rifle, killing 2 and wounding 25. As part of a plea bargain, Kinkel confessed to his killings and assaults, reducing the charges to 4 counts of aggravated murder, 26 counts of aggravated attempted murder, and 1 count of assault on a detective at the police station (Kip was trying to provoke the detective into killing him). A note found on the coffee table in the Kinkel living room after his arrest read,

> I have just killed my parents! I don't know what is happening. I love my mom and dad so much. I just got two felonies on my record. My parents can't take that! It would destroy them. The embarrassment would be too much for them. They couldn't live with themselves. I'm so sorry. I am a horrible son. I wish I had been aborted. I destroy everything I touch. I can't eat. I can't sleep. I didn't deserve them. They were wonderful people. It's not their fault or the fault of any person, organization, or television show. My head just doesn't work right. God damn these VOICES inside my head. I want to die. I want to be done. But I have to kill people. I don't know why. I am so sorry! Why did God do this to me. I have never been happy. I wish I was happy. I wish I made my mother proud. I am nothing! I tried so hard to find happiness. But you know me I hate everything. I have no other choice. What have I become? I am so sorry.

In November 1999, after a protracted 6-day sentencing hearing, in which both sides presented evidence to Judge Jack Mattison to argue for a more severe or more lenient sentence, Kip Kinkel was sentenced to more than 111 years in prison, without a chance of parole. Although Kip and his lawyers plea-bargained to the lesser offenses rather than face the possibility of a first-degree murder conviction and death or life without parole should their "not guilty by reason of insanity" fail to persuade a jury, Kip's public defender, Jesse Barton, argued and presented psychological experts who testified to Kinkel's mental health.

During the proceedings, a number of experts, including two psychologists and one psychiatrist, were called by the defense to testify. Only one doctor testified that Kip was not mentally ill. He was Jeffrey Hicks, a child psychologist, who had treated Kip on nine occasions between January and June 1997. He had also recommended that the Kinkels have their son try an antidepressant. Hicks was further aware that Kip often for no apparent reason felt angry and would set off explosives to vent his feelings. After a short period during which Kip took Prozac, Dr. Hicks had concluded that Kip was better and that he no longer needed counseling or his antidepressant drug. Drs. Bolstad and Sac, who had not examined Kip before the murders, had very different diagnoses of Kinkel's mental condition.

Orin Bolstad, a psychologist who worked with juvenile killers in the Oregon penal system, met with Kip for over 32 hours. Bolstad, in some 4 hours of testimony, stated "that it was clear to him that Kip suffered from a psychotic disorder with major paranoid symptoms, potentially some forms of early onset schizophrenia." Tests indicated that Kip had a major learning disorder (of which the mother and father, as high school teachers, were aware; they had worked on it with Kip since he was in grade school). Other tests revealed "a very depressed, alienated child who sees adults as unfair, arbitrary and untrustworthy. He had very low self-esteem, and is manipulative and paranoid." Dr. Bolstad, in addition, described a number of delusional beliefs that Kip had related, and Bolstad's testimony revealed evidence of auditory hallucinations that were documented in an English course Kip had taken in 1998.

Dr. Sack testified that he believed Kip was a "very very sick psychotic individual." Although he was reluctant to definitely diagnose Kip because of his young age, Sack thought it was quite possible that as Kip grew older he might fall into one of two psychological categories: schizoaffective or paranoid schizophrenia. Asked whether or not Kip could be faking, Sack responded that he was as sure as he could be, based on the details of the stories and the emotional reactions that he had observed, that Kip was not.

Noteworthy testimony also came from Dr. Richard J. Konkol, a pediatric neurologist. Konkol shared images of computerized scans of Kinkel's brain, which showed "holes" that accounted for reduced blood flow to the frontal lobe, the area of the brain associated with emotional control and decision making. He further indicated that other aspects of Kip's behavior, such as his secretiveness and the lucid moments between killing each of his two parents and the students the next day, were not inconsistent with emerging schizophrenia.

Despite the formidable evidence, which was undisputed by the prosecution and favored a more lenient sentence, Judge Mattison focused on the 1996 change to the Oregon State Constitution requiring that a sentence should be sufficient to hold a person accountable for his actions. Hence, he sentenced Kinkel to "consecutive" rather than "concurrent" punishments. A concurrent sentence would have made Kip eligible for parole after 25 years of serving his sentence. On May 18, 2001, the public defender from Grants Pass filed an appeal to the Oregon Court of Appeals to reduce the sentence, arguing that the judge erred in giving more weight to the "protection of society" than to the "principle of reformation" as called for in the law.

Source: Kirk, M., Navasky, M., & O'Connor, K. (Producers). (2000, January 18). The killer at Thurston High [Television series episode]. In D. Fanning (Senior Executive Producer) & M. Sullivan (Executive Producer), *Frontline*. Boston: WGBH.

Box 2.12 The Smiling Gunman

The weekend before he carried out his Monday morning assault, which killed two students and wounded 13, Charles Andrew Williams had talked excitedly about the shootings at Columbine High in Littleton, Colorado, where two students had killed 12 fellow students and a teacher before committing suicide. He also talked about taking a

(Continued)

Box 2.12 (Continued)

weapon to school, but other kids thought he was joking around. Charles even said that he was joking when questioned by a friend of his mother's boyfriend. Williams was very small for his age, subject to getting picked on a lot, and thought to be dumb. People called him such names as "freak," "dork," and "nerd."

As Williams emerged from the restroom where he had just shot and killed two students at close range, and before he randomly began spraying the cafeteria with bullets, he could be seen looking around and smiling while brandishing his weapon. One student claimed that "he had an evil kind of sadistic demeanor to him" (CNN, 2001). At one point, when Andy ran back into the bathroom, he was followed by a security person and one student. He pointed the gun at both of them, and as they left, he fired one shot into the security person's back.

Williams, who moved to California with his father and brother after his parents divorced, rarely saw his mother, who was still back in rural Maryland. In a home video that was shown on the syndicated program *Inside Edition,* Williams could be seen playfully showing off his Santee home for his friends back in Maryland. Andy, who, since coming to Santana High, had been subject to much bullying, could also be heard on the video commenting about his life: "My school is horrible. I hate it here, everyone is horrible to me" (Tippit, 2001).

Mary Nederlander, the mother of Williams' former Maryland girlfriend Kathleen Seek, was quoted as saying, "He emailed us and told us that he just wanted to come home and that it was just awful over there. They were teasing him, calling him 'country boy.' He didn't dress right, he didn't look right. He was skinny, they called him gay" (Tippit, 2001). When Mary saw Andy in the police car on TV, he looked empty. "That wasn't the boy who came and ate dinner at our house and called me mom." That wasn't the boy she knew with "a gentle kind of heart" (Tippit, 2001).

Sources: CNN. (2001, March 6). *Shooting suspect reloaded "at least 4 times."* Retrieved September 18, 2002, from http://www.cnn.com/2001/US/03/06/school.shooting/index.html
Tippit, S. (2001, March 8). *Suspect teen nervous in first court hearing.* Retrieved March 9, 2001 from http://dailynews.yahoo.com

From 1984 to 1993, the risk of nonfatal violent victimizations, which include rape, robbery, aggravated assault, and simple assault, increased 17% for youth between 12 and 17 years old, compared to 24% for those between 18 and 24 years and with no change for those older than 24 years old. However, this grouping of nonfatal violent victimizations is misleading. If one factors out simple assaults from more serious violent behaviors (e.g., rape, robbery, and aggravated assault), then no statistically significant changes occurred in the nature of juvenile victimizations. In fact, the proportion involving serious injury declined slightly, although the percentage of serious violent incidents resulting in injury remained essentially the same. Once again, the changes in a juvenile's risk of violent crime differed by ethnicity and race. For example, the rate of victimization for non-Hispanic whites increased 21% during this period, from 57 to 69 per 1,000; for Hispanic whites it increased 40%, to a level equal to that of whites; and for blacks, the rate remained constant at 84 per 1,000 (Snyder & Sickmund, 1995).

Overall, numerous juvenile violence studies reveal that violent offenses are overwhelmingly committed by males, that the majority of juvenile victims of violence are male, and that African American males are disproportionately involved as both offenders and victims. Girls, however, appear to be getting more involved in violent behavior, with one study finding that, at age 13, slightly higher rates of violent behavior were reported for females than for males. Most officially recorded violent juvenile offenders live in impoverished neighborhoods and are involved in gangs. However, the majority of youth who live in high-risk environments are not involved in serious delinquency or violence, nor are they gang members. In sum, the research on juvenile violence has found that "there is a small group of offenders responsible for a large percentage of violent crime but that the majority of youth in these neighborhoods are not involved in violent offending" (Bilchik, 1999, p. x).

PHYSICAL AND SEXUAL CHILD ABUSE

Based on an analysis in 1991 of incarcerated violent offenders serving time in state prisons, approximately 61,000 offenders, or 1 out of 5, were convicted of a crime against a victim under age 18. More than half of the violent crimes committed against children involved victims 12 years old or younger. Seven out of 10 of those offenders reported that they were imprisoned for a rape or sexual assault. Similarly, two thirds of all prisoners convicted of rape or sexual assault committed their act against a child. Ninety-seven percent of violent child victimizers were male. Comparatively speaking, other characteristics of these offenders included

- On average, offenders who had victimized a child were 5 years older than those violent offenders who had committed their crimes against adults. Nearly 25% of child victimizers were 40 years old or older, whereas only 10% of the inmates with adult victims were over 40.
- Whites accounted for almost 70% of those serving time for violent crimes against children and for 40% of those imprisoned for violent crimes against adults.
- Inmates who had victimized children were less likely than other inmates to have had a previous criminal record. About 33% of the former had never been arrested prior to the current offense, compared to fewer than 20% of those who had victimized adults.
- Although the majority of all violent offenders, regardless of age, did not have a history of being physically or sexually abused when they were children, violent child victimizers were substantially more likely than those with adult victims to have experienced such violence.
- About 14% of child victimizers carried a weapon during the violent crime, compared to nearly half of those who victimized adults.
- Child victimizers experienced somewhat shorter average sentences (11 years) than offenders against adults.
- Three out of 10 child victimizers reported that they were more likely than adult victimizers to have had multiple victims. (Greenfeld, 1996, pp. 1-2)

Three out of four child victims of violence were female. Three quarters of the violent victimizations of children took place in either the victim's home or the offender's home. Four in ten child victims of violence suffered either a forcible rape or another injury. The vast majority of child victimizers in state prisons knew their victim before the crime. In fact, one third of these victimizers abused their own child; about half had a relationship with the victim as a friend, acquaintance, or relative other than parent; only 1 in 7 child victimizers reported that their victim had been a stranger to them (Greenfeld, 1996).

The literature on sexual offenders generally reveals problems of intimacy and loneliness stemming from inadequate child-parent experiences. Seidman, Marshall, Hudson, and Robertson (1994), for example, found in their study that "sex offenders showed greater deficiencies in intimacy than both control subjects and wife batterers. Furthermore, within sex offenders, rapists and nonfamilial child molesters appeared to be the most deficient in intimacy" (p. 547). Loneliness also significantly distinguished sex offenders from controls and batterers, but there were no significant differences in loneliness among the various sex offender groups. Rapists reported a far more violent family background than did any of the other sex offenders, and they were among the most deficient in intimacy. They were not, however, any more lonely, angry, or hostile toward women than other kinds of sex offenders. Most interestingly, wife batterers did not show any greater lack of intimacy than controls, and they did not have greater violence in their family of origin. Finally,

Seidman et al.'s research showed that violent nonsexual offenders, compared to non-violent and nonsexual offenders, child molesters, and rapists, scored significantly higher on measures of anger traits.

In a computer-administered interview, self-reports of past criminal behavior were obtained from 99 institutionalized sex offenders. The sample contained both rapists and child molesters. All of these sex offenders had been mandated to receive specialized treatment. Consistent with other self-report studies, offenders disclosed an enormous amount of undetected sexual aggression (e.g., sex offenses). The findings from this study also revealed an extensive overlap between sexual and nonsexual offenses, the latter involving crimes against both people and property: "nearly 20,000 nonsex crimes were committed during the year prior to institutionalization, with rapists contributing a disproportionate share [see Box 2.13]. Still, child molesters, including those whose only known crime was incest, were very active in assault and property crime" (Weinrott & Saylor, 1991, p. 286).

Box 2.13   Rapist Returns

Samuel Cusperte, 29, was charged with a brutal rape in Queens, New York, in the spring of 2001. Cusperte had a long criminal history, including charges of drug possession, arson, assault, and robbery. In this instance, he was charged with rape and robbery. He was also under suspicion for a similar rape and robbery in the Bronx.

In this case, after the accused had apparently followed the victim home from the train, he first assaulted her in the vestibule of her home and then proceeded to push her inside. According to Sgt. Jacob Brown, Cusperte demanded her money, and she handed him $70. "Then he took a pair of tweezers out of the victim's purse and jabbed it at her neck, saying, 'Give me more. What else do you have?' She then handed her attacker her cell phone, and Cusperte allegedly growled: 'I want what's behind the pocketbook'." The assailant then ripped off her pants and sexually assaulted her. At this point, the victim did not resist, as she feared for her life.

What was revealing in this particular case was the extent to which Cusperte regarded his behavior as not necessarily offensive or inappropriate. Ultimately, his cavalier attitudes about assault, robbery, and rape contributed to his being set up by the victim and caught by the police. Cusperte was lured back to the scene of the crime by the cell phone he had stolen from the victim. Investigators at the scene of the crime had persuaded the victim, a 29-year-old woman, to dial her own cell phone number to reach the attacker. When Cusperte, on his way back home to the Bronx, answered the phone, the victim told him, "I am not mad . . . Why don't you come back and meet me? I have some beer." Forty minutes later, Cusperte strode up her street drinking a 40-ounce beer. In his right pocket was the victim's cell phone; in his left pocket were her panties and $67 in cash. A positive identification by the victim resulted in the arrest of Cusperte.

Source: McPhee, M. (2001, April 26). Suspect lured into his arrest. *New York Daily News,* p. 6. Retrieved September 18, 2002, from http://nydailynews.com

As Weinrott and Saylor (1991) underscored, "Even the pedophiles were engaged in a significant amount of nonsexual criminal activity, far more than clinical staff had envisioned. It would appear, at least among this group of institutionalized 'sex psychopaths,' that specialization in sex crimes only is relatively rare" (p. 297). Some researchers with a psychoanalytic orientation have speculated that nonsexual crimes committed in conjunction with a sex crime or an attempt, or even the more removed auto theft, burglary, selling of drugs, kidnapping, assault, drunkenness, and so on and so forth, could be part of some men's sexual modus operandi (Weinrott & Saylor, 1991).

Sociologically, however, it would appear that the number and variety of nonsexual offenses have far exceeded the number of sexual offenses. Also, working against the Freudian interpretations that these behaviors share some kind of underlying motivation are the high frequency of aggravated assaults reported as not connected to any type of sexual offense. Whether these nonsexual offenses were or were not committed with sexual intent, most of them were relatively minor or trivial. This is true for both categories of offending. Most nonsexual offenses involve some minor transgression, such as public intoxication, carrying a concealed weapon, or petty theft. Most sexual offenses are also petty. That is to say, the majority of these sexual offenses do not involve any physical contact between the perpetrator and the victim.

RAPE

Rape or sexual assaults of nonchildren are, typically, criminal offenses in which victims who may be known or unknown to their offenders are forced or coerced to participate in sexual activity, including but not limited to acts of anal, oral, or vaginal penetration. According to the findings from the National Violence Against Women Survey, not only have 52% of women surveyed reported having been physically assaulted at some time in their lives, 54% have reported having experienced a completed or attempted rape, usually before their eighteenth birthday (Tjaden & Thoennes, 1998a). Most of these acts involved partners rather than strangers. Once more, the prevalence of reported rape and physical assault varied significantly among women of different racial and ethnic backgrounds.

Depending in part on the characteristics of both the perpetrators and the victims and in part on the relationship between the two parties to the conflict, physical violence may or may not be involved in rape or sexual assault (Douglas et al., 1992). For example, are the rapists and the victims of rape strangers, acquaintances, lovers, friends, spouses, or fathers and daughters? Most perpetrators of sexual assault are motivated less, if at all, by sex and more by an underlying emotional conflict or psychological issue that propels the interpersonal aggression in whatever form (e.g., molestation, rape, voyeurism) it takes.

It takes perhaps its most extreme expression in the case of serial rape-homicides (see Box 2.14). Today, most researchers, as well as the general public, regard sexual assaults as stemming primarily from sexual pathologies, behavioral disorders, and aggression management problems, rather than from some kind of sexual release and/or sexual need (Finkelhor & Yllo, 1985; Groth, 1979). A. Nicholas Groth (1990) has explained it this way:

> Rape is not primarily the aggressive expression of sexuality but rather the sexual expression of aggression. It is a pseudosexual act prompted more by retaliatory and compensatory motives than by sexual ones. It is complex and multidetermined, but involves issues of control and hostility more than those of passion and desire. The rapist is not assaulting because he is sexually frustrated or deprived, any more than the alcoholic is drinking because he is thirsty. (p. 74)

At the same time, this is not to argue that rapes or sexual assaults may not, in fact, be related to a person's identity or sexuality.

Box 2.14 Elder Rape and Murder

Through the use of DNA testing conducted in 1998 and 1999, investigators were able to connect Michael D. Harris, 37, to two murders in 1982: the September 30th slaying of 85-year-old Marjorie Upson and the October 1 death of 84-year-old Louise Köebnick. Although Harrison is serving a life sentence in the Brooks Correctional Facility in Muskegon County, Michigan, for the separate rapes and neck-slashing murders of two elderly women, 77 and 78, in Lansing in November and December 1981, he was also a suspect in the rape and murder of four elderly women in Ann Arbor and Ypsilanti during 1980 and 1981. These cases involved either slashing or strangulation. In addition, Harris was a suspect for four other nonfatal attacks on elderly women in Lansing. At the time of these acts, the alleged serial killer-rapist was only a teenager.

In late December, 1982, Harris was captured and charged with beating, raping, robbing, and the attempted murder of a 68-year-old woman in her Jackson, Michigan home. Five months later, he was convicted of first-degree rape and attempted murder. A few days after receiving a sentence of 60 to 90 years for his first conviction, Harris attempted suicide in his Jackson County Jail cell. Harris has been a suspect or may be considered responsible for as many as 15 killings statewide.

Harris grew up in Muskegon Heights, Michigan, and was 18 when he was sentenced to a 4-month jail term for breaking into the homes of two elderly women in Ingham County. After his release from jail, Harris first lived in Lansing and then in Jackson. It had appeared that the deaths and rapes of several elderly women conformed with his living patterns, but there was no DNA technology available that could establish the necessary links. At 19, labeled a drifter and found staying at the Interfaith Shelter for homeless men in Jackson, Harris was arrested once more and ultimately charged with the crimes that led to his 60- to 90-year sentence.

For the past 20 years, Harris and his mother, Betty, have both proclaimed his innocence. After each of his convictions, Harris told reporters that he was innocent and that he would appeal the verdicts. He never has. In a letter to the *Ann Arbor News,* mailed during the week of January 21, 2001, Harris (who changed his name while in prison to Malcolm Hakeem Abdul Ali) said that he was "totally innocent" of the DNA-related cases (i.e., Koebnick and Upson) in Washtenaw County. He also wrote,

> This is a very sad day for justice. I can only say that I am so sorry that the families of the victims, and my family, are being taken through the process of having the wounds reopened. I am not the scared 19-year-old boy that police railroaded in 1983. I am the 37-year-old man that will prove that there is a police cover-up in this matter. (Nash 2001a, p. A11).

Sources: Nash, A. (2001a, January 27). DNA connected to 2 deaths. *Ann Arbor News,* pp. A1, A11.
Nash, A. (2001b, January 26). 2 local deaths linked to serial killer. *Ann Arbor News,* pp. A1, A12.

There are a number of other characteristics that sexual assaulters tend to share in common (see also Chapter 7). First, they lack emotional empathy, the ability to feel for other persons or to put themselves in their victims' place. Unlike nonrapist heterosexual males, whose sexual arousal is frequently inhibited when they are presented with descriptions or pictures of violence during a sexual encounter, rapists may, in fact, experience increased sexual arousal associated with victim distress and violence during rape (Malamuth, 1992; Rice, Chaplin, Harris, & Coutts, 1994). Second, they possess cognitive factors associated with beliefs in rape myths or in various sexual and/or sexist stereotypes that not only help to justify their sexual behavior, but seem to be interconnected with a variety of risk factors for sexual assault (Kandel Englander, 1997). Third, sexual assaulters demonstrate psychological factors such as low self-esteem, doubts about masculinity, and a greater likelihood of distant and superficial personal relationships than nonrapists. Finally, many sexual offenders reveal childhood histories of sexual and/or physical abuse.

In conceptualizing rape as the sexual expression of aggression, Groth (1979, 1990) has identified three patterns of different yet overlapping dynamics of sexual violence at work. In other words, some rapes are about anger and violence, some are about control and domination, and some are about eroticized aggression. Nevertheless, "in every act of rape, there is present a combination of all these facets of aggression, but one will usually predominate" (Groth, 1990, p. 75).

Comparatively, the behavior of anger rapists seems to be the least sexual of the three forms. In anger rape, the sexual behavior of the offender appears as a means of expressing and discharging feelings of suppressed hostility and rage. The act is not really about sexual intercourse, as the assault is characterized by both physical brutality and force in excess of what would be necessary if the intent were merely to overpower the victim and achieve sexual intimacy. The objective in these sexual assaults is not the offenders' sexual gratification, but the satisfaction of their needs to hurt, punish, and/or humiliate their victims: "Sex becomes the means by which the offender can degrade his victim; through rape he retaliates for what he perceives to be wrongs experienced at the hands of others" (Groth, 1990, p. 75).

Anger rapes appear to be unplanned, impulsive, and spontaneous acts that come with little or no warning. Typically, these assaults are of short duration, some lasting only a few minutes. At the time of their offenses, these rapists have reported that they were not sexually aroused, nor did they anticipate raping anyone. On the contrary, some of these offenders reported that they could not achieve or sustain an erection. They did, however, report that they experienced feelings of anger and depression at the time of their assault. Hence, anger rapes are viewed as vehicles for discharging the offender's pent-up aggression and providing temporary relief from inner turmoil. In anger rape, a "frustration-aggression" reaction persists: tensions build and eventually explode into a violent sexual encounter ("climax"), and then the process repeats itself (Groth, 1990).

By contrast, power rapes are not about harming victims, but about dominating women sexually. The objectives of power rapists are to satisfy their needs to feel powerful and in control. At the same time, power rapists need to feel sexually wanted; they especially desire their victims to embrace their sexuality. Accordingly, their aggressive sexuality becomes a means of compensating for their underlying feelings of inadequacy. In other words, power rapes represent attempts to deny or combat feelings of helplessness and vulnerability.

Although power rapes may be opportunistic in origin, they are usually planned to the extent that these rapists' modus operandi involve capturing, controlling, and conquering their prey. Concerned about their sexual adequacy and competence, power rapists usually experience moods of high anxiety at the time of their assaults. As a result, like anger rapists, power rapists often find the act to be sexually unsatisfying, as their attempts at gaining sexual control of someone else leave them with no greater sense of control over their own lives, wherein the origins of their problems lie. Hence, one unsuccessful sexual encounter can often lead to a compulsion or need to try to sexually validate oneself through a repetition of power rapes.

In contrast to anger and power rapists, sadistic rapists experience a great deal of sexual satisfaction. In fact, they reveal countless ways of finding sexual pleasure. Despite their sexual fulfillment, sadistic rapists are considered the most "sick," or psychologically disordered, of the three groupings of rapists. Characterizations of sadistic rapists are made more complex by the fact that there are at least three kinds of sexually motivated sadists—*power*, *anger*, and *violent*. What these three sadist types share in common is that their sexuality and aggression have become fused or merged. In brief, the aggressive component of their psyches has become eroticized. Often, the conflation of sex and aggression is further aided by the victim's serving as a symbolic representation of some deep-seated and unresolved personality conflict.

In the case of power-sadist rapists, it is the power components of aggression that become eroticized; in the case of anger-sadist rapists, it is the anger components that become eroticized. Rapes by the former are typically characterized by both symbolic and ritualistic acts, such as bondage and domination. Rapes by the latter are characterized by sexual abuse and torture. As for the violent-sadist rapists, they specifically require aggression or some other form of violence to achieve sexual satisfaction. Their sexual excitement or arousal involves some kind of physical resistance on the part of the victim. The "taking of the woman" must, in other words, be against her will. These sexual assaults might require the use of objects or instruments (e.g., sticks, knives, bottles) to accomplish the deed. Finally, sadistic rapes in general are more planned and organized than anger or power rapes, and sadistic rapists have a "richer" fantasy life than do other rapists.

What about the characteristics of rape victims? Although it is often stated that any woman can be a victim of rape, the truth is that the risks of rape are not the same for all people. "As with any interpersonal violence, certain individuals are at higher risk than others of being vulnerable to sexual victimization" (Kandel Englander, 1997, p. 113). For example, statistical relationships have been found between childhood sexual victimization and sexual victimization with dating partners. Similarly, research has shown not only that earlier victimization experiences were a risk factor for later victimization, but that the more severe those earlier victimizations were, the more likely were subsequent episodes of sexual violence. Studies of a variety of ethnic women have found that a prior history of incest or rape for all groups of women was a risk factor for later sexual victimization. Still other studies have suggested that certain women, such as sorority members, women with psychiatric

or developmental difficulties, the homeless, prostitutes, and runaways were at greater risk of sexual victimization than were those women who did not belong to any of these groups (Kandel Englander, 1997; Totten, 2000).

What most, if not all, of these women share in common is a lack of physical, psychological, and cultural power in relation to their particular sexual abusers, whether the abusers are fraternity members, custodial staff, or sexual clients. In a study of teenage girls and sexual assault in Memphis, for example, the picture of sexual assault there mirrored the picture nationally. Young women from 14 to 17 years old were at the highest risk for sexual assault, including what the authors referred to as "statutory" rape (in which victims are less than 18 years old and perpetrators are at least 4 years older) and sexual battery, including fondling and other forms of molestation (Betts, 2000).

More specifically, 20% of the young women in the Memphis study were sexually assaulted by relatives, friends of relatives, or other "family-like" perpetrators. Another 20% of these female victims believed themselves to be involved in serious relationships; their parents and guardians were the primary complainants, and they were uncooperative daughters. In other words, these cases were brought to court over the protests of the adolescent girls, who believed that they were in consensual relationships with their boyfriends. Whatever might be the truth of these relationships, in cases that did not involve family-like perpetrators and in which suspects were identified, 35% of the male "perpetrators" were at least 25 years old. Some have argued that these sexual assaults are more about environmental and cultural or situational factors than about psychodynamic factors: "Much of the sexual assault in this city occurs in a social and economic context where resources others may take for granted are scarce; adults are working two and three jobs to make ends meets; and young people must fend for themselves in the hours after school" (Betts, 2000, p. 7). As important, if not more so, are the underlying attitudes of misogyny and sexism that are regularly expressed toward powerless girls and women in society:

> The contempt for women and girls displayed in so many of these assaults is all too common to women of all races and classes. In the majority of cases, young women are assaulted and abused by casual acquaintances who appear to have no reservations about self-gratification and no respect for their victims. While most perpetrators do not fit the image of the murderous sexual psychopath, they appear to have a distorted view of sexual relationships and demonstrate little empathy for girls and women. (Betts, 2000, p. 7)

STALKING

Since the early 1990s, antistalking laws have been established in all 50 states and the District of Columbia. Legal definitions of stalking vary from state to state. Although most states "define stalking as the willful, malicious, and repeated following and harassing of another person," some states "include in their definition such activities as lying-in-wait, surveillance, nonconsensual communication, telephone harassment, and vandalism" (Tjaden & Thoennes, 1998b, pp. 1-2). Most states require further that the acts not be one-time occurrences, some stipulating how many acts are required (usually two or more). Some states require that the alleged stalker's course of conduct constitute only an implied threat; others require that the alleged stalker have made a credible threat of violence against the victim or the victim's immediate family. The definition of stalking used by the National Violence Against Women Survey (1995-1996) was "a course of conduct directed at a specific person that involves repeated visual or physical proximity, nonconsensual communication, or verbal, written or implied threats, or a combination thereof, that would cause a reasonable person fear" (Tjaden & Thoennes, 1998b, p. 2).

The findings from the National Violence Against Women Survey revealed that stalking was a significant social problem: 8% of women and 2% of men in the United States had been stalked at some time in their life. However, if less stringent definitions of stalking are used, such as "requiring victims to feel only somewhat frightened or a little frightened by their assailant's behavior," then rates rise to 12% and 4%, respectively (Tjaden & Thoennes, 1998b, p. 4). Annually, it is estimated that 1,006,970 women and 370,990 men are stalked. Based on U.S. census estimates, 1 out of every 12 women (8.2 million) and 1 out of every 45 men (2 million) have been stalked at some time in their lives. According to the survey, three quarters of stalking victims (74%) were between 18 and 39 years old.

Compared to other violent behaviors, stalking is considered to be a "gender-neutral" crime. For example, the National Violence Against Women Survey tallied responses from 8,000 men and 8,000 women regarding rape, physical assault, and stalking. In a 1-year period, women were three times more likely to be stalked than raped and two times more likely to be physically assaulted than stalked. Men were more than four times as likely to be stalked than raped and 8.5 times as likely to be physically assaulted than stalked. Nevertheless, women were still the primary victims of stalking (78%) and men were the primary perpetrators (87%). The survey also confirmed the fact that most victims knew their stalker. For example, stranger stalkers were involved in 23% of female stalking cases and in 36% of male stalking cases. The most common stalker is an intimate or former intimate (e.g., spouse or exspouse, cohabitant or excohabitant, lover or exlover). But this too varies significantly by gender. Female victims were stalked by intimate partners 59% of the time, compared with 30% of the time for male victims: a ratio of almost 2 to 1 (Tjaden & Thoennes, 1998b).

Interestingly, in terms of antistalking laws that require overt threats, "the survey found that less than half the victims—both male and female—were directly threatened by their stalker" (Tjaden & Thoennes, 1998b, pp. 7-8). Based on victims' perceptions (rather than perpetrators' reports or responses), the motivations surrounding stalking behavior in rank order were (1) 21% of stalkers wanted to control the victim, (2) 20% of stalkers wanted to keep the victim in the relationship, (3) 16% of stalkers wanted to scare the victim, (4) 7% of stalkers were mentally ill or abusing drugs or alcohol, (5) 5% of stalkers wanted or liked the attention, and (6) 1% wanted to catch the victim doing something wrong. In the other cases, victims were not sure why.

The survey provided "compelling evidence of the link between stalking and other forms of violence in intimate relationships" (Tjaden & Thoennes, 1998b, p. 8). Eighty-one percent of women who were stalked by a current or former intimate were also physically assaulted, and 31% had been sexually assaulted. Comparatively, "husbands or partners who stalk their partners are four times more likely than husbands or partners in the general population to physically assault their partners, and they are six times more likely than husbands and partners in the general population to sexually assault their partners (Tjaden & Thoennes, 1998b, p. 8). The survey also found that about two thirds of all stalking cases lasted a year or less, about a quarter lasted 2 to 5 years, and a tenth lasted more than 5 years (average, 1.8 years). The three most prevalent reasons

given by victims for the stopping of stalking were (1) 19% of the victims had moved away, (2) 8% of the stalkers had found a new love interest, and (3) 15% said the stalking ended after the perpetrator received a warning from the police.

Similarly, compelling links were found between stalking and controlling and emotionally abusive behavior. The survey's Exhibit 14: Percentage of Ex-Husbands Who Engaged in Emotionally Abusive or Controlling Behavior, by Whether They Stalked revealed significant differences across 11 indicators. For example, percentages of stalking and nonstalking exhusbands who were "jealous or possessive" were 83.7% and 46.3%, respectively; who "tried to provoke arguments," 90.3% and 45.3%; who "tried to limit her contact with family and friends" or "prevented her from working outside the home," 77.1% and 32.3%, and 30.7% and 13.0, respectively; who "insisted on knowing where she was at all times," 80.7% and 34.4%; who "made her feel inadequate," 85.5% and 40.9%; and who "frightened her," 92.2% and 33.1% (Tjaden & Thoennes, 1998b).

Finally, in terms of the psychological and social consequences of stalking, there was evidence of a negative impact on mental health. In general, "about a third of the women (30%) and a fifth of the men (20%) said they sought psychological counseling as a result of their stalking victimization. In addition, stalking victims were significantly more likely than non–stalking victims to be very concerned about being stalked, to carry something on their person to defend themselves, and to think personal safety for men and women had gotten worse in recent years" (Tjaden & Thoennes, 1998b, p. 11). In fact, 26% of the stalking victims reported that their victimization caused them to lose time from work; 7% reported that they never returned to work. On the average, victims who lost time from and returned to work missed 11 days.

SUMMARY

This chapter has presented a demographic overview of five common forms of interpersonal violence. These include homicide, juvenile victimization, physical and sexual child abuse, rape, and stalking. Although these acts of interpersonal violence have different and overlapping characteristics and pathways to actual performance, the perpetrators all, to varying degrees, share a lack of empathy or identification with their victims, known or unknown. Actions of interpersonal violence and conflict are also about feelings of inadequacy, shame, and disrespect. Finally, interpersonal acts of violence seem to reflect the inabilities of persons to control their emotions of abandonment, loss, depression, anger, embarrassment, and/or narcissism.

For the purposes of enhancing the depictions of interpersonal violence, real-world "cases" were used to describe the contextual nature of these actions. These examples tended to reflect the availability of mass-media coverage of interpersonal violence, such as it is. That is to say, the case illustrations were drawn primarily from narratives about murder and sexual assault rather than from narratives of child molestation or adult stalking. There are certainly more news and entertainment stories of the former than of the latter, and the illustrations provided were not meant to suggest that rape and homicide, for example, were or are more prevalent or serious than juvenile victimization or physical and sexual child abuse. In fact, the more prevalent and more serious cases of interpersonal violence would be those associated with child abuse and juvenile victimization rather than with adult rape or homicide. Past or present, these demographic relations hold true in terms of both the incidents of and pathways to violence.

As was pointed out in the previous chapter, the worlds of interpersonal, institutional, and structural violence are interactive and reciprocal worlds that blend into each other. It is as difficult to distinguish between the interpersonal and institutional aspects of sexual harassment and sexual assault (see Box 2.1) as it is to distinguish, for example, between all of the cultural and social-psychological aspects shared in the sexual "objectification" of females as cheerleaders, lap dancers, and calendar pin-ups, and what could be thought of as a rather rare or unusual and extreme form of collective or institutionalized "stalking" (see Box 3.1). In the next chapter, the descriptions of violence move from the interpersonal to the institutional level of analysis.

REFERENCES

Aitken, R. (2001, June 1). *Inside McVeigh's mind*. Retrieved September 18, 2002, from http://news.bbc.co.uk/1/hi/world/americas/1382540.stm

Baker, A. (2001, May 17). The search for a Hofstra sophomore becomes a college murder case. *New York Times*, p. B1.

Becker, E. (2000, May 12). Women in military say silence on harassment protects careers. *New York Times*, p. A1.

Betts, P. (2000). Something to think about . . . Reflections on teen girls and sexual assaults. *Center News, 18*(2), 2, 7-8.

Bilchik, S. (1999). *Report to Congress on juvenile violence research*. Washington, DC: U.S. Department of Justice.

Brown, R. M. (1987). *Religion and violence* (2nd ed.). Philadelphia: Westminister.

CNN. (2001, March 6). *Shooting suspect reloaded "at least 4 times."* Retrieved September 18, 2002, from http://www.cnn.com/2001/US/03/06/school.shooting/index.html

Cobbs, L. (2000, August 4). Convicted murderer gets life in prison. *Ann Arbor News*, pp. C1, C4.

Dead men tell no tales [Television series episode]. In S. Zirinsky (Executive Producer), *48 hours*. New York: CBS News.

Douglas, J. E., Burgess, A. W., Burgess, A. G., & Ressler, R. K. (1992). *A pocket guide to the crime classification manual: A standard system for investigating and classifying violent crimes*. New York: Lexington.

Finkelhor, D., & Yllo, K. (1985). *License to rape: Sexual abuse of wives*. New York: Holt, Rinehart and Winston.

Fleming, A. T. (2002, March 17). Ideas and trends: Crime and motherhood; maternal madness. *New York Times*, §4, p. 3.

Gifis, S. H. (1975). *Law dictionary*. Woodbury, NY: Barron's Educational Series.

Gilligan, J. (1997). *Violence: Reflections on a national epidemic*. New York: Vintage.

Greenfeld, L. A. (1996). *Child victimizers: Violence offenders and their victims* (Bureau of Justice Statistics NCJ 153258). Retrieved September 18, 2002, from http://www.ojp.usdoj.gov/bjs/abstract/cvvoatv.htm

Groth, A. N. (1979). *Men who rape: The psychology of the offender*. New York: Plenum.

Groth, A. N. (1990). Rape: Behavioral aspects. In N. A. Weiner, M. A. Zahn, & R. J. Sagi (Eds.), *Violence: patterns, causes, public policy*. New York: Harcourt Brace College.

Kandel Englander, E. (1997). *Understanding violence*. Mahwah, NJ: Lawrence Erlbaum.

Kirk, M., Navasky, M., & O'Connor, K. (Producers). (2000, January 18). The killer at Thurston High [Television series episode]. In D. Fanning (Senior Executive Producer) & M. Sullivan (Executive Producer), *Frontline*. Boston: WGBH.

Loper, A. B., & Cornell, D. G. (1996). Homicide by juvenile girls. *Journal of Child and Family Studies*, 5(3), 323-336.

Luckenbill, D. F. (1990). Criminal homicide as a situated transaction. In N. A. Weiner, M. A. Zahn, & R. J. Sagi (Eds.), *Violence: Patterns, causes, public policies*. Fort Worth, TX: Harcourt Brace College.

Malamuth, N. (1992). Evolution and laboratory research on men's sexual arousal: What do the data show and how can we explain them? *Behavior and Brain Sciences*, 15, 394-396.

McPhee, M. (2001, April 26). Suspect lured into his arrest. *New York Daily News*, p. 6. Retrieved September 18, 2002, from http://nydailynews.com

Menninger, K. (1938). *Man against himself*. New York: Harcourt, Brace.

Miller, A. (1990). *For your own good: Hidden cruelty in child-rearing and the roots of violence*. New York: Farrar, Straus and Giroux.

Nash, A. (2001a, January 27). DNA connected to 2 deaths. *Ann Arbor News*, pp. A1, A11.

Nash, A. (2001b, January 26). 2 local deaths linked to serial killer. *Ann Arbor News*, pp. A1, A12.

Pokorny, A. D. (1990). Human violence: A comparison of homicide, aggravated assault, suicide, and attempted suicide. In N. A. Weiner, M. A. Zahn, & R. J. Sagi (Eds.), *Violence: Patterns, causes, public policy*. Fort Worth, TX: Harcourt Brace College.

Rice, M., Chaplin, T. C., Harris G. T., & Coutts, J. (1994). Empathy for the victim and sexual arousal among rapists and non-rapists. *Journal of Interpersonal Violence*, 9(4), 435-449.

Ross, B., & Hutchinson, B. (2000, December 15). Slay trial's t-shirt twist. *New York Daily News*, p. 22. Retrieved September 18, 2002, from http://nydailynews.com

Ross, B., Peterson, H., & Goldiner, D. (2000, December 21). Kee guilty in rape-slay spree, faces life term. *New York Daily News*, p. 4. Retrieved September 18, 2002, from http://nydailynews.com

Ross, B., & Standora, L. (2000, December 14). Rape-slay defendant denies guilt on stand. *New York Daily News*, p. 17. Retrieved September 18, 2002, from http://nydailynews.com

Salamon, J. (2001). *Facing the wind: The true story of tragedy and reconciliation*. New York: Random House.

Saulny, S. (2001, June 14). Man who killed 2 outside gay bar remains mentally ill, a jury finds. *New York Times*, p. B8.

Seidman, B. T., Marshall, W. L., Hudson, S. M., & Robertson, P. J. (1994). An examination of intimacy and loneliness in sex offenders. *Journal of*

Interpersonal Violence, 9(4). 518-534.

Skoloff, B. (2001, March 22). *Jury split on rape, murder sentence.* Retrieved September 18, 2002, from http://www.cbsnews.com

Sky News. (2001, April 28). *The McVeigh letter in full.* Retrieved September 19, 2002, from http://www.sky.com/skynews

Snyder, H., & Sickmund, M. (1995). *Juvenile offenders and victims: A national report.* Washington, DC: U.S. Department of Justice.

Stewart, J. (2001, April 1). A case of insanity: A review of *Facing the wind. New York Times Review of Books,* p. 10.

Thomas, E. (2001, July 2). Motherhood and murder. *Newsweek,* pp. 20-25.

Tippit, S. (2001, March 8). *Suspect teen nervous in first court hearing.* Retrieved March 9, 2001 from http://dailynews.yahoo.com

Tjaden, P., & Thoennes, N. (1998a). *Prevalence, incidence, and consequences of violence against women: Findings from the national violence against women survey* (National Institute of Justice and Centers for Disease Control and Prevention NCJ 172837). Retrieved September 18, 2002, from http://www.ojp.usdoj.gov/nij/pubs-sum/172837.htm.

Tjaden, P., & Thoennes, N. (1998b, April). *Stalking in America: Findings from the national violence against women survey.* Washington, DC: U.S. Department of Justice, National Institute of Justice. Retrieved September 23, 2002, from http://www.ncjrs.org/pdf-files/169592.pdf

Totten, M. D. (2000). *Guys, gangs, and girlfriend abuse.* Peterborough, Ontario, Canada: Broadview.

Weiner, N. A., Zahn, M. A., & Sagi, R. J. (Eds.). (1990). *Violence: Patterns, causes, public policy.* Fort Worth, TX: Harcourt Brace College.

Weinrott, M. R., & Saylor, M. (1991). Self-report of crimes committed by sex offenders. *Journal of Interpersonal Violence,* 6(3), 286-300.

Wolfgang, M. E. (1958). *Patterns of criminal homicide.* Philadelphia: University of Pennsylvania Press.

Wolfgang, M. E., & Zahn, M. A. (1990). *Homicide: Behavioral aspects.* In N. A. Weiner, M. A. Zahn, & R. J. Sagi (Eds.), *Violence: Patterns, causes, public policy.* Fort Worth, TX: Harcourt Brace College.

REVIEW QUESTIONS

1. Provide a comprehensive definition of interpersonal violence.

2. What, if any, are the similarities and differences between mass killer Timothy McVeigh, serial rapist and killer Arohn Kee, and family killer Bob Rowe?

3. What, if any, are the similarities and differences between Kip Kinkel, Charles Williams, and Andrea Yates?

4. Of the five types of violence examined in this chapter, rank order from most to least serious or most to least dangerous to society. Explain your answer.

5. Compare and contrast the typical perpetrators and victims of child abuse, sexual assault, and stalking.

CHAPTER 3

Institutional Violence

Like interpersonal forms of violence, institutional forms include physically or emotionally abusive acts. However, institutional forms of violence are usually, but not always, impersonal: that is to say, almost any person from the designated group of victims will do (see Box 3.1). Moreover, abuses or assaults that are practiced by corporate bodies—groups, organizations, or even a single individual on behalf of others—include those forms of violence that over time have become "institutionalized," such as war, racism, sexism, terrorism, and so on. These forms of violence may be expressed directly against particular victims by individuals and groups or indirectly against entire groups of people by capricious policies and procedures carried out by people "doing their jobs," differentiated only by a myriad of rationales and justifications. Finally, institutional violations cannot be thought of as separate or distinct from other spheres of violence. These acts of violence, even more so than acts of interpersonal violence, take on their meanings from their larger social and ideological contexts. Institutional forms of violence also serve as conduits between interpersonal and structural forms of violence.

Box 3.1   Rampage in Central Park

At least 16 young men were arrested for participating in a frenzy of sexual assaults on 48 women during gatherings in Central Park after the National Puerto Rican Day Parade along Fifth Avenue, June 16, 2000. These assaults consisted of chasing, spitting, yelling, throwing and pouring ice and water, tearing off clothes, and groping breasts, buttocks, and genitals. Eventually, all the men would be charged with first-degree sexual abuse and first-degree riot. The actions occurred an hour or so after the parade was officially over, around 6:00 p.m. Explanations for the rampage in the park ranged from nonresponsive police behavior to "spontaneous combustion." A relatively small number of participants and observers were involved, compared to the parade crowd, which was estimated to be about 1 million.

(Continued)

Box 3.1 (Continued)

A number of ingredients may have contributed to the worst of the violence, such as the alchemy of alcohol, drugs, oppressive weather, testosterone, and even the overlapping police jurisdictions in the Manhattan borough. At the same time, the collective violence perpetrated that late afternoon in the park was primarily directed against young women by groups of unrelated young men. It also reflected an extreme version of patriarchal-marginal culture and the objectification of women as sexual targets. The sexual assaults were neither premeditated nor organized but were, rather, a function of institutionalized beliefs and gender relations moving beyond or "out of control." According to several eyewitness accounts and a number of home video cameras, the scenario unfolded as follows:

It was about 5:15 P.M., still above 90 degrees, when a burly young man stole a bag of ice from an ice van that had stopped on the Avenue of the Americas just south of the park. Witnesses said the man, a distinctive figure with a lion's face tattooed across his bare back and the words "Puerto Rico" shaved into the back of his head, began pressing the ice bag against the backs of young women. Someone punctured the ice bag, and young men began dropping ice cubes down women's shirts. Several women laughed and smiled and sassed the young men. But at least one woman grew angry when men surrounded her and trapped her against a storefront, dousing her with water.

There were several police officers in the area, and one, a supervisor in a white shirt, was seen by passers-by leading off a young man who had been involved in the ice cube horseplay. Things quieted for a bit, but then . . . the group re-formed just inside the park, on Center Drive. Now self-appointed "scouts" began to signal to the larger group when they spotted women who fit their calculus of sexual appeal. "Yo, yo, here comes a good one!" they would call out, as unsuspecting women approached. Several older women got through. For the young and attractive, nearby fences helped form a natural chute into which they were steered.

Many [women] said they had no idea what they were entering until it was too late. Men would close around them from all sides, spraying water on their heads, their backs, and everywhere.

Some women said they tried to stay near friends, but they were quickly separated by the crowd. They screamed their friends' names, to no avail. Some women tried to run, only to be chased down and surrounded once more. The men yelled, "Get 'em, get 'em," chanted "Go, go, go," and shouted misogynistic curses. More young men joined the mob—men who wore crucifixes.

Some of these men began to tear at the women's shirts, to pull on their bras, to tug on their shorts. The women, of course, fought to stay clothed. They clutched torn shirts to their chests and tried to swat sweaty hands away from their straps and zippers. But they were hopelessly outnumbered, and several of them suddenly found themselves half-naked in a bleary, swirling crowd of strange men.

One young woman, her hair matted with beer and water, her top torn off, huddled against a wall, and still men tried to grope at her. Some women said they were groped and grabbed and prodded so violently that their genitals were scratched or bruised. Some of the women began to fear that they were going to be gang raped right there in the shadow of Trump Tower, right there inside the crown jewel of New York City.

As more men were drawn to the mob, some took pictures, some took videos, and some robbed the women of their cell phones, purses, and jewelry. Few if any offered assistance, called 911, or went for help. Perhaps the men with the strangest reactions were those who seemed bored by the whole scene. "It was as if the crowd had turned a patch of Central Park into an outdoor version of a topless bar, only it was worse; the women were not willing participants, and there were no bouncers to protect them." Again, the fact that this gruesome and pathetic display of violence and abuse happened with at least the tacit approval of numerous bystanders raises fundamental questions about the social forces of patriarchy and gender, especially as these intersect with the masculinities of marginalized males.

Source: Barstow, D., & Chivers, C. J. (2000, June 17). A volatile mixture exploded into rampage in Central Park. *New York Times*, p. A1. Retrieved September 24, 2002, from http://www.nytimes.com. Reprinted with permission.

Comparatively, acts of institutional violence have been less visible than acts of interpersonal violence and more visible than acts of structural violence. Nevertheless, historically, the United States has paid little attention to the institutionalized nature of family, economic, military, religious, and state violence, or to thinking about these expressions of violence as "social problems" worthy of amelioration and reform. Unawareness, disinterest, acceptance, and denial have been the cornerstones upon which the invisibility and silence regarding these forms of violence are based.

Only since the early 1960s, for example, has the United States taken family violence seriously. Other forms of institutionalized violence, however, remain fairly hidden, occasionally rising into public consciousness. In this chapter, attention is focused on the following five representative forms of institutional violence:

- Family violence
- Childhood maltreatment
- School violence
- Gang violence
- Police and penal violence

Before turning to an examination of these institutional forms of violence, two historical illustrations of institutionalized racial violence, nearly a century apart, are presented as a way of underscoring the social and reciprocal interaction of conditions and acts of violence (see Boxes 3.2 and 3.3). Both of these cases of institutionalized violence, in related ways, expose the interconnected relations between the overt perpetrators of the deeds and the various roles played by authority figures in the selective and nonenforcement patterns of law and order. Legacies of the Hamburg riot in South Carolina, July 8, 1876, and of the Birmingham church bombing in Alabama, September 15, 1963, and of other acts of violence like them, North and South, may be seen today in various forms. These include institutionalized racism and marginalized examples of white supremacy (i.e., hate violence), which are related to other forms of bias violence that still persist across the American landscape, such as homophobic assaults against lesbians and gay men.

Box 3.2   The Hamburg Riot, 1876

The biography of Ben Tillman written by Stephen Kantrowitz (2000) is an excellent book from which to gain understanding of how racism took hold in the post–Civil War South and gradually spread to the rest of the country. The keys, Kantrowitz argues, are located in the ideologies and foundations of white supremacy. For close to half a century, Tillman was one of America's foremost ideologues and architects of racism and white supremacy. In fact, it is due to his early leadership role as commander of Edgefield County's Sweetwater Sabre Club, a paramilitary unit dedicated to terrorizing Republican officeholders and restoring white rule in South Carolina, that he established his political career, first as governor of South Carolina and then (for the next 24 years) as one of their U.S. senators.

On July 8, 1876, the 29-year-old Tillman, with his red-shirted troopers, participated in the Hamburg riot, which was marked by the cold-blooded, execution-style murders of a number of black militiamen who had had the audacity to conduct a celebratory parade through the predominantly black town of Hamburg, SC, 4 days earlier on the Fourth of July. For the record, none of the perpetrators of the murders were ever brought to justice. Quite the contrary. Tillman, for example, bragged constantly about his role in the events of that day. More important, he developed and proved himself a master of social discourse when it came to pillorying his well-bred political opponents, referring to them as "white Negroes" and "dudes."

In the 1890s, while he was governor, an epidemic of mob violence broke out in South Carolina, and lynchings for the decade outnumbered legal executions.

On these matters, Governor Tillman has been historically remembered for saying at least two things: First, there was his famous "lynching pledge," in which he "coupled a statement opposing lynching with a declaration that he would 'willingly lead a mob in lynching a Negro who had committed an assault upon a white woman'" (Dew, 2000); second, there was his often-quoted line that the black man "must remain subordinate or be exterminated." As for Tillman's supporters, at least one group in Abbeville, SC, arranged a banner acclaiming the governor as the "Champion of White Men's Rule and Women's Virtue."

Throughout his political career, and up until his death in 1918, Tillman was a highly paid national speaker on the lecture circuit. His lecture on "the race problem" was by far his most popular. Tillman preached "the gospel of white supremacy straight from the shoulder" and a "witches' brew of bare-knuckled, no-holds barred racism" (Dew, 2000). Kantrowitz underscores the legacy that these teachings have left behind and how

Tillman and his political allies at the time significantly undermined any chance of developing a race-neutral language of manhood and citizenship in the South and beyond. In different words, in the post–Civil War South, which was ripe with the cultural reconstruction of white supremacy, white men were determined to reclaim what they had lost through the emancipation of the black man and the white experience of Reconstruction.

Many white men, Kantrowitz argues, were yearning for a past that included a relatively independent and unfettered manhood. Given the blow to white southern manhood, Tillman sought to make the slogan "white supremacy" into a social reality. He did so, throughout his political career, by trying to reconstruct white male authority in every sphere of society, from the individual household to state and national politics. Tillman's constituency believed that the end of slavery and the enfranchising of blacks had set loose a threat to white society that had to be checked by whatever means necessary. It took a man like Tillman—"an ideologue, an organizer and a terrorist" (Dew, 2000)—to give voice to their fears and to translate their determination into physical and political action.

Sources: Dew, C. B. (2000, May 21). Tightening the noose: *Ben Tillman and the reconstruction of white supremacy*, by Stephen Kantrowitz. *New York Times Review of Books*, p. 31. Retrieved October 2, 2002, from http://www.nytimes.com

Kantrowitz, S. (2000). *Ben Tillman and the reconstruction of white supremacy*. Chapel Hill, NC: University of North Carolina.

Carry Me Home, written by journalist and Birmingham born and raised Diane McWhorter (2001), picks up historically where Kantrowitz's portrayal leaves off. McWhorter's story begins in the 1920s and moves across time to the church bombings in Birmingham during the height of the civil rights era, the 1960s. Her analysis of the context and of the conditions or states of violence at this time period and beyond is comprehensive. For example, she highlights the collaboration between the Klansmen, local and national law enforcers (including the Federal Bureau of Investigation), and the barons of southern business or, as they were known at the time, the Big Mules. Her book masterfully weaves through both the segregationist and integrationist sides of Birmingham. In the process, she indicts just about everyone for the bombing of the 16th Street Baptist Church, including the *New York Times*, CBS, John F. and Robert

---

Box 3.3   The Birmingham Church Bombing, 1963

Depicting Birmingham as sitting at the crossroads of some of this country's momentous antagonisms—between black and white, Jew and gentile, Roman Catholic and Protestant, labor and industry, communist and anticommunist—McWhorter explains how as early as the 1920s, the Ku Klux Klan's anti-Catholicism had taught the coal and

(Continued)

Box 3.3   (Continued)

---

steel industrialists the value of "divide and conquer" as a means of defeating union solidarity even among whites, let alone across color lines. For example, the antiunion vigilantism committed by the Klan, which was on the payroll of U.S. Steel and other corporations, set the patterns that lasted decades. Unwilling to dirty their own hands or to give specific orders calling for racial violence, these industrialists promoted and employed racism by delegating political intermediaries to oversee the actual deeds of violence.

Chief among those intermediaries was Eugene "Bull" Connor, Birmingham's notorious commissioner for public safety. Not only did Bull run the Klan-based vigilantes on behalf of the Big Mules, his vigilantes included such people as Robert Chambliss, who organized the church bombings, and Troy Ingram, who rigged the exploding devices. Both of these men were miners and on the payroll of the Charles DeBardeleben coal mining company. McWhorter's book skillfully exposes the intricacy of segregationist alliances among corporations, judges, politicians, local newspaper editors, the police, and the Klan.

Source: McWhorter, D. (2001). Carry me home: Birmingham, Alabama: The climactic battle of the civil rights movement. New York: Simon and Schuster.

F. Kennedy, and Martin Luther King, Jr., all as parts of the foundation of bigotry.

A fundamental difference, then, as these recent and not so recent historical events reveal, between interpersonal and institutional violence has to do with the ways in which systematic violations can become, de facto, legitimate or acceptable through a covert consensus of cultural denial, accompanied by overt political and social inaction. Often, institutionalized behavioral patterns of violence are also sanctioned by both the perpetrators and the victims of the abuse. In the contemporary period, during the relatively recent decline of patriarchy and the rise of sexual equality in the workplace, a classic illustration of these cultural blinders to abuse can be seen in the numerous instances, official and unofficial, of sexual harassment in those occupations worked traditionally by men, such as in the Wall Street financial industry (Antilla, 2002).

FAMILY VIOLENCE

Among institutional forms of violence in the United States, family or domestic violence is the most publicly recognized and delegitimized form of violence. Initially, this form of violence pertained to the physical abuse, victimization, and exploitation of children and wives. In particular, there were the discoveries of battered child syndrome in the early 1960s and battered wife syndrome in the early 1970s. Although the past 30 years have seen institutionalized social service and welfare responses to these forms of abuse, the historical legacies of family violence die hard. "Violence between family members has enjoyed a long tradition of legal legitimization. In 1824, the Mississippi Supreme Court was the first of several states to grant husbands immunity from assault and battery charges for moderately chastising their wives"

(Gelles, 1990, p. 106). These statutes were consistent with the "rule of thumb," traceable to the older English common law that gave husbands the right to strike their wives with a stick no wider than their thumb. Similarly, "historical evidence indicates legal precedents allowing for the mutilation, striking, and even killing of children as part of the legal parental prerogative" (Gelles, 1990, p. 106).

Gradually, notions of family violence expanded beyond physicality per se to include notions of child abuse and neglect, sexual abuse, emotional neglect, child maltreatment, mental abuse, marital rape, and elder abuse. Today, there is still very little attention paid to violence between siblings or to child-to-parent violence. Some of the known facts or social characteristics of family violence that have been derived from national surveys include (a) mothers are more physically abusive of young children than fathers as a function of their generally more invested role and commitment to parenting; (b) sibling violence for boys (83%) is slightly higher than for girls (74%); (c) there is a generational relationship between child abuse and parental abuse—what has been called "the cycle of family violence" by some and the need to express a "repetitive compulsion" by others; (d) research has generally supported the hypothesis that family or domestic violence is more prevalent in low-socioeconomic-status families, but that it occurs across the spectrum of socioeconomic status and that it is least common in middle-class families where parents are more equally dependent—psychologically and economically—on each other; (e) ethnically and racially, evidence is mixed or inconclusive with respect to different forms of family abuse; (f) other related conditions include social stress and social isolation (Gelles, 1990; Kandel Englander, 1997; Schwendinger & Schwendinger, 1983; Straus, Gelles, & Steinmetz, 1980).

As with most discussions of violence by intimates, this one is not relegated only to family relations but also incorporates incidents of violence against a current or former spouse, boyfriend, or girlfriend. Thus, the use of the broader term—domestic violence. Each year, according to the National Crime Victimization Survey (1992-1996), more than 960,000 incidents of violence occur between former spouses, boyfriends, and girlfriends. Nationwide, intimate murder accounts for about 9% of all murders annually. Although the number of female victims declined in the 1990s generally, they still accounted for about 85% of the victims of domestic violence. There were about 2,000 murders attributable to intimates in 1996 and 1,830 in 1998, down from nearly 3,000 in 1976 (Rennison & Welchans, 2000). The only category of victims to have experienced a small increase in the number of murders between 1976 and 1996 was white females murdered by nonmarital intimates (Greenfeld et al., 1998).

Data from as far back as the 1985 National Family Violence Survey indicated that about 1.8 million wives were being beaten by their husbands and that about 1 out of 8 husbands carried out at least one violent act toward his wife (Straus & Gelles, 1988). Subsequent surveys reported in *Violence by Intimates* (Greenfeld et al., 1998) have indicated that incidents of violence are often more severe when perpetrated by current boyfriends, current girlfriends, former spouses, or former cohabitants. Although data reveal that both males and females engage in intimate violence, male violence tends to be more "offensive" and female violence more "defensive" (DeKeseredy, 1993). Also, male violence has consistently been found to have more detrimental effects than female violence. For example, wives are more likely than husbands to suffer severe physical injuries and depressive symptoms (Holtzworth-Munroe & Stuart, 1994).

Domestic violence also includes same-sex violence and abuse. Although bias or hate violence against gay men and lesbians, such as the 1998 murder of Matthew Shepard in Wyoming, attract more media attention, abuse within same-sex relationships is far more widespread, if not more severe. The National Coalition of Anti-Violence Programs, a network of 24 nonprofit gay and lesbian organizations, reported in July 2000 that same-sex or homosexual violence was on par with that of abuse between heterosexual couples (Leland, 2000) (see Box 3.4). So far, relatively little research has been conducted on homosexual violence. For example, the National Coalition's report noted that studies' results were mixed as to whether there is as much violence and abuse among lesbians as there is among gay men.

Box 3.4   Abuse in Gay Relationships

One researcher, Claire Renzetti, a criminologist from St. Joseph's University in Philadelphia, has studied lesbian violence extensively and is the author of *Violent Betrayal: Partner Abuse in Lesbian Relationships* (1992). Renzetti has underscored the emotional as well as the physical abuse in these same-sex relationships: "One woman was a diabetic . . . her partner never hit her, but forced her to eat sugar. Two women, who were disabled, reported that their abusers took them to isolated, wooded areas and left them without their wheelchairs. One woman quit her job before her partner could out her at work" (Leland, 2000). Exposure of one kind or another seems to be central to the institutionalized expression of same-sex violence.

At least traditionally, homosexual abuse had been to some extent a product of institutionalized neglect by both the straight and gay communities. In short, same-sex violence had remained firmly locked up in the "homosexual closet," so to speak. Victims of such abuse have customarily been in various states of denial, as the following examples illustrate.

When Benjamin DeLanty's partner started hitting him, he did not think of the attacks as domestic violence. After all, DeLanty, 32, did not regard himself as a battered woman, but as a fit man, a bit larger than his partner. As the relationship progressed, so did the violence, and twice he went to the emergency room with bruised or broken ribs. DeLanty either was not willing to confront the truth or he was too embarrassed "to tell his friends or colleagues at the L.A. Gay and Lesbian Center, where he managed the mental health care program" (Leland, 2000). It wasn't until 1999, when DeLanty's partner assaulted him with a frying pan, opening a cut that required stitches in the forehead, that he finally moved out and sought an "order of protection" from the other man.

Another case of same-sex abuse denial involved a woman, Bekki Ow-Cuevas, 40, who had escaped from an abusive marriage to a women's shelter in Kansas in the late 1980s. She found herself sexually victimized by a female partner but was reluctant to recognize the violence as abuse: "There was a piece of me that really wanted to believe that women are safe people" (Leland, 2000).

Many young homosexuals who have only recently informed their parents and friends that they are gay or lesbian, and who find themselves in abusive relationships, are reluctant to report this to their families because, as J. T. Brix, cochairman of the Seattle Commission for Sexual Minorities, has stated, "I wanted to show [my parents] that my relationships could work" (Leland, 2000). Victims of same-sex abuse also face even more stigma, disbelief, and denial from courts and legal systems than do straight victims. They face a lack of services to meet their special needs, as well. When police do respond, they commonly do so inappropriately, confused by stereotypes that assume the smaller gay man or the more feminine lesbian cannot be the abuser. Consequently, the police may arrest both parties, at times placing the abused and the abuser near each other, even in the same cell.

Sources: Leland, J. (2000, November 6). Silence ending about abuse in gay relationships. *New York Times*, p. 18. Retrieved October 2, 2002, from http://www.nytimes.com
Renzetti, C. (1992). *Violent betrayal: Partner abuse in lesbian relationships*. Newbury Park, CA: Sage.

In 1996, the number of violent victimizations, including murder, rape, sexual assault, robbery, and aggravated and simple assault, broke down by intimates as follows: 837,899 female victims and 147,896 male victims (Greenfeld et al., 1998). Overall, for the period of 1993 to 1998, the number of female victims of intimate violence declined from about 1.1 million to about 900,000. For the same years, the significantly smaller number of intimate violent acts against men remained fairly constant at about 160,000 (Rennison & Welchans, 2000). During this period, approximately 85% of the victimizations of intimate partners were against women, down from about 88% a decade earlier.

Rates of violence, nonlethal and lethal, are highest among black women, women 16 to 24 years old, women in households in the lowest economic categories, and women residing in urban areas. Three out of four women experienced their violence at or near their own home. Similarly, 3 out of 4 female victims of intimate violence defended themselves during the incident. Half reported that it occurred in the evening hours, between 6:00 p.m. and midnight. About half of the female victims reported the incident to the police (black female victims being more likely than others to call). About half of all female victims reported an injury of some type, and 20% of those sought medical assistance. In 1994, hospitals recorded nearly a quarter million visits resulting from intimate violence. Medical expenses and other costs to victims of domestic violence totaled about $150 million that year. Annually, it is estimated that about 160,000 female victims of violence receive services from a victim service agency (Greenfeld et al., 1998).

Because most domestic violence researchers believe that "men are the problem," they also believe that it is more productive, for the understanding of husband-to-wife violence or intimate violence generally, to examine men, and they have done so. They have discovered that what violent men and boys share in common are such features as an acceptance of violence, negative attitudes toward women, and various skill deficits. Nonetheless, research has shown that the relative importance of the common features varies across subtypes of batterers and that abusive men and boys therefore constitute a heterogeneous group of male batterers.

Accordingly, the literature contains several typologies of male batterers that were reviewed in "Typologies of Male Batterers: Three Subtypes and the Differences Among Them" by Holtzworth-Munroe and Stuart (1994).

Based on an analysis of 15 typologies, the authors concluded, among other things, that "across existing typologies, including those developed with a rational/deductive approach and those developed with an empirical/inductive approach, three major dimensions have been used to distinguish among subtypes" (Holtzworth-Munroe & Stuart, 1994, p. 481). Primarily descriptive in nature, these dimensions are (a) the severity of marital physical violence and related abuse, such as frequency of the violence and psychological and sexual abuse; (b) the generality of the violence (i.e., family-only or extra-familial violence) and related variables such as criminal behavior and legal involvement; and (c) the batterer's psychopathology or personality disorders. Using these dimensions, Holtzworth-Munroe and Stuart came up with three hypothesized major subtypes of batterers: *family-only, dysphoric/borderline,* and *violent/antisocial.*

Comparatively, family-only batterers should engage in the least-severe forms of intimate violence. They should also be the least likely to engage in psychological and sexual abuse. The violence committed by these men is generally restricted to members of the family; they are not likely to engage in violence outside the home, nor are they likely to be involved in other legal problems. They possess little evidence of psychopathology or mental illness. They have no personality disorders, or if they do, these are of the passive-dependent types. Relative to other subtypes of batterers, the family-only batterer has generally liberal attitudes toward women and the least positive attitudes toward violence.

As the label suggests, dysphoric/borderline batterers are the most dysphoric, psychologically

distressed, and emotionally volatile. These batterers "may evidence borderline and schizoidal personality characteristics and may have problems with alcohol and drug abuse" (Hotzworth-Munroe & Stuart, 1994, p. 482). They can be expected to engage in moderate to severe wife abuse, complete with psychological and sexual abuse. These men's violence is mostly confined to the family, but some extrafamilial violence and criminal behavior may be present. As for their attitudes toward women, these tend to be more conservative; their attitudes toward violence are less clear.

As their label implies, violent/antisocial batterers possess the most positive attitudes toward violence as well as the most conservative attitudes toward women. These batterers are most likely to engage in all kinds of violence, including moderate to severe intimate violence—physical, psychological, and sexual—extrafamilial violence, and criminal violence. They will have the most conflicts and problems with the law. They are also likely to have alcohol and drug abuse problems and are the most likely subtype to have an antisocial personality disorder or other psychopathy.

Familicide, as one form of family violence, is particularly revealing in regard to gender differences and violence. Family homicide, as it is also known, has been defined as a multiple-victim incident in which the killer's spouse or exspouse and one or more children are slain (Daly & Wilson, 1988). In one of the few studies on the subject, Wilson, Daly, and Daniele (1995), using data from British (i.e., English and Welsh) and Canadian archives for homicides in 1977 to 1990 and 1974 to 1990, respectively, found that "men were responsible for 95% of all familicidal killings, compared to 78% of other spouse killings and 49% of other filicides," or the killing of children by parents (excluding in this study those killings by foster as opposed to genetic, adoptive, and stepparents). Of the

109 familicide cases, just 12 of the 249 victims were killed by women.

Key questions to unraveling the complexities of familial and gender violence, then, would include answers to "What accounts for the variation in these three forms of male violence?" and "What are the overlapping factors between marital conflict/violence, parent-child conflict/violence, and other forms of family conflict/violence?"

Part of the answer may lie in an analysis of psychological processes that may include, on the one hand, evolutionary-based psychological perspectives on human emotions and, on the other hand, socially and culturally constructed norms of sexuality and gender that suggest that familicides have more in common with uxoricides (the killing of wives) than they do with filicides. For example, in terms of the data, "the ages of familicidal men were more similar to those of other uxoricidal men than to those of other filicides. Familicides were also somewhat more like other uxoricides than other filicides with respect to method of killing" (Wilson et al., 1995, p. 286). Widening the discussion even further, two distinct subtypes of familicide scenarios seem to prevail in which men are the perpetrators, differing with respect to the killer's motivation. Both of these reflect masculine attitudes of proprietariness, yet each is expressed differently, and each is related to other forms of lethal violence, such as those involving suicides, nonfamilicidal uxoricides, or filicides committed by mothers.

In the first type of familicide, the killer professes a grievance against his wife, usually with respect to alleged infidelities and/or her intending or acting to terminate the marriage. These cases usually involve a history of violence, including overt and even public expressions of the man's aggrieved hostility. In the second type, the killer is a depressed and gloomy man who may apprehend impending disaster for himself and his family (see Box 2.7). Expressions of hostility toward the victims are generally absent in these cases, and the despondent killer may even characterize his deed as an act of mercy or rescue. Similar to these familicides by men are those few cases by women (see Box 2.8) in which the killers see the killing of the children and themselves as "the only way out" of an impossible situation (Wilson et al., 1995, pp. 287-288).

As different as these two categories of familicide appear, they have at least one thing in common:

> The killer's professed rationale for his actions invokes a proprietary conception of wife and family. The hostile, accusatory familicidal killer is often enraged at the alienation of his wife, and may declare that "if I can't have her, no one can." The despondent familicide perpetrator instead appears to believe that his victims could not persist or cope in his absence, and that their deaths are therefore necessary, perhaps even merciful, corollaries to his [or her] suicide. In either case, the killer apparently feels entitled to decide his victims' fates. (Wilson et al., 1995, p. 289)

CHILDHOOD MALTREATMENT

Some 2,000 or more severe cases of child abuse and neglect end tragically in death each year. This is but a tiny fraction of the majority of child maltreatment cases that occur each year and that have been correlated with increases in the risk of problems during adolescence, including serious and violent delinquency, teen pregnancy, drug abuse, low academic achievement, and an assortment of mental health problems. The term *childhood maltreatment* encompasses a fairly broad spectrum of abuse and neglect scenarios (see Box 4.1), with seven subtypes: physical abuse, sexual abuse, physical neglect, lack of supervision, emotional maltreatment, educational maltreatment, and moral-legal maltreatment.

At this point in time, it is not clear which forms of child maltreatment are more damaging to youth development. For example, in one study of a sample of 1,575 court cases of child maltreatment, the experience of neglect appeared to be as damaging as physical abuse. Victims of both abuse and neglect were more likely as teenagers and young adults to be arrested for and involved in violent crimes than the nonmaltreated control group (Widom, 1994).

The National Committee to Prevent Child Abuse (NCPCA) estimated that in 1995, one million children suffered maltreatment by parents or caretakers in the United States (Kelley, Thornberry, & Smith, 1997). However, a substantial but unknown proportion of childhood maltreatment is never reported or brought to the attention of state or local child protective services. Other annual estimates, derived from surveys for all 50 states and the District of Columbia, have been collected by the NCPCA since 1986. For 1995, their estimates were as follows:

- Child protective services received 3,111,000 children who were reported to have been alleged victims.
- Between 1986 and 1995, there was a steady increase in the number of reported child maltreatment cases, amounting to a 49% increase over the period.
- The number of reported child victims rose from a reported rate of 33 per 1,000 in 1986 to 46 out of 1,000 in 1995.
- Approximately 1 million children were found to be victims of maltreatment.
- Fifteen of every 1,000 children were substantiated to be victims of maltreatment.
- About one third of the alleged cases of child maltreatment were confirmed.
- Of the substantiated reports, 54% involved neglect, 25% physical abuse, 11% sexual abuse, 3% emotional maltreatment, and 7% other forms of maltreatment (Kelley et al., 1997, p. 2).

These figures were generally true for the years 1992 through 1995, as well.

In spring, 1988, a sample of 1,000 youths (75% boys and 25% girls) was drawn from public school students in the seventh and eighth grades in Rochester, New York, as part of a larger, longitudinal research project (the Rochester Youth Development Study) sponsored by the Office of Juvenile Justice and Delinquency Prevention's Program of Research on the Causes and Correlates of Delinquency. Of the total sample, 14% had a record of childhood maltreatment and 86% did not. "These subjects were maltreated in a total of 219 separate incidents (an average of 1.5 incidents per maltreated subject). This rate [was] somewhat higher than prevalence rates reported in national data . . . and [was] probably related to the urban population of youth in the sample" (Kelley et al., 1997, p. 3). Demographically, the prevalence of maltreatment did not vary significantly by sex or race, although it did significantly differ by social class and family structure:

> Twenty percent of youth reared in disadvantaged families—those in which the principal wage earner was unemployed, welfare was received, or income was below the poverty level—were victims of maltreatment, while only 8% of the non-disadvantaged respondents were maltreated. The largest difference observed is in family structure. Only 3% of the boys and girls who resided with both biological parents at the beginning of the Rochester study (spring 1988) had a history of maltreatment, but 19% of those in other family situations had been maltreated. (Kelley et al., 1997, p. 3)

In terms of the prevalence and frequency of delinquency, based on an examination of both official police records and self-reports, across six delinquent categories (i.e., official, minor, moderate, serious, violent, and general), the maltreated were significantly more likely to be involved in delinquent behavior. For example, while 32% of the nonmaltreated youth had official records of delinquency, the figure rose to 45% for those with a history of maltreatment. Similarly, when researchers divided the childhood maltreatment experiences into "more," "medium," and "less," based on the number, severity, duration, and subtypes of maltreatment, there were also notable differences, with the more-maltreated subjects "arrested about twice as often as the less-maltreated subjects along each of the four dimensions" (Kelley et al., 1997, p. 7). With respect to violent delinquency, the figures were 70% for maltreated youths and 56% for nonmaltreated youth. The same general relationships held for female pregnancy, drug use, lower grade-point averages, and mental health problems.

Although empirical links between childhood maltreatment and later problem behavior have been found in the Rochester Study, "these data do not imply that maltreatment leads directly or inevitably to later problems" (Kelley et al., 1997, p. 13). Pathways between the two are, for example, subject to various intervening variables such as the emergence and role of protective factors and the provision of effective services for children. Nevertheless, it is fairly safe to assume that maltreated youth make up a disproportionate number of those adolescents involved in school and gang violence.

SCHOOL VIOLENCE

There is both a growing literature and a sociopolitical movement in the United States concerned with the declining quality of American public education. In part, concern is focused on order, disorder, and misbehavior in and around the classroom. On and off campus, issues of "control" have, correctly

or incorrectly, been associated with lower test scores and more incidents of conflict and violence. Reactions to minor infractions, as a result, have been swift and severe, involving corporal punishment, suspensions, and other forms of discipline, including the expelling of an 11-year old, Shannon Coslett, for mistakenly picking up her mother's lunch box, which contained a paring knife (Cummins, 1998). What is missing from most of these discussions on institutional safety, discipline, punishment, and fear of abuse is perspective, especially regarding the relationship or connections between school violence and the larger social, cultural, and economic environments.

Initial reports on school violence focused their attention on the violence committed by teachers against students. The culprits were those teachers and disciplinarians (e.g., counselors and vice principals) who imposed a form of discipline called corporal punishment, or "the infliction of pain or confinement as a penalty for an offense committed by a student" (Regoli & Hewitt, 2000, p. 207). Historically, the tradition of corporal punishment dates back to 17th-century Jesuit schools, and it was commonplace during the colonial era in America. Following the Old Testament and a statement attributed to Solomon—"He that spareth his rod hateth his son; but he that loveth him chastiseth him betimes" (Proverbs 13:24, King James Version)—the Puritans expected teachers to physically punish unruly students. "By the end of the 19th century and into the 20th century, discipline problems in schools were a daily occurrence. Teachers tried to control students through threats, intimidation, and beatings" (Regoli & Hewitt, 2000, p. 208).

Today, with the exceptions of the United States, Canada, and one state in Australia, corporal punishment is illegal in every developed nation. Despite the fact that the U.S. Supreme Court has twice (in *Baker v. Owen,*

1975, and *Ingraham v. Wright,* 1977) upheld its constitutionality, once on the grounds that schools and teachers have the right to administer reasonable corporal punishment for disciplinary purposes, and once on the grounds that corporal punishment did not violate the Eighth Amendment's "cruel and unusual" punishment clause, 27 states have banned the practices and the spirit of corporal punishment. It is interesting to note that convicts cannot be legally beaten nor can persons in mental hospitals or any branch of the U.S. military. Yet, in an opinion poll from 1990, 48% answered yes, 44% answered no, and 8% had no opinion to the question: "Do you agree with teachers' being allowed to inflict corporal punishment?" (Hyman, 1991).

In terms of institutionalized school violence, the U.S. Department of Education reported that more than 470,000 children received corporal punishment from teachers, principals, coaches, or bus drivers in 1996. Some 5,000 of those youths were beaten so badly that they required medical attention (Marklein, 1997). Males and African Americans are struck and victimized most often. Males constitute 51% of students nationwide but are the recipients of corporal punishment in 80% of all cases; for African Americans, the figures are roughly 25% and 37%, respectively (Shaw & Braden, 1990). In the early 1990s in the South, 10% of the children in Alabama, Arkansas, Mississippi, and Tennessee had been corporally punished at some point in their schooling (Hyman, 1991).

Combined with the maltreated children from "dysfunctional" families, who may harbor intense feelings of anger toward or alienation from their parents, and who are most likely to act out in the classroom or the hallway, are those corporally punished children who harbor feelings of anger and fear as well as humiliation and shame. With time, feelings of anger and humiliation are less likely to fade than feelings of fear and shame. The point is that students who are angry are more likely than students who are not to strike out at whomever and whatever they blame for their pain and suffering (see Boxes 2.11 and 2.12). But student violence is not only a negatively or pathologically based set of behaviors stemming from child maltreatment and corporal punishment; it can also be viewed as positively and righteously based social and cultural activity—as, for example, when it is associated with actions related to certain sports (see Box 3.5). In fact, violence can at the same time constitute both negative and positive sets of behavioral interaction. For example, limited research has concluded that "the more children are spanked, the more anger they report as adults, the more likely they are to spank their own children, the more likely they are to approve of hitting a spouse, and the more marital conflict they experience as adults" (Regoli & Hewitt, 2000).

Box 3.5   Youth Sports and Violence

During the 1990s in the United States, violence associated with institutionalized sports for kids, especially that kind of violence involving parent attacks on other parents, referees and umpires, coaches, and children, both their own and others, rose. Bob Still, a spokesman for the National Association of Sports Officials, which represents some 19,000 umpires and referees in professional as well as high school and youth sports, says that his organization saw a sharp increase in the number of violent incidents perpetrated by parents between 1996 and 2000. Although some of this violence has involved mothers and girls, it is predominantly fathers and boys who account for these assaults.

Rarely, however, do these assaults result in murder and charges of manslaughter as they did when a suburban Boston father, Thomas Junta, 42, following a pickup game of youth hockey, fatally beat another father, Michael Costin, 40, over the rough play that ensued between their two 10-year-old sons.

According to the police investigation, Costin had been on the ice monitoring play when "Mr. Junta, watching from the stands, shouted at him, demanding that he stop some body checking and fighting" (Butterfield, 2000a). As Costin (175 lbs.) left the ice, Junta (275 lbs.) assaulted him. The rink manager then ordered Junta to leave; instead, he turned around and slammed Costin head first into the concrete floor (where the blow apparently caused brain death almost immediately), pushed his knee into Costin's chest, and continued to pummel him in the head.

On parental sports violence, Fred Engh of the National Alliance for Youth Sports had this to say: "Whether it's living through their children or looking ahead to scholarships and professional riches, parents are getting caught up in children's games" ("Violence in youth," 2000). William Pollack of Harvard Medical School, a psychiatrist and authority on father-son relationships, has argued that the increased violence by male athletes and their fathers stems from the fact that parents are encouraging their children to play more aggressively (Butterfield, 2000a). One articulate multisport athlete at Bell High School in Texas, T. J. Dibble, has the following to say about the increasing violence involving young athletes and their parents:

> Everyone's out there being competitive, but some people don't know how to be competitive and keep their composure. It's just pure emotion when you're out there on the field, but some people don't know how to keep it between the whistles. It kind of seems society has become more violent and with that something in sports has changed as well. It's kind of an everyone-for-themselves attitude. No one seems to have respect for anyone anymore. ("Violence in youth," 2000)

Sources: Butterfield, F. (2000a, July 11). A fatality, parental violence and youth sports. *New York Times*, p. A14. Retrieved October 2, 2002, from http://www.nytimes.com
Violence in youth sports spreads beyond the field. (2000, May 14). *Ann Arbor News*, p. C3.

Even more important, the majority of students involved in violent altercations ascribe to norms and values that find this behavior acceptable. For example, middle school and high school students in one violence study rationalized their violent-incident behavior as legitimate: it punished their antagonist for something that he or she did (40%); it convinced their antagonist to desist from an offensive course of action (22%); or it defended their image by saving face, defending their honor, or enhancing or maintaining their reputation (8%). As the principal researcher of this study noted: "What is perhaps most troubling is the finding that the students' violent behavior did *not* stem from a lack of values. Rather it was grounded in a well-developed set of values that holds such behavior to be a justifiable, commonsense way to achieve certain goals" (Lockwood, 1997, p. 1). Instead of the "conflict-management"–prescribed values of nonviolent forms of redress, larger cultural messages pervade the school environment, where a preference for violent retaliation, a strong belief in punishment, and a sensitivity to perceived injustice and mistreatment become the "core values at the heart of these students' violent responses. Students adopt the styles of parents, teachers, and other adults around them, and students' norms will not change unless these models change" (Lockwood, 1997, p. 8). Many of those students adopt fear-based perspectives, some realistic, some not. In any event, each school day, 160,000 students stay home from school because they are afraid to attend.

Nearly 4 million school crimes are committed annually, and more than $600 million is lost annually in damage to schools from theft, vandalism, and arson (Regoli & Hewitt, 2000). An estimated 16% of all high school students in this country have been in one or more physical fights on school property in the course of a year. Victimization rates for simple assault are highest among young people 12 to 19 years old (Lockwood, 1997). Although, for example, 57% of public school principals report one or more incidents of crime or violence to police during the school year, only 10% reported at least one serious incident each year, including a murder, rape, fight or armed attack, or sexual assault (Regoli & Hewitt, 2000). During the period 1996 to 1997, more than 400,000 incidents of crime were reported in public schools.

Of those, only 4,170 involved rape or sexual battery, and only 10,950 involved a weapon of some kind, compared to the number of 12- to 18-year-olds in 1996 who were victims of about 255,000 incidents of nonfatal serious violent crime at school and about 671,000 incidents away from school.

In 1997, 40 school shootings were reported, compared to 3,000 students who died from gunfire *off* school grounds. In other words, "these numbers indicate that when students were away from school they were more likely to be victims of nonfatal serious violent crime including rape, sexual assault, robbery, and aggravated assault than when they were at school. Moreover, between 1976 and 1996, the percentages of 12th graders who were injured (with or without a weapon) at school did not change, although those who had been threatened with one showed a very slight overall upward trend" (Kaufman, Chandler, & Rand, 1998; Regoli & Hewitt, 2000). At the same time, the presence of reported street gangs in schools increased from 15% to 28% between 1989 and 1995 (Kaufman et al., 1998).

Students in urban areas, compared to students in suburban and rural areas, were more vulnerable to serious violent crime. Although there is no comprehensive data here, one set of interviews with school counselors, school guards, parents, and community leaders suggested that only about 10% of the students are responsible for most of the vandalism and violence even in the worst schools. Although these troublesome students did not seem to belong to any specific racial, ethnic, or socioeconomic background, they did seem to share difficulties in terms of their academic performance, trouble in the wider community, and tendency to come from troubled and dysfunctional homes.

Lockwood's study of middle and high school students found that the average number of incidents per student was about the same for the 40 girls and 70 boys in his sample. "While boys tended to fight mainly with other boys, girls were involved in almost as many fights with boys as with other girls. Moreover, girls were the offenders in all incidents in which knives were used" (Lockwood, 1997, p. 3). Nationally, between 1993 and 1996, there was a decline (from

14% to 9%) in the percentage of male high school seniors who reported carrying a weapon to school at least 1 day within the 4 weeks before the survey. For females, however, the number rose from 2% to 3% (Kaufman et al., 1998).

One out of every 11 teachers has been attacked at school. From 1992 to 1996, teachers were the victims of 1,581,000 non-fatal crimes at school, including 619,000 violent crimes (e.g., rape or sexual assault, robbery, and aggravated and simple assault). Per year, there were about 316,000 nonfatal crime victims. Teachers were most in danger of being victims of violent crime from middle and junior high students; they were safest from elementary students, with high school students falling in the middle. Although levels of violence in general and gang violence in particular are variable and differ from city to city and from school to school, odds are that teachers are more in danger of becoming victims of violence from gang members than from non–gang members (Howell, 1998).

GANG VIOLENCE

Gangs are by no means a new social phenomenon in the history of the United States. They have been around at least since the American Revolution, although their various roles and behaviors have changed over time. Public stereotypes and mass-produced images of teenage ganging are predominately of males, especially African American males; nevertheless, gangs are actually of multicultural composition and involve the participation of both sexes. At the same time, the experiences and behaviors of male and female gang members have varied in relation to how masculinities and femininities are socially constructed and how they are influenced by gender and class (Joe & Chesney-Lind, 1993).

Girls and boys growing up in poor and violent families and neighborhoods turn to gangs for obvious reasons, not the least of which is protection:

> Many youth are drawn from families that are abusive, and particularly for girls, the gang provides the skill to fight back against the violence of their families. The marginalization of working and lower working class communities has specific meaning for young men as well. The displays of toughness and risk taking . . . are a source for respect and status in an environment that is structurally unable to affirm their masculinity. Their acts of intimidation and fighting are rooted in the need for protection as well as the need to validate their manliness. (Joe & Chesney-Lind, 1993, p. 30)

The gang as refuge, then, helps to insulate its members from their very real insecurities and vulnerabilities at the same time that it sets a significant minority of them up for an escalation in violent interaction.

Adolescent and older gangs are products of social, political, and economic forces, their members having grown up primarily in communities marked by poverty, racism, and rapid population growth. More specifically, "a gang" usually refers to a locally based social organization of youths whose status is derived from engaging in illegal and/or conflict behavior with other gangs and the authorities (Thrasher, 1927; Miller, 1980). Gangs also specialize in offenses that are often related to the members' ethnic backgrounds.

Gangs are antisocial in nature, but also social, in that they provide outlets and tonics for the chronic boredom of low-income life. In other words, there are many gang members who are not engaged directly in illegal activities while they pass the time of day. Nobody knows the actual breakdowns in the comparative data between licit and illicit gang members, but most researchers agree that the majority of gang members do not fit the popular images of drug-selling, weapons-brandishing hoodlums.

Between 1980 and 1996, the United States experienced rapid growth in the number of youth gangs and the level of gang violence, much of it related to competition in the drug markets (Howell, 1998; Regoli & Hewitt, 2000). During this period, the number of gangs grew by a factor of around 15 and the number of gang members by a factor of about 8. In 1980, there were an estimated 286 jurisdictions with more than 2,000 gangs and nearly 100,000 gang members. By 1996, the figures had risen to 4,800 jurisdictions, with more than 31,000 gangs and approximately 846,000 gang members (Howell, 1998).

A couple of significant differences between contemporary youth gangs and gangs of the 1950s and 1960s have been noted by a number of gang researchers. Comparatively, today's gangs are exceedingly well armed and significantly more violent than gangs of the past. In many urban areas, a small proportion of gang violence has spilled over into school settings, involving not only rival gang members but teachers and fellow students. For the most part, however, gang-related violence involving serious assaults—shootings, stabbings, beatings—has remained outside of school settings. For perspective, it should be kept in mind that "except for gangs that specialize in violence," violence "is a rare occurrence in proportion to all gang activities" (Howell, 1998, p. 8). Finally, it should be noted that in the 1990s, gang homicide rates mirrored national homicide patterns: both experienced a downturn.

In addition to the situational violence associated with such gang activities as drug trafficking, gang norms also contribute to the elevated levels of youth gang violence:

> Most gangs are governed by norms supporting the expressive use of violence to settle disputes and to achieve group goals associated with member recruitment, defense of one's identity as a gang member, turf protection and expansion, and defense of the gang's honor. Gang sanctioning of violence is also dictated by a code of honor that stresses the inviolability of one's manhood and defines breaches of etiquette. Violence is also a means of demonstrating toughness and fighting ability and of establishing status in the gang. (Howell, 1998, p. 9).

Interestingly, some of the values sanctioning gang violence as normative overlap with those values sanctioning school violence as normative, especially as these revolve around issues of honor and retaliation. Both sets of values for violence include a "vocabulary of motives" that serves to justify the behavior as rational and just. Listen to the words of one 17-year-old homeless "homeboy" reflecting on the world of gangbanging violence among the Bloods and Crips of South Central Los Angeles (see Box 3.6). Similar vocabularies of motive or rationale surround police killings and penal interventions.

Box 3.6 *Do or Die*

His name is Faro and he lives from couch to couch, or in a sleeping bag, or in the back seat of a parked car. A couple of days here, a week or two there. He does not remember the last time he went to school. Neither can he read or write. As León Bing writes in her book *Do or Die*, Faro "is as close to invisibility as it is possible to be." In spite of his invisibility, Faro wears his hair sectioned into a myriad of tiny braids with blue rubber bands at the tips. "He is wearing shabby sweats and busted-down Nike high-tops. He is very thin; the bones of his wrists stick knobbily out of the elastic cuffs of his hooded jacket, which is at least two sizes two small for him." As Faro informs Bing and her readers about his upbringing,

> My mother, she died from a drug overdose. I got a grandmother, but she gonna go the same way—she just wanderin' the streets day and night, lookin' for handouts so she can fix herself a pipe. My brother got killed in a holdup three years ago. Most people think he was holdin' the gun . . . he wasn't but eight years old. He was lookin' at comic books in a 7-eleven and some dude come in to rob the place . . . The homies [gave] him a nice funeral. I used to have a picture of him, laid out, in my scrapbook. It got lost.

In the following exchange, which occurred as Faro and Bing were cruising the "hood" in her car, he said to her, regarding two guys driving in a car beside them, "I'm gonna look crazy at 'em. You watch what they do."

> He turns away from me, and I lean forward over the wheel so that I can watch the faces on the two guys. The driver, sensing that someone is looking at him, glances over at my car. His eyes connect with Faro's, widen for an instant. Then he breaks the contact, looks down, looks away. And there is no mistaking what I saw there in his eyes: it was fear. Whatever he saw in Faro's face, he wasn't about to mess with it.

> Faro giggles and turns back toward me. He looks the same as he did before to me: a skinny, slightly goofy-looking kid . . . I ask Faro to "look crazy" for me. He simply narrows his eyes . . . and everything about his face shifts and changes, as if by some trick of time-lapse photography. It becomes a nightmare face, and it is a scary thing to see. It tells you that if you return his stare, if you challenge this kid, you'd better be ready to stand your ground. His look tells you that he doesn't care about anything, not your life and not his.

> I ask Faro what would have happened if the guy had looked crazy back.

> "Then we woulda got into it . . . Never woulda happened. That was just some damn preppy out on his lunch hour."

> "But if he had returned the challenge. What then?"

> "Then I woulda killed him."

> My eyes slide over his skinny silhouette. No way can he be hiding a weapon under that sweatshirt. He smiles slyly and pats the top of his right shoe. I peer down and there, unbelievably, is the glint of metal.

> "Like there was this fool, this enemy nigger from our worst enemy set, and he was with his wife and his baby. They was walkin' down there near Vermont, where he had no business bein.' He was slippin' bad and we caught him. We was in a car, all homies, and I was like, 'Let's pop this dumb nigger, let's empty the whole clip [referring to an AK-47 automatic rifle]. . . . I just wanted to make him pay.

(Continued)

Box 3.6   (Continued)

"For all our dead homeboys. For bein' our enemy. . . . You gotta understand—enemy got to pay just for being alive. . . . So I strapped it [the AK-47] to the seat . . . and we circled around and pulled up on this nigger from two blocks away, crept up on him slow like, and I just gave it to him . . . Pah-pah-pah-pah-pah-pah-pah! You know, just let him have it. Just emptied the whole . . . I lit his ass up! I killed him—shot his baby in the leg—crippled his wife!"

We are silent for a moment; when Faro speaks again his voice is a fusion of bad feelings: despair, remorse, a deep, biting resentment.

"It was like, damn,' cuz—I killed him, that was my mission, but still—his whole family."

He shakes his head several times, as if he cannot will himself to believe his own story. Then he places the tip of one index finger on the glass next to him and taps it in a nervous, rhythmic beat.

"That's a crazy world out there, and we livin' it."

"Dying in it, too."

[The finger stops tapping.] "If you die, you die. Most gang-bangers don't have nothin' to live for no more, anyway. That why some of 'em be gangbangin' . . . I tell you this—you see enough dyin', then you be ready to die yourself, just so you don't have to see no more of death."

Source: Bing, L. (1991). *Do or die.* New York: Harper Collins. ©1991. Reprinted by permission of HarperCollins Publishers Inc.

Unlike law enforcement or the military, gangs, despite their public image to the contrary, are not particularly well organized and cohesive, with strong and charismatic leadership or with an esprit de corps of "all for one and one for all" when it comes to turf protection. At the same time, research has found that gang members tend to have important problems as adolescents, learn to cope by being aggressive, and are able to be "enticed" or "seduced" by gangs because they think they will receive various kinds of emotional and cultural compensation. First, gangs are enticing or attractive because being a member can enhance one's prestige or status among friends and peers. This is true for males and females. Gangs also provide opportunities for excitement, making money, selling drugs, making social connections, and acquiring other personal advantages that come from "in-group" behavior. Second, gangs are perceived as seductive or welcoming because marginalized youth, minority and otherwise, are in the market for social relationships that give them a sense of identity, family, and belonging, if not outright purpose.

In terms of gang victimization, the data suggest that gang members are not as safe as nongang members. For example, recent studies conducted in Denver and Pittsburgh of delinquent behavior and victimization suggest that the two are inextricably linked for some individuals. Comparatively, 1 in 2 males who were serious, violent, juvenile offenders were violently victimized, compared with 1 in 10 of their nondelinquent peers, suggesting a cycle of violence, or that being victimized leads to victimizing others (Loeber, Kalb, & Huizinga, 2001).

Compared to the general population, a gang member's risk of being killed is 60 times greater. In St. Louis, it was found that the gang member homicide rate was 1,000 times higher than the U.S. homicide rate. Of course, these figures would come down significantly if only similar age brackets were compared. Yet, gang homicides have characteristics that distinguish them from other homicides, suggesting the reasons that gang members have greater vulnerability to fatal violence. Gang homicides are more public or visible, often occurring in the middle of the street. They typically involve strangers, multiple participants, and the use of automobiles (e.g., drive-by shootings accounted for 33% of Los Angeles' gang-related homicides from 1989 to 1993). Gang homicides are also three times more likely than nongang homicides to involve motives of fear or retaliation. In fact, among rival gangs, promoting fear and intimidation is more important than the intent to kill somebody (Hutson, Anglin, & Eckstein, 1996).

In sum, studies by Esbensen, Thornberry, and Battin and their colleagues (Battin, Hill, Abbott, Catalano, & Hawkins, 1998; Esbensen & Huizinga, 1993; Esbensen, Huizinga, & Weiher, 1993; Thornberry, Krohn, Lizetta, & Chard-Wierschem, 1993; Thornberry & Burch, 1997) have consistently found clear differences in delinquency rates between gang and nongang members. For example, in the Rochester Youth Development Study, one third of the youths reported that at some time before the end of high school, they had been members of a street gang. At the same time, gang members accounted for 86% of all serious delinquent acts, 69% of violent delinquent acts, and 70% of drug sales (Thornberry & Burch, 1997). Regarding female delinquency, the data is less conclusive; however, it appears from the Office of Juvenile Justice and Delinquency Prevention studies in Denver and Rochester (Loeber et al., 2001) and from Fagan's (1990) study of female gang members in Chicago, Los Angeles, and San Diego that the rates in all behavior categories, including violent offenses, were higher when compared to nongang females. Fagan (1990) also found that across all categories of behavior, rates were higher among female gang members than among nongang males.

POLICE AND PENAL VIOLENCE

In some ways, police and penal violence are not unlike gang and school violence. Perpetrators of these four types of institutionalized violence seem to share common concerns about issues of honor, esteem, and solidarity. Also, they have often experienced harassment, intimidation, and exploitation in their social worlds, but not usually in the same way. The fundamental difference between these forms of violence is that school and gang violence are strictly taboo, but police and penal violence often have had tacit if not sanctioned approval from society (Nelson, 2000).

Unfortunately, the data surrounding police and penal violence is sparse at best and nonexistent at worst. Most information on these forms of violence comes from news media and reports issued by various activist organizations concerned with social and international justice, such as the American Civil Liberties Union, Amnesty International, or Human Rights Watch (see Box 3.7). It is very difficult, therefore, to evaluate the extent of police and penal abuse, and whether and to what degree these situations are improving or deteriorating. At the same time, enough evidence and reports of institutionalized abuse and violence exist to conclude that such behavior, although not uniform across jurisdictions (not unlike gang and school violence) in the United States, does systematically occur.

In June 1999, the U.S. Department of Justice held a national summit on police brutality as one of a number of planned initiatives designed to improve police-community relations and to increase police accountability. During September and October of the same year, Amnesty International held hearings on police brutality in Los Angeles, Chicago, and Pittsburgh. The organization "documented patterns of ill treatment across the USA, including police beatings, unjustified shootings and the use of dangerous restraint techniques to subdue suspects" (Amnesty International, 1999). Moreover, although

> only a minority of the many thousands of law enforcement officers in the USA engage in deliberate and wanton brutality, [AI] found that too little was being done to monitor and check persistent abusers, or to ensure that police tactics in certain common situations minimized the risk of unnecessary force and injury. The report also noted that widespread, systemic abuses had been found in some jurisdictions or police precincts. It highlighted evidence that racial and ethnic minorities were disproportionately the victims of police misconduct, including false arrest and harassment as well as verbal and physical abuse.

Box 3.7   Police Torture

In one of the more infamous cases of police brutality, the City of New York and the Police Benevolent Association tentatively agreed to pay Abner Louima $9 million in damages for physical injuries they unjustifiably caused the civil-suit plaintiff while he was in police custody in 1997. For dropping the case, Louima also agreed to drop his "demand for reform in the way the New York City Police Department deals with officers accused of crimes" ("Report: Tentative," 2001). In 1998, the plaintiff had filed a $155 million civil suit in Brooklyn federal court, claiming that officers at the 70th Precinct had conspired to create a "blue wall of silence and lies to obstruct justice" and that police and officials from the Police Benevolent Association condoned an "environment in which the most violent police officers believed they would be insulated" from prosecution.

In three previous criminal trials, which had resulted in six criminal convictions, Louima had testified about his ordeal. After his arrest, stemming from a street brawl outside a Brooklyn nightclub, he was handcuffed and taken as a prisoner to Brooklyn's 70th Precinct. Once there, Officer Justin Volpe, under the mistaken belief that Louima had punched him, sought revenge in a bathroom by sodomizing the victim with a broken broomstick and threatening to kill him if he reported it. Volpe pleaded guilty and is serving a 30-year sentence. A jury found patrolman Charles Schwarz guilty of pinning Louima down during the assault. In addition, four other officers were convicted of lying to authorities who had conducted investigations into what had happened.

Source: Exclusive torture suit settled; Louima gets $9M. (2001, March 22). *New York Daily News*, p. 1. Retrieved October 12, 2002, from http://www.nydailynews.com

Abuse of police authority and discretion ranges from verbal slurs and racial profiling to brutality and murder. These acts may be committed by rogue officers, by small teams, or by larger groups. Some of this behavior is more spontaneous and personal, and some of it is more planned and organizational (see Box 3.8). Reports are widely circulated about the misuse of pepper spray and police dogs, about deaths resulting from dangerous restraint holds, and about police shootings in disputed circumstances. Moreover, several police forces, including the Detroit, Los Angeles, and New York police departments, have been under federal investigation for systematic human rights abuses, especially related to members of minority groups and to cases involving mentally or emotionally disturbed individuals who were killed under questionable circumstances.

Box 3.8 The Rampart Scandal

In a case involving the Rampart Division of the Los Angeles Police Department (LAPD), a federal judge ruled in August 2000 that the government's antiracketeering statute, known as the RICO (Racketeer Influenced and Corrupt Organization) Law and created for the purpose of dealing with drug bosses and organized crime figures, could be applied to the LAPD. This ruling, by Federal District Court Judge William J. Rea, was a first of its kind. In effect, the judge converted a civil rights lawsuit into a racketeering lawsuit, suggesting that the LAPD was essentially a "criminal enterprise." Statutes of limitations for civil rights cases are 1 year; for racketeering cases, they are 10 years. There is no telling what this will ultimately cost the City of Los Angeles.

By late 2000, some 100 criminal cases had been "overturned as a result of the scandal, in which officers are said to have planted evidence and beaten people in a struggling Latino neighborhood for sport and profit" (Terry, 2000). Damages are estimated to be as high as $150 million for the 68 cases filed so far against the city, but the potential number of claimants could run as high as 200 or more. If this turns out to be the case, damages could approach half a billion dollars. The corruption and violence perpetrated by the Rampart Division (and beyond) not only led to the investigation of 70 Los Angeles police officers, it ultimately resulted in an "astonishing consent decree that for the first time in history put the fiercely independent L.A.P.D. under the supervision of the federal government" (Cannon, 2000). Had it not been for the actions of one crooked police officer in particular, Rafael Perez, and a few of his close associates from the Rampart Division of Community Resources Against Street Hoodlums (Crash), the biggest scandal in the history of Los Angeles policing might never have seen the light of day. In a nutshell, Perez was found to be dealing cocaine, which he would steal from that which he and other cops had confiscated from drug deals gone awry in their precinct area.

In recognition of Perez's illegal drug dealing, on September 8, 1999, his lawyer, Winston Kevin McKesson, a protégé of Johnnie Cochran, Jr., "negotiated an agreement in which his client promised to expose misconduct within Rampart Crash in exchange for a five year prison sentence, immunity from further prosecution and total immunity for his wife," a civilian employee with the department whom the prosecutors claimed

(Continued)

Box 3.8   (Continued)

knew of Perez's illegal activities (Cannon, 2000). In more than 50 hours of interrogation, Perez sang to the authorities about how he and his comrades beat, framed, and engaged in other violent and corrupt practices, including murder and cover-ups.

Today, after spending 16 months in isolation in a local jail rather than in a state prison, Perez has been paroled and is "free" to walk the streets. He may even have access to $722,000 from a bank robbery in which it is suspected but has never been proven that he was an accomplice. The money was never recovered, even though two other police officers are now behind bars for the crime (see below).

To place these extreme abuses of police authority, such as the shooting, paralysis, and framing of Javier Ovando (who was sentenced to 23 years in prison and later freed when the truth came out), into their institutional perspective, some context is called for. The Rampart area, west of downtown, is considered one of the most dangerous neighborhoods in Los Angeles. Traditionally, it leads the city in homicides, narcotics sales, and violent crime. Encompassing 7.9 square miles, Rampart has the highest population density of any urban area west of the Mississippi, officially 36,000 people per square mile. Beginning in the late 1970s, life on the streets there was controlled by more than 60 gangs. Most of these gangs were organized along ethnic lines (e.g., El Salvadoran, Nicaraguan, Guatemalan).

Ovando, who had no criminal record, was a marginal member of the 18th Street Gang, noted for its brutality and its unique multiethnic and sometimes interracial membership. "The gang terrorized neighborhoods, sold narcotics and rented space to drug dealers. But it also functioned as a haven for jobless Latinos who lived on the streets during the severe recession of the early 90's" (Cannon, 2000). In 1993, Ovando was 16, on his own and with no roof over his head, so he joined the gang as they became "*mia familia.*" During the 1980s, the LAPD, who had a relatively small number of officers to police a vast area and who had always relied on technology and aggressive tactics to handle "the crime problem," created two elite antigang forces: one was Crash, and the other was Operation Hammer. The latter was the brainchild of former police chief Daryl Gates, and it rounded up suspected gang members en masse. Under attack by civil libertarians, Operation Hammer was totally discredited and disbanded in 1988 when its officers destroyed four apartment buildings that they mistakenly thought were crack houses.

Though criticized from time to time for excesses and for too much independence, Crash units survived. After all, "Crash officers worked in tough places and expected to confront violence with violence." (Cannon, 2000). Rampart Crash became even more independent in 1995 when, because of overcrowding, the unit moved out of the main Rampart station house and into a substation nearly two miles away:

> There, the cowboy cops were almost entirely on their own, and they weren't shy about expressing their separateness. While most of the city's Crash officers were required to work in uniform, Rampart members made a point of showing up in street clothes. When [David] Smith [an LAPD captain who had had several encounters with the unit] responded to a call

from a Rampart resident who had been roughed up by police officers, he was told to mind his own business. "There were all sorts of warning signals coming out of Rampart," he said. (Cannon, 2000)

For example, Rampart Crash, which varied in size from a dozen to about 20 officers, depending on the time of year and amount of gang activity, was a tight-knit group; its members gave plaques to each other for shooting gang members. They also wore logos and patches, including a skull with a cowboy hat and a poker hand of a pair of aces and a pair of eights. This is the famous dead-man's hand that the frontier outlaw Wild Bill Hickok was holding when he was gunned down. Over the door of the Rampart Crash substation was the saying, "We intimidate those who intimidate others." Finally, they solidified their independence by rekeying the lock to their precinct to 888, invalidating the 999 key that all Los Angeles police officers receive, along with their badge and gun, that grants them access to all the police stations in the city.

To make a very long story a bit shorter, Perez and his buddies (including David Mack, 39, who was convicted on federal charges of bank robbery and is currently serving 14 years in prison, and Perez's former partner Nino Durden, who allegedly fired the first of four shots at Ovando while he was handcuffed and *not* firing a semiautomatic at the officers, as they claimed during the trial) each enjoyed his dual role of criminal and cop. On the topic of framing persons, for example, Perez told investigators that in Rampart Crash it was commonplace to set up gang members on weapons and drug charges. He added that such tactics had the approval of his commanding officer, Sgt. Edward Ortiz. In Perez's view, there was nothing wrong with this activity, and he never once felt bad about it. On the contrary, he felt good about it because he was taking the "bad guys" off the street. He rationalized it this way: "These guys don't play by the rules; we don't have to play by the rules" (Cannon, 2000).

At his sentencing in early 2000, however, Perez was singing a different tune. To hear Perez tell it then, he had been a victim of the aggressive LAPD and its corrupt culture. In a tearful statement, Perez said that he had become consumed after transferring to Rampart Crash by the "us-against-them ethos of the overzealous cop." His cautionary tale to other cops, especially rookies, was that they should not be seduced by the "pressure of status, numbers and impressing supervisors." As he stated it, his job had become "an intoxicant that I lusted after. I began to lust also for other things of the flesh. The end result: I cheated on my wife, I cheated on my employers and I cheated on all of you, the people of Los Angeles" (Cannon, 2000).

There can be no doubt that Perez is playing every which way he can with the truth. Nevertheless, five Los Angeles County judges interviewed for Lou Cannon's article all said that they had presided over trials in which they suspected that police officers were lying. Like the other judges, who insisted that they not be named, one with many years of experience reflected that perhaps unwittingly judges (as well as prosecutors) were complicit in the Rampart scandal:

(Continued)

Box 3.8 (Continued)

It's said we need to change the police culture, and that's absolutely necessary. But we have to change the judicial culture too. The judicial culture is hostile to the defense. You'll hear judges talking at lunch about some stupid thing a defense attorney did—they rarely talk about a prosecutor. I don't think they're aware how biased they sound. (Cannon, 2000)

Although it's hard to know exactly how widespread the abuse of police power was (or is) in Los Angeles, recent chief Bernard Parks has pointed out that more credit should have been given to his "watch" and the LAPD for reforming an "unhealthy" department:

In three years, although people say the civil-service system is very difficult to work with, we [had] disciplined over 800 officers and terminated 113. We . . . had 200 officers leave the department while being investigated. We . . . had a number of officers that we refused to promote, because of their disciplinary history. (Cannon, 2000)

These numbers are significant and are undoubtedly related to the decision to place the Los Angeles police under the control of the federal government. However, as Cannon (2000) points out, "What distinguishes the Rampart scandal from other Los Angeles police scandals is not just its scale but the sheer lack of public outcry in response to it." There were no citizens inside or outside of the Rampart area of L.A. demanding to be part of an oversight or reviewing body. In other words, most people in the inflicted area were—perhaps still are—resigned to a police force that uses and abuses its force and that applies violence in the name of combating the violence and abuse of others, especially those identified as "dangerous" gangbangers.

Sources: Cannon, L. (2000, October 1). One bad cop. *New York Times*, §6, p. 32. Retrieved September 24, 2002, from http://www.nytimes.com
Terry, D. (2000, August 30). Rackets law can be used against police in Los Angeles. *New York Times*, p. A14. Retrieved October 3, 2002, from http://www.nytimes.com. Reprinted with permission.

There were reports that police ill-treated demonstrators, both in the street and in custody in jail, who were in Seattle protesting during the World Trade Organization talks in Seattle in December 1999. Allegations, under investigation, included indiscriminate police use of pepper spray and tear gas against nonviolent protesters, unresisting residents, and bystanders, and the excessive use of force by police against people held in the King County jail after arrest. Similar complaints were lodged in response to the police handling of demonstrators at the 2001 Biotechnology Industry Organization trade show in San Diego. As one member of the BioJustice Legal Team stated, police worked "to squash public debate over genetic engineering by harassing, intimidating and otherwise criminalizing the public for our concern with these issues" (McDonald, 2001).

A number of lawsuits were also filed against the police for a variety of abusive and discriminatory behaviors in 1999 (see Box 3.9). In April, the U.S. Justice Department filed a federal lawsuit against the New Jersey State Police for an alleged pattern and practice of discrimination or "racial profiling" involving traffic stops. Various state and local police departments are also facing similar lawsuits filed by civil rights groups in several states, including Colorado, Illinois, Maryland, Michigan, Oklahoma, and Pennsylvania. In October of the same year, the Justice Department also sued the Columbus (Ohio) Police Department for tolerating a pattern of civil rights abuses, including excessive use of force, false arrests, and improper searches.

Box 3.9   New Jersey Turnpike Shootings

When Judge Smithson dismissed the criminal charges against two white state troopers for the shooting of three unarmed black and Hispanic men in 1998, the case became a symbol in the national debate over racial profiling. It also raised serious questions about police use of discretion and became a political "hot potato" involving local law enforcement and prosecutors, judges, civil rights leaders, a state's attorney general, a governor, and the U.S. Department of Justice. On October 31, 2000, Smithson ruled that the prosecutors had made several errors in presenting their evidence to the grand jury. Three days later, the Justice Department announced that it would intervene to see whether or not the New Jersey state troopers should be prosecuted for violating the three wounded men's federal civil rights.

In fact, a joint statement, issued the same day as the Justice Department's decision to intervene, by New Jersey's Republican attorney general John F. Farmer, Jr., and U. S. Attorney Robert Clear said that "the Federal Bureau of Investigation would work with state officials to investigate both the shooting and criminal charges that the two troopers, John Hogan and James Kenna, falsified documents to cover up their alleged practice of singling out black and Hispanic drivers." At the same time, Republican governor Christine Todd Whitman of New Jersey, who had been previously criticized by civil rights leaders for responding too slowly, stated that she welcomed the Justice Department's intervention.

Until 1999, Governor Whitman had defended New Jersey's police, even though a Gloucester County judge had ruled in 1996 that there was compelling evidence of widespread profiling on New Jersey highways. In February 1999, she ordered her own investigation and 2 months later became "the first New Jersey official to acknowledge that troopers engaged in racial profiling." Although the Justice Department's investigation of this matter is still pending at the time of this writing, the undisputed facts of the case were simply these: As Keyshon Moore of the Bronx drove his three friends to a basketball camp in North Carolina, troopers Hogan and Kenna stopped their van for speeding near Exit 7A in Cranberry, New Jersey. Within 1 minute, the troopers fired 11 times at the van's unarmed occupants, seriously wounding three of them. The officers said that they fired their weapons because the van had begun moving backward and they feared it might run over Trooper Kenna.

Source: Kocieniewski, D. (2000, November 4). U.S. to open civil rights inquiry in New Jersey turnpike shooting. *New York Times,* p. A1. Retrieved October 2, 2002, from http://www.nytimes.com

When it comes to police violence more generally, data and studies center around such things as police-citizen encounters and police shootings. Although some of the violence may be attributed to disturbed officers, alcohol abuse, the game of "cops and robbers," and especially to the role of fear, the bulk of this behavior has more fundamentally to do with issues of respect. As Hans Toch (1990) has written about the shape of police violence, when used, it is often in response to taunts. This is so

> because the officer's self-love is gauged by "respect" from others. "Respect" for law, when a man feels he embodies law, inspires private wars under color of law. Few officers may be violent, but these are backed by others—by peers who see police bonds as links to survival. . . . violent suspects often tend to be counterparts of violent officers. These suspects also prize respect, and view it as a measure of self-esteem. This suggests that much police violence comes about when either party to a confrontation engages the other in a test of respect. Violence becomes probable where issues of self-esteem are mobilized for both contenders. (p. 230)

Finally, where police forces are obsessed with real and imagined dangers, and where various communities are in fear of the police, polarization and distance between the two are inevitable. Fear, on both sides, increases in-grouping and/or protective behavior among police and increases alienation and distrust among citizens, which leads to further isolation, cynicism, and police violence. The evidence, for example, is quite consistent across the United States that African Americans represent a disproportionate share of police shooting victims and that "this disproportion is greatest where elective shootings of non-assaultive, unarmed people are concerned" (Fyfe, 1990, p. 238).

Penal violence associated with incarceration and punishment for criminal convictions is probably a more significant and certainly a more common experience than police violence. The range and variety of penal violence is also much broader and more diverse than the violence associated with law enforcement. For example, in October 1999, 5 years after ratifying the United Nations' Convention Against Torture and Other Cruel, Inhuman and Degrading Treatment or Punishment, the United States submitted its initial report to the United Nations' Committee against Torture. The report acknowledged that there were areas of concern but stated that "torture did not occur except 'in aberrational situations and never as a matter of policy'" (Amnesty International, 2000).

Though the United States does not engage in systematic torture as a matter of either formal or informal policy, the nation is in violation of international standards regarding death penalty trials and appeals, the prohibition on the use of the death penalty for crimes committed by children under 18 years of age, and the imprisonment of delinquent children with adult criminals. At the same time, the United States has been known to violate some of the human rights of its prisoners, adult and juvenile, especially with the advent of the privatization of prisons: the legal etiquette of private prisons is less circumscribed by the U.S. Constitution than are public institutions (see Box 3.10). Much more common is the ill treatment in jails and prisons, including the physical and sexual abuse of inmates as well as the abusive use of electroshock weapons.

Box 3.10 Private Youth Prisons

In the fall of 2000, an agreement was reached to settle several lawsuits against the state of Louisiana, including one brought by the U.S. Justice Department, which charged that teenage inmates were being deprived of goods, clothing, and medical care. The staff was also charged with routinely beating the youth. The agreement effectively ended Louisiana's experiment with privately run juvenile prisons, where the worst abuses had occurred, according to the director of the Louisiana Juvenile Justice Project, which provides legal services for incarcerated juveniles in the state.

In finding that teenagers had been deprived of underwear, sweaters, blankets, and food, a juvenile court judge also shared one of the severest forms of abuse found by the investigators working for the Justice Department. This incident involved a 17-year-old boy who had recently undergone stomach surgery for a gunshot wound and was wearing a colostomy bag. He had been forced to lie face down on the concrete floor with a guard's knee pressing into his back.

The agreement prohibited the state from placing any more young inmates in a prison at Jena, Louisiana, which had been run by Wackenhut Corrections Corporation. It also established timetables and mechanisms for improving the quality of services in juvenile lockup facilities, specifying (in more than 100 pages) detailed obligations and responsibilities for the state to meet. Under the settlement, doctors from Louisiana State University's School of Medicine "would provide medical, mental health and dental care at the state's five juvenile prisons, and independent monitors would have the right to inspect the facilities to make sure guards were not beating the inmates." If the problems continue, the agreement allows the Justice Department and other independent monitors to file motions to reopen the lawsuits in federal district court in Baton Rouge.

Source: Butterfield, F. (2000b, September 8). Settling suit, Louisiana abandons private youth prisons. *New York Times,* p. A14. Retrieved October 2, 2002, from http://www.nytimes.com

---

During the 1990s, in overcrowded prisons across the nation, penal violence was pervasive. In 1997, for example, there were 69 inmates killed by other inmates, and thousands were injured seriously enough to require medical attention. Mentally ill inmates, estimated to constitute from 6% to 14% of the prison population nationally, are rarely adequately monitored and treated for their conditions. And, although federal law and 13 states prohibit, on humanitarian grounds, the putting to death of mentally handicapped persons, the United States has knowingly executed 34 mentally retarded people since the Supreme Court reinstated the death penalty in 1976, according to the Death Penalty Information Center (Bonner & Rimer, 2000).

In short, abuse and violence behind bars, in jails or prisons, comes in a variety of forms, shapes, and practices. Inmates and staff alike experience both abuse and violence as perpetrators and victims (see Box 3.11). Penal violence, however, is pretty much hidden or invisible from public scrutiny. Prison life, culture, and behavior take place almost as a surrealistic experience for the majority of people who are not directly or indirectly involved with a penal institution. A prison may be considered a "total institution" or "closed system," and within such, both the order of the prison and penal practices of abuse and violence become highly controlled and structured. The various forms of abuse and violence, including extreme kinds, can become ritualized exercises in dehumanization and humiliation. At another level, the institutionalization of penal violence cannot be divorced or separated from the structural conditions residing inside and outside the confining walls. As Angela Davis (1998) has reflected, the "prison industrial system materially and morally impoverishes its inhabitants and devours the social wealth needed to address the very problems that have led to spiraling numbers of prisons" (p. 2).

Box 3.11 Danger on Death Row

In California, a 63-year-old law makes it mandatory that all death row inmates in the state be housed at San Quentin. There are some 589 death row prisoners, the most dangerous of whom, 85 killers, are known as Grade-B condemned and are housed in the Adjustment Center, a three-story-high building. In a recent 18-month period, October 1999 to April 2001, it was reported that Grade-B inmates had tripled their number of attacks on guards, from 22 to 67. These included attempted stabbings, kicks, slashes and cuts with razors, firing small objects from makeshift slingshots, and "gassings" (inmates hurl cups filled with feces and urine or even infected blood at security).

The unprecedented number of assaults on officers working in the Adjustment Center, always a dangerous place, has increased, according to correctional authorities, because of the recent overcrowding there. At the same time, inmates said in response to questions asked by Robert Navarro, an attorney representing the family of a death row inmate who died after he was pepper sprayed and dragged from his cell by officers, that the violence cuts both ways. They said also that their assaults are often in response to taunts and provocation by officers, including racist jokes and slurs on people's ethnic backgrounds. Finally, inmates claim that prison officials routinely ignore convict complaints of excessive use of force by guards.

As the violence has appeared to escalate at San Quentin's Adjustment Center, the prison response has been to further tighten up an already tight security system of riot gear, stab-proof vests, plastic shields for face and chest, and biohazard body suits. In such an atmosphere, with danger and fear permeating everywhere, dehumanizing of both keepers and kept seems to be the order of the day. "Being gassed," for example, "turns you into a different person," said Tony Jones, president of San Quentin's 800-member correctional officers union: "It is the most disgusting thing you can ever imagine. The first time it happened to me, the stuff got in my eyes and ears. I took fifteen showers that day and couldn't get clean."

Gassings and other forms of humiliation are not unique to death row or to adult institutions. Bullying, intimidation, and same-sex rape and exploitation, especially in male institutions, juvenile and adult, are far more common than the type of assaults that occur in the Adjustment Center. Most of the more common forms of penal violence occur between inmates and, if not provoked and encouraged on occasion, are tacitly approved as a way of keeping "order in the asylum."

Source: Glionna, J. M. (2001, April 21). Guards on death row face escalating dangers. *Los Angeles Times*, p. A1.

In terms of the U.S. Constitutional prohibition of cruel and unusual punishment, several state and federal investigations and injunctions against the use of stun belts and beatings, especially in high-security and "super-maximum security" units, were ongoing in a number of penal jurisdictions at the time of this writing, including Florida, Texas, California, Pennsylvania, and Virginia. Increasingly, penal authorities, especially those operating private prisons (where the rights of prisoners are less regulated), were relying on administrative segregation or isolation. Accordingly, prisoners deemed to be particularly disruptive and dangerous are secured in small, often windowless cells for 23 hours a day. It is estimated that at any given time in the United States, more than 24,000 prisoners are being kept in this modern form of solitary confinement (Human Rights Watch, 1999).

In Pennsylvania in 1998, dozens of guards from the State Correctional Facility at Greene were under investigation for beatings, slamming inmates into walls, racial taunting, and other mistreatment of inmates. Eventually, the state's Department of Corrections "fired four guards, and twenty-one others were demoted, suspended or reprimanded" (Human Rights Watch, 1999). In February 1998, federal authorities indicted eight correctional officers from the Corcoran State Prison in California for deliberately pitting unarmed inmates against each other in gladiator-style fights. After a while, guards would break up these fights by firing on them with rifles. In July, California announced another investigation into at least 36 serious and fatal shootings of Corcoran inmates since the facility had opened, 10 years earlier. In September of the same year, more than 40 prison staff were reported to be under investigation for sexual misconduct in several California women's prisons.

Sexual and other abuses of inmates, particularly male inmates by other male inmates,

female inmates by male staff, and juvenile inmates by both, continue to present serious problems in adult and juvenile institutions across America. As of 1998, 42 states allowed for the detaining of juveniles in adult jails while they awaited trial, and another 40 states had adopted legislation making it easier for children to be tried and punished by criminal rather than juvenile courts. In light of the "tough on crime" policies toward juveniles in the United States, the minimum age to be treated as an adult is 14 years in Massachusetts, 12 in Oregon, and 10 in Wisconsin. In some states, such as Michigan, there is no minimum age.

Recent changes in state laws are in the process of overturning a century-old juvenile justice system whose very reason for existence was to protect children from contact with adult prisoners. Despite the fact that most juvenile crimes are committed by whites, 3 out of 4 youths admitted to adult courts, jails, and prisons are children of color. In spite of the fact that penologists and criminologists almost all agree that these children are more likely to be physically and sexually abused in these institutions than in juvenile institutions, and that they are more likely to continue committing crimes after their release, more and more prosecutors are moving young offenders into the adult system without any regard for the child's age or circumstances. "In 1994 alone, 45 children met their deaths in adult prisons, and to this date, the number continues to climb as over 18,000 children are incarcerated annually" in adult institutions (American Civil Liberties Union, 2000, p. 69).

Overall, it seems to make little difference whether one is talking about the United States' illegitimate use of police violence (e.g., abuse of force) or its legitimate use of penal violence (e.g., executions of those convicted of capital crimes): the victims of these acts are, in the vast majority of cases, persons with little power, status, or stake in

American society. In fact, because of clerical errors and bureaucratic snafus, abuse of these persons is so commonplace that in August 2001, Los Angeles County admitted to illegally detaining over 5 years some 400,000 people in county jails. To settle five class-action lawsuits, the county supervisors agreed to pay claimants $27 million in damages (Larrubia & Riccardi, 2001).

SUMMARY

This chapter has presented a demographic overview of five common types of institutional violence, including family violence, childhood maltreatment, school violence, gang violence, and police and penal violence. Once again, the cumulative and reciprocal relationships between the interpersonal and institutional acts of violence have established normative guidelines that directly and indirectly reinforce subcultural violence by tacitly sanctioning abuse, neglect, injury, or harm to large minorities of the population.

Over the life course of individuals, there are interactions between the five types of violence examined here. These interactions not only contribute to the pathways to violence, they reproduce reciprocal relations of life-course experiences of violence. For example, infants who are first victimized by child neglect and/or family violence are more likely in later childhood and adolescence to become involved in school and/or gang violence and to subsequently experience police and penal violence.

What differentiates institutionalized expressions of violence from interpersonal and structural expressions of violence is that the former are often interwoven with the normative pathways of socialization found in the home, at school, in the street, at the workplace, and in the criminal justice system. In other words, these institutional forms of violence are part and parcel of the cultural attitudes, social statuses, and relations of power and conflict that parents and children, teachers and students, adolescents and adults, and agents and enemies of the established legal and social orders occupy in their various roles as members of society. At the same time, most of the acts that constitute the five representative types of institutional violence are supported by ideologies that rationalize, justify, or excuse such behavior by helping to blur or cloud the distinctions between abuse and discipline, harassment and teasing, assault and defense, and punishment and reform.

Institutional acts of violence, however, do not survive because the majority formally or overtly endorses these kinds of behavior. On the contrary, typically these acts of violence are denied, ignored, or dismissed as exceptional events rather than general patterns of institutional behavior. Historically, it has only been less than four decades since the United States and other developed nation-states began to challenge the various forms of institutionalized violence in society. To date, the battering of women and the physical and sexual abuse of children has received the most condemnation. For some 500 years previously, at least in terms of Anglo-Saxon common-law tradition, the separation of the "public" and "private" spheres had not only shielded family violence from common exposure but had provided policies for upholding such practices. Meanwhile, the other forms of violence—school, gang, police, and penal—discussed in this chapter are still primarily thought of as interpersonal rather than as group, organizational, or subcultural problems. Thus, most attempts at reducing these forms of violence are aimed exclusively at controlling and/or changing the individual perpetrators, or "bad apples," all the while ignoring the larger social and cultural roots of these institutionalized patterns of violent behavior.

Finally, as with interpersonal forms of violence, institutional forms of violence are consumed with emotional issues of esteem and respect. However, the issues of shame associated with institutional abuse are less about individual characteristics and more about group characteristics associated with such variables as class, race, and gender. These variables, and other social indicators of value, serve in turn as means for differentiating the forms of abuse and nonabuse that are institutionally viewed as appropriate for men, women, boys, girls, heterosexuals, homosexuals, whites, African Americans, Asians, Hispanics, the rich, the poor, the homeless, and so on. In the next chapter, the types of violence move from interpersonal and institutional to interpersonal and structural levels of analysis.

REFERENCES

American Civil Liberties Union. (2000, August 6). They finally found an answer to overcrowded prisons. Smaller prisoners [Advertisement]. *New York Times Magazine*, p. 69.

Amnesty International. (1999, January 9). *United States of America: Race, rights, and police brutality* (AI index AMR 51/147/1999). New York: Author. Retrieved September 24, 2002, from http://web.amnesty.org

Amnesty International. (2000). *Amnesty International: Annual report 2000*. Retrieved September 24, 2002, from http://www.web.amnesty.org/web/ar2000web.nsf/ar2000

Antilla, S. (2002). *Tales from the boom-boom room: Women vs. Wall Street*. Princeton, NS: Bloomberg Press.

Baker v. Owen, 395 F. Supp. 294 (D.C. NC. 1975).

Barstow, D., & Chivers, C. J. (2000, June 17). A volatile mixture exploded into rampage in Central Park. *New York Times*, p. A1. Retrieved September 24, 2002, from http://www.nytimes.com

Battin, S., Hill, K., Abbott, R., Catalano, R., & Hawkins, J. D. (1998). The contribution of gang membership to delinquency beyond delinquent friends. *Criminology, 36*(1), 105-106.

Bing, L. (1991). *Do or die*. New York: Harper Collins.

Bonner, R., & Rimer, S. (2000, August 7). Executing retarded poses troubling questions. *Ann Arbor News*, p. A4.

Butterfield, F. (2000a, July 11). A fatality, parental violence and youth sports. *New York Times*, p. A14. Retrieved October 2, 2002, from http://www.nytimes.com

Butterfield, F. (2000b, September 8). Settling suit, Louisiana abandons private youth prisons. *New York Times*, p. A14. Retrieved October 2, 2002, from http://www.nytimes.com

Cannon, L. (2000, October 1). One bad cop. *New York Times*, §6, p. 32. Retrieved September 24, 2002, from http://www.nytimes.com

Cummins, C. (1998, June 14). Busted students try to cope. *Rocky Mountain News*, pp. A14, A26.

Daly, M., & Wilson, M. (1988). *Homicide*. Hawthorne, NY: Aldine de Gruyter.

Davis, A. (1998). What is the prison industrial complex? Why does it matter? *Color-Lines Magazine, 1*(2), 1-8.

DeKeseredy, W. (1993). *Four variations of family violence: A review of sociological research*. Ottawa, Ontario: Health Canada.

Dew, C. B. (2000, May 21). Tightening the noose: *Ben Tillman and the reconstruction of white supremacy*, by Stephen Kantrowitz. *New York Times Review of Books*, p. 31.

Esbensen, F.-A., & Huizinga, D. (1993). Gangs, drugs, and delinquency in a survey of urban youth. *Criminology, 31*(3), 565-589.

Esbensen, F.-A., Huizinga, D., & Weiher, A. (1993). Gang and non-gang youth: Differences in explanatory factors. *Journal of Contemporary Criminal Justice, 9*(1), 94-111.

Exclusive torture suit settled; Louima gets $9M. (2001, March 22). *New York Daily News*, p. 1. Retrieved October 12, 2002, from http://www.nydailynews.com

Fagan, J. F. (1990). Social process of delinquency and drug use among urban gangs. In C. R. Huff (Ed.), *Gangs in America*. Newbury Park, CA: Sage.

Fyfe, J. L. (1990). Blind justice: Police shootings in Memphis. In N. A. Weiner, M. A. Zahn, & R. J. Sagi (Eds.), *Violence: Patterns, causes, public policy*. New York: Harcourt Brace College.

Gelles, R. J. (1990). Domestic criminal violence. In N. A. Weiner, M. A. Zahn, & R. J. Sagi (Eds.), *Violence: Patterns, causes, public policy*. New York: Harcourt Brace College.

Glionna, J. M. (2001, April 21). Guards on death row face escalating dangers. *Los Angeles Times*, p. A1.

Greenfeld, L. A., Rand, M. R., Craven, D., Klaus, P. A., Perkins, C. A., Ringel, C., et al. (1998, March). *Violence by intimates: Analysis of data on crimes by current or former spouses, boyfriends, and girlfriends* (Bureau of Justice Statistics NCJ 167237). Washington, DC: U.S. Department of Justice, Bureau of Justice Statistics. Retrieved September 24, 2002, from http://www.ojp.usdoj.gov/bjs/abstract/vi.htm

Holtzworth-Munroe, A., & Stuart, G. L. (1994). Typologies of male batterers: Three subtypes and the differences among them. *Psychological Bulletin, 116*(3), 476-497.

Howell, J. C. (1998, August). Youth gangs: An overview (Juvenile Justice Bulletin NCJ 167249). Washington, DC: U.S. Department of Justice, Office of Juvenile Justice and Delinquency

Prevention. Retrieved October 2, 2002, from http://www.ojjdp.ncjrs.org/jjbulletin/9808/contents.html

Human Rights Watch. (1999). *Human Rights Watch world report 1999: United States*. Retrieved October 2, 2002, from http://www.hrw.org/worldreport99/usa/

Hutson, H. R., Anglin, D., & Eckstein, M. (1996). Drive-by shootings by violent street gangs in Los Angeles: A five-year review from 1989 to 1993. *Academic Emergency Medicine, 3*, 300-303.

Hyman, I. (1991). *Reading, writing, and the hickory stick*. Lexington, MA: Lexington Books.

Ingraham v. Wright, 430 U.S. 651 (1977).

Joe, K., & Chesney-Lind, M. (1993, November). *Just every mother's angel: An analysis of gender and ethnic variations in youth gang membership*. Paper presented at the annual meetings of the American Society of Criminology, Phoenix, AZ.

Kandel Englander, E. (1997). *Understanding violence*. Mahwah, NJ: Lawrence Erlbaum.

Kantrowitz, S. (2000). *Ben Tillman and the reconstruction of white supremacy*. Chapel Hill, NC: University of North Carolina.

Kaufman, P., Chandler, K. A., & Rand, M. R. (1998, October). Indicators of school crime and safety, 1998: Executive summary. Washington, DC: U.S. Department of Justice,

Office of Educational Research and Improvement.

Kelley, B. T., Thornberry, T. P., & Smith, C. A. (1997, August). In the wake of childhood maltreatment (Juvenile Justice Bulletin NCJ 165257). Washington, DC: U.S. Department of Justice, Office of Juvenile Justice and Delinquency Prevention. Retrieved October 2, 2002, from http://www.ncjrs.org/txtfiles1/165257.txt

Kocieniewski, D. (2000, November 4). U.S. to open civil rights inquiry in New Jersey turnpike shooting. *New York Times*, p. A1. Retrieved October 2, 2002, from http://www.nytimes.com

Larrubia, E., & Riccardi, N. (2001, August 15). County to pay inmates millions. *Los Angeles Times*, p. A1. Retrieved October 2, 2002, from http://www.latimes.com.

Leland, J. (2000, November 6). Silence ending about abuse in gay relationships. *New York Times*, p. 18. Retrieved October 2, 2002, from http://www.nytimes.com

Lockwood, D. (1997, October). *Violence among middle school and high school students: Analysis and implications for prevention* (National Institute of Justice NCJRS 166363). Washington, DC: U.S. Department of Justice, Office of Justice Programs. Retrieved October 2, 2002, from http://www.ncjrs.org/txtfiles/166363.txt

Loeber, R., Kalb, L., & Huizinga, D. (2001, August). *Juvenile delinquency and serious injury victimization*

(Juvenile Justice Bulletin NCJ 188676). Washington, DC: Office of Juvenile Justice and Delinquency Prevention. Retrieved October 2, 2002, from http://www.ncjrs.org/html/ojjdp/jjbul2001_8_1/contents.html

Marklein, M. B. (1997, June 6). More educators sparing the rod. *USA Today*, p. D9.

McDonald, J. (2001, August 18). Some question police tactics at biotech protest. *San Diego Union-Tribune*, p. A1. Retrieved October 2, 2002, from http://www.signonsandiego.com

McWhorter, D. (2001). *Carry me home: Birmingham, Alabama: The climactic battle of the civil rights movement.* New York: Simon and Schuster.

Miller, W. (1980). Gangs, groups, and serious youth crime. In D. Shichor & D. Kelly (Eds.), *Critical issues in juvenile delinquency.* Lexington, MA: Lexington Books.

Nelson, J. (Ed.). (2000). *Police brutality: An anthology.* New York: W. W. Norton.

Regoli, R. M., & Hewitt, J. D. (2000). *Delinquency in society* (4th ed.). Boston: McGraw-Hill.

Rennison, C. M., & Welchans, S. (2000, May). *Intimate partner violence* (Bureau of Justice Statistics Special Report NCJ 178247). Washington, DC: U.S. Department of Justice, Office of Justice Programs.

Retrieved October 3, 2002, from http://www.ojp.usdoj.gov/bjs/abstract/ipv.htm

Renzetti, C. (1992). *Violent betrayal: Partner abuse in lesbian relationships.* Newbury Park, CA: Sage.

Schwendinger, J., & Schwendinger, H. (1983). *Rape and inequality.* Newbury Park, CA: Sage.

Shaw, S., & Braden, J. (1990). Race and gender bias in the administration of corporal punishment. *School Psychology Review, 19*, 378-383.

Straus, M. A., & Gelles, R. J. (1988). How violent are American families? Estimates from the National Family Violence Resurvey and other studies. In G. T. Hotaling, D. Finkelhor, J. T. Kirkpatrick, & M. A. Straus (Eds.), *Family abuse and its consequences: New directions in research.* Newbury Park, CA: Sage.

Straus, M. A., Gelles, R. J., & Steinmetz, S. K. (1980). *Behind closed doors: Violence in the American family.* New York: Doubleday.

Terry, D. (2000, August 30). Rackets law can be used against police in Los Angeles. *New York Times*, p. A14. Retrieved October 3, 2002, from http://www.nytimes.com

Thornberry, T., & Burch, J. (1997). *Gang members and delinquent behavior* (Juvenile Justice Bulletin NCJ 165154). Washington, DC: U.S. Department of Justice, Office of Juvenile Justice

and Delinquency Prevention. Retrieved October 3, 2002, from http:// www.ncjrs.org/txtfiles/ 165154.txt

Thornberry, T., Krohn, M., Lizotte, A., & Chard-Wierschem, D. (1993). The role of juvenile gangs in facilitating delinquent behavior. *Journal of Research in Crime and Delinquency, 30*(1), 55-87.

Thrasher, F. (1927). *The gang: A study of 1,313 gangs in Chicago.* Chicago: University of Chicago Press.

Toch, H. (1990). The shape of police violence. In N. A. Weiner, M. A. Zahn, & R. J. Sagi (Eds.), *Violence: Patterns, causes, public policy.* New York: Harcourt Brace College.

Violence in youth sports spreads beyond the field. (2000, May 14). *Ann Arbor News*, p. C3.

Widom, C. S. (1994). Childhood victimization and risk for adolescent problem behavior. In M. E. Lamb & R. Kettlerlinus (Eds.), *Adolescent problem behaviors.* New York: Lawrence Erlbaum.

Wilson, M., Daly, M., & Daniele, A. (1995). Familicide: The killing of spouse and children. *Aggressive Behavior, 21*, 275-291.

REVIEW QUESTIONS

1. Discuss the ways in which institutional forms of violence overlap with interpersonal forms of violence.

2. Explain how the rampage in Central Park can be viewed as institutionalized rather than interpersonal or group violence.

3. What were some of the similarities and, if any, the differences in the ways that institutionalized racism worked during and after the Hamburg riot of 1876 and during and after the Birmingham church bombing of 1963?

4. Rank the five types of institutional violence discussed in this chapter in terms of most to least serious or most to least dangerous to society. Explain your answer.

5. Discuss the cumulative and reciprocal effects of the violence outside and the violence inside of prison in relation to both penal violence and life-course histories.

CHAPTER 4

Structural Violence

Structural violence is the most basic or fundamental form of violence. It is expressive of the conditions of society, the structures of social order, and the institutional arrangements of power that reproduce mass violations of personhood 24 hours a day, 7 days a week. Such violence is accomplished in part through "policies" of informal and formal denial of civil, criminal, and basic human rights for all people. Although institutional and structural forms of violence may work hand in hand with each other, they may also be differentiated. *Institutional violence*, as illustrated in the cases in Chapter 3, refers to those actions or inactions that "deviate" from prescribed institutional norms and have a negative and differential impact on certain underprivileged groups. By contrast, *structural violence* refers to the established patterns of organized society that have been institutionalized—rationalized and sanctioned—yet result in systematic harm to millions of victims annually, including, disproportionately, members of the marginal classes of society. Robert Brown (1987) has discussed structural violence as "the violence of the status quo" and as the violence against extraordinary numbers produced by *the way things now are*. Poverty and homelessness in affluent societies such as the United States, for example, represent a classic form of structural violence.

In addition, structural violence includes the actions or inactions of both the public and private sectors. With respect to governments, corporations, or politics, structural harm or injury refers to "business as usual" and to the bureaucratic realities of social, political, and economic interaction. Consequently, structural forms of violence may be thought of as very complex varieties of violence. Interpersonal forms of violence are generally the products of actions taken; institutional forms are usually the products of actions taken, but may also be the products of actions not taken (e.g., as in asserting positive rights or as in remedial legal actions). Structural forms of violence, by contrast, may be the products of actions taken, actions not taken, or both. Structural violence, in other words, may include violence by commission and violence by non-commission or omission.

Structural violence may also be about individuals acting abusively or violently in their private lives, or about individuals acting abusively or violently within the context of their institutionalized roles or public lives. More fundamentally, structural violence reinforces adversarial social organization that incorporates both personal and impersonal ideologies of difference, privilege, and inequality. Finally, like interpersonal and institutional violence, structural violence occurs in forms that include both physical suffering and emotional pain. In addition, structural violence generates and exacerbates other forms of interpersonal and institutional violence.

As introduced in Chapter 1, structural violence happens in the context of establishing, maintaining, extending, or reducing hierarchical relations or as a consequence of the hierarchical order of categories of people (Iadicola & Shupe, 1998). These hierarchies of privilege or systems of stratification appear to be universal, and they have served to organize societies around the world. In the United States and elsewhere, the three most common hierarchical relationships have revolved around class, gender, and ethnic or racial identity. In the contemporary age of globalization, each of these systems of stratification, in different but related ways, has become a structural feature of the post–Cold War, new world political-economic order dominated by advanced forms of capitalism:

> These systems of stratification (class, gender, and race) intersect to create positions along a hierarchy of life chances and patterns of victimization for violence. We can think of the dominant positions in [the United States] and in the rest of the world in general as occupied by whites of European ancestry, males, capitalists who reside in countries referred to as the center of the world political economy (United States, Western Europe, Japan, Canada, and Australia). Those who occupy this position

have the greatest power within societal institutions and have the greatest ability to fulfill their potentials as measured in terms of life expectancy, illness rates, educational level, control over resources, and so on. Those who occupy the most dominated positions in [U.S.] society and the world in general are female, ethnic minority group members (i.e., African, Hispanic, Asian or Native American), and members of the working class or another subservient position within a subordinate mode of production (peasantry). (Iadicola & Shupe, 1998, p. 304)

Moreover, globalization has increased the polarization of wealth and income, as well as intensified disease, poverty, and hunger—both within and between rich and poor nations (see Box 4.1). Developmental studies by the United Nations reveal that the upper fifth economic level of those living in high-income countries accounts for 86% of all the world's private expenditures. At the same time, 10s of millions of people succumb annually to famine and preventable diseases. For hundreds of millions of others, mostly in developing but also in developed countries, "life is a daily preoccupation with obtaining safe water, rudimentary health care, basic education, and sufficient nutrition" (Weiss, 2000, p. 2).

Looked at globally, structural violence in the 21st century expresses itself in how societies have naturally organized themselves—intellectually, physically, and emotionally—into

---

Box 4.1 Child Slave Labor

The U.S. State Department estimates that 15,000 young boys are enslaved in the Ivory Coast, a place where nearly half of all the world's cocoa beans—chocolate's essential ingredient—are produced. On small farms, "young boys pick cocoa beans from dusk to dawn. Recently, a number of factors—including razor-thin profit margins and the desperation of migrant workers—have all combined to tempt plantation owners into renewing an age-old cost-cutting method: child slave labor." How does this form of child slavery persist in the 21st century?

Traffickers, or "locateurs," as they are called, approach young boys offering toys and good-paying jobs. The boys are then sold to unscrupulous growers, who force them to work long hours harvesting the cocoa beans. These growers are also known to beat their child laborers with branches, bicycle chains, and other objects. The cocoa beans are then sold to "silent conspirators," the chocolate industry, represented in the United States by Hershey and M&M/Mars. Other silent conspirators include the federal contracts and taxpayer subsidies for the cocoa and chocolate industry. At the time of this writing, a silent battle was taking place in the U.S. Congress.

On one side were the forces to end child slave labor in the Ivory Coast, led by Congressman Eliot Engel (D-NY) and Senator Tom Harkin (D-IA). On the other side were the "business as usual" forces, led by the Chocolate Manufacturers Association and their hired gun, former vice-president and Viagra pitchman Bob Dole (R-KS), and many other Washington-based lobbyists. First, Engel sponsored a measure in the House that passed with overwhelming bipartisan support. The amendment would fund the Food and Drug Administration to "establish a labeling system to certify cocoa beans and chocolate products as having involved 'no child slave labor'." Second, Harkin was prepared to offer an amendment in September 2001 that would cut off funds for contracts and subsidies unless the industry adopted a credible action plan of their own to end this form of child slavery. Evidently, that bill, like so many others post–September 11th, was tabled.

After years of ignoring the evidence of child slave labor practices in the cocoa industry, the Chocolate Manufacturers Association, in the wake of mass-media attention to the problem in July 2001, finally was forced to acknowledge these serious human rights abuses. However, Dole and many other lobbyists oppose any legislation or labeling approach. Instead, they talk the talk of "free trade" and "self-regulation" while thousands of young boys toil in subhuman conditions. Unfortunately, even before the terrorist attacks of 2001, it seemed as though the chocolate industry was poised to succeed in the defeat of necessary legislation, as there were few people speaking up for those youngsters enslaved on cocoa plantations in the Ivory Coast.

Source: Working for Change. (2001, August 2). Help end child slave labor. Retrieved October 9, 2002, from http://209.15.12.20/csny/action.htm.

independent-dominant and dependent-dominated nations, especially in regard to life chances or access to opportunities for individuals to realize their full potential. With globalization, the most recent stage of postindustrial capitalism, has come the further polarization of the wealthy and the poor. Globally, if we use a planetary population figure of 5.5. billion inhabitants, then 14% of expenditures on private consumption are divided among at least 5 billion people (90% of the world's inhabitants), and the other 500 million are the source of the remaining 86% of expenditures (Cohen, 2001). This type of gross inequality worldwide not only accounts for all kinds of daily suffering, but it is often at the root of the variety of atrocities committed by rich and poor nations alike. As Stanley Cohen (2001) argued in his book, *States of Denial,* it takes many states of denial to perpetuate these forms of abuse and violence.

Of course, it should go without saying that in the wealthiest nation of all, the United States—with its thousands of impoverished and hungry people, including 1 out of every 5 children; the 10s of thousands of homeless mentally ill; the children in schools without books and technology across urban America; and the 45 million Americans without health care insurance—the forms of violence experienced by these people are the result of their structural victimization through political omission, indifference, and inaction. The disconnected policies of "compassionate conservatism," for example, are every bit as or more harmful to the well-being of marginal peoples as are their victimizations from the more conventional forms of interpersonal and institutional violence. Domestically, the violence in the ghettos or slums of the United States is usually referenced by the popular media with discourse about acts of physical abuse and havoc perpetrated by dangerous muggers, hooligans, or predators rather than by victims of impoverishment and institutional discrimination.

Discussions of structural violence raise the ante considerably because they stress the nature of violence in the structural orders of the ghetto, the slums, poverty, and other forms of oppression rather than in the people residing in these social milieus or geographical locales. In short, all of those persons who inhabit impoverished environments, even if they have never been mugged, raped, or robbed by others living in their victimized neighborhoods, have been structurally violated every day of their lives.

They are denied the possibility of achieving full personhood, since living in the slum means that they will probably not get the health care to which human beings are entitled; their children will almost certainly go to inferior schools; because of their inferior schooling, their children will almost certainly have to take inferior jobs; as a result, they too will have to live in inferior neighborhoods; their children, in turn, . . . and the vicious cycle will be repeated each generation. (Brown, 1987, p. 36)

As already noted, structural forms of violence both intersect and interact with interpersonal and institutional forms of violence. This occurs in two basic ways.

First, there are the individuals acting outside of any institutional roles to establish, maintain, extend, or reduce privilege and inequality. In relationship to ethnic or racial or to hetero- or homosexual hierarchies in the United States, there have been the violent actions of such hate groups as the Ku Klux Klan and the Posse Comitatus, or gay bashers more generally. On the other side, there have been nonviolent groups as well as various militant factions for social change to end, for example, racism or heterosexism, such as the Black Panther Party for Self-Defense or The AIDS Coalition to Unleash Power.

Second, there are those individuals acting in accord with or in reaction to governmental or other institutional policies that serve to establish or maintain the status quo as they defend or extend hierarchies of gender, race, and class. Such violent activities might include, human service bureaucrats denying food stamps to hungry but ineligible people, penal authorities confining inmates to sensory-depriving holding cells 23½ hours per day, or capitalists displacing 10s of thousands of workers in the pursuit of cheaper labor costs and larger bottom lines. They might also include runaway girls selling their bodies for food and shelter or unemployed workers seeking compensation in the illegal marketplaces and underground economies.

Generally, though, with an increase of social inclusion and diversity over the past 30 years or so, and through the legal resolution over some conflicts of hierarchy, sources of collective labor, racial and urban violence have been reduced. Conversely, during the postindustrialism of the past quarter century, there has evolved an excluded "underclass" of disenfranchised Americans who are not only marginalized, but who also experience very high levels of interpersonal, institutional, and structural violence. What ties these structural expressions of violence together are the intersecting forces of the political economy and a myriad of violent and nonviolent roles that are either adopted or denied by nation-states in the course of their historical patterns—bureaucratic, strategic, or otherwise—of social development and victimization. In the rest of this chapter, attention is focused on five representative forms of structural violence:

- Postcolonial violence
- Corporate violence
- Underclass violence
- Terrorist violence
- Institutional-structural violence

POSTCOLONIAL VIOLENCE

To understand the nature of structural violence, one needs to understand the nature of the systems of inequality within and between societies. In other words, even though this book focuses on the pathways to violence and nonviolence in the United States, its examination of these pathways is grounded within a cross-cultural and comparative perspective. Even before the early emergence of mercantile capitalism in the 12th century, the driving forces among nation-states have been those of imperialism. As a system of

international relations, imperialism refers to the institutionalized patterns of domination by some countries over other countries.

Imperialism is older than capitalism. However, imperialism developed into a worldwide system of domination as capitalism blossomed, facilitating the development of empires as the most dominant form of nation-states. In this sense, imperialism as an economic and political system was strengthened as the system for the organization and distribution of capital emerged and developed—a system in which, for example, the wealthiest fifth of the world's population controls 85% of global income, the poorest fifth lives off 1.4%, and the remaining three fifths share 13.6% (Iadicola & Shupe, 1998).

One result of these relations of extreme inequality has been the human-created levels of poverty, hunger, famine, and violence found throughout the developing world. A billion persons are subject to and victimized by this kind of economic-structural violence or by the systems of productive appropriation and exploitation. As a modern-day system, advanced imperialism, or "globalism," is grounded in processes whereby multinational corporate oligarchies seek to preserve and increase their capital through the extension of markets and production to locations outside of their native nations. The driving force behind this extension of capitalist relations is the worldwide competition between multinational conglomerates for "surplus" (or profits) in its two basic forms:

Owners must seek ways of generating and realizing increasing levels of surplus and must find additional outlets for the productive use of this increasing surplus to keep extending the process. In the first case, owners search the globe for cheaper costs of materials and labor, and for ways of making the process of production more efficient by reducing the amount of time required to reproduce the labor power of the workers. In the second case, they search the globe for new investment opportunities where their capital can produce more surplus. (Iadicola & Shupe, 1998, p. 306)

In short, capitalist development depends on continued expansion and exploitation (Dowd, 1993). As an evolving system, imperialism-capitalism has three broad and overlapping stages: plunder, trade, and invest. During each of these stages of development, the dominated or victimized societies have played significant roles in the advancement of the dominant or imperialist societies. In the first stage of plundering, which began in the 15th through the 17th centuries, the dominant European powers (joined in the 19th and 20th centuries by the United States) were able to accumulate vast sums of capital as they divided up the societies in Africa, Asia, and Central and South America. The dominated or colonized societies provided sources for cheap resources as well as for the labor necessary to extract raw materials for the rapid expansion of industries in the dominant home countries. In the beginning, populations were slaughtered and enslaved to enrich those persons who were dominant within the dominating nations (see Box 4.2). The colonized societies saw their formerly prospering agricultural systems and primitive industries destroyed and refitted into the exploitive relations of imperialism, in which these peoples also became politically and economically dependent on the colonizing powers.

Box 4.2   Genocide in the Americas

During the period of merchant capitalism (1500-1750), long-distance trade was the main instrument of profit making. At the beginning of the capitalist era, the strong nations of Europe, including Spain, Portugal, France, England, and the Netherlands, were dependent for their economic well-being on the "precious mineral ores from Latin America, the sugar from the Caribbean islands, the 'ebony flesh' from Africa, and the spices of Asia" (Salmi, 1993, p. 27). In short, the gold, silver, tin, and mercury mined in the West Indies, Mexico, Peru, Brazil, and Bolivia; the sugar cultivated in the West Indian, Peruvian, Brazilian, and Javanese plantations; the West African slaves involved in the triangular trade; and Asian spices and textiles "all constituted an enormous source of profits and wealth for the European states, banks, and trading companies" (Salmi, 1993, p. 27).

For example, on the island of Hispañola under the governorship of Christopher Columbus, 50,000 native people died within a matter of months after the establishment of the first Spanish colony in the Caribbean. The "civilizing process" used by the early explorers included enslaving the native people, "chaining them together at the neck and marching them in columns to toil in gold and silver mines, decapitating any who did not walk quickly enough" (Stannard, 1992, p. 430). The barbaric cruelty of these early capitalists involved the slicing off "women's breasts for sport and [feeding] their babies to the packs of armored wolfhounds and mastiffs that accompanied the Spanish soldiers" (Stannard, 1992, p. 430) Wrote one Spanish eyewitness to the massacres, the soldiers "would test their swords and their manly strength on captured Indians" and "place bets on the slicing off of heads or the cutting of bodies in half with one blow" (Stannard, 1992, p. 430).

Take the case of Hernando Cortez and his accompanying conquistadors. In November 1519, they became the first Westerners to gaze upon the magnificent Aztec city of Tenochtitlan. This island metropolis was far larger and more impressive than any city they had seen in Europe. At the time, Tenochtitlan's population was five times the population of either London or Seville. Less than 2 years later that incredible city was a smoldering ruin:

> Tenochtitlan, with its 350,000 residents, had been the jewel of an empire that contained numerous exquisite cities. All were destroyed. Before the coming of the Europeans, central Mexico, radiating out from those metropolitan centers over many tens of thousands of square miles, had contained about 25 million people—almost ten times the population of England at the time. Seventy-five years later hardly more than 1 million were left. And central Mexico, where 95 out of every 100 people perished, was typical. In Central America the grisly pattern held, and even worsened. In western and central Honduras 95 percent of the native people were exterminated in half a century. In western Nicaragua the rate of extermination was 99 percent—from more than 1 million people to less than 10,000 in just sixty years. (Stannard, 1992, p. 430)

When the Caribbean holocaust had exhausted itself, around 1535, the genocide then spread to South America. For example, before the arrival of the Europeans in what are today Peru and Chile, the population was somewhere between 9 and 14 million. A century later, the population had been reduced to a little over 500,000. In Brazil and all across the South American continent the same story repeated itself. Comparatively speaking, the number of deaths and proportion of the populations affected by these earlier holocausts far exceeded that of any of the more recent genocides, including those perpetrated against the Armenians, Jews, Gypsies, Ibos, Bengalis, Timorese, Cambodians, Ugandans, and others.

All in all, before the 17th century had arrived, between 60 million and 80 million Amerindians had perished at the hands of the civilizing Europeans. By the time of the Industrial Revolution (1750-1850) in England and the period of imperialist expansion (1850-1950), the mass killings had subsided not only because there were relatively few persons left to exterminate but because what the developing economies of the world now desired was cheap sources of labor. Inhuman working and living conditions were thus substituted for the previous bloodshed and slaughter of innocent persons.

Sources: Salmi, J. (1993). *Violence and democratic society*. London: Zed.
Stannard, D. E. (1992, October 19). Genocide in the Americas: Columbus's legacy. *The Nation, 255*, 430-434.

Following the industrialization of the capitalist nations of Western Europe came the stage of acquiring new markets and world trade. During this stage, capitalists viewed less-developed societies not only as sources of raw materials, but also as locations for disposing of surplus populations and production. The peak period of colonialism was from the latter part of the 19th century to the end of the Second World War, when all the world was divided up, as it were, among Western European and North American powers.

In general, this form of capitalist development is of a dependent nature, characterized by unequal trade, minimal industrial development, and out-of-balance capital flows favoring the dominant over the dominated countries. For example, at least through the mid-1980s, according to the United Nations, 79% of the exports of developing countries was food, mineral fuels, and crude materials. In contrast, 75% of the exports of developed capitalist nations was machinery and equipment, chemicals, and other finished products (Sherman, 1987). Among the consequences of these material relations are the facts that people in the poorest nations die from diseases associated with malnutrition and starvation, but people in the richest nations die from diseases like high cholesterol and heart attacks associated with gluttony and overconsumption.

The postcolonial urges for colonies to liberate themselves and become independent nation-states, were strongly affected by the two world wars and by the Russian and Chinese revolutions. These events all helped to spark revolutionary movements and violent struggles that eventually led to the freedom of hundreds of millions of colonized people throughout Asia and Africa.

The third stage of imperialism, investment, emerged during the second half of the 20th century. When the "pax Britannica" was assumed by the "pax Americana," the United States had become the dominant military, economic, and political force in the worldwide system of imperialism. As the proprietor of contemporary global capitalism, "its responsibility and interests are in maintaining the hierarchy between the center and the periphery for the benefit of its capitalist class" (Iadicola & Shupe, 1998, p. 309). With the assistance of "free trade" agreements, the World Bank, and the World Trade Association, policies are adopted which permit the dominating nations in the world to extract more capital than they invest in the dominated nations. These policies also allow for the capitalists within the dominated countries to export their investment capital to banks and investment houses within the dominant countries for purposes of security and higher returns in the currency of the dominant economies.

By this stage of capitalist development, the indigenous populations of the first stage of conquest and domination have either been destroyed or make up the most impoverished classes of these neocolonial regimes and governments. And although settlers exported from the dominant countries during the second stage may have experienced upward mobility in their adopted countries, the control and domination remains within neocolonial structures subject to capitalist penetration and the interests of multinational corporations. In other words, during the third stage of imperialism, the underlying political and economic relations that have long been established and institutionalized are simply transformed from overt to covert forms of political domination. At the same time, the perpetual need for capitalist accumulation—more markets, greater surpluses, and continued exploitation of peoples around the world—marches on.

As a consequence of these imperialistic-capitalistic relationships, the dominated countries fall deeper into debt as they act to subsidize the wealthy of both the core and the periphery (or their own) nations. Between 1982 and 1985, in Latin America alone, capital inflows (e.g., aid and investment) came to less than $38 billion, while Latin American countries paid back $144 billion in debt service, for an overall net transfer of $106 billion to the rich (George, 1988). All of this was occurring during times when the per capita GNP was declining and unemployment and poverty were increasing. In the process, the workers of both the dominant and dominated societies, relative to the wealthy of those societies, became worse off. In the larger scheme of things, since the 1960s, global income disparity has more than doubled. During the same period, the richest 20% of the world's population was receiving 150 times the income of the poorest 20%, and 1.3 billion people were living in absolute poverty as the inequality and disparity within and between developed and developing nations continued to grow (Iadicola & Shupe, 1998; see also the Human Development Reports available at http://hdr.undp.org/).

Finally, the role of political violence, state-sponsored terrorism, and other forms of low-intensity conflict or warfare should not be underestimated in maintaining the relations of domination in the imperialist-capitalist system (Barak, 1991). For example, throughout the 20th century, the United States regularly used force to maintain its relationship of dominance in Central America. Since the invasion of Cuba in 1898, the United States has sent troops to protect American (capitalist) interests in Central America and the Caribbean 27 times, the invasions of Panama and Grenada being the most recent. Moreover, throughout most of the second half of the century, the United States engaged in covert operations and sponsored violence and terrorism in such countries as Guatemala, Chile, and El Salvador (Bodenheimer & Gould, 1989).

In the case of Nicaragua, the United States, beginning in 1981, organized, funded, and directed the contra invasion and campaign of terrorism against the popularly elected Sandanista government and the Nicaraguan population. By 1989, the United States had spent between $4 and $6 billion in training and arming the contras, and 30,000 Nicaraguans had been killed (Sharkey, 1990). Ultimately, this resulted in the U.S.-backed "free-market" candidate winning power after a couple of national elections.

CORPORATE VIOLENCE

Corporate violence and harm "may just as easily be a product of dangerous factory conditions, polluted air, or unsafe motor vehicles as [they are] of bullet wounds, knifings, or beatings" (Swiggert & Farrell, 1990, p. 271). For the past five centuries, however, capitalist law has been slow to criminalize the actions of corporations or the persons in charge. Recently, as the vocabulary surrounding harms and injuries has changed, so have notions of corporate and ethical responsibility. Corporate violence includes fatal and nonfatal assaults; for example, those resulting from unsafe working conditions, defective products, environmental pollution, food and drug adulteration, and other institutionalized corporate behavior that makes mass victimization possible. Eventually, corporate violence may come to be viewed side by side with other forms of criminal and not merely those of regulatory and civil liability (see Box 4.3). Laws criminalizing corporate violence have been slow to arrive not only because of the obvious resistance from deeply entrenched political and economic interests, but also, instrumentally, because of the positive social and material differences associated with the violence of corporate production and consumption.

Box 4.3   The Tobacco Industry

In the late summer of 2001, in Los Angeles, Judge Charles W. McCoy of the California Superior Court rejected the $3 billion damage award against the tobacco giant Philip Morris as excessive. Instead, he offered dying smoker Richard Boeken, 56, $100 million—the largest award ever in an individual lawsuit against a tobacco company. In a 27-page ruling, Judge McCoy denounced the tobacco giant's actions as "reprehensible in every sense of the word, both legal and moral," and for refusing "to accept even a scintilla of responsibility for the harm it has done." The judge also reprimanded Philip Morris for going to "extraordinary lengths to hide its own scientific information" about the associated health risks of smoking.

McCoy further said that the company would get a retrial only if the cancer-stricken plaintiff did not accept the $100 million settlement. Philip Morris, of course, has argued that it could not afford to pay $100 million, let alone $3 billion, for every plaintiff that sues the company. Boeken's attorney explained that $100 million was the equivalent of one week's earnings for Philip Morris, or fining somebody $1000 who makes $50,000 a year. Putting the compensation issue aside and getting back to the harm caused by hundreds of thousands of people dying from cancer-related smoking diseases, William S. Ohlemeyer, vice president and associate general counsel for Philip Morris, had this to say about the ruling:

> This case became an exercise in punishing an unpopular industry. Our appeal will request a complete reversal and retrial on multiple grounds, not the least of which was the passion and prejudice the jury displayed in reaching its verdict. It's simply not believable that anyone living in America for the past 40 years could testify under oath that they were unaware of the risks of smoking.

Among other things, Boeken claimed, as many other individual and state-wide class-action lawsuits have, that he was a victim of a tobacco industry campaign that portrayed smoking as "cool" while concealing its dangers. The greater social issues here are that the tobacco industry is permitted to simply negotiate with states and individuals through large cash settlements for the right to continue to peddle its killing substance to forewarned consumers. This kind of structural violence, like many other forms, counts its greatest number of victims among the poor and minimally educated people of society.

In today's global world of "free trade," complete with the World Trade Organization, the Free Trade for the Americas Act, G-8 summits,[1] and more, multinational tobacco interests find themselves struggling against those who are trying to resist the spread of this insidious commodity. For example, many nations around the world are currently working on the development of a global tobacco-control treaty backed by the World Health Organization. In opposition to better health, the United States, Britain, and Japan are using the WTO as a club to force open markets in poor countries to tobacco pushers. Like other forms of "corporate dumping," the victims of these forms of corporate violence are disproportionately poor and from the less-developed nation-states.

Source: Peyton, C. M. (2001, August 7). Judge reduced settlement against tobacco company." *Ann Arbor News*, p. A7.

As Friedrichs (1996) has enumerated, corporate violence differs from interpersonal violence in five ways: (1) it is indirect in the sense that victims are assaulted not by other persons, but by policies and actions undertaken on behalf of the corporation that result in the exposure of people to harmful conditions, products, or substances; (2) its effects are often quite removed in time and distance from policies and actions that harm individuals, and thus the establishment of injury to health, including death, is often difficult to prove legally; (3) the corporate actions that cause nonfatal and fatal injuries are often the product of large numbers of persons acting collectively rather than those of a single individual or a couple of people; (4) the motivation behind corporate violence is to maximize corporate profits rather than to intentionally harm people, although the consequences of the economic motivations are structurally as or more harmful; and (5) the legal responses to corporate violence have been more circumspect and less emotional than the legal responses to either interpersonal or institutional violence.

What also makes corporate violence different from interpersonal and institutional violence is that the former is a more comprehensive form of violence in terms of its victims. In other words, corporate violence is about "equal opportunity" victimization. Counted among its victims are the general public, consumers, workers, employees, citizens, and taxpayers. Some of the most common forms of corporate violence are unsafe environmental practices; unsafe products; unsafe working conditions; and the abuse of power, fraud, and economic exploitation.

Probably the most common form of corporate violence involves the mass polluting and poisoning of the environment. For example, the production and improper disposal of deadly, hazardous, and toxic wastes by corporations are among the most infamous forms of environmental violence. Whether in the form of chemicals (e.g., pesticides,

herbicides, oil) spilling on land, in the water, or evaporating into the air we breathe, the "fallout," or devastation, from these toxins is enormous. "The overall harmful consequences of such practices for the health of Americans seem evident to many observers. An estimated one-quarter of the U.S. population (56 million people) will develop cancer, and by some (admittedly controversial) estimates 80-90 percent of all cancers may be environmentally related" (Friedrichs, 1996, p. 71).

Beyond the growing rates of cancer associated with environmental pollution during the last century, other serious U.S. health problems and maladies associated with corporate violence have included heart and lung diseases, birth defects and genetic disorders, and sterility (Brownstein, 1981; Regenstein, 1986). Consumers and the general public have been victimized by unsafe foods, drugs and medical devices, motor vehicles, household products, and cosmetics. At the turn of the 21st century, the production, promotion, and distribution of cigarettes were estimated by reputable scientists to cause the premature death of over 400,000 Americans annually (Cowley, 1990; Rosenblatt, 1994). Aside from the direct harm to smokers, there are the indirect harmful effects of "passive smoke" that have been implicated in birth defects and other health problems.

Whether one is talking about unsafe environmental practices or unsafe products, both are prime examples of structural violence. As Friedrichs (1996) has underscored about the latter, and which is just as true about the former, "although corporations hardly wish to inflict harm on consumers [or the environment], they have in fact all too often done so when the drive to maximize profit or survive in the marketplace has taken precedence over a concern with consumer [or environmental] safety" (p. 75) (see Box 4.4). In short, competitive bottom lines and rates of return on capitalist investment impose these and other forms of violence.

Box 4.4   The ValuJet Crash

In the case of the ValuJet Airlines crash in the Everglades that killed 110 people in 1996, a now defunct jet-repair contractor, SabreTech, was ordered to pay $11 million in penalties. Judge James L. King of the Federal District Court in Miami imposed a $2 million fine and ordered Sabreliner Corporation (SabreTech's parent company) to pay $9 million in restitution. Its insurers had already paid out $262 million to settle lawsuits by the families of the victims. In connection with this crash, SabreTech also faces pending charges in Florida's criminal court for murder. Investigators in these cases had believed that 144 canisters in the cargo hold of the DC-9 ignited a fierce blaze that caused the plane to crash a few minutes after takeoff from Miami International Airport.

As federal prosecutor Caroline H. Miller said, "we must not lose sight of the crime in this case. . . . This is a case of unspeakable harms." As a result of the federal lawsuit, SabreTech became the nation's first aviation company to be convicted of criminal charges stemming from a commercial jet crash. Specifically, the maintenance contractor for ValuJet "was convicted of illegally causing the transportation of hazardous waste— the oxygen generators—and failing to train its crews in its handling." Investigators had concluded that the five cartons (144 canisters) of used generators, which were not labeled as hazardous cargo by SabreTech, were delivered to ValuJet even though the airline was not cleared for carrying hazardous materials. Prosecutors in the case pointed out that the generators did not have safety caps on them. Moreover, the canisters, which use an extremely hot chemical reaction to generate oxygen, were wrapped in plastic bubble wrap and packed in a cardboard carton.

Although this case does not necessarily constitute a pattern of "business as usual," the temporary shutting down of ValuJet Airlines as a whole was a historical first in the industry. Moreover, the National Transportation Safety Board, in its report, split the blame for the crash among SabreTech, ValuJet, and the Federal Aviation Administration. The Safety Board charged all three with lax oversight of the fast-growing discount airline. Of course, for all kinds of reasons, it is difficult to know what exactly constitutes "business as usual" or even to know about the magnitude of abuse and harm caused by the vagaries of an air transporting marketplace. Public ignorance is a function, at least in part, of the degree to which private (yet public) corporations struggle to keep their workings secret and outside legal action or incrimination.

Source: Service company must pay $11 million in ValuJet crash. (2000, August 15). *New York Times.* Retrieved October 11, 2002, from http://www.nytimes.com

---

In the United States, worker-related accidents and diseases are the leading causes of disability and premature death. For example, it is estimated by governmental and private studies alike that work-related accidents cause some 10,000 to 11,000 deaths annually and work-related diseases account for about 100,000 deaths and 1.8 million disabling injuries annually (Cullen, Maakestad, & Cavender, 1987; Michalowski, 1985; Reiman, 1990). More generally, corporate violence against workers refers to exposing laborers and others to dangerous conditions. Workers and employees of many industries, especially in mining, textiles, and the chemical fields, are regularly subjected to toxic materials without regard to proper safety standards. The effects of asbestos, "black lung," and "brown lung" are probably the most well-known of the injuries and damages done to specific groups of workers. Once again, corporate harm and violence against workers stems fundamentally from the structural realities of capitalism, which necessitate the maximization of profit and the minimization of

costs (see Box 4.5). In the end, "the absence of direct intent to do harm, the difficulty of pinpointing the specific cause of harm, the diffusion of responsibility for harm-producing corporate decisions, and the economic and political clout of corporations have all tended to shield corporate employees from full-fledged liability for work-related injuries and deaths" (Friedrichs, 1996, p. 83).

Box 4.5   The Auto Industry

In the massive auto-defect cover-up scandal of 2000 in Japan—"Police Raid Mitsubishi Headquarters" (Coleman, 2000)—company president Katsuhiko Kawasoe was forced to resign when it became known that the automaker had been hiding flaws in its products for 20 years, even though the flaws had garnered some 64,000 consumer complaints. Although there were no known deaths to date, the revelations of the concealment by Mitsubishi and pressure from Japan's transport ministry forced the company to recall 620,000 vehicles for defects such as failing breaks, fuel leaks, and malfunctioning clutches (Coleman 2000).

The situation at Mitsubishi Motors can be contrasted with the abuses and violations of Ford and Firestone, which, as of July 18, 2002, had resulted in their having settled over 600 death and injury claims without any of these ever being tried in a court of law. By that date, 346 people had reportedly died when Ford Explorers rolled over after the treads had separated on their Firestone Tires. In addition, there were some 800 serious injuries caused from these "accidents." At the time of the public scandal in the United States, back in the summer of 2000, Bridgestone-Firestone and Ford Motors each did their best to blame the other for the situation. They ended up dissolving a 100-year-old working relationship over the matter.

The U.S. Congress was quick to accuse both companies of ignoring public safety and of perhaps even conspiring to do so. As Sen. Richard C. Shelby (R-AL) said, "both failed to bring this issue to consumers' and the federal government's attention (Bradsher & Wald, 2000). Likewise, "an ongoing *CBS News* investigation [had] uncovered evidence that both Ford and Firestone documented problems with the tires years before they were recalled." Nevertheless, had the potential lawsuits ever reached trial, the cases would have revolved around the classic issues of "what did they know, and when did they know it?"

At the time of the hearings in September 2000, and after lawmakers on Capitol Hill had come up with all kinds of proposals for reform, including some that emphasized harsher punishments for those who violate safety rules and some that focused on closer government monitoring of the auto industry, no specific legislation was ever broached on the subject of new safety rules for tires, as recommended by the National Highway

(Continued)

Box 4.5 (Continued)

Traffic Safety Administration. In fact, as of winter 2002, no member of Congress had ever introduced a bill with any of the measures recommended by this agency—a case no doubt related to the power of auto manufacturing lobbyists and "politics as usual" in Washington, DC.

In sum, it is doubtful whether the operating spheres of the auto industry will undergo any significant change as a result of the Firestone blowouts and the Ford Explorer rollovers, which caused injury, paralysis, and death. Although Sen. Herb Kohl (D-WI) had promised that he would use the scandal "to seek quick passage of legislation barring companies from sealing information relevant to public safety in court settlements of lawsuits," such a law has never materialized (Bradsher & Wald, 2000). One would have thought that such laws would have already been on the books. Until such laws and mechanisms are in place, corporations will be able to continue to keep their consumers and the public in the dark about life-threatening "accidents."

Sources: Bradsher, K., & Wald, M. L. (2000, September 7). More indications hazards of tires were long known. *New York Times*, p. A1. Retrieved October 8, 2002, from http://www.nytimes.com
Coleman, J. (2000, August 25). Police raid Mitsubishi headquarters. *Ann Arbor News*, p. A9.

Finally, corporate abuse of power, fraud, and economic exploitation refers to an ensemble of outrageous behaviors that are not in and of themselves dangerous or directly violent. However, these kinds of corporate violations are indirectly responsible for the impoverishment of a growing number of Americans and thereby contribute to the risks of victimization and to other incidents of violence. These various forms of corporate theft are costly to the body politic, both symbolically and materially, whether one is discussing corporate tax evasion, the undue influence of lobbyists favoring the interests of corporations over those of ordinary citizens, the usurpation and corruption of the political process itself, or more specific economic violations such as unfair labor practices, restraints of trade, misrepresentations in advertising, or price-fixing. These patterns of behavior are also damaging to the physical and psychological well-being of the American people.

UNDERCLASS VIOLENCE

As argued throughout this book, those who are most victimized by violence in any nation-state are those marginal and powerless persons who are located where there is a convergence of interpersonal, institutional, and structural violence in society. Deprived of the basic opportunities and necessities of life, adults of the underclass are subject to illegal markets, such as those for drugs and sex, for the acquisition of some of their goods and services. Children of underclass families are more likely not to develop marketable occupational skills than are children who grow up in working-, middle-, and upper-class families. Both of these types of structural victimization place adults and children of the underclass at greater risk for other forms of violence than any other group in society. These overlapping forms of violence and the cross-fertilization of victimization contribute further to the economic dependency, psychological despair, and social isolation of the underclass.

In the scheme of things, the cycles of dependency, violence, and poverty have been reinforced by public apathy and policies of indifference that work hand in glove with the requirements of capitalist expansion, which take precedence over social capital or basic human needs and development. Among the most negatively affected institutions of underclass life are education and the nuclear family. Some have argued that because corporations and governments have created conditions of deprivation that lead indirectly to a group's destruction, the victims are subjects of genocide, not unlike those who have been directly exterminated (Staub, 1989). Without education and legitimate economic prospects, family life becomes a pretty dismal reality.

For example, three quarters of urban poor families residing in the ghettos and barrios across America are single-parent, female-headed households. In this regard, girls and women of the underclass experience more victimization than any other societal group. In the case of mothers, the victimization may come in the form of physical or sexual abuse from their lovers or ex-spouses; in the case of daughters, it may come from parents— present or absent—boyfriends, acquaintances, or strangers. What often becomes ordinary and normative for underclass females is, in other words, impoverishment, physical and

psychological beatings, jailed boyfriends and spouses, single motherhood, welfare dependency, and so on and so forth. In turn, these girls and women are more likely to become neglectful and abusive of others.

Underclass children living in the poverty and despair of urban or rural America sense the political impotence of their parents and communities. This is especially the case for homeless people, young or old, who find themselves the objects of all kinds of insults and injuries, physical and emotional (see Box 4.6). The underclasses also sense the larger society's indifference as the economic, social, and educational conditions around them continue to stagnate. Abused, neglected, and maltreated by their families, schools, and social service bureaucracies, these underclass children are more at risk for engaging in juvenile delinquency and young adult criminality. These children are similarly at greater risk for experiencing violence as both victims and victimizers. As discussed in Chapter 3, gang life and gang violence become viable alternatives for many boys and for a much smaller number of girls. Even if one's chances (sooner or later) of an early death on the street or of incarceration in a juvenile reformatory and/or adult prison will subject these gangbangers to a greater likelihood of various forms of penal violence, in their fatalistic worlds, such an option is preferable to "no option" at all.

Box 4.6   Hate Crimes Against the Homeless

As the most marginal members of the underclass, homeless persons are especially vulnerable to violent and hate street crimes. In the late 1990s, for example, because of what the National Coalition for the Homeless characterized as a dangerous trend across the United States of hate crimes committed against homeless adults, the group's Civil

(Continued)

Box 4.6 (Continued)

Rights Organizing Project began to document these hate crimes. The National Coalition for the Homeless found that acts of violence and hate perpetrated against the homeless had become daily affairs across the country. The "widespread nature of these increasingly violent acts [is] seemingly being perpetrated by younger adolescent members of society." These brutally violent acts, including homicides involving decapitation, skull crushing, multiple stabbing, drowning, use of flammable chemicals, and shooting, have been documented in such diverse places as Denver, Colorado; Jeffersonville, Indiana; Rapid City, South Dakota; Anchorage, Alaska; Seattle, Washington; Chicago, Illinois; and Los Angeles and San Francisco, California.

In a 6-week period, October to November 1999, there were seven violent killings in Denver. In North Seattle, three teenagers were charged in the killing of a sleeping 46-year-old man whom they allegedly stabbed 18 times. Prosecutors in the case said that they overheard one of the youths bragging about the killing, telling his friends: "Let's just say there's one less bum on the face of the earth." In one of the more gruesome hate crimes against the homeless, Henry Northington, 39, living on the streets of Richmond, Virginia, was found beheaded in a local cemetery. Police believed at the time of the murder that the killer or killers carried his head nearly a mile, carefully placing it on a footbridge as a message. Some people told police that they believed Northington was targeted because he was a homeless person; others thought it was because he was a gay man.

Source: Record numbers of hate crimes committed against men and women homeless in the U.S. (1999). *Safety Network: The Newsletter of the NCH: National Coalition for the Homeless*, 18(3), 1, 4.

Hate groups more generally are often the products of marginal and underclass existence combined with a negative politics of difference spawned by the civil rights movements of decades past, a "crisis of identity," especially in the context of the meaning and place of whiteness, and a profound sense of dislocation brought about by the inclusion of non-Whites, non-Christians, nonheterosexuals, and even nonmales into the multiculturalism of the United States. Hate violence, as Barbara Perry (1998) has argued, is supported culturally by ideologies of racism, homophobia, and sexism that "condition human action, identity and place in such a way as to maintain hierarchies of difference" (p. 33). These ideologies, as incorporated by such intolerant groups as the National Alliance, Christian Identity, and World Church of the Creator, are used to construct such dualistic categories as us versus them, good versus evil, strong versus weak, superior versus inferior. In turn, these dualisms provide the essential and legitimate foundation upon which these groups can marginalize and victimize the Other, all in the name of a White Racial Holy War. Of course, in other parts of the world, Muslim extremists belonging to such terrorist organizations as al Qaeda also talk about holy wars and eliminating the infidels of the West.

TERRORIST VIOLENCE

Terrorism is a complex and multifaceted phenomenon characterized by political passions and deep-seated emotionalism, resulting in varying points of view and disagreements about what constitutes "terrorism," "terrorists," or "terrorist violence."

In the same way, there are numerous definitions of terrorism and characterizations of terrorists. Many of the definitions of terrorism are one-sided, biased, or politically and legally restrictive, indicting some behaviors and ignoring others. As the old adage goes, "one man's terrorist is another man's freedom fighter." In other words, some forms of terrorism have been illegitimated and others have been legitimated. Terrorist violence of the first kind involves kidnapping, torturing, and killing; terrorist violence of the second kind involves freedom fighting, national liberation, and social justice. Hence, there has been a fair amount of disagreement about the accuracy and application of these terms, especially if one is looking for a definition that "works" universally over time.

A more generic definition of terrorism and terrorist violence would try to employ standards that showed no political favoritism, did justice to the social relations of inequality, and was inclusive of all forms of terrorism, "retail" and "wholesale," without regard to victims or perpetrators. One rather wordy definition was provided by George Rosie (1987) just before the end of the Cold War. It is obsolete in this day of suicidal terrorists and invisible "bioterrorists" who are not necessarily negotiating demands but who are, instead, attempting to create widespread panic and despair or engage in a totally new kind of terrorism as warfare; nevertheless, it meets the criteria of a generic definition of terrorism: Rosie defined terrorism as "the use and/or threat of repeated violence in support of or in opposition to some authority, where violence is employed to induce fear of similar attack in as many non-immediate victims as possible so that those so threatened accept and comply with the demands of the terrorists" (p. 7).

There are traditionally three basic types of terrorism or terrorists: religious, political,

and racial or ethnic. Each of these may express different and overlapping kinds of grievances, real or imagined. Terrorist motivations are too numerous to count. Generally, the motivations of most terrorists have been separated into "rational," "psychological," and "cultural" types. With rare exceptions, most terrorists believe their "cause," or the actions that flow from it, are not only justified, but that it is a necessary means for achieving some end that will better society.

In examining the various kinds of terrorism and terrorist violence, it helps to think about whether these acts are domestic or foreign-based and whether they are carried out by governments or by citizens—from "above" or from "below" (Simonsen & Spindlove, 2000). Historically, when terrorism is carried out from above (by the state) in some kind of systematic way, it has been labeled as "wholesale," or state, terrorism. This is the type of governmental abuse and terror perpetrated by traditional dictatorships, from Europe to Central and South America, that in the popular vernacular have often been referred to as a "reign of terror." By contrast, when terrorism is carried out from below (by groups of citizens or noncitizens) in quasiorganizational cells or sporadic outbursts, it has been labeled "retail" terrorism, or guerrilla warfare, and is often referred to as a "state of siege" (Falk, 1988; Herman, 1982; Marighella, 1990). Finally, making things even more complex is the social reality that terrorist tactics have been and are used during times of peace, conflict, and war.

Compared to countries in Europe, Asia, the Middle East, Africa, and Central and South America, the United States has been a nation relatively free of terrorist violence or terrorism. In other words, there have been a limited number of domestic-based terrorist attacks such as the one carried out by Timothy McVeigh in Oklahoma City in

1995, and of internationally based terrorist attacks like the ones carried out against the World Trade Center and the Pentagon in 2001. Most of the other lesser-known acts of terrorism have been relatively unsophisticated, involving local, right-wing militia or hate groups or special-interest extremists engaged in violence against abortion clinics or providers. While this book was in press, a "psychotic terrorist" and marksman of an entirely different constitutional makeup [e.g., nonpolitical] was on the loose in the greater Maryland-Washington, DC area. As of October 20, 2002, over a 19-day stretch, this individual had shot with a high-powered rifle 11 unknowing victims, killing 9 of them with a single bullet each.)

As a sponsor of state-organized or wholesale terrorism outside the United States, however, the Central Intelligence Agency has had a rather dubious history of supporting repressive dictators in countries such as Cuba, Iran, the Philippines, Brazil, South Korea, and Argentina and of overthrowing or destabilizing democratically elected governments in countries such as Guatemala, Chile, Jamaica, and Nicaragua (Bohenheimer & Gould, 1989). These international actions on the part of the CIA and the U.S. Department of Defense have had little to do with the rights of national sovereignty, freedom, and democracy and much to do with whether the involved nations were seen as contributing to or resisting "American interests." Nevertheless, in spite of the historical record, and because of the fact that the United States is the most prosperous and powerful country in the world, even before September 11th many scholars of terrorism had been arguing that America was in danger of becoming a prime target of international terrorism (Simonsen & Sprindlove, 2000).

Finally, if one leaves the realms of conventional terrorism, then historically one can point to the terrorist violence employed by a number of groups in American society during the 20th century. First, there were the actions of both capitalists and workers engaged in the struggle to organize labor. During Prohibition, in the late 1920s, there were organized gangsters who preyed on society and each other with deadly violence: "Mobsters gunning down those who opposed or interfered with their bootlegging traumatized all that witnessed such carnage" (Simonsen & Spindlove, 2000, p. 277). More recently, especially in the late 1980s, street gang activities involving drug trafficking and drive-by shootings were fairly commonplace. All of these examples of terrorist violence share in common a tactic for creating fear and danger. Terror strikes at the basic need for safety in anyone who hears about it or observes it. By applying this notion to describe terrorist violence, one can well imagine the terror experienced by those children and others who have had no choice but to consume, suppress, and remain silent about the abuse that they have observed and experienced.

INSTITUTIONAL-STRUCTURAL VIOLENCE

Institutional-structural violence refers to violence that is a product of political and economic arrangements working in tandem or symbiotically. The interests of the political economy are regarded as lying at the roots of institutional-structural violence. These forms of violence have the intended effect of maintaining or extending the structures of dominance as well as the privileges and inequalities that accompany such order. In other words, threats to the status quo or legal order, including violence or nonviolence, real and imagined, will be portrayed as dangerous. Without examining the causal relations of social violence, the war on youth and related efforts to control or suppress the alleged transgressions of young people are enforced by institutional-structural biases not to juxtapose the violence by youth with the violence against youth (see Box 4.7). In different words, the social constructions of what constitute dangerous or vulnerable youth and the actions to contain or to liberate them reflect the competing interests of governing elites and their representative "talking heads," on the one hand, and of activists-advocates and their clients, on the other hand. The contested policies of social intervention that have been created to "deal with" violence and nonviolence have also been identified as involving the institutional interactions of the developing "social-industrial" complexes.

Box 4.7   The War on Kids

By the mid-1990s, curfews for minors had been established in a number of cities throughout the United States. According to the dominant rhetoric at the time, youth was out of control, and the rates of some forms of juvenile violence were rising. Therefore, the prevailing logic reasoned that young people were in need of better social control, which meant increased surveillance by people and technology. To those politicians and advocate groups that were responsible for the passage of curfew laws, it mattered little, if at all, that there was no evidence that curfews had ever been instigators of parental responsibility or of curbing youth violence, and it made even less difference whether or not such laws represented an infringement on the lives of young people generally or on the lives of inner city youth in particular. As one social anthropologist, writing about the cultural politics of "youth in crisis," put it, the war against kids "combines the popular images of television as monster corrupter, the delinquent child, and the absent parent" and ignores the millions of youth in this country who experience actual rapes and beatings during their grammar school years by parents, peers, and others (Acland, 1995, pp. 135-136).

Alexander Cockburn (1996) tried to place the issue of youth violence in perspective when he emphasized that young people are victims first and perpetrators second:

> With films like *Kids* making the rounds, we're now back in William Golding country, with youth depicted as feral in essence. Yet Golding did at least concede in a commentary on his novel *Lord of the Flies* that " . . . adult life appears dignified and capable, but in reality is enmeshed in the same evil as the symbolic life of the children on the island."

> Even this statement elides the connection between adult and juvenile evil. Notoriously, murderers and other violent criminals are almost invariably abused as children. Violence is handed down in the form of blows, sexual predation, and punishment inflicted by adults on the young. The U.S. Advisory Board on Child Abuse and Neglect . . . reported in April 1995 that violence, mostly by parents and caretakers, kills 2,000 children and seriously injures 140,000 more per year. (p. 7)

Without trying to oversimplify, although there was an increase in teenage violence in some areas, on the whole the 1990s witnessed reductions in both youth and adult violence. Nevertheless, in mass media portrayals, the tendency was and is to extend the

(Continued)

Box 4.7 (Continued)

problem of "youth violence" too inclusively. In other words, all youth is presented as in danger of becoming out of control or contaminated by youth violence. It is as if there is a youthful plague of violence going around that all teenagers will be exposed to. In the context of a generalized fear of youth, there has been an overflexing of energy spent to survey and control the activities of youth.

In one sense, there is something familiar here, universal perhaps. Historically, the dangers of the "evils" of youth reach back to antiquity. In the United States, "wild" teenagers have been the subject of public scrutiny at least since the end of World War II and James Dean in *Rebel Without a Cause* in the 1950s. In another sense, as part of the more recent "criminalization of youth" (i.e., treating child offenders as adults) and the abandoning of the more empathic environs of the juvenile justice system, there is a recognition that with new forms of media, the youth of today are no longer "innocent" because they have the same access to adult and previously hidden subject matter as adults do, including sex and violence. So if they have the same knowledge and are committing the same acts as adults, why not treat them as adults?

Mass culture has, in effect, demonized youth. In the demonic state, youth are profiled by the ways they express themselves in dress and language. That is, they are identified by their presentation of themselves as being affiliated with various subcultures and, by implication, with crime and violence. For example, in the early 1990s, there were "links among [Oakland] Raider gear, black style, and black crime [that] immediately inspire[d] worry that as Raider gear proliferate[d], so, too, would the possibilities of youth crime" (Acland, 1995, p. 136). The hysteria about youth has included a preoccupation with violence, with "babies having babies," with teenagers contracting AIDS/HIV or some other sexually transmitted disease, and with youth as simply more reckless, more stupid, and more in need of tough controls than adults. Data on teen lifestyles belie these stereotypes. For example, the groups at risk for contracting STDs are not teenagers, but rather people in their 20s and 30s.

As adolescents are often social agents from beyond the ideological confines of the dominant or hierarchal structures of power, youth represents many states of being, including but not limited to crisis, spectacle, affectation, and the sublime. During the 1990s, catalyzed by the "wave" of school shootings, there was a consensual moment where youth were viewed in a collective state of crisis. In response, this crisis was met with despair, fear, and calls for more surveillance and discipline. With all the concern about youth in crisis, however, the real threats to youth at risk, such as the increasing levels of childhood poverty and the lack of proper day care, health care, or education, seem to all take a back seat to issues of controlling youthful violent behavior.

Perhaps what the war on kids, or the wars on drugs, pornography, terrorism, poverty, AIDS, and so on and so forth do best is to oversimplify the world into dualities of "good" and "bad" as they obscure the social realities of these complex phenomena. For example, in regard to violence, rap music, and the white-dominated mass media, bell hooks (1994), writing at the peak of the most recent "war on youth," had this to say: "[The] controversy over gangsta rap makes a great spectacle. Besides the exploitation of these issues to attract audiences, a central motivation for highlighting gangsta rap continues to be the sensationalist drama of demonizing black youth culture in general and the contributions of young black men in particular" (p. 26). She has argued further that the modern or contemporary remakes of *Birth of a Nation* encourage us all "to believe it is not just vulnerable white womanhood that risks destruction by black hands but everyone" (p. 26).

hooks wants to locate gangsta rap in the center, rather than at the margins, of what this country is fundamentally about. Ultimately, her point is that rather than being viewed as a reflection of the dominant culture, gangsta rap has been viewed as an aberrant pathology of the ghetto. In the process, young black males assume the role of the violent Other and are forced to accept blame for all the violence in society, deflecting attention away from the patriarchal sources of rape and violence against women. In other words, as part of the antifeminist backlash of the 1980s and early 1990s, gangsta rap had perhaps far less to do with young black males' manhood than it did with their "subjugation and humiliation by more powerful, less visible forces of patriarchal gangsterism" (hooks, 1994, p. 27).

hooks also wanted people to examine such questions as why huge audiences, especially young white consumers, were so turned on by the music, the misogyny and sexism, and the brutality. Where was the anger and rage at females expressed in the music coming from? Why the glorification of violence, death, and destruction? By avoiding these tough questions and those related to all the other forms of violence—interpersonal, institutional, and structural—and by turning its focus to the simpler task of attacking gangsta rap as the culprit and its musicians as the villains, the mass media facilitates the mass denial of the material culture having produced the need for such "trash" in the first place.

Sources: Acland, C. R. (1995). *Youth, murder, and spectacle: The cultural politics of "youth in crisis."* Boulder, CO: Westview.
Cockburn, A. (1996, June 3). The war on kids. *The Nation, 262,* 7-8.
hooks, b. (1994, February). Sexism and misogyny: Who takes the rap? *Z Magazine, 7,* 26-28.

Complexes, such as the police-industrial complex or the penal-industrial complex, are suggestive of the mutually reinforcing interests and needs of state and economic ruling orders (Mills, 1956). Historically, state violence has been directed at, for example, racial and ethnic minorities, worker movements, and politically dissident groups who have challenged or resisted the proverbial status quo. It has never been directed with the same zeal against racist, homophobic, violent antiabortionist, or other hate organizations. These individuals and groups do not represent a threat to the maintenance or extension of the structures of dominance, privilege, and inequality that the prevailing political and economic arrangements have created. In similar ways, some of the acts of police and penal violence perpetrated against the "dangerous classes" have also been a function of stratification and marginality. Of course, this "secret of violence" must remain in a state of denial, otherwise the entire order of the political economy of inequality could become a "house of cards," subject to renegotiation and reconstruction.

The same social forces are at work in the covert and overt interventions of dominant national and international powers into the affairs of other sovereign nations. With very few exceptions, throughout U.S. history, military interventions and the accompanying violence and terror "have been designed to maintain the imperialist relations (often defined in terms of preserving a free market and defending the right of private property) threatened by political movements within the dominated country" (Iadicola & Shupe, 1998, p. 337). This was certainly the case in several interventions by the United States into Central and South America during the 20th century. The primary victims of these encounters were the peasants and workers of those nations, not the landed gentry, bankers, and political dictators of those societies who tended to "cooperate" with their imperialist benefactors.

Similarly, regarding the economic-ecological violence that has become institutionalized within the United States, especially the corporate kind discussed above, those who are most victimized tend to be the most economically disadvantaged and racially marginal groups. Toxic waste and dumping sites, for example, pollute first and foremost the environmental living areas of the poor. When it comes to institutional and structural injuries in the various lines of production, the same rules apply. The most dominated or oppressed persons in society are also the most likely victims of economic fraud and product injuries.

Finally, the institutional-structural nature of family or domestic violence, in the past and the present, has been related both to material inequalities and to the hierarchies of power rooted in the social relationships of patriarchy. Patterns of victimization, in other words, occur with respect to class, age, and gender. As already discussed at length in the previous two chapters, young boys and girls and women of all ages are more likely than adult men to become victims of violence and abuse. Ethnic and racial discrimination

may further contribute to the pathways to victimization and to the cycle of victims becoming perpetrators of violence.

SUMMARY

This chapter has presented a demographic overview of five common forms of structural violence: postcolonial violence, corporate violence, underclass violence, terrorist violence, and institutional-structural violence. Traditionally, within scholarly and popular circles alike, the recognition of, attention to, and examination of structural violence has been almost nonexistent compared to the scrutiny of interpersonal and institutional violence. Because of this lack of attention, it may not seem as if the commissions and omissions of structural violence are inclusive of both interpersonal and institutional forms of violence—but so it is.

On the one hand, the fact of this relationship makes little sense if the goal of humanity is to prevent or reduce violence. On the other hand, it makes perfect sense because tackling the structural realities of violence necessitates tackling the political, economic, and social arrangements of hierarchy and inequality. Of course, denying that these structural relationships or the social policies driven by them have anything to do with violence is in the vested interests of those who benefit most from the status quo. Therefore, the less said about, for example, corporate violence, mass impoverishment, or the toxic environment, the "better off" the privileged sectors of this world remain. These paradoxical relationships in the pathways to violence and nonviolence are confronted in the later portions of the book, which specifically address not only the pathways to recovery from violence, but the pathways or models and policies of nonviolence.

Finally, the fundamental difference between interpersonal and institutional forms of violence and structural forms of violence is that the latter are normative or rational from the perspective of the dominant power arrangements. Common to the expressions of most forms of postcolonial violence, corporate violence, underclass violence, terrorist violence, and institutional-structural violence are the cultural denials of harm, injury, and victimization that accompany "business as usual." These commissions and omissions of violence, in other words, are the products of a complex development of social and psychic forces that have allowed masses of people the ability to deny, with only minimal, if any, feelings of shame and guilt, the humanity of whole groups of people that their actions or inactions victimize. In sum, these states of cultural and institutional denial of victimization contribute to the socialized lack of empathy for, and dehumanization of, the Other, each a prerequisite for the social reproduction of structural violence.

REFERENCES

Acland, C. R. (1995). *Youth, murder, and spectacle: The cultural politics of "youth in crisis."* Boulder, CO: Westview.

Barak, G. (Ed.). (1991). *Crimes by the capitalist state: An introduction to state criminality.* Albany, NY: State University of New York Press.

Bodenheimer, T., & Gould, R. (1989). *Rollback! Right-wing power in U.S. foreign policy.* Boston: South End.

Bradsher, K., & Wald, M. L. (2000, September 7). More indications hazards of tires were long known. *New York Times,* p. A1. Retrieved October 8, 2002, from http://www.nytimes.com

Brown, R. M. (1987). *Religion and violence* (2nd ed.). Philadelphia: Westminster.

Brownstein, R. (1981). The toxic tragedy. In R. Nader, R. Brownstein, & J. Richard (Eds.), *Who's poisoning America: Corporate polluters and their victims in the chemical age.* San Francisco: Sierra Club Books.

Cockburn, A. (1996, June 3). The war on kids. *The Nation, 262,* 7-8.

Cohen, S. (2001). *States of denial: Knowing about atrocities and suffering.* Cambridge, UK: Polity.

Coleman, J. (2000, August 25). Police raid Mitsubishi headquarters. *Ann Arbor News,* p. A9.

Cowley, G. (1990, June 11). Secondhand smoke: Some grim news. *Newsweek, 115,* 59.

Cullen, F., Maakestad. W. J., & Cavender, G. (1987). *Corporate crime under attack.* Cincinnati, OH: Anderson.

Dowd, D. (1993). *U.S. capitalist development since 1776.* Armong, NY: M. E. Sharpe.

Falk, R. (1988). *Revolutionaries and functionaries: The dual face of terrorism.* New York: E. P. Dutton.

Friedrichs, D. O. (1996). *Trusted criminals: White collar crime in contemporary society.* Belmont, CA: Wadsworth.

George, S. (1988). *A fate worse than debt.* New York: Grove.

Herman, E. S. (1982). *The real terror network: Terrorism in fact and propaganda.* Boston: South End.

hooks, b. (1994, February). Sexism and misogyny: Who takes the rap? *Z Magazine, 7,* 26-28.

Iadicola, P., & Shupe, A. (1998). *Violence, inequality, and human freedom.* Dix Hills, NY: General Hall.

Marighella, C. (1990). Mini-manual of the urban guerilla. In N. A. Weiner, M. A. Zahn, & R. J. Sagi (Eds.), *Violence: Patterns, causes, public policy.* New York: Harcourt Brace College.

Michalowski, R. J. (1985). *Order, law, and crime.* New York: Random House.

Mills, C. W. (1956). *The power elite.* New York: Oxford University Press.

Perry, B. (1998). Defenders of the faith: Hate groups and ideologies of power in the United States. *Patterns of Prejudice, 32(3),* 32-54.

Peyton, C. M. (2001, August 7). Judge reduced settlement against tobacco company. *Ann Arbor News,* p. A7.

Record numbers of hate crimes committed against men and women homeless in the U.S. (1999). *Safety Network: The Newsletter of the NCH:*

National Coalition for the Homeless, 18(3), 1, 4.

Regenstein, L. (1986). *How to survive in America the poisoned.* Washington, DC: Acropolis.

Reiman, J. (1990). *The rich get richer and the poor get prison.* New York: Macmillan.

Rosenblatt, R. (1994, March 20). How do tobacco executives live with themselves? *New York Times Magazine,* pp. 34, 76.

Rosie, G. (1987). *The directory of international terrorism.* New York: Paragon House.

Salmi, J. (1993). *Violence and democratic society.* London: Zed.

Service company must pay $11 million in ValuJet crash. (2000, August 15). *New York Times.* Retrieved October 11, 2002, from http://www.nytimes.com

Sharkey, J. (1990, May/June). Nicaragua: Anatomy of an election. *Common Cause Magazine,* 20-29.

Sherman, H. J. (1987). *Foundations of radical political economy.* Armonk, NY: M. E. Sharpe.

Simonsen, C. E., & Spindlove, J. R. (2000). *Terrorism today: The past, the players, the future.* Upper Saddle River, NJ: Prentice Hall.

Stannard, D. E. (1992, October 19). Genocide in the Americas: Columbus's legacy. *The Nation, 255,* 430-434.

Staub, E. (1989). *The roots of evil: The origins of genocide and other group violence.* New York: Cambridge University Press.

Swiggert, V. L., & Farrell, R. A. (1990). Corporate homicide: Definitional processes in the creation of deviance. In N. A. Weiner, M. A. Zahn, & R. J. Sagi (Eds.), *Violence: Patterns, causes, public policy.* New York: Harcourt Brace College.

Weiss, R. (2000). Introduction: Criminal justice and globalization at the new millennium. *Social Justice, 27*(2), 1-15.

Working for Change. (2001, August 2). *Help end child slave labor.* Retrieved October 9, 2002, from http://209.15.12.20/csny/action.htm.

REVIEW QUESTIONS

1. Discuss the ways in which structural forms of violence overlap with both interpersonal and institutional forms of violence.

2. Discuss the various forms that imperialist violence has taken over the past five centuries.

3. Discuss genocide as both an institutional and structural form of violence.

4. Discuss the similarities and differences between wholesale and retail terrorism. Provide examples of each.

5. What are some of the relationships between corporate violence and underclass violence?

NOTE

1. "G-8" refers to the "Group of Eight" major market democracies: Canada, France, Germany, Italy, Japan, Russia, the United Kingdom, and the United States of America. The European Union also participates in G-8 summits as a permanent nonhosting member.

Part II

PATHWAYS TO VIOLENCE

CHAPTER 5

Explanations of Violence

In Part II, "Pathways to Violence," the emphasis moves from types and descriptions of violence to analyses and critiques of violence. In a nutshell, each of the discussions that follows revolves around such questions as "why do we have the violence that we have?" and "why do people kill?" Each of these chapters specifically addresses various explanations of violence and of violent behavior that have been popularized in scientific and mass communications. This chapter, Chapter 5, provides a general overview of the most prominent scientific or academic theories of violence; the next two chapters explore theoretically relevant and nonrelevant ideas pertaining to violence in the mass media and sexually motivated violence.

It is my contention that the pathways to violence are more or less inversely related to the pathways to nonviolence. Stated differently, the pathways to violence and the pathways to nonviolence each exhibit supporting and reciprocal interactions that mutually reinforce the dialectical or contradictory trajectories of violence and nonviolence. Over the course of this explanatory chapter, I try to develop a satisfactory picture of the individual and collective pathways to violence by, first, presenting an overview and critique of the "ad hoc"

theories of violence; second, highlighting the valuable contributions of "life-course" analyses of the pathways to violence; third, introducing my own reciprocal theory of violence; and fourth, offering a narrative proof of reciprocal violence. In the remainder of the book, I try to develop a satisfactory picture of the individual and collective pathways to violence and nonviolence and reveal the inverse relationships between these two sets of pathways.

Nearly all explanations of violence begin as "ad hoc" explanations that try to account for the observed regularity of various forms of isolated and self-contained violent events in such singular entities as gender, class, or ethnicity as these are, in turn, related to differences in biology, psychology, sociology, culture, and mass communication. Most explanations of violence, unfortunately, remain partial and incomplete because they separately emphasize different yet related phenomena of violence without ever trying to provide for a comprehensive explanation that encompasses the full range of interpersonal, institutional, and structural violence. In fact, most of the ad hoc explanations of violence underscore the violence seen in behavioral expressions of persons, to the relative exclusion of institutional and structural expressions of violence.

	Origin of Cause	
	External	Internal
Nature of Cause		
Motivation		
	External/Motivation	Internal/Motivation

Figure 5.1 Typology of Interpersonal Explanations of Violence

These interpersonal explanations of violence can typically be classified into 1 of 4 kinds, based not only on the etiology of individual violence as either internal or external, but on the particular focus or orientation assumed about the relationship between human nature and violence. Traditionally, ad hoc explanations of violence are associated with theories that locate the origins of violence within the person or within the social environment. Concurrently, some ad hoc theories maintain that humans are naturally inclined to act violently, requiring little in the way of stimulation or motivation, and that violence is, ultimately, the product of a failure of constraint or control. Other ad hoc theories maintain that humans are naturally inclined to conform to the rules of custom and order (nonviolence), requiring much in the way of stimulation or motivation, and that violence is, ultimately, the product of unusual or "deviant" impulses. From this dualistic (either/or) perspective, violence is normative in the former case and aberrant in the latter case. Dialectically, however, it may very well be that various forms of violence and nonviolence are normative and aberrant at the same time.

By cross-classifying the external and internal motivations and constraints, a fourfold typology of interpersonal violence can be created (see Figures 5.1 through 5.3). These ad hoc explanations of violence break down into those theories that explain violence, on the one hand, (1) in terms of "properties" that are (a) external to individuals, and that stimulate them to act violently—*externally motivated*—or (b) inside people, and that stimulate them to act violently—*internally motivated*—and, on the other hand, (2) in terms of the failure or absence of (a) *internally* or (b) *externally* grounded *constraints* that inhibit or prohibit people from acting on their violent impulses, represented typically as self-control and social control.

There are at least six problems with most of these types of ad hoc explanations of interpersonal violence. First, they are overly deterministic and one-dimensional, focusing on a limited rather than a broadened number of specific empirical regularities of violence. Second, they overemphasize one of the four binary combinations (externally motivated, internally motivated, externally constrained, internally constrained) to the relative neglect of the other three. Third, they represent one-directional and linear formulations of violence that split "causation" into either/or categories of internally and externally motivated or constrained acts of violence. Fourth, they are generally static and stable models of violence, locating the etiology of violence or antisocial behavior mostly in the early years of life. Fifth, they ignore and lack any explanation for the interconnections between individual forms of violence, on the one hand, and institutional and structural forms of violence, on the other hand. Sixth, they fail to consider the factors or properties involved in the cessation of antisocial behavior and violence.

To varying degrees and with differing degrees of success, the problems associated with ad hoc interpersonal theories of prosocial and antisocial behavior are being tackled by the social and behavioral sciences with the emergence and development of both *integrative modeling* and *life-course perspectives*. These epistemological approaches, when applied to violence, assume a complexity of human interaction that cuts across both the behavioral motivations and cultural constraints existing inside or outside the person. When compared to the earlier and more traditional ad hoc explanations of violence, these integrative and life-course explanations of violence constitute models that conceptually are more dynamic, developmental, and multidimensional in both process and action.

Integrative explanations focus attention on the dynamic relationships between the internal and external influences of violence and nonviolence and the pushes (motivation) toward and pulls (constraints) away from violence or nonviolence. Life-course models of violence and nonviolence focus attention on the developmental trajectories of persons toward and away from specific courses of behavior. These models recognize the cumulative nature of violent and nonviolent behaviors, the reciprocal consequences of

abusive and nonabusive behavior, and the integral relationships between events, situations, and conditions in the course of one's life. In a similar and related way, the criticisms raised about ad hoc explanations of interpersonal violence can be reduced, or these theories can be improved upon, by incorporating models of interactive human behavior that are convergent, contingent, and integrative in their examinations.

Moreover, as alternatives to ad hoc interpersonal explanations of violence, there can be explanations of violence that are more heuristic and general because, in addition to the individual life histories, they include the social histories of institutional and structural patterns of violence. For example, the reciprocal model of violence introduced toward the end of this chapter emphasizes obvious links or connections between interpersonal, institutional, and structural pathways of violence or nonviolence. This reciprocal theory of violence and nonviolence is derived from an extension of the same logics upon which integrative, pathway, and multidimensional analyses of interpersonal violence are based. The *general explanation of reciprocal violence* does not reject ad hoc relationships between violence and such factors as variable "a," "b," or "c," or "a" and "c," or so on and so forth, per se, but it does prefer to incorporate these properties and others into the larger institutional and structural relationships that constitute the interactions between the spheres of and the pathways to violence.

AD HOC EXPLANATIONS: GENERAL AND FAMILY VIOLENCE

What these explanations of violence all have in common is the tendency to reduce violence to one primary variable or set of variables. These one-dimensional explanations

<u>Origin of Cause</u>

Nature of Cause	External	Internal
Motivation	*Sociobiological* *Social Learning* *Subcultural* *Patriarchal*	*Psychological*
Constraints	*Evolutionary* *Exchange* *Resource*	

Figure 5.2   Typology of Interpersonal Explanations of Violence: Single-Cell Explanations

of violence often acknowledge the importance of other variables, but rarely do they factor them into their examinations and analyses, preferring not to demonstrate so much that A causes B but rather that A and B often show up together. In reality, correlation rather than causation or prediction is generally the empirical test or outcome of choice for these explanations of violence. From my perspective, however, this may not necessarily be a bad thing. As one who views these ad hoc explanations of violence as less about causation and more about the identification of the properties of violence, I consider that so-called predictions about violence and nonviolence are simply vulnerable, in most instances, to too many contingent variables to be of any practical value.

For example, several explanatory frameworks have been advanced to make sense out of violence in general and out of family violence in particular. These include exchange theory, subcultural theory, resource theory, patriarchal theory, ecological theory, social learning theory, evolutionary theory, sociobiological theory, pathological conflict theory, psychopathological theory, general systems theory, and inequality theory. Out of these 12 theories, 8 of them address only 1 of the 4 cells from the typology of interpersonal explanations of violence (see Figure 5.2). Of the four remaining explanations of violence, pathological conflict theory takes into account both internally motivated and constrained variables; ecological theory takes into account both externally motivated and constrained variables; inequality theory takes

Origin of Cause

Nature of Cause	External	Internal
Motivation	*Inequality* *Ecological* *General Systems*	*Inequality* *Pathological Conflict* *General Systems*
Constraints	*Ecological* *General Systems*	*Pathological Conflict*

Figure 5.3   Typology of Interpersonal Explanations of Violence: Multi-Cell Explanations

into account both internally and externally motivated variables; and general systems theory takes into account both internally and externally motivated variables, as well as externally constrained variables (see Figure 5.3).

Externally motivated explanations of family violence are represented (not exclusively) by the disciplines of social psychology, social anthropology, and sociology. These explanations of violence, aggression, and vulnerability stress the importance of structural functionalism and the processes of socialization. As categorized above, these explanations of violence are most commonly expressed by sociobiological, social learning, subcultural, and patriarchal theories. For example, sociobiological theories are used to explain rape, child abuse, infanticide, and other forms of domestic violence (Alexander, 1974; Daly & Wilson, 1981; Lightcap, Kurland, & Burgess, 1982). These explanations of intimate violence are based on the inclusive fitness theory, which postulates that individuals will behave in ways that will increase the probability that their genes will be transmitted to future generations. There are, indeed, associations between cases of child abuse and paternal uncertainty and handicapped or stepchild status, as well as among poor families when allocations of limited resources require the hierarchical ranking of offspring.

By contrast, the social learning or sociocultural theories of violence, of which the subcultural and patriarchal theories are simply a variation, are less about nature than nurture. These explanations of aggression and violence address issues of gendercentric attitudes and maintain that these behaviors are learned and precipitated by a combination of contextual and situational factors (O'Leary, 1988). The social context of the "dysfunctional" family, for example, produces stress, aggressive personalities, and violent behavior. Situational factors such as alcohol or drug abuse, financial problems, or marital infidelity accommodate exercises in aggression and violence. Probably the most familiar of these social learning theories is the "intergenerational transmission of family violence" explanation, which contends that people who have witnessed or suffered physical family violence when growing up have a greater likelihood of living in a violent domestic situation later on in life. Also, associations have been found between the sexual abuse of children, especially boys, and the likelihood of those children becoming sexually abusing teenagers and adults (Groth, 1983; Kaufman & Zigler, 1987; Pagelow, 1981; Straus, Gelles, & Steinmetz, 1980).

The subcultural theories of violence, such as the "culture of violence" theory (Wolfgang & Ferracuti, 1967), argue that within large, complex, and pluralistic societies, subgroups learn and develop specialized norms and values through differential associations and organizations that emphasize and justify the use of physical force above and beyond that which is regarded as "normative" for the culture as a whole. Family and street violence, for example, are viewed as the products of an exaggerated ethos of masculinity or machismo characteristic of "lower-class" society. The various patriarchal theories have been advanced mostly, but not exclusively, by feminist social and behavioral scientists, who argue that violence is used by men to control women, to suppress the latter's rebellion and resistance to male domination, and to enforce the differential status of men and women that has traditionally been translated into laws and customs to serve the collective interests of men. These theories argue that, both in the past and present, but less so today, the unequal distribution of power between the sexes has resulted in societies that have been dominated by men and that most women occupy subordinate positions of power, increasing their vulnerability to violence, especially within the family (Dobash & Dobash, 1979; Martin, 1976).

Externally constrained explanations of family violence are represented (not exclusively) by anthropologists, sociologists, and economists (Berreman, 1978; Lenski & Lenski, 1970; Pryor, 1977). Evolutionary theories maintain that aggression and violence in, for example, technologically developed and highly stratified societies are used during childhood socialization as means of securing youngsters' obedience and conformity within both the family and the larger society. The argument assumes that

> In simpler and less technologically advanced societies, independence and self-reliance are encouraged in youngsters. This also means less adult supervision, more individual freedom, and therefore less demand for obedience and submission and fewer occasions for punishment. Instead, in complex, advanced, and hierarchical societies, compliance and obedience are the preferred traits. One has only to think of an industrial assembly line or of a large legal firm working on an important case to realize the pressure toward unquestioning acceptance of assignments and directions along rank lines. (Viano, 1992, p. 9)

The two other externally constrained explanations of family violence are of a negative kind. That is to say, exchange theory is essentially a cost-benefit analysis of violence. "People hit and abuse other family members because they can" (Gelles, 1983, p. 157).

Similarly, the resource theory argues that the family member with the most power or aggregate value of resources (e.g., money, property, prestige, strength) in society, traditionally the male, commands higher power in the marital and family relationships than other members, namely, women and children who are in subordinate and vulnerable positions (Blood & Wolfe, 1960). Like exchange theory, resource theory views violence in the nuclear family as a product of a lack of external constraints.

Internally motivated explanations of family violence are represented (not exclusively) by the fields of psychology, psychoanalysis, psychiatry, physiology, and biology. These explanations of family and domestic violence range widely in scope and may include explanations favoring internalized feelings of shame and humiliation leading to feelings of anger, hostility, and rage (Hale, 1994); Freudian systems of ego pathology and impaired object relationships in the development of sexuality, or concerns about dominance, submission, and control as unresolved conflicts originating during the anal period of development (Janssen, 1995); pathophysiological models such as "cognitive fracture," in which it is hypothesized that "hyperaroused orbitofrontal and medial prefrontal cortices tonically inhibit the amygdala and are no longer regulated by visceral and somatic homoeostatic controls ordinarily supplied by subcortical systems" (Fried, 1997, p. 1845); abnormal trace-metal concentrations, such as the presence of elevated serum copper and depressed plasma zinc in the blood of violence-prone individuals (Walsh, Isaacson, Rehman, & Hall, 1997); and general psychopathology models such as those involving the *Diagnostic and Statistical Manual* (4th ed.) label of "conduct disorder," in which repetitive acts of patterned aggression toward animals and people are significant to the diagnosis (American Psychological Association, 1994).

All of these explanations, despite their differences, share in common the attempt to account for personality dynamics and psychopathology that are unique to violent assailants. In other words, affected individuals, regardless of the particular origin of their violence, are suffering from some kind of physiological and/or psychological imbalance(s) expressed by combinations of obsessive ideation, compulsive repetition, poor impulse control, rapid desensitization to violence, diminished affective reactivity, failure to adapt to changing stimulus-reinforcement associations, hyperdependence, depression, anxiety, low self-esteem, paranoia, dissociation from their own feelings, antisocial tendencies, failure to empathize, fear of intimacy, and so on.

As already noted, all of these one-dimensional ad hoc explanations of violence are too narrowly focused, each excluding more variables of importance to violence than they include. With respect to some forms of violence, each of these explanations may be partially correct, plausible, and in some way or another empirically demonstrated (i.e., correlated); however, there remain many cases with respect to each explanation that do not square with their models. In sum, the dynamics of violence are far more complex in nature than any of the ad hoc explanations imply. It may, therefore, make more sense to talk about these ad hoc relationships (correlations) as properties of violence. As a prelude of things to come, violence should be viewed as a product of the relationship between the pathways created by the interactions of the four cells of interpersonal violence and a reciprocal set of cells operating at the institutional and structural levels of society.

Moving in a more inclusive direction, then, are the four other explanations of violence. Three of these consider two cells and one considers three cells from the typology of interpersonal violence. Each of these theories—pathological conflict, ecological, inequality, and general systems—is an improvement over the one-dimensional ad hoc theories of violence already discussed.

Pathological (social conflict) theories are represented (not exclusively) by social psychologists, cultural anthropologists, and sociologists. These models of "violence as pathological conflict," whether addressing marital disputes or large-scale conflicts, focus attention on communication processes and the tensions between, on the one hand, the internal constraints, or bonds and attachments, among individuals, especially families (but the larger communities, as well), and, on the other hand, the internal motivations of abandonment, shame, and alienation. Pathological or emotional conflict, in the forms of aggression and violence, occur, whether individual or collective, when unacknowledged humiliation, dissociation, or depression is transformed into reactive anger and rage (Gilligan, 1997; Retzinger, 1991).

Ecological theories are represented (not exclusively) by such disciplines as mental health, social work, ecology, sociology, and criminology. These explanations of aggression are sensitive to social milieus such as neighborhood context, social support networks, poverty, and value systems that may coalesce to break down the external constraints to violence while simultaneously legitimating the external motivations to violence. For example, child abuse has been associated with both the isolation of the nuclear family in contemporary advanced societies and the associated rationales for using violence against children (Garbarino, 1977).

Inequality theories are advanced by virtually all of the disciplines of the behavioral and social sciences. These explanations of aggression and violence are related to the differential ways in which inequalities, privileges, hierarchies, discriminations, and oppressions, on the one hand, externally motivate some people to abuse, exploit, and generally take advantage of those labeled as socially inferior and, on the other hand, internally motivate those persons subject to the labels of inferiority to resist and rebel violently against their inferior status. These explanations of violence are grounded in the political economies of private property and capitalist development (Iadicola & Shupe, 1998).

Finally, general systems theories are also advanced by several of the social and behavioral sciences. These explanations of aggression and violence focus on positive feedback loops involving the interactions of individuals, families, and societal spheres (Straus, 1978). These theories assume that optimal levels of violence are necessary to maintain and reproduce the system, and they take into account various sets of behavioral factors (with the exception of internally constrained mechanisms of violence), including high levels of conflict inherent in the family, the integration of violence into personality and behavioral scripts, cultural norms that legitimate violence, and the sexist organization of families and society (Viano, 1992).

LIFE-COURSE MODELS OF HUMAN BEHAVIOR: CAUSATION, TIME, AND VIOLENCE

It has been written that "life-course theories systematically examine the multitude of causal influences that shape offending behavior over time" (Piquero & Mazerolle, 2001, p. 87). As part of the development of a newly emerging and dynamic paradigm in the study of human behavior and social change, the life-course and integrative explanations bring together the interdisciplinary nature of the interaction between biography and history. At the same time, these reciprocal explanations of human interaction reject the ad hoc, one-dimensional, and overdetermined explanations of antisocial and violent behavior.

Life-course (developmental), as well as integrative, studies of human behavior and social structure have tried to address the ongoing interaction between individuals and their social environments over time. These overlapping and converging orientations to the interplay of human agency and historical conditions appreciate the diverse ways in which individual lives are linked and connected through social integration with, and unlinked and disconnected through social separation from, families, communities, nations, and the world. In contrast to the ad hoc theories discussed above, each of the developmental models or theories of human behavior and social interaction provides an explanation capable of taking into account the four dimensions of the interpersonal typology of violence (see Figure 5.2).

Robert Sampson and John Laub, who were among the first in the early 1990s to popularize the life-course perspective in the field of criminology, have consistently focused their developmental work "on continuities and discontinuities in deviant behavior over time and on the social influences of age-graded transitions and salient life events" (Sampson & Laub, 2001a, p. 21). Life-course studies of violence are similarly interested in both the persistence and the desistance of this kind of antisocial behavior, not to mention the possible transitions from violence to nonviolence. The life-course perspective argues that there is both stability of individual differences over time and changes in adolescence or adulthood that cannot be explained by early childhood development or by the pathways first traveled and experienced in life.

One of the first post–World War II sociologists to bring attention to the importance of life-course studies was C. Wright Mills (1959), in his methodological classic *The Sociological Imagination*, when he argued

persuasively not only about the connection between the "personal" and the "public," but for "the study of biography, of history, and of the problems of their intersection within social structure" (p. 149). Almost half a century earlier, the first wave of life-course studies was ushered in by Thomas and Znaniecki (1918-1920), who had focused their investigations on Old- and New-World Polish peasants in terms of (a) the processes of lives embedded in family contexts and in intergenerational relations of the life cycle and (b) the social psychology of macrochanges within people's everyday lives. Presently, life-course perspectives may be found throughout the social and behavioral sciences, including in such obvious disciplines as social history, developmental psychology, and gerontology.

Today, the earlier emphases on families have been augmented by studies on age and the life course. These types of conceptual examinations of human lives and social change have made the study of time, context, and process more salient to theory and analysis (Elder, 2001). Two central concepts currently lie beneath the analysis of life-course dynamics: *trajectories* and *transitions*. A trajectory is a pathway or a line of development over the life span. Trajectories might include, for example, the growth (or depletion) of self-esteem, depression, aggression, passivity, marriage, parenthood, or a career. Trajectories or pathways by definition refer to long-term patterns and sequences of behavior. By contrast, transition refers to a change of state or condition that is abrupt or involves a shorter time span. Transitions, such as a first marriage, a first child, or a first job, are specific life events that are viewed as embedded in trajectories or pathways of longer duration.

More specifically, the life course "can be viewed as a multilevel phenomenon, ranging from structured pathways through social institutions and organizations to the social trajectories of individuals and their developmental pathways," both subject to changing conditions and future options, as well as to short-term transitions that are usually chronologically grounded (Elder, 2001, p. 4). In the developmental scheme of things, life-course analyses assume that earlier trajectories and transitions have implications for subsequent experiences and events. In fact, theoretically informed panel studies have already begun to "document the mechanisms of reciprocal influence between social and developmental trajectories" (Elder, 2001, p. 5). At the same time, however, the majority of young antisocial children do not become adults who engage in antisocial behavior. Hence, the contradictory realities of continuity and change "are best seen as two aspects of a single dialectical process in which even major transformations of individuality emerge consequentially from the interaction of prior characteristics and circumstances" (Sampson & Laub, 2001a, p. 33).

Glen Elder (2001), one of the life-course pioneers from the field of family studies, has identified four themes which he believes are central to this still-emerging paradigm: the interplay of human lives and historical times, the timing of lives, linked or interdependent lives, and human agency in choice making. The inclusion of "interplay between lives and history" acknowledges the cohort effect in terms of when people were born into this world, what was going on at the time, and how cultural sentiments are acquired. "The timing of lives" refers to the incidence, duration, and sequence of roles that people adopt based on age-appropriate expectations and beliefs. "Interdependent or linked human lives" refers to life-spanning or existing social relationships, real and symbolic, that involve individuals, kin, and friends. Finally, within the constraints of people's worlds, human agency, will, choice, or whatever, refers to the importance of individuals socially constructing their own life courses in the

pathways that are created from the interactions with those people and events around them.

Like life-course studies of human behavior in general and of antisocial and violent behavior in particular, integrative studies have also covered a wide range of perspectives within and across academic disciplines. In the process, these multidimensional or multidisciplinary, and even interdisciplinary and transdisciplinary, analyses of, for example, crime and violence, have concurred about the inadequacy or limitations of those ad hoc explanations that divide human beings and society into biological, cultural, or psychological entities. Actual approaches to the integration or synthesizing of these dynamics of the human condition, however, have varied significantly by their epistemological orientations (Barak, 1998, 2002).

When it comes to explanations of crime and punishment, for example, "modernist" constructions of integrative theory have tended to emphasize models that focus on microsocial processes, macrosocial structures, or micro-macro cultural syntheses. These models of integration focus on linear and multiple causality, striving for some kind of cause-and-effect prediction of human behavior in the future (Box, 1983; Colvin, 2000; Quinney, 1977; Tittle, 1995; Wilson & Herrnstein, 1985). By contrast, the "postmodern" constructions of integration focus on interactive or reciprocal causality or on dialectical or codetermination causality (Arrigo, 1995; Barak & Henry, 1999; Laub & Sampson, 1993; Sampson & Laub, 1993). Recently, there have been efforts among the criminological postmodernists to reconcile the differences and similarities between modern empiricism and postmodern interpretivism (Henry & Milovanovic, 1996; Messerschmidt, 1997). As sociologist Richard Brown (1989) has explained: "The conflict that exists in our culture between the vocabularies of scientific discourse and of narrative discourse, between positivism and romanticism, objectivism and subjectivism, and between system and lifeworld can be synthesized through a poetics of truth that views social science and society as texts" (p. 1).

Taken together, the developmental and integrative perspectives on antisocial behavior, regardless of orientation, share in common a concern for the dynamic, interacting, and unfolding nature of biological, psychological, and social processes through time. In opposition to the time-invariant or static interpretations of the ad hoc explanations of violence, the life-course perspectives focus "on systematic change, especially how behaviors set in motion dynamic processes that alter future outcomes" (Sampson & Laub, 2001b, p. 147). Nevertheless, within this research there has been a tendency to attribute continuity to time-stable personality traits and social-psychological processes over structured mechanisms of social allocation or inequality, even though both are capable of producing differentiating tendencies in successive cohorts (Dannefer, 1987). Let us now turn to three articulations of the life-course perspective and to some of the related research findings on delinquent, criminal, and violent behavior.

Terrie Moffitt

Terrie Moffitt (2001), a psychologist, has offered a two-pronged theory of "adolescence-limited" and "life-course–persistent" antisocial behavior. Her contentions are that each of these types of antisocial offenders has unique natural histories and etiologies. She argues that

> For delinquents whose criminal activity is confined to the adolescent years, the causal factors may be proximal, specific to the period of adolescent development, and theory must account for the *dis*continuity in their lives. In contrast, for persons whose

adolescent delinquency is merely one infliction in a continuous lifelong antisocial course, a theory of antisocial behavior must locate its causal factors in early childhood and must explain the continuity in their troubled lives. (p. 92)

In the case of the adolescence-limited theory of antisocial behavior, "a contemporary maturity gap encourages teens to mimic antisocial behavior in ways that are normative and adjustive" (Moffitt, 2001, p. 91). In the case of the life-course–persistent theory of antisocial behavior, "children's neuropsychological problems interact cumulatively with their criminogenic environments across development, culminating in a pathological personality"(p. 91). Comparatively, the antisocial behavior of the teens is temporary, situational, and less extreme than the antisocial behavior of the adults who were children with neuropsychological and environmental problems, represented by a relatively small number of males whose behavioral problems are acute, stable, and persistent over the life course.

Research studies have shown that antisocial behavior is stable across time and circumstances for a small percentage of people, ranging from 3% to 9%. It is decidedly unstable for most but not necessarily all other birth cohorts, such as those regarded as being at moderate risk (Fergusson, Horwood, & Lloyd, 1991). Epidemiological research has also shown that there are virtually no persons diagnosed with adult antisocial personality disorder who did not have conduct disorder as children (Robins, 1966, 1978). Other research has found a progression from disobedient and aggressive behavior at age 3 to later childhood conduct disorder and, finally, to arrest in early teen years (White, Moffitt, Earls, Robins, & Silva, 1990), and a correlation between first arrest between the ages of 7 and 11 years and arrest in adulthood (Loeber, 1982). Moreover, research reveals that life-course–persistent antisocial persons lie at home, cheat at school, fight at bars, steal or embezzle at work, drive drunk, batter spouses, and abuse and neglect children (Farrington, 1991; Farrington & West, 1990; Loeber & Baicker-McKee, 1990; Sampson & Laub, 1990). Finally, research has also born out the relative distinctions between life-course–persistent and adolescent-limited wrongdoers and the career relationships of serious, violent, and chronic juvenile and adult offenders (Kempf-Leonard, Tracy, & Howell, 2001).

In sum, "continuity is the hallmark of the small group of life-course–persistent antisocial persons. Across the life course, these individuals exhibit changing manifestations of antisocial behavior: biting and hitting at age 4, shoplifting and truancy at 10, selling drugs and stealing cars at age 19, robbery and rape at age 22, and fraud and child abuse at age 30; the underlying disposition remains the same, but its expression changes form as new social opportunities arise at different points in development" (Moffitt, 2001, p. 100). At the core of Moffitt's explanation of life-course–persistent antisocial behavior is a theory that "emphasizes the constant process of reciprocal interaction between personal traits and environmental reactions to them" (p. 111). Although she does not mention it as such, what Moffitt describes becomes an interactive-reciprocal "self-fulfilling" socially constructed prophecy of antisocial behavior that may begin in vitro or even earlier.

Moffitt locates the roots of stable antisocial behavior in factors that are present before or soon after birth. She hypothesizes that "the etiological chain begins with some factor capable of producing individual differences in the neuropsychological functions of the infant nervous system" (Moffitt, 2001, p. 102). Whether such factors as disruption in the ontogenesis of the fetal brain due to physical injury, poor prenatal nutrition, maternal drug abuse during pregnancy, or pre- or postnatal exposure to toxic agents are the proximate elements associated with elevated rates among violent offenders and subjects with antisocial personality traits (Fogel, Mednick, & Michelson, 1985; Kandel, Brennan, & Mednick, 1989; Paulhus & Martin, 1986), or whether neuropsychological development is disrupted later by neonatal deprivation of nutrition, stimulation, and even affection (Cravioto & Arrieta, 1983; Kraemer, 1988; Meany, Aitken, van Berkel, Bhatnagur, & Sapolsky, 1988), or later yet by more deliberate child abuse and neglect associated with brain injuries (Lewis, Shanok, Picus, & Glaser, 1979; Milner & McCanne, 1991; Tarter, Hegedus, Winsten, & Aterman, 1984), Moffitt (2001) argues that there is good evidence to believe that "children who ultimately become persistently antisocial do suffer from deficits in neuropsychological abilities" (p. 102).

When Moffitt discusses neuropsychological variation and the "difficult" infant, she is talking broadly about the extent to which anatomical structures and psychological processes within the nervous system influence psychological characteristics such as temperament, behavioral development, cognitive abilities, or all three. At one end of the continuum of children with neurological difficulties would be those with severe autism, physical handicaps, or mental retardation: those with a clinical problem recognized by professionals and many parents. On the other end of the continuum are those infants with mild impairments, who have subclinical levels of problems or compromised neuropsychological functions that may include clumsiness and awkwardness, overactivity, inattentiveness, irritability, impulsiveness, and late development. These latter children, those with cognitive and temperamental disadvantages, as Moffitt refers to them, are not generally born into supportive environments, nor do they get a fair chance of being randomly assigned to good or bad environments. "Vulnerable infants are disproportionately found in environments that will not ameliorate because many sources of neural maldevelopment co-occur with family disadvantage or deviance" (Moffitt, 2001, p. 105).

Moffitt goes on to cite research demonstrating the intergenerational transmission of severe antisocial behavior, especially that involving aggression; the resemblance between parents and children in temperament and personality as well as in cognitive ability; and the stacking of the social and structural aspects of the environment against those children who enter the world at risk. She refers to this negative covariation in the nature of the child-environment relationship as providing a source of interactional continuity. She then turns her attention to the reciprocal relationships between the emergence of antisocial behaviors and what she refers to as the problem of parent-child interactions:

> I believe that the juxtaposition of a vulnerable and difficult infant with an adverse rearing context initiates risk for the life-course–persistent pattern of antisocial behavior. The ensuing process is a transactional one in which the challenge of coping with a difficult child evokes a chain of failed parent-child encounters. (Moffitt, 2001, p. 106)

✱Moffitt identifies three person-environment interactions that she believes are important in promoting an antisocial style and maintaining its continuity across the life course. These interactions are *evocative, reactive,* and *proactive.* Of the three types of interactions, Moffitt suggests that evocative interaction is perhaps the most influential. Evocative interaction is defined as that which occurs when a child's behavior evokes distinct responses from others. The point here is that children with neuropsychological problems create challenges for even

the most resourceful, loving, and patient families (Tinsley & Parke, 1983). Similarly, numerous studies have shown that the problem behaviors of toddlers, for example, affect parents' disciplinary strategies as well as subsequent interactions with adults and peers (Bell & Chapman, 1986; Chess & Thomas, 1987). The other two types of interaction are triggered by early behavioral difficulties and are maintained through the development of persistent and repetitive antisocial behavior, a function over time of the evoked responses exacerbating the child's tendencies. In other words, "the child acts; the environment reacts; and the child reacts back in mutually interlocking evocative interaction" (Caspi, Elder, & Bem, 1987, p. 308).

Moffitt continues that once the evocative interactions are set in motion, reactive and proactive interactions promote the further extension or continuity and pervasiveness of antisocial behavior throughout the life course, as long as the same underlying constellation of traits that got a person into trouble as a child remain intact. In other words, reactive interactions over time become conditioned defensive responses. In new or ambiguous interpersonal situations, for example, hyperactive or aggressive children are more likely (than nonaggressive children) to attribute harmful intent to others and to act accordingly (Dodge & Frame, 1982). Proactive interactions refer to the fact that antisocial individuals appear to selectively affiliate with others of similar personality configurations, such as that affiliation seen in the nonrandom mating patterns of spouses who have both been convicted of crimes (Baker, Mack, Moffitt, & Mednick, 1989; Buss, 1984). Finally, Moffitt's theory of life-course–persistent antisocial behavior argues that these early causal sequences are dominated by chains of cumulative and contemporary continuity that restrict a person's behavioral repertoire.

Life-course–persistent persons miss out on opportunities to acquire and practice prosocial alternatives at each stage of development. Children with poor self-control and aggressive behavior are often rejected by peers and adults. In turn, children who have learned to expect rejection are likely in later settings to withdraw or strike out preemptively, precluding opportunities to affiliate with prosocial peers. Such children are robbed of chances to practice conventional social skills. (Moffitt, 2001, p. 109)

Robert Sampson and John Laub

Criminologists Sampson and Laub (2001b) have provided a theory of "informal social control and cumulative disadvantage" that I believe nicely complements Moffitt's two-pronged theory of antisocial behavior. Their explanation of antisocial behavior argues that there are important events and conditions that alter and redirect deviant pathways. Their theory is built upon three related themes or arguments. First, structural factors or conditions such as poverty or racism affect the development of social bonds. Second, a combination of social conditions and labeling processes can lead to cumulative disadvantage and the stability of antisocial behavior across the life span. Third, the development of social capital later in life, especially during adulthood, can alter antisocial trajectories toward conformity. What holds this theory of cumulative disadvantage together is "a dynamic conceptualization of social control over the life course, integrated with" what they argue is "the one theoretical perspective in criminology that is inherently developmental in nature—labeling theory" (Sampson & Laub, 2001b, p. 147).

It is certainly true that the labeling perspective is developmental in nature because of its emphasis on processes such as "primary" and "secondary" deviance, but to say that there are no other theories in criminology that are developmental is to reflect narrowly on that field. Such a theory focuses only on the sociological contributions to crime and deviance, ignoring the biological, psychological, and evolutionary contributions, which can be found in models that are more often than not developmental in their structural approaches. Nevertheless, I believe that Sampson and Laub are correct to emphasize the interactive nature of labeling, identity formation, exclusion from normal routines and conventional opportunities, and the increased contact with and relative support from other deviant or antisocial subgroups, as converging to create a cumulative disadvantage.

Specifically, these researchers argue that "the cumulative continuity of disadvantage is thus not only a result of stable individual differences in criminal propensity, but a dynamic process whereby childhood antisocial behavior and adolescent delinquency foster adult crime through the severance of adult social bonds" (Sampson & Laub, 2001b, p. 155). In the process, they link the pathways of cumulative disadvantage and the constraints of subsequent development to four key institutions of social control—family, school, peers, and state sanctions—and to the causal sequential link in a chain of adversity between early childhood delinquency and adult criminal behavior. Following the lead of Gerald Patterson and his colleagues (Patterson, 1993; Patterson, DeBaryshe, & Ramsey, 1989; Patterson & Yoerger, 1993), Sampson and Laub talk in terms of a "cascade" of secondary problems (e.g., school failure, peer rejection, depressed mood, and involvement with deviant peers) and of antisocial traits as a "chimera" of socially constructed and interactive aspects of racial, socioeconomic, and structural locations.

The Social Development Model

The social development model (SDM) of the etiology of conforming and nonconforming behavior hypothesizes parallel developmental processes leading to prosocial and antisocial behavioral outcomes. This model is holistic to the extent that it recognizes that biological, psychological, and cultural factors, operating at multiple levels and in different social domains, contribute to the development of institutionalized problems such as delinquency, alcohol abuse, or violence. The SDM is also holistic in the sense that it not only accounts for the risk factors associated with antisocial behaviors but incorporates "protective factors" believed to mediate or moderate the effects of risk exposure. In a similar vein, the SDM is consonant with Goldstein's (1986) relational theory of aggression (see Chapter 7).

More specifically, the SDM specifies mechanisms by which identified risk and protective factors interact in the etiology of behavior. As shown in Figure 5.4, two general pathways are indicated in this life-course model that depict adolescent interactions as predicated on earlier and later development periods. One set of paths delineates the processes that encourage prosocial behavior; the other set delineates those processes that encourage antisocial behavior. Although the model "suggests how involvements and interactions lead to bonds hypothesized to have an inhibitory or promotional effect on antisocial behavior" (Huang, Kosterman, Catalano, Hawkins, & Abbott, 2001, p. 78), both sets of pathways are characterized generally by similar causal processes explaining how, for example, many young people experience or engage in prosocial and antisocial behavior at the same time. In other words, "through separate paths whose processes of reinforcement, learning, and bonding are independent but influence one another over time, the social development model allows for this variation in experience" (Huang et al., 2001, p. 78). It is also worth noting in Figure 5.4 that although there are four pathways conducive to antisocial behavior, three

during and one before adolescence, there are only three inhibitory pathways to prosocial behavior, one occurring before and two during adolescence. As in most other developmental models of antisocial behavior, the key seems to be whether one has experienced prosocial or antisocial behavior during early childhood development.

Potentially, the SDM represents the most inclusive of the life-course, developmental, and integrative pathway models of antisocial behavior. So far, however, the theory has been overly solicitous of or dependent on propositions stemming from control theory, social learning theory, and differential association. That is to say, the SDM has been tested in terms of the processes of socialization, for example, and found to adequately predict violence at age 18 based on measured constructs for ages 10, 13, 14, and 16 (Huang et al., 2001). Conceptually, however, it should be understood that the SDM does take into account other factors, internal (e.g., temperament, hyperactivity, cognitive abilities) and external (e.g., ethnicity, gender, class, neighborhood, social policies), that are hypothesized to influence the socialization process itself (Catalano & Hawkins, 1996).

Silver (2000), for example, examined the structural correlates of "neighborhood social disorganization" in relationship to the variation of violence committed by psychiatric patients who had been treated and discharged from an acute inpatient facility. He found that living in socially disorganized neighborhoods increased the likelihood of violent behavior among the people in his samples, as there was a lack of comparative social support in these areas, which might have mediated such violence. Similarly, Savolainen (2000) tested "institutional anomie theory" as articulated in Messner and Rosenfeld's book *Crime and the American Dream* (1997). Institutional anomie theory argues essentially that crime, violence, and antisocial behavior are

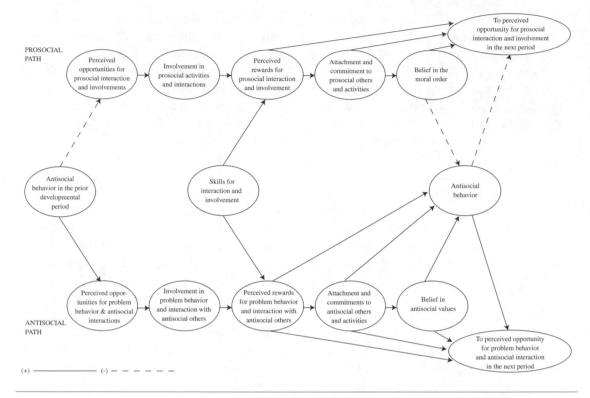

Figure 5.4   The Social Development Model of Prosocial and Antisocial Behavior

Source: Huang et al. (2001). Modeling mediation in the etiology of violent behavior in adolescence: A test of the social development model. *Criminology, 39*, 75-108. ©2001. Reprinted with permission.

dependent in the aggregate on an imbalance between the elements, properties, and sentiments of culture, on the one hand, and the structural relations of various institutional contexts, including the family, education, and politics, on the other hand. Moreover, the theory contends that

> An institutional balance of power in which the economy dominates other institutions is assumed to be the most conducive to high rates of serious crime because such an arrangement is the least capable of restraining criminal motivations stimulated by the logic of egalitarian market capitalism. At the level of culture, institutional imbalance of this description generates value orientations that emphasize efficiency norms at the expense of moral considerations; the "mood" of the society becomes more predatory. At the level of social structure,

> weak noneconomic institutions are less capable of providing stakes in conformity in the forms of meaningful social roles. (Savolainen, 2000, p. 1022)

In the spirit of these interacting spheres of violence and public policy, Savolainen examined the relationships between inequality, welfare development, and homicide. In short, he tested the moderating effect of the institutional context. Cross-nationally, he found that "nations that protect their citizens from the vicissitudes of market forces appear to be immune to homicidal effects of economic inequality" (Savolainen, 2000, p. 1021). Specifically, it was shown that in those societies characterized by a developed welfare state, or with strong institutions of social protection, economic inequality was a less salient factor in relation to national homicide rates than in those nations with an under-developed welfare state or weaker institutions of social protection.

ON THE RECIPROCITY OF VIOLENT AND NONVIOLENT PATHWAYS

No theory of violence or nonviolence will ever evolve that is capable of predicting future violence or nonviolence based on some kind of formulaic expression that if A, B, C, and so forth, then X, Y, Z, and so on. This is so in part because the possible sources and origins of violence and nonviolence at the interpersonal, institutional, and structural levels are so numerous and subject to change over time. It is also so in part because most explanations of the etiology of violence and nonviolence—ad hoc, integrative, or developmental—emphasize the interpersonal spheres to the virtual exclusion of the institutional and structural spheres. Nevertheless, comparative analyses of human development and individual-social interactions reveal common pathways that are conducive to both violence and nonviolence. By not incorporating these interpersonal experiences with the two other sets of violent and nonviolent spheres, these nonreciprocal analyses fail to track the intersecting pathways between the individual, the institutional, and the structural. In turn, these types of analyses not only miss the mutually reinforcing interactions between the three spheres; they overlook any cumulative effects that the interrelated spheres might have on violence or nonviolence.

A Violence and Nonviolence Continuum

Sooner or later, most students of violence come to the conclusion that whether the object of examination is emotional, physical, and/or psychological, there are connecting and overlapping patterns that involve the repetitious or habitual acts of perpetrators, victims, and agents of social control. Although the same kind of conclusion could be reached or drawn about the connecting and overlapping patterns engaged in by those involved in nonviolence, relatively few have bothered to systematically study these relations. That is to say, most social and behavioral scientists are asking questions about the how and why of violence, not the how and why of nonviolence. In the context of the latter set of questions, the reader might jump ahead and consult Part III of this book, especially Chapter 9. In the context of the former set of questions, let's consider acts of sexual coercion, for example, as representative of the sameness and difference involved in many acts of violence.

Sexual coercion can take a variety of forms and expressions. Among the most common are heterosexual rape, child molestation, and gender harassment. Although at first these acts may seem very different, upon further reflection, they may each correspond to the same kind of related and underlying tension or dynamic. In each of these types of sexual coercion, the perpetrators share a common need to compensate for a lack of an adequately secure sexual identity. Varying only by degree, heterosexual rapists, child molesters, and gender harassers, whether diagnosed as "normal" or "pathological" actors, are persons who consciously and unconsciously use their situations or relative positions of power to control, force, trick, or pressure relatively weaker persons through fear, intimidation, and what often amounts to a sexual terror of other human beings so that they may feel some kind of temporary relief or release from their sexuality anxiety.

Acts of sexual misuse or abuse are primarily committed by men against women and children, and secondarily by women against children. Those who perpetrate these kinds of sexual activities were often victims of child abuse themselves. As children, their acquired abilities to trust, empathize, and identify with others were undeveloped as a consequence of their abuse or neglect. As adults, if alienation from both self and others continues, this is enough to "help" violators disassociate from their victims or suppress any ability they might have to mutually identify with others. With respect to the weakening institutions of patriarchy and the legacy of a "double standard" of sexuality, however, coercive activities by men may still be associated with the abuse of prostitutes and a misogynist culture more generally. After all, sexual harassment sometimes includes rape, as does child sexual abuse, and prostitution often involves rape and sexual harassment (Grauerholz & Koralewski, 1991).

In terms of the overlap between "normative" and "deviant" sexual interactions, there are also the issues of power, aggression, and control (see Chapter 7). Issues of dominance and submission reside inside and outside of the bedroom. That is to say, in everyday life, issues of sadomasochism permeate the full spectrum of human behavior. Yet these behaviors need not ever express themselves in violent form—physical, sexual, or otherwise. There are plenty of solid, peace-loving, and nonviolent citizens who have mentally tortured their spouses, children, and elderly parents for years and years but have never so much as raised a finger to physically assault anyone. In sum, noncoercive and coercive sexual activities "occur along a continuum that stretches from intense fantasies and private, noncriminal sexual acts between consenting partners, to the more publicly deplorable behaviors of rape and the baroque and bizarre sexual fantasies that lead to ritualized, serial, sexually sadistic murders" (Simon, 1996, p. 9). These cases are indicative of some of the contradictions that cut across the continua of violence and nonviolence.

In similar fashion, there is no single variable or set of variables that can account for the full range of other forms of violence, such as homicide, terrorism, penal abuse, economic slavery, and so on. In short, because all of the factors that contribute to violence reside in such diverse realms as biology, psychology, or culture, their complex, multidimensional, and interactive pathways need to be sorted out. In other words, whether the manifestations of sexual violence in particular or of violence in general are reflected or not in various internal and external factors, there are pathways or developmental themes that can be identified and used to reveal overlapping etiologies among the varieties of violence.

Despite the diversity of violent and nonviolent expressions found throughout neighborhoods, classrooms, families, workplaces, country clubs, or in a variety of other settings and groupings, there are established pathways to violence and nonviolence that cut across the interpersonal, institutional, and structural spheres of social and cultural organization. Therefore, it makes sense to view violence or abuse, and nonviolence or nonabuse, as happening along a kind of two-sided continuum where the actions of individuals, organizations, or nation-states are capable of stimulating, accommodating, or resisting various pathways to both violence and nonviolence (see Figure 5.5). The terms "mild," "moderate," and "extreme" refer to such indicators as the prevalence, severity, intensity, directness, or duration of such activities, suggesting that there is a relativity of violent and nonviolent behaviors or of violent and nonviolent conditions.

In terms of time and place, I am also referring to the spatial webs of violence and nonviolence expressed at the familial, subcultural, and cultural levels of social, political, and economic organization (see Figure 5.6). All combined, there are nine possible

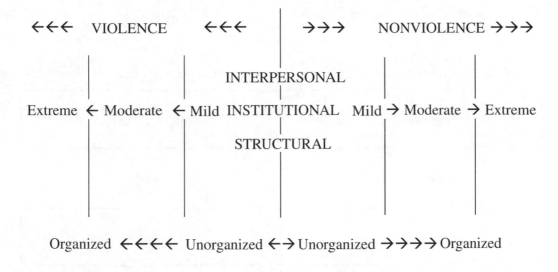

Figure 5.5   A Two-Sided Continuum of Pathways to Violence and Nonviolence

pathways to violence and nine possible pathways to nonviolence. In the structural spheres of violence and nonviolence alone, for example, there are the same informational, financial, and media networks that form an underside of global capitalism, global terrorism, and global peacemaking. Whether operating for prosocial, antisocial, or no particular social purposes, these expanding global infrastructures have created virtual realities in which once-secure societies now find themselves becoming "permeable webs that both allow and require new communication systems, circulation patterns and organizational structures" (Taylor, 2001, p. B14).

As societies and people adapt, as we move from industrial organization to network organization, and as the new technologies interact with the "global village" of cultures, it is as if we are moving from a world of modules to a world of nodules. In the "old" world, things are "modular": separate, distinct, and linear. They are also hierarchically ordered and sequentially arranged. In the "new" world, things are "nodular": relational, connected, and nonlinear. They are

also not only nonhierarchically organized, but connected to and formed by intersection with many other nodules, which may or may not be hierarchically or egalitarian oriented. In the spheres of both violence and nonviolence, these nodules consist of constellations of properties and pathways to violence and nonviolence (see Figure 5.7).

Accordingly, each of the spheres of violence and nonviolence may be thought of as more or less organized, ranging from strongly organized to disorganized. These distinctions do correspond to the two-sided continuum's arbitrarily labeled categories of extreme, moderate, and mild, but by definition, interpersonal violence is the least organized and structural violence is the most organized, with institutional violence falling somewhere in between. Moreover, human history continues to teach that the extreme acts of violence, including mass killings, wars, and genocides, are typically the most organized. As for interpersonal, institutional, and structural actions of nonviolence, comparatively speaking, these seem to be historically underorganized.

Violence	Nonviolence
←Cultural→Subcultural←Familiar→	←Familiar→Subcultural←Cultural→
Interpersonal	Interpersonal
Institutional	Institutional
Structural	Structural

Figure 5.6   Pathways to Violence and Nonviolence

In describing the Nazi atrocities, Hannah Arendt (1963) used the term *banality of evil* to refer, at least in part, to the infrastructure that facilitated the genocidal execution. She referred not only to the sadistic functionaries who tortured their victims, but to the administrators and all of the bureaucrats that performed the day-to-day tasks necessary to keep the killing machine running on schedule. On a continuum of violence ranging from, for example, executioners at one end, to bureaucrats somewhere in the middle, to public citizens at the other end, the "property of violence" that the average Nazi and the average German shared in common were varying states of denial and disassociation. Minds and behaviors were "split" or compartmentalized as feelings of empathy for the Other were buried within warm and fuzzy feelings of love and affection for one's family and tribe.

The expressions of mild, moderate, and extreme violence or nonviolence may also be thought of as interdependent spheres of violence or nonviolence. For illustrative purposes, think about lethal abuse in relation to each of the three spheres of violence. Despite the unique differences between the spheres, there are overlapping or mutually reinforcing pathways across each.

Interpersonal killing, for example, even though committed by an isolated individual, may range in nature from a highly unorganized, warm-blooded act of passion, such as the unplanned second-degree murders of an adulterous spouse and her lover caught in the married couple's bed, to the highly organized and cold-blooded serial murders of a number of strangers. Somewhere between these "mild" and "extreme" expressions of deadly violence would fall the "moderate" case of a battering husband who ends up one evening beating his wife to death. There may also be some etiological overlap in the pathways between these forms of interpersonal killings; however, there are enough pathways of difference between them to call for a range of societal responses.

Similar distinctions can be made within the lethal ranges of institutional and structural killings. Institutional violence involving the killing of gang members by other gang members may be characterized as "mild"

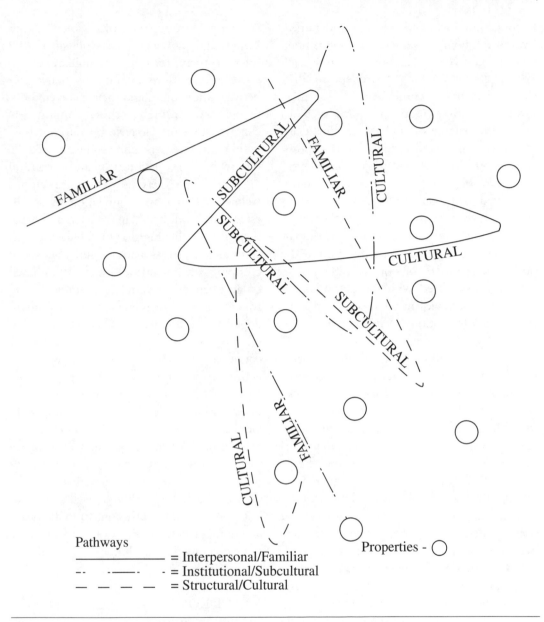

Figure 5.7   Constellation of Pathways and Properties to Violence and Nonviolence

when two warring or rival groups in combat indiscriminately kill one of their enemies, "moderate" when a drive-by shooting kills a member of an opposing organization in retaliation, and "extreme" when a contract for assasination put out by one group ends in the death of a particular individual. Structural violence connecting the toxic killings of workers, consumers, and the public at large

may also be thought of as culturally mild, moderate, or extreme when such labels as "accidental," "negligent," or "deliberate" are applied to the deaths involved.

Properties of Violence

Properties of violence refers to the essential attributes, characteristics, elements, factors, situations, and conditions identified by the ad hoc, life-course, developmental, and integrative explanations of antisocial and violent behavior. More specifically, those properties conducive to violence include negative emotional states such as alienation, shame, humiliation, mortification, rejection, abandonment, denial, depression, anger, hostility, and projection, as well as a lack of the positive emotional states associated with such properties of nonviolence as love, security, attachment, bonding, identification, altruism, compassion, empathy, mutualism, and reciprocity. As already noted, the properties of violence and nonviolence are associated with the pathways to violence and nonviolence that consist of constellations of emotional states conducive to violence and nonviolence.

Developmentally, the build-up of negative emotions acts as a catalyst or motivator for injury, abuse, and violence, and the lack of an accumulation of positive emotions fails to inhibit, control, or constrain antisocial and violent inclinations. Notice that the properties of violence and nonviolence have not been identified per se in Figure 5.7. Instead, there are blank circles that represent or symbolize the positive and negative emotional states or properties of violence and nonviolence suggested above. However, these psychological labels are not exhaustive; there are other labels that could be used to describe the same or similar phenomena. For example, in place of denial, one could talk in terms of disassociation or compartmentalization. At the same time, there are those inverse cognitive pictures or mirror images of violence and nonviolence that people can acquire, such as detachment/attachment or disassociation/association. In sum, there is no shortage of (mostly) psychological concepts with which to describe the whole range of emotional states that is inextricably caught up in both violent and nonviolent behavior.

These properties of violence, or "emotional pathogens," as Gilligan (1997) refers to them, form in the familiar, subcultural, and cultural interactions that occur between individuals and their social environments. Accordingly, these emotionally charged states of violence operate not only within the interpersonal psyches of people, but within the institutional and structural "psyches" of society as well. For example, feelings of shame and humiliation, or of self-esteem and well-being, may be felt and experienced by individuals or by families, gangs, communities, tribes, nations, and other social groupings or subcultural stratifications based on age, gender, class, religion, ethnicity, and so on. In other words, persons may feel abandoned by or bonded with parents, families, schools, churches, communities, media, or countries; likewise, small groups of people or entire nation-states may feel estranged from or attached to other groups of people or other nation-states. To the extent that individuals and groups feel and experience connection or disconnection, they will be prone to relate or not relate, to identify or not identify, to empathize or not empathize, to take or not take responsibility, as well as to project hostility and aggression, to make peace and nonviolence, to be anxious and angry, or to be contented and calm.

A RECIPROCAL THEORY OF VIOLENCE

With respect to the two-sided continuum of violence and nonviolence, the pathways and their trajectories and transitions may be both linear and nonlinear in evolution, or they may zigzag. At times these pathways are moving in parallel fashion, at times they may be in opposition, and at times they approach perpendicularity. On the interpersonal level, these dialectical situations are understandable because from birth people are exposed to interactions and conditions that reflect varying opportunities and risks for the development of both prosocial and antisocial behavior. Similarly, on the institutional and structural levels involving policy making and implementation, dialectical relations may prevail: There are starts and stops, zigzagging, forward and backward movement, privatizing and publicizing, and regulating and deregulating.

Not only are the pathways to violence and nonviolence dialectical in nature, so too are the properties of violence. In other words, any person is capable, more or less, of acquiring the properties for and developing the pathways to both violence and nonviolence. The same may be stated about groups, organizations, nation-states, and the larger global order. In the relative scheme of cross-cultural and multinational relations, most individuals, institutions, and structures have been less likely to have engaged in the extremes of the two-sided continuum of violence and nonviolence than in the milder forms of each.

Pathways that involve extreme expressions of violence or nonviolence may be best represented by straight lines. In the majority of instances that involve moderate or milder expressions of violence, however, the pathways may be better represented by curving lines (see Figure 5.7). These social interactions do not exactly correspond to the ideals of positivist science and linear development. Nor are these interactions as predictable as social scientists would like, yet relationships do emerge between the properties and pathways, and patterns of both violent behavior and violence develop subject to life courses and historical events. Moreover, according to the reciprocal theory of violence, it is not necessary for interactions involving all, or even most, of the properties and pathways to violence to be present and accounted for in order for violence to occur. Of course, as the number of properties increases and the

pathways accumulate, the reciprocal forces of these social relations multiply and enhance the likelihood that violence will happen.

More specifically, the reciprocal theory of violence also assumes that, as the number of properties and pathways to violence converge in time and space, at least three things happen: First, the severity or intensity of these mild, moderate, and extreme forms of violence swell in magnitude. Second, these expressions become more prevalent among the mild, moderate, and extreme categories of violence. Third, the distinguishing factors of the spheres of interpersonal, institutional, and structural violence become less distinct. A reciprocal theory of nonviolence also assumes that the same kinds of relationships hold for the properties and pathways to nonviolence.

In sum, at the interpersonal, institutional, and structural levels of interaction, the reciprocal theory of violence hypothesizes three things about violence and nonviolence: first, that the properties of violence and nonviolence are cumulative. The more (or fewer) properties characteristic of violence or nonviolence that are present, the more (or less) likely it is that violence or nonviolence will occur. Second, as the familial, subcultural, and cultural pathways to violence and nonviolence combine, overlap, and interconnect, expressions of violence and nonviolence will become more or less intense and, conversely, more or less common. Third, both the properties of and the pathways to violence and nonviolence are mutually and inversely related. That is to say, social relationships exist within and between the levels of interpersonal, institutional, and structural violence and nonviolence, and when those properties and pathways common to individuals, organizations, and nation-states converge in everyday reality, they work to reinforce and support the reproduction of violence or nonviolence.

A NARRATIVE PROOF OF
RECIPROCAL VIOLENCE

In the narrative descriptions that follow, the reciprocal social relations linking the properties and pathways of violence are described. As explanations of different expressions of lethal violence—interpersonal, institutional, and structural—are related thematically, there is a disclosure of the cumulative interactions among families, subcultures, and culture that construct pathways to violence and nonviolence. In the first instance, the scenarios of boys that kill are full of stories that have to do with abandonment or with disconnected youths who have been victimized in one form or the other as infants and young children, by their parents and/or their communities. These stories are also about youths who have lost their childhood and who have, at a very early age, been exposed to, rather than protected from, the dark side of violent realities. Last but not least, these stories of violent boys are about the efforts of youths to overcome their feelings of shame, humiliation, and rejection.

In the second example that follows, the nature of suicidal terrorists is shown to involve scenarios that have to do with the exclusion from or disaffection with political and economic participation. This occurs primarily among young adult males. The pathways taken to these particular forms of lethal violence are numerous and emanate from larger histories of religious, ethnic, and cultural conflicts involving an array of secular and nonsecular groups. The subcultural acts of suicidal terrorists have typically been aimed at harming, destroying, or remaking the prevailing political, economic, and social relationships of their enemies. In the process, these acts of violence have served as a means of establishing the terrorist as a martyr.

In the third example, genocide has to do with an entire people's, tribe's, or nation's cultural disassociation from and rationalization of the mass extermination of groups of different human beings. Rather than the Holocaust, for example, being the product of a perverted, pathological, or diseased handful of collaborators suffering from despair and acting in isolation, this episode of systematic and planned execution was more accurately the product of exterminators who belonged to supportive groups of well-wishers and sympathizers. The collective emotions of onlookers and bystanders, all of whom possessed degrees of prejudice, bigotry, and hostility toward non-Aryan races, were not only enduring elements of the normal state of affairs; these sentiments of insensitivity to other humans were quite often celebrated by nonviolent, law-abiding citizens.

Killer Boys: A
Case of Lost Childhood

In both the rash of relatively unusual rural and suburban school shootings across America in the 1990s and the more steadily occurring and common inner-city drive-by shootings committed in association with gang activities during the late 1980s and early 1990s, there are profound emotional and psychological similarities that link these acts of lethal violence. In the scheme of socialization and social relationships, gender, far more than either race or class, is etiologically connected to these expressions of violence. As there are shared pathways between these forms of youthful killing, there are also different, and overlapping, pathways. Familial and/or social abandonment, for example, may be experienced by adolescent boys, leading to multiple pathways to killing. Those who experience only the former or only the latter types of abandonment will differ from those who accumulate both types of experience.

From the beginning of life and even possibly before birth, human development has required the interplay of biology and culture. Child development, for example, is about "the characteristics children bring with them into the world *and* the way the world treats them, nature *and* nurture" (Garbarino, 1999, p. 72). By combining the perspectives of exchange theory, resource theory, ecological theory, and sociobiology, it can be argued that children "face different opportunities and risks for development because of their mental and physical make up *and* because of the world they inhabit *and* because of how well their inborn traits match up with what their social environment offers, demands, rewards, and punishes" (Garbarino, 1999, p. 72). What this kind of developmental model assumes about lethal youth violence is that natural or biological predispositions to aggression will only translate into behavior when they occur in social situations that allow or promote their expression. In other words, social contexts matter very much in the impact, expression, and mediation of temperamental characteristics associated with violence.

Whether a baby is characterized as "difficult" or "easy" or predisposed to be "hyper," "hypo," or somewhere in the middle of a continuum of temperament, for optimal development, all newborns possess essentially the same needs. On their own, without social interaction, human infants can neither survive physically nor develop normally. "To begin the process of human development, a child needs not so much stimulation as responsiveness; children need to make connection through entering into a relationship" (Garbarino, 1999, p. 38). Making a connection or an attachment with another human being during the first year of life is a critical step in the process of human development.

During infancy, according to most psychological models of development, we are all natural narcissists—it's a matter of survival. If we are not to become sufferers of classic narcissism, a personality disorder in which the symptoms include lack of empathy, grandiose fantasies, excessive need for approval, rage, social isolation and depression, psychoanalytic theory informs us that we must more or less successfully negotiate the uneven transition from the natural narcissism of infancy to a more realistic view of our place in the world by the age of 4 years. The psychological adjustment away from narcissism begins around month 3, when most babies come to know and love the people who care for them. By 9 months, most babies have formed a specific attachment to one or more caregivers.

Attachment is a mixture of at least two properties, *knowing* and *feeling*. Positive connections are supposed to exist when infants know their caretakers in their particularity as individuals and when they are able to feel for them as special individuals. When both of these conditions occur, there is said to be a sense of affirmative connection and a foundation for sound emotional development. When one, the other, or both of these properties are missing from early childhood development, there is a greater likelihood of detachment, disconnection, disassociation, and/or denial. Although there are varieties of attachment, it is generally concluded that in the presence of their "objects" of attachment and desire, infants become free to explore and to develop their skills in mastering the world. Conversely, it is also concluded that

> In the absence of the beloved object, they become wary and withdrawn, defensive rather than exploratory, captured by their anxiety. This relationship becomes one of the important mediators between a child's temperament and the challenges of entering and mastering the world outside the family. Good attachment does not inoculate a child against later misfortune, but it does get the child off on the right foot. (Garbarino, 1999, p. 39)

In terms of human development, then, what does get the child off on the wrong foot, or on a pathway to violence? It should be clear by now that there is no one thing, but rather a series of things: an accumulation of things that are both inside and outside a young person's head. At the interpersonal level, these may include early childhood trauma, abuse, neglect, or family disruption. At the institutional or structural levels, these may include toxic environments, economic deprivations, communities of violence, racism, and other systems of cultural discrimination and oppression, such as the intense pressure that most boys feel, by virtue of the dictates of masculine socialization, to be tough, to suppress tender emotions, and to be powerful.

Interpersonally, youths suffering from abuse, neglect, or disruption are more likely to experience shame, rejection, alienation, rage, and a bloated sense of self-centeredness. On top of this, if they are experiencing the damage or injury inflicted by living in the ecological communities most victimized by other forms of institutional and structural violence, these youths (especially males) are more susceptible or vulnerable to victimization and to longer careers of violence, to committing lethal violence, and to being institutionalized first as juveniles and then as adults, for life. By contrast, those young males who have been supported by a parent or significant other and insulated from institutional and structural forms of violence tend to be relatively protected from the darker sides of life, at least during their early infancy and toddlerhood. Having bonded, attached, or connected in their formative social relationships, these individuals are more likely to empathize and relate with other people in a positive fashion. Young people who have been deprived politically and economically, but not socially or emotionally, are also less likely to experience desensitization and to dehumanize others near and far, making

them less likely to engage in violence throughout the life cycle, with most violent activity on their parts peaking (if it exists significantly at all) during late adolescence and, shortly after that, disappearing altogether.

As for killer boys, although most will have a history of victimization, this need not be the case. Some boys who mange to kill have not been obvious victims of physical abuse, emotional neglect, or environmental toxins. However, through "normal" human developmental processes, these boys end up feeling terribly inferior, rejected, and/or humiliated, even when they have grown up in the ideal family setting. Whether based on reality, fantasy, or some combination of the two, killer boys, from the school corridors to the ghetto streets, engage in toughness and aggression as a means of adaptive survival or as a defense mechanism against overwhelming feelings of personal vulnerability. Whether these killer boys are withdrawn or acting out, most of them have experienced overwhelming feelings of abandonment and intense bouts of depression that they typically do their emotional best to suppress, deny, and avoid altogether.

Psychoanalytically, of course, such feelings stem from the shared fear of mother-child abandonment common to all newborn humans. If these feelings of abandonment do not dissipate normally, or if they remain as unresolved issues of rejection (e.g., when a boy concludes that his addicted mother chose crack and other drugs over him), then strong feelings of humiliation are often the result:

> What shame a boy feels when he is abandoned by his mother! What lengths he will go in order to defend himself against these feelings. Inside, he "forgets" so that he doesn't have to feel. Outside, he punishes the world so that he feels avenged. Shame at abandonment begets covert depression, which begets rage, which begets violence. That is one of the powerful equations of life for lost boys. (Garbarino, 2000, p. 44)

At the same time, not knowing your biological father can also lead to severe feelings of abandonment associated with the usual feelings of shame, rejection, and negative self-worth.

Where repressed feelings of early childhood coalesce in a context of persistent poverty and deprivation, accompanied by feelings of alienation from society's broader institutions, such as schools and law enforcement, then a "code of the street" often develops as a means of psychological adaptation. Organized around a desperate search for "respect" and a credible threat of vengeance, this code credits the possession of both respect and credibility with the ability to shield the ordinary person from the interpersonal violence of the street. In the form of a kind of "people's law," or "street justice," the code involves a "primitive form of social exchange that holds would-be perpetrators accountable by promising an 'eye for an eye,' or a certain 'payback' for transgressions. In service of this ethic, repeated displays of 'nerve' and 'heart' build or reinforce a credible reputation for vengeance that works to deter aggression and disrespect, which are sources of great anxiety on the inner-city street" (Anderson, 1999, p. 10).

In sum, whether the killer boys are lost in early childhood due to parental abuse, neglect, or maltreatment, or in early adolescence due to economic deprivation, racial prejudice, and/or societal stigmatization, the interactive search for individual and social respect may, sooner or later, erupt into lethal violence that, although it appears random and senseless to most law-abiding citizens, has an intrinsic logic of its own. This logic is rarely understood by victims, victimizers, or society at large, which are all too often too busy dismissing these violent deeds as the inexplicable acts of crazy or evil people.

Suicidal Terrorists: A Case of Secular Despair

Terrorism and terrorists come in all sizes and shapes. For example, there are political terrorists, religious terrorists, ethnic terrorists, ecoterrorists, narcoterrorists, state terrorists, counterterrorists, and international terrorists, to identify the socially most prominent. These different terrorist groups may consist of political anarchists, religious extremists, nationalist-separatists, governmental agents, hired mercenaries, and/or organized criminals. While there are no "terrorist personalities" or even "terrorist mind sets" per se, there are subcultural worlds of terrorism that are motivated by political calculus, by nationalist fervor, or by religious hate. These different subcultural groups of terrorists, such as those involved in suicidal terrorism, have their own unique social psychologies and dynamics that help to reinforce a pattern of one-dimensional groupthink. This form of thinking does not accommodate the other person's point of view and often amounts to little more than clichés to express one's own "point of view", which is more often than not simply the reflection of a social construction of reality capable of engaging in what Arendt (1963) referred to as "the word-and-thought-defying banality of evil."

Historically, those who become members of violent sectarian groups or extremist cults have been mostly young adult males. Suicidal, homicidal, or both, in the case of suicidal terrorists who kill themselves and others, the composition of these subcultural organizations varies from nation to nation according to social conditions, religious traditions, and historical factors. In Europe of the 19th and 20th centuries, for example, there were working-class and elite-born terrorists, respectively. In the Muslim world of today, terrorists are likely to come from two classes. Either they are unemployed and from poor families, or they have been educated at universities or seminaries but are also unemployed. What is shared by Western and Eastern terrorists across the modern periods are collective feelings: of betrayal by authorities and elders; of social, psychological, and political, if not spiritual, despair; and of shame and humiliation at their own inefficacy to alter or transform their situation.

Terrorists, secular and nonsecular, East and West, are generally not psycho- or sociopaths, but they are often persons with unresolved psychological tensions, unfulfilled spiritual yearnings, and feelings of isolation and loneliness. Joining a terrorist subculture provides members with self-confidence, certainties, and a sense of belonging to a closely knit, exclusive community engaged in a "righteous" struggle against some omnipresent enemy. What these subcultural terrorist groups possess in common are fantasies of evil and dreams of victory over conspiring evil agents, whether they are political, religious, ideological, or cultural.

Often these beliefs in conspiracies, intensified by a group mentality, border on paranoid delusions capable of facilitating fanaticism, self-deception, and violent behavior. Every religion has had its share of fanatic proponents, especially during its formative stages. But the spirit of fanaticism has not been confined to the religious sphere only:

> Fanaticism was one of Adolf Hitler's favorite terms, and it appeared again and again in his speeches. It has appeared in every religious and political creed, especially the radical ones, in one way or the another. It is not the same as fundamentalism, because the fundamentalist is (or anyway should be) bound by the holy texts, whereas the fanatic frequently feels free to provide his own interpretations. Fanaticism can turn inward and express itself in asceticism or self-flagellation, as it still does, for example, among the Shiites. But in our

day and age it shows itself more frequently as hostility toward an outside enemy, an unwillingness to compromise, and an eagerness not just to defeat the enemy but to destroy him. The modern fanatic is more eager to castigate the flesh of others than his own. (Laquer, 1999, p. 98)

Although the century that has just ended and the one that has just begun have not experienced a rise in Christian or Islamic fundamentalism per se, there has been, especially in the autocratically ruled countries of Central Asia and elsewhere, a revival of Zoroastrian and Manichean theology. Dating back to the third century and to the ancient religions of the Middle East that believed in an eternal struggle between divine powers of good and evil, both of these early religious traditions profoundly influenced the extreme warrior visions of Islamic and Judeo-Christian thought alike (Warner, 2001).

In a way that is not dissimilar to the code of the street subscribed to by youthful killers of the inner cities, members of secular and nonsecular terrorist subcultures also subscribe to the code of their sect or cult. Perhaps what differentiates terrorists who kill from kids who kill is the degree to which the former are able to better compartmentalize and control their violence. What these offensive and defensive fanatics, religious zealots, political soldiers, and gangbangers all share in common is "an absolute certainty as to the justness of their cause, legitimacy of their leader, the inability to recognize other moral values and considerations, and the abdication of critical judgment" (Laquer, 1999, p. 99).

Historically, suicide has played an important role in a number of religious sects and terrorist groups. These acts, committed by both individuals and groups en masse, may stem from a variety of psychological sources, rational and irrational. A tradition of collective suicide in the history of religious sects can be traced back to a wing of the

Donatists, a fourth-century Christian sect in North Africa, and it has continued into the present day. At their extremes, these suicidal sects have regarded life on earth as relatively unimportant, a prelude to life after death—to paradise, a place of material and sexual fulfillment where as martyrs the sect members will be reunited with their families and stand in front of God as innocent as newborn babies. Hence, their suicides are often thought of as joyful occasions. It is not unusual for living family members to be proud of and to even celebrate their dead relative's suicidal-homicidal exploits.

In 2002, in the West Bank or Gaza Strip, suicidal terrorists may be protesting the Israeli occupation, showing their hate and contempt for America and for Jews, and trying to liberate all of Palestine, but they may also be on a pathway to paradise. Other Palestinian candidates for suicide may be more fatalistic, less theological, about dying, maintaining that since they are bound to die violently sooner or later, they might as well die sooner for a good cause. In the case of the World Trade Center suicidal terrorists of September 11, 2001, Mohamed Atta and several of his coconspirators were said to be driven and incensed by an American-backed repressive Egyptian regime, the Gulf War, and the Oslo peace accords. More generally, when it comes to suicidal bombers, it is often difficult, if not impossible, to disentangle religious from nationalist motives.

Genocidal Exterminators: A Case of Cultural Denial

On the dark side of cultural existence, anything is possible, even the mass exterminations of fellow human beings.

> During the Nazi period of the 1930s and 1940s, millions of people (particularly, but not exclusively, Jews) were systematically rounded up and shipped to concentrations camps, where they were worked to death, starved to death, tortured to death, or simply executed. Three decades later, the Khmer Rouge Party, under the leadership of Pol Pot, did much the same thing to the people of Cambodia. Just after the turn of the [20th] century, the Turks attempted to exterminate the Armenian people. (Garbarino, 1999, p. 112)

Genocide usually involves the cultural denial that any "real harm" is being done. Mass killings of "other" human beings are socially rationalized as necessary either to overcome evil of some kind or to accomplish some greater collective good for those who are not being eliminated. Generally, genocidal killings represent extreme forms of hate and intolerance. By comparison, institutionalized discriminations such as "redlining" geographical areas as uninsurable or selective employment practices represent moderate forms of hate and intolerance. Individual bigotries, in the form of expressed ideologies, written, spoken, or portrayed, represent mild forms of hate and intolerance.

Histories of genocide, past and present, reveal that the buildup of a collective or cultural denial of other groups' right to exist requires generations of family and community members passing along or instilling, at both the conscious and unconscious level, attitudes conducive to actions of intolerance. Stories of genocide also disclose, for example, that the genocidal denial of personhood requires the cultural support and accumulation of prejudice and hatred across the spheres of interpersonal, institutional, and structural violence. For example, during the Nazi era of the 1930s, tens of thousands of German citizens reacted to Hitler's interpretation of a terrible economic situation by helping to transform their historical sympathy for anti-Semitism into mass murder (Goldhagen, 1996).

However, cross-national comparisons reveal that in the late 19th and early 20th centuries, there were variations in the degree and types of anti-Semitism across Europe, for example. Some countries such as Bulgaria had traditions of religious tolerance and diversity and were thus less susceptible to anti-Jewish policies and practices, even during hard economic times. In other countries such as Romania, Great Britain, Italy, and France, between 1879 and 1939, when economic prosperity was deteriorating and the level of immigration of Eastern European Jews was increasing, anti-Semitism grew. It all depended "on the extent to which Jews were perceived as a threat to non-Jews" (Levin 2001, p. 149). In Poland, for example, evidence was recently revealed that a massacre of Jews in the town of Jedwabne, in 1941, involved ordinary farmers who herded 1,600 of their Jewish neighbors into a barn and set it on fire (Stylinski, 2001).

The point is that the policies and practices of genocide were carried out and encouraged not by ideological fanatics and schizophrenics, but by ordinary citizens. In other words, histories of cultural hate that culminate in genocide have not depended on individual pathology or abnormal psychology. Rather, these genocides are simply the extreme manifestations of the shared normative and traditional values of hatred and intolerance. The combination of a long history of anti-Semitism and a strong desire or need to protect the Fatherland, as each of these were connected to one's individual self-interest, accounted for the creation and enactment of the "final solution" in Nazi Germany:

> Hitler's condemnation of the Jews reflected not only his personal opinion, but also the beliefs of hundreds of thousands of German and Austrian citizens. While the police looked on approvingly, university students joined together to beat and batter their Jewish classmates. Faculty members and students voiced their demands to rid the universities of Jews and cosponsored lectures on "the Jewish problem." Because of

their genuine conviction, thousands of German soldiers and police helped to murder Jews. Civil service bureaucrats aided in doing the paperwork to expedite carrying out Hitler's extermination program. Many important business, banking, and industrial firms cooperated in the task of enslaving and murdering Jewish citizens. Thousands of German physicians cooperated in sterilizing or eliminating the "undesirables." Finally, whereas the church in other European countries denounced racist anti-Semitism, Germany's religious leaders (both Catholic and Protestant) failed to protest the final solution. (Levin, 2001, p. 47)

Hence, genocidal exterminators refer not only to those folks who constructed the ovens and filled them with people and gas, but to the hundreds of thousands of civilians and noncivilians alike who aided and abetted, or did not resist, the extermination of whole groups of people.

Collectively, genocide represents the familiar, subcultural, and cultural depersonalization and desensitization of Others, to the extent that the perpetrators fail to see the individuality and humanity of their victims. That is, to the extent that the genocidal exterminators lack the ability to empathize, they lose their ability to control their inhumanity. They also become objects and subjects of unlimited possibilities for violence. The same kinds of reciprocal relations of violence, for different as well as for overlapping reasons, engulf killer kids and suicidal terrorists, as these too have become vulnerable to interpersonal and subcultural forms of depersonalization and desensitization.

SUMMARY

This chapter has presented an overview of ad hoc, life-course, developmental, and integrative models of explaining violence and violent behavior. It was argued that the ad hoc theories—exchange, subcultural, resource, patriarchal, ecological, social learning, evolutionary, sociobiological, pathological conflict, psychopathological, general systems, and inequality—are inadequate explanations because they each ignore, for the most part, more relevant variables than they explore. Eight of these explanations address only one of the four interpersonal dimensions of internal as well as external motivation and constraint. Explanations derived from models of inequality, ecology, and pathological conflict address two of the four interpersonal dimensions, and general systems explanations address all but the internal constraints.

By contrast, the life-course, developmental, and integrative models were judged to be superior explanations, as most of these tried to account for all four dimensions of the interpersonal typology of violence. Such models as Moffitt's two-pronged theory of adolescence-limited and life-course–persistent antisocial behavior, Sampson and Laub's theory of informal social control and cumulative disadvantage, and the more general social development model of the etiology of conforming and nonconforming behavior all recognize the interactive, reciprocal, and dialectical relationships leading to prosocial and antisocial behavioral outcomes. Although these models are, indeed, an improvement over the primarily one-dimensional ad hoc models, these explanations also reveal themselves to be incomplete. They do usually account for internal as well as external motivations and constraints at the interpersonal level, but they generally ignore similar interactive, reciprocal, and dialectical relationships involving the institutional and structural domains of violence. Finally, omitted from these explanations of violence are the reciprocal or mutually reinforcing relationships between the spheres of interpersonal, institutional, and structural violence.

As a more comprehensive explanation of violence and violent behavior, the reciprocal theory of violence was introduced. This model argues that both the properties of and pathways to violence or nonviolence, across the spheres of interpersonal, institutional, and structural relations as well as across the domains of family, subculture, and culture, are cumulative, mutually reinforcing, and inversely related. To provide a proof of the theory of reciprocal violence, narrative examples were used to depict the parallel social realities of killer boys, suicidal terrorists, and genocidal exterminators. Their reciprocal properties of and pathways to lethal violence included depersonalization, desensitization, and dissociation.

Similarly, the same kinds of reciprocal relations, involving the constellation of properties of and pathways to violence, apply to other forms of interpersonal violence, ranging from mild expressions like verbal abuse and emotional neglect to moderate expressions like physical battery and sexual coercion to extreme expressions like serial rape and murder. These reciprocal relations also apply to the institutional and structural spheres of violence. In the case of the former, these forms of violence might include racial profiling and sexual harassment at the milder end of the continuum, state execution and the abuse of deadly force at the extreme end of the continuum, and penal and police brutality somewhere in between. In the case of the latter, the forms of violence might include exploitation and abuse of workers, consumers, and the general public, resulting in harms, injuries, or deaths vis-à-vis the reproduction of unsafe goods and polluted or toxic environments through negligence, malfeasance, silence, intent, or conspiracy.

In the end, like Anthony Giddens' (1984) *structuration theory* more generally, the reciprocal theory of violence does not treat individual action and social structure as separate and dualistic phenomena. The interpersonal, institutional, and structural levels of society are, indeed, part and parcel of the same set of cultural relations. Thus, to "bring off" violent or nonviolent interactions, most individuals, groups, or nation-states make use of their knowledge of cultural behavior in such a way as to render their interchanges "meaningful." By invoking institutional orders in this way, persons and whole nations alike reproduce the reciprocal orders of violence and nonviolence that they know, subject only to the alternative interventions of "new" and radically different theories and practices.

REFERENCES

Alexander, R. D. (1974). The evolution of social behavior. *Annual Review of Ecology and Systematics, 5,* 325-383.

American Psychological Association. (1994). *Diagnostic and statistical manual of mental disorders* (4th ed.). Washington, DC: Author.

Anderson, E. (1999). *Code of the street: Decency, violence, and the moral life of the inner city.* New York: W. W. Norton.

Arendt, H. (1963). *Eichmann in Jerusalem: A report on the banality of evil.* New York: Viking.

Arrigo, B. (1995). The peripheral core of law and criminology: On postmodern social theory and conceptual integration. *Justice Quarterly, 12,* 447-472.

Baker, L. A., Mack, W., Moffitt, T. E., & Mednick, S. A. (1989). Etiology of sex differences in criminal convictions in a Danish adoption cohort. *Behavior Genetics, 19,* 355-370.

Barak, G. (1998). *Integrating criminologies.* Boston: Allen & Bacon.

Barak, G. (2002). Integrative theories. In D. Levinson (Ed.), *Encyclopedia of crime and punishment.* Thousand Oaks, CA: Sage.

Barak, G., & Henry, S. (1999). An integrative-constitutive theory of crime, law, and social justice. In B. Arrigo (Ed.), *Social justice/criminal justice: The maturation of critical theory in law, crime, and deviance* (pp.152-175). Belmont, CA: Wadsworth.

Bell, R. Q., & Chapman, M. (1986). Child effects in studies using experimental or brief longitudinal approaches to socialization. *Developmental Psychology, 22,* 595-603.

Berreman, G. E. (1978). Scale and social relations. *Current Anthropology, 19,* 225-237.

Blood, R. O., & Wolfe, D. M. (1960). *Husbands and wives: The dynamics of married living.* Glencoe, IL: Free Press.

Box, S. (1983). *Power, crime, and mystification.* London: Tavistock.

Brown, R. H. (1989). Texuality, social science and society. *Issues in Integrative Studies, 7,* 1-19.

Buss, D. M. (1984). Toward a psychology of person-environment correspondence: The role of spouse selection. *Journal of Personality and Social Psychology, 53,* 1214-1221.

Caspi, A., Elder, G. H., & Bem, D. J. (1987). Moving against the world: Life-course patterns of explosive children. *Developmental Psychology, 23,* 308-313.

Catalano, R. F., & Hawkins, J. D. (1996). The social development model: A theory of antisocial behavior. In J. D. Hawkins (Ed.), *Delinquency and crime: Current theories* (pp. 29-43). New York: Cambridge University Press.

Chess, S., & Thomas, A. (1987). *Origins and evolution of behavior disorders: From infancy to early adult life.* Cambridge, MA: Harvard University Press.

Colvin, M. (2000). *Crime and coercion: An integrated theory of chronic criminality.* New York: St. Martin's.

Cravioto, J., & Arrieta, R. (1983). Malnutrition in childhood. In M. Rutter (Ed.), *Developmental neuropsychiatry* (pp. 32-51). New York: Guilford.

Daly, M., & Wilson, M. I. (1981). Abuse and neglect of children in evolutionary perspective. In R. Alexander and D. Tingle (Eds.), *Natural selection and social behavior: Recent research and new theory* (pp. 405-416). New York: Chiron.

Dannefer, D. (1987). Aging as intracohort differentiation: Accentuation, the Matthew effect, and the life course. *Sociological Forum, 2,* 211-236.

Dobash, R. E., & Dobash, R. P. (1979). *Violence against wives.* New York: Free Press.

Dodge, K. A., & Frame, C. K. (1982). Social cognitive biases and deficits in aggressive boys. *Child Development, 53,* 629-635.

Elder, G. (2001). Time, human agency, and social change. In A. Piquero & P. Mazerolle (Eds.), *Life-course criminology: Contemporary and classic readings* (pp. 3-30). Belmont, CA: Wadsworth.

Farrington, D. P. (1991). Antisocial personality from childhood to adulthood. *Psychologist, 4,* 389-394.

Farrington, D. P., & West, D. J. (1990). The Cambridge study of delinquent development: A long-term follow up of 401 London males. In H. J. Kerner & G. Kaiser (Eds.), *Kriminalitat* (pp. 117-138). New York: Springer-Verlag.

Fergusson, D. M., Horwood, L. J., & Lloyd, M. (1991). A latent class model of child offending. *Criminal Behavior and Mental Health, 1,* 90-106.

Fogel, C. A., Mednick, S. A., & Michelson, N. (1985). Minor physical anomalies and hyperactivity. *Acta Psychiatrica Scandinavica, 72,* 551-556.

Fried, I. (1997). Syndrome E. *Lancet, 350,* 1845-1847.

Garbarino, J. (1977). The human ecology of child maltreatment: A conceptual model for research. *Journal of Marriage and Family, 39,* 721-735.

Garbarino, J. (1999). *Lost boys: Why our sons turn violent and how we can save them.* New York: Anchor.

Gelles, R. (1983). An exchange social theory. In D. Finkelhor, R. J. Gelles, G. T. Totaling, & M. A. Straus (Eds.), *The dark side of families: Current family violence research* (pp. 151-165). Beverly Hills, CA: Sage.

Giddens, A. (1984). *The constitution of society: Outline of the theory of structuration.* Cambridge, UK: Polity.

Gilligan, J. (1997). *Violence: Reflections on a national epidemic.* New York: Vintage.

Goldhagen, D. (1996). *Hitler's willing executioners: Ordinary Germans and the Holocaust.* New York: Basic Books.

Goldstein, J. H. (1986). *Aggression and crimes of violence* (2nd ed.). New York: Oxford University Press.

Grauerholz, E., & Koralewski, M. A. (1991). *Sexual coercion: A sourcebook on its nature, causes and prevention.* Lexington, MA: D. C. Heath.

Groth, A. N. (1983). Treatment of the sexual offender in a correctional institution. In J. G. Greer & I. R. Stuart (Eds.), *The sexual aggressor: Current perspectives in treatment* (pp. 160-176). New York: Van Nostrand Reinhold.

Hale, R. (1994). The role of humiliation and embarrassment in serial murder. *Psychology: A Journal of Human Behavior, 31,* 17-23.

Henry, S., & Milovanovic, D. (1996). *Constitutive criminology: Beyond postmodernism.* London: Sage.

Huang, B., Kosterman, R., Catalano, R. F., Hawkins, J. D., & Abbott, R. (2001). Modeling mediation in the etiology of violent behavior in adolescence: A test of the social development model. *Criminology, 39,* 75-108.

Iadicola, P., & Shupe, A. (1998). *Violence, inequality, and human freedom.* Dix Hills, NY: General Hall.

Kandel, E., Brennan, P. A., & Mednick, S. A. (1989). Minor physical anomalies and parental modeling of aggression to predict violent offending. *Acta Psychiatric Scandinavica, 78,* 1-5.

Kaufman, J., & Zigler, E. (1987). Do abused children become abusive parents. *American Journal of Orthopsychiatry, 57,* 316-331.

Kempf-Leonard, K, Tracy, P. E., & Howell, J. C. (2001). Serious, violent, and chronic juvenile offenders: The relationship of delinquency career types to adult criminality. *Justice Quarterly, 18,* 449-478.

Kraemer, G. W. (1988). Speculations on the neurobiology of protest and despair. In P. Simon, P. Soubrie, & D. Widlocher (Eds.), *Inquiry into schizophrenia and depression: Animal models of psychiatric disorders* (pp. 101–147). Basel, Switzerland: Karger.

Laquer, W. (1999). *The new terrorism: Fanaticism and the arms of mass destruction.* New York: Oxford University Press.

Laub, J., & Sampson, R. (1993). Turning points in

the life course: Why change matters to the study of crime. *Criminology, 31,* 301-325.

Lenski, G., & Lenski, J. (1970). *Human societies: An introduction to macrosociology.* New York: McGraw-Hill.

Levin, J. (2001). *The violence of hate: Confronting racism, anti-semitism, and other forms of bigotry.* Boston: Allyn & Bacon.

Lewis, D. O., Shanok, S. S., Picus, J. H., & Glaser, G. H. (1979). Violent juvenile delinquents: Psychiatric, neurological, psychological and abuse factors. *Journal of American Academy of Child Psychiatry, 2,* 307-319.

Lightcap, J. L., Kurland, J. A., & Burgess, R. L. (1982). Child abuse: A test of some predictions from evolutionary theory. *Ecology and Sociobiology, 3,* 61-67.

Loeber, R. (1982). The stability of antisocial and delinquent child behavior: A review. *Child Development, 53,* 1431-1446.

Loeber, R., & Baicker-McKee, C. (1990). The changing manifestations of disruptive/antisocial behavior from childhood to early adulthood: Evolution or tautology? Unpublished manuscript, Western Psychiatric Institute, University of Pittsburgh, PA.

Martin, D. (1976). *Battered wives.* San Francisco: Glide.

Meany, M. J., Aitken, D. H., van Berkel, C., Bhatnagur, S., & Sapolsky, R. M. (1988). Effect of neonatal handling on age-related impairments associated with the hippocampus. *Science, 239,* 766-768.

Messerschmidt, J. (1997). *Crime as structured action: Gender, race, class and crime in the making.* Thousand Oaks, CA: Sage.

Messner, S., & Rosenfeld, R. (1997). *Crime and the American dream.* Belmont, CA: Wadsworth.

Mills, C. W. (1959). *The sociological imagination.* New York: Oxford University Press.

Milner, J. S., & McCanne, T. R. (1991). Neuropsychological correlates of physical child abuse. In J. S. Milner (Ed.), *Neuropsychology of aggression* (pp. 131-145). Norwell, MA: Kluwer Academic.

Moffitt, T. (2001). Adolescence-limited and life-course–persistent antisocial behavior: A developmental taxonomy. In A. Piquero & P. Mazerolle (Eds.), *Life-course criminology: contemporary and classic readings* (pp. 91-145). Belmont, CA: Wadsworth.

O'Leary, D. K. (1988). Physical aggression between spouses: A social learning theory perspective. In V. B. Van Hasselt (Ed.), *Handbook of family violence* (pp. 31-55). New York: Plenum.

Pagelow, M. D. (1981). *Women-battering: Victims and their experiences.* Beverly Hills, CA: Sage.

Patterson, G. (1993). Orderly change in a stable world: The antisocial trait as a chimera. *Journal of Consulting and Clinical Psychology, 61,* 911-919.

Patterson, G. R., DeBaryshe, B. D., & Ramsey, E. (1989). A developmental perspective on antisocial behavior. *American Psychologist, 44,* 329-335.

Patterson, G. R., & Yoerger, K. (1993). Developmental models for delinquent behavior. In S. Hodgins (Ed.), *Mental disorder and crime* (pp. 140-172). Newbury Park, CA: Sage.

Paulhus, D. L., & Martin, C. L. (1986). Predicting adult temperament from minor physical anomalies. *Journal of Personality and Social Psychology, 50,* 1235-1239.

Piquero, A., & Mazerolle, P. (Eds.). (2001). *Life-course criminology: Contemporary and classic readings.* Belmont, CA: Wadsworth.

Pryor, F. L. (1977). *The origins of the economy.* New York: Academic.

Quinney, R. (1977). *Class, state, and crime.* New York: David McKay.

Retzinger, S. M. (1991). *Violent emotions: Shame and rage in marital quarrels.* Newbury Park, CA: Sage.

Robins, L. N. (1966). *Deviant children grown up.* Baltimore, MD: Williams and Wilkins.

Robins, L. N. (1978). Sturdy, childhood predictors of adult antisocial behavior: Replications for longitudinal studies. *Psychological Medicine, 8,* 611-622.

Sampson, R., & Laub, J. (1990). Crime and deviance over the life course: The salience of adult social bonds. *American Sociological Review, 55,* 609-627.

Sampson, R., & Laub, J. (1993). *Crime in the making: Pathways and turning points through life.*

Cambridge, MA: Harvard University Press.

Sampson, R., & Laub, J. (2001a). Crime and deviance in the life course. In A. Piquero & P. Mazerolle (Eds.), *Life-course criminology: Contemporary and classic readings* (pp. 21-42). Belmont, CA: Wadsworth.

Sampson, R., & Laub, J. (2001b). A life-course theory of cumulative disadvantage and the stability of delinquency In A. Piquero & P. Mazerolle (Eds.), *Life-course criminology: Contemporary and classic readings* (pp. 146-170). Belmont, CA: Wadsworth.

Savolainen, J. (2000). Inequality, welfare state, and homicide: Further support for institutional anomie theory. *Criminology, 38,* 1021-1042.

Silver, E. (2000). Extending social disorganization theory: A multilevel approach to the study of violence among persons with mental illness. *Criminology, 38,* 1043-1074.

Simon, R. (1996). *Bad men do what good men dream: A forensic psychiatrist illuminates the darker side of human behavior.* Washington, DC: American Psychiatric.

Straus, M. (1978). Wife-beating: How common and why? *Victimology, 2,* 443-459.

Straus, M. A., Gelles, R. J., & Steimetz, S. K. (1980). *Behind closed doors: Violence in the American family.* New York: Anchor.

Stylinski, A. (2001, March 16). Polish role is admitted in 1941 massacre. *Boston Globe,* p. 15.

Tarter, R. E., Hegedus, A. M., Winsten, N. E., & Aterman, A. L. (1984). Neuropsychological personality and familiar characteristics of physically abused delinquents. *Journal of American Academy of Child Psychiatry, 23,* 668-674.

Taylor, M. C. (2001, December 14). Unplanned obsolescence and the new network culture. *Chronicle of Higher Education,* pp. B14-B16.

Thomas, W. I., & Znaniecki, F. (1918-1920). *The Polish peasant in Europe and America* (Vols. 1-2). Urbana, IL: University of Illinois Press.

Tinsley, B. R., & Parke, R. D. (1983). The person-environment relationship: Lessons from families with preterm infants. In D. Magmusson & V. I. Allen (Eds.), *Human development in interactive perspective* (pp. 93-110). San Diego, CA: Academic.

Tittle, C. (1995). *Control balance: Toward a general theory of deviance.* Boulder, CO: Westview.

Viano, E. (Ed.). (1992). *Intimate violence: Interdisciplinary perspectives.* Washington, DC: Hemisphere.

Walsh, W. J., Isaacson, H. R., Rehman, F., & Hall, A. (1997). Elevated blood copper/zinc ratios in assaultive young males. *Psychology and Behavior, 62,* 327-329.

Warner, M. (2001, December 16). Ideas and trends: Fantasy's power and peril. *New York Times,* §4, p. 5.

White, J., Moffitt, T. E., Earls, F., Robins, L. N., & Silva, P. A. (1990). How early can we tell? Preschool predictions of boys' conduct disorder and delinquency. *Criminology, 28,* 507-533.

Wilson, J., & Herrnstein, R. (1985). *Crime and human nature.* New York: Simon and Schuster.

Wolfgang, M., & Ferracuti, F. (1967). *The subculture of violence: Toward an integrated theory of criminology.* London: Tavistock.

REVIEW QUESTIONS

1. In terms of interpersonal ad hoc explanations of violence (refer to Figures 5.2 and 5.3), discuss any four of these in relation to family violence.

2. In terms of the "life-course" models of human behavior, discuss the similarities and differences in the arguments of Terrie Moffitt, Sampson and Laub, and the social development model (SDM) of prosocial and antisocial behavior.

3. In terms of the reciprocity of violent and nonviolent spheres, discuss "the properties of violence" in relation to the two-sided continuum of the pathways to violence and nonviolence.

4. What does the reciprocal theory of violence assume, argue, and/or hypothesize about the relationships of violent behavior?

5. Apply the reciprocal theory of violence to the actions of killer boys, suicidal terrorists, and genocidal exterminators as discussed in the three cases at the end of the chapter.

CHAPTER 6

Media and Violence

In the previous chapter, nine pathways to and an infinite number of properties of violence and nonviolence were identified. In the context of interpersonal, institutional, and structural violence, some of these pathways and properties linking violent events in time and place are difficult to miss. In most instances, the particular forms or expressions of violence associated with the emotional states of the mind of the individual, the group, the community, the tribe, or the nation are easy to discern. In other instances, those properties of and pathways to violence that connect the mind's cognitive recognition and imagination with acts of abuse, violence, and exploitation are less obvious, more subtle or indirect.

In Chapters 6 and 7, two of the more subtle, influential, and yet misunderstood institutional and structural pathways to violence are explored. I refer specifically to those pathways to violence that may or may not flow from that violence channeled through the mass media ("mass-mediated violence"), from culturally learned sexuality and gender, and from the complex and interacting relations involving both of these sets of behaviors. In the process of examining in detail these particular social interrelations between the interpersonal, institutional, and structural spheres of violence, an "indirect

effects" model of media and violence and of media and sexuality is endorsed as the "best" approach to understanding these intricate relationships (Malamuth & Briere, 1986).

In this chapter, after a critical film review of *Schindler's List* and *Saving Private Ryan*, I will try to place America's fascination with mediated violence into perspective, followed by a fairly elaborate discussion on the effects of the mass media's model of violence ("mediated violence") in general and of sexually mediated violence in particular, ending the chapter with an examination of media ownership, mass advertising, and ideological distortion, as well as the productive and consumptive values of the pathways to violence. As a way of setting up the chapter, I will now briefly entertain some of the more subtle and complex issues involved in mass-mediated violence.

MASS MEDIA, COLUMBINE, AND THE MIDDLE EAST

There have been more than 3,000 reports on the effects of televised violence on American consumers. Most of these have concluded that there is some kind of *correlation* between mediated violence and societal violence; none have proven a *cause-and-effect* relationship between the two. Of course, today's screen violence is no longer confined to cinema and television: It increasingly includes videos, DVDs, and the Worldwide Web. These technological innovations and others raise serious doubts not only about what is being correlated, but about short-term and immediate consequences versus long-term and lasting consequences.

Today's "video games make available to any child in America a killing simulator that will train him or her to shoot without a moment's hesitation" (Bellesiles, 2000, p. B8). But are these kinds of interactive advances in technology and communication, which employ violence to market ideas or to sell products while instructing audiences on the selective intricacies of violence, really the problem? That depends on one's interpretation of a myriad of ideas on the relationships between media and violence (see Box 6.1).

For example, these "first-person shooter" games reward players for killing and eviscerating victims in gory and bloody detail. In the game Carmageddon, the rules encourage players "to think of new and humorous ways of pulping pedestrians," and as one reviewer for *Wired* magazine commented: "It's not whether you win or lose, it's how many innocent bystanders you smear down the sidewalk in the process" (Bok, 1999, p. 55). As for students of violence and media, the question becomes: Does a fascination with simulated violence and interactive video translate into real-life assaults or killings?

High-profile mass killers Eric Harris and Dylan Klebold, who stormed Columbine High School on April 20, 1999, executing 13 and wounding 21 others before they killed themselves, were alleged to be excellent players of these "first-person shooter" games like Doom and Quake. Such games, however, have been consumed by tens of millions of teenage youths across this nation and elsewhere. How many of these players have become homicidal-suicidal killers? Perhaps something on the order of one in five million. In other words, other factors would need to be marshaled to explain why Harris and Klebold did what they did. Only one month before the Colorado shootings, Dylan had gone on a tour of the University of Arizona, where he was supposed to begin his freshman year, with his parents and had picked out his dorm room for the upcoming fall semester. Obviously, there was a lot more going on in Dylan's life than had met the eyes of his parents, counselors, and teachers.

The Columbine incident is used not as an illustration to imply that media violence and societal violence are without any relationships. On the contrary, it has been my contention and that of other media scholars of crime and justice that the relationships between media and violence are quite different than the ways in which most people have been taught to think about them (Barak, 1996; Hunter, 1995; Jenkins, 1994; Kidd-Hewitt & Osborne, 1998; Malamuth, 1989; Rafter, 2000; Sharrett, 1999; Surette, 1994). Briefly, there are no one-to-one or direct relationships between reel violence and real violence. In other words, while the mass media does provide context as well as a conduit for both simulated and nonsimulated violence, it does not unleash, stimulate, or teach violence and aggression per se. In conjunction with the marketing of products and identities for mass consumption, however, it does influence the way people feel and think about themselves, other people, and the world in which they live. Finally, when well-conceived, mediated, or "designer" violence, executed in news, documentaries, films, and video games, leverages creativity, fascination, and repulsion in such a fashion, the three overlap. The consumer's imagination is thus allowed to emotionally and intellectually interact with very real and complex human tensions in ways that some would characterize as pathological and others would characterize as cathartic (Brown, 2002; Leland, 2002).

Box 6.1   A Dialogue on Media and Violence

We are fascinated by the darkness in ourselves. It's part of our mechanism, the duality in our psyche, the light and the dark. Hannibal Lecter—he is the pure paradox of human nature.

Anthony Hopkins, actor

I guess you walk a very thin line when you write about a serial killer in a satirical way.

Bret Easton Ellis, author of *American Psycho*

Crime films offer us contradictory sorts of satisfaction: the reality of what we fear to be true and the fantasy of overcoming that reality; the pleasure of entering the realm of the forbidden and the illicit and the security of rejecting or escaping that realm in the end.

Nicole Rafter, professor of criminology and author of
Shots in the Mirror: Crime Films and Society

Popular art, movies, best-selling books and television shows function as a kind of communal dream or nightmare, and you can read a lot into what's going on in the back of culture's mind by analyzing that material.

Harold Schechter, professor of American literature and author of
The A to Z Encyclopedia of Serial Killers

What becomes clear is the extraordinary preeminence of the violent image in the extreme alienation of late twentieth-century America.

Christopher Sharrett, professor of communication and editor of
Mythologies of Violence in Postmodern Media

Where the traditional horror film invited, however ambiguously, an identification with the return of the repressed, the contemporary horror film invites an identification (either sadistic or masochistic or both simultaneously) with punishment.

Robin Wood, film critic and author of *Hollywood from Vietnam to Reagan*

One woman's misery is another man's pleasure; one man's pleasure is another man's crime; one man's crime another man's beat; one man's beat is another man's T.V. show. And all of these pieces of the drama become one big paycheck for the executive producer.

Debra Segal, writer and former employee of "reality-based" TV police shows

It's sort of like "sex sells"—in this case, violence sells. There's a meanness aesthetic being developed.

William Stumpf, inventor of the Aeron chair

The news media have delivered more vivid horror—both real and fiction—than we can absorb, and out of self-protection from this onslaught, we tend toward disengagement.

Roxana Robinson, writer and novelist

(Continued)

Box 6.1   (Continued)

The media's disproportionate emphasis on violence and mayhem contributes to skewing the perspective of unsuspecting viewers. And their skewed perspective may in turn lead to faulty reasoning and deliberation about choices in their own lives and in their communities, as well as in their views about collective policymaking with respect to crime and justice.

Sissela Bok,
Harvard Center for Population and Development Studies
and author of *Mayhem: Violence as Public Entertainment*

When violent crimes hit the headlines, people want to lash out at something, anything, and assign blame. The media is too often that something, even though, as our report found, there is no causal link between the violent content in the media and real violence.

David Horowitz, executive director of the
Media Center

It would appear, therefore, that we will save a considerable amount of time if we replace the question: "Does the media lead to crime?" with a reflection on why a culture identifies—in emotional, intellectual, and practical terms—with the criminal element, and especially with serial killers.

Denis Duclos, Paris-based sociologist and author of
The Werewolf Complex: America's Fascination with Violence

I am not indicting the media. I don't have the answers. I'm a filmmaker, not a politician. I'm just asking . . . Is the TV media feeding the public's appetite for violent stories, or are they encouraging it?

John Herzfeld, writer and director of *15 Minutes*

I've reached the point where I think violence should be an assault on the audience—realistic, unrelenting, with severe and lasting psychological aftershocks—or it shouldn't be shown at all.

David Chase, series creator of HBO's *The Sopranos*

Hypothetically, it may be the case that Harris and Klebold (for example) were suffering from the same kind of delusions and paranoid fantasies that homicidal-suicidal terrorists in the Middle East are suffering from. That is to say, in the context of selected mass-mediated images and texts about "good" and "evil," both Harris and Klebold, as well as the Palestinian "human bombs," were each experiencing their own unique feelings of pain, humiliation, and vulnerability. For very different reasons, these American high school seniors and their Middle Eastern counterparts were both in the market for, and vulnerable to, those rationales and justifications that are about seeking some kind of "collective" revenge and sense of "justice." A secular and nonsecular social despair, if you will; analogous kinds of retaliation against their respective enemies and oppressors who, they felt, left them no alternatives to pursue other than cold-blooded murder and personal death.

Although there could be some kind of indirect, remote, or tangential relationship between mass-mediated violence and the deviant actions of these exceptional youths from Colorado and Palestine, the direct sources of their violence reside elsewhere. In short, the sources have little, if anything, to do with the techniques or knowledge of violence and the explicit or graphic depictions of violence—real or imaginary—that matter, cause, or result in real-world acts of private or public violence. Far more important are the mass-mediated images or portrayals of violence and nonviolence, the socially constructed contexts and the delicately communicated messages about the appropriateness or inappropriateness of violent conditions, and the extent to which these mediated relations exploit their audiences' psychic investments in both desire for and fear of violence. In short, it is all about context (see Box 6.2).

Box 6.2   Tania Modleski's Take

In a review that appeared in *The Chronicle of Higher Education,* film critic Tania Modleski questioned the mass media's "free passes" for two of Steven Spielberg's award-winning film productions, in what she otherwise characterized as the media's "wholesale denunciation of Hollywood violence." She argues that these particular two films of violence were excepted from public criticism allegedly because of the historical events portrayed and the morally instructive and enriching stories conveyed. In deconstructing the appropriateness or inappropriateness of the lack of criticism about the films, Modleski not only exposes the media's short-sightedness regarding violence and other social values, but their role in and contribution to the rise in a new kind of American militarism.

Modleski contends that *Schindler's List* was lauded because of its "supposedly praiseworthy treatment of violence" even though it could be argued that the movie had the "potential to make us worse human beings by enabling us to engage in some rather questionable voyeurism, and then to take pride in the experience." She continues that this kind of realism provides the psychic alibi for "indulging in morally dubious pleasures, assuring us that we're not just having a little sadistic fun but participating in the solemn act of bearing witness" (pp. B15-B16). She also points out that *Schindler's List* received a "bye" (a pass) of sorts by the critics because of its historical veracity.

That is to say, Modleski argues that the film was praised for convincing "doubters" that the Holocaust actually occurred. In a twist of social reality, Hollywood documents and provides proof of history, rather than vice versa, or some variation of "life imitating art." Concerning the film's artistic production of history, she asks:

> Isn't it a trifle worrisome if we seem more comfortable with ourselves for having responded in kind to the self-congratulation the film oozes (the way it calls attention to itself in its artsy, *vérité* use of black-and-white film, with greeting-card touches of red; its moment of silence at the end; Spielberg's personal appearance, as if he were taking a bow) than we do after taking in the latest Jean-Claude Van Damme flick? Shouldn't a morally instructive film

(Continued)

Box 6.2   (Continued)

---

encourage self-scrutiny by asking us to look at our own weaknesses and capacity for evil? (p. B15)

In examining both *Schindler's List* and *Saving Private Ryan,* Modleski articulates the ideological role served by both of these films in psychologically preparing its audiences for the next just war, like World War II, and how the heroic formulas of such Hollywood-directed films about war allow the artists to reconstruct the same old tired and simplistic character types of "good guys" versus "bay guys." The latter film, for example, has been acclaimed for being a masterful antiwar film. At the same time, most critics ignored any mention of the sexist and racist treatment in parts of the film.

For example, when Private Ryan (Matt Damon) says that he cannot remember what his brothers look like, his captain counsels him to picture them doing something. Ryan pictures them involved in a misogynous context that is dismissed as funny and a product of innocence. The brothers are in a barn with an exceptionally ugly girl who is about to have sex with one of them who is all of a sudden knocked unconscious. This film is also critiqued for its sentimental and propagandistic celebration of motherhood, God, and nation, and for its historical amnesia of the mixed motives for entering the war and the racism that fueled the fighting, to say nothing of the Allies' own questionable acts of devastating violence. Instead, when the audience tries to picture these things, they are seen through hazy nostalgic glows.

Furthermore, "embedded in a sanctimonious mom-and-apple-pie vision of us good old Americanos fighting for truth, justice, and the American way," these narratives do little to "encourage reflective thinking about humans' propensity for violence, including our own." They simply make "our side look all the nobler for enduring the hellishness of battle" (p. B16). In other words, bring on the next Afghanistan, bring on Iraq, bring on the next just war—another war that can justify a mindlessly jingoistic attitude toward collateral damage and destruction, and that allows us to claim that this attitude has everything to do with our "evil" enemies' dissimilarities, all the while shielding us from or denying us the opportunities of seeing their human faces and similarities.

Source: Modleski, T. (2001, April 27). The context of violence in popular culture. *Chronicle of Higher Education, 47,* B15-B16. Reprinted with permission.

AMERICA'S FASCINATION WITH MEDIATED VIOLENCE

In the summer of 2002, 5-year-old Samantha Runnion from Stanton, California, was the fifth little girl to be snatched away in a split second from a place that seemed to be "normally" safe. As the suspect, Alejandro Avila, was being arrested for the sexual assault, murder, and desecration of the tiny body (3 feet 6 inches, 40 pounds), as mourners were still coming to the sheltered courtyard where Samantha had lived, and as arrangements were being made for a huge funeral, news

Table 6.1   Prime-Time Crime Shows That Debuted in Fall 2002

- ABC

  Dragnet (a revival of the classic Jack Webb series from the 1950s and 1960s)

- CBS

  Without a Trace (FBI agents who investigate missing persons)

  CSI: Miami (forensic police investigators; a spin-off from the popular *CSI*, dealing with the same subject in a different city)

  Robbery Homicide Division (law-abiding Los Angeles police)

  Hack (a disgraced Philadelphia cop who becomes a vigilante cab driver)

- FOX

  Fast Lane (two hip cops and lots of gunplay)

- NBC

  Kingpin (a "Soprano"-like protagonist/antagonist Hispanic drug lord)

reports from traumatized Stanton were intercut with titillating promos for *She Spies,* NBC's syndicated clone of *Charlie's Angels,* staring Natasha Henstridge and two gorgeous friends wearing skintight outfits who spend their time karate-kicking and punching the bad guys. At the same time, during the summer TV tour at the Ritz-Carlton in Pasadena, TV "suits" and stars were arriving in limos "to hawk shows exploiting America's morbid fascination with the erotic and psychotic" (Dowd, 2002, p. 13).

Only those without television sets could have any doubts about the fact that violence and sex drive TV ratings day-to-day. Check out the listings of the "new" crime shows introduced during the fall 2002 season (see Table 6.1). As for sex, it is virtually incorporated into every medium. On TV, it resonates across advertisements, sitcoms, serious dramas, entertainment news, talk shows, and, last but not least, reality TV shows, which are certainly more sex-driven than real life has ever been (and that's saying a lot). A sampling of some of the more recent newcomers will have to suffice, as there are far too many programs to include: the pilot of CBS's *Bram and Alice,* a sitcom about a

womanizing New York writer who meets his young, blond daughter, whom he had not previously known, complete with incest jokes; Fox's *Girls Club,* about three sexy female lawyers in San Francisco; and ABC's *8 Simple Rules for Dating My Teenage Daughter,* a sitcom staring John Ritter with two nubile roommates, only this time they are not girl "friends" (*Three's Company*), but his teenage daughters, who flaunt their hot high school romances and thong underwear during "prime time" viewing.

This preoccupation with sex and violence begs the questions: how unique are Americans' fascinations compared with those from other parts of the world? Without any data other than having personally lived and worked as an American in Europe and having traveled and viewed mass media in a few dozen countries, I would suggest that Americans highly overrate sex. Perhaps this state of affairs has something to do with Americans' repressed sexuality compared to, say, that of Europe, where naked bodies (male and female) on public billboards and beaches alike are both more common than they are over here. And, while the United States still leads the world in violent image depictions (see below), there is data to suggest that with globalization, other nations might be playing "catch up." One empirical piece of evidence for this speculation was the acquisition of *The Shield* in 2002 by Britain's Channel 5. After other stations in that nation had acquired the distribution rights to such American series as the highly successful *CSI: Crime Scene Investigation* and the long- running *Law and Order,* Channel 5 picked up the new but critically acclaimed series as "part of a strategy to boost its 'quality' image" in the United Kingdom (Wells, 2002).

The Shield is about Detective Vic Mackey, a leader of a corrupt and violent team of officers in a tough Los Angeles neighborhood. In only one short season, the show was credited with moving an obscure cable channel (FX) to the top of the local TV ratings. The show, based on the activities of the infamous Ramparts Division (see Box 3.8), though likened to *LAPD Blue* and *The Sopranos* by media critics, angered the Los Angeles police department. It also sparked an advertising boycott that resulted in Burger King and MasterCard pulling their advertisements from the series.

The point is, the fascination with and repulsion to, for example, sexual violence is far more universal than is usually acknowledged. Of course, a fascination with either sex or violence, or both, does not necessarily translate into higher or lower rates of sex and violence. Higher rates of fantasies, however, are something else. In any event, the fascination of the United States with violence, if not sex, predates the era of mass communication. This fascination also includes an attraction to guns, mobsters, crime fighters and other violence-oriented actors. As Michael Bellesiles (2000), founding director of Emory's Center for the Study of Violence and author of *Arming America: The Origins of a National Gun Culture,* has written:

> It is not just a small minority of individuals who idolize and even fetishize firearms.

Guns are central to the identity of Americans, to their self-perception as a rugged and violent people, as well as their perception of others. Most of the world associates the United States with firearms, if not as the world's leading maker of guns, then for such global cultural icons as the cowboy, the gangster, the street thug, and the heroic cop.

Although the exported icon of choice has recently become the serial killer, "organized crime" remains the staple of violent films, exemplified by those mini-series or soap operas made especially for TV, as well as the small and big screen features repeatedly shown on cable. Just as the Mafia has always been big business in the underworld, it has always been big business on the television, and before that, at movie box offices. As one TV reviewer writing about the hit series, *The Sopranos,* expressed it: "the mob has always fascinated people and TV got married to getting 'whacked' in order to cash in." (Cutler, 2001 p. 9)

Moreover, in the blurred realities of fiction and non-fiction violence, it seems to make little, if any, difference to the mass consumption of these images, whether the violence is based in social reality or not. Nor does it matter if the violence has actually occurred or not, or if it is real or imaginary, for it to be ingested into the authentic worlds of individual and collective fantasy. The "relationship between the imagined violence and 'real' violence is unclear, contested, negotiable, unstable, and radically unpredictable; and yet, imagined and real violence is not simply a binary formulation. Precisely because we cannot predict what action representations will give rise to, it is impossible to describe the boundary that divides imagined violence from real violence in any detail." (Halberstam, 1993, pp. 187-188)

For example, visit the Web sites of three mainstream television programs reviewed in *Entertainment Weekly* (Hart, 2001): *Murder in Small Town X* (http://www.fox.com/smalltownx), *Autopsy* (http://www.hbo.com/

autop), and *CSI* (http://www.cbs.com/csi). Warning—none of these Web sites are for the particularly squeamish! At the homepage of *Murder in Small Town X*, one reads about a new groundbreaking series that immerses the viewer into a deadly game of murder and suspense: "Follow the unraveling mystery on Fox, then come back here to track suspects, dig up clues and match wits with the killer." Simply click on the cigarette-smoking man to enter the killer's own site, which includes taunting messages and streaming snuff videos shot from the slayer's perspective. Or, at HBO's *Autopsy* Web site, hosted by none other than America's most famous real-life post-mortem examiner, Dr. Michael Baden, one can "go inside a real life murder investigation, examine crime scene photos, collect and analyze evidence and watch fascinating interviews with forensics experts who," for example, had "convicted Delaware's first serial killer" ("Casebook #1, The Corridor Killer"). Finally, at the Web site for the most popular new television show for the 2000-2001 season, CBS's *CSI*, one can access the "computer" belonging to the fictional Crime Scene Investigation boss Gil Grissom, take a dead-serious cram course in forensic science, or easily explore the illustrated glossary of more than 100 technical terms.

The facts are that violent and shocking images abound on the screen, and many people cannot seem to get enough of them. For example, within 30 hours of the debut episode of *Murder in Small Town X*, Fox's Web site had already drawn 3 million page views for this program (Hart, 2001). Whether one is talking about computer games, motion pictures, pro-wrestling stomp fests, or such "adult" cartoon fare as *Celebrity Death Match* or *Beavis and Butthead*, these forms of entertainment seem to have enormous audience appeal.

In a nutshell, cynical and noncynical people alike find these mediated representations of violence to be fun, exciting, engaging, stimulating, and even empowering.

Seldom asked and unanswered questions still remain, however, such as: Why are these horror and criminal lineups so popular? How do the repetitive images of, say, serial killers and their perverse inclinations help to reassure viewers or readers of their sanity at a time when their world seems to be breaking up and traditional signs of their identities seem to be shattering?

In one of the more sophisticated treatments to come from across the Atlantic Ocean, Duclos (1998) argues, among other things, that American culture epitomizes the reincarnation of the ancient Nordic myth or Anglo-Saxon legend of civilization as a self-regulating form of barbarism. He also argues that the circulation of such myths as the "werewolf myth," the "myth of the mad warrior," and the "myth of vampires" in combination with a preoccupation or attraction to uncommon killers (i.e., serial or mass murderers) are not only symbolic of the United States' image of itself as an uncommon society but reflective of its well-known tales in which violence has always had a central role as something at once desired and feared. After surveying and analyzing an impressive list of films and writings on crime and especially serial murderers, Duclos is able to make his case that the representation of on-screen violence in the U.S. media mirrors America's deep-seated belief that society is only a fragile barricade holding at bay the beast latent in us all.

By repetitively showing us both fictional and nonfictional atrocities, "American culture is in fact reminding us that we all wish for the pain and death of others, and that it is a slim borderline that separates the community of 'normal' people who resist this impulse from the blood-thirsty heroes whose acts are a reflection of all people's propensity for evil" (Duclos, 1998, p. 11). Accordingly, "abnormal" people who give in to these impulses should be appropriately reprimanded, and society should take action to build elaborate mechanisms of surveillance and control to protect itself from inevitable wickedness. Finally, within the context of the artificial binary dualities of nature/culture, barbarism/civility, good/evil, and so on and so forth, that are replayed over and over again in mass-mediated forms of American narrative, Duclos is able to reveal how the ideology of extreme individualism without any genuine concern for the collective well-being of all people has become a self-fulfilling prophesy of failure and despair inherent in this kind of one-dimensional thinking.

Thus, Duclos would like to see the United States change direction in its questioning of the cultural relationships between societal violence and mass-mediated violence. Instead of asking whether and how Hollywood and the imaginary violence created by other mass media are to blame for the fictional and non-fictional violence running amok in America, he wants Americans to ask themselves the opposite kinds of questions, such as: What accounts for the large numbers of people living in a fantasy world of violence and disorder who find the mediated triumph of force or aggression over perversity and deviant desires so reassuring? What encourages large audiences, as well as authors, artists, and journalists, to envision violent actions before they happen? For instance,

When Joel Schumacher foreshadows Timothy McVeigh in the lead character in *Falling Down,* is he guilty? When Stephen King imagines a pro-life activist crashing an airplane full of explosives into a pro-choice meeting [in *Insomnia*], should he be accused of inciting the Oklahoma City incident [or World Trade Center destruction]? Of course not. In fact, the censorship rules that certain Senators propose to apply to television and movie violence can be seen as a form of denial and a refusal to accept criticism which maintains that the cult of violence is deep-rooted and widespread, even among the most virtuous. (Duclos, 1998, p. 7)

The confrontation of real (as opposed to fantasized) violence that is based on historical events, in the cinema or other multi-medium, as well as the exploration of the roots of the relationships between non-fictional and fictional violence, has become increasingly rare in mass-mediated forms of entertainment. The number of films, for example, that seriously and meaningfully examine violence occurring in this or any society are hard to find indeed (see Box 6.3). When these mediated efforts do materialize, such as in *Bowling for Columbine* (2002) or *Bloody Sunday* (2002), they make lasting connections with audiences large or small. These two films, virtually free of the exploitation of violence for the sake of titillation, fear, or stimulation, provide political, social, and economic interpretations of violence and nonviolence such that their narrative commentaries are usually challenged by the political status quo and the mainstream media and dismissed as either excessive or illogical. If they are not so dismissed, then the violent events depicted in the films are regarded by the media and politicians as exceptional rather than general cases. Typically, these reconstructions or critiques of the kind of serious analysis of violence and nonviolence found in such films act to absolve the institutional and structural nature of the outbursts of violence dealt with therein, pinning the blame, once again, on the alienated individual rather than the "powers that be."

VIOLENCE AND MEDIA CONTEXT: THE DIRECT AND INDIRECT EFFECTS

Conclusions regarding the mediated representations of aggressive and violent behavior, both sexual and nonsexual, are difficult to draw in the abstract, absent context.

Box 6.3   When Reel Violence Captures Real Violence

Two films from 2002, *Bowling for Columbine* (a Cannes Film Festival winner) and *Bloody Sunday* (featured at the Lincoln Center Film Festival in New York), represent documentary works that capture the complexity of violence and nonviolence. Both films, for very different reasons, are tours de force. Both films are ideological works that present multiple sides of issues in very direct and unbalanced ways. Neither film exploits violence for the sake of violence, yet each uses techniques of cinema vérité; the first incorporating news footage and surveillance video shots of the actual assault at Columbine in combination with a series of interviews with various known and unknown Americans, the second employing hand-held cameras and a Brechtian newsreel technique that invites the audience into the action of murder and mayhem. Both films are also disturbing, if not infuriating, and each is intensely emotional and political. Yet, these two films are quite different; one is presented as a comedy of sorts and the other as a Shakespearian tragedy. One will be a box office hit and go on to be a contemporary classic antiviolence film; the other, with little popular audience other than Irish people worldwide, will quickly fade from repressed obscurity into artistic oblivion.

Bowling for Columbine, written, produced, and directed by Michael Moore, is a provocative and complex examination of violence, culture, and American social structure. Moore's brilliance in delving into the relationships between the layers of interpersonal, institutional, and structural expressions of violence are unmatched by other commentators. It matters little whether you agree with Moore's analysis or not, because either way you are appalled by or caught up in his message. Moore actually raises questions and makes his audience think. He has few answers and does not preach per se. However, in his narrative, he does away with all of the simple explanations of violence offered up by media pundits, politicians, and experts alike. More important, he addresses the repressed histories and the denied social realities of America that envelop its relative propensity for violence, especially lethal violence, in both the individual and the nation-state as a whole.

Moore brings a passion and sensibility to his work that resonates with the little guy or girl; a class consciousness that energizes the popular masses and infuriates the power elites. Certainly, Moore is "over the top" and "in your face" because he realizes that if one is going to tackle such issues as gun violence, foreign policy, health care, community development, paranoia, racism, and more, one had better "bury the message" (as it were) in a barrage of scattered bits of humor. After all, we live in an age in America where *Jackass: The Movie*, a spin-off from a much-maligned MTV series, can become a number-one box office smash. Accordingly, Moore reaches the masses with serious questions about controversial issues vis-à-vis the medium of pop entertainment, incorporating the likes of *South Park*, contemporary arms manufacturers and military installations, classic media footage from eras past, and inserted lessons of history rarely found in traditional texts. In the process, Moore captures an American culture that is as belligerent and callous as it is immune to compromise or compassion.

(Continued)

Box 6.3   (Continued)

By contrast, writer-director Paul Greengrass's magnetic and impassioned melodrama *Bloody Sunday*, a story about the 1972 massacre in Northern Ireland in which British troops shot and killed 13 civil-rights marchers and IRA sympathizers, succeeds with strong and shocking images of violent horror. There are no laughs of any kind in this serious docudrama, which takes the side of the 15,000 Irish Catholic demonstrators who turned out to make a nonviolent statement on their grievances against the Protestant majority in the Ulster Government. Indirectly, Greengrass captures the real-life tragedy of that day, a day that was inevitably taken over by historical circumstances and by the institutional and structural forces of violence.

Greengrass is able to tap into the unconscious movements attached to other timeless civil-rights struggles from around the world. For example, the protagonist in this movie, Ivan Cooper, is a Protestant member of Parliament. His behavior is full of gestures and nuances associated with the likes of Gandhi and the Rev. Dr. Martin Luther King, Jr. Cinematically, the director's work is reminiscent of such classic political–civil-rights films as Costa-Gavras's *Z* and Gillo Pontecorvo's *Battle of Algiers*. All in all, the artistry of Greengrass's work is plain, as he is able to move his audience beyond the bloody bodies of the 13 unarmed civilian marchers to the rush of the blood within the institutionalized hearts and minds of the unprepared British paratroopers who were assigned, that fateful day, to police a situation that had already been established as volatile.

In the end, both *Bowling for Columbine* and *Bloody Sunday* work because they capture the interchange between the politics of violence and the violence of politics. Both films, although very different, are nevertheless able to make the necessary connections between the private and the public domains of violence as they examine the everyday relationships between the interpersonal, institutional, and structural levels of social engagement.

Nevertheless, in the aggregate, the findings from a series of experiments—laboratory and naturalistic—suggest, for example, that a PG-rated film screening rape in a positive light could be more socially detrimental than an X-rated film that does not transport any sexual violence (Malamuth, 1989). In other words, the degree of sexual explicitness may be less relevant than the message conveyed by the portrayals of sexual aggression. "Context is everything."

Perhaps more important, studies of mediated violence or aggression of a sexual or nonsexual nature have been able to differentiate among media consumers. These studies have also been able to examine the effects of media in relation to the reciprocal roles of other contributing factors to violence. As Neil Malamuth (1989) and his colleagues have shown, "no influence works in a vacuum, and media influences are viewed as combining and interacting with a variety of other individual and cultural factors—sometimes counteracting them, sometimes reinforcing them, and at other times, not having much of any effect" (p. 162). Nevertheless, as Brownmiller (1975) suggested some time ago about the relationship between rape and mass media, it makes sense to think in terms of a "cultural climate" and of the effects that

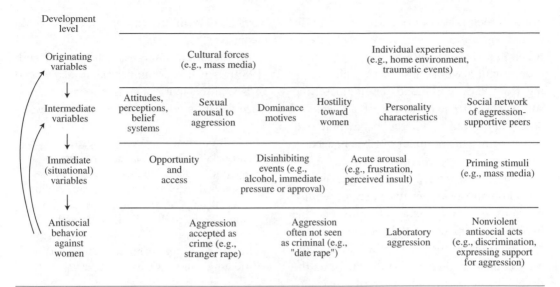

Figure 6.1   Indirect-Effects Model of Mediated Violence

Source: Malamuth, N.M. (1989). Sexually violent media, thought patterns, and antisocial behavior. *Public Communication and Behavior, 2,* 159-204. Reprinted with permission.

do not necessarily produce immediate or direct violence but rather yield harmful and indirect long-term consequences.

In response to their general findings on the problem of violence against women, Malamuth and Briere (1986) constructed an "indirect-effects" model of hypothesized environmental influences on the development of antisocial behavior against women (see Figure 6.1). Malamuth (1989) has succinctly summarized their model as follows:

Individual conditions and the broader social climate are postulated as the originating environmental influences on the individual. The mass media are considered one of the *many* social forces that may, in interaction with a variety of other cultural and individual factors, affect the development of intermediate attributes, such as thought patterns, sexual arousal patterns, motivations, emotions, and personality characteristics. These immediate variables, in complex interactions with each other and with situational circumstances, such as alcohol consumption or acute arousal, may precipitate behaviors ranging from passive

support to actual aggression. In addition to having relatively long-term influences, the mass media may temporarily increase the recall of (or may "prime") antisocial thoughts, or behavioral urges that were previously formed. (pp. 164-164)

As the name implies, the indirect-effects model does not assume some direct or linear cause-effect relationship between violence and any other variables, media included. Rather, this general model assumes a reciprocating system of mutually influencing factors where behavioral outcomes are not overly determined but may vary considerably, both directly and indirectly, especially in relation to the complexity of violence. That is to say, the same exposure to violent media could result in a variety of direct antisocial forms of violence for some people, including those forms that would come to the attention of the law, such as sexual harassment or discrimination against women. For other people, such exposure could result in desires to act that are suppressed and/or redirected in the support of those who do act, vis-à-vis their covert or overt reactions to the sexual aggressions—verbal or physical—of others. Finally, depending on and in combination with a whole host of variables, ranging from early childhood development and socialization to experiences of adolescence and young adulthood, the behavioral outcomes or responses might not be changed or altered in any way, direct or indirect.

More specifically, the indirect effects model on antisocial behavior against women has posited two connected and testable hypotheses which have demonstrated that "(1) exposure to some sexually violent media may contribute in some individuals to the development of thought patterns that support aggression against women, and (2) such patterns, in combination with other influences and circumstances, may contribute to sexually violent acts in some cases and to other antisocial, but not necessarily violent, responses in others" (Malamuth, 1989, p. 165). Yet, many others will have no reactions whatsoever, violent or otherwise, and still others will become defensive against antisocial actions of a violent or nonviolent nature. The point is that the human experiences of the audience and the contexts of the sexually violent media content are interacting in a real-world sense.

For a concrete example related to allegedly nonsexual aggression, think of media depictions of violent vigilantes as heroes or antiheroes. Films like the *Death Wish* series or *Falling Down* may certainly contribute to a cultural climate conducive to or condoning similar behavior in real-world settings. Of course, the story lines of these narratives can also set up and frame vigilantes as antiheroes. Once again, what people or audiences bring to these films or to any media interaction must also be entered into the equation of what they take away. The degree and kinds of violence depicted are almost beside the point. What is key is the contextualization and the portrayal of the particular form or expression of violence mediated.

In the final analysis, what Malamuth (1989) concluded about mass media and antisocial behavior against women is also true of mass media and violence in general:

> As with many behaviors, it is apparent that antisocial behavior against women is a function of many interacting causal factors. It is very difficult to gauge the relative influence, if any, of media exposure alone. However, by itself, it is likely to exert only a small influence, if any. But, this may be true, to some degree, for all potentially contributing causes. Only in interaction with other factors might they have substantial influences. (p. 198)

Televised Violence

Before discussing the effects of televised violence, there are at least two other sets of factors that should be considered. First, there are factors related to the kinds and frequencies of violence that audiences are exposed to. Cross-cultural or comparative studies of televised violence reveal both similarities and differences among nations. For example, the United States, Japan, the United Kingdom, and Spain have each devoted more time to interpersonal than to property, institutional, or structural violence. Differences between three of these countries include, for example, the range or variation in the number of violent acts per hour of programming: 18.5, 7.0, and 1.7, respectively in the United States, Japan, and the United Kingdom (Sutil, Esteban, & Takeuchi, 1995).

Second, there are factors associated with what audiences value or find entertaining. For example, a study of Dutch and U.S. children 6 to 11 years old found that children of both nations were very much alike in what they valued. In both countries, the most favored programs were those that were comprehensible and action oriented, followed by humor, interestingness, and innocuousness. The least favored programs were those given to realism, violence, and romance. Both the Dutch and U.S. boys gave more value to action and violence than did the girls of both countries. Romance had a similar lack of appeal for girls and boys alike in the two nations (Valkenburg & Janssen, 1999).

Other studies of youthful attitudes, violence, television viewing, and aggressive behavior have found that (1) those adolescent boys and girls between 11 and 16 years old who watched an average of about 25% more television daily than their peers had less negative attitudes toward violence, and they possessed a higher sense of personal risk and suspicion and were more likely to perceive the world as a scary place (Hough & Erwin, 1997; Singer, Singer, & Rapacynski, 1984); (2) as children progress from kindergarten through elementary school they are less frightened by fictional representations of violence and more frightened by news representations of violence, especially stranger violence (Cantor & Nathanson, 1996); and (3) violent programming may influence negatively those individuals who are already violence prone, or some children during vulnerable periods in their development, but that violent content per se has no significant effect on most young or adolescent viewers (Palermo, 1995).

More generally, with respect to both short-term and long-term consequences, there have been a variety of laboratory and naturalistic studies conducted on the effects of televised violence on real violence. These studies of mediated violence have ranged from broad investigations to very specific examinations, such as those involving homicides and suicides. The inconsistencies of the research findings on these televised and other forms of mediated violence make it difficult to draw any firm conclusions. The majority of scholars who have reviewed the relationships between mediated violence and real violence believe there is some kind of effect (Centerwall, 1989; Cook, Kendzierski, & Thomas, 1983). However, other scholars disagree and believe that the effects of televised violence on real violence have not been demonstrated (Freedman, 1984; McGuire, 1986). As Richard Felson (1996) has concluded, "the reason that media effects are not consistently observed is probably because they are weak and affect only a small percentage of viewers" (p. 123).

At the same time, Felson reasons that weak effects of mediated violence may still have some practical, if not significant, importance in large populations, contributing to some of the deaths and injuries. Despite this small reality, most violent crime rates mirror changes in crime rates generally. What is more, those folks who tend to engage in criminal violence also engage in other types of antisocial behavior, suggesting that there are factors other than socialization and mediation involved. And even though it seems reasonable that some people are more susceptible to media influence than others, the failure to find individual difference factors that condition the effects of media exposure on aggressive behavior contributes to further skepticism about media effects. Finally, as Felson (1996) cautiously noted,

> It is not clear what lesson the media teaches about the legitimacy of violence, or the likelihood of punishment. To some extent that message is redundant with lessons learned from other sources of influence. The message is probably ambiguous and is likely to have different effects on different viewers. Young children may imitate illegitimate violence, if they do not understand the message, but their imitative behavior may have trivial consequences. Out of the millions of viewers, there must be some with highly idiosyncratic interpretations of television content who intertwine the fantasy with their own lives, and as a result have an increased probability of engaging in violent behavior. (p. 124)

A very comprehensive review and analysis of the real-world impact of mass-mediated stories on suicides and homicides was carried out by David Phillips in the mid-1980s. He examined both media-based and alternative explanations in relation to incidents of suicide, including vehicle fatalities and plane crashes as well as homicides. Phillips (1986) presents 16 findings that were both statistically significant and persisted after he corrected for the influence of extraneous variables:

1. United States monthly suicides (1946-1968) increase significantly just after publicized suicide stories. This finding has been replicated with daily United States suicide data (1972-1976).

2. The greater the publicity devoted to the suicide story, the greater the rise in United States suicides thereafter.

3. The rise is greatest in those geographic areas where the suicide story is most heavily publicized.

4. California motor vehicle fatalities increase significantly (by 31%) just after a publicized suicide story. This finding has been replicated with Detroit data (increase in fatalities, 35%). In both data sets, motor vehicle fatalities rise most steeply on the third day after the publicized suicide.

5. Single-vehicle fatalities increase more than other types of fatality.

6. The driver in these single-vehicle crashes is usually similar to the person described in the suicide story (but the passengers are not).

7. The greater the publicity devoted to the suicide story, the greater the rise in motor vehicle fatalities.

8. The rise in motor vehicle fatalities occurs mainly in the geographic regions where the suicide story is publicized.

9. Automobile crashes occurring after suicide stories are often lethal, as one would expect if these crashes have a suicidal component.

10. United States private plane crashes increase significantly just after publicized murder-suicide stories. The increase is strongest on the third day after the story appears.

11. The more publicity devoted to these stories, the greater the increase in plane crashes.

12. The increase in plane crashes is particularly large in those states in which the murder-suicide story is publicized.

13. U.S. homicide did not increase significantly following the John F. Kennedy assassination or the Speck and Whitman murder stories.

14. However, United States homicides (1973-1978) did increase significantly just after heavyweight championship prizefights. The increase was strongest on the third day following the fight.

15. Homicides rose particularly strongly after more heavily publicized prizefights.

16. There was a strong, significant relationship between the characteristics of the losing boxer and the characteristics of those killed during the experimental period. (Phillips, 1986, pp. 295-296)[1]

Sexually Violent Media

Before examining the effects, I need to mention some basic similarities and differences between sexual and nonsexual mediated violence, as well as issues about availability and frequency of exposure. For example, when it comes to sexually aggressive depictions of violence, males are exclusively acting against females (Smith, 1976a, 1976b; Yang, 1987). When it comes to "nonsexual" violence, both the perpetrators and victims are males (Gerber, 1972;

Slocum, 2001). Moreover, when sexual violence is portrayed, "there is frequently the suggestion that, despite initial resistance, the victim secretly desired the abusive treatment and eventually derived pleasure from it" (Malamuth, 1989, p. 167). Not only is sexual violence often presented without negative consequences for either victim or perpetrator, but in the process, subtle and not-so-subtle excuses or justifications are generated for aggressive behaviors that would otherwise be unacceptable or unthinkable. As Smith (1976a, 1976b) found in his survey of rapists in "adult" books, fewer than 3% suffered negative consequences. Rape victims were also seldom shown having regrets about having been raped.

By contrast, perpetrators of nonsexual violence not only experience consequences for their aggressive behavior, they may suffer from the violence the same as their victims. Whether or not their victims suffer, these victims of nonsexual aggression are almost always outraged by their experiences. In addition, they are intent not only on punishing their aggressors but in avoiding future victimization or interaction with their attackers. Another distinction between sexual and nonsexual violence involves the element of sexual arousal.

Regardless of whether sexual violence is portrayed negatively or positively at the cognitive level, it may, in either case, elicit sexual arousal because of the explicitness of the representation (of rape, for example). In short, people may find the images and behavior immoral, but they may nonetheless be "turned on." This arousal could prove to have harmful or beneficial effects depending on how this energy is brought to fruition. In one sense, sexually violent pictures, by associating physical pleasure with violence, might result in subliminal conditioning and cognitive changes in the consumer. In turn, these changes could help to provide a rationale for

the consumer's sexual aggression or victimization through the minimization of its seriousness or consequences for others. Or, these changes could motivate or stimulate nonviolent sex and sexuality.

There is yet another finer distinction that needs to be made between explicit and non-explicit sexually violent material. Most but not all research that has been conducted on media stimuli has focused on the former rather than the latter. As was pointed out earlier in the chapter, the content and context are even more important than the explicitness of the sexual violence. Availability of such explicit and nonexplicit sexual violence varies considerably from medium to medium. For example, content analyses of sexual explicitness range from a high of around 30% for "adult" books, 10% to 15% for "adult" movies, and some 5% for "soft-core" magazines (Smith, 1976a, 1976b; Yang, 1987).

When it came to analyzing daytime "soap operas," content analyses were mixed on their findings. Sexual aggression was the second most common form of sexual activity depicted. Most of these, however, were implied rather than actually portrayed. Sexual aggression, according to one study, found that references to rape occurred about once in every 11 hours of broadcasting, compared to references of consenting sexual intercourse, which occurred every 45 minutes (Greenberg & D'Alessio, 1985). In a study of MTV in the early 1980s (Baxter, DeRiemer, Landini, Leslie, & Singletary, 1985), it was found that portrayals of violence, sex, and sexuality were very available. When it came to the music videos, the violence and sexuality were rarely fused together; sadomasochism and sexual bondage occurred 5% and 2%, respectively. Another study on exposure to gender-stereotyped music video imagery on MTV (Kalof, 1999) found that, although men scored higher than women on each of the sexual attitude subscales, indicating men's greater endorsement of adversarial sexual beliefs, gender-role stereotyping, and rape myths, women had slightly higher scores than men on the acceptance of interpersonal violence subscale.

In terms of exposure, limited research as far back as the 1980s revealed that more than one third of youths between 12 and 17 years old reported viewing sexually explicit films at least once a month (Roth, 1985). In his study, Roth also found that among undergraduate males, 36% reported viewing sexually violent pornography (i.e., depicting either a male raping a woman or a man forcing a woman to perform a sexual act against her will) at least once during the past year, and 13% more than twice. In addition, this study suggested that as many as 45% of children acquire their first knowledge of sexual life "from viewing films in which sexual conduct is inextricably entwined with violence, hatred, coercion and the humiliation of women in particular" (Roth, 1985, p. 3).

The question becomes, of course, Does sexual violence stimulate arousal in its audiences? The research on males suggests that about 30% of men are aroused by sexual violence, and that for 70% of men, the presence of aggression inhibits sexual arousal. But these outcomes were affected by whether the portrayals of sexual aggression were negative or positive. When women were portrayed as abhorring the sexual assault, there was little sexual arousal from most consumers. However, when victims were portrayed as becoming involuntarily aroused sexually, viewers' sexual arousal from observing portrayals of rape was as high, and even tended to be higher (but not significantly), than arousal from observation of depictions of consensual sexual activity (Malamuth, 1989). Once again, context seems to be more important than the actual images and representations of sexual

violence per se. As Malamuth (1989) has concluded, data on direct media effects of sexual violence on real violence are not supportive.

On the other hand, data on the indirect media effects of sexual violence on real violence, along with other influencing factors including family background, social class, educational attainment, war experience, peer behavior, and personal attitudes toward sexual aggression, appear to demonstrate "a synergistic process whereby the combined action of several variables yielded considerably higher levels of sexual aggression than would be expected by the combination of them" (Malamuth, 1989, p. 191). More specifically, Malamuth's findings suggested that the most important factor related to sexual aggression was having a peer culture (e.g., fraternities, sport clubs) of sexually supportive and aggressive friends (see also DeKeseredy & Schwartz, 1998), followed by personal attitudes legitimating such behavior, and then military service (at the time of Malamuth's study, this was associated with Vietnam War veterans).

Audience Reception of Mediated Violence

Although most of us are consumers rather than producers of mediated violence, audiences are not merely passive receptors of transmitted messages, images, and narratives (Barak, 1988; Ferguson, 1998; Potter & Kappeler, 1998). Audiences rely on other experiences and interactions as well as mediated ones to reinforce their individual and collective desires and fears. Audiences have also demonstrated some ability to resist the power of media representations and even to deconstruct various versions of violent reality, such as during the Vietnam War. More recently, however, in the Gulf War of the early 1990s, there was very limited coverage, and in Afghanistan (2001-2002), there was virtually a blackout on what American viewers could see, reducing the chances of their resisting the "manufactured consensus" favoring violence, especially under the banner of the "new war on terrorism."

More generally, examinations of mediated stories on crime, law enforcement, and violence, especially in the news, are perceived and interpreted differently by age, gender, class, and racial or ethnic social experiences (Barak, 1999; Gray, 1999; McPhail, 1999; Valdivia, 1999; Young, 1996). In ultramodernity, there is often confusion as well as conflation of semblance and substance, and these have marked viewers' experiences of violence not only with literal truths of the various images consumed, but with allegorical truths, with truths that speak to the psychoanalytically derived pleasure of reading about or viewing serial homicide, and with the "unspoken" truths of the Others or the marginal. Consequently, groups tend to read different things into the same messages and images and hence take away different interpretations from essentially the same representations. For example, as this book goes to press, John Allen Muhammad and John Lee Malvo have just been arrested and have not yet been tried for the sniper killings of fall 2002—we can only speculate about the forthcoming mediated portrayals, representations, and interpretations of these homicides to and of different audiences.

In one of the more sophisticated studies of "audience effects" of fear of crime and its relationship to news coverage, Chiricos, Eschhol, and Gertz (1997) surveyed 2,092 adults in Tallahassee, Florida, at the height of a media-driven "panic" about violent crime in 1994. The findings of this study both confirmed other findings and introduced new ones. In terms of replication, the frequency of listening to radio news and watching television news was significantly related to fear; reading newspapers and newsmagazines, even about highly publicized violent acts, was unrelated to fear. When the audiences were disaggregated by gender, race, and other attributes, fear from watching televised news was only related significantly to white females between the ages of 30 and 54. The authors believe that the best explanation for the concentration of media effects among white women had to do with an affinity of these audience members with the victims most often represented on television news.

Another study of "A Serendipitous Finding of a News Media History Effect" by Ray Surette (1995) revealed the interactive nature and differential impact of a particular news story of a police shooting, wherein the officer's ethnicity became a central issue, on Hispanics and non-Hispanic police recruits during their pre- and post-training at the academy. It also revealed how the similarities of police academy experiences narrowed their differences in perception, regardless of ethnicity. For example, the attitudes of both Hispanics and non-Hispanics toward the news media became more cynical, skeptical, and less believable after their study at the academy. Such study also significantly reduced their trust in people, increased their concerns about crime, and weakened their support for civil liberties. These studies and others reveal the importance of social experiences in the reception of audiences and in their interpretations of what they are consuming. Finally, these sets of relations demonstrate the reciprocal interactions between reception and interpretation.

MASS MEDIA: PRODUCTION, DISTORTION, AND CONSUMPTION

Whereas "the media are frequently pointed to as culprits in fostering a climate of violence, little effort is made to determine what exactly the media are, the political and economic interests they represent, and the ideological assumptions they perpetuate" (Sharrett, 1999, p. 10). It is not only that most public discussions about power and the influence of mass communications ignore the political and economic interests of the media; these discussions about "the media" assault on all of us remain essentially divorced from the concept of the media's primary relationship with the development of advanced capitalism. To put it succinctly, the media, in an age of global capitalism, with its intensification of profits and its penetration into all areas of public, private, and cultural space, increasingly become little more than advertising venues for the stimulation of mass consumption. In effect, the aftermath of 9/11 became, among other things, a marketing tool used to urge consumers to spend, spend, spend rather than think, think, think. Thus, it makes little difference if the media is perceived to be biased to the political "left" or "right" because both sides not only ascribe to, but for their very existence they are dependent on, the dominant ideologies of free enterprise and extreme individualism. This is not to deny the importance of the recent emergence of a National Entertainment State (NES) or of the ownership and monopolization of the distribution of newspapers, books, magazines, films, radio, video, television, software, and the Internet, at home and abroad. Among the mega–corporate conglomerates, there are such media fiefdoms as General Electric (GE), Disney/Cap Cities (DCC), Westinghouse, and AOL/Time Warner.

For example, in addition to its interests in transportation, turbines, electrical equipment, motors, communications, plastics, lighting, appliances, retail, medical services, music, financing, insurance, and software, GE owns cable and network television stations, including NBC. DCC, in addition to its interests in multimedia, home video, book publishing, films, magazines, retail, athletic franchises, newspapers, theme parks and resorts, insurance, and oil, owns radio, cable, and television stations, including ABC. In addition to its interests in communications and information, insurance, financing, banking, managing, electricity, nuclear power, and refrigeration, Westinghouse owns radio, cable, and television stations, including CBS. And AOL/Time Warner, in addition to its interests in liquor, electric utilities, coal, software, the Internet, films, book publishing, magazines, multimedia, entertainment and resorts, athletic franchises, retail, television programming, and home video, owns Turner Broadcasting and its assorted interests, including CNN, TNT, and TBS.

In terms of the production, consumption, and circulation of mass culture, both the intensification of the "bottom line" across all of these shared economic interests and the emergence of "infotainment," or the triumph of entertainment over "pure" news as exemplified by such television news shows as ABC's *20/20*, CBS's *60 Minutes,* and NBC's *Dateline,* tend to reproduce a homogenization of images, texts, and narratives that shape and influence our collective dreams and nightmares. This is accomplished essentially as the political and news analyst, Walter Lippmann, argued a half century ago, through the formal and informal relations that limit public discourse and manufacture mass consent. In short, the commodification of the NES and its pursuit of advertising dollars act as buffers, if not censors, on our cultural understandings of "social reality." As a "user friendly" Big Brother, the NES's mass communication selectively plays to the attractions, desires, fears, and repulsions of its audiences' preoccupations and fascinations, including those of its own creative artists and "talking heads," involving mostly interpersonal forms of violence, to the exclusion, omission, downplaying, or dismissal of institutional and structural forms of violence.

The rise of the NES, or of the huge commercial media empires, has also spelled doom for those efforts aimed at establishing publicly controlled broadcasting stations and networks. One outcome of the privatization of the public media has been the nearly complete integration of the mass-consuming audience into the bourgeois value system (Smythe, 1981). Another outcome has been that the multiple-sided nature of discourse has increasingly become a popularized two-sided discussion of the same coin. In short, as the transnational interests of capital that lie elsewhere than in the nurturing of pluralistic discourse have blossomed, there has been an atrophy of or a significant reduction in the ratio of public service programs to private-time programming (Aufderheide, 1987).

In his instructional video *Advertising and the End of the World,* Sut Jhally (1997), professor of communications, demonstrates the critical nature or importance of advertising's contradictory relations with the survival of both advanced capitalism and the welfare and future of all of humanity. In this fascinating video, Jhally provides both a tour de force and a powerful application of "the medium is the message," as he dissects and deconstructs the role of advertising as the indispensable and ever-expanding force necessary for the mass consumption of accumulated commodities. The time, energy, and money that goes into contemporary advertising in the United States has become an enormous empire that is virtually colonizing American culture in the process.

For example, in 1980, the average American was exposed to 1,500 commercial images daily. By 1996, that figure had risen to 3,600 commercial images. In the same year, the advertising industry spent $175 billion to sell us products. No longer confined to billboards, radio, and TV, commercials are literally everywhere. As their numbers over the past quarter of a century have increased exponentially, they have begun to literally eat up everything in their path in search of "free" space. Films, sports, schools, and the Internet—each and every one of these institutions, and others, have become an advertising medium. In the process, advertisements have become integrated into all spheres of public and private life.

In the traditional arenas of mediated advertising, revenue breakdowns are as follows: TV and radio, 100%; magazines, 50%; and newspapers, 80% (Jhally, 1997). However, in an era of global capital, advertising is more important than competition and media revenues per se. Otherwise, how does one explain, in an age of multinational conglomeration and shrinking competition, the expansion of both advertising and expenditures on advertising? In the mid-1990s, for example, the cost of making a 30-second TV commercial for prime-time showing was $264,000, compared to a cost of $236,000 for 30 seconds of making the film *Jurassic Park* (Jhally, 1997). Generally, a lot more money is spent on television advertising than on television programming.

As Jhally has demonstrated, these spending realities are, in part, a product of the fact that advertising today is primarily about selling a cultural way of living, thinking, and identifying. These expenditures also reflect, in part, the fact that advertising has become an adjunct of production, engaging in slick narratives of individual consumption. Consistently, the same kinds of images and stories portraying the "good life" (of material and narcissistic affluence) and the same, limited sets of social and political ideas that ignore collective responsibility are one-dimensionally promoted. Moreover, because of the ever-expanding number of commercial images being marketed or because of the growing "noise and clutter" of mass-mediated advertising, promos must increasingly connect with their audiences in emotive rather than in cognitive ways.

The best way for advertising to connect emotionally with consumers has always been through the bodies, senses, and imaginations of its audience. It's not news that sex is used to sell, for instance (if not necessarily), all kinds of products, but to the chagrin of advertising executives, sexual images often disassociate the viewer from the pitched product (Jhally, 1997). Today, however, to be seen or noticed, sex still represents the best approach. Increasingly, though, as the advertising ingestion builds up, the emotional connections being used, sexual or otherwise, must be "over the top"; they must smack consumers in their emotional "faces." Again, Jhally (1997) has pointed out that advertising has become a virtual fantasy factory, and ads have become the creators of illusions. In other words, advertising is not about the real world; ads do not mirror how people act, but what they dream. Ads tap into our emotions and repackage them into desires that can be satisfied through the consumption of things. This was certainly the case with Victoria's Secret's advertising of its "very sexy" collection of lingerie, introduced in fall 2002 and marketed in its special Christmas edition catalog for that year and in its primetime fashion show that aired on CBS November 20th. In a market society, then, the key to happiness, success, love, friends, and so on is the acquisition of valuable commodities, whether one is talking about a new BMW or "reindeer thong" underwear. Finally, advertising plays with our desires and our fears, as both of these become translated over and over into dreams of delight or nightmares of fright.

Since the invention of advertising a little over a century ago, the industry has been transformed away from selling the content (or value) of a product to selling the content of a "lifestyle" that can allegedly be obtained through the acquisition of more and more goods and services. Beyond appealing to the egocentric needs and feelings of isolated and alienated individuals, advertising narratives also perform ideological functions as they help to define people and shape society and its future. With respect to each of these functions, capitalist advertising narratives repeatedly convey to us that we are all a bunch of unrelated individuals rather than members of some kind of social order. Thus, social values, interests, and concerns become subordinate to matters of egotistical growth and self-satisfaction. In the process, collective needs or social responsibilities such as the quality of ecosystems, the growing scarcity of natural resources, or domestic and world homelessness, for example, are all pushed to the margins, if not totally off the "monitoring" screens, of our Dow Jones–dominated society.

Violent Content and Its Distortions

The "bread and butter" ideologies of extreme individualism that drive contemporary advertising are also reinforced by the mass-mediated and distorted representations of violence and society. These misrepresentations owe their roots to several things, including an often moralistic conflation of the erotic with violence, dating at least as far back as complaints about the "pornography of violence" associated with the repetitive images of the political assassinations of the Kennedys, Martin Luther King, Jr., and Malcolm X in the 1960s. Arthur Schlesinger (1968), in his delimited liberal public discourse, equated the sexual image with sin, and the violent image as a blemish on the American character. The problem, he argued, was the availability and easy access to guns, not the manufacturing, advocacy, and cultural usage of these weapons. Images of lone violent acts and of serial killers in particular also serve the politics of scapegoating and the demonization of these semihuman "monsters" as some kind of excrescence of society's underbelly:

Perhaps the fetish status of the criminal psychopath . . . is about recognizing the serial killer/mass murderer not as social rebel or folk hero (as often suggested in gore film fanzines of the last two decades) but as the most genuine representative of American life. If [Charles] Manson was the "dark side of Aquarius" [in the 1960s], he was also, as he argued with fractured eloquence, a pure product of America that America needs simultaneously to destroy through propitiatory ritual, and, as if out of guilty conscience, make sacrosanct. (Sharrett, 1999, p. 13)

In the fictional (e.g., television soaps, films) and nonfictional (e.g., news, documentaries) arenas alike, representations of "good" and "evil," "nonviolent" and "violent," "control" and "out of control" usually distort the pictures and images that consumers use to imagine the realities of crime and punishment (Surette, 1993, 1994). For example, when it comes to "violence," there is generally an exaggeration in the proportion of interpersonal violence depicted compared to that of institutional or structural violence. Violence may occur in the home, but it typically occurs in the street, and rarely in boardrooms or executive suites. In the process, myths and stereotypes of various kinds of violent "offenders" and "nonoffenders" are projected onto the screens and into our heads.

Concerning news gathering and reporting on violence, the products are often the result of "procedures not to know" (Fishman, 1978; Kasinsky, 1994). When it comes to "serious" stories on violent crime, for example, selective information provided by law enforcement and politicians serves a gatekeeping function in the social construction of violence. By interacting with and relying almost exclusively on "official" sources, news organizations invoke and reproduce prevailing views of "serious violence" (Barak, 1994; Ericson, Baranek, & Chan, 1987). The point is that out of a glut of violent stories, those that are selected and played over and over

again, literally or figuratively, are highly reflective of particular versions of social reality, violent and nonviolent.

One-dimensional constructions of violence are contributed to by news stories that, for example, decry the mugging of elderly women, but do not include a description of the same elderly women "who may be surviving in a cold room, undernourished and frail, because a corporation deprived [them] of [their] pension" (Claire Culhane, quoted in Burtch, 1986, p. 141). In other words, one form of violence is visible and condemned; the other form is invisible and ignored. Similarly, Stuart Hills (1987), in his examination of *Corporate Violence: Injury and Death for Profit,* called attention to the serious lack of news coverage on this kind of behavior and for the need to "heighten awareness of the vast scope of serious harm caused by the illegal acts of 'respectable' business executives who impersonally kill and maim many more Americans than street muggers and assailants" do (p. vii).

Mediated messages may, in fact, relay different stories and narratives, especially in relation to gender and less so in terms of race, ethnicity, and class (Barak, Flavin, & Leighton, 2001). In terms of "color," fictional accounts on television or in the movies are fairly undistorted, and representative, for example, of the official rates of violent criminal activity. In terms of televised news coverage and tabloid shows of mysteries, crimes, and cops, a distortion of violence and violent acts appears to the detriment of African American males, illegal aliens from Mexico, and working-class girls from broken homes. It is not the 16-year-old boy and girl from next door, a college student that one is dating, or a corporate executive that society needs to worry about. Instead, the images of the former Others, as portrayed on such shows as *COPS,* reinforce stereotypes that violent people, particularly "criminals," are not like the rest of us:

They are a strange and dangerous breed driven to crime [especially violent] not because of poverty or injustice, but because they suffer from biological or psychological flaws. Consequently, politicians [along with mediated violence] have no difficulty selling the idea of an increasingly punitive criminal justice system with fewer constitutional restraints to keep neighborhoods safe from the demonic "Other" we have constructed as criminal. (Kooistra, Mahoney, & Westervelt, 2000)

Similarly, Romer, Jamieson, and de Coteau (1998) found, based on an examination of three stations in Philadelphia and an analysis of homicide rates, that local television news coverage engaged in a discourse of "ethnic blame" that was independent of realistic group conflict. Specifically, they found that persons of color were heavily represented in stories about crimes of violence, and that within those stories, they were more likely to be presented as perpetrators rather than as victims or persons reacting to or suffering from violence. In contrast, not only were white persons overrepresented as victims of violence, people of color were overrepresented as perpetrators against white persons.

Gender, however, works altogether differently in its portrayals and resolutions, especially in terms of fictional accounts of violence. Filmmaking is particularly revealing here. As Frus (2001) has argued in "Documenting Domestic Violence in American Films," because "Hollywood films are expert at providing illusion of reality, no matter how fantastic the story, they are an important source of our mythology about family violence" (p. 227). What she documents, and what other analyses of the portrayal of women in American cinema have shown, is that, for the most part, this depiction still communicates eight myths about domestic violence:

- Beatings leave no permanent damage, and there are no consequences.
- Batterers are not like us—they're mobsters, or immigrants, or lower class.
- Women enjoy rough sex and secretly want to be raped.
- Women who are battered are asking for it.
- Women as batterers are as abusive as male batterers.
- Ordinary men don't batter or abuse mates and children.
- Women can stop the abuse by leaving the batterer.
- Women who successfully escape their batterer do it all by themselves.

Moreover, as Frus and other film scholars have argued, by including action, thriller, and suspense genres, it can be shown that films, through their constant depiction of misogyny and violence against women, contribute to a cultural context that has, until very recently and with the exception of the new female adventure-warrior heroines, encouraged the subjugation and battering of women.

Perhaps no group in recent memory was more maligned by media stereotypes than were African American females during the height of the war against "welfare queens" and mothers giving birth to crack-addicted babies in the late 1980s and early 1990s. Whether discussing primetime and local news stories or the more full-blown entertainment versions viewed from shows like *60 Minutes, Dateline, Nightline,* and so on, portrayals zoomed forth of African American women trading sex for crack, rather than of middle-class white women snorting the more expensive powder cocaine. While the former group of women became appropriate targets for criminal prosecution and lock-up, the latter escaped negative scrutiny by having access to medical personnel and the confines of private detoxification facilities (Humphries, 1999).

Finally, when stories of upper class violence reflective of economic and political arrangements are occasionally broached, they are done so in a comparatively subdued fashion, so that these violent actions are viewed as less threatening than those actions associated with lower class violence. In any event, whether portraying interpersonal, white-collar, or corporate violence, mass-mediated representations of the "causes" of these actions are rarely, if ever, located within social relations or cultural productions. As for the morals of these news stories, they are almost always dissociated from or free of any communications on the organizational, institutional, or structural nature of the conditions underlying these violent encounters. Inevitably, the narratives are about the need to rationalize the use of force to contain violently alienated and isolated individuals who have gone "mad," "crazy," or "insane."

In the mediums of films and literature specifically, violence is often put to use, through shifting mythic and ideological imperatives, in the service of constructing an audience consciousness and a worldview sympathetic with the political and economic assumptions of extreme individualism and free enterprise. Implicitly, this is not about artistic conspiracies or conscious efforts to politically manufacture consensus. This is about reflexivity, reification, and reproduction, and it is derived from a changing and integrating political economy and collective unconscious.

Violence and Cinema in Postmodernism

Cinema review in the contemporary period examines mediated violence from the points of view of both historical materialism and psychoanalysis. These examinations focus on the primacy and valorization of bloodletting within existing representational practices. At least two themes of postmodern representation have emerged from these types of analysis: First, that within the current narrative, a flattening of affect has occurred within the presentation and acceptance of violent imagery; second, that the contextualization of these images is closely associated with the legacies of patriarchy, rugged individualism, and laissez-faire capitalism. For example, Annalee Newitz (1999) has provided a distinct economic strategy in her analysis of the serial killer cinema in general and in *Henry: Portrait of a Serial Killer* (1990) in particular. She argues that the "body count" of this cinema is "a caustic rebuke to an atomized society of consumption in which cravings are constructed so as never to be fulfilled" (Quoted in Sharrett, 1999, p. 14). The question posed by Newitz (1999) is: "What exactly is it about the narratives of serial killers which makes them so seductive, particularly when their seductiveness is so easily and quickly criticized?" (p. 56). She answers by suggesting that "the serial killer—in both allegory and reality— acts out the enraged confusion with which Americans have come to regard their postwar economic and social productivity" (p. 56). Likewise, Jhally (1997) has responded in kind that Americans' confusion and unsatisfied cravings are byproducts of the material dream pushed by the advertising industry. He has underscored that even if the American dream could be realized worldwide, it is devoid of those social amenities that make people truly happy, such as autonomy, control, positive self-esteem, warm families, leisure time, romance and love, and close and meaningful friends. One of the more "far out" postmodern analyses of the relationship between mediated violence and television and films has been Ilsa Bick's examination of *The X-Files*.

Bick suggests (Sharrett, 1999) that this show's immense popularity had to do with some kind of profound collective trauma, about which the public seems to be in a state of denial. Obliquely, *The X-Files* took on such issues as the death of the family, the Holocaust, political and serial murder, child abuse, and sexual violence, especially against the female body. The show's continuing saga unfolded by way of an insistent repression of history and the denial of an endemic psychological crisis. Bick argues that the series "is very much in tune with postmodernity's disingenuousness in replacing historical consciousness with fractal, subjectivist, hallucinatory, conspiratorial fictions that seem to pass for a new skepticism, one that obtains legitimacy from the sophomoric postmodernist acknowledgment of the slipperiness of truth" (Sharrett, 1999, p. 17).

Perhaps no book or film (in this case both) has captured the dilemma of the postmodern imagination and mediated violence better than Bret Easton Ellis' twisted satire on serial murder, *American Psycho*. This best-selling novel was first published in 1991, and in 1999 it was released as a semisuccessful film. Despite the book's controversial reception, the film has become a cult classic as a video rental and can often be seen on cable television. In a *New Times* piece that was published in a variety of alternative weeklies almost a decade after the book's release, Ellis made this observation: "it's weird that *American Psycho* in many ways is mainstream now . . . we're long past the point of people believing this book was really written by the devil" (Quoted in Lippman, 2000, p. B4). That doesn't mean that there are not more than a few persons who wish that the devil had been the author.

In the related violence genre of "gore culture," it has been argued that the media frenzy around the trial of Jeffrey Dahmer functioned as a "vicarious thrill and religious ritual for the spectator-consumer, but in ways that showed the inefficacy of cathartic sacrificial ritual in postmodern society" (Sharrett, 1999, p. 14). Similarly, it has been argued that the way the apocalyptic rhetoric worked in such films as *Seven, Kalifornia,*

and *Natural Born Killers* was to reinforce a religious-mystical view of violence and social disintegration. Neither in the case of trial footage nor in films are viewers' psyches ever really reassured or put at ease.

In the related contexts of gender construction and family interaction, and in terms of the implementation of violent ideological narratives, the conventional use of "female" genres like the soaps or melodrama assists the action thrillers to reconcile the hyperviolence of Arnold Schwarzenegger-style blockbusters with the "family values" grounded in a neoconservative and patriarchal culture. For example, in "Mutilating Mel: Martyrdom and Masculinity in *Braveheart*" (Luhr, 1999), several of Gibson's pictures are criticized for resurrecting the old-fashioned, charismatic, supremely competent epic hero in narratives that depict vicious homophobia, antifeminism, and hysterical castration anxiety.

With respect to violence in relation to issues of social control and the new technology, the postmodern media apparatus functions as a virtual kind of "policing" and "imprisoning." Here, cultural analysis and visual theory together describe how the technical depictions of violent images have changed over the last quarter of a century, especially as these were related to the recent transformations in consciousness, representational practice, and ideological demand. In addition, mediated versions of violence can only become public when the "separate worlds of professional and lay person, of controller and controlled, are brought into relation with one another and appear, for a time at least, to occupy the same space" (Hall, Critcher, Jefferson, Clarke, & Roberts, 1978, p. 145).

To put it succinctly, mass media provides the means by which the public space is created, and it is in this space where the social constructions of violence and social control emerge for popular consumption and legitimation. For example, Elayne Rapping

(1992) examined television shows like *COPS* and found that the criminals portrayed in these narratives were not only subjects to be pathologized, controlled, and treated; they were also viewed as incorrigible and subhuman Others to be demonized, contained, and destroyed. Similarly, Ken Morrison (1999) has focused his attention on the trajectory of violence from modernism to postmodernism. He specifically studied the shower murder in *Psycho* and the fatal head wound of President Kennedy as portrayed in Oliver Stone's *JFK*. He concludes that psychiatry, law, science, conspiracy, and more had been inadequately used in these and other films not only to explain violent action, but to recognize the value and currency that the violent image continues to have outside of real, lived experience.

SUMMARY

This chapter has provided an overview of the diverse roles and effects played by mass media in the commodification or circulation of real/reel violence. It has also subscribed to an indirect-effects model of violence mediation and provided a critique of one-dimensional views of mediated violence. I have argued that both within and beyond various postmodern interpretations of mass-mediated violence are the institutional and structural relationships between motion pictures and television, on the one hand, and the construction of advertising and news-making, on the other. When taken as a whole, this political economy of the fictional and nonfictional, not to mention the blurred representations of these two mediating violent genres, have communicated a distorted and underdeveloped picture of the various forms and dangers of interpersonal, institutional, and structural violence.

As a result, violence and violent behavior are often reduced to a function of "evil" people, and the danger stems from the street rather than the executive suite. Together, these values, narratives, and vocabularies of individual motivation surrounding violence have shaped a particular way of seeing and relating to violence (and nonviolence) in our society, if not in other societies as well. These social constructions of violence and the remedies or policies established on their behalf have been primarily retributive rather than restorative (see Chapters 8 and 10) in nature.

What is more, these constructions are almost always framed within the paradigms of adversarialism rather than within the paradigms of mutualism. Hence, the dominant representations of mediated violence that are authorized and valorized, as well as the acts of violence that are forbidden and vilified in contemporary popular narratives, help to reproduce cynical, untrusting, and pessimistic views of the human condition. In turn, these types of mediated-violence perspectives help to perpetuate the kinds of antagonistic and adversarial pathways to violence, aggression, and conflict resolution that are not only not conducive to decreasing violence, but antithetical to those mutualistic and caring alternatives of peacemaking and nonviolence that are actually capable of bringing down levels of violence throughout society.

REFERENCES

Aufderheide, P. (1987, June 24-July 7). Media beat. *In These Times*, p. 20.

Barak, G. (1988). Newsmaking criminology: Reflections on the media, intellectuals, and crime. *Justice Quarterly, 5*(4), 565-587.

Barak, G. (Ed.). (1994). *Media, process, and the social construction of crime: Studies in newsmaking criminology.* New York: Garland.

Barak, G. (Ed.). (1996). *Representing O.J.: Murder,*

criminal justice, and mass culture. Gilderland, NY: Harrow and Heston.

Barak, G. (1999). Reflexive newsmaking and represen-tation. *Critical Studies in Mass Communication, 16*(4), 480-482.

Barak, G., Flavin, J., & Leighton, P. (2001). *Class, race, gender, and crime: Social realities of justice in America.* Los Angeles: Roxbury.

Baxter, R. L., DeRiemer, C., Landini, A., Leslie, L., & Singletary, M. W. (1985). A content analysis of music videos. *Journal of Broad-casting and Electronic Media, 29,* 333-340.

Bellesiles, M. (2000, September 29). Exploding the myth of an armed America. *Chronicle of Higher Educa-tion,* pp. B7-B10.

Bok, S. (1999, October). Violence, free speech, and the media. In *Perspectives on Crime and Justice: 1998–1999 Lecture Series* (pp. 51-72). Washington, DC: U.S. Department of Justice.

Bradsher, K. (2000, July 23). The latest fashion: Fear of crime design. New York Times, §4, p. 5. Retrieved October 27, 2002, from http://www.nytimes.com

Brown, J. (2002, October 27). Designers incorporate com-plex payoff systems as part of milieu. *Taipei Times,* p. 12.

Brownmiller, S. (1975). *Against our will: Men, women, and rape.* New York: Simon & Schuster.

Burtch, B. (1986). Interview with Claire Culhane. *Crime and Social Justice, 26,* 135-150.

Cantor, J., & Nathanson, A. (1996). Children's fright reactions to television news. *Journal of Communication, 46*(4), 139-152.

Centerwall, B. (1989). Exposure to television as a cause of violence. *Public Communi-cation and Behavior, 2,* 1-58.

Chiricos, T., Eschhol, S., & Gertz, M. (1997). Crime, news and fear of crime: Toward an identification of audience effects. *Social Problems, 44*(3), 342-357.

Cook, T. D., Kendzierski, D. A., & Thomas, S. V. (1983). The implicit assumptions of television: An analysis of the 1982 NIMH report on television and behavior. *Public Opinion Quarterly, 47,* 161-201.

Cutler, J. (2001, July 29-August 4). Offer they can't refuse: TV gets married to mob.: *Ann Arbor News: TVWeek,* pp. 3, 9.

DeKeseredy, W. S., & Schwartz, M. D. (1998). *Women abuse on campus: Results from the Canadian National Survey.* Thousand Oaks, CA: Sage.

Dowd, M. (2002, July 21). A tale of two cities. *New York Times,* §4, p. 13.

Duclos, D. (1998). *The were-wolf complex: America's fascination with violence* (A. Pingree, Trans.). New York: Oxford University Press.

Ericson, R. V., Baranek, P. M., & Chan, J. B. (1987). *Visualizing deviance: A study of news organization.* Toronto, Ontario, Canada: University of Toronto Press.

Felson, R. (1996). Mass media effects on violent behavior. *Annual Review of Sociology, 22,* 103-128.

Ferguson, R. (1998). *Repre-senting "race": Ideology,*

identity, and the media. London: Arnold.

Fishman, M. (1978). Crime waves and ideology. *Social Problems, 25,* 531-143.

Freedman, J. L. (1984). Effects of television violence on aggression. *Psychological Bulletin, 96,* 227-246.

Frus, P. (2001). Documenting domestic violence in American films. In J. D. Slocum (Ed.), *Violence and American cinema* (226-244). New York: Routledge.

Gerber, G. (1972). Violence in television drama: Trends and symbolic functions. In G. Comstock & E. A. Rubinstein (Eds.), *Tele-vision and social behavior* (Vol. 1). Washington, DC: U.S. Government Printing Office.

Gray, H. (1999). A different dream of difference. *Critical Studies in Mass Communi-cation, 16*(4), 484-487.

Greenberg, B. S., & D'Alessio, D. (1985). Quantity and quality of sex in the soaps. *Journal of Broadcasting and Electronic Media, 29,* 309-321.

Halberstam, J. (1993). Imagined violence/queer violence: Representation, rage, and resistance. *Social Text, 11*(4), 187-201.

Hall, S., Critcher, C., Jefferson, T., Clarke, J., & Roberts, B. (1978). *Policing the crisis: Mugging, the state and law and order.* London: MacMillan.

Hart, H. (2001, August). A view to a killer. *Entertain-ment Weekly, 11,* 139.

Hills, S. (Ed.). (1987). *Corporate violence: Injury and death in profit.* Totowa, NJ: Rowman and Littlefield.

Horowitz, D., & Chernela, R. (2000, August 24). *Shooting*

the messenger debunks link between media violence and real violence. Retrieved October 27, 2002, from http://www. mediacoalition.org/reports/press_release.htm

Hough, K., & Erwin, P. G. (1997). Children's attitude toward violence on television. *Journal of Psychology, 131*(3), 411-415.

Humphries, D. (1999). *Crack mothers: Pregnancy, drugs, and the media*. Columbus: Ohio State University Press.

Hunter, S. (1995). *Violent screen: A critic's 13 years on the front lines of movie mayhem*. New York: Delta.

Jenkins, P. (1994). *Using murder: The social construction of serial homicide*. New York: Aldine De Gruyter.

Jhally, S. (1997). *Advertising and the end of the world*. Boston: Media Education Foundation.

Kalof, L. (1999). The effects of gender and music video imagery on sexual attitudes. *Journal of Social Psychology, 139*(3), 378-385.

Kasinsky, R. G. (1994). Patrolling the facts: Media, cops, and crime. In G. Barak (Ed.), *Media, process, and the social construction of crime* (pp. 203-236). Gilderland, NY: Harrow and Heston.

Kidd-Hewitt, D., & Osborne, R. (1998). *Crime and the media: The postmodern spectacle*. London: Pluto.

Kooistra, P., Mahoney, J., & Westervelt, S. (2000, November). *The world of crime according to COPS*. Paper presented at the Annual Meetings of the American Society of Criminology, Toronto, Ontario, Canada.

Leland, J. (2002, October 27). Mafia video game raises the ante, fires up the crowd. *Taipei Times*, p. 12.

Lippman, L. (2000, April 24). Time catches up with outrages of Ellis' provocative psycho. *Ann Arbor News*, p. B4.

Lombardi, K. S. (1999, March 28). Author and expert on serial killers who relishes his work. *New York Times*. Retrieved October 27, 2002, from http://www.abjectfilms.com/news2.html

Luhr, W. (1999). Mutilating Mel: Martyrdom and masculinity in *Braveheart*. In C. Sharrett (Ed.), *Mythologies of violence in postmodern media* (pp. 227-247). Detroit, MI: Wayne State University Press.

Malamuth, N. M. (1989). Sexually violent media, thought patterns, and antisocial behavior. *Public Communication and Behavior, 2*, 159-204.

Malamuth, N. M., & Briere, J. (1986). Sexual violence in the media: Indirect effects on aggression against women. *Journal of Social Issues, 42*, 75-92.

McGuire, W. J. (1986). The myth of massive media input: Savagings and salvagings. *Public Communication and Behavior, 1*, 173-257.

McPhail, M. (1999). Trialogues along the color lines: (Re)reading resistance at the end of the twentieth century. *Critical Studies in Mass Communication, 16*(4), 478-480, 488-491.

Modleski, T. (2001, April 27). The context of violence in popular culture. *Chronicle of Higher Education, 47*, B15-B16.

Morrison, K. (1999). The technology of homicide: Constructions of evidence and truth in the American murder film. In C. Sharrett (Ed.), *Mythologies of violence in postmodern society* (pp. 301-317). Detroit, MI: Wayne State University Press.

Newitz, A. (1999). Serial killers, true crime, and economic performance anxiety. In C. Sharrett (Ed.), *Mythologies of violence in postmodern media*, (pp. 41-64). Detroit, MI: Wayne State University Press.

Palermo, G. (1995). Adolescent criminal behavior: Is TV violence one of the culprits? *International Journal of Offender Therapy and Comparative Criminology, 39*(1), 11-22.

Phillips, D. (1986). The found experiment: A new technique for assessing the impact of mass media violence on real-world aggressive behavior. *Public Communication and Behavior, 1*, 259-307.

Potter, G. W., & Kappeler, V. E. (1998). *Constructing crime: Perspectives on making news and social problems*. Prospects Heights, IL: Waveland.

Rafter, N. (2000). *Shots in the mirror: Crime films and society*. New York: Oxford University Press.

Rapping, E. (1992, August). Tabloid TV and social reality. *Progressive*, pp. 35-37.

Romer, D., Jamieson, K., & de Coteau, N. (1998). The treatment of persons of color in local television news: Ethnic blame discourse or realistic group conflict? *Communication Research, 25*(3), 286-305.

Roth, M. (1985). Introduction: The social-psychological phenomenon of violence. In G. Barlow & A. Hill (Eds.), *Video violence and children* (pp. 1-24). London: Hodder and Stoughton.

Schlesinger, A., Jr. (1968). *Violence: America in the sixties.* New York: Signet.

Sharrett, C. (Ed.). (1999). *Mythologies of violence in postmodern society.* Detroit, MI: Wayne State University Press.

Singer, J. L., Singer, D. G., & Rapacynski, W. S. (1984). Family patterns and television viewing as predictors of children's beliefs and aggression. *Journal of Communication, 34,* 73-89.

Slocum, J. D. (Ed.). (2001). *Violence and American cinema.* New York: Routledge.

Slotek, J. (2002, September 29). "Hannibal" goes back for thirds. *Toronto Sun.* Retrieved October 27, 2002, from http://www.canoe.ca/JamMoviesArtistsH/hopkins.html

Smith, D. G. (1976a, August). *Sexual aggression in American pornography: The stereotype of rape.* Paper presented at the Annual Meetings of the American Sociological Association, New York.

Smith, D. G. (1976b). The social context of pornography. *Journal of Communication, 26,* 16-33.

Smythe, D. (1981). *Dependency road: Communication, capitalism, consciousness, and Canada.* Norwood, NJ: Ablex.

Surette, R. (1993). *Media, crime, and criminal justice: Images and realities.* Pacific Grove, CA: Brooks/Cole.

Surette, R. (1994). Predator criminals as media icons. In G. Barak (ed.), *Media, process, and the social construction of crime* (pp. 131-158). New York: Garland.

Surette, R. (1995). A serendipitous finding of a news media history effect. *Justice Quarterly, 21*(2), 355-364.

Sutil, C., Esteban, J., & Takeuchi, M. (1995, December). Televised violence: A Japanese, Spanish, and American comparison. *Psychological Reports, 77,* 995-1000.

Valdivia, A. (1999). La vida es loca Latina/o. *Critical Studies in Mass Communication, 16*(4), 482-484.

Valkenburg, P., & Janssen, S. (1999). What do children value in entertainment? A cross cultural investigation. *Journal of Communication, 49*(2), 3-21.

Wells, M. (2002, July 22). Channel 5 builds hopes on tough US crime drama. *Guardian Unlimited.* Retrieved October 26, 2002, from http://media. guardian.co.uk/Print/0,3858,4466000,00.html

Yang, N. (1987). *Sexual, violent, sexually violent, and prosocial behavior in R-, X-, and XXX-rated films and videos.* Unpublished doctoral dissertation, Newhouse School of Publication Communication, Syracuse University, New York.

Young, A. (1996). *Imagining crime: Textual outlaws and criminal conversations.* London: Sage.

REVIEW QUESTIONS

1. From "A Dialogue on Media and Violence" (see Box 6.1), select two statements that you agree with and two that you disagree with. Explain why.

2. What do you think of Barak's speculation that the Columbine school killers and some of the Palestinian suicide bombers may be suffering from some common maladies?

3. Provide a summation of Malamuth and Briere's "indirect-effects" model of mediated violence and its application to antisocial behavior against women.

4. How is the mass production and consumption of media involved in distorted representations of violence? Provide examples.

5. What is one of your least favorite and one of your most favorite violent films, books, or TV series? Explain what you dislike and like about these.

NOTE

1. Reprinted with permission.

CHAPTER 7

Sexuality and Violence

In Chapter 5, I introduced the concept of "a violence and nonviolence continuum" by organizing the ideas of "mild," "moderate," and "extreme" forms of violence and nonviolence and connecting these to their interpersonal, institutional, and structural pathways (see Figure 5.5). In the context of violence, I also discussed sexual coercion and identified some of the "properties" shared in common by heterosexual rapists, child molesters, and gender harassers. In so doing, I raised questions about these individual perpetrators using their power over others and even inflicting sexual terror on their victims so that they might, in effect, compensate for or feel some kind of temporary relief from their own sexual and identity maladies.

This pathologic or sympathetic interpretation and analysis of these perpetrators' sexuality as "sick" or compulsive, or of their behavior as the product of weakness, vulnerability, and underdevelopment (i.e., the perpetrators are also victims), is one viable view, among others, of what motivates these offenders. Other viable analyses include the idea that the different pathways of these coercers originate in a need for sexual gratification, control, domination, or some combination of these. From this latter perspective, the ordinary occurrences of acquaintance, date, and marital rape, for example, are viewed as extensions or exaggerations of conventional sexual relations and the power differentials between men and women, boys and girls. These violations are not the result of some kind of aberration or deviant response on the part of so many normative "offenders." According to this view, rape is not about pathology, it's "a form of socially conditioned sexual aggression that stems from traditional gender socialization and sexual learning" (Berger, Free, & Searles, 2001, p. 250). In the end, there is plenty of data to support the positions that both "mentally ill" and "culturally normative" offenders and victims comprise the perpetrators of sexual violence.

The relationships between sexuality and violence go beyond the interpersonal actions of the sexual perpetrators themselves. Hence, analyses of sexuality and violence must also encompass those institutional and structural relations that exist across the interactions of these offenders and the larger cultural order of which they are a part. Once again, all expressions of violence and nonviolence or of violent or nonviolent behavior need to be examined with respect to both their symbolic and real meanings, as these are constantly shaped and redefined by societies' responses to specific behaviors and conditions, on the one hand, and in the context of the interaction between these reactions and the mediated representations of sex and violence, on the other hand. When this kind of examination is made, one is better able to grasp that similar, different, and contradictory messages are concurrently attached to violence and the lack of nonviolence in everyday mass communication.

In other words, from an institutional or structural pathways perspective on violence, acts such as a "moderate" flashing or an "extreme" rape may also function to reassure the perpetrators of their power and potency over women because both of these acts "include, as a crucial factor in that reassurance, the fear and humiliation of the female victims" (Cameron & Frazer, 1987, p. 164). From the perspective of victimized females, this is certainly happening to varying degrees. Many times, however, the perpetrators are not actually reassured by their actions; on the contrary, they may feel even more frustrated and ashamed than before they sexually violated somebody, creating a proverbial recycling of angry emotions and sexual aggressions. More often than not, these male perpetrators, regardless of their motives, are unaffected by the pain and suffering they cause their victims, and they are indifferent to what women and girls want.

Culturally, however, the abusers' lack of empathy or mutuality with their victims' needs may also reflect the larger world of the politics of sexual violence. That is to say, depending on the "value" or "innocence" placed on the victims of sexual abuse, society may be indifferent or unaffected, as evidenced by its lack of empathy, compassion, and aid. From this perspective, the legacies of patriarchy and misogyny may work hand in hand with an androgenic bias about male-female heterosexual relations that gathers both ideological and social strength from its various synergistic forms of inequality, which function to keep "good" and "bad" women "in their place."

Moreover, the sheer numbers of the interpersonal acts of sexual violence against women, combined with a mélange of mass-mediated images of sexual danger looming over the "weaker" gender—ranging from serial rape and "snuff" pornography to mainstream news and mass advertising—have created a cultural climate of fear and intimidation, if not victimization, for many women, girls, and boys. As Catherine MacKinnon (1983) has written about rape law and its reform: "From a women's point of view, [it] is not prohibited, it is regulated" (p. 653). Whether these sexual violations are verbal, visual, or physical, they are *expected* within the arrangements of the existing legal and political order. What's more, these reel and real violations "serve to remind women and girls that they are at risk and vulnerable to male aggression just because they are female" (Sheffield, 1989, p. 484). As Berger, Free, and Searles (2001) point out:

> Since men's sexuality is presumed to be naturally aggressive, women's fear of sexual violence seems inevitable. Society even places responsibility on *women* to monitor their behavior so they won't be violated. If they are violated, they may be blamed for their victimization or find that their suffering is "trivialized, questioned, or ignored." (p. 247)

Herein lies a key relationship or connection between the "concept of a sexual violence continuum" (Kelly, 1987) and the "concept of a sexual intimacy continuum" (Schmalleger & Alleman, 1994), as the two of these overlap or converge at the point of appropriate and inappropriate behavior, bringing together some forms of sexual violation with the more common behaviors or everyday expressions of masculine sexuality.

As Betsy Stanko (1985) suggested early on in her study of female victimization, women "who feel violated and intimidated by typical male behaviour have no way of specifying how or why typical male behaviour feels like aberrant male behaviour" (p. 10). In part, this has to do with the way in which mass media both trivializes and eroticizes violence against women and children. Moreover, in terms of trying to establish separate pathways to consensual and nonconsensual sex, Liz Kelly (1987) and others have found that women often experience heterosexual sex not as an either/or (i.e., consent or not, yes or no) thing, but as a continuum that moves from choice to pressure to coercion to force. Unfortunately, far too many men have also approached heterosexual sex not as an either/or matter. If they had, women probably would not have come up with the slogan: "What about *no* don't you understand?"

Even more fundamentally, MacKinnon (1983) has challenged altogether the notion of consent. She too finds it problematic, within the cultural patterns of sexual interaction, where males initiate and often dominate the transactions, but within which they have also been socialized not to be too concerned about the needs of women or others, to seriously entertain the idea of real consent or the idea that men really care about it. In addition, under the prevailing conditions of male-female sexual relations, as Berger et al. (2001) assert:

> It's difficult for women to assess how much resistance is necessary to convince men that they haven't been granted consent or that they've withdrawn it . . . and the fact that the man may not have used physical force doesn't guarantee that the woman had freely agreed to sex. He may fail to distinguish acquiescence and consent, and so may she. She may consider it rape, or she may be confused by the fact that she stopped resisting and *not* define the encounter as rape, even though she experienced it as unwanted and nonconsensual. (p. 252)

The principal objectives of this chapter are not only to try to understand how gender, media, and other relations constituting the "battle of the sexes" have evolved over time but to expose common properties or pathways between sexual and nonsexual violent behavior. The efforts here are primarily anthropological, sociological, and psychological, as the focus shifts between an examination of sexuality and violence and the social relations of sex, aggression, and gender as these have emerged and developed more or less universally over time. To understand the intricate relationships of sexuality, violence, and human nature, one must appreciate that although the individual and society are inseparable, they are not identical—the individual does not disappear in the social whole, nor is the social whole reflected in the individual. In sum, to unravel the complexities of sexuality and violence, one must address both the real and symbolic interactions of individuals and society.

PHILOSOPHIZING ABOUT SEX AND SEXUALITY

One can think about love, hate, aggression, violence, nonviolence, peace, and cooperation as separate phenomena, yet one can also think about the unity or totality of the relations between all of these. Analysts of human behavior have studied aggressive patterns in general and the type of aggression that occurs in particular between and within the sexes. Researchers have also addressed the similarities and differences in the violence of both sexes (Dobash & Dobash, 1998c; Godenzi, Schwartz, & DeKeseredy, 2001; Hatty, 2000; Messerschmidt, 1993; Miller, 1991; Renzetti, 1992; Stanko, 1985; Totten, 2000). Many of these findings will be reviewed later in the chapter. For now, I turn to a more general discussion of how sex and sexuality have been philosophically viewed over the past century or so.

When it comes to heterosexual relations, there is a popular saying used by both men and women to describe the opposite sex that captures the interplay of aggressive and libidinal forces: "You can't live with them, and you can't live without them." Consciously or subconsciously, this aphorism addresses the issue of "sexual antagonism," or what various scholars of human sexuality have referred to as "sexual ambivalence," "sexual hostility," or "sexual animosity" (Schoenewolf, 1989).

There is another popular saying that addresses the more generic question of "sexual and nonsexual aggression." It includes and yet transcends sexual dyads at the same time: "Make love, not war." In psychoanalytic language, this aphorism conveys the duality of Eros (forces of life and love) and Thanatos (forces of destruction and death). It contends that in the most intimate sense, acts of copulation are the ultimate victories of Eros over Thanatos and the place where an individual's aggression is neutralized (Klein, 1932). Perhaps in some ideal or abstract world, the act of love or sexual intercourse might be a pure expression of Eros. But in the real world, as no one is without aggression, Eros and Thanatos may be said to intermingle, more or less, in every heterosexual interaction.

In *The Art of Loving*, Erich Fromm (1956) contended that strong emotions of virtually any kind could readily blend with sexual desire. He was not only referring to love and vanity, but to the wish to vanquish or be vanquished, to hurt or be hurt, and even to the anxieties of depression and loneliness. Others, from the perspectives of physiology and endocrinology, have similarly examined the relationships between romantic love, sexual desire, and what is called "peripheral arousal," or the assumption that something (e.g., anger, a fetish) other than emotional attraction can enhance sexual interaction (Berscheid & Walster, 1974). Moreover, to the extent that sexual desire is influenced by the feedback of peripheral ("indirect") arousal such as through pornography, any emotions capable of producing a flow of adrenaline are capable of exciting sexual arousal, including violence. And because adrenaline controls peripheral arousal, it can not only fuse with sex and/or aggression, it can make the heart grow fonder or angrier.

Conflicts and conflations over sexuality and violence in general, and the "battle of the sexes" in particular, raise questions of similarities and dissimilarities about battering, incest, rape, and other assaults, sexual and nonsexual, in relation to power and conflict, dominance and submission, male and female psychologies, illness and wellness, life and death. Conflicts over or about sexuality also revisit some of the indirect-effects kinds of questions raised about mediated violence, pornography, erotica, and other graphic portrayals of sexuality (see Figure 6.1 and Box 7.1). In trying to make sense of the various ways that aggression and hostility work in general and in relation to sexual intimacy and violence in particular, responses within and across the disciplines have varied.

Those with a psychoanalytic orientation see most, if not everything, as related to sex. For example, the 19th-century philosopher Arthur Schopenhauer (1896) underscored the importance of male-female relations and the impact of sexual conflict on society. He argued essentially that the relation of the sexes was the invisible central point of all action and conduct. This was the case not only between men and women, but between women and women and between men and men. He contended that the causes of war and peace were also about the relations of the sexes. He went so far as to argue that these relations were the basis of jests, wit, allusions, and hints. Such relations, he maintained, were behind the daily thoughts of the chaste and unchaste, of the young and often the old. Schopenhauer argued that sexual passion was at the root of an individual's identity, and that sexual discord was at the root of one's misery.

Carl Jung (1951) is credited with being the first person to use the word *animosity* with regard to the male-female dyad. His formulation was based on a physiological explanation of male-female disharmony located in the "collective unconscious" of humankind and passed on from generation to generation. He saw sexual animosity as rooted in the anima-animus relationship between men and women: the man's anima (i.e., unconscious female component of his personality) and the woman's animus (i.e., unconscious male component of her personality) produce feelings of repulsion toward members of the opposite sex as a result of negative projections based on feelings of genital anxieties. Jung argued that this sexual duality affected the internal harmony of each individual as well as the relations of men and women in general.

Though Sigmund Freud (1918, 1925/1957, 1931/1957), like Jung, believed in the primary bisexuality of humans, he approached the subject of sexual animosity from the angle of psychosexual development rather than from biology. He concentrated on the psychodynamics of the phallic stage, during which males and females (raised by heterosexual couples) first become attracted to their parents of the opposite sex. In his formulation, animosity stems from man's castration complex and woman's penis envy and from their feelings of guilt and/or unresolved Oedipal and Electra complexes. Contemporary psychology has had much to say in critiquing and modifying these and other concepts related to mechanistic, Freudian models of sexuality and development.

Feminist psychoanalysts in particular, such as Alfred Adler (1927/1977) and Karen Horney (1926/1977) early on and Carol Gilligan (1982) more recently, have questioned both the methods and assumptions of

Freudians; however, they have not abandoned the idea of sexual animosity. Rather, they have argued that the cultural differences or inequalities between men and women have been the outcomes of patriarchy and the conscious and unconscious subjugation of—and hostility toward—women by men. Hence, sexual animosity is attributed largely to cultural values of hierarchy that favor men and oppress women.

Many other feminist scholars have also questioned the rigidly defined categories of sexual and gender differences, challenging as well the very notion of a naturally expressed animosity or unconscious hostility between men and women. Their emphases are on the social construction of sex and gender roles, as well as sexual identities, and how these express themselves in everyday relations. For example, Gayle Rubin (1975) from social anthropology has argued fundamentally that "the social organization of sex rests upon gender, obligatory heterosexuality, and the constraint of female sexuality." In other words, "gender is a socially imposed division of the sexes," "a product of the social relations of sexuality" (p. 179). Similarly, MacKinnon (1987) from law and jurisprudence critiques the idea of gender difference in the law because it "legitimizes the way gender is imposed by force" and "helps keep the reality of male dominance in place" (p. 3).

Finally, from sociology and philosophy, Michel Foucault (1980) critiques the notion of a "naturalness" of sexual relations and warns that "sexuality must not be described as a stubborn drive, by nature alien and of necessity disobedient to a power which exhausts itself trying to subdue it and often fails to control it entirely" (p. 103). In his broad and engaging discussion of sexuality and its expressions throughout social organization, he argues that it "appears rather as an especially dense transfer point for relations of power: between men and women, young people and old people, parents and offspring, teachers and students, priests and laity, [and] an administration and a population" (p. 103). Foucault concluded that sexuality was not among the most intractable elements in power relations, but rather one of those endowed with the greatest instrumentality. For example, as James Messerschmidt (1993) from criminology has observed, although sexuality has recently become "a domain of extensive exploration and pleasure for women," it still remains "a site where gendered oppression may occur" (p. 76).

NATURE, NURTURE, AND HUMAN EVOLUTION

Regardless of their particular takes on the "battle of the sexes," most contemporary students of human violence and sexual aggression view these conflicts primarily as socially established, yet they function or operate through the interaction of both nature and nurture. As human evolution occurs, however, we are not free agents in this process of social development because we are forever subject to the specific, yet flexible, determinations of our cultural histories. The roots of this kind of anthropology are in the double contentions: we are of nature, and we are more than nature.

For example, other animals use nature, but humans master nature as self-conscious organisms. Other animals may have changed, adapted, or evolved over time in response to environmental changes, but they have not transformed their environments as they have evolved. Humans possess a superiority over other animals because of our abilities to comprehend the laws of nature and to apply them in practice. So although "a spider conducts operations that resemble those of a weaver, and a bee puts to shame many an architect in the construction of her cells . . . what distinguishes the worst architect from the best of bees is this, that the architect raises his structure in the imagination before he erects it in reality" (Marx, 1906/1940, p. 198). The point is that, because we have the power of imagination or the power of the ideal, we can transcend any immediately given social reality or material condition. However, because we are natural beings, too, we cannot transcend nature any way we please. We can reconstitute ourselves and the world only by reconstructing the current personal, social, and cultural environments of which we are all a part.

Perhaps the most fundamental lesson about evolution is that, as an ongoing force, it has shaped attributes and behaviors shared by all human beings, and at the same time, it has given every single individual a different nature. We are all the same and yet we are all uniquely different. Why? The background necessary to answer this question lies within the intersecting domains of biological and cultural evolution. The answer itself lies within the gradual alterations, over some 6 million years, of genetic and cultural information possessed by humanity.

Biological evolution refers to that part of evolution that causes changes in our genetic endowment. This evolution has helped to shape human natures, including human behavior, in many ways. These behaviors are shaped in very general ways, however, as there are simply not enough genes to program all of the behavioral variations. In short, genes are not destiny. As Paul Ehrlich (2000b) explains:

> Human beings have something on the order of 100,000 genes, and human brains have more than one *trillion* nerve cells, with about 100-1,000 trillion connections (synapses) between them. That's at least one *billion* synapses per gene, even if each and every gene did nothing but control the production of synapses (and it doesn't). Given that ratio, it would be quite a trick for genes

typically to control more than the most general aspects of human behavior. (p. B7)

Cultural evolution refers to that part of evolution that passes on nongenetic information and that is unique to human beings. This evolution consists of the socially transmitted behaviors, beliefs, institutions, arts, and sciences that are shared and exchanged among people. Comparatively, cultural evolution can be much more rapid than genetic evolution. Since the invention of agriculture some 10,000 years ago, our evolution has been overwhelmingly cultural in nature.

There are also important "co-evolutionary" interactions between cultural and biological evolution, such as how farming practices changed the environment in ways that altered the evolution of blood cells. In terms of nature (i.e., genetic and biological) or nurture (i.e., learning and culture), it makes sense to view these as coproducers of social evolution rather than a case of "nature versus nurture." For example, the ability to speak human languages is a result of a great deal of genetic evolution. At the same time, the diversity of languages around the world speaks just as loudly to the power of cultural evolution. The point is that both genetic and nongenetic information are important for our understanding of the evolution of human nature:

> Not only is the evolution of our collective non-genetic information critical to creating our natures, but also the rate of that evolution varies greatly among different aspects of human culture. That, in turn, has profound consequences for our behavior and our environments. A major contemporary human problem, for instance, is that the rate of cultural evolution in science and technology has been extraordinarily high in contrast with the snail's pace of change in the social attitudes and political institutions that might channel the uses of technology in more beneficial directions. (Ehrlich, 2000b, B8)

Evolution theory holds that virtually every attribute of every organism is the product of the interaction between its genetic code and its environment. The relative contributions of heredity and environment are difficult, if not impossible, to specify. It is much like trying to assess the contributions of length and width in the area of a rectangle. Moreover, the contributions of nature and nurture vary from attribute to attribute. So when it comes to aggregated attributes or to the variations in adult human behavior, there is not a lot to detail. What scientists know is that genes do not shout commands to us about our behavior. It seems more as if genes "whisper suggestions, and the nature of those whispers is shaped by our internal environments (those within and between our cells) during early development and later, and usually also by the external environments in which we mature and find ourselves as adults" (Ehrlich, 2000b, p. B9).

In another vein, geneticists are busy trying to sort out some of the ways genes and environments, as well as hereditary endowments, interact in making their contributions to the development of the individual. They have learned, for example, that even within experimental environments, it is often very difficult for genetic evolution to change just one characteristic or gene at a time. This is especially worthy of consideration in light of the claims that "natural selection" has programmed humans to be selfish and greedy or altruistic and compassionate. Other hereditary studies criticize those who have made claims about genetic differences between males and females, such as that the former are naturally dominant, violent, aggressive, controlling, or sadistic and the latter are naturally subordinate, submissive, passive, accommodating, or masochistic.

From this evolutionary perspective, it seems to make sense, as Ehrlich (2000a) argues, to think in terms of both human natures and human nature. The latter term, or singular human nature, for example, should be employed when we are discussing things that all humans possess, such as the ability to communicate through language or the capacity to develop complex penal systems. Talking in terms of more than one human nature also makes sense, as (a) most aspects of our natures and our genomes (genetic endowments) are nearly universal, and (b) the variations or differences within our hereditary endowments are small compared with those between humans and chimpanzees.

At the same time, the plural use of human natures recognizes the cultural diversity within *Homo sapiens,* the variations from society to society, from individual to individual, and from place to place in time and space. For example, the human natures of Chinese living in Beijing are slightly different than the human natures of Chinese living in San Francisco. These Chinese natures are also slightly different than they would have been for Chinese living in either city 50 years ago or than they will be 50 years from now. The human natures of great inventors, musicians, athletes, or artists may be similar, but they are not identical. Inner-city gang members' natures are different than the natures of those youths raised in an affluent suburb. The natures of those, even those who are identical twins, who habitually vote Republican are different from those who habitually vote Democrat. All of these subtle differences or variations are products of the power of cultural evolution, the super-rapid kind of evolution that only our species excels at. In sum, different cultural environments—local, regional, and international—have the power to shape and alter human nature over time.

ON AGGRESSION AND NONAGGRESSION

During the last quarter of the 20th century, studies of violence moved away from individualistic and toward social or relational models of aggression (Dobash & Dobash,1998b; Malamuth, 1998; Smuts, 1992). The earlier individual models of aggressive behavior tended to divide up between those that favored nature and those that favored nurture. In his classic book *On Aggression,* Lorenz (1966) argued that animals and humans shared an instinct for aggressive behavior. He also argued that humans, unlike other species, lack developed mechanisms for the inhibition of aggression. Subsequent research and analysis repudiated both of these positions and basically put the "killer ape" myth to rest (Barnett, 1983; Binford, 1972; Montagu, 1968, 1976).

On the side of nurture were the psychologists, who developed frustration-aggression hypotheses and studied the effects of role models and authorities. Proponents on both sides of the nature-nurture divide, however, were in agreement on the *antisocial nature or character* of aggressive behavior. However, the evidence from neither animal and psychophysiological research nor from psychoanalytic and anthropological research has justified the conclusion that *Homo sapiens* have passed along aggressive genes or instincts that are compelled to find expression of one kind or another when stimulated by specific environmental cues.

The first problem with these individual models of aggression is that they are oblivious to social contexts. The second problem is that they are one directional. The models focus on a myriad of different influences on aggression, both internal (e.g., hormones, genes, drives) and external (e.g., frustration and pain, alcohol, learning), but they do so without examining the social consequences of aggression. In effect, they analyze individual aggression in a real social vacuum. At best, these models can tell us how aggression starts, but not how it ends or how it is kept under control. Such models are unable, for example, to offer any insights into peacemaking or conflict resolution, or to address what contemporary anthropology refers to as a range of conflict-of-interest responses, including "tolerance" (e.g., sharing or exchanging of resources), "avoidance" (e.g., submission or withdrawal), and "aggression" (e.g., infliction of harm or humiliation).

By contrast, the more recent social or relational models of violence view aggressive behavior as one of several interactive ways that conflicts of interest can be settled. Initially inspired by studies of primate societies and later by the study of children and adults, anthropologists and other behavioral scientists discovered that both nonhuman and human primates use aggression as a tool of competition and negotiation. At the same time, both of these species engage in various practices of cooperation and reconciliation. These reconciliations are usually after, but may occur any time in, the "cycles of violence" as aggression becomes an enduring phenomenon (de Waal, 2000). For example, in the case of preschoolers, two forms of conflict resolution have been noticed:

> Peaceful associative outcomes, in which both opponents stay together and work things out on the spot, and friendly reunions between former opponents after temporary distancing. These two complementary forms of child reconciliation, expressed in play invitations, body contacts, verbal apologies, object offers, self-ridicule, and the like, have been found to reduce aggression, decrease stress-related agitation (such as jumping up and down), and increase tolerance. The striking similarity of these findings to those on nonhuman primates suggests causal, as well as functional, parallels. (de Waal, 2000, p. 589)

In the days before there were relational models of aggression and nonaggression, the rarity of violence, especially lethal violence, was attributed exclusively to the physical differences between the potential combatants'

fighting abilities. In many social animals, however, including humans, both parties to a conflict stand to lose if fighting escalates out of control. Recent research of de Waal (2000) and others demonstrates, without denying the human heritage of aggression and violence, that there is an equally old heritage of countermeasures designed to protect cooperative arrangements against the undermining effects of competition. In Part III, the implications of these findings will be explored in terms of erecting individual and collective pathways to social, political, and economic nonviolence.

At the cross-cultural level, even without those studies on the natural heritage for conflict resolution, there are and have been a number of human societies in the world that cannot be characterized as aggressive or violent (Montagu, 1978). Even if these nonaggressive cultures represent only a small portion of humanity, they offer more than enough proof to conclude that the human species has acquired the means to do away with its "violent impulses." Even in those societies which can be (or are) characterized as aggressive or violent, relatively few boys or men, and even fewer girls or women, actually kill or seriously wound anybody during the course of their lives. In social reality, no matter how angry or mad most people become even in the so-called violent societies, they have learned to control their "aggressive natures." This is not to deny that we are all born with the potential and capacity for learning both violence and nonviolence.

A Relational Model of Aggression

If we are to examine the relations of violence, sexuality, and culture, it is useful to have a relational model of aggression as reflected in the anthropological and sociological evidence on violence. One such model views violent acts as the product of two sets of opposing tendencies operating in any potentially aggressive situation. Jeffrey Goldstein's (1986) "relational model of aggression" maintains that in any social situation, there are opposing tendencies to be aggressive and not to be aggressive. Succinctly, Goldstein argues that any aggression overtly expressed as violence is a product of pro-aggression factors triumphing over anti-aggression factors:

> The decision of whether or not to aggress in any particular situation depends upon the relative strength of these two opposing tendencies. When the number and strength of all the pro-aggression factors outweigh the number and strength of the anti-aggressive factors, aggression will ensue. When the anti-aggression factors are stronger than the pro-aggression forces, no aggression will result. (p. 24)

Finally, Goldstein's relational model views aggressive behavior as a complex act involving three simultaneously interacting elements. "There must be some impetus to aggress, inhibitions against aggressing must be overcome, and the situation—in terms of the opportunity and ability to aggress and the availability of a target—must be appropriate" (Goldstein, 1986, p. 24). In turn, this integrative model divides pro- and anti-aggressive features into *long-term* and *situational* factors.

Long-term factors promoting aggression are those which are relatively enduring, such as individual and cultural norms, attitudes, and values supportive of aggression and violence, positive prior experiences with aggression and violence, and knowledge of and the ability to use aggressive and nonaggressive strategies in disputes of all kinds, real and imagined. Enduring factors in aggression find their source in socialization and selective reinforcement by parents, peers, teachers, and cultures. For example, in the United States and elsewhere, long-term cultural

values that facilitate aggression include the teaching that aggression is desirable when used in defense of country, self, property, or the law.

Situational factors that facilitate aggression are immediate and consist of circumstances—idiosyncratic, habitual, or otherwise—conducive to violence. These include any factors that momentarily raise a person's (or nation-state's) tendencies to be aggressive or to lower a person's (or nation-state's) restraints against aggression. Such factors include the presence or absence of friends and relatives, levels of emotional arousal and frustration, availability of weapons or witnesses, and physical environments conducive to anonymity or exposure.

There are long-term and situational factors conducive to nonaggression, as well. Just as we learn which situations, targets, and means are appropriate for violence and aggression, we learn which situations, targets, and means are inappropriate for such actions. There are, for example, locations in most societies conducive to aggression and nonaggression: the former type includes taverns, sporting events, public streets, vacant lots; the latter includes other people's homes, workplaces, theaters, churches, and so on. Situational factors conducive to nonaggression or to the reduction of aggression are the presence of punishing agents (e.g., parents, teachers, police), unfamiliar environments, lack of potential victims, identifiability of the actors or actions, and the presence of nonaggressive others. For example, very few batterers or aggravated assaulters, habitual or occasional, rarely (if ever) lift so much as a finger to anyone else when they believe there is any chance of getting their own "ass whipped."

In sum, according to this relational model of aggression, violence is the product of conflicts—personal and social. This model assumes that violence is not simply a matter of pro- and anti-aggressive factors, but that it also consists of the relative importance of each of these factors to the involved parties. Moreover, we can talk about violence or aggression as long-term and short-term conflicts or as high-conflict and low-conflict situations. Whatever the case, antisocial aggression or violence is not viewed as the result of too few norms or values, as functional sociologists have argued for more than 150 years, but quite simply as a "power play" based on the perpetrator's reasonable expectation that he will get away with his abusive behavior.

An Evolutionary Perspective on Sexual Aggression

The vast literature on rape and male sexual assault leaves no doubt that violent action may continue and even escalate after sexual access has been accomplished or sexual frustration has allegedly dissipated. In many other instances of sexual violence, aggressive impulses may dominate sexual ones. In less coercive sexual scenarios, sex may become a means of expressing aggression in the form of debasing or humiliating one's victim. Of course, motivations for these actions will vary. On the continuum of an aggression-sexual fusion between "consenting" partners, the sexual art of flagellation and bondage involved in the contemporary practices of sadomasochism (S&M), or the use of pain and control in the service of sexual pleasure, appears to be a normative way of experiencing intimacy between many sexually active adults (Chancer, 1992; Hunt, 1974; Presdee, 2000).

These and other forms of sexual and aggressive fusion apply to both women and men as they exchange places and roles in these S&M scenarios of mutual love, respect, and identification without doing harm or violence. However, even where trust has been established between intimates, S&M scenes have sometimes resulted in very real physical or mental anguish, even to those who thought they were enjoying it. Such are the dialectics of pain, pleasure, and sexuality. Although these types of consensual sexual and aggressive acts are not my concern here, they do speak to the abilities of heterosexual and homosexual dyads alike to negotiate pleasure and pain fully and mutually within the terrains of intimacy and sexuality. In contrast to the relatively positive and nonabusive aggressive-sexual fusions, my primary focus in this section is to try to account for the social evolution of negative, abusive, and violent male aggression toward women and others. In short, where does controlling or dominating male sexual aggression come from?

In her examinations of male aggression against women, Barbara Smuts (1991, 1992) uses a biological, evolutionary perspective. She makes it clear that such a framework need not rest on any type of genetically deterministic assumptions, nor does it have to result in conclusions that are necessarily supportive of the status quo. On the contrary, Smuts argues that evolutionary perspectives can be quite useful for rendering costs-benefits analyses of different courses of action. Finally, to the extent that these perspectives can identify those situations and conditions that favor male aggression toward women, they can contribute both to political strategies and to the formulation of social policies that may alter those situations and conditions.

Using evidence from research on both human and nonhuman primates, Smuts (1992) argues that historically "men use aggression to try to control women, and particularly to try to control female sexuality, not because men are inherently aggressive and women inherently submissive, but because men find aggression to be a useful political tool in their struggle to dominate and control women and thereby enhance their reproductive opportunities" (p. 30). She also argues that male use of aggression as a tool is not inevitable but conditional. Under some circumstances, coercive control of women pays off; under other circumstances, it does not. What underpins Smuts' idea about the conditional nature of male aggression against women is its emphasis on individual reproductive success as the ultimate goal of both male sexual coercion and female resistance to it.

Evolutionary analyses begin with the successful reproduction of the human species from the interests of both males and females. Through sexual intercourse, it is assumed that male eagerness to mate, combined with female reluctance to reproduce with any male who comes along, creates an obvious sexual conflict of interest that is virtually universal (Hammerstein & Parker, 1987). In terms of resolving or negotiating an exchange over sexual reproduction, males could overcome female resistance and improve their chances of mating by one of three means. They could offer females benefits, such as meat, or protection from other males. They could provide assistance to females in rearing the young. Or, they could employ force or the threat of force. In turn, women restricted their sexual promiscuity and provided limited sexual access to one male or a few. In the larger scheme of social relations, what evolved were *pair bonds:* long-term, more-or-less exclusive, mating relationships.

Pair bonding has long been considered a critical development in human social evolution, especially since it is unique among primates. Smuts suggests that as males and females developed long-term mating associations, men formalized the kind of tolerance seen among male allies in nonhuman primates. This was beneficial at some point during hominid evolution, when male cooperation became increasingly important in terms of hunting and intragroup competition for power, resources, and mates. It was also beneficial to women, as it reduced their vulnerability to sexual coercion, including

the perpetration of infanticide by males. In Smut's (1992) speculative scenario, "Human pair bonds, and therefore human marriage, can be considered a means by which cooperating males agree about mating rights, respect (at least in principle) one another's 'possession' of particular females, protect their mates and their mates' children from aggression by other men, and gain rights to coerce their own females with reduced interference from other men."

Evolutionary theorists and cultural anthropologists of a functionalist orientation tend to emphasize the cooperative nature of the division of labor in humans. Women gather and harvest, men hunt and plow. Those evolutionists with a conflict orientation tend to stress the widespread existence of sexual asymmetries in the control of resources (e.g., food, property, tools, weapons) that allow men to control women. They also recognize how once women became dependent on men for resources, their vulnerability to male coercive control also increased. As men expended more resources on their mates and offspring, they were motivated to control female sexuality because of issues of paternity. As women became more dependent on men for resources, the alternatives to remaining with a coercive mate declined, further reducing the power of women to negotiate the terms of the relationship. Cross-cultural analyses generally support the hypothesis that male control of resources makes women more vulnerable to male aggression, involving cases such as rape (Schlegel & Barry, 1986) or wife beating in developing (if not necessarily developed) societies (Levinson, 1989).

In sum, evolutionary perspectives vary, but they all assume that male aggression against women reflects selective pressures that began operating during the social evolution of our ancestral hominids (Burgess & Draper, 1989; Daly & Wilson, 1988). Most also assume that male domination of women is not genetically determined, and that frequent male aggression toward women is a changeable feature of human nature. In fact, there is dramatic variation in male aggression toward women throughout the world. And although there are still a sizable number of men who resort to the use of aggression and sexual violence toward women, it can be shown that roles culturally scripted around sex, gender, and violence in the past and present have helped to reproduce male sexualities that are more or less likely to engage in violence against other men and women. Research, however, generally demonstrates that even with an association between higher levels of androgens, especially testosterone, and some forms of violence, there are still no significant behavioral differences between men and women with respect to aggression, dominance, and competition that can be linked to heredity or biology (Richmond-Abbott, 1992).

MARKING THE SEXUALITIES OF DIFFERENCE AND HIERARCHY

Sexualities of difference and hierarchy are both physical and mental. In other words, female and male sexualities are a function of both corporal bodies and constructed images. As Rubin (1975) has commented: "Sex is sex, but what counts as sex is equally culturally determined and obtained. Every society also has a sex/gender system—a set of arrangements by which the biological raw material of human sex and procreation is shaped by human social intervention and satisfied in a conventional manner, no matter how bizarre some of the conventions might be," (p. 165) such as the ones involving female circumcision (genital mutilation).

In contemporary sexual discourse, *sex* refers to nature and the biological components that characterize male and female— chromosomes, hormones, anatomy and physiology. By contrast, *gender* typically refers to nurture and the psychological, social, and cultural components that "encapsulate the dominant ideas about feminine and masculine traits and behaviors prevalent in any society at one time" (Hatty, 2000, p. 111). Sexualities may be thought of as combining elements of sex and gender as well as a person's subjective sense of him- or herself, or what is usually referred to as gender identification or the engendering of a "masculine" or "feminine" personality.

Under the older regimes and studies of sexology, the Western heritage of a Cartesian duality or split between the mind and body required a situation in which the former was allegedly in control of the latter. In the newer regimes of multiplicity and integration, "we now acknowledge that subjectivity and corporeality are intimately entwined, and that the body mediates the experience of the external world" (Hatty, 2000, p. 119). In other words, in the postmodern culture, the body is viewed as contributing to subjectivity and as central to the experience of self.

These two accounts of gender and sexuality represent modernist (traditional) and postmodernist (revisionist) explanations of difference and hierarchy. The traditional models stress the idea that masculinity and femininity are embedded in fixed and stable gender identities, expressing an inner essence of maleness and femaleness. These models view masculinities and femininities as deep-seated, resilient, and persistent aspects of individual identities or personalities, a function and a reflection of an organism's biological plumbing and constitutional make up. Gender and sexuality are reduced to the differences of *m/f* based on chromosomal sex (i.e., XY males or XX females), gonadal sex (i.e., testes or ovaries), hormonal sex (e.g., androgens or estrogens), and the sex of the internal (i.e., prostate glands and ejaculatory ducts or uterus and fallopian tubes) and external (i.e., penis and scrotal sacs or clitoris, labia, and vagina) organs.

The revisionist models, by contrast, stress the idea that the taking up of gender identity and sexuality is a highly flexible, contextually sensitive, and relational enterprise.

In these models, physiology and genitals are not necessarily destiny. As studies of the relative importance of chromosomes, hormones, physical appearance, and the manner in which a child has been reared have revealed, the sex of rearing is almost always found to be the primary factor. "Even when the external genitals contradicted the sex of rearing," for example, one study "reported that twenty-three of twenty-five [subjects] believed themselves to be the sex which they were raised" (Richmond-Abbott, 1992, p. 40).

Money and Ehrhardt (1972) argued that children acquire their gender identities from the age of 6 months to 3 or 4 years, and that it is relatively difficult to change children's primary orientation after the age of 2 years without emotional trauma and even permanent damage to their gender or sexual identity. The historical record actually reveals that there have been successful and unsuccessful sex and gender reassignments of both children and adults. Either way, revisionists generally hold that gender and sexuality represent processes of becoming rather than states of being. In sum, there is a tendency in traditionalists to treat sexuality as a "noun" and in revisionists to treat sexuality as a "verb."

Once again, Foucault (1980) is instructive when he says that "sexuality must not be thought of as a kind of natural given which power tries to hold in check, or as an obscure domain which knowledge tries gradually to uncover" (p. 105). Instead, he argues that the production of sexuality is a historical artifact or social construction. It is "not a furtive reality that is difficult to grasp, but a great surface network in which the stimulation of bodies, the intensifications of pleasures, the incitement to discourse, the formation of special knowledges, the strengthening of controls and resistances, are linked to one another" (p. 106). Historically, even the most cursory examination of bodies, sexualities, and genders discloses that ideas about each of these or about sex and gender systems as a whole are quite malleable and subject to change.

What has constituted feminine and masculine traits and behaviors has varied over time. In fact, throughout history the cultural images and the living expressions of maleness/femaleness or masculinity/femininity (*m/f*) have assumed a variety of forms. Notions about the attributes and characteristics of each of these have provided a range of possibilities that are to be achieved through culturally specific processes or rituals in which one becomes the ideal man or woman. Cross culturally, ideas of *m/f* have not only contradicted themselves, disappeared, and reappeared; they have also normally involved a wide range of meanings and behaviors. Surprisingly, perhaps, the very configurations of sexed bodies and of the nature of male and female gender have even reversed themselves at certain times (Hatty, 2000).

In most traditional prestate societies where evidence of hierarchy between the sexes prevailed, femaleness was associated with self-sufficiency and maleness with dependency; in other more egalitarian formations, images of sexual androgyny prevailed (Hatty, 2000). Contrast these with most modern, industrial societies, which have associated maleness with strength and independence and femaleness with weakness and dependence. Yet, women (or some classes of women) to varying degrees have always been presented sexually as dangerous, polluting, and threatening to the well-being of societies. Female bodies have also tended to be characterized more negatively than male bodies.

In terms of the Western ideologies that emerged in the 17th century regarding the closed, controlled, and well-mannered "positive" bodies associated with civil societies, the "privatized and contained body, modeled on a masculine ideal, can be contrasted against the 'grotesque body,' which is characterized by its openness and its orifices, which lack closure" (Hatty, 2000, p. 147). Women's bodies, with their cyclical nature and reproductive potential, past and present, threaten to "spill over" into social space, threatening or breaching its order. As sexed objects in contemporary Western society, the unbounded or unrestrained character of women's bodies incites fear in most, if not, all masculine imaginations, as feminists and others often say. At the same time, many men and women today characterize female sexuality as both lower in intensity and less oriented toward sexual variety than male sexuality but acknowledge women's greater empirical capacities for intensity and frequency of orgasm (Richmond-Abbott, 1992).

Moreover, an abundance of anthropological evidence, past and present, exists to suggest that female sexuality, especially in male-dominated systems of interaction, may not yet have "evolved" into its own and is still captive of male needs and desires rather than subject to its own needs and desires (Rubin, 1975). Numerous examples pertain to the negative sanctions, including physical punishment as well as body mutilation, that certainly put a damper on female sexuality. As Smuts (1992) cautions,

> both the objective, observable expression of female sexuality and women's subjective experience of their own sexuality are so influenced by repression and fear of violent coercion that, in most societies, it is impossible to identify the "intrinsic" nature of female sexuality based on female behavior. It seems premature, for example, to attribute the relative lack of female interest in sexual variety to women's biological nature alone in face of overwhelming evidence that women are consistently beaten for promiscuity and adultery. (p. 29)

Similarly, labels or ideologies attached to various connotations of sexuality, especially those associated with "safety" and "danger," are often split around class and ethnic lines. For example, the "pure" labels of female sexuality have been reserved for middle and upper class white women; the "dirty" labels (e.g., sluts, whores) of female sexuality have been allocated to poor and working class women and women of color. For men, there have been no similarly negative stigma. On the contrary, because men are all assumed to be desirous of sexual variety, they are awarded labels of "stud" or the less flattering "womanizer," statuses aspired to consciously or subconsciously by most adolescent and adult heterosexual males. These ideologies of sexual difference, which depict some women as "whores," allow boys and men, especially those of higher socioeconomic status, to "attribute their sexual exploits to ["bad"] women's voracious sexuality, drawing attention away from the coercive tactics they employ to gain access to these women" (Smuts, 1992, p. 26).

More generally, the frequent construction of many, if not all, women or the female gender as the dangerous sex serves to reinforce a gendered threat that relies heavily on

> the utilization of violence by men—in intimate relationships, in public places, and on a national and international scale. Violence, as a prerogative of the dominant gender, is invoked to sustain this position of social superiority. . . . Violence is also invoked in transactions between men. Displays of hegemonic masculinity involving violence assert the primacy of this version of manliness and marginalize alternative versions. (Hatty, 2000, p. 148)

In a related way, it may also be true that what we identify as the "intrinsic" nature of male sexuality may also be a distortion or a reflection of a different kind of sexual repression and fear associated with the various meanings of *m/f*. Men, in separate and yet related ways, may also be captives of a sexuality that they are either not fully one with or that they are alienated from. In short, it appears that sexualities for many males and females are still relatively repressed.

Historically, we could talk about specific medieval, Enlightenment, New World, or postmodern masculinities and femininities. For example, during the Middle Ages (12th to 14th centuries), heroic masculinity was associated with action and movement, with slaying enemies and conquering malevolent powers. In addition, this masculinity was detached from the institutions of marriage and antithetical to the sphere of domesticity. A few centuries later, modern civilizations of greater stability and order arose, derivative of self-control and self-discipline. A bit later, during the Enlightenment period or Age of Reason, a developing individualism of heroic proportions reinforced and supported the sexualities of married couples only; it condemned or marginalized the sexualities of everybody else (Foucault, 1980).

In 20th-century America, *m/f* was affected by many developments, including the ideologies of militarism associated with World Wars I and II; the struggles of feminism and the crises in masculinity associated with both Vietnam-related anxieties and the Sexual Revolution of the 1960s and after; the "backlash" response to these and the associated emphasis on exaggerated masculine values and behaviors during the "get tough" era of President Reagan and politics of Cold War; and, most recently, in the "transgender" cultural attitudes of hardness and aggression for men and women, which first began to appear thematically on television and in films during the 1990s. Today, as Connell (1987) and others have argued, we find ourselves living in a world, domestically and internationally, that relies on diverse and heterogeneous constructions of *m/f*, ranging from a "hegemonic masculinity" to various

subordinated masculinities and femininities. While there may be a preferred or prominent version of femininity, "there is no femininity that is hegemonic in the sense that the dominant form of masculinity is hegemonic among men" (Connell, 1987, p. 183).

Hegemonic masculinity, in other words, is the cultural manifestation of men's ascendancy over women, dependent on the circulation of mass-mediated ideologies and images for its survival and prosperity, and not at all divorced from the uses of force or violence. For example, J. Gilligan (1996), Totten (2000), and others have discussed in different and related ways how crimes, particularly crimes of violence, often revolve around issues of male sexuality and identity and proving that one possesses the required hegemonic masculinity. When adolescent boys are unable to comfortably express their sexualities, for example in the case of young males coming to terms with their or somebody else's homosexuality, the chances of their physically abusing another person, male or female, becomes more likely (Totten, 2000). In the forms of some male homicides, issues of identity formation and sexual intimacy have been germane to the type of person who became the target of these kinds of killers (Gilligan, 1996).

Similarly, Messerschmidt (1993, 1997) has emphasized the relational and hierarchical character of masculinities. He argues essentially that excluded or marginalized male youth, especially African American or Hispanic American, who have not been able to demonstrate their manliness in more conventional or legitimate ways (e.g., social achievements) may adopt a masculinity of resistance or opposition. Middle class white male adolescents, by contrast, may embrace an accommodating masculinity in the short run as they assume that in the not too distant future they will acquire some of the semblances of hegemonic masculinity and the rewards that come with it.

Box 7.1 The Dialectics of Sexuality and the New Pornography

In postmodern culture, the traditional distinctions between "erotica" and "pornography" no longer apply, even if they once may have. As Brian McNair (1996) has pointed out, "the dramatic increase in sexually explicit images which has characterized the post-1960s period in the west is not the cause of sexism and patriarchy, but the reflection of broader social developments, some negative (HIV/AIDS), others positive (the achievements of feminism and gay rights)" (p. 174). Today, it makes more sense, is less ideological or moralistic, and is more representational of the diverse, overlapping, and contradictory images and texts of sexuality to speak in terms of the content or intent of a variety of pornographies. In a nutshell, there are pornographies that are and are not misogynistic and sexist.

Even in the context of those "old" pornographies that operate out of male desire or from a male point of view, and where there are frequently distasteful, crude, and offensive sexual representations supportive of hierarchy, inequality, and patriarchy, nothing has precluded the development of other caring, trusting, and mutually satisfying representations of explicit "hardcore" (e.g., erections, penetrations, and "money shots" in film or video) sexualities derived from the desires and points of view of male, female, gay, or straight audiences or some combination thereof. These "new" pornographies may also be politically correct or incorrect, but like their older counterparts, should only be censored or banned on "the basis that illegal acts have been committed in the process of [their] production, for which the pornography is the evidence, as well as being the crime itself" (p. 174).

Philosophically, the new pornographies do not deny the fact that there are pornographies, especially among the "old" pornographies, which denigrate women and girls and which may or may not be destructive of the building of trusting sexual relations among people. It also seems that not a few serial sexual murderers, such as Ted Bundy in the United States or Peter Sutcliffe (the "Yorkshire Ripper") in England, claim to have been avid consumers of this kind of material. Such self-justificatory statements, of course, should not be taken as some kind of "proof" that pornography causes sex crimes. One would, not surprisingly, hypothesize or expect to find that those who commit sexual crimes are consumers of such pornography. Once again, however, these kinds of correlations between mediated sex or violence and real sex and violence are tenuous at best in an indirect-effects kind of way and spurious at worst in terms of avoiding the sources or etiology of the pathways to their sexual violence.

The new pornographies are part of the different sexual lifestyles that were publicly emerging in the West at the turn of the 21st century. As such, these new pornographies service a diverse set of consumers and subcultural tastes. They may also be used as educational tools and, of course, for purposes of masturbation and the arousal of other sexual activities. More specifically, what are some of the meanings, gratifications, and different uses of the new pornographies in general and by those who consume them in particular?

(Continued)

Box 7.1 (Continued)

First, these have been attached to the sexual revolution as it has affected straight and gay men and women. Second, they have been attached to mediated sex and to the associated eroticizing of violence; for example, in the forms of S&M and for the purposes of distinguishing between "real" and "representative" sexual coercion. Third, meanings have ceased to be carriers of uniform, universally agreed-upon connotations; they are now polysemic, shifting signifiers. In short, "gays can read straight porn, and vice versa; images can vary in their meaning according to the social semiotic of their reception; pornography can be decoded or encoded 'subversively'" (p. 105).

Moreover, with respect to such new pornographies as "porn for women" and to the proliferation of "soft-core" mainstream pornography, from cable to satellite to the Internet to mass advertising, perhaps (a real stretch?) those on the pathways to future sexual violence might desist from and alter their violent courses of behavior as they become compulsive consumers of explicit and mutualistic nonviolent sexuality, rather than of the adversarial or misogynistic kinds. The unlikelihood of such indirect and mediated sexualities altering the behavioral courses of these individuals could be enhanced if they were incorporated into some kind of individual and group therapy. Although I am not necessarily suggesting, let alone arguing for, a "therapeutic pornography" per se, I do believe that such policies of treatment for sexually violent offenders would do more to decrease their negative kinds of behaviors than would policies of "pornographic censorship."

In summation, while acknowledging and not dismissing the potential use and abuse of pornography in relation to coercive sexual activity, the perspective adopted here has "proceeded from the assumption that, in many of the contexts in which it is used, pornography is neither the cause nor the conduit of antisocial violent behaviour," but "a form of sexual representation or exposure to which people have freely entered into" (p. 104). Because of the inherent abuse of power and lack of even a semblance of consent on the part of children, child pornography should be regarded as an exception to the general rule that pornographies, depending on their content, can be used in the pursuit of sexual violence or nonviolence. Thus, the notion that all pornography must somehow treat the body as an object to be controlled and dominated for violent purposes, or that there is some kind of inevitable abuse and degradation associated with soft- or hard-core texts and other sexually explicit materials, is simply wrong. Pornography, in other words, like erotica, can also be about autoerotic or mutually gratifying pleasure and, at the same time, be free of sexual conduct that is insulting, disrespectful, or abusive of other people.

Source: McNair, B. (1996). *Mediated sex: Pornography and postmodern culture.* London: Arnold.

Bodies and Sexualities

In discussing sexualities, Foucault showed how bodies come alive through the intervention of historically specific institutional processes and practices. More specifically, bodies and sexualities are the workings of power in relation to the Self—self-regulation, supervision, and discipline—and the Other—scrutinized, categorized, judged, and even violated. As both Foucault and Elizabeth Grosz (1994) have contended, sexualities and bodies "cannot be adequately understood as ahistorical, precultural, or natural objects in any simple way; they are not only inscribed, marked, engraved, by social pressures external to them but are the products, the direct effect, of the very social constitution of nature itself" (Grosz, 1994, p. x). In today's world, of course, images of sex and sexuality—mediated sex—are everywhere: in popular cinema and TV, the press, pop music, advertising (see Chapter 6), and in the proliferation of sexual discourses and the "new pornographies" that cut across sex and gender boundaries.

Historically, male bodies have often been depicted as instruments acting in the service of some kind of political or social end. This is why men in the public sector are often shown as "talking heads," divorced from their physicality and sexual desires. In addition, male bodies have often been thought of as weapons. The very meaning of *masculinity* conjures up the embodiment of force (Connell, 1983). In fact, violence or the threat thereof has always been wrapped around masculinity: Men have been "taught to occupy space in ways that connote strength, potency, and assertiveness" (Hatty, 2000, p. 120).

In many ways, the male body becomes a project subject to the will and motivation of its "possessor." In turn, body-reflexive practices such as bodybuilding lead to an achievement-oriented approach to masculinity that includes, among other things, sports, military combat, and sexual assault (Connell, 1995). Accordingly, the ideal male body becomes one that is hard as a rock, free of looseness and flaccidity (Bordo, 1996). As part of an achievement-oriented masculinity, the ideal ("hegemonic") male body is one that is solid, resistant, and self-sufficient. It is also a body to be desired and feared. With respect to the presentation of the "naturalized" heterosexual male body, Jackson (1990) has noted how heterosexual relations have shaped him "to embody superiority over women in [his] bodily relations. Practically, this means holding [his] body in a firmly decisive way that marks [him] off from an imaginary woman" (p. 57). These bodily actions may involve such means as thrusting, driving, and pushing, and such ends as angry presentations of controlling behaviors and animated selves. At the cultural extreme of masculinity in the United States are the images associated with the black male body as an icon of danger, conjuring up extreme levels of personal harm against others, creating high levels of social anxiety and fear, and threatening the overturn of social order (Gray, 1995; Hutchinson, 1996; Russell, 1998).

In reality, male bodies have proven over and over to be fragile creations, marked by their own failures to measure up (Connell, 1995). The discourses of the self-built and carefully engineered male body, from classical Greece onward, have often clashed head on with the lived experiences of unpredictable and undisciplined physicality. Related to the differences between ideal and real male bodies is the fact that living in a male body can often be a semidetached or "out of body" experience. "Men's experience of the body is often epitomized by feelings of alienation and absence. Indeed, men will frequently speak of the foreign character of their own bodies, as if they are referring to a physical entity that is not integral to their identity as male subjects" (Hatty, 2000, p. 120).

In a very general way, males may be little invested in their bodies and view them as low-maintenance propositions (Updike, 1996). At the same time, even if the male body and penis do measure up and perform well, in other ways, both will always be a source of great anxiety when compared to the mythical or symbolic power of the phallus and the masculine ideal that "dominates, restricts, prohibits, and controls representations of the male body" (Lehman, 1993, p. 71). In terms of sexuality, the alienation from the body may manifest itself in a strange kind of way. On the one hand, there can be a sense of the semiautonomous penis, often with a physicality and a mind of its own. On the other hand, in preparation for sexual activities there can be a sense of coconspiracy. In fact, many men have been known to name this part of their anatomy and to engage the penis in silent or private conversations before and during sexual acts. These conversations about "body parts" differ in both form and substance from those typically engaged in verbally by participants involved in sexual intimacies.

Like men, women are alienated from their bodies. However, their estrangements are of a different kind, as, historically, the personal and social experiences of female bodies have been of a different nature. Although there is some debate over Laqueur's (1990) theory of a one-sex model in pre-Renaissance Europe, in which male and female bodies were simply viewed as mirror images of each other, there is little disagreement over the lack of a precise medical nomenclature for female genitals and the reproductive system until well after the Middle Ages. Before the Renaissance, males were considered to be "the measure of all things," and femaleness did not exist as an ontologically distinct category. Finally, when the female body emerged in its "own right," it did so in terms of an incorporation of the male gaze.

As the Other of the male gaze, women's bodies as experienced become severed from the social meanings attributed to their bodies. The rupture between the lived body for females and the female body as object of desire and/or repulsion renders women's perceptions of their bodies problematic: "The body is transformed into a foreign entity, one *inside* social relations but *outside* the self" (Hatty, 2000, p. 124). In the scheme of things, maleness and the male body become the healthy norm, and femaleness and the female body become the "diseased" norm. In terms of this "difference as pathology," a woman's reproductive capacity transforms her body into a public abnormality, where it is viewed as assembled bits and pieces that can never measure up to some ideal female body.

The focus on the female body as fragmented and diseased is matched by an obsession with the surface area of the female body. This cultural construction or objectification of the female body translates into a vocabulary of deficiency and desire and into a social project of corrective actions to shore up the lack. Corrective actions include a wide range of normalized practices, such as efforts to reduce body size and to contain female desire so it will not overwhelm the woman's body or encroach on other, male bodies. Anorexic women, for example, have taken extreme corrective steps, to the point of extinguishing their female desire altogether, represented by the absence of hunger. At the same time, many anorexics still experience physical hunger; they just ruthlessly suppress it. They also may believe (consciously, at least) that their bodies are sexy (although their libidos are virtually nonexistent). They may even claim that their avowed reason for starving themselves is about being attractive and (theoretically, if not practically) desirable. This form of repressed sexuality, however, rarely if ever expresses itself in sexual mutualism. More generally, social institutions such as psychiatric facilities, prisons, hospitals, and the health and diet industries have historically extolled or shaped the female body by force—confining, constraining, watching, and categorizing it. In the process, the female body has been reorganized again and again into themes that have resonated with patriarchal and chauvinistic narratives.

Historically, the female body and its interior and exterior have continually been the object and subject of the male's (Other) project. Today, it seems as though the male body, at least with respect to its exterior, is becoming less of a "talking head," as it increasingly has become the object and subject of the Other's (female) gaze, as in, "He's a hunk." The growing universality of sexed bodies and the tendency to sexually objectify and exploit the ideal of both female and male bodies over the past quarter century are reflective of an emerging process of transgendering in which the traditionally drawn public lines between *m/f* have started to blur, and sexualities have become more fluid and flexible (see Box 7.2).

Box 7.2 Sexualities, Androgyny, and Sadomasochism

When it comes to sexualities, people often think about the various traits or characteristics associated with the identities of *m/f* as oppositional. Studies, however, have demonstrated that men and women generally overlap in regard to many gender stereotypes, especially as these are related to sexual paraphernalia (e.g., body piercing, sex toys, S&M) and sexual orientations (e.g., heterosexual, homosexual, bisexual, transsexual). Among all of these sexual groups, for example, there can be found persons who are assertive or passive, independent or dependent, emotional or unemotional, nurturing or non-nurturing, and so on and so forth. In short, within and across sex and gender, connections exist among sexualities and between those attributes traditionally associated with women ("femininity") and with men ("masculinity").

Sandra Bem (1975), who did some of the pioneering work on measuring androgyny, developed the Bem Sex Role Inventory scales. Depending on the differences in one's masculinity and femininity scores, one can be considered to be "more masculine," "more feminine," "undifferentiated," or "androgynous." In actuality, however, Bem's inventory was not a true measurement of *m/f* but at best only a reflection of gender stereotypes. Some have argued that her scales were really measuring expressive and instrumental personality traits rather than gender roles. So, like other forms and expressions of sexuality, androgyny is a loose concept involving social, psychological, and biological dimensions.

Androgyny is an ancient word taken from the Greek "andro" (male) and "gyn" (female). It refers to a condition under which the human impulses expressed by men and women and the characteristics of the sexes are not rigidly differentiated. More generally, "androgynous" has come to be understood as referring to an individual of either the male or female sex who is capable of calling forth elements of both masculinity and femininity. Others have maintained that androgynous persons are those who identify with the desirable characteristics of both masculinity and femininity and who are also comfortable with the behavioral aspects of these across a wide variety of social conditions (Jones, Chernovitz, & Hanson, 1978). In short, one can think of androgyny as a blending of both masculine and feminine traits and behaviors.

For example, male and female bodily alterations are common fare throughout North America, Britain, Europe, and most places throughout the world, past and present. In the

(Continued)

Box 7.2   (Continued)

modern nation-states of the West, such as Germany or the United States, tattooing and piercing establishments no longer restrict themselves to simple ear piercing but specialize in tongue, nipple, scrotum, labia, and more. It is estimated that throughout Britain there are a few thousand erotic piercings weekly, including some 600 genital piercings performed in London alone, with a 50/50 gender split (Presdee, 2000). The connections between sexuality, tattooing, and erotic piercings are made visible not only in magazines such as *Savage* and in sex shops and lingerie stores alike, such as Victoria's Secret and Frederick's of Hollywood, but in mass marketing as well. Moreover, these and other emerging unisexual trends and customs are expressive of a growing androgynous sensibility in both popular culture and mass communications.

Popular tastes in the "new" sexualities, involving both pleasure and pain, are also indicative that "S&M activities are now firmly embedded in the cultural fabric of everyday life at an international level and have become part of the consciousness and life experiences of millions of citizens" (Presdee, 2000, p. 98). The use of handcuffs, whips, and restraints or the infliction of pain and humiliation, for example, between consenting or nonconsenting sexual dyads for the purposes of mutual or self-gratification have moved from the domains of "art" or "battered chic" and into the mainstreams of commercial advertising and mass communications.

Whether marginal or conventional, "playing with power" seems to be an essential ingredient of S&M relationships, as does consensus, sexual arousal, and an unequal sharing of a balance of power (Taylor & Ussher, 2001). As Lynn Chancer (1992) has explained, S&M can be about pleasure, diversity, and mutual self-exploration between consenting persons, based on extreme need and a trust not usually found in the wider society. S&M can also be placed on a continuum from extreme violence to extreme nonviolence. Sadomasochism, like destructive (adversarial) and constructive (mutualistic) pornography, can also be about the reification of or the resistance to patriarchy, sexism, and inequality. On converging contradictory pathways, then, pornography and S&M can, at one end of the continuum, be repressive and conducive to violence, and at the other end, liberating and conducive to nonviolence.

S&M relations that are primarily consensual in nature may also share some aspects in common with other abusive and nonabusive behaviors. However, what differentiates S&M expressions of sexuality from their exploitative counterparts is the presence of mutual consent (or love) rather than intimidation, manipulation, and degradation. In the context of trying to understand the pathways toward and away from violence and nonviolence, it is useful to briefly characterize these emerging democratic forms of sexuality, aggression, power, and control as they converge and blend with the older and established forms of patriarchal sexuality.

To say the least, there is much confusion, misunderstanding, and a lack of basic knowledge of the area of S&M. For example, sadomasochism as a form of sex play is about the mutual pleasure of both the "dominant" and "submissive" partners. Often times, partners switch roles, possessing control in one encounter and being controlled in the next encounter. Another common misconception is that S&M is some kind of male power game. In practice, however, there are women who dominate men, men who dominate women, women who dominate women, and men who dominate men.

Despite the recent democratization of the practices of S&M, they are still viewed by the medical establishment primarily as some kind of sexual pathology. As for the prevailing sexual discourse on the subject, the World Health Organization, for example, lists S&M as a mental disorder, even though the psychiatric community's knowledge of sadomasochism, as well as empirical data on the subject, remain virtually nonexistent (Presdee, 2000). In the same vein, S&M is described in the current psychological textbooks as a mental illness, often discussed alongside behaviors such as child sexual abuse and rape. This "illness" is regarded in the most general way as some kind of intrapsychic conflict related to the sexual drive. In one of the few empirical studies, researchers questioned 24 self-identified sadomasochists and found that the motivations and purposes between S&M and other sexual practices were essentially the same: intrapsychic, dissidence, pleasure, escape, transcendence, learning, and so on (Taylor & Ussher, 2001).

SEXUAL DIFFERENCE, GENDER IDENTITY, AND VIOLENCE

In this book, the examination of sexuality and violence employs a social relations or interactive approach. If nothing else, this perspective has revealed the importance of the "context-specific approach" to the study of mediated sex and violence—sexual and nonsexual—and to the value of an "indirect-effects" approach to both media and sexuality as these are blended from the real and reel pathways of violence or nonviolence. Apart from the mediated natures of sex and violence, Dobash and Dobash (1998a) have appropriately commented about the material nature of sexual violence in particular:

> While accumulating evidence does suggest the existence of "male" violence against women in all societies and across time, which might in turn suggest an inherent, universal male characteristic, research also shows variation in both the nature and level

of this violence between men and women across [and within] different societies and/or cultures. This variation suggests cultural specificity and the importance of different contexts rather than an unvaried, universal behavior. (p. 16; see also Dobash & Dobash, 1983)

In the context of gender differences and sexuality, the rest of this chapter explores some of the similarities and dissimilarities of males and females engaged in a variety of violent activities. These types of violence include (a) nonlethal relationship violence, (b) familiar and unfamiliar lethal violence, (c) gang violence, (d) child sexual abuse, and (e) serial murder. Before turning to these comparative pathways to violence, it is important to underscore the cultural differences of male and female violence in relation to *m/f* identities, sexually scripted roles, and the sex-gender systems more generally.

In most cultures around the world, the propensity to use lethal and other forms of violence has been greater among boys and men than among girls and women. From a culture of gender perspective, violence and aggression are more accessible to men than to women because of the embedded nature of violence "in a net of physicality, experience, and male culture such that it is more easily used and more readily available as a resource" (Dobash and Dobash, 1998c, p. 164). Simply stated, in many cultures of masculinity, past and present, aggressive and violent behavior have been highly valued and rewarded. In a few words, contemporary boys and young men learn to "do" violence in a number of formal and informal arenas that allow them to cultivate aggression and to use their bodies as instruments of force, intimidation, and success. Some of these expressions of male violence cannot be disconnected from their social places nor from the vital roles they play in the formation of masculine identities (Newburn & Stanko, 1994; Toch, 1992).

When it comes to male violence, the Dobashes and others have documented meaningful distinctions in the acts of violence between men and in the acts of violence against women. The former have been characterized as involving valor, heroism, masculine pride, and a focus on the act. Win or lose, these are righteous or "heroic" acts that possess reaffirming qualities about personal identity. By contrast, the latter acts of violence have been characterized as involving masculine power, control, domination, and a focus on the outcome. These acts of violence are not about process but about conquest ("winning") or defeating women whether the purpose is one of shutting her up, getting a meal, or having sex. These acts of violence do not bring a sense of masculine pride and status, but they do reconfirm a masculine identity to the extent that the male is not subordinated to the female.

Although there may be some commonality between male and female violence, especially in terms of the costs and benefits to the individuals concerned, "in a wider cultural sense, feminine identity is not valorized by female-to-female violence or by violence to men" (Dobash & Dobash, 1998c, p. 168). Of course, this does not mean to imply that women are innately incapable of aggression and violence. Rather, it simply underscores that males and females have both been objects and subjects of the cultural differences of *m/f*, gendered behavior, and identity formation. In short, girls and young women have been nurtured or socialized away from violence. In spite of these cultural biases against female violence, women's capacities for, initiated actions, and perpetrations of intimate violence, especially involving the least serious levels of violence, tend to equal or surpass those of men (Bland & Orn, 1986; Brinkerhoff & Lupri, 1988; DeKeseredy & Schwartz, 1998; Kwong, Bartholomew, & Dutton, 1999; Stets & Straus, 1990). Also, both genders have reported that women do initiate violence and are sometimes the sole perpetrators of aggression in relationships. Thus, it appears that a sizable proportion of women's violence against men cannot be explained merely as acts of self-defense against physically assaultive males. Nevertheless, in terms of serious injuries, danger, and victimizations, men are the predominant offenders and women the predominant victims.

Nonlethal Relationship Violence: Heterosexual Battering

In marital and marital-like relations, men and women have interests and conflicts in common. In the context of families, although parents and children, as well as husbands and wives, share goals, they are also in competition for the resources of the domestic arena, including time, physical space, freedom of movement, and the fruits of domestic labor. In intimate heterosexual relationships generally, there is relative parity when it comes to the number of incidences of battering between the sexes, if not in the severity of those acts of violence. Women rarely, if ever, beat to death their heterosexual partners. As for sex-related violence, this is essentially a male problem, as sexually based abuse of men by women is virtually nonexistent. Even if one were to include S&M dominatrixes, the argument can be made that these are consensual rather than exploitative sexual relations.

When it comes to the use, frequency, type, and prevalence of violence used between men and women, several studies in the United States, Canada, and Britain (already cited in Chapters 1 or 2) confirm "that a large minority of both men and women commit violent acts within their intimate relations" (Kwong et al., 1999, p. 156). The Violence Aggressive Index, for example, reveals little difference between the sexes regarding the less serious rates of violence (e.g., pushing and grabbing, slapping face or body, restraining her or him, punching walls, and throwing objects). In other words, men and women report similar acts of petty violence perpetration and victimization. The greatest differences are found in the context of the more serious types of interpersonal violence, including rape and forced sex, punching and kicking the body or face, choking, using or threatening to use weapons, and attempting to kill a person. Men are the more prevalent and frequent perpetrators of these acts of violence, but women are more likely to be the persons who suffer serious injuries as a consequence of their abuse.

In studies on relationship violence that the Dobashes and their colleagues have carried out for more than 20 years, they have consistently found that conflicts or arguments between men and women revolve around four major themes. Each of these is related to patriarchal notions of masculinity: men's possessiveness and jealousy, men's sense of the right to punish "their" women for

perceived wrongdoing, and the importance to men of maintaining or exercising their power and authority. Other sources of conflict include money, sex, the man's use of alcohol, and children.

Lethal Violence: Familiar and Unfamiliar Homicide

When it comes to both familiar and unfamiliar killings, men are as likely to be perpetrators as they are to be victims. Women are more likely to be victims of current or former sexual intimates than of strangers. Women are also more likely to be murderers of their own children than men are. When it comes to the murders of other people's children, however, men account for more than 80% of those killings. The world of stranger homicide, then, is truly a man's world. Women perpetrators of unfamiliar lethal violence are relatively rare.

When it comes to lethal violence, gender affects not only who the perpetrators are likely to be in a given type of homicide scenario but the means by which the victims are likely to die. Generally, men are as likely to be involved in familiar as in unfamiliar ("stranger") murders. Men's involvement in homicide is "total": It extends across all relational boundaries in society. By contrast, women's involvement in homicide is primarily limited to the relational spheres of family and/or sexual intimacy.

For example, an examination of homicide incidents in England and Wales (1986-1996) revealed that 27% of male victims were killed in the context of familiar or sexual intimacy, compared to 68% of female victims. Moreover, almost 2 out of 3 (64%) male victims knew their killer; among women, nearly 7 of 8 (84%) did (Smith & Stanko, 1999). In fact, this examination found that the most common homicides against females were perpetrated either by their parents when they were young girls or by their current or former partners or boyfriends when they were adult women. Among adults, a current or ex-partner accounted for 6 out of every 10 women killed. Similarly, when women killed adult males, 65% of killings involved the murder of a current sexual partner.

As discussed in Chapter 2, gender is also related to the means of lethal violence selected by men and women. Men kill with guns, fists, and knives. Women kill mostly with knives. In terms of intergender homicide, the analysis by Smith and Stanko (1999) found that nearly 3 out of 4 (73%) women used knifes on their current or ex-partners, as compared to 3 out of 10 (29%) men.

Finally, the motivations associated with male and female homicides involving familiar and sexual situations may overlap, especially where histories of violent domestic conflict exist. However, the "battered women's syndrome" murder defense underscores at least one motivational difference in relationship lethal violence. Another gender dissimilarity is that men's motives for killing at home and away from home are more diversified and encompassing than women's. These motives have been identified as involving sexual dominance, jealousy, proprietariness, saving of face, and masculine honor (Polk, 1994; Wilson & Daly, 1998).

Gangs and Violence-Related Behavior

Traditionally, gangs and gang violence in particular were associated with adolescent males and "masculine" acts of vandalism, violence, and other serious threats. Not until the late 1980s and early 1990s did adolescent females and gang behavior become a topic in their own right. Before then, female gang members were viewed primarily in terms of their relations to male gang members. Images of female gang members focused almost exclusively on their sexual activities,

portraying them as "bad girls," meaning that they were neither modest nor feminine (Campbell, 1984, 1990). These female gang members were regarded as threatening and shocking because they not only engaged in real deviance like the boys, but in the process, they also seriously challenged gender-role norms for girls.

Nationwide surveys and estimates of the percentage of girls involved in gang behavior in the United States have varied from a low of 3% to a high of 11% over the past three decades. Today, females may belong to all-female gangs allied or not allied with other male gangs, or they may belong to fully integrated male-female gangs. Although males and females may both join gangs for friendship, family, and self-affirmation as well as for the economic gains to be made, gangs also seem to provide a place of refuge and protection for young women who have been sexually abused at home and/or subjected to drug dealing and other illicit activities (Moore & Hagedorn, 2001).

As with male gang members, not all female gang members are involved in some kind of delinquency and criminality. Nevertheless, youth surveys have consistently shown that delinquency rates for female gang members are higher than those of nongang females or males (Bjerregard & Smith, 1993; Esbensen & Huizinga, 1993; Fagan, 1990). Overall, "female gang members commit fewer violent crimes than male gang members and are more inclined to property crimes and status offenses" (Moore & Hagedorn, 2001, p. 5). Keeping in mind that girls constitute around 7% of all gang members nationwide, male-to-female ratios based on arrest records from 1965 to 1994 reveal that boys accounted for about 94% of the nonlethal violence, 96% of drug offenses, and 99% of gang-related homicides (Moore & Hagedorn, 2001, p. 5).

Although these statistics suggest that female gang violence is at most a nuisance to police and authorities, and certainly more than a nuisance to victims, an 11-city survey of eighth-grade gang members conducted in the mid 1990s suggested more violent activity than the official arrests would indicate. In a previous 12-month period, for example, 90% of both male and female gang members reported having engaged in one or more violent acts. Moreover, it was reported that 78% of female gang members had been involved in gang fights, 65% had carried weapons for protection, and 39% had attacked someone with a weapon (Deschenes & Esbensen, 1999; Esbensen & Osgood, 1997).

In the formative years of female gang delinquency (1970s), female gangs tended to be more autonomous from male gangs. For example, female gang members would fight rival female gang members, but they did not fight side by side with males as they more commonly do today. Hard drug use among contemporary female gang members also seems to be more likely than it was in the past. Finally, gangs seem to have become more integral or central to female gang members' lives today, much the same as they have always been for male gang members (Moore & Hagedorn, 2001).

Child Sex Abusers

Gender and sexual representations of males and females suggest that men are sexually more aggressive than women and that women are more emotionally demanding.

Such gender-differentiating norms allegedly encourage women to value emotional intimacy over sexual intimacy and to attach less significance than men to direct sexual satisfaction. These same norms allegedly encourage men to value such masculine characteristics as sexual competence and the satisfaction of intimacy needs through direct sexual pleasure. These gender-differentiating perspectives have also been used to explain why men, more than women, sexually abuse children. Typically, the arguments are that

> Men, sexually aggressive and dominant, are motivated to use children to satisfy their sexual needs when they fail to have these needs met in relationships with adult partners. Blocked in their access to socially accepted outlets for meeting their sexual needs, men turn to children, who are easily dominated and coerced. Women, on the other hand, are passive and sexually receptive . . . [they are] oriented towards older, not younger, sexual partners. Warm and nurturant, women, unlike men, have no sexual motives or tendencies toward children. (Allen & Pothast, 1994, p. 74)

Certainly, as Chapter 2 described, many more males than females sexually abuse young children. These facts, however, should not allow us to deny the fact that women do also sexually molest children. And, in terms of explanatory power, it should be kept in mind that most men will complain at one or more times during the course of their lives that their sexual satisfaction is not what they would like it to be. Yet the overwhelming majority of men do not sexually abuse children.

To test various gender-stereotyping biases and to distinguish between the characteristics of male and female child sex abusers, Allen and Pothast (1994) explored relationships among gender, role identity, and the emotional and sexual needs of child abusers and nonabusers in their adult relationships. In trying to sort out the relations of sex, gender, and role identity, their scores for masculinity and femininity were derived from the Bem Sex Role Inventory; emotional and sexual needs were measured by the Partner Relationship Inventory (Richmond-Abbott, 1992). Their sample consisted of 71 male and 58 female offenders and 38 male and 52 female nonoffenders.

As expected, the findings revealed that abusers in general had higher levels of emotional and sexual need than nonabusers. Contrary to expectations, however, female abusers and nonabusers had higher levels of both emotional and sexual need than their male counterparts. From the point of view of gender stereotypes, the most interesting results were that "higher levels of masculinity were associated with *lower,* not higher, levels of sexual need for all groups, men and women as well as abusers and nonabusers" (Allen & Pothast, 1994, p. 85).

Serial Murderers

Serial murderers, serial rapist-killers, and to a lesser extent, serial violent offenders are sensationalist creations of mass media and the collective imagination more than they are a representative reflection of the severity or prevalence of these particular forms of violence. In fact, by the end of the 20th century, these socially constructed cold-blooded, predominantly white and male murderers had become a cultural and media phenomenon well beyond any tangible harm and injury they might have actually inflicted. Serial killers as icons of danger and fascination have certainly become staples of books, film, and television (see Chapter 6).

Just as there are differences in the means, kinds, and motives of female and male homicide, differences by gender seem to be even more dramatic when it comes to serial murderers. As with homicides in general, for which females constitute only about 10% of those arrested, the representation of females among serial killers seems to be even smaller. In fact, some researchers (Egger, 1990; Leyton, 1986) in the area have stated that serial murder is an almost exclusively male behavior. Hickey's (1991) research has suggested otherwise and that female representation for homicide and serial homicide is about the same.

Definitions might have something to do with this discrepancy, as well as the reluctance of law enforcement and the general public to suspect women as perpetrators of serial killing. One comparative study on gender differences in serial murder defined it "as the premeditated murder of three or more victims committed over time, in separate incidents, in a civilian context, with the murder activity being chosen by the offender" (Keeney & Heide, 1994, p. 384). Like the FBI's definition, this one excludes killing by military or police personnel as part of their jobs, as well as assassinations by political terrorist groups. However, this definition does include health-care workers who murder their patients, parents who murder their children, professional assassins who operate under the confines of organized crime syndicates, and persons who kill multiple spouses or lovers.

Using a sample of 14 women serial killers and comparing them to composite analyses of 11 serial killer studies, Keeney and Heide were able to find useful information on 14 variables. With respect to behavior patterns, psychosocial history, and demographics, there were fewer similarities than there were differences. Similarities between male and female serial murderers included broken homes, childhood abuse, race (i.e., white), education level (i.e., low to average), and occupation (i.e., nonprofessional). Differences between the two groups included victim damage, victim torture, weapon and method, stalking versus luring behavior, crime-scene organization, motive, substance abuse history, psychiatric diagnosis, and household composition.

As groups of violent offenders go, male serial killers tend to be "sicker" individuals than female serial killers: male motives revolve around emotional issues of power and domination; female motives are divided between affective or emotional issues and instrumental goals (e.g., collecting insurance).

For example, unlike males who commonly engage in "overkill" or in actions above and beyond what is necessary to cause death, there were no females from the sample who sexually assaulted, mutilated, or dismembered their victims. Moreover, none of the female serial murderers tortured their victims, nor did they experience their victims' suffering as some kind of sexual turn-on or release.

Male serial killers tend to be "loners," as contrasted with females, who tend to be living with others at the time of their murders. Women serial killers use poisons as their first weapon of choice (57%), smothering as their second (29%), and firearms as their third (11%). By contrast, males tend to be almost exclusively "hands-on" killers, using knives, blunt objects, and their hands to kill their victims. Male serial killers tend to be quite mobile during their killing sprees; female serial killers tend to be sedentary and confine their killings to the same geographical area. Similarly, unlike males, females rarely moved their victims' bodies, cannibalized them, or fetishized any of their body parts. Also, unlike male serial killers, whose crime scenes tend to be either "organized" or "disorganized" affairs, females' crime scenes often appear to have characteristics of both.

Finally, there are differences between male and female serial murderers and their relationships to their victims. Comparatively, females killed few persons that they did not know. Their victims are typically family members or other persons in their charge, such as patients or infants. By contrast, males often kill strangers or casual acquaintances who satisfy some kind of fantasy-world criteria.

SUMMARY

This chapter extended and incorporated the mass-mediated sex and violence analyses from Chapter 6 by providing an overview of the "battle of the sexes" as it has physiologically and cross culturally evolved over some 6 million years. In the process, common properties and pathways within and between sexual and nonsexual violent behaviors were discussed. Examination shifted between sexuality and violence and the social relations of sex, aggression, and gender as these revealed differential pathways to violence.

Philosophically, anthropologically, and psychoanalytically situated, this chapter concluded that the differences between the levels of aggression in general and in relation to sexual violence in particular between men and women are primarily social and cultural phenomena and only secondarily a biological phenomenon. Sexualities of difference and hierarchy, for example, were presented at different points in history to reveal the cultural pathways of sexual interaction. These in turn were directly related to sexual differences and gender identities in relation to assault, rape, murder, gang violence, and child abuse. The conclusion reached was that both violence and sexual violence are predominantly problems related to issues of masculinity and male sexual identity.

In the "close-ups" for this chapter, one on pornography and one on androgyny and S&M, the dialectics of sexuality were explored in the context of postmodern culture and the political economy of mass consumption. Although not spelled out in the body of this chapter, I would argue that sexual violence is primarily the product of an unhealthy sexual development that cannot be separated from cultural production. I also agree with those ideas first raised more than a half century ago by Reich (1945/1961) and Marcuse (1955/1966) of the Frankfurt School, and more recently by Lichtman (1982) and Fellman (1998), who have attempted to connect or integrate the models of Marx and Freud as these have pertained to both fascism and everyday life in relation to "sexual alienation" and "sexual repression."

Each of these analysts, and others, have tied these particular sexual maladies to political and economic domination, and each has called for some form of sexual revolution of liberation in which Eros would triumph over Thanatos. Once again: Make love, not war!

REFERENCES

Adler, A. (1977). Sex. In J. B. Miller (Ed.), *Psychoanalysis and women* (pp. 40-50). New York: Penguin. (Original work published 1927)

Allen, C. M., & Pothast, H. L. (1994). Distinguishing characteristics of male and female child sex abusers. In N. J. Pallone (Ed.), *Young victims, young offenders* (pp. 73-88). Binghamton, NY: Haworth.

Barnett, S. A. (1983). Humanity and natural selection. *Ethology and Sociobiology, 4,* 35-51.

Bem, S. (1975). Sex role adaptability: One consequence of psychological androgyny. *Journal of Personality and Social Psychology, 31,* 634-643.

Berger, R. J., Free, M. D., & Searles, P. (2001). *Crime, justice, and society: Criminology and the sociological imagination.* Boston: McGraw-Hill.

Berschield, E., & Walster, E. (1974). A little bit of love. In T. L. Huston (Ed.), *Foundations of interpersonal attraction* (pp. 355-381). New York: Academic.

Binford, S. (1972). Apes and original sin. *Human Behavior, 1(6),* 64-71.

Bjerregard, D., & Smith, C. (1993). Gender differences in gang participation, delinquency, and substance abuse. *Journal of Quantitative Criminology, 9,* 329-355.

Bland, R., & Orn, H. (1986). Family violence and psychiatric disorder. *Canadian Journal of Psychology, 1,* 129-137.

Bordo, S. (1996). "Reading the Male Body." In L. Goldstein (Ed.), *The male body: Features, desires, exposure* (pp. 256-307). Ann Arbor, MI: University of Michigan Press.

Brinkerhoff, M. B., & Lupri, E. (1988). Interpersonal violence. *Canadian Journal of Psychology, 13,* 407-434.

Burgess, R. L., & Draper, P. (1989). The explanation of family violence: The role of biological, behavioral, and cultural selection. In L. Ohlin & M. Tonry (Eds.), *Family violence, crime and justice: A review of research* (pp. 59-116). Chicago: University of Chicago Press.

Cameron, D., & Frazer, E. (1987). *The lust to kill: A feminist investigation of serial murder.* New York: New York University.

Campbell, A. (1984). *The girls in the gang.* Oxford, England: Basil Blackwell.

Campbell, A. (1990). Female participation in gangs. In C. R. Huff (Ed.), *Gangs in America* (pp. 76-94). Newbury Park, CA: Sage.

Chancer, L. S. (1992). *Sadomasochism in everyday life: The dynamics of power and powerlessness.* New Brunswick, NJ: Rutgers University Press.

Connell, R. (1983). *Which way is up?* Sydney, Australia: Allen and Unwin.

Connell, R. (1987). *Gender and power: Society, the person, and sexual politics.* Cambridge, MA: Polity.

Connell, R. (1995). *Masculinities.* Sydney, Australia: Allen and Unwin.

Daly, M., & Wilson, M. (1988). *Homicide.* Hawthorne, NY: Aldine de Gruyter.

DeKeseredy, W. S., & Schwartz, M. D. (1998). *Women abuse on campus: Results from the Canadian National Survey.* Thousand Oaks, CA: Sage.

Deschenes, E. P., & Esbensen, F. (1999). Violence in gangs: Gender differences in perceptions and behavior. *Journal of Quantitative Criminology, 15,* 63-96.

de Waal, B. M. (2000, July 28). Primates: A natural heritage of conflict. *Science, 289,* 586-590.

Dobash, R. E., & Dobash, R. P. (1983). The conflict-specific approach. In D. Finkelhor, R. Gelles, G. Hotaling, & M. Straus (Eds.), *The dark side of families: Current family research* (pp. 261-276). Beverly Hills, CA: Sage.

Dobash, R. E., & Dobash, R. P. (1998a). Cross-border encounters: Challenges and opportunities. In R. E. Dobash & R. P. Dobash (Eds.), *Rethinking violence against women* (pp. 1-21). Thousand Oaks, CA: Sage.

Dobash, R. E., & Dobash, R. P. (Eds.). (1998b). *Rethinking* violence against women. Thousand Oaks, CA: Sage.

Dobash, R. E., & Dobash, R. P. (1998c). Violent men and violent contexts. In R. E. Dobash & R. P. Dobash (Eds.), *Rethinking violence against women* (pp. 141-168). Thousand Oaks, CA: Sage.

Egger, S. (1990). *Serial murder: An elusive phenomenon.* New York: Praeger.

Ehrlich, P. (2000a). *Human natures: Genes, cultures, and the human project.* Covelo, CA: Island.

Ehrlich, P. (2000b, September 22). The tangled skeins of nature and nurture. *Chronicle of Higher Education,* pp. B7-B11.

Esbensen, F., & Huizinga, D. (1993). Gangs, drugs and delinquency in a survey of urban youth. *Criminology, 31,* 565-589.

Esbensen, F., & Osgood, D. W. (1997). *National evaluation of G.R.E.A.T.* Washington, DC: U.S. Department of Justice.

Fagan, J. (1990). Social processes of delinquency and drug use among urban gangs. In C. R. Huff (Ed.), *Gangs in America* (pp. 108-124). Newbury Park, CA: Sage.

Fellman, G. (1998). *Rambo and the Dalai Lama: The compulsion to win and its threat to human survival.* Albany: State University of New York Press.

Foucault, M. (1980). *The history of sexuality: An introduction.* New York: Vintage.

Freud, S. (1957). The taboo of virginity. In J. Strachey (Ed. & Trans.), *The standard edition of the complete psychological works of Sigmund Freud* (Vol. 11, pp. 192-208). Oxford, England: Oxford University Press. (Original work published 1918)

Freud, S. (1957). Some psychical consequences of the anatomical distinction between the sexes. In J. Strachey (Ed. & Trans.), *The standard edition of the complete psychological works of Sigmund Freud* (Vol 19, pp. 243-260). Oxford, England: Oxford University Press. (Original work published 1925)

Freud, S. (1957). Female sexuality. In J. Strachey (Ed. & Trans.), *The standard edition of the complete psychological works of Sigmund Freud* (Vol 21, pp. 223-246). Oxford, England: Oxford University Press. (Original work published 1931)

Fromm, E. (1956). *The art of loving.* New York: Harper.

Gilligan, C. (1982). *In a different voice: Psychological theory and women's development.* Cambridge, MA: Harvard University Press.

Gilligan, J. (1996). *Violence: Reflections on a national epidemic.* New York: Vintage.

Godenzi, A., Schwartz, M. D., & DeKeseredy, W. S. (2001). Toward a gendered social bond/male peer support theory of university woman abuse. *Critical Criminology: An International Journal, 10*(1): 1-16.

Goldstein, J. H. (1986). *Aggression and crimes of violence* (2nd ed.). New York: Oxford University Press.

Gray, H. (1995). Black masculinity and visual culture. *Callaloo, 18,* 401-404.

Grosz, E. (1994). *Volatile bodies: Toward corporeal feminism.* Sydney, Australia: Allen and Unwin.

Hammerstein, P., & Parker, G. A. (1987). Sexual selection: Games between the sexes. In J. W. Bradbury & M. B. Andersson. (Eds.), *Sexual selection: Testing the alternatives* (pp. 119-142). New York: Wiley.

Hatty, S. (2000). *Masculinities, violence, and culture.* Thousand Oaks, CA: Sage.

Hickey, E. (1991). *Serial murderers and their victims.* Belmont, CA: Wadsworth.

Horney, K. (1977). The flight from womanhood: The masculinity complex. Women as viewed by men and by women. In J. B. Miller (Ed.), *Psychoanalysis and women* (pp. 5-20). New York: Penguin. (Original work published 1926)

Hunt, M. (1974). *Sexual behavior in the 1970s.* New York: Dell.

Hutchinson, E. O. (1996). *Beyond O.J.: Race, sex, and class lessons for America.* Los Angeles: Middle Passage.

Jackson, D. (1990). *Unmasking masculinity.* Winchester, MA: Unwin Hyman.

Jones, W., Chernovitz, E., & Hanson, R. (1978). The enigma of androgyny: Differential implications for males and females. *Journal of Consulting and Clinical Psychology, 46*(2), 298-313.

Jung, C. (1977). *The portable Jung* (J. Campbell, Ed.). New York: Viking. (Original work published 1951)

Keeney, B. T., & Heide, K. M. (1994). Gender differences in serial murderers: A preliminary analysis. *Journal of Interpersonal Violence, 9*(3), 383-398.

Kelly, L. (1987). The continuum of sexual violence. In J. Hammer & M. Maynard (Eds.), *Women, violence, and social control* (pp. 110-128). Atlantic Highlands, NJ: Humanities International.

Klein, M. (1975). *The psycho-analysis of children*. New York: Delacorte. (Original work published 1932)

Kwong, M. J., Bartholomew, K., & Dutton, D. G. (1999). Gender differences in patterns of relationship violence in Alberta. *Canadian Journal of Behavioural Science, 31*(3), 156-160.

Laqueur, T. (1990). *Making sex: Body and gender from the Greeks to Freud*. Cambridge, MA: Harvard University Press.

Lehman, P. (1993). *Running scared: Masculinities and representation of the male body*. Philadelphia, PA: Temple University Press.

Levinson, D. (1989). *Family violence in cross-cultural perspective*. Newbury Park, CA: Sage.

Leyton, E. (1986). *Compulsive killers: The story of modern multiple murder*. New York: New York University Press.

Lichtman, R. (1982). *The production of desire: The integration of psychoanalysis into marxist theory*. New York: Free Press.

Lorenz, K. (1966). *On aggression*. New York: Harcourt Brace World.

MacKinnon, C. (1983). Feminism, Marxism, method, and state: Toward feminist jurisprudence. *Signs, 8*, 635-658.

MacKinnon, C. (1987). *Feminism unmodified: Discourses in life and law*. Cambridge, MA: Harvard University Press.

Malamuth, N. M. (1998). An evolutionary-based model integrating research on the characteristics of sexually coercive men. In J. G. Adair, D. Belanger, & K. L. Dion (Eds.), *Advances in psychological science* (Vol. 1, pp. 33-55). Hove, England, UK: Psychology Press.

Marcuse, H. (1966). *Eros and civilization*. Boston: Beacon. (Original work published 1955)

Marx, K. (1940). *Capital* (Vol. 1). New York: Modern Library. (Original work published 1906)

McNair, B. (1996). *Mediated sex: Pornography and post-modern culture*. London: Arnold.

Messerschmidt, J. W. (1993). *Masculinities and crime: Critique and reconceptualization of theory*. Landham, MD: Rowman and Littlefield.

Messerschmidt, J. W. (1997). *Crime as structured action: Gender, race, class, and crime in the making*. Thousand Oaks, CA: Sage.

Miller, B. D. (1991). Wife-beating in India: Variations on a theme. In D. Counts, J. K. Brown, & J. L. Campbell (Eds.), *Sanctions and sanctuary: Cultural perspectives on the beating of wives*. Boulder, CO: Westview.

Money, J., & Ehrhardt, A. (1972). *Man, woman, boy and girl: The differentiation and dimorphism of gender identity from conception to maturity*. Baltimore, MD: Johns Hopkins University Press.

Montagu, A. (1968). *Man and aggression*. New York: Oxford University Press.

Montagu, A. (1976). *The nature of human aggression*.

New York: Oxford University Press.

Montagu, A. (Ed.) (1978). *Learning non-aggression: The experience of non-literate societies*. New York: Oxford University Press.

Moore, J., & Hagedorn, J. (2001, March). *Female gangs: A focus on research* (OJJDP Juvenile Justice Bulletin NCJ 186159). Retrieved November 3, 2002, from http://www.ncjrs.org/html/ojjdp/jjbul2001_3_3/contents.html

Newburn, T., & Stanko, E. A. (Eds.). (1994). *Just boys doing business? Men, masculinities and crime*. London: Routledge.

Polk, K. (1994). *Why men kill: Scenarios of masculine violence*. Cambridge: Cambridge University Press.

Presdee, M. (2000). *Cultural criminology and the carnival of crime*. London: Routledge.

Reich, Wilhelm. (1961). *The sexual revolution*. New York: Orgone Institute. (Original work published 1945)

Renzetti, C. (1992). *Violent betrayal: Partner abuse in lesbian relationships*. Newbury Park, CA: Sage.

Richmond-Abbott, M. (1992). *Masculine and feminine: Gender roles over the life cycle* (2nd ed.). New York: McGraw-Hill.

Rubin, G. (1975). The traffic in women: Notes on the "political economy" of sex. In R. Reiter (Ed.), *Toward an anthropology of women* (pp. 157-210). New York: Monthly Review.

Russell, K. (1998). *The color of crime: Racial hoaxes, white fear, black protectionism, police harassment, and macroaggressions*.

New York: New York University Press.

Schlegal, A., & Barry, H. (1986). The cultural consequences of female contributions to subsistence. *American Anthropologist, 88,* 142-150.

Schmalleger, F., & Alleman, T. (1994). The collective reality of crime: An integrative approach to the causes and consequences of the criminal event. In G. Barak (Ed.), *Varieties of criminology: Readings from a dynamic discipline.* Westport, CT: Praeger.

Schoenewolf, G. (1989). *Sexual animosity between men and women.* Northvale, NJ: Jason Aronson.

Schopenhauer, A. (1896). *The world as will and idea* (R. B. Haldane & J. Kemp, Trans.). London: Kegan, Paul, Trench and Trubner.

Sheffield, C. (1989). The invisible intruder: Women's experiences of obscene phone calls. *Gender and Society, 3,* 483-488.

Smith, J., & Stanko, E. (1999, November). *Rage, quarrels and temper tantrums: A critique of official explanations of homicide incidents in England and Wales.* Paper presented at the Annual Meetings of the American Society of Criminology, Toronto, Canada.

Smuts, B. (1991). The origins of gender inequality: An evolutionary perspective. In A. Zagarell (Ed.), *The foundations of gender inequality.* Kalamazoo, MI: Western Michigan University Press.

Smuts, B. (1992). Male aggression against women: An evolutionary perspective. *Human Nature: An Interdisciplinary Biosocial Perspective, 3*(1), 1-44.

Stanko, E. (1985). *Intimate intrusions: Women's experience of male violence.* Boston: Routledge and Kegan Paul.

Stets, J. E., & Straus, M. A. (1990). Gender differences in reporting marital violence and in medical and psychological consequences. In M. A. Straus & R. J. Gelles (Eds.), *Physical violence in American families: Risk factors for and adaptations to violence in 8145 families.* New Brunswick, NJ: Transaction.

Taylor, G. W., & Ussher, J. M. (2001). Making sense of S&M: A discourse analytical account. *Sexualities: Studies in Culture and Society, 4*(3), 12-21.

Toch, H. (1992). *Violent men: An inquiry into the psychology of violence* (2nd ed.). Chicago: Aldine.

Totten, M. (2000). *Guys, gangs, and girlfriend abuse.* Petersborough, ON, Canada: Broadview.

Updike, J. (1996). The disposable rocket. In L. Goldstein (Ed.), *The male body: Features, desires, exposures* (pp. 8-11). Ann Arbor, MI: University of Michigan Press.

Wilson, M., & Daly, M. (1998). Lethal and nonlethal violence against wives and the evolutionary psychology of male sexual proprietariness. In R. E. Dobash & R. P. Dobash (Eds.), *Rethinking violence against women* (pp. 199-230). Thousand Oaks, CA: Sage.

REVIEW QUESTIONS

1. In the context of sexual violence against women, discuss the similarities and dissimilarities between the motives of "culturally normative" and "mentally ill" offenders.

2. Regarding philosophies of sex and sexuality, whose ideas do you agree and disagree with from the following list? C. Gilligan, Foucault, Fromm, Freud, Jung, MacKinnon, and Rubin. Explain why.

3. What are the parallels between Jeffrey Goldstein's relational model of aggression and Barbara Smuts' evolutionary perspective on sexual aggression?

4. Explain the differences in point of view on sexuality, gender, and *m/f* from the traditional (modernist) and the revisionist (postmodernist) perspectives.

5. In terms of the differences between the old and new pornographies (Box 7.1) or between the violent and nonviolent practices of S&M (Box 7.2), what do you think about these late-20th-century developments in sexuality and violence?

Part III

PATHWAYS TO NONVIOLENCE

CHAPTER 8

Recovering From Violence

P art III of this book tackles the transformative processes involved in moving away from the reciprocal relations of violence and toward the reciprocal relations of nonviolence. As the properties and pathways to violence have been shown to function across the personal, familiar, and cultural milieus of everyday life, it is assumed that the properties and pathways to nonviolence are similarly situated, but otherwise constructed. In different words, both of these sets of relations can be viewed as derived from the dialectics of adversarialism and mutualism (see Chapter 5). It is also assumed that as "emotional states of being," pathways to both violence and nonviolence operate across the same kinds of interpersonal, institutional, and structural terrains (or "psyches") of individuals and societies alike. Lastly, it is assumed that the interactions of the pathways and properties of nonviolence, like the interactions of the pathways and properties of violence, are both cumulative and reciprocal as they work their way across the interpersonal, institutional, and structural relationships of existence real and imaginary.

It follows, therefore, that to "recover" from rather than merely "survive" violence, there must be comprehensive efforts to deal not only with those victims and perpetrators

of interpersonal abuse but with those bystanders to violence and the myriad policies that tend to ignore, dismiss, or deny the actual harm, injury, pain, or suffering experienced by millions of people daily as a result of the prevailing institutional and structural arrangements. Moreover, in the context of discovering the cultural relations of the properties and pathways to nonviolence and the related "mutualisms of recovering" among individuals and their social relationships, including those involving victims, perpetrators, bystanders, and the rest of society, Chapter 8 specifically addresses the connections between recovery, violence, and nonviolence. It also provides a variety of representative examples of recovering from interpersonal, institutional, and structural forms of violence.

Chapters 9 and 10 link the processes of "recovering subjects" not only to the violent relations of the past but to the nonviolent relations of the future. In so doing, the ninth chapter provides an overview of representative models of nonviolence as these have emerged and developed and as they have been infrequently, but successfully, used as a means of decreasing "cycles" of violence. The tenth chapter provides a summary and recapitulation of the findings on violence, a critique of the "counterviolence" policies used predominantly in the United States and elsewhere, and an overview of what future policies of nonviolence could look like across the interpersonal, institutional, and structural spheres of society.

A RECIPROCAL APPROACH TO VIOLENCE RECOVERY

As already suggested, a reciprocal approach to violence recovery is viewed as an integral component of the dialectical relations of violence and nonviolence as these are derived from the political economy of social change and social order. What often connects the pathways to violence and nonviolence are various overlapping public and private discourses that are spoken (and unspoken) on behalf of each set of relations. Comparatively, what is missing from the efforts to resist violence and counterviolence or to reproduce nonviolence is a lack of mediated messages critiquing the current regimes of violence and marketing nonviolent alternatives. The difficulties of this transformative agenda involve finding the necessary political will as well as individual and collective voices to help change the professional languages, cultural images, popular discourses, and policy practices that are crucial to the process of producing and reproducing violent and nonviolent behavior as both have changed in the evolution of human intercourse. Nevertheless, a reciprocal approach to recovery has the potential to be a viable means for individuals or nation-states alike to move away from the practices of violence and counterviolence and toward the practices of nonviolence and peacemaking.

To break with those cyclical pathways of violence and violence recovery that do little, if anything, to suppress or to decrease violence and that may even exaggerate the reproduction of violence, it is necessary not only to incorporate the interpersonal, institutional, and structural aspects of recovery into some kind of functional whole, but to evolve a transformative practice of social organization based on a fundamental belief in and commitment to the satisfaction of the needs of all humanity. Historically, the constellation of violence and violence recovery in the United States has been the object of a political economy of extreme individualism and laissez-faire exemplified by greed, narcissism, and self-aggrandizement. In their totality, the artifacts of these cultural habits often have not only been antisocial and violent in and of themselves; they have been violence generating, as they repeatedly fail to address the institutionalization of the hierarchies of privilege and inequality throughout society in general, and as these relations intersect with the domains of violence and nonviolence in particular. In short, the prevailing models for addressing violence and violent behavior have been separated from the beliefs and practices of nonviolence.

These policies have fundamentally been tied to or based on the ideological models of "distributive" and "retributive" justice or on a system of meritorious "rewards" and "punishments" that perpetuate the reproduction of violence at the interpersonal, institutional, and structural levels of social organization. Both the distributive ("rights-based") and the retributive ("desserts-based") models of individual justice are supportive of widespread hierarchy and inequality. Specifically, rights-based approaches believe that all people, regardless of their class, age, gender, ethnicity, and so on, should "receive benefits, privileges, burdens, hold rights, and have access to resources solely on the basis of [their] rank or place" in society (Sullivan & Tifft, 2001, p. 99). Similarly, desserts-based approaches believe that people should receive benefits, privileges, and burdens or have access to resources on the basis of the contributions they have made or the injuries they have inflicted. At the most basic level, these models of positive and negative entitlements view the political economy of social relationships as being constituted by the relative value and worth that society assigns to us and that we assign to ourselves.

As Dennis Sullivan and Larry Tifft (2001) point out:

> When we develop a rights- or desserts-based political economy, we create a classification or ranking system whereby we situate some people as more worthy and others as less worthy; some of more, and others of less, value. And person worth here is defined in terms of the degree to which a person is considered worthy of our attention: that is, of having his or her needs met in everyday situations and especially in terms of crisis. (p. 102)

Moreover, it should be kept in mind that these relationships of hierarchy and inequality apply differentially to perpetrators, victims, and bystanders alike. That is to say, these systems of reward and punishment apply to those that harm, to those that are harmed, and to all those who directly or indirectly observe, represent, or tend to the public and private crises of violence.

According to these ideological scripts of rights, privileges, and punishments, individual offenders and victims of interpersonal violence are to experience pain, suffering, or recovery appropriate to their positions in society. Not surprisingly, these individually based models of "differential justice" focus primarily, if not exclusively, on the relations of interpersonal violence divorced from relations of institutional and structural violence. Alternative ideological scripts are based on equity throughout society or on "social justice" models for all. By contrast, these approaches to violence reduction focus their attention across the three spheres of violence

and nonviolence. A comparative difference between these traditional and alternative analyses is that the latter addresses the interpersonal, institutional, and structural spheres of both violence and nonviolence, while the former rarely addresses more than the interpersonal sphere of violence. That amounts to six out of six spheres versus one out of six.

Alternative and comprehensive approaches to violence reduction call for a "needs-based" political economy of social relations that does not necessarily replace rights- and/or desserts-based systems of reward or punishment. Rather, the attempts are aimed at transforming violence recovery processes from approaches that include only interpersonal expressions of violence to those that include all forms and spheres of violence and nonviolence. This needs-based or reciprocal approach to violence, recovering from violence, and nonviolence recognizes in both its discourse and practice the necessity of addressing the full constellation of the properties and pathways to violence and nonviolence.

The reciprocal theory of violence introduced in Chapter 5 and its complement, a reciprocal theory of nonviolence, as loosely articulated here and in the next chapter, resonate with both the notion of *recovering subjects* and the theory of *constitutive criminology*. The former recognizes the overlapping needs or similarities of the victims and perpetrators of violence. It also recognizes the common pathways that each needs to travel to overcome their respective experiences ("feelings") of humiliation, stigmatization, anger, and revenge. More generally, recovering subjects may achieve closure on their victimization; however, the processes of "healing" and "growing" are ongoing, life-course projects that everyone experiences to one degree or another. Finally, the philosophy of recovering subjects encourages the use of "self-help" organizations, local support groups, and narrative-based forms of therapy for both abusing and abused persons (Parry & Doan, 1994; White & Epston, 1989).

Constitutive criminology, as developed by Stuart Henry and Dragan Milovanovic (1996), is

> a theory proposing that humans are responsible for actively creating their world with others. They do this by transforming their surroundings through interactions with others, not least via discourse. Through language and symbolic representation they identify differences, construct categories, and share a belief in the reality of that which is constructed that orders otherwise chaotic states. It is towards these social constructions of reality that humans act. In the process of investing energy in their socially constructed, discursively organized categories of order and reality, human subjects not only shape the world, but are themselves shaped by it. They are co-producers and co-productions of their own and others' agency. They are channeled and changed, enabled and constrained, but all the time, building [socially carved pathways to violence and nonviolence, both consciously and unconsciously]. (p. ix)

Similarly, Barak and Henry (1999) argue in their integrative-constitutive theory of crime, law, and social justice that an adequate theory of these relations "must address, rather than accommodate, the production of inequalities and the law's part in their continuation" (p. 160). These authors further argue that in contemporary postmodern society, "while the class relations of capitalism remain a central source of inequality contributing to injustice [and violence], these are intertwined with and accompanied by other sources of inequality, principally gender and race" (p. 163). Each of these alone and together

have had consequences for both victims and perpetrators (see Box 8.1).

Briefly, recovering from violence may be thought of as not unlike the constitutive view of recovering from harms and injuries. Both of these are enveloped by and need to be released from inequalities, discriminations, and, in effect, punishments. Accordingly, violence could be viewed from the perspective of constitutive criminology and defined "as an expression of energy to make a difference over others who, in the instant, are rendered powerless to make their own difference" (Henry & Milovanovic, 1996, p. x). Violence, in other words, may be thought of as the power to deny others their basic human needs, whether expressed interpersonally, institutionally, or structurally. Moreover, the sources of violence may refer to those who are powerless and denied their basic human needs. These expressions of violence are repetitive and self-referential activities—recursive productions.

As historically and culturally specific discourses and practices, these coproduced expressions of real and imaginary violence have attained a relative degree of stability. Materialistically and ideologically rooted, they become pathways for social action whereby violence and nonviolence are excessive investments in either the accumulation and expression of adversarial power and control or in the democratization and mutualistic sharing of power and control. Finally, violence recovery may be thought of as involving the power of the offender to refrain from violence, the power of the offended to escape violence and powerlessness, and the power of the bystander to facilitate the efficacy of both the perpetrator and the victim to obtain their respective goals of healing.

Box 8.1   Battered Women, Welfare, Poverty, Reciprocal Violence, and Recovery

The percentage of battered women on welfare and in poverty is comparatively high. Published reports indicated in the late 1990s that more than half of the participants in welfare-to-work programs were victims of domestic violence, compared to only 6% of all households (Raphael, 2000). In *Saving Bernice: Battered Women, Welfare and Poverty*, Jody Raphael tells the story of many women who have spent much of their lives as victims of abuse and most of their adult lives as recipients of welfare. Like so many of these abused women, Bernice, the protagonist of Raphael's narrative, finds herself trapped by welfare benefits that are not sufficient to help her leave her abuser, as well as a larger system of poverty and discrimination that does not help batterers to meet their economic needs or cope with their feelings of shame and inadequacy and thus encourages battery.

The cycle of poverty, violence, and insufficient welfare and employment assistance has all kinds of reciprocal effects in play. For example, Raphael has concluded that for many of the battered welfare mothers living in poverty and with the constant fear of abuse, getting on or staying off welfare seems to be of little consequence in their decision-making process. Struggling to be "good" parents, these women often find themselves at home, unemployed and pregnant, and in (h)arm's reach of their abusers. For many, their lives become impossible roads to recovery as their self-esteem, confidence, and very sense of worth or being are taken away from them over and over.

Raphael also underscores poverty and ethnic discrimination's roles and reciprocal effects on the production and reproduction of domestic violence: "By not helping men to meet [their economic] needs, we shame them for having the desire that all people have" (p. 148). In turn, these men abuse not because it necessarily makes them feel good, providing them with a true sense of worth and esteem, but because it demonstrates that as lousy as life might be, they are at least not controlled or "pussy whipped" by some female. As Mark Totten's (2000) research on the behavior of marginal young men and their fathers toward their respective girlfriends, wives, or cohabitants has shown, these abusive patterns become ingrained in peer cultures of abusing males where battering becomes, in effect, institutionalized.

Raphael goes so far as to say that "to prevent domestic violence, then, we must work to eliminate relative poverty and race discrimination" (p. 148). In revealing and making the connections between the intersections of welfare and battering, her recommendations help to address the individual lives of battered women on welfare. These policies, such as those supporting early intervention teen programs, screening by welfare workers for domestic violence, and programs of education and support for employers of women escaping domestic violence, are certainly appropriate and called for. They are not, however, likely to reduce poverty, nor do they address the economic or psychological needs of the recovering abuser or batterer in the situation.

Sources: Raphael, J. (2002). *Saving Bernice: Battered women, welfare, and poverty*. Boston, MA: Northeastern.
Totten, M. (2000). *Guys, gangs, and girlfriend abuse*. Petersborough, ON: Broadview.

INTERPERSONAL RECOVERY

After a brief set-up, this section begins with four cases of individuals dealing with their experiences of victimization and recovery. These narratives of recovery include a woman philosopher writing about the aftermath of her firsthand experience with trauma-inducing violence and the remaking of herself (Case 8.1); a father who goes on an investigative journey to make sense out of the killing, in large and small ways, of his 18-year-old son (Case 8.2); a freshman theater major at Louisiana State University who takes solace in the "wake-up" calls by such notorious students as Eric Harris and Dylan Klebold of Columbine High School infamy (Case 8.3); and the parents of a slain daughter and the mother of the son accused of doing the killing, who exchanged kind words and prayers of comfort for each other amid the murder trial (Case 8.4).

All of the victims involved in these scenarios of violence, in their own unique and yet similar ways, portray the emotional journeys that they have taken in their hearts and minds on their roads to recovery. Despite the diversification of their scenarios of violence and victimization, each of the four narratives of recovery reveals the extent to which those harmed directly and even indirectly by violence, from insults to murder, may all experience episodes of the kinds of loss and emotional disruption that tend to leave indelible marks. With regard to the more extreme and direct forms of violence and sexual assault, some persons "recover" and some do not, but most are never quite the same persons they once were.

Next, the discussion on interpersonal recovery moves to perpetrators; to representative samples of aggressive, violent, and abusive offenders; and to some of the treatment modalities and strategies (e.g., medical, psychological, and cultural) employed to curb the various forms of personal violence.

There are also those people who are at the same time victim and offender, who must struggle with recovery for both of these aspects of themselves. This was certainly revealed in the intriguing case of the "altruistic killings" by Bob Rowe and the story of his recovery as a victim-offender (see Box 2.7). In any event, the recovery of the offender may be as or more important than the recovery of the victim, especially because the status of the latter is generally dependent on the production and reproduction of the former. The last part of this section on bystanders touches on the roles of family members and others, such as "self-help" groups, in the recovering or healing processes.

What this section makes known is that at a minimum, diagnostic prescriptions for intervention are diverse, can be unique, are often general, and may be contradictory. Then from a reciprocal perspective, the inclusive modalities of amelioration and change are preferable over those that rely on relatively one-dimensional approaches. This is even more important when those singular approaches downplay or ignore altogether the processes or contexts of cognitive development.

Scenarios of Victim Recovery

Case 8.1: A Sexual Assault and Attempted Murder Victim[1]

Susan J. Brison is a professor of philosophy and the author of *Aftermath: Violence and the Remaking of a Self,* a book about her recovery from a stranger's attack in the summer of 1990. The sexual assault and attempted homicide occurred on the side of a country road in a village outside of Grenoble, France, as Susan was out taking her morning constitutional one beautiful summer day. In an abridged essay about her experiences, she describes her ordeal:

> I had been grabbed from behind, pulled into the bushes, beaten, and sexually

assaulted. Helpless and entirely at my assailant's mercy, I talked to him, trying to appeal to his humanity, and, when that failed, addressing myself to his self-interest. He called me a whore and told me to shut up. Although I had said I'd do whatever he wanted, as the sexual assault began I instinctively fought back, which so enraged my attacker that he strangled me until I lost consciousness. When I came to, I was being dragged by my feet down in the ravine. I had often thought I was awake dreaming, but now I was awake and convinced that I was having a nightmare. But it was no dream. After ordering me to get on my hands and knees, the man strangled me again. This time I was sure I was dying. But I revived, just in time to see him lunging toward me with a rock. He smashed it into my forehead, knocking me out. Eventually, after another strangulation attempt, he left me for dead. (Brison, 2002, p. B7)

Susan relates many of the thoughts and feelings she had while negotiating her victimization and post-trauma experiences. She does so from the vantage points of victim, woman, feminist, philosopher, and mother.

She begins her story of recovery in the Grenoble hospital where she spent 11 days following her attack. During her stay, she repeatedly heard from doctors and nurses about how "lucky" she was to be alive. Initially, Susan believed them, but it was not long before she discovered what she had not previously known: "I did not yet know how trauma not only haunts the conscious and unconscious mind but also remains in the body, in each of the senses, in the heart that races and the skin that crawls whenever something resurrects the buried terror. I didn't know that the worst—the unimaginably painful aftermath of violence—was yet to come" (Brison, 2002, p. B7). In examining the experience of trauma, hers and others', Susan confronts the ambivalent feelings of going on (or not) with life:

Many trauma survivors who endured much worse than I did, and for much longer, found, often years later, that it was impossible to go on. It is not a moral failing to leave the world that has become morally unacceptable. I wonder how some people can ask of battered women, Why didn't they leave? while saying of those driven to suicide by the brutal and inescapable aftermath of the trauma, Why didn't they stay? Jean Amery wrote, "Whoever was tortured, stays tortured," and that may explain why he, Primo Levi, Paul Celan, and other Holocaust survivors took their own lives decades after their physical torture ended, as if such an explanation were needed. (Brison, 2002, p. B10)

More than 10 years after the event, Susan has "recovered" as much as any victim of physical and sexual assault can. As she tells it, "While I used to have to will myself out of bed each day, I now wake gladly to feed my son, whose birth gave me reason not to have died. Having him has forced me to rebuild my trust in the world, to try to believe that the world is a good enough place in which to raise him" (Brison, 2002, p. B10).

For the first several months after the attack, Susan felt a sense of unreality and disorientation. She didn't know exactly where she was and how or if she fit into the world. It was "as though I'd outlived myself, as if I'd stayed on a train one stop past my destination" (Brison, 2002, p. B7). She explains how her sense of unreality was fed by the massive denial of those around her, a common reaction from loved ones and others toward those who have been victims of rape. Inadvertently, some people would communicate how the violent act might have been avoidable or somehow her fault.

Susan then explores why she found herself keeping her attack secret from all but medical and legal personnel. Shame was part of it; not wanting to be stereotyped a victim was also a motivation. In addition, she found herself in a professional dilemma. Having previously done some academic work on pornography and violence against women, she did not want her work to be discussed as the ravings of a "hysterical rape victim." Susan did, eventually, go public as a rape "survivor," but only after she had come to terms with what little control she had over the meaning of the word "rape." In other words, "using the term denied the particularity of what I had experienced and invoked in other people whatever rape scenario they had already constructed" (Brison, 2002, p. B8).

As a philosopher, Susan tried to make sense out of her experience, realizing that sometimes knowledge sets one free, and at other times it fills one with incapacitating terror or uncontrollable rage. Turning to philosophy for meaning and consolation proved to be of no assistance to Susan. In fact, she discovered that there was virtually nothing in the philosophical literature about sexual violence. About all Susan knew for sure was that she was not feeling herself. For a time, she even believed that she might have incurred permanent brain damage as a result of her head injuries.

> Had my reasoning broken down? Or was it the breakdown of Reason? I couldn't explain what had happen to me. I was attacked for no reason. I had ventured outside of the human community, landed beyond the moral universe, beyond the realm of predictable events and comprehensible actions, and I didn't know how to get back. (Brison, 2002, p. B8)

Years later, after Susan had spent time off from teaching doing a full-time research gig, had returned to teaching at Dartmouth College, and had been speaking publicly on the topic of sexual violence, she would find herself losing her voice, both literally and figuratively:

> It was one thing to have decided to speak and write about my rape, but another to find the voice with which to do it. Even after my fractured trachea had healed, I frequently had trouble speaking. I lost my voice, literally, when I lost my ability to continue my life's narrative, when things stopped making sense. I was never entirely mute, but I often had bouts of what a friend labeled "fractured speech," during which I stuttered and stammered, unable to string together a simple sentence without the words scattering like a broken necklace. (Brison, 2002, p. B9)

During the first year or so of her recovery, Susan found that although her abilities to speak would come and go, her ability to sing seemed to be more resilient:

> For about a year after the assault, I rarely, if ever, spoke in smoothly flowing sentences. I could sing, though, after about six months and, like aphasics who cannot say a word but can sing verse after verse, I never stumbled over the lyrics. I recall spending the hour's drive home from the weekly meetings of my support group of rape survivors singing every spiritual I'd ever heard. It was a comfort and a release. Mainly, it was something I could do, loudly, openly (by myself in a closed car), and easily, accompanied by unstoppable tears. (Brison, 2002, p. B9)

CASE 8.2: A Father Who Lost His 18-Year-Old Son to Murder

Gregory Gibson, an antiquarian book-seller and a first-time author with *Gone Boy: A Walkabout* (2000), provides a poignant and insightful chronicle of a father's successful attempt to come to terms with, if not make sense of, his son's murder. It was December 14, 1992, when Gibson's son, a freshman at a small college in Great Barrington, Massachusetts, was shot and killed by another student who had gone on a random shooting campaign. When it was over, Wayne Lo had killed two persons, including a professor, and he had wounded several other students and a security guard. Lo was subsequently found guilty on two counts of first-degree murder and sentenced to life in prison.

These facts alone were not enough for Gregory. As he has written, "I had a story with characters and events but nothing connecting them" (Zengerle, 2000, p. 42). So he set out on a "walkabout" to see if he could make the connections, if he could understand what had happened. On his journey, he went to the "scene of the crime" at Simon Rock College, an affiliated institution of Bard College, to the gun store where the killing weapon was purchased, to the two psychiatrists that Lo's lawyers relied on for their failed insanity defense, and to Lo's parents. Initially, Gregory was motivated and driven by anger and the need to get even (or revenge), but over time, his need for retribution faded as he came to see that those he might blame were also mostly victims, too. Gregory came to appreciate that nobody is deserving of revenge—not the college, the gun-store owner, the Wayne Lo family, or Wayne himself. Finally, as Gregory reconstructed his walkabout in narrative form, the book became a venue or opportunity to process his grief and reclaim his life.

This is another journey of an altogether different kind than Susan Brison's recovery. Nevertheless, both Gregory and Susan had to travel for some time, years in fact, before they were able to "come out the other side" of their pain and suffering. During the intervening periods, their bodies, minds, and spirits had to undergo consolation and repair. At first, Gibson's anger was focused on the college administration and its negligence and culpability in Galen Gibson's death. Gregory Gibson conducted his own interviews with students and staff, filed a civil lawsuit, and settled with Simon Rock's insurance company for an undisclosed sum. As he explains, he would assemble an airtight case against the college and send it to his lawyers or get it published in the *New York Times*.

In the early period of his recovery (during the stage of retribution), Gregory visited the proprietor of the store where Lo bought the gun, as well as the person who had previously owned and modified the cheap Chinese semiautomatic SKS rifle. Eventually, Gregory viewed the gun itself, and the object became demystified: "It seemed an oddly insubstantial thing to have displaced so many lives" (Quoted in Zengerle, 2000, p. 42). Later on, Gregory talked with Lo's psychiatrists, and he and his wife met with Wayne Lo's parents. After these visits, he concluded that despite what the jury decided, Lo was "indeed truly, deeply crazy" and that what went wrong with him will forever remain a "terrible mystery, a holy mystery." In the end, Gregory Gibson remarks, his inability to understand what happened that day in December 1992 is understandable, and that in itself becomes its own kind of understanding.

Case 8.3: Insults, Outcasts, and Intolerance Toward a Non-Christian Radical Student

R. Brian Blake and his friends, self-identified pagans and atheists, had been subject to insults, harassments, intimidations, and interrogations for their outcast status while attending both high school and Louisiana State University. In a letter to the editor of the student newspaper, *Reveille,* also published online at http://reveille. stumedia.lsu.edu/archive, Blake relates in a letter marking the 2-year anniversary of the Columbine High School shooting (April 19, 2001) how he and others have become victims of suspicion and false accusations. In the wake of the shootings, not only were those students who had been wearing long coats suspended and/or interrogated by their Colorado school administrations for fear of a copycat killing, but halfway across the country, Blake had been "interrogated by my vice principal for wearing a long green coat the entire year" and questioned about his family life and emotional state (Blake, 2001).

Blake relates further that even though his mother and the vice principal had been friends, he and his friends were nevertheless being targeted by school officials "because they didn't share Christian beliefs, fashions, or opinions of the administration, student body, teachers, and parents. It was, like the Crusades, a witch hunt to destroy the non-Christians" (Blake, 2001). He argues that he was similarly targeted by the LSU Department of Residential Life in the wake of his only other letter to the editor. He believes that his atheist views were also responsible for his having been spit on, called numerous names, and physically abused. He further maintains that his life was threatened and that rather than the administration assisting him and pursuing the culprit, they held him responsible for instigating the confrontation.

Blake (2001) draws an analogy between the abuse to which Eric Harris and Dylan Klebold were subjected and the abuse he and his friends endured:

> They, like me, dressed differently; had intellectual, "nerdy" interests; shared alternate, non-Christian approaches to religion and spirituality; and had a similar, more alternate taste in music. My friends are also similar in some of those respects. The outcasts of our school society do band together, not making them individuals, like the Columbine killers and their Trenchcoat Mafia, but the support given by that close-knit group of friends cannot cancel out the agony inflicted by the general student body. Therefore, certain people go to extremes.

He goes on to suggest that society should use such tragedies as the Columbine shooting to teach lessons about difference, tolerance, and kindness. By writing publicly of his own experiences as a victim, Blake finds a sense of solace and empowerment against his abusers. But he is really less concerned about himself than about those who are mentally ill and abused by their peers. Recognizing the inevitable public hysteria over these killings and the backlash of security and repression that has followed in the wake of the 1990s school shootings, Blake wants us to realize that these shooters are troubled youngsters, suffering from mental illnesses, and that they require both treatment and relief from the ridiculing and abuse delivered by peers and administrators alike.

CASE 8.4: *The Parents of a Killed Daughter Meet the Mother of the Accused Killer*[2]

The fourth scenario of recovery from interpersonal violence raises the importance of forgiveness, prayer, redemption, and empathy in the context of those persons associated with both the "perpetrators" and "victims" of violence. This particular case of mutualism involved the parents of Amy Watkins, a 26-year-old social-work student who died in 1999 on a Brooklyn street with a knife in her back, and the mother of 28-year-old David Jamison, the man on trial for the killing. Though at "opposite ends" of a murder trial, Lawrence and Gayle Greene Watkins and Margo Jamison found a way to comfort each other and themselves as they shared their mutual pain and suffering. For example, at least once a day during the 2-week trial, the parents shook hands and talked about life. They called each other by their first names and stated that they prayed for one another.

The interaction between the parents of the victim and the mother of the accused being tried for first-degree murder and robbery, needless to say, had caught the attention of other courtroom participants and observers.

Michael F. Becchione, the assistant district attorney and the lead prosecutor in the trial, had this to say: "In as many cases as I've tried, I've never seen this kind of kindness shown. One of them has already suffered a loss, and the other is facing a potential loss. It speaks volumes about them that they can do this," especially in light of the fact that Jamison believed her son was innocent of the murder charge and the Watkins wanted the jury to find him guilty (Christian, 2001). In their own words:

Mr. Watkins: We are two families hurting. . . . It's obvious he came from a loving family, but at this point in David Jamison's life he is dangerous. [Although Watkins believed that he should be in prison, he did not wish to see the young man spend the rest of his life there.] I've taught in prisons; I know people can change. And if David Jamison could have the opportunity to really change, I wouldn't object to him on parole.

Mrs. Watkins: I can't think of anything more terrible than losing a child, but for Margo to sit there and see her boy come in each day in handcuffs must be so painful. How can I not care about his family?

Mrs. Jamison: It helps knowing that they don't look at me with vengeance. Sometimes Gayle, Larry and I just exchange nods, or they'll ask how I slept. It is a big help. They are good people who have suffered through a horrendous crime. [Whatever the verdict, she intended to] keep praying that God helps all of us to heal and find peace. (Christian, 2001).

Perpetrators

Perpetrators are made up of diverse groups of violent people with a variety of pathways to their violence. One of those pathways to violence is under the feet of those persons with organic illnesses. For example, certain expressions of interpersonal violence, such as those associated with the habitual acting out of pathological aggression and anger, have been linked to persons who have experienced some kind of neurochemical imbalance or physiological disturbance. That is to say, individuals with persistent aggressive, abusive, or violent behavior "show a much higher prevalence of overt and covert neurologic and neurophysiologic abnormalities than nonviolent control subjects or in the population at large" (Fishbein, 2000, P7-1). This physiological condition or "property of violence" may be more common among habitually violent persons than among nonviolent persons, but it is still not representative of the overwhelming majority of violent people whose pathways are more psychological than biological.

This increasing awareness of the close connections between recurrent interpersonal violence and anatomical, chemical, and neurological abnormalities in serious and habitual perpetrators has begun to result in the assessment and pharmacological treatment of these individuals, whether they are clinical patients or prison inmates. The correctional chemistry of "anger management" has involved pharmacological approaches to treatment intervention alone or in combination with other psychosocial treatment, as a means of stabilizing the violence so that the individual becomes more in control of his or her own behavior, minimizing the need for external controls.

From a reciprocal-neurological perspective, "there is abundant evidence, collected over a century of research, that damage to specific structures in the brain can lead to recurrent attacks of destructive aggression in formerly equable individuals, that this and other disinhibited behaviors can also be associated with covert neuro-developmental defects incurred before or after birth and that *the liability to violence in such individuals is usually increased by childhood exposure to social adversity, emotional deprivation, and physical/mental abuse*" (Elliott, 2000, p. 19-2, italics added). Two applicable groups of perpetrators are "predatory" and "affective" violent offenders. Although the violent predators often tend to congregate in one kind of institutional confinement or another, these actors are not representative of the more typical and less predatory forms of interpersonal violence. Similarly, those individuals suffering from intense attacks of rage, without reflective delay, also known as "intermittent explosive disorder" victims, often express themselves in various forms of domestic violence, yet they are not typical of, for example, most wife-batterers. Affective aggressors, like their predatory violent counterparts, often have "biogenic" defects that can be effectively managed through pharmacotherapy.

Thus, for that small segment of the violence population that is estimated to be responsible for over 60% of "recurrent criminal violence," there is an impressive array of agents that can not only control specific types of violence, but can make recalcitrant offenders more accessible to psychotherapy by reducing their hostility (Elliott, 2000; Fava, 2000). There are, for example, several drugs that are apparently effective in treating pathological anger and aggression associated with a number of neurological and psychiatric disorders (e.g., organic brain syndrome, biopolar disorder, psychoactive substance intoxication and withdrawal, premenstrual dysphoric disorder, post-traumatic stress disorder). These drugs may include lithium for the treatment of aggression among nonepileptic prison inmates, mentally retarded and handicapped patients, and among conduct-disordered children with explosive disorder, as well as for those bipolar patients suffering from excessive irritability and anger outbursts; anticonvulsant medications for patients with outbursts of rage and abnormal electroencephalogram (EEG) findings; beta-blockers such as propranolol for intermittent explosive disorder and other organic defects; serotonergic agents for both organic and functional conditions; and clomipramine to reduce aggressive thoughts.

Other expressions of interpersonal violence, such as the battering of intimate partners by males or the sexual assault and murder of children and women, are generally not related to biochemical factors and how these influence the range of the form and intensity of emotional responses, the threshold of arousal, the readiness to learn certain stimuli as opposed to others, and the patterns of sensitivity to additional environmental factors. Instead, these violent behaviors are typically reflected in a heterogeneity of pathways including, but not limited to, paternalistic and patriarchal cultural traditions, cognitions justifying physical and sexual aggression, personality problems, and affective dyscontrol. The reciprocal relations between these and other negative emotional states and the normal inhibitors of physically and sexually aggressive behaviors such as victim empathy, guilt, moral conviction, and the anxiety about or fear of adverse consequences require a multidimensional, if not an integrated or holistic, approach to "violence recoveries" (Finkelhor, 1984; Hall & Hirschman, 1991).

For example, as violence against women by male intimates has revealed, there are subgroups of abusers. Their properties of difference revolve around issues of power and control, attitudes toward women, notions of male authority, and other controlling aspects of behavior. These cannot be separated from the wider social conditions of which they are constituted. In other words, whether or not these abusive relationships are related to problems of anger management, emotional stress, or low self-esteem, programs of recovery should be aimed at connecting the "psychogenic" and "sociogenic" sites of violence. Male recovery from abusing women, therefore, is viewed as inseparable from and related to the prevailing political, social, and economic relationships of hierarchy and inequality. Accordingly, the overall aim of recovery should not only be about the transformation of those offending individuals, but about the transformation of the institutional, organizational, and cultural relationships that support violence as well (Dobash, Dobash, Cavanagh, & Lewis, 2000).

In their more sophisticated forms, for example, men's programs against domestic violence are embedded in a wider network of community and governmental action, such as the multifaceted program in Duluth, Minnesota. This program aims at both protecting women victims and holding male abusers accountable for their behavior. These kinds of programs, such as those considered in the Violent Men Study in the United Kingdom, involve court-ordered or mandated programs of recovery for the abusers. Ideologically, many of these programs are both profeminist in their ideals and educational in their formats, grounded in an overall framework of gender and power domination:

> Instead of a traditional therapist-client relationship, the approach is closer to that of teacher-pupil, with a pedagogical format, albeit one that is augmented with many of the techniques of counseling. These programs include group work and role playing meant to be two way, with program workers communicating disapproval of the violence [and] at the same time providing a generally supportive context in which abusive men can begin to learn new ways of thinking and acting. . . . men are urged to talk about their violent behavior and associated beliefs in order to begin the transformative process of taking responsibility for their own behavior and for its elimination. (Dobash et al., 2000, p. 180)

Research by R. Emerson Dobash, Russell P. Dobash, and others (Andrews et al., 1990; Gendreau, Cullen, & Bonta, 1994; Marshall & Eccles, 1991) has produced a growing body of evidence indicating that structured and holistic approaches to recovery are more productive than those unstructured programs targeting general mental health problems such as anger, self-esteem, and stress management. In other words, those programs that focus their attention and energy on the offending behavior and the associated beliefs and attitudes underpinning such behavior have better records of successful intervention into patterns of male violence against intimate partners. In short, these programs work on improving internal controls, developing social skills, increasing critical reasoning about the offending behavior, and enhancing empathy or insight into the pain and suffering of their victims. In addition, many abusers need to address their own feelings and experiences of powerlessness, as well as their tolerance for being controlled and for being controlling (Petrik, Olson, & Subotnik, 1994).

When examined earlier in the book, murder was shown to be not a uniform or one-dimensional behavior. Once again, there are different internal and external sources of homicide. At one end of a spectrum of homicide would be those exogenous killings that tend to be sociogenic or situational in nature. At the other end of the spectrum would be those endogenous killings that tend to be psychogenic in nature. Though statistically rare, sexually motivated homicides, for example, tend to be more impulsive, catathymic, and compulsive. If those persons responsible for such acts in the past or the future, or—perhaps even more important—if those who harbor such thoughts and fantasies in the present are not to become potential serial murderers, then different treatment modalities should be realized for actual or potential murderers, almost all of whom have been men.

Even among the sexually motivated killings, the repetition of such acts is rare among the impulsive and catathymic killers.

Repetition is only common to those killers falling into the group of compulsive sex murderers. Recovering from these psychodynamic violations will also vary, because the psychogenic processes or properties of these violations vary. For example, the origins of the catathymic killer are thought to reside in specific psychic vulnerabilities associated with early infantile traumatization. Used to explain various unprovoked episodes of severe violence, "a catathymic reaction is the transformation of the stream of thought as the result of certain complexes of ideas that are charged with a strong affect, usually a wish, a fear, or an ambivalent striving" (Wertham, 1937, p. 975). The incubation stage, especially in those experiencing chronic depression, loose schizophrenic-like thinking, and obsessive preoccupation with ideas of doing violence to family members and especially to girlfriends, may precede the acts for weeks, months, or even years.

By contrast, the compulsive murderer, or the potentially compulsive murderer who engages in other types of compulsive antisocial behavior (e.g., harming animals, voyeurism, breaking and entering not for the purpose of theft), experiences overwhelming feelings and urges that are often so strong that attempts to resist bring on extreme forms of anxiety with somatic manifestations, such as migraine headaches and severe perspiration over the entire body. Almost all compulsive forms of murder, whether overtly sexual or not, have an underlying basis of sexual conflicts (e.g., preoccupations with maternal sexual conduct, overt or covert incestuous preoccupations, feelings of sexual inferiority, guilt over and rejection of sex as impure). The incubation periods for these compulsive (or potentially compulsive) murderers may be short or long, and they may be expressed in ritualistic or nonritualistic behaviors (Schlesinger & Revitch, 1990).

In addressing the recovering needs of these diverse kinds of sexual killers (or potential killers) who are evidencing psychological symptoms and are seeking treatment, Schlesinger and Revitch (1990) argue that "it is not specific techniques that have proved helpful to clinicians, but, rather, an overall plan with some practical suggestions" (p. 176). They explain, furthermore, that the treatment involved here is not materially different from the treatment involved in other difficult psychological cases, except for the fact that in these cases the need to establish control is greater. In short, rapport and patient support in treating these perpetrators or potential perpetrators cannot be overemphasized. At the same time, in helping individuals gain insight into their problems and treatment, therapists and the recovery process must also allow, or encourage, patients, because of the cathartic effect, to express their feelings and emotions about these violent acts and fantasies. This approach to recovering from sexual murder is often easier said than done because of the defensive reactions of therapists to the repellant nature of the acts or fantasies involved and because of the legal liability problems facing those persons who treat very disturbed and/or dangerous people.

Bystanders

Part of the irony of the reciprocity of recovery in relationship to gender and violence has to do, on the one hand, with the inequitable distribution of pain perpetrated by men against men and women, and, on the other hand, with the inequitable distribution of care and support required by women for both men and women. In terms of recovering perpetrators, for example, regardless of the sex of the inmates, the burden of assisting their healing through sentencing and its aftermath of confinement falls disproportionately on women family members. As Lori Girshick (1996) has pointed out, "men in prison are visited by their wives and mothers, whereas women in prison are visited by their mothers and sisters" (p. 25). In arguing for a "women-wise penology" and discussing the value of not brutalizing law-breaking men during their prison stays, Pat Carlen (1990) emphasized the importance of not encouraging the oppression of women because the men associated with them are being punished.

As a group, the partners or families of prisoners—those "on the outside"—have remained fairly invisible and marginal, although some self-help groups have emerged to see to their special needs. Most of the support and services for these families have not come from government-based or -sponsored programs, but from voluntary or charitable organizations. The activities, structures, and philosophies of these self-help groups vary widely, but all focus on a mutual response to common difficulties, usually founded on shared experiences. Most of these groups, especially those associated with victims, such as MADD (Mothers Against Drunk Drivers) in the United States or SAMM (Survivors After Murder and Manslaughter) in the United Kingdom, engage in vocal campaigns for legislative reforms and changes in sentencing. There are also self-help groups for prisoners' partners and families such as Aftermath (United Kingdom), organized on behalf of those accused and convicted of serious offenses, which are far more circumspect in their political and ideological dealings with the media and the public.

In one study of individuals who received help from a range of organizations, including the Prison Reform Trust, Victim Support, Prison Fellowship, and local churches, the benefits (e.g., attending drop-in sessions, meetings, or social events) of membership that accrued to those women who had been in regular contact were significant (Codd, 2000). Interviews revealed that these women were more positive in their outlook compared to those women without the contact. In addition, participation provided

information, practical assistance, empowerment, and the promotion of self-esteem. This type of recovering for the bystanders of violence is not generally found among the more formal and institutional responses of the criminal and legal systems. Unlike those formal organizations, self-help groups hold out the potential for providing an extended "kin" of sorts. For example,

> It's not just having someone to talk to, you need the friendship, and it is like a family, it really is . . . when I say to them "do you know what I mean?" and they say "yes" then I know they're not lying to me, because they do know what I mean because they've been there, they've done it, they've seen it, they've read the book, seen the picture. (Codd, 2000, p. 14)

Perceived as less threatening, hierarchical, and power-based, the strength of these self-help groups lies in the emphases on shared experiences and empathy, combined with nonjudgmental, welcoming attitudes. "For women who have experienced harassment and hostility as a result of their partner's [violence and] imprisonment, self-help groups provide a valuable safe environment in which feelings and experiences can be revealed and shared" (Codd, 2000, p. 8). What these and other self-help groups for addicts, victims, perpetrators, and their families all share in common is the adoption and belief of inclusion for all their members. In the end, such groups provide not only emotional support to the partners and families of inmates, but the potential for building and reconstructing the egos of those members whose self-esteem and confidence can certainly use a boost of empowerment.

INSTITUTIONAL RECOVERY

Recovery from institutionalized violence involves a complexity of action plans and systems involving persons and policies designed for the delivery of a wide spectrum of programs and interventions. Institutional recoveries may also be thought of as proactive initiatives that overlap and converge with, or spill over into, other areas of comprehensive (e.g., primary, secondary, and tertiary) health-care provision and violence prevention. What these activities share in common is the social mobilization of resources, services, and politics for the aggregated care of groups of victims, including those at risk for future violence. When it comes to the institutionalization of providing for the needs of victims and survivors of violence, for example, the National Criminal Justice Reference Service identifies "resources of recovery" at its Web site (http://www. ncjrs.org/recovery/serv4.html).

In reference to victim assistance, a number of publications and educational videos from the Office for Victims of Crime (U.S. Justice Department) are available. Among these titles are four that I will briefly describe. *First Response to Victims of Crime* (NCJ 176971) was designed as a field guide and discusses how law enforcement officers should approach and help victims of crime. *Meeting the Mental Health Needs of Crime Victims* (video; NCJ 167235) was designed to improve the criminal and juvenile justice systems' responses to the needs of traumatized crime victims. In a comprehensive way, findings from current mental health research on the immediate and short-term trauma associated with crime victimization and factors related to victims' healing and recovery are presented. *Working with Grieving Children* (video; NCJ 165927) provides interviews with children who have lost loved ones through violence, discusses the effects on these children, and suggests ways to help them cope with their loss. *From Pain to Power: Crime Victims Take Action* (NCJ 166604) chronicles the many ways in which crime victims have healed themselves by channeling their pain into helping others and serving their communities.

Institutional recovery can refer to a broad range of activities: government-organized efforts that target children who have been abused, neglected, and/or exposed to domestic violence; diversification and availability of legal remedies for victims of sexual assault or sexual harassment; provision of shelters and refuges for battered women and their children; grassroots antiviolence work with the homeless and other marginal groups such as homosexuals and women of color; or reformation of police departments and correctional units that have engaged in habitual patterns of abuse in their interactions with citizens, suspects, and convicts. Let's look more closely at some of these different modes of institutional recovery.

The institutionalized responses to youth victimization in general and to children that have been exposed to violence in particular provide an assortment of community-based, federally sponsored programs and interventions. Three examples:

- Child Development-Community Policing Program
- Child Witness to Violence Project
- Green Book Initiative on Domestic Violence and Child Maltreatment

The Child Development-Community Policing Program implemented in New Haven, Connecticut, in 1991 was designed "to address the psychological impact of chronic exposure to community, family, or school-related violence on children and families" (Osofsky, 2001, p. 5). The program, funded by the Office of Juvenile Justice and Delinquency Prevention (OJJDP), is a partnership between the Yale University Child Study Center, the New Haven Department of Police Services, and the New Haven County Office of Juvenile Probation. Together, they coordinate the efforts of mental health professionals and community police officers to "reduce the impact of violence on children and their families by providing interdisciplinary interventions to children who are victims, witnesses, or perpetrators of violent crime" (Osofsky, 2001, p. 5). At the heart of the program is the training of community police officers in the principles of child development so that they may incorporate these principles into their daily work.

The Child Witness to Violence Project was established in 1992 in Boston, Massachusetts. It operates through the Department of Pediatrics at Boston Medical Center. The project is designed to help heal young children who, as bystanders to and victims of community and domestic violence, are in need of overcoming the trauma of having witnessed violence. Specifically, intervention occurs as a means of providing developmentally appropriate counseling to these children, their families, and other caregivers in their lives. In addition to direct services, the multicultural and multilingual staff of social workers, psychologists, early childhood specialists, and a child psychiatrist has implemented a national and statewide training program for healthcare professionals, police, educators, and other social service practitioners who come in contact with children who have witnessed violence.

The Green Book Initiative on Domestic Violence and Child Maltreatment is a multiagency demonstration project in six sites across the United States. The project started in 2000 and was funded for 3 years at about $1,000,000 per site. Countywide initiatives may be found in five states: Colorado, New Hampshire, Oregon, Missouri, and California. The goal at each site is "to improve responses that protect and empower women who are victims of abuse and their children" (Osofsky, 2001, p. 6). Applying the recommendations set forth in *Effective Intervention in Domestic Violence and Child Maltreatment Cases: Guidelines for Policy and Practice*, published by the National Council of Juvenile and Family Court Judges, the sites strive to implement a collaborative approach between the courts and service providers to facilitate the safety and well-being of battered women and their children. Such goals are realized through the protection and counseling of, and advocacy for, abused women.

What these programs and others like them share in common is a network and teamwork approach to recovering from community violence. A "manifesto" with eight operating principles—work together, begin earlier, think developmentally, make mothers safe to keep children safe, enforce the law, make adequate resources available, work from a sound knowledge base, and create a culture of nonviolence—was published in an OJJDP document *Safe from the Start: Taking Action on Children Exposed to Violence* (2000). This action plan and its guiding philosophy or set of principles were the product of 150 practitioners and policy makers who convened at The National Summit on Children Exposed to Violence in June 1999.

Their approach is highly interdisciplinary and multiprofessional. It recognizes the importance of prevention, intervention, and collaboration among persons from the public and private sectors who represent a host of institutional relations, including but not limited to child protective services, domestic violence services and advocacy, juvenile and family courts, law enforcement and prosecution, mental health, substance abuse, healthcare services, family violence prevention, childhood education and services, and legislative branches of government. Perhaps the most interesting principle is number 8, create a culture of nonviolence. This principle recognizes the importance and necessity of viewing neighborhood communities as integrated wholes or as "social ecologies" of violence that should experience comprehensive pathways to recovery. It also appreciates efforts to restructure or transform the present violent relations into nonviolent relations.

> The greatest success will be achieved when specific actions are taken within a larger social environment that can help sustain them. A culture of nonviolence that supports children, women, and families is the vital context to ensure success in preventing and reducing the impact of children's exposure to violence. New studies are revealing two important facts: that the presence of "protective factors" (e.g., strong family relationships and alternative supports, among others) can guard children against the negative effects of exposure to violence and that "collective efficacy" (the willingness of neighbors to intervene on behalf of others) is the one characteristic that can account for less violence in a community. There is evidence to suggest, then, that a culture supportive of families, women, and children would inherently provide the protective factors and the collective efficacy needed to keep children safe from violence. (Office of Juvenile Justice and Delinquency Prevention, 2000)

Unfortunately, these community-based, prosocial programs are not too "sexy," and the principles articulated by the OJJDP, especially the one about creating a culture of nonviolence, has to compete with the more popular, mass-mediated cultures of violence and vigilantism (see Box 8.2).

Institutional responses to women who have been physically battered by their intimate partners, and to girls and women who have been physically and/or sexually assaulted more generally, have expanded significantly over the past 30 years. As a phenomenon, violence against women has been recognized as a widespread problem and crisis locally, nationally, and internationally. Shelters, emergency housing, reforms in the criminal and civil laws, protective orders, recovery programs, and interventions of all kinds and sizes exist for victims and, to a lesser extent, for perpetrators. Nevertheless, such institutional responses may have backlash effects, may not go far enough, and may have become too professionally or service oriented.

For example, at the expense of suppressing gender differences, with respect to the asymmetry of violence between men and women, the U.S. Supreme Court ruled in the spring of 2000 that compensation for gender-motivated violence could only be pursued in state rather than in federal courts. Despite data supplied by Congress showing gender discrimination and the effects of violence against women on interstate commerce, and the endorsement of 38 attorney generals supporting the right of women victims to sue in federal court, the justices ruled 5 to 4 that rape victims could not sue their attackers under the Violence Against Women Act. In effect, Chief Justice William H. Rehnquist, writing the majority opinion, concluded that the issue was one of local rather than national importance, and that there were enough remedies available in state courts (Tolme, 2000).

At the expense of suppressing the ethnic differences of women of majority and minority status, with respect to the asymmetries in both responding to and recovering from gendered and state-based violence, it has been argued that the organizing efforts against racial and sexual injustice and the focus on services have ignored the forms of racism and sexism that women of color face:

> Over the years, the anti-violence movement has also become increasingly reluctant to address sexual and domestic violence within the larger context of institutional inequality and violence. For example, many state coalitions on domestic/sexual violence have refused to take stands against the anti-immigration backlash, arguing that this is not a sexual/domestic violence issue. However, as the anti-immigration backlash intensifies, many immigrant women do not

report abuse—from the INS, police, employers or family members—for fear of deportation. (Smith, 2001, p. 2)

Consequently, many women of color (e.g., Native Americans, African Americans, Hispanics, Asians, and Middle Easterners) must often go outside of their communities to receive services from domestic violence shelters and rape crisis centers.

These criticisms are leveled mostly at the turn away from an antiviolence movement based on grassroots political mobilization toward one that has gradually become increasingly professionalized as a means of securing accreditation and funding from both public and private sources. In the process, the lack of advocacy has resulted in practices that have tended to exclude many women, especially those of color and

poverty, from full participation in these programs of intervention. In short, it is often argued that the professionalization of domestic violence services has eclipsed the former role of political organizing in the movement against male violence:

> This narrow approach toward working against violence is problematic because sexual/domestic violence within communities of color cannot be addressed seriously without dealing with the larger structures of violence, such as militarism, attacks on immigrants and Indian treaty rights, police brutality, the proliferation of prisons, economic neo-colonialism, and institutional racism. It is simply futile to attempt to combat interpersonal violence without addressing the fact that we live in a world structured by violence. (Smith, 2001, p. 2)

Box 8.2   Films, Recovery, and Vigilantism

Long before the terrorist attacks on the United States and the collective call for retribution and for a "war on terrorism," one staple of American cinema had been scenarios of injury and vengeance: "Shorn of spouses and offspring, forced to hug their guns for warmth, our mythic vigilantes reside in the multiplexes and the art houses, on the jingoist right and the bleeding-heart left" (p. AR15). Historically, vigilantism has been restricted almost exclusively to white males threatened by a multiracial, murderously parasitical underclass. In the movie *Death Wish* (1974), for example, the protagonist enthusiastically guns down urban thugs after the rape and murder of his wife. Eventually, however, vigilantism also became accessible to the African American male, in (for example) *A Time to Kill* (1986), in which the main character's preadolescent daughter is violated by privileged whites. Vigilantism was also alive and well in the studio releases of *Collateral Damage* and *John Q* in 2002. What each of these and other films like them share in common are the lessons that violence is the primary, if not the only, way to solve human problems, and isolationism and extreme individualism rather than collective action and social responsibility are the pathways to temporary periods of order amid the growing "breakup" or "breakdown" of society.

All of these films work at the level of primal or basic instincts as they relentlessly come at their audiences and bulldoze right over their other values of nonviolence, making them feel antihuman if they resist their retributive urges. Cinema representations of individual

(Continued)

Box 8.2   (Continued)

violent vengeance have been so successful that they have been able to conflate the political and the personal, the patriotic and the unpatriotic. For example, what could have been more subversive of patriotism than the motion picture *The Patriot* (2000). After all, the patriarch of the family in this film was not motivated by any sense of patriotism. His involvement in the revolutionary effort was not about self-sacrifice for the nation-state but rather about the sorts of tribal blood feuds that characterize gangster films. In other words, his beef had nothing to do with patriotism and the "collective good," it was simply about personal loss, family loyalty, and payback. In fact, the protagonist, played by Mel Gibson, wants nothing to do with the war and strongly advises his sons not to get involved. When one son disobeys and then is killed in battle, our "patriot" changes his mind. These types of extreme forms of individualistic retribution and punishment generally tend to perpetuate systems of vengeance begetting vengeance.

Oftentimes, vigilante-vengeance scenarios in films tend to blur the differences between heroism and sociopathic behavior. Such was the case in two classic films, *The Searchers* (1956), directed by John Ford, and *Taxi Driver* (1976), by Martin Scorsese and Paul Schrader. More recently, in *In the Bedroom* (2001), the climactic scene of the film captures our love-hate affair with vengeance when the audience is confused about whether they are to endorse or reject the act of retribution by the mild and humane protagonist. That is to say, when the trigger is pulled by the murder victim's father, one feels satisfaction even though one pays for such satisfaction with a melancholy denouement. From the perspective of evolutionary psychology, this duality is understandable, as it recognizes various forms of retribution, vengeance, and punishment as both adaptive and-counteradaptive. In the latter cases, such interventions are not only useless, but more likely than not, they tend to perpetuate violence and conflict at the expense of conciliation and nonviolence.

Unfortunately, the vigilante spirit is not confined to the films of Hollywood and to the mass-mediated consumption of Western communications. It is discernible throughout American culture as a whole, from incidents of road rage to those school-age children and adult workers who have regarded themselves as some kind of righteous avenger to the majority of U.S. citizens who still favor the death penalty or state-sanctioned murder in the name of war. Thus, the more fundamental issue or question of violence recovery pertains to the reality that a significant portion of popular and political culture is devoted to an imagination that is reinforcing—even aggravating—our most primitive angers and fears. Playing to the imaginary fantasies of vigilantism does little, if anything, to discharge or neutralize such impulses. On the contrary, these and other mediated forms of vengeful violence tend to provide their "addicted audiences" with desire for more, rather than fewer, of these kinds of vigilante fantasies. The problem, then, with these scenarios of recovering, in film and politics alike, is that neither cultural expression either alleviates our fears or addresses the roots of these violent acts. In a democratic society, of course, this is not the purpose, nor should it be the role, of entertainment and mass media; the same, however, cannot be said of the body politic and the nation-state as a whole.

Nevertheless, in the scenarios of vengeance films and vengeance politics, each works at excluding the "other," and both play at exploiting our feelings of vulnerability. In neither case does the culture or politics of vengeance "help us to work through our fear of losing loved ones, our impatience at not being recognized, [or] our sense of impotence" (p. 29). In fact, rather than aid us in recovering from the violence, the terrorism, or whatever, these representations of vengeance, fictional or nonfictional, "prey on those primitive emotions for the sake of softening us up, enraging us, leaving us open to jolt after gratifying jolt—payback" (p. 29). These messages are loud and clear, whether dealing with domestic or international threats of violence: "Anyone who threatens a spouse or child must die, die in pain, die many times if possible, die in recognition of our power. Until tomorrow, that is, when they're back on their feet and we're powerless" all over again (p. 29). Ironically, the very conditions that contribute to the insecurities and downward mobility of some males are linked to the rising rates of these forms of violence.

Source: Edelstein, D. (2002, February 10). Vigilante vengeance, Hollywood's response to primal fantasies. *New York Times*, pp. AR 15, AR 29. Retrieved November 14, 2002, from http://www.nytimes.com

Lastly, as one example of a police department trying to escape ("recover") from its recent histories of institutionalized abuse, racial and nonracial, the city officials of Los Angeles decided in September 2000 to accept a federal court agreement that would require a series of long-sought "changes in police management and training to head off a threatened civil rights lawsuit over what the Justice Department ha[d] called a systemic pattern of abusive conduct by officers" (Purdum, 2000, p. 1). At least since the videotaped beating of speeding motorist Rodney G. King in 1991, police conduct had been a major civic and political issue in Los Angeles. Throughout the 1990s, tensions between some communities and some police divisions in the "city of angels" remained stressed. Finally, matters of police corruption, such as evidence-tampering and testifying falsely at trial, the shooting of an unarmed suspect, the sudden resignations of 20 active duty officers, and the more than 100 criminal convictions tossed out by local judges and prosecutors associated with the Rampart antigang unit scandal of 1999 (see Box 3.8), brought the crisis in policing in Los Angeles to a head.

In 1996, the U.S. Department of Justice began conducting an inquiry centering on excessive use of force by Los Angeles police officers. Operating according to a 1994 federal law inspired by the King beating, the law authorizes federal prosecutors to go to court to force changes in the operations of local police departments that have been found to be engaging in patterns and practices of misconduct. The consent decree, overseen by an independent monitor and supervised by a federal judge, requires that the department "collect data on the race of people stopped by officers in an effort to determine the extent of racial profiling, install a computerized tracking system to track [citizen] complaints and disciplinary actions against officers, strengthen the civilian board of commissioners that oversees the police and create a special department unit to investigate shootings and use of force by officers" (Purdum, 2000, p. 1). Other elements of the agreement included tightening controls over the police units that monitor gangs, using stricter guidelines for the use of confidential informants, and developing a campaign of "community outreach" aimed at restoring public confidence.

"I think it's just terrific as a first step to police reform," said Erwin Chemerinsky, a constitutional law professor and the author of a report for the police union that recommended accepting the consent decree and adopting similar changes. "My only caution is that it's just a first step. . . . I think that it's very important that this not be the occasion for declaring victory and moving on, because there's a lot it doesn't do" (Purdum, 2000, 1-2). Equally important to this effort in police reform and recovery will be the spirit and cooperation of the Los Angeles Police Department, whose record had been one of not incorporating similar recommendations put forth by the Warren M. Christopher Commission after the commission's inquiry into police misconduct following the 1992 riots sparked by the acquittal of the accused officers in the King case.

STRUCTURAL RECOVERY

Recovery from structural violence involves the modification, reconstruction, and transformation of not only the conditions of violence and violence production but the various systems of injustice and inequality—economic, political, and social. These forms of recovery represent intractable and sweeping changes because they challenge and involve a restructuring of social and cultural relations that are traditionally "fixed" and in place. In other words, structural recoveries involve changing the historically and institutionally established "order of things" when this is acknowledged to be antisocial, injurious, harmful, violent, abusive, and so on by so many people that it can no longer be tolerated as politically acceptable.

Structural recovery could refer to (for example) all of those processes involved in addressing the legacies of racism in the United States or apartheid in South Africa. In both instances, attempts have been made to recover from institutionalized systems and practices of violence that eventually came to be viewed not only as repressive, inhumane, obsolete, barbaric, and unacceptable, but as violating an evolving notion of inalienable human and civil rights. Whether these efforts of recovery have involved civil wars and conflicts, legal restructurings, changed forms of government, apologies, reparations, affirmative actions, Truth Commissions, or the like, they have not only pursued fundamental social change and institutional reform, but have scooped up in their collective pathways the emotional and community sensibilities that the mass of the people experiences in everyday life.

In terms of "recovering" from other forms of institutionalized violence, such as the religious-based terrorism of September 11, 2001, the American people as a whole experienced the attack live or near live vis-à-vis the replayed video of the plane crashing into the second of the Twin Towers. The events of that infamous day in American history can be viewed as dramatically affecting the lives of everyday Americans in a variety of ways:

> For the first time, every American has been touched by terrorism—whether in the financial markets, travel inconvenience, or direct loss of a loved one. The court system is not immune to the effects of September 11 either. The manner in which the federal courts will be affected is just beginning. Although new security measures are being put into place, the real changes will be most notable in fundamental judicial procedures. (Smith, Damphousse, Jackson, & Sellers, 2002, p. 335)

In the aftermath of the mass killings came the shared grief and respect for the loss of more than 3000 lives, as well as varying kinds of resolve that ranged from rage, anger, and retaliation to peace, forgiveness, and reconciliation.

From a reciprocal perspective on violence and nonviolence, it is important to reemphasize that people, politicians, and institutions alike are "free" to reconstruct, from the same terrorist-generated mayhem, pathways to retribution, vengeance, and violence or pathways to forgiveness, peacemaking, and nonviolence. For those individuals who took the extreme and immediate pathways to retribution, they may have driven their car at high speeds into a mosque, as one Indiana man did, or they may have engaged in assaultive acts of ethnic profiling, as several hundred Americans across the country did. Most people turned to families, expressed their anger and grief, reflected on it for a period of time, and then moved on more or less depending on their direct and/or indirect involvement with those who lost their lives that infamous day. Other individuals waged a low-profile campaign of restraint and nonviolence, over the Internet and at various peace and civil liberties rallies (which gained little in the way of mass media coverage) to protest the retaliatory strikes and the immediate escalation of the war on terrorism. As for the extreme pathways to peace and nonviolence, there were small groups of U.S. Buddhists and other pacifists who, during the aftermath of the crisis, relied on inner calmness and strength so that "true courage" and compassion for others could come forth in these times of crisis.

Institutionally, opinion makers and politicians, mass-mediated discussions, and corporate America, if not yet the law and the U.S. Supreme Court, have in effect colluded with the U.S. attorney general and the Bush administration to (a) engage in governmental forms of ethnic profiling and (b) reduce in size certain constitutional protections guaranteed to American citizens as well as the outright elimination of certain legal safeguards for noncitizens. Internationally, it appears that the current Bush administration, both before and after September 11th, was busy breaking treaties dealing with both arms control and environmental protection and was already moving into adversarial directions with our European allies by rejecting an international court of law and granting itself the sole authority to declare war and launch preemptive strikes.

This type of "go it alone" approach to the world and to globalization, which tries to hide behind a questionable war on terrorism at best and an indefensible one at worst, is quite literally another case of the United States embarking on one of its naked power grabs. But in most of the world, our empire has "no clothes"—and no support for its offensive wars, such as the projected one with Iraq in the winter of 2003. It also seems that the United States in general and the current administration in particular is slowly and surely losing its credibility on issues other than war, such as the deadly pursuits of global warming, ozone depletion, population explosion, and destruction of rain forests.

Comparatively, structural forms of recovery are the most difficult forms of recovery to accomplish because they permeate all institutions and social spaces of life—material, spiritual, and emotional—and they challenge the traditional ways of doing things. As was shown in the previous section on institutional recovery, a case certainly can be made in the mediated (if not in the real) world that the pathways of violence, vengeance, and vigilantism are representative of the American way. In the dialectics of recovery, structural recovery can vary depending on whose properties and pathways of violence one is addressing (see Box 8.3). Moreover, structural recoveries are resisted consciously and unconsciously by those politically involved persons who have been and/or are benefiting from the prevailing social arrangements or who are still in various states of denial about the existence or impact of structural violence.

In the context of the "dichotomies of recovering" that cross the spheres and pathways of violence and nonviolence alike, it is interesting to see how far Americans are willing to go to "fight terrorism." According to the political pundits and to several polls conducted not long after the terrorist attacks, U.S. citizens' support for the war against terrorism was so solid that a majority backed assassination, one in three supported government-sanctioned torture of suspects, and one in four agreed with the use of nuclear arms. The largest gap in attitudes came, not surprisingly, from the category of gender, with women supporting assassinations, for example, at 53% compared to men's support of 68%. Another difference of significance in support of assassinations was between Democrats and Republicans, with the former at 54% and the latter at 69%.

These figures surely reveal a less-than-overwhelming endorsement of assassination as a legitimate form of vengeance or retribution. Although it might have been an exaggeration, as a religious studies professor said in an interview with *The Christian Science Monitor* (McLaughlin, 2001) 2 months after the September attack, "the American soul is in turmoil," with most Americans feeling caught between the kind of primitive warfare among tribes that elicits forthright and aggressive response and the more reasoned approaches that appear over time once the initial crisis or trauma has passed. In other words, it is probably not an exaggeration to suggest that the events of September 11 did not create a warmongering nation per se, even if the terrorist attacks did untether an American impulse to strike back. It should be noted, for example, that even at the peak of feeling after the attacks, the American people still maintained a disdain for the use of chemical and biological weapons.

Box 8.3   Terrorism, Counterterrorism, Energy, and Recovery

The crime against humanity that took place on September 11th was so horrific and shocking that for several months it dominated media discussions until such time as Enron and other corporate scandals of the spring and summer of 2002 knocked it into second place, at least for a while. In any event, for those victims of the incidents in New York, including those who died and their living relatives and friends, as well as for those who were only in the area, such as those Long Island residents who experienced post-traumatic, biological reactions in the form of dreams, hallucinations, and/or phobias about leaving home and returning to work in Manhattan, roads to recovery from this crisis have varied. For the greater group of Americans, who know Ground Zero only from the news and other media, recovery is of a different and yet overlapping kind than that of those directly victimized. These forms of recovery tend to be more institutional and structural in nature than individualistic or interpersonal.

When turning to the institutional and structural relations involved in the ideologies and practices of terrorism and to the "recovery" from all that constitutes the mentalities of those who engage in such behavior, Michael Kimmel (2002) has addressed the links between misogyny, homophobia, and the masculinity of this behavior. He discusses the similarities between Timothy McVeigh from Lockport, NY, Adolf Hitler from Austria and Germany, and the Taliban and Al Qaeda in Afghanistan, as well as associated belief systems in society at large, including anti-Semitism and a belief in an international Jewish conspiracy. Among the other commonalities shared by these terrorists and their associates are downward mobility and economic insecurity, a preoccupation with emasculation or masculinity, and a focusing on, blaming of, and anger toward "others."

Any faction of people that competes with the position of such people in society, especially for secondary-level or low-skilled jobs, including women, members of minority groups, immigrants, gay men, and lesbians, may receive the wrath of these marginalized groups of terrorists, sexists, racists, and homophobes. The restoration of manhood and the repression of sexual diversity are central to many terrorists' ideologies. With the exception of the "downward mobility" pathway of these "antiestablishment" terrorists, governmental counterterrorists share similar sentiments of disdain for or indifference to the lives of "others." Both kinds of terrorists or terrorist activities use parallel techniques of, for example, neutralization, adopting the discourse of "collateral damage" to justify their avenging violence with more violence against people who are close to those whom they claim have injured, harmed, or threatened their respective ways of life.

The recovery of the terrorists involves addressing their exclusion from full participation in their societies and the larger world order. In a different but related way, the recovery of counterterrorists also involves addressing those same exclusionary conditions. In other words, as long as conditions of extreme and comparative inequality exist at home and abroad, it is safe to assume that cycles of terrorism and counterterrorism will exist. Those conditions that not only prohibit full participation by more than half the world's population but know no particular ethnic or religious limits to violence are all subject to the forces of patriarchy and market capitalism. Thus, the origins of the making or marking of mass murderers and terrorists alike are to be found within the patterned and gendered feelings of "masculine" shame, humiliation, and inadequacy connected to the political economies of globalization. As Kimmel (2002) recognizes:

> The events of September 11, as well as of April 19, 1995 (the Oklahoma City bombing), resulted from an increasingly common combination of factors—the massive male displacement that accompanies globalization, the spread of American consumerism, and the perceived corruption of local political elites—fused with a masculine sense of entitlement. Someone else—some "other"—had to be held responsible for the terrorists' [exclusion] and failures, and the failure of their fathers to deliver their promised inheritance. The terrorists [and counterterrorists] didn't just get mad. They got even. Such themes were not lost on the disparate bands of young, white supremacists. American Aryans admired the terrorists' courage and chastised their own compatriots. "It's a disgrace that in a population of at least 150 million White/Aryan Americans, we provide so few that are willing to do the same [as the terrorists]," bemoaned Rocky Suhayda, the chairman of the American Nazi Party. "A bunch of towel head/sand niggers put our great White Movement to shame." (p. B12)

Structurally, it is difficult to recover from these attitudes, beliefs, and values and from their counterparts involved in "America Strikes Back," for both are interconnected with

(Continued)

Box 8.3 (Continued)

and inseparable from the exclusionary effects of late modernization and the globalization of production and consumption (Young, 1999). Moreover, these expressions of structural terrorism and counterterrorism are reciprocal, perpetuating, and self-defeating responses of meeting vengeance with vengeance. These relationships silently scream out for a different order of things, but the "old" and "new" ways of warring die hard, as evidenced by the at least temporary unification of political censorship and cultural representations of "terrorist" violence from Hollywood to the District of Columbia.

Finally, in terms of the geopolitics of energy, Central Asia, the Middle East, and the war on terrorism, what holds out a promise for nonviolent alternatives is the recent emergence of Russia as a world-class supplier of oil and gas, second only to Saudi Arabia. As Europe distances itself as much as it can afford from the United States' foreign policies, especially in such important matters as the environment, nuclear weapons treaties, and the international criminal court, and as the United States would like to reduce its energy dependency on the Middle East and Central Asia, Russia's recent expansion in the market can help ease the present and projected dependency on Saudi Arabia, Venezuela, and others. More important, as Russia gains power in geopolitical affairs, it becomes a broker between China and the United States, the United States and the Arab states and the Middle East, and Europe and the United States. As more nations enter into these global relations as "power" (as opposed to "superpower") players, the possibilities for pursuing the collective and nation-state interests of the world simultaneously grow.

In the end, as the United States finds itself in the middle of balancing its needs (interests) for energy with the interests of both the Saudis and the Russians, who both desire American markets, it could be in a position to pressure Israel, the Palestinians, and the undemocratic regimes in the Middle East and Central Asia to recognize the human rights of all, and in turn, these nation-states could pressure the United States as well to conform to, abide by, and develop more internationally based cooperative agreements that globally take into account the collective and individual state interests of developing and developed nations alike.

Sources: Kimmel, M. (2002, February 8). Gender, class, and terrorism. *Chronicle of Higher Education*, pp. B11-B12. Reprinted with permission.
Young, J. (1999). *The exclusive society: Social exclusion, crime and difference in late modernity*. London: Sage.

Alternative Forms of Structural Recovery

Finally, what do alternative forms of structural recovery from violence, be it from the terrorist or the nonterrorist variety, look like? Whatever differences in approach to recovery there may be in the structural alternatives to the old-fashioned wars between states, the commonality in approaches lies in a crucial recognition that everything on the world stage is being played out in the context of globalization and geopolitical conflict. It also lies in the recognition that the so-called new wars involve transnational networks, based on political claims in the name of religion or ethnicity, through which ideas, money, arms, and mercenaries are organized:

> These networks flourish in those areas of the world where states have imploded as a consequence of the impact of globalization on formerly closed, authoritarian systems, and they involve private groups and warlords as well as remnants of the state apparatus. In the new wars, the goal is not military victory; it is political mobilization. Whereas in old-fashioned wars, people were mobilized to participate in the war effort, in the new wars, mobilizing the people is *the aim* of the war effort, to expand the networks of extremism. In the new wars, battles are rare and violence is directed against civilians. The strategy is to gain political power through sowing fear and hatred to create a climate of terror, to eliminate moderate voices and to defeat tolerance. And the goal is to obtain economic power as well. These networks flourish in states where systems of taxation have collapsed, where little new wealth is being created. They raise money through looting and plunder, through illegal trading in drugs, illegal immigrants, cigarettes and alcohol, through "taxing" humanitarian assistance, through support from sympathetic states and through remittances from members of the networks. (Kaldor, 2001, p. 15)

Given this transnationalization or internationalization of violence and terrorism that "takes no innocent civilians" and knows no limits to its destructive extremism, vengeance, retributive justice, terrorism and counterterrorism, or whatever label one uses to describe these actions will only stimulate more of the same. Obviating those conditions responsible for socially, politically, and economically breeding the kinds of institutionalized arrangements that result in "structural standoffs" of violence and counterviolence

becomes the alternative way to escape these reciprocal pathways to violence. In other words, the need is not merely to escape these pathways, but to plant the structural seeds of nonviolence as substitutes for the structural seeds of violence.

To step out of the old and anachronistic paradigm of violence and warfare is to act on the realization that the world (strangely enough) is being shaped less today by military power than by complex political processes involving international institutions, multinational corporations, citizens' groups, fundamentalists, terrorists, and others. Under these new conditions, structural recovery becomes a process of working toward the transformation of a global politics based on the nonviolent negotiations of balancing the basic human needs of people from around the world with the needs of capitalist accumulation and development.

Toward these ends, I finish this section with visions of structural recovery articulated by the Labor Committee for Peace and Justice and the National Lawyers Guild. Although both groups condemned the attacks of September 11th in unequivocal terms as crimes against humanity, they also had this to say on the subject:

> Much of the substance and tone of the US government's response to these events has also troubled us. We fear that blind anger and violent retaliation will only result in further loss of innocent lives, both American and foreign, and perpetuate a destructive cycle of violence that has already gone on too long. We also do not believe that such violence will result in justice that most Americans are truly seeking. (Labor Committee for Peace and Justice, 2001, p. 19)

> The National Lawyers Guild reaffirms our commitment to our guiding principle, that human rights shall be regarded as more sacred than property interests, by continuing to support the struggle of poor and working people for freedom, justice,

education, health care, social security, job security, and a safe environment. We encourage all Guild members to participate in community teach-ins on the mandates of the U.N. Charter, and on the right to conscientious objection to participation in war, to represent those seeking peaceful alternatives to war, and to help our nation envision a 21st Century free from the violence and retributive approaches of the past. (National Lawyers Guild, 2001)

In "A Time for Justice, Not Vengeance: An Open Letter to the Labor Movement," the Labor Committee for Peace and Justice (2001), in keeping with their tradition of working for fairness and justice in the United States and across the globe, called on people to incorporate six basic principles as part of their recipe for structural recovery from the events of September 11, 2001:

Six Basic Principles

1. **Promote Solidarity.** We cannot let the acts of a few extremists be used to justify hostility towards other Muslims, Arab-Americans, immigrants in general, or any other targeted group. We must be willing to speak out publicly against any acts of discrimination or intimidation based on race, ethnicity, religious affiliation, national origin, or immigration status. We must stand in solidarity with all working people.

2. **Support Working People.** We must insist on a relief package for displaced workers and compensation for the injured and families of the lost, paying particular attention to the needs of undocumented workers and those not protected by union representation. We must also be vigilant for attacks on organized labor, ranging from employers exploiting the situation to undermine organizing and bargaining, to legislators passing anti-labor legislation in the name of the "war effort."

3. **Protect Civil Liberties.** Domestic security is necessary to protect our freedoms and way of life. But we cannot let the quest for such security actually undermine those very freedoms and liberties that the U.S. has selectively repressed. Especially in this time of crisis, civil liberties must be maintained.

4. **Stop the Cycle of Violence.** Nothing excuses the attacks. We must take seriously the threat of terrorism and develop an effective response. To do so, we must recognize that the violence did not begin on September 11. Instead, those terrible events were merely the latest in a long-standing cycle of violence. To perpetuate that cycle with a lengthy series of overt and covert military operations will merely result in the loss of more innocent lives and will pave the way for more retaliations and assaults on other innocent Americans in the future.

5. **Address the Sources of Violence.** Instead of more violence, we must be willing to seriously examine the conditions and policies that have provided the soil within which terrorism germinates. We must reexamine U.S. foreign policy, the stationing of massive numbers of US troops abroad, and US support for undemocratic regimes. We must be willing to hear the cries for justice and freedom that come from the world's poor, and to act to support efforts that promote justice.

6. **Seek Justice, not Vengeance.** We should reject the crude calls for frontier "justice" of "dead or alive." Instead, we should affirm the importance of international law and seek civilized justice through multinational mediating bodies like the creation of an international criminal court. Justice is a global issue that requires the cooperation of many nations. It cannot be imposed on the world by a single "super-power." True justice will punish those responsible for injustice while providing insurance against future violence. (p. 19)

SUMMARY

This chapter has provided an overview of interpersonal, institutional, and structural recovery from violence. The process of recovery includes a wide array and diversity of services, programs, resources, and perspectives aimed at the three spheres of violence. There are the actions to assist individual perpetrators, victims, and bystanders in the processes of rehabilitating, reaffirming, or reconstructing their personal sense of self-worth and value. There are the institutional policies and practices that try to respond to aggregated victims and perpetrators of violence from an ecological model of community-based illness prevention and collaborative intervention. Finally, there are the structural relations or the political and economic arrangements that underpin, establish, and change the physical and emotional conditions of life (e.g., high rates of infant mortality, child maltreatment, poverty, or homelessness in a nation like the United States with its unprecedented wealth and affluence) in which most interpersonal and institutional violence resides.

In sum, just as the three spheres of violence are interdependent and have cumulative effects in their production and reproduction of pathways to violence, the three spheres of violence recovery are also interdependent and have cumulative effects of their own in the efforts to decrease those pathways that reproduce violence and increase those pathways conducive to the production of nonviolence. As I have argued in this chapter, the pathways to recovery and nonviolence are derived, in part, both from assuaging the pain and suffering of violent victims as well as violent offenders and, in part, from altering the sources of institutional and structural violence that intersect with the sources of interpersonal violence. Thus, what are called for are reformative strategies of recovery that work across the spheres of violence and that incorporate pathways for establishing and facilitating a needs-based system of individual ("private") and social ("public") justice.

To proceed further with this discussion on the dialectical and reciprocal relations between the pathways to violence, violence recovery, and nonviolence, an overview and dissection of the various models and policies of nonviolence are called for. In the final two chapters of this book, I provide detailed examinations of the philosophies and arguments underpinning the models and policies of nonviolence.

REFERENCES

Andrews, D., Zinger, I., Hope, R. D., Bonta, J., Gendreau, P., & Cullen, F. T. (1990). Does correctional treatment work? A clinically relevant and psychologically informed meta-analysis. *Criminology, 28*, 369-404.

Barak, G., & Henry, S. (1999). An integrative-constitutive theory of crime, law, and social justice. In B. A. Arrigo (Ed.), *Social justice/criminal justice: The maturation of critical theory in law, crime, and deviance* (pp. 152-175).

Belmont, CA: West/Wadsworth.

Blake, R. B. (2001, April 19). Columbine shooting "Should be considered a blessing, not a tragedy." *Reveille.* Retrieved April 20, 2001 from http://reveille.stumedia.lsu.edu/archive.

Brison, S. J. (2002, January 18). Violence and the remaking of a self. *Chronicle of Higher Education,* B7-B10.

Carlen, P. (1990). *Alternatives to women's imprisonment.*

Milton Keynes, Buckinghamshire, England: Open University Press.

Christian, N. M. (2001, May 18). Kindness shared amid murder trial. *New York Times.* Retrieved November 14, 2002, from http://www.nytimes.com

Codd, H. (2000, November). *"Sometimes it's hard to be a woman": Gender, kinship and self-help groups for prisoners' partners.* Paper presented at the Annual Meetings of the American

Society of Criminology, San Francisco.

Dobash, R. E., Dobash, R. P., Cavanagh, K., & Lewis, R. (2000). *Changing violent men*. Thousand Oaks, CA: Sage.

Edelstein, D. (2002, February 10). Vigilante vengeance, Hollywood's response to primal fantasies. *New York Times*, pp. AR 15, AR 29. Retrieved November 14, 2002, from http://www.nytimes.com

Elliott, F. A. (2000). A neurological perspective of violent behavior. In D. H. Fishbein (Ed.), *The science, treatment, and prevention of antisocial behaviors: Application to the criminal justice system* (pp. 19.1-19.21). Kingston, NJ: Civic Research Institute.

Fava, M. (2000). Drug treatment of pathologic aggression. In D. H. Fishbein (Ed.), *The science, treatment, and prevention of antisocial behaviors: Application to the criminal justice system* (pp. 20.1-20.7). Kingston, NJ: Civic Research Institute.

Finkelhor, D. (1984). *Child sexual abuse: New theory and research*. New York: Free Press.

Fishbein, D. H. (Ed.). (2000). *The science, treatment, and prevention of antisocial behavior: Application to the criminal justice system*. Kingston, NJ: Civic Research Institute.

Gendreau, P., Cullen, F. T., & Bonta, J. (1994). Intensive rehabilitation supervision: The next generation in community corrections? *Federal Probation, 58*(1), 72-78.

Gibson, G. (2000). *Gone boy: A walkabout*. New York: Kodansha.

Girshick, L. (1996). *Soledad women*. Westport, CT: Praeger.

Hall, G.C.N., & Hirschman, R. (1991). Towards a theory of sexual aggression: A quadripartite model. *Journal of Consulting and Clinical Psychology, 59*, 662-669.

Henry, S., & Milovanovic, D. (1996). *Constitutive criminology: Beyond postmodernism*. London: Sage.

Kaldor, M. (2001. November 5). Wanted: Global politics. *The Nation, 273*(14), 15-18.

Kimmel, M. (2002, February 8). Gender, class, and terrorism. *Chronicle of Higher Education*, pp. B11-B12.

Labor Committee for Peace and Justice. (2001, November 12). [Paid advertisement]. *The Nation, 273*(15), 19.

Marshall, W. L. & Eccles, A. (1991). Issues in clinical practice with sex offenders. *Journal of Interpersonal Violence, 6*(1), 68-93.

McLaughlin, A. (2001, November 14). How far Americans would go to fight terror. *Christian Science Monitor*, pp. 1-3. Retrieved November 12, 2002, from http://www.csmonitorarchive.com/csmonitor/archivesearch.jhtml;jsessionid=A3RURIFCM4NW1KGL4JASFEQ

National Lawyer's Guild. (2001, October 15). *NLG resolution on the current crisis*. Retrieved November 14, 2002, from http://venus.soci.niu.edu/~archives/CRIT-L/jan01/0122.html

Office of Juvenile Justice and Delinquency Prevention. (2000, November). *Safe from the start: Taking action on children exposed to violence* (NCJ 182789). Retrieved November 14,

2002, from http://www.ncjrs.org/html/ojjdp/summary_safefromstart/index.html

Osofsky, J. D. (2001, October). Addressing youth victimization. *Coordinating Council on Juvenile Justice and Delinquency Prevention Action Plan Update* (NCJ 186667). Retrieved November 14, 2002, from http://www.ncjrs.org/html/ojjdp/action_plan_update_2001_10/index.html

Parry, A., & Doan, R. (1994). *Story re-visions: Narrative therapy in the postmodern world*. New York: Guildford.

Petrik, N. D., Olson, R. E., & Subotnik, L. (1994). Powerlessness and the need to control: The male abuser's dilemma. *Journal of Interpersonal Violence, 9*(2), 278-285.

Purdum, T. S. (2000, September 21). Los Angeles agrees to changes for police. *New York Times*. Retrieved November 14, 2002, from http://www.nytimes.com/2000/09/21/national/21ANG.html.

Raphael, J. (2002). *Saving Bernice: Battered women, welfare, and poverty*. Boston, MA: Northeastern.

Schlesinger, L. B., & Revitch, E. (1990). Outpatient treatment of the sexually motivated murderer and potential murderer. *Journal of Offenders, Counseling, Services, and Rehabilitation, 15*(2), 163-178.

Smith, A. (2001, Winter). Colors of violence. *ColorLines, 3*(4). Retrieved November 16, 2002, from http://www.arc.org/C_Lines/CLArchive/story3_4_01.html

Smith, B. L., Damphousse, K. R., Jackson, F., & Sellers, A. (2002). The prosecution and punishment of international terrorists in federal courts: 1980-1998. *Criminology and Public Policy, 1*(3), 311-338.

Sullivan, D., & Tifft, L. (2001). *Restorative justice: Healing the foundations of our everyday lives.* Monsey, NY: Willow Tree.

Tolme, P. (2000, May 16). Advocates: Ruling hurts rape victims. *Ann Arbor News,* p. A5.

Totten, M. (2000). *Guys, gangs, and girlfriend abuse.* Petersborough, ON: Broadview.

Wertham, F. (1937). The catathymic crisis: A clinical entity. *Archives of Neurology and Psychiatry, 37,* 974-977.

White, M., & Epston, D. (1989). *Literate means to therapeutic ends.* Adelaide, Australia: Dulwich Centre.

Young, J. (1999). *The exclusive society: Social exclusion, crime and difference in late modernity.* London: Sage.

Zengerle, J. (2000, September 17). Something happened. *New York Times Review of Books,* p. 42.

REVIEW QUESTIONS

1. Both in terms of recovering from the cycles of terrorism and counterterrorism and in the context of reducing the actions of terrorists and counterterrorists, design a nonviolent alternative strategy to the "war on terrorism" based on the new geopolitics of oil and gas, Central Asia, and the Middle East. (Hint: Think of the "collective" and "nation-state" interests of the United States, Saudi Arabia and other Arab countries, Europe, Russia, China, Israel, and the Palestine Liberation Organization.)

2. Expound on the reciprocal approaches to recovery and nonviolence.

3. What conclusions do you draw from the four cases of victim recovery?

4. Discuss the similarities and dissimilarities between interpersonal, institutional, and structural recovery.

5. In terms of the reciprocity between violence and violence recovery, discuss either the relationship between battering, welfare, and recovery or between films, vigilantism, and real life.

NOTES

1. Brison, S. J. (2002, January). Violence and the remaking of a self. *Chronicle of Higher Education, 18,* B7-B10. Reprinted with permission.

2. Christian, N. M. (2001). Kindness shared amid murder trial. *New York Times* [retrieved online]. www.mytimes.com, May 18:1-2.

CHAPTER 9

Models of Nonviolence

There is a tendency in peace studies to view and discuss conflict and power primarily in terms of social groups and material interests. However, it should be noted that these social, political, and economic interests are also psychological. Many of these interests, which tend to be quite personal in nature, are experienced as unresolved psychic conflicts and desires. In other words, these personal-political conflicts or desires are often as, or more, emotional than they are material. Whatever the case, these unsettled public and private matters have consciously and unconsciously promoted, in the name of peace and justice, both violence and injustice. As a consequence, a basic principle shared by both peace studies and models of nonviolence has been that

> one of the most important tasks for humanity in the new millennium is to learn how to handle individual, social, and national or international strife in more constructive and peaceful ways. The toll in human misery and the threat to our survival on this planet have become far too great. Rather than continuing to rely on entrenched procedures, we need to find less destructive, less violent ways of dealing with conflict at every level, from the family and the neighborhood all the way up to the community of nations and states. (Brunk, 2000, p. 12)

In this chapter, models of nonviolence will be shown primarily in two contexts: first, as alternative or competing visions to the paradigm of adversarialism, and second, as expressions of the shared visions of the paradigm of mutualism. In the final chapter, practices and policies that have developed and that are consistent with both the prevention of violent conflict resolution and the inducement of nonviolent behavioral interaction are presented.

In neither chapter am I suggesting that there is some kind of natural or linear evolution from adversarialism to mutualism or from violent to nonviolent relationships between people. Nor am I suggesting that these competing cultural states or conditions are mutually exclusive or that they do not coexist in time and space. On the contrary, my argument has been that both have existed in some kind of relationship to each other for thousands of years. Hence, both paradigms need to be taken into account as expressing real parts of self and society or of character and social structure.

Moreover, in the context of political praxis or social action, each of these paradigms needs to be continually reevaluated and reconstructed in light of the evolving human condition. For example, in his brilliant book *Rambo and the Dalai Lama: The*

Compulsion to Win and Its Threat to Human Survival, Gordon Fellman (1998) contends:[1]

> I see the shifting of relative emphasis from adversarialism to mutuality as essential to the survival of our species, of other species, of nature itself. I am not predicting that in the face of possible human-engineered extinction, we will opt for life; I am only suggesting that with the proper analysis and appropriate behaviors that follow from it, we can find our way to renouncing the predominance of adversarial ways and creating a fully elaborated mutuality as an essential piece of a survival strategy. (p. 6)

In different words, each of these paradigmatic models for viewing human nature provides plenty of meaning and orientation to the world. In the adversarial model, human interaction "is based on conflicts of interests, wars, and the opposition of people to each other and to nature"; in the mutuality model, "cooperation, caring, nurturing, and loving" are viewed "as equally viable ways of organizing relationships of humans to each other and to nature" (Fellman, 1998, p. 5). Historically, the model of adversarialism has been the dominant one and the model of mutualism has been the alternative one. As suggested below, however, it may turn out that in the 21st century, the subordinate ideas of mutualism expressed, for example, in the recent worldwide concern for human rights grows in both its attractiveness and attainability as it becomes more familiar and more routine in global affairs.

The "battle" to develop a fuller and richer mutualism and the challenge to reign in and to control our adversarial tendencies, especially when they are destructive of others as well as ourselves, involves individuals, families, communities, nation-states, and, ultimately, the planet, all working together to alter traditional as well as international patterns of social interaction. The struggles for peacemaking and nonviolence are not about negating competitiveness or conflict per se. After all, at various levels of individual and group interaction, conflicts are normal and to be expected. In this sense, conflict can be defined as what results from the existence, real and imagined, of incompatible beliefs, interests, goals, or activities:

> Conflict is itself inevitable among beings who live together in situations where common interests meet finite resources, and where different interests lead to incompatible activities. There is nothing particularly bad, or even undesirable, about the inevitability of conflict. It is, in itself, neither bad nor good, though it can lead to misunderstanding, hostility, alienation, and violence. But conflict can also be a stimulus to creative thinking and the development of new ideas, new technologies, or new forms of social interaction, all of which can make things better for everyone. (Brunk, 2000, p. 17)

The rest of the body of this chapter is divided into three parts. In the first part, an elaboration of Fellman's adversarial and mutual paradigms is presented, with emphases on the "rituals of coercion" and the "seeds of mutuality," on the one hand, and on the "dialectics of ambivalence," on the other hand. The second part is a short and sweeping overview of the historical development of 20th-century nonviolent movements and practices that have been relatively successful in obtaining their political, economic, or social objectives without having to resort to much, or any, violence in the process. In the third part, some of the more prevalent models of nonviolence such as "mutuality," "altruistic humanism," "positive peacemaking," and "resilience" are described and connected to the spheres of interpersonal, institutional, and structural interaction.

ON THE PARADIGMS
OF ADVERSARIALISM
AND MUTUALISM

As the next section underscores, there were a number of successes in nonviolent social change for the improvement of humankind during the 20th century. Despite these successes and the development of the theory and practice of nonviolence over the past century, the historical reality was that violent confrontations and deaths grew at an unprecedented rate at the same time. In fact, there are many historians who argue that the 20th century was the bloodiest in recorded history. Such claims are surely justified, judging simply from the numbers of people who suffered violent death or the many other terrors of warfare and social strife. The majority of those killed in World War I and World War II, as well as the majority of victims of the many regional wars that followed, were noncombatant civilians. The bloody stories of the last century included border wars between smaller nations and ethnic, religious, and revolutionary conflict in which acts of terrorism, guerilla war, and even genocide figured prominently. Moreover, the past half century saw most of the nation-states of the planet, whether part of the First, Second, or Third Worlds, experience a general increase or expansion in acts against property and persons alike (Barak, 2000).

At the same time, the latter half of the century was dominated by a "cold war" in which two superpowers, the United States and the Union of Soviet Socialist Republics (USSR), threatened massive genocide of each other's population. Although the Cold War came to an end, its weapons of mass destruction—nuclear, chemical, and biological—remain in existence and continue to place the people of the world at risk. There is also the danger that other nation-states will, in the not too distant future, add their names to the list of countries with weapons of mass

destruction. The perils of nuclear combat need not mean the end of war or complete annihilation. More likely, wars in which the use of nuclear weapons was considered an option would still involve the use of "conventional" weaponry plus a few limited and targeted nuclear devices—which would still pose an enormous danger to our species and others. Writing about the nature of peace studies and the shaping of a vision, Conrad Brunk (2000) has stated the problem succinctly: "The human race has achieved many apparent economic, scientific, and political advances in the modern era, but when it comes to managing our conflicts our most recent record demonstrates that we have made little, if any, progress. Indeed, it appears that the human race has a decided penchant for turning its most impressive technological achievements to the task of finding ever more painful and destructive ways of dealing with its conflicts" (pp. 11-12). All of which begs the question, "What can we do more than we have done to reduce human suffering and enhance human fulfillment?"

The tendency to oppose—adversarialism—is by no stretch of the imagination confined to the domains of war or large-scale social and political conflicts. On the contrary, adversarialism as a paradigm of social interaction operates in essentially all spheres of life and in all human relationships. At the institutional and cultural levels of interaction, the tendencies to oppose or compete rather than connect and cooperate (mutualism) are revealed in ecology, sports, law, economics, education, sex, politics, race, religion, class, consumption, and perception. Although adversarialism is the dominant mode of interaction in "free market" societies, mutualism as an alternative or subordinate mode of interaction is becoming a "competitive" paradigm that offers a way out of the violence-begets-violence trap. By simply acting on the assumption that peaceful (as opposed to unpeaceful) relations between individuals and nations alike are preferable, the mutualistic or alternative paradigm, derivative of communal and basic needs for all, calls for a fundamentally different kind of social organization and delivery of goods and services or of rewards and punishments.

From the levels of the individual or the interpersonal to the levels of the international and global, the paradigms of adversarialism and mutualism are reflective of opposing assumptions or of the dialectics of such thinkers as Thomas Hobbes and Buddha. The former believed that the creation of civil states always and inevitably involves a war of everyone against everyone; the latter believed that "victory" between individuals or nations generates hatred and that "defeat" generates suffering: a "lose-lose" situation. So Buddha "optimistically" argues that, in effect, those who are wise strive for neither victory nor defeat, but for mutually benefiting exchanges. Hobbes "pessimistically" argues that neither victory nor defeat can be avoided because a "war" of all against all is a given. In a fundamental way, "life is about the tension between adversarialism and mutuality. Both sets of forces are inevitable; the question is how they are expressed and in what degree of saliency" (Fellman, 1998, p. 25). It becomes important, then, to grasp the relative emphases and consequences of each paradigm for behavioral interactions and to strive toward some kind of balance between them.

To begin, adversarial assumptions include the beliefs that one engages in adversarial behavior to overcome another, to achieve revenge, and/or to arouse envy. It is also assumed under adversarialism that parties oppose each other's interests more than they share anything in common. Seen from this perspective, the adversary school

> forecloses all options but antagonism and one form or another of battle. It means that self and relationship are defined in terms of winning and losing, conquering and submitting. It is as if conflicts are the essence of life, and living means enduring them, winning as many as possible and learning how, when it comes to that, to live with failure. (Fellman, 1998, p. 24)

Mutualism assumes deep fulfillment in social connections. It assumes that there are pleasures to be derived from sharing and from cooperation. Mutualism also assumes that both individuals and societies can reside in peaceful relationships with themselves and others. Erik Erikson has emphasized the reciprocal relations between, for example, infant and mother as epitomizing the potential for reciprocal relations between the self and others and the self and society. When Erikson (1964) used the term *mutuality*, he was referring to the processes by which two or more persons support and nourish each other, to the enhancement of all.

By contrast, adversarialism, especially "compulsive adversarialism" (i.e., competition for the sake of competition), represents a cultural defense system that promotes the denial or circumvention of the necessary work to overcome the unnecessary and destructive tensions in the self and in the larger society (Kohn, 1992). Adversarialism, in short, promotes extreme individualism and isolationism. In a similar vein, Fellman (1998) captures the dialectical and reciprocal relations of adversarialism and mutualism when he writes:

> Adversarialism culminates, individually, in feelings of rage that can escalate into total hatred and violence. Mutuality culminates in love: love for self, love for lover, love for parents, love for children, love for friends, love for group, love for humanity, love for nature, love for planet, love for life—love for a work of art, a sunset, a seascape, a walk in the woods. Whereas hatred wants to destroy, love wants to celebrate, to embrace, and finally, to merge. Adversarialism expresses

Thanatos, the death force, the determination to separate, to distance, to define the self in terms of what one is not. Mutuality is Eros; it flowers in the subtle, caring, loving recognition of parent and child delighting in each other. Mutuality, like love that is its essence, expresses the yearning to merge with something higher. Some people call this spirituality, the sense that there is a higher, inclusive force in the universe. This force may be named God, Jesus, Allah, Buddha, Brahman, spirit, love, transcendence, enlightenment, nirvana. The names are numerous and reflect the striving, the yearning for union. (pp. 25-26)

In true dialectical style, the two paradigms are not exclusive. That is to say, within each paradigm there may be features of the other paradigm. For example, in war and during other times of intense competition, people take pleasure in cooperating against those they oppose. In business, sports, or politics, people coordinate actions with their teammates against their competitors, opponents, or enemies. Together, they enjoy the thrill of victory; together, they share the agony of defeat. At the cultural level, pleasures of cooperation need not be organized, whether they are adversarial or mutual. For example, group hatred like racism or sexism that can potentially result in genocide or mass rape is a stylized way of *opposing* the "other" as well as of enjoying *solidarity* with similarly inclined people. Group love, like holism or environmentalism, that can potentially result in healthier communities or more balanced ecosystems, is a stylized way of *connecting* with the "other" and of striving for solidarity with all human beings and other species, including one's "enemies." At the same time, there is still an aspect of adversarialism in holism and environmentalism in that participants are, at least superficially or initially, working against not only individual and organizational adversaries, but some aspects of nature such as diseases of both humans and vegetation. The point is that humans construct meanings, including what is possible and what is not. They have also socially constructed adversarialism and mutualism, which is not to deny that both are products of the human condition. To the extent that one is more true than the other, it is more likely a historical outcome or a self-fulfilling prophesy that has favored the adversarial over the mutuality model of human interaction. Thus far, models by which the world is understood have tended to take adversarialism as the "real" and to take mutualism as the "ideal." In fact, alternative models to competition, such as those that have advocated cooperative ownership of capital and nonviolence at all levels of social organization, have been marginal both to behavioral science and to the popular understanding of how the world could work. Mutualism as an idea, concept, or practice is not only ridiculed and belittled by the ideologies of adversarialism, but typically viewed with suspicion and a high degree of cynical disbelief.

According to the adversary paradigm, people are defined as dangerous, potential competitors, and inevitable combatants. According to the mutuality paradigm, people are defined as potential friends "who can be trusted to respect feelings and vulnerabilities and who can be known partly through knowing oneself" (Fellman, 1998, p. 27). Adversarialism sees human interactions as primarily a series of "zero-sum" games with only winners and losers; mutualism sees human interactions as potentially a series of "win-win" exchanges, or negotiations and compromises, where all parties to a conflict can become benefactors.

Adversarial values tend to give greater importance to battle and tough-mindedness than to friendship and serenity. Nonadversarial or mutual values, such as enjoying good health, feeling secure and comfortable in one's environment, exploring sensuality, caring for others, and finding pleasure in a great range of people and diverse experiences, gives greater importance to peacemaking and social justice and to flexibility of mind rather than to structured conformity, vilification, and revenge. In short, a situation of making love rather than making war.

Historically, one can argue that women have more experience with mutualism than men do because friendship, nurturance, and compassion have been more central to most females' socialization in most societies than to that of most males. One can also argue that traditionally there have been both nonsecular efforts in compassion and giving and secular efforts in volunteerism and restoration. As the subordinate, alternative, or marginal paradigm, the actualization of mutualism requires all kinds of stimuli, as it still resides in a state of arrested development:

> To live more harmoniously with others would mean developing potentials of the self to enjoy emotional interdependence. These pleasures depend on adjusting needs and desires to those of others. That adjustment is possible by virtue of the capacity to take the role of the other, a central form of which is empathy. (Fellman, 1998, p. 27)

The problem is that such identification with the feelings of the other (i.e., empathy) is anathema to the adversarial paradigm, with its associated practices of dehumanizing, humiliating, and/or denigrating the other.

Empathy may be thought of as the opposite of competition: the mutualism of empathy reveals the necessary projections of adversarialism, which at their base stem from two constituents—anger and rage—that are central to the psychology of social opposition. Without the demonization of the adversarial other, one is unable to mock one's enemy in favor of one's own supposed superiority. Setting aside momentarily the fundamental differences between empathy and adversarialism, one should recall that both of these modes of relating may be expressed in

mild, moderate, and extreme forms. In short, both paradigms represent tendencies of conflict and cooperation that range in intensity from slight to compulsive.

In the areas of economics and politics, for example, the spirit of adversarialism fumes supreme in the name of winning profits and power at any cost. As part of the dynamics of winning, any respect for and trust in someone or something else must be undermined as much as possible. "Desires for justice, safety, and non-exploitation are sacrificed for 'victory.' In its most virulent forms, adversarialism is murder, war, and environmental destruction" (Fellman, 1998, p. 28). Although most people conform more or less with both paradigms, to date, people who are compulsive about mutuality have rarely had the influence of people who are compulsive about adversarialism. Or, as Fellman (1998) informs us:

> Most people go along with all these forms of adversarialism because they are socialized into doing so. The key players in such behavior are a minority of people, the compulsive adversaries, whose personalities are so constituted as to drive them, as if addicted, to fight and win or lose. Their insistence, and their leadership, solidify and reproduce norms of adversarialism that most people are taught not to question and with which they learn to play along. There are corresponding degrees of intensity— and, consequently, effect—in mutuality. In its most limited expression, people cooperate for self-interest, simply to gain something for themselves that they consider desirable. A further stage of mutuality is cooperation for mutual interest, where goals and feelings of others with whom one identifies, as well as one's own, are taken into account. The next step is love of family and friends. Then collaboration with and feelings of love for others for the common good, the good of the community, small or large. Mutuality at its fullest involves feelings of unity and love, and actions to realize those feelings for the human

species, other species, nature, the entire planet. (p. 28)

At its core, mutualism rejects the idea of an adversary impulse or imperative to seek advantage over others as either "natural" or "moral." To enhance the human condition, mutualism assumes that people need to draw from their own subjective histories as well as from objective history and compassion. Specifically, in the context of violence, recovery, and nonviolence, mutualism understands the importance of and advocates that people identify with the hurts of others by recognizing their own hurts and the energies of resentment and rage that are bound up with them. Adversarialism, by contrast, especially the compulsive kinds represented by "competition addicts," assumes both material and emotional scarcity, whether one is referring to money, medals, honor, promotions, acceptance, love, or some other icon. Mutualism rejects the adversarial belief in the necessity of competition and the addiction to winning: "As with any addict, the person acting under the adversary compulsion hints at something repressed, something avoided. Just as the alcoholic is not really looking for yet another chemical high, but rather for peace, so compulsive adversaries do not know what inner issues are driving them to win-lose strategies in politics, business, sport, or anything else" (Fellman, 1998, p. 44).

Underlying the dynamics of adversarialism are, often, the transferences of unresolved personal problems. For example, anger, if not rage as well, is problematic for just about everyone, even though most people do not succumb to its influences. At the same time, rather than confront these repressed feelings and dealing in a spirit of mutualism with the anger found in families, at work, or in public life, a spirit of adversarialism redirects this anger at other opponents. Anyone or anything can be defined as or turned into a legitimate enemy, including ideas, structures, subcultures, or groups of people that are viewed negatively or that are associated with evil. By projecting anger onto others, such as minorities, police, the media, or pedophiles, people are able to preserve images of themselves not as angry, but as reasonable and moral. Such dualistic thinking about "good" or "bad" and "loving" or "hating" denies the fuller and more complex realities of self, other, and society.

The point is that through transference and projection, people are able to avoid facing their own anger as they displace this anger onto others. In the process, they often help to create more anger in others, and then they self-righteously congratulate themselves when the anger comes back at them. This kind of "sadomasochism in everyday life" (Chancer, 2000), or socially and politically sanctioned displacement, is often effective because those victims of anger, even if unable to confront their own abusers, gain seeming control over their humiliation and anger by dumping these onto others. In turn, their own passive victimization becomes seemingly bearable as they become active victimizers. At its most extreme,

> The gleeful hatred radiated by white racists, the macho brutality of mercenary soldiers, the sickening obsession of serial rapists—all suggest not only warped consciences but overflowing reservoirs of bitterness. Unbound, they brutalize traditional scapegoats, national enemy groups, and random passers-by. Societies are fascinated by these dramatic figures because they caricature "normal" behavior. Burning a cross on a lawn, raping a woman, shooting a stranger are but exaggerations of everyday acts of cruelty and thoughtlessness so normative as to be unacknowledged by their perpetrators. (Fellman, 1998, 46-47)

Ritualizing Adversarialism and Mutualism

Rituals represent stylized ways of behaving that cultures adopt for a variety of reasons, such as binding anxiety, enjoying the familiar, celebrating unity, or avoiding new ways of doing things. Rituals can be adversarial as in squabbles and arguments or as in trials by ordeal, combat, or jury; they can also be mutual as in friendly greetings and conversation or as in weddings, baptisms, and burials. Rituals fulfill normative expectations of what will be said or done. At the same time, they are mutually affirming, serving as a basis of the human need for recognition.

Adversarial rituals are used by cultures to bind anger and accusation, defamation and humiliation, subjugation and victory. The value of these rituals is that they sustain hostility in structured and predictable ways. These rituals do something else as well: They represent collective clichés or ways of avoiding possibilities of real dialogue and real change. In examining adversary rituals, Fellman distinguishes between *rituals of coercion* and *rituals of resistance*. The goals of the former are to force, harass, distance, humiliate, or subdue; the goals of the latter are to overcome rituals of coercion. Fellman specifically identifies four sets of rituals of coercion. I have labeled these rituals of killing, rituals of undermining, rituals of deprecation, and rituals of denial.

In their more extreme and collective form, rituals of killing have traditionally been thought of as war; however, today, wars can also be conducted without the consent or enthusiasm of the masses. In more limited arenas, rituals of killing would include the extermination of convicted offenders by a nation-state, mafia murders, gang killings, school shootings, terrorist bombings, and other forms of homicide. Rituals of undermining refer to the patterned ways of insulting, frightening, abusing, and unnerving

others. Rituals of deprecation involve parties or interests presenting images of superiority and inferiority to others by comparing or contradicting or by constricting feelings of identification. And finally, rituals of denial are perhaps the most complex: They involve mistrusting, blaming, and displacing the other as at fault and identifying the self as innocent and fair in behavior. Each of these sets of rituals of coercion is proactive in the sense that it initiates fights in one form or the other; once in motion, it sustains itself through the ritualistic reactions to the fight underway.

By contrast, rituals of resistance oppose forces that inhibit freedom and life itself, and they can be divided up into adversary rituals of resistance and mutuality rituals of resistance. The former rituals include revolutions, strikes, and humiliation of one's opponent. In these adversarial forms, resistance tends to perpetuate coercion by seeking to win encounters. Mutuality rituals of resistance include civil disobedience, demonstrations, and other challenges that "maintain the humanity and dignity of the other, speak to maximizing integrity of all parties involved, and seek solutions that are least harmful to everyone. The goals of such rituals include efforts to change all parties rather than overcoming anyone" (Fellman, 1998, p. 67). These mutuality rituals, in other words, use cooperation and assume nonviolence as a framework for action, and they build from respect for the other and the desire to relate to the other mutualistically. They also assume that there is an abundance of surplus emotionality waiting for constructive appropriation and distribution.

In mutuality, people cultivate feelings of pleasure and joy in all of their relationships. Whatever the context—family, lovers, friends, groups, species, the cosmos—no one is debased, no one is made to feel inferior or superior. The logic of mutuality is that each relationship can be enhancing; the goal is to bolster others rather than to embarrass, humiliate, or otherwise overcome them. All parties can benefit; all can be strengthened. The desire is to develop selves that are so well integrated that they need not attribute unwanted or unmet parts of themselves to others. Mutuality does not strive to end tension but to cultivate those tensions that produce growth and pleasure. Indeed, there is tension in mutuality. But it is not the tension of confrontation and defeat, it is the tension of efforts to expand and to connect. It is about the tensions involved in finding alternatives to the unnecessary destructiveness fostered by adversary assumptions. It is about finding out how to relate to others and nature as friend rather than foe. It is about finding out how to live a life of balance rather than of excess.

The seeds (not yet rituals) of mutuality may be identified in familiar institutions. They may also refer to emerging patterns and institutions organized around cooperation as the main mode of relating. Mutuality rituals, then, are not as evolved as adversary rituals. Nevertheless, they are developing as stylized ways of enjoying the humaneness of others, empathy, support, and caring. More systematically, Fellman (1998) identifies seven elements that minimally constitute the philosophy of mutuality:

1. The other is experienced as fully human or the other's full personhood is retained in one's consciousness, emotions, and action.

2. Compromise and harmony, openness and growth are prized, and contrasting realities are accommodated to each other.

3. Power is shared among all parties and all people.

4. Mutuality replaces subordination to hierarchy with interdependence of equals, the shared connectedness of human lives.

5. Emotional responsiveness is essential.

6. Giving is a primal way of connecting.

7. Love and community are prime aspirations. (pp. 135-138)

Mutuality means realizing, directly or through sublimation, the full range of one's own feelings, fears, and inclinations. It means connecting with one's own emotions and, in turn, trying to understand them and allowing for their full recognition and (where appropriate) expression. It is the denial of emotions' centrality in organized social existence that gives virtually free rein to their destructive possibilities. Mutuality also calls for a liberation of the self from the tyranny of an overly rigid conscience and from overly rigid people who threaten to disapprove of or punish the self. It is a morality of insight into and compassion for the self and others and their interrelationships. Finally, mutuality is not about sentimental declarations of unity, idealism, or utopianism, or about clinging to early internalized authorities. Rather, it is an empathetic act of putting oneself in the place of another and then reflecting critically.

In empathizing, people not only use their own feelings and experiences to deduce the feelings of others, they do so to allow themselves the opportunity to feel those feelings with the others. Empathizing allows us to understand what might motivate the behavior of others as well as ourselves. Empathy is the apprehending of another's feelings as well as feeling those same feelings for a better understanding of both the other and the self. Empathy, in short, is a process whereby people recognize others as human and see themselves and the other as part of the same humanity. Empathy is not about and does not call for identification, however. It simply desires understanding and an appreciation of the fact that others listen and understand, too.

By its nature, empathy is inclusive rather than exclusive; it is about substituting the mutual "and" for the adversarial "but." Empathy has also been thought of as both a "form of receptivity" and as "vicarious introspection." In contrast to the distancing and dehumanization central to adversarialism, empathic mutuality connects and unites people.

> In empathy, one recognizes distress, joy, any condition in another person and allows oneself to face the corresponding feelings in oneself. To do so means to enjoy access to the full range of one's feelings. If that is defined as a major criterion of adulthood, then the species as a whole, and societies as subunits of the species, have yet to achieve it in broad, useful ways. (Fellman, 1998, p. 158)

Moreover, empathy "is anathema to killing, to torture, and to the waging of war. It stands in contrast and in contradiction to the demonization of the enemy, to scapegoating, to that polarization of good and bad which creates a world" divided up into "heroes and villains, and little else" (Moses, 1985, p. 136). Empathy carries with it support and caring patterns of social interaction; it also suppresses and curtails ritualistic patterns of undermining. Hence, such behaviors as insulting, frightening, abusing, and unnerving are reduced, and other forms of dehumanization, such as ridicule, sarcasm, cursing, posturing, hostile looks, contradicting, negating, debasing, ignoring, caricaturing, scolding, reproaching, humiliating, trivializing, mocking, and so on and so forth, are less tolerated.

Empathy, then, is the other side, or inverse, of projection, which is the situation in which people attempt to escape or deny their own unwanted feelings by attributing them to other people. The aftermath of projection is distance. The aftermath of empathy is closeness, or a feeling of common humanity. In other words, empathy allows feelings to be shared, aired, and relieved through mutual recognition. Except in intimacy and friendship, however, numerous cultural taboos work against opening up conversations to various emotional mine fields, providing instead safe, and yet not secure, defense mechanisms against ego integration.

> For many people, keeping others away by fighting feels safer than inviting them to join in feeling emotions in their complexity, variety, and intensity. Fighting is protection against vulnerability, against unconsciously anticipated pain; it means ignoring the liberation of releasing pain and joining with another who can acknowledge and accept it. Opposition of individuals and groups to each other preserves the isolation of the self on the assumption that the self really cannot handle all its feelings. This misconception of ego and reality is understandable in the child and tragic in the adult. Bad feelings can be most fully relieved when recognized and accepted by other people. This happens in love, good parenting, good therapy, and good friendship. Drugs, alcohol, nicotine, and other numbing devices like compulsive television viewing and compulsive consuming all provide ways of not revealing feelings to other or self, of trying to stifle rather than deal with them. (Fellman, 1998, pp. 158-159)

On the Dialectical Ambivalence of Adversarialism and Mutualism

Competition can be thought of as a compromise between conflicting desires to merge with others and to separate from them. Unconsciously, ambivalence may underlie mutualism as well as adversarialism; each may be premised on combating others. If psychoanalysis is correct that we are all inevitably ambivalent toward parents, others, self, and even life itself, then people can face and enact both positive and negative valences, favor positive and negative valences, or act on some positive and some negative valences. Whether some behavior is noble or crude, the usual resolution to ambivalence that is adopted by most people is to decry or admire others who express what they dare not allow themselves. When others act virtuously, admiration is public and disparagement is private. Conversely, when others act despicably, disparagement is public and admiration is private.

The idea that humans are fundamentally ambivalent toward people or phenomena about which they have strong feelings helps to make sense of seemingly contradictory behavior. As Fellman (1998) observes, a "common meaning of opposition is the warding off of attraction to the other's virtues, accomplishments, wickedness, élan, body. Often in relationships inside and outside of families, a stylized 'picking on' the other can be seen as both a form of intimacy and as disguised adversarialism suggesting unfaced ambivalence" (p. 52). The same can be said of impersonal bullying involving adolescents, tribes, or nation-states.

The point is that for many people, affection for its own sake may be experienced as too threatening to bear, especially among highly competitive folk. Consequently, a lot of people are more comfortable opposing than connecting, competing than caring, hating than loving, ridiculing than respecting, and so on. Recognizing ambivalence in ourselves and in our normative adversaries allows us to see the mutualism as we transcend the adversarialism. It also allows us to integrate the full range of our humanity, including what Jungians refer to as the "shadow parts" of our psyches or collective unconscious. Genuine mutuality, in other words, finds useful ways to express the "bad" and "good" parts of the self and society, as both are viewed as being essential and integral to the human condition.

In sum, compulsive adversarialism and compulsive mutualism are both inauthentic orientations to life. Similarly, both of these forms of compulsion result in the destruction of something of value. In the case of adversarialism, there is the unrealistic repression of mutuality inclinations. In the case of mutualism, there is the unrealistic repression of adversarial inclinations. To be authentic, the entire range of both must be accounted for. Nevertheless, the two compulsions are not parallel in their consequences, as at least one fundamental distinction remains between them: Compulsively mutualistic persons are usually trying to create something of value; compulsively adversarial persons are usually trying to destroy something of value.

Most people are neither compulsive adversaries nor compulsive mutualists. However, most people have not confronted their ambivalence toward people who are either close to or distant from themselves. And, most of the public's animus or "surplus destructiveness" is willingly displaced onto structures beyond the contexts that evoked them in the first place. Internationally, nations package the repressed hatred of their people and indulge in war with other countries. Domestically, so-called wars against criminals, drug users, and other immoral threats, or cultural wars between the "left" and the "right" over such issues as taxation, racism, and abortion, also allow for the management and release of inner forces of destructiveness. The challenge, then, is for citizens to take back the violence from the state and to figure out more constructive things to do with it. Thus, the reappropriation by individuals of "the aggressiveness saved by [them and] deposited into the state, as if into a bank . . . appears to be the path that must be taken if the state is to be liberated from the accumulation of private violence which it has monopolized, capitalized, and finally increased to nuclear proportions" (Fornari, 1974, xxvii).

A BRIEF HISTORY OF NONVIOLENT STRUGGLE (1900-2000)

Histories of nonviolence usually focus on the philosophies and techniques of nonviolence as a means of social change. Histories of nonviolence also refer to a way of life that "might preempt the causes of conflict rather than merely solving existing crises, thus providing a route by which to move closer to positive peace—that is, towards the freeing of the potential of all" (Vellacott, 2000, p. 103). Thus, nonviolent practices refer to more than the strategic adoption of nonviolent measures or approaches used against overwhelming power and force. In addition, nonviolent practices refer, in and out of crisis, to a different state of mind and orientation to the world. In short, nonviolence is about practicing certain principles of living and relating that are expressive of a preference for mutualism rather than a preference for adversarialism.

The philosophies and techniques of political nonviolence are typically associated with celebrated individuals, social movements, and historical events. The stories of these episodes in history reveal how nonviolent resistance has overcome violence and force and brought about constructive social change. In the 20th century, the institutional rearrangements of several nation-states were impressive: "Tyrants were toppled, governments were overthrown, occupying armies were impeded, and political systems that withheld human rights were shattered. Entire societies were transformed, suddenly or gradually, by people using nonviolent resistance to destroy their opponents' ability to steer events" (Ackerman & Duvall, 2000, p. 2). Time and again, popular movements battled entrenched regimes or military forces with weapons very different than guns and bullets. Their ammunition consisted of petitions, parades, walkouts, demonstrations, and other forms of noncooperation such as strikes, boycotts, resignations, and various forms of civil disobedience.

Historically, nonviolent political actions or sanctions have been used to overcome three types of social conflict. First, there have been the various uses of nonviolent sanctions to bring about self-rule, empowerment, and democracy. Three of the 20th century's great nation-changing popular movements included the campaigns against the imperial dynasty in turn-of-the-century Russia, the British colonial command in India mid-century, and the Soviet-style system in Poland in the 1980s. Second, there have been the nonviolent efforts to resist state and militaristic terrorism. Such actions include civilians who have confronted occupiers as well as oppressive regimes. For example, there were Germans who hindered the invading French and Belgians in 1920, Danes and other Europeans who subverted Nazi activities during the occupation and World War II, Salvadoran people who ousted General Martinez in 1944, and Argentines and Chileans who weakened autocratic rulers and militaristic regimes that terrorized their peoples in the 1970s and 1980s. Third, during the last half of the 20th century, there were the nonviolent campaigns used against a variety of governments to achieve specific rights or benefits. These have included, for example, the American civil rights movement to outlaw segregation and discrimination; the movement to upend the apartheid structure in South Africa; and the popular movements in such places as China, Eastern Europe, and Mongolia to contest one-party regimes in those countries.

Each of the nonviolent struggles that succeeded (or did not) delegitimated the adversarial fallacies that only violence can overcome violence and that those battles with the greatest stakes have to be settled by force of arms. The continuities represented by these nonviolent triumphs in history and the lessons learned from these encounters have been recognized and incorporated by subsequent leaders and persons engaged in each of the aforementioned struggles. For example,

Gandhi was inspired by what happened in Russia in 1905. African American leaders traveled to India to study Ghandhi's tactics. When Chileans organized against the dictatorship of General Augusto Pinochet in the 1980s, and Filipinos organized against Ferdinand Marcos, they were influenced by Richard Attenborough's motion picture *Gandhi*. (Ackerman & Duvall, 2000, p. 6)

What all of these struggles have shown is that power is not only derived by the threat of violence; it also derives from the nonviolent consent of those it would control.

This was certainly the case of the recent struggle by the Soviet-dominated Polish nation to liberate itself from the authoritarian-imposed regime. In December 1981, when Lech Walesa and other leaders of Solidarity were arrested after a meeting in Gdansk, their free trade union movement had already for 16 months shaken the foundation of communist power in Poland by occupying factories and staging strikes. At the time of their imprisonments, Solidarity had looked as though it would be defeated by gun barrel diplomacy and the imposition of martial law. However, when arrested, the defiant Walesa challenged his captors: "At this moment, you [have] lost . . . We are arrested, but you have driven a nail into your communist coffin . . . You'll come back to us on your knees" (Ackerman & Duvall, 2000, p. 1). If only violence is power, and if nonviolence was not a response to repression, then Walesa's words would have been foolhardy to say the least. But Walesa knew better. He realized that Solidarity had already defined, if it had in fact not yet won, the course of the conflict. It did so "simply" by stripping the regime of the Polish people's consent:

When the state had run out of ways to coerce their compliance, it would have to come to terms. Seven years later General Wojciech Jararuzelski, who had jailed Walesa, invited him and other Solidarity leaders to join round table talks that led to elections and the formation of a new government. In 1990 Walesa, a shipyard electrician only ten years before, became president of Poland. He had never fired a shot, nor had anyone in Solidarity. But together they threw back the shroud of authoritarian power and gave freedom to every Pole. (Ackerman & Duvall, 2000, pp. 1-2)

Generally, these nonviolent popular movements for freedom have interwoven a developing theory and analysis of nonviolence (Vellacott, 2000). There are, of course, streams of nonviolent thought that predate the 20th-century experiences and the 19th-century philosophy and duty of conscientious disobedience, first identified with Henry David Thoreau's essay *Civil Disobedience* (1848/1986). Early on, there were the writings and philosophies of such thinkers as Socrates, Jesus, and Buddha; more recent political theorists have included Gandhi, Hannah Arendt, and Gene Sharp. All of these thinkers share in common a questioning of the traditional equation of power and violence. They introduce concepts of positive power, cooperation, and nonviolence. They usually distinguish between conflictive or destructive power and cooperative or constructive power, preferring the latter over the former.

Although Thoreau's essay is often cited as a classic in nonviolence, he was actually writing on the relationship of law, rights, the government, and citizens. As an anarchist who believed in living simply with nature, Thoreau (1817-1862) argued that the rights of people were more important than laws and property and that all persons should have the opportunity (the right) to follow their consciences regardless of what the majority decides. Specifically, Thoreau was opposed to both Massachusetts' slaveholding policy and the Mexican war. He protested by refusing to pay his taxes, for which he briefly went to prison.

Another 19th-century writer of renown and wealth, Leo Tolstoy, was over 50 years old when he introduced his radical philosophy of Christian anarchism. Tolstoy (1828-1910) rejected all institutions based on violence, including governments, legal courts, the police, armies, private property, and money. He further believed that people were commanded not to resist even these "evils" by force. Tolstoy's social philosophy was grounded in a vision of "society based on a maximum of consent... social life reorganized on the basis of voluntary consent" (Quoted in Vellacott, 2000, pp. 129-130). In his ideal society, free of government, all should labor for the necessities of life, but without hierarchical compulsion.

The doctrine most clearly associated with Tolstoyan thought today is "passive nonresistance" to evil, although he never engaged in direct action himself. Practices of passive nonresistance have included noncooperation as well as conscientious objection to military service or to other force-based functions of government. The approaches to nonviolence stemming from the beliefs of anarchists like Thoreau and Tolstoy are about resisting and not contributing to violence. They are not about attempting to influence or improve upon government or societal relations. The actions founded in these approaches are ones of nonintervention, as contrasted with the active nonviolent resistance advocated by Mahatma Gandhi.

Gandhi (1869-1948) was an admirer of Tolstoy, but the two saw nonviolence very differently. The former was not an anarchist, but rather a lawyer and politico who constantly interacted with the state in an effort to transform it through nonviolent resistance. Moreover, Gandhi's philosophy appears to be both strategic and spiritual, secular and nonsecular, as his two related concepts of *Satyagraha* (truth-force), deeper in meaning than the English negative *nonviolence*, and *Ahimsa* (avoidance of violence or causing harm because all life is sacred) still allow for the option of audacious violent resistance to wrongs over a nonviolence based only on weakness.

Catherine E. Marshall, a suffragist, who was well educated and well read, developed a philosophy of anti-militarism and nonviolence not only as a strategy but as a principle to live by. Marshall (1880-1961) believed that war was in large part the result of a male monopoly of power. She opposed patriarchy, hierarchical rule, domination, colonialism, and the perpetuation of social injustice. She favored equality, and she believed that it was essential for national and international peace and justice that women share power with men. At a personal level, Marshall worked during her lifetime with male conscientious objectors to compulsory military service and with the newly formed Women's International League for Peace and Freedom.

Her brand of anti-militarism, like nonviolence, more generally involved struggles for gender equality, social justice, and political power for the common folk. More important, perhaps, Marshall is associated with the themes of "positive peace" in which she saw the struggles for individual and collective justice as

> embodying an attitude which respected the humanity in all, refusing to demonize the opponent, and which approached conflict resolution, whether between individuals or nations, as something to be negotiated with the interests of both sides taken into consideration. (Vellacott, 2000, p. 131)

Dorothy Day, a journalist and founder of the influential paper the *Catholic Worker,* also helped to organize Catholic Nonviolent Action for Social Justice. Day (1897-1980) was influenced by both Thoreau and Marshall. Her advocacy combined Christian nonviolence with communist idealism, and it is credited with helping to liberate many Catholics to adopt positions more radical than those traditionally supported by the Church. The causes that she espoused included "women's suffrage, opposition to fascism, support for the unemployed and homeless in the Depression, conscientious objection to war service, [César] Chavez's campaign to unionize farm workers, reconciliation between the USA and Cuba, opposition to the Vietnam War, and support for nuclear disarmament" (Vellacott, 2000, p. 132).

Martin Luther King, Jr. incorporated the ideals of both nonviolent direct action and Christian love. Although he was influenced by the likes of Thoreau and Gandhi, King (1929-1968) forged his own particular philosophy of nonviolent resistance and confrontation. Like Gandhi, King was both a spiritualist and a strategist. His form of aggressive nonviolent direct action in the face of racial (and other forms of) oppression was to call upon those who believed as he did to engage first in "self-purification" and self-examination so that at the moment of actual violence and physical abuse, they would not resort to violent actions in kind. King defended his right to provoke the oppressor into violent responses as a necessary means for making the transition from "an obnoxious negative peace, where the Negro passively accepted his unjust plight, to a substance-filled positive peace, where all men [would] respect the dignity and worth of every human personality" (Quoted in Vellacott, 2000, p. 133).

No contemporary discussion of nonviolence and nonviolent theory would be complete without mentioning the work of Gene Sharp. Both a theorist and a practitioner, Sharp is the founder of the Albert Einstein Institution in Cambridge, Massachusetts, a center for nonviolent action. Considered to be one of the foremost Gandhi scholars and advocates, he has authored several books on nonviolent theory, methods, and dynamics, including *Exploring Nonviolent Alternatives* (1970), *The Politics of Nonviolent Action*

(1973), *Gandhi as a Political Strategist* (1979), and *Social Power and Political Freedom* (1980). A believer in the redistribution and democratization of power, Sharp, like Gandhi and other nonviolence theorists, works from the premise that governments rest, at bottom, not on force but on cooperation.

Accordingly, Sharp (1980) has classified the methods of nonviolent action into three broad groups: (1) nonviolent protest and persuasion; (2) noncooperation with institutions that use social, economic, and political force; and (3) nonviolent intervention. Like Gandhi, Sharp believes that ceasing to play the part of the ruled or engaging in nonviolent noncooperation is the most viable path to securing beneficial social change. Finally, Sharp (1980) has categorized the three outcomes to nonviolent action as consisting of "conversion," which is rare; "accommodation" through negotiated change; and "coercion," whereby oppressive systems are no longer able to function without conceding to the demands of the resisters.

MODELS OF NONVIOLENCE

All models of nonviolence, whether addressing interpersonal, institutional, or structural levels of conflict and peacemaking, ascribe to the spirit, theory, and practice of what has generally been cast above as the paradigm of mutualism. For example, when Robert Aitken Roshi, a Zen practitioner, wanted to bring Buddha's teaching of infinite compassion outside the monastery walls, he founded the Buddhist Peace Fellowship (BPF) in 1978. Located in Berkeley, California, BPF publishes the award-winning magazine *Turning Wheel,* a venue for thoughtful and personal perspectives on social justice and peace activism.

BPF is involved in a number of other projects that explore and practice "loving kindness." Some of these activities include

(a) the Buddhist Alliance for Social Engagement, which focuses on, among other things, race and diversity in our lives; takes inner-city children on wilderness trips; sits with people who are dying; and prepares meals in soup kitchens for homeless people; (b) the BPF Prison Project, which is attempting to transform the prison system through reforming the prison-industrial complex, abolishing the death penalty, and bringing the teachings of "dharma" to those persons confined in prisons and jails; and, more generally, (c) feeding children around the world, offering low-interest loans to displaced Tibetans in Nepal and India, underwriting medical services for refugee victims of the civil war in Burma, and peacemaking efforts in such areas of regional conflict as Israel and Palestine, Guatemala, Sri Lanka, and, more recently, Afghanistan.

In a solicitation dated February 28, 2002, the BPF's executive director, Sibylle Scholz, Ph.D., opened her letter with the following lines:

> I participated in premeditated, cold-blooded murder. That is how I felt last month when I sat at the vigil at San Quentin, while yet another being was executed. The Buddhist Peace Fellowship was there. Over 100 Buddhists from different traditions sat in silence as part of a demonstration that included other faith groups and activists.

Further on in the letter, Scholz explained how the BPF takes seriously the Buddhist precept of not taking life and how "we recognize our interdependence with all beings." Hence, members of the Buddhist Peace Fellowship "allow themselves to deeply and completely explore what loving kindness means. Please join us on this path" (Scholz, 2002).

Like other models of nonviolence, the BPF engages in a theory and practice that tries to negate the adversarial paradigm and to undo, where possible, the rituals of killing or revenge, of undermining, of acting superior, and of faulting and blaming others. In the case of revenge, for example, nonviolent models recognize that revenge—from ridicule to murder—is a form of reactive hurting, an effort to negate the hurt self, to compensate for it, as if by displacing the hurt to someone else—either the person who caused it or a substitute—one could alleviate, if not eliminate, the hurt. At best, these adversarial rituals offer temporary or momentary relief. At worst, they offer little, if anything, in terms of positive, proactive, or constructive ways for dealing with the hurt. In most instances, these "rituals of coercion" simply perpetuate and/or escalate the pain (and violence). As Fellman (1998) so aptly puts it:

> Hurt and rage are twinned—two aspects of one experience. People insulted, negated, humiliated, respond in rage. Attacked, one either replies in kind, imagines doing so, joins in cultural metaphors for assault, or turns the anger inward. Or one leaves the adversary system and finds constructive ways to deal with hurt. (p. 82)

Whether or not one can actually leave the adversarial system remains in doubt, but nonviolent models of mutualism represent alternative and constructive ways for dealing with hurt, pain, harm, and violence. Situated in the academy, in the community, and in the cultural mass media, these models represent a growing perspective from a diversity of persons who are struggling with the development of mutuality in the context of adversarialism. In the popular domain, for example, there is the myriad of "self-help" groups for dealing with problems of addiction and violence.

In the academic arenas of psychology and criminology, there are "cognitive therapists" and "peacemaking criminologists," respectively, who engage in mutualistic enterprises as alternatives to adversarial enterprises. These social and behavioral scientists recognize that most perpetrators of violence are vulnerable to patterns of anger, rage, and shame, and/or they are imprisoned by patterns of hate, hostility, and violence.

They also recognize the linkage or connection between these patterns of interpersonal violence and the larger institutional and structural relations of violence. Moreover, these academics understand that the revenge or vengeance which occurs between individuals, between individuals and the state, or between nation-states represents both a "failure to communicate" and a "failure to empathize."

Vengeance happens when apologies, forgiveness, and restitution are repudiated or thought to be impossible. That is, fantasies of annihilating one's antagonist do not follow merely from the antagonist's insults but, more typically, from their refusal to talk about something or to own up to some type of responsibility. Stated differently, the rage in revenge reveals a failure to connect in ways other than revenge with the objects of one's wrath. This profound and fundamental insight seems to be assumed and shared by all those persons who espouse, advocate, or engage in nonviolent theory and practice. In the rest of this section, I will provide an overview of four streams of nonviolent consciousness and action. These include mutuality, altruistic humanism, positive peacemaking, and resilience.

Mutuality

Fellman (1998) has demonstrated that the seeds of mutuality are already alive, if underdeveloped, in everyday life. Thus, he argues that the present struggle of the human condition involves nurturing the old and new seeds of mutuality in the old and new institutions of social organization. Dialectically, the family is (and can be) the primary site

for training in both adversarialism and mutualism. In "functional" families, feelings of caring, respecting, responding, supporting, loving, and other such behaviors flourish. People from these families are better equipped or able to deal with the realities of adversarialism and mutualism. By contrast, "dysfunctional" families have not learned how and/or are unable to move back and forth between these two paradigmatic modes of social interaction.

The general argument is that mutuality and its delicate tunings are learned early on by both infants and children. It is further argued that love between consenting adults represents the essence of mutuality, with its giving and taking, its experiencing of the needs and hurts and hopes of the other, as well as its emotional and sexual fusion at moments of joy. Finally, it is argued that the attitudes of mutuality learned by the child, first inside the family, then outside, can be extended to groups, communities, nation-states, and ultimately, to the entire planet: "Good child-rearing and good education would focus on these processes as essential not only for personal satisfaction but for survival of species and planet" (Fellman, 1998, p. 179).

Mutualism can be found in institutions and spheres of everyday adversarialism. That is to say, from the worlds of entertainment, sports, and leisure to the worlds of nationalism, politics, business, and law, people take pleasure in both individual and team excellence, appreciate the values of cooperation, coordination, and competition, and employ loyalty and solidarity to their advantage. Often, however, to avoid the potential of adversarial tensions between people—families, communities, nations—on the same side, these are projected, displaced, or defused by a myriad of convenient enemies and scapegoats. Of course, it is a shame that so much mutuality is subject to the dominant paradigm of adversarialism and contingent on collective opposition to others.

The seeds of mutuality can also be found in organized religion and sport, in international and domestic politics, in business, education, architecture, and music, and in the growing globalization of nonviolence, expressed in the worldwide politics and teaching of mutuality. Old and new, organized religion with the binding together of worshippers depends to some extent on their feelings of mutuality for each other and to ideas shared in common. At the same time, all of the world's religions encompass messages of both mutualism and adversarialism. Interestingly, these dialectics are found in both the East and the West: "Buddhism was as much a reaction to Hinduism's contradicting its mutuality tradition as Christianity was to Judaism's doing the same. The distortions of Hindu values at the time of Buddha sound like what Jesus objected to in the spiritual rigidity and corruption of the Pharisees" (Fellman, 1998, p. 183).

Combining the seeds of mutuality from both Western and Eastern religions can provide what Charlene Spretnak (1991) refers to as a "meta-religion" that interconnects, without replacing, the world religions and integrates their mutualistic tendencies into some type of emerging world culture. For example, the emphases on community, mending, healing, repairing, fixing, transforming, peace and social justice in Judaism, Christianity, and Islam can connect with the Buddhist traditions of introspection and release from unnecessary inner pain, the Native American legacy of comfort and oneness with the cosmos, and the earth- and body-centeredness of Goddess spirituality.

In another example of the cross-fertilization of utility and pleasure, organized sport provides seeds of mutualism and even the subversion of the dominant paradigm of winning at any cost. Whether or not play is "democracy in action," as Philip Slater (1991) contended because of its nontotalitarian structure, play and sport can be beautiful and provide meaning apart from the contest of winning and losing. In fact, both play and sport can provide a temporary and limited perfection that transcends the competitive, moving toward the noncompetitive as a mutuality ritual—appreciated, if not thoroughly enjoyed, by both sides in an adversarial contest. The "slam dunk" in basketball is said to epitomize this relationship, taking on an importance that far exceeds its role in the game (Cotton, 1984). Although the slam dunk may be a surer way to score two points, it seems to have taken on a pleasurable quality of its own involving an act of proud display. This is especially true of the breakaway dunk, when a player intercepts a pass or steals the ball, drives half court or longer without the interference of an opponent, and completes this show of dexterity with an uninhibited flight and design culminating with the ball going through the hoop:

> The moment of take-off signals a glimmer of brief celebration, a respite from the intense adversary strivings of sport, a moment when athlete and spectator are reminded of a time in their lives when it was considered all right to play, to experience joy at no expense to another. The dunk transcends team loyalties, geographic sympathies, and the adversary parameters of sport. It is not altogether unique, though. The appreciation in any sport for the move expertly executed—the successful long pass in football, the winning home run in the last half of the last inning in baseball, the brilliant scoring of a goal in hockey or soccer— all partake of admiration for play performed at its highest level as well as for adversary victory. (Fellman, 1998, p. 185)

In the world of international and domestic politics, nonviolence and civil disobedience represent the seeds of mutuality. Following Gandhi and others, the goal becomes to recognize and respect the enemy as human. The challenge for nonviolent activists becomes finding those points of connection between people or locating vulnerabilities within the self and the other where human connection can be made. Such actions require that people recognize all humans as a single species and give up the practice of demonizing the "other"—a very tall order to say the least. After all, the seeds of mutuality in both the international and domestic arenas are often suppressed as leaders of nations or of parties put the interests of their populations or constituencies ahead of those of other nations-states or parties.

Nevertheless, the United Nations today and the European Community, for example, stress at least on the surface interdependence over independence. Hopefully, this represents a transitional stage between the *realpolitik* of the nation-state and a planet predominantly based on global mutuality. It is important here not to confuse the ends with the means. Empires, for example, from the Roman to the United States', have stressed the value of interdependence, but they are far cries from being mistaken for mutuality associations, let alone as facilitating positive peace and social justice for all. Even after the Cold War, the UN continues in many ways to still be an adversary organization, with all the downsides that that implies, including the perpetuation of human exploitation, hunger, and suffering. This is not to deny that the United Nations "moves in mutuality directions when it creates the UN Declaration of Human Rights, sponsors the International Court of Justice, works for children's issues in UNICEF, and promotes general interests through WHO and UNESCO. These are its positive directions, in laying the infrastructure for a world in which conflicts are resolved peacefully and peoples work together for the common good" (Fellman, 1998, p. 187).

Briefly, in other institutional realms such as education, business, and architecture, similar seeds have been planted. For example, the vision of Education 2000 (Global

Alliance for Transforming Education, 1993) emphasized five beliefs concerning cooperative education. These included (1) students rather than curriculum driving the system; (2) teachers acting as facilitators of learning and knowledge rather than imparters of information; (3) active student participation in the democratic process; (4) students encouraged to participate in community-service projects; and (5) students developing feelings of connectedness, love, and compassion for the needs of people.

In the areas of economics and business, efforts are certainly alive that are altering attitudes and patterns of behavior. For example, cooperation among people has emerged in relation to the natural environment through respect for its limits and vulnerabilities. Socially responsible investing, characterized by decisions on the part of firms not to invest in companies that are not good for the environment and people, such as those companies making alcohol, tobacco, and weapons, is growing. Although capitalism remains intact, deviations from its classical mode are growing: "companies that develop positive relations with their community and employees, fair treatment of women and minorities, product quality, and a caring attitude towards consumers have found a rapidly increasing number of investors" (Fellman, 1998, p. 193). In addition, there are the socially responsible businesses like Ben and Jerry's ice cream or Stoneyfield Yogurt that give a portion of the profits back to employees and a portion to organizations like Oxfam America or National Public Radio.

Last but not least, with the end of the Cold War came calls for a scaling back of the military-industrial complexes and the wasteful production of weapons and warfare. Mikhail Gorbachev (1987), especially, articulated the need for the world's superpowers to reinvest their resources for the purposes of meeting real human needs:

The arms race, just like nuclear war, is unwinnable. . . . All of us face the need to learn to live at peace in this world, to work out a new mode of thinking, for conditions today are quite different from what they were even three or four decades ago. The time is ripe for abandoning views on foreign policy which are influenced by an imperial standpoint. . . . From the viewpoint of long-term, big-time politics, no one will be able to subordinate others. . . . Along with the above-said realities of nuclear weapons, ecology, the scientific and technological revolution, and informatics, this also obliges us to respect one another and everybody. (p. 138)

Domestically, in the wake of the rising number of U.S. gun-related homicides in the 1980s, special-interest groups emerged calling for gun control, and this helped contribute to a loss in the status and popular image of the gun and in the demise of such a legendary manufacturer as Colt 45.

Art, architecture, and music, in their own and related ways, can each expand on and encourage the mutualism and environmental messages of the postindustrial age. These have to do with moving toward a celebration of the cooperation between ecosystems and away from the celebration of power over matter and life. Contemporary architecture, for example, has become absorbed by the rediscovery of "humanity's debt to the earth and connecting this awareness into a new iconography" (Wines, 1993, p. 23). And from Article 5 of the International Union of the Architects/ American Institute of Architects World Congress of Architects' Preamble to the *Declaration of Interdependence for a Sustainable Future*:

A planetary culture of interdependence requires that . . . environmental auditing, monitoring, and forecasting are used to ensure that the well-being of both present and future generations and of other species is adequately protected and nurtured . . . [and that similar] standards are applied to all countries and locations, irrespective of their socio-economic status. (Wines, 1993, p. 23)

Altruistic Humanism

In *Prisoners of Hate: The Cognitive Basis of Anger, Hostility, and Violence*, Aaron Beck (1999) discusses "The Brighter Side of Human Nature" in the context of attachment, altruism, and cooperation. Beck concludes that "evidence from statistical surveys, anecdotal reports, observations of children, experimental studies, and practical applications in the classroom [indicates] that people in general have an innate capacity for altruistic behavior that can balance or override hostile tendencies" (p. 227). Beck also believes that we all have great capacities for rational thinking on which we can correct our biases and distortions, including the various "values and ideologies that divide people and make them mistrustful and antagonistic toward each other" (p. 227). This goes for "healthy" and "unhealthy" individuals as well as for nation-states. Accordingly, Beck's "cognitive theory" of behavior holds out the potential for modification and change. In other words, although "anger and hostility thrive on rigid, egocentric beliefs and biased perspectives, . . . it is possible to reshape the images and beliefs that drive these feelings and consequently to weaken the disposition for violence" (p. 227).

For example, at the macro or global level, the dualistic modes of adversarialism and mutualism can and have reversed directions in terms of assigning other nations to unfriendly and friendly categories. That is to say, because of a change in circumstances, the image of an adversary changes from implacable enemy to ally or friend, from malevolent to benevolent, and from dangerous to safe:

America's image of Joseph Stalin and the Soviet Union changed from negative to positive when Germany attacked the Soviet Union in World War II. Indeed, our adversaries in World War II—Germany, Japan, and Italy—became staunch allies after the war was over. The Soviet Union, in contrast, was switched back to the negative track as we entered several decades of cold war; then, after its breakup, it regained a more positive image. In other parts of the world, feuding neighboring states have learned to swallow their differences and engage in constructive reciprocal relationships. (Beck, 1999, p. 229)

Beck contends that images and beliefs regarding other individuals, groups, and nations can be similarly influenced by both preventive and interventionist strategies. In the international arena, Beck would like us to broaden our perspective of the adversary so that we are able to see the "alien" as human, like ourselves. Having such a perspective can arouse empathy for the other's vulnerability and suffering. Whether abroad or at home, Beck would like to see the development of programs based on the brighter side of human nature: that is, on its benevolent and rational components. Hence, Beck wants us to create or reinforce prosocial structures that resist or counteract hostility and violence: "The innate qualities of empathy, cooperation, and reason, which are just as intrinsic to human nature as hostility, anger, and violence, can provide the building blocks for prosocial structures. Understanding and empathy are more readily extended to members of one's own group than to outsiders, but there is no immovable block to expanding them to all humankind" (Beck, 1999, p. 230).

In allowing for the formation of an empathetic understanding of the opponent's perspective, Beck argues that one is able both to distance oneself from the egocentric construction of a conflicted situation and to adopt the decentered position of reframing the meaning of a situation with the objectivity of an impartial observer. He writes further that through "responding with body movements or emotional distress, humans seem to be hardwired to [act in response] to other people's painful experiences. In contrast to sympathy, which may involve feeling sorry for another person without experiencing his distress, true empathy consists of sharing another person's perspective and his specific distress" (Beck, 1999, p. 254). This is not to deny that people who, for example, are exposed to killing, or who kill or engage in torture, are not capable of desensitization or of distancing themselves from their empathetic impulses.

The "turning off" or nullification of empathy can occur within the narrow confines of a conflicting family, or more broadly, in terms of conflicting nation-states.

At both the individual-private and group-public levels, the development or support of the "unempathetic" occurs both consciously and unconsciously. When this occurs, one person's antipathy toward another person or one nation's toward another allows not only for the inflicting of pain and suffering without feelings of guilt or identification, but for feelings of how one is doing the right thing in the process—the doctrine of what has been traditionally called "retributive justice."

Within the adversarial paradigm, retributive justice predominates as the preferred mode of intervention. At least since the Enlightenment period of the 17th century, this has been the case for both the state and individual alike. In the same way as authorities or representatives of the state believe that they are enforcing the law by incarcerating a thief, a person tricked in a game of cards or a spouse deceived by an adulterous partner invokes the principle of retribution to reduce the stress of being violated. In addition, Beck's analysis of "the perversion of the moral domain" explains how people, children and adults, may consciously believe that they are just, although their actions are often driven by egocentric beliefs:

> The desire to punish, to exact justice, provides a sense of power, self-righteousness, and freedom from restraint. Consequently, individuals tend to take it on themselves to punish others for their supposed wrongdoing. Instead of trying to clarify probable sources of conflict, their conscious rationale is that they are asserting their own right to get angry and retaliate. In actuality, their claim for justice emanates from a primal reflex pattern: their hurt feelings automatically trigger the impulse to retaliate. Their justification is the belief bridging the hurt feeling and the punitive impulse: "Since I am hurt, I am entitled to punish the offender." Further, they try to control or even eliminate others in order to alleviate their own sense of frustration or impotence. (Beck, 1999, p. 237)

Beck's analysis of the pathways to nonviolence turns next to the "moral concepts of justice and caring." Combining Lawrence Kohlberg's six stages of moral development, which culminates in a humanistic version of justice, with Carol Gilligan's concept of caring (as an equally moral voice), Beck argues that the universality of humankind "is an antidote to the rigid perspective characteristic of tribalism, nationalism, and self-serving morality. If the value of the human life overshadows one's political or social ideology, it is more difficult to carry out harmful behavior" (Beck, 1999, p. 240). Hence, for Beck, what needs to be done is to move from the "separateness" to the "connectedness" perspective.

Like other models of nonviolence, Beck's involves the transition away from a "moral justice" based on adversarial interaction and toward justice based on mutualistic interaction. Adversarial models have an individualistic orientation that emphasizes rights and entitlements, such as life, liberty, and the pursuit of happiness; equal opportunities; fair treatment and justice. These models revolve around the central assumption that people have competing claims and are in conflict with each other for personal reinforcement and available resources. By contrast, mutualistic models have a caring orientation that revolves around the sensitivity to others' (and one's own) needs and a sense of responsibility for everyone's welfare. All people, then, when confronted with virtually any situation, have "to decide whether to assert their rights, to express caring, or simply to pursue their self-interest" (Beck, 1999, p. 240). It is at this point of decision making that *altruism* enters the picture.

Altruism exists on a continuum that ranges from making basic services or necessities available to making significant sacrifices or partaking in serious risks to intervene in the saving of other people's lives. Altruism involves the emotional strands of empathy, caring, identification, and a benevolent self-image. Altruistic behavior is said to be its own reward; the pleasure is derived not from any tangible benefit but rather from knowing that one "did the right thing." Beck distinguishes between "narrow" and "enlightened" altruism or between "limited" and "unlimited" altruism, advocating on behalf of the latter "altruistic-humanistic" mode over the former "narcissistic-expansive" mode.

Narrow forms of altruism are generally an expression of group narcissism as well as altruism. "The members of the group show commitment to the cause, loyalty to fellow members, and a willingness to risk or give up their lives, but have little concern for the lives of people on the other side" (Beck, 1999, p. 243). This contradiction expresses how group narcissism can be the antithesis of altruism. For example, missionaries, militarists, and revolutionary groups

> emphasize intangible institutionalizing values such as religion, country, and home

and resort to violence to enforce their program. Pursuing the philosophy that "the end justifies the means," they declare war on adversaries within and outside of their group. Internal dissidents are persecuted as heretics or traitors, and outside opponents as enemies. The follower's identity is subordinated to the goals of the group, which are formulated by the leaders. In this context, self-sacrifice by the followers represents a naïve and circumscribed altruism. (Beck, 1999, p. 243)

Enlightened altruism, by contrast, is not only universal and humanistic, but represents an antidote to group narcissism.

Representing opposite sides in our dualistic personality structures, narcissism favors the self while altruism favors the other. The narcissistic mode perpetuates and reinforces separateness, difference, and inequality; the altruistic mode seeks connection, sameness, and equality. The former mode promotes self-interest and expands personal domains. It is competitive with other people, assertive of personal rights and privileges, and strives to maintain individuality and self-identity. The latter mode promotes the general welfare of all living things, derives pleasure from subordinating personal interests to the needs of other people, and is on guard to protect the rights of the underprivileged and disadvantaged. Individuals and groups of people representing a demographic cross-section will reveal themselves along the altruism continuum. Those exemplifying "pure altruism," such as the "Just Christians" who risked their lives to save Jews during the Holocaust, in a controlled study displayed a number of characteristics that differentiated rescuers from those who had not attempted to save Jews (Oliner & Oliner, 1988).

The authors found that not only were the rescuers (compared to the nonrescuers) more empathetic and more susceptible to feeling other people's pain, they also possessed a greater sense of responsibility and commonality with alien groups. For example, on an itemized questionnaire, the rescuers were more likely than the nonrescuers to indicate that they regarded Turks, Gypsies, and Jews as very much like themselves. Oliner and Oliner (1988) attributed the differences between the two groups' altruistic dispositions to their child-rearing experiences and to their parents' emphasis on the values and practice of moral and ethical behavior. Rescuers had been exposed to a childhood socialization that praised good behavior and relied on reasoning and explanation more than on harsh discipline. Their home environments consisted of caring people who inculcated tolerant attitudes toward people different from themselves.

Beck argues, from the literature of social psychology as well as from substantial experimental evidence, that the altruistic mode of behavioral interaction can be "tuned up" by appropriate interventions. More generally, contemporary neobehaviorists and cognitive-behavioral theorists emphasize the development of *social cognition,* or the awareness of one's own attitudes, beliefs, and values "about other people and their actions" in relationship "with one's own social functioning in relation to others" (Hollin, 1993, p. 62). Prosocial training, empathy training, and taking the perspective of the other can be applied throughout early childhood development and the life cycle—the earlier the better, of course. In the final chapter, some of the cognitive interventions both for individuals and groups experiencing violence will be spelled out in more detail.

Positive Peacemaking

A distinction has been made between "negative" and "positive" peace. The former is viewed as stemming from the mere absence of overt conflict, the latter from humanism and mutual understanding. In discussing the criminology of peacemaking, both Richard

Quinney and Harold Pepinsky maintain that it is grounded not only in humanism, but in existentialism, Buddhism, pacifism, and socialism. Quinney explains that at the roots or very foundation of peacemaking criminology are compassion and love: "A love that not only allows us to identify ourselves with others, but allows us to know that we are one with another, that we are one with each other. Such loves makes a different world, a world without crime" (Quinney, 2000, p. 25).

In assuming an intersubjectivity of social reality and by approaching peacemaking from an interdisciplinary and integrative stance, Quinney (2000) articulates that for his imagined world without crime or violence to become a reality, there has to be

> the interconnection between the inner peace of the individual and the outer peace of the world. The two develop and occur together. The struggle is to create a humane existence, and such an existence comes only as we act peacefully toward ourselves and one another. (p. 21)

These ideas, taken as a whole, help to construct a positive peace. Going beyond the traditional debate of objective and subjective reality, Quinney follows Albert Camus and submits that it is the absurd that is the essential concept of our lives. He further maintains that it is existentialism that allows us to entertain the ambiguity of our existence, with its uncertainty and the fear of life and death.

The novelist Milan Kundera, in *The Unbearable Lightness of Being* (1984), referred to this as "the wisdom of uncertainty." In the absence of such wisdom, humans have created worlds that are cruel and oppressive. As Kundera (1984) has observed: "Man desires a world where good and evil can be clearly distinguished, for he has an innate and irrepressible desire to judge before he understands. Religions and ideologies are founded on this desire" (p. 7).

Unfortunately, as he notes again, we humans have "an inability to tolerate the essential relativity of things human, an inability to look squarely at the absence of the Supreme Judge." Quinney (2000) adds that the modern law and the administration of criminal justice are also products of our collective inabilities to tolerate the essential relativity of things human. In the larger scheme of things, these represent various "states of denial" (Cohen, 2001).

In the same way, Erich Fromm (1965), in discussing "a godless religion" and in his pursuit of a nontheistic perspective, offered up his vision of social humanism. In its most basic form, Fromm claimed that social humanism was the belief in the unity of the human race and the potential of human beings for self-actualization through their own individual and shared collective efforts. He further assumed that the urgent issue in the world was the establishment of peace, and that this was inseparable from the realization of the human developmental project. Fromm (1976) argued in his last book, *To Have or to Be,* that *radical hedonism*—seeking maximum pleasure and trying to satisfy the desire to possess—and *egoism*—selfishness and greed—are the products of the economic contradictions of capitalism that promote a *having* mode of existence over a *being* mode.

Fromm argued that it was imperative that individuals and societies be based on the being mode of existence. For him, it was simply a matter of survival. For Fromm and many others, "love" is the essence of being human. In *The Art of Loving*, he argued that love opens us to the fullness of our being. Love is about activity, not passivity; it is primarily about giving rather than receiving. In his opening chapter, "Love and Its Disintegration in Contemporary Western Society," Fromm observes that love is difficult to find and to practice:

If love is a capacity of the mature, productive character, it follows that the capacity to love in an individual living in any given culture depends on the influence this culture has on the character of the average person. If we speak about love in contemporary Western culture, we mean to ask whether the social structure of Western civilization and the spirit resulting from it are conducive to the development of love. To raise the question is to answer it in the negative. No objective observer of our Western life can doubt that love—brotherly love, motherly love, and erotic love—is a relatively rare phenomenon, and that its place is taken by a number of forms of pseudo-love which are in reality so many forms of the disintegration of love. (Fromm, 1989, p. 75)

Unfortunately, this reality of pseudo and disintegrating love also seems to characterize contemporary civilizations in the East, especially in the contexts of late modernity and globalization.

The establishment of authentic love and positive peace can be derived, then, from the awareness, consciousness, and compassionate sense of the interconnectedness of all things, including people, animals, plants, clouds, and stones. As Quinney (2000) points out, the truth of our *interbeing* is "beyond the dualistic thinking of the Western mind" (p. 25). And Fromm (1976) underscores that

Our understanding of the quality of knowing in the being mode of existence can be enhanced by the insights of such thinkers as the Buddha, the Hebrew prophets, Jesus, Master Eckhart, Sigmund Freud, Karl Marx. In their view, knowing begins with the awareness of the deceptiveness of our common sense perceptions, in the sense that our picture of reality does not correspond to what is "really real" and, mainly, in the sense that most people are half-awake, half-dreaming, and are unaware that most of what they hold to be self-evident is illusion produced by the suggestive influence of the social world in which they live. . . . Knowing does not mean to be in possession of the truth; it means to penetrate the surface and to strive critically and actively in order to approach truth ever more closely. (p. 28)

Moreover, the search for truth and the retreat from "false consciousness" involves a recognition of the impermanence of everything and everyone and, at the same time, a recognition that actual knowledge begins with the shattering of illusions—with "disillusionment."

In other words, "everything is everything else" and "everyone is responsible for everything that happens in life," or "when you produce peace and happiness in yourself, you begin to realize peace for the world" (Hahn, 1988, pp. 51-52). Thus, Quinney (2000), like A. J. Muste (1942), Gandhi (1957), and others before him, argues that peace *is* the way:

Social action—our service—comes out of the informed heart, out of the clear and enlightened mind. We act with an understanding of our own suffering and the suffering of others. If human actions are not rooted in compassion, these actions will not contribute to a compassionate and peaceful world. "If we cannot move beyond inner discord, how can we help find a way to social harmony? If we ourselves cannot know peace, be peaceful, how will our acts disarm hatred and violence?" The means cannot be different from the ends; peace can come only out of peace. (pp. 26-27)

Similarly, in *The Geometry of Violence and Democracy*, Pepinsky (1991) has held that it is "crucial to peacemaking that confrontation and anger not become violence and punishment" (p. 323). In the context of the Vietnam War and the Iran Contragate Affair, for example, Pepinsky writes about how he didn't want to see our political leaders go to jail for their various crimes. However, he didn't believe that he would "object to their going through a few years of mediation sessions with all the people whose fears they have increased and reinforced, or with the countless families of the countless victims U.S. officials and their private allies have killed" (Pepinsky, 1991, p. 323). Pepinsky further stressed that

> The object is neither to obtain revenge nor to minimize the true suffering caused by street crime. Once one recognizes the magnitude of crime, retribution becomes absurd. If we give a president with a life expectancy of twenty years a life sentence for first-degree murder of say 2,000,000 people (the number of Vietnamese killed in our war), how many microseconds of jail do we give a kid for stealing a $400 stereo from someone's home? Do we then do nothing about the burglary? (Pepinsky, 1991, p. 323)

Moreover, punishment, deterrence, retribution, revenge, and retaliation are not the ways of peace. Such punitive responses are fueled by anger and hate, the antitheses of love and compassion. These responses to violence are simply other forms of violence. As I have argued throughout this text, both of these "proactive" and "reactive" forms of violence simply beget more violence. Thus, most practices of criminal justice are merely efforts in negative peacemaking, reactions aimed at suppressing, controlling or processing antisocial acts through the threats and applications of force. Usually, these are not acts involving prevention or the elimination of those social relations responsible for violence in the first place.

By contrast, positive peacemaking as a pathway to the actual reduction of violence is quite different. It is not about the punishment of certain forms of violence, nor is it about the absence of terrorism and war. Rather, positive peacemaking is affirmative. It refers to the affirmative absence of those conditions that foster crime and violence before they occur. Positive peace, then,

conveys political and economic arrangements "in which exploitation is minimized or eliminated altogether, and in which there is neither overt violence nor the more subtle phenomenon of structural violence" (Barash, 1991, p. 8). Positive peace, in other words, will only exist as a social reality when the sources of violence—alienation, humiliation, shame, inequality, poverty, racism, sexism, and so on—are no longer present. In sum, without the construction of peace and the establishment of social justice worldwide, the violence of the individual, the family, the community, and the nation-state will continue, more or less, as we have known them for at least the past century.

Resilience

In *Pathways to Peace: Forty Steps to a Less Violent America*, Victor LaCerva (1996) discusses those pathways that lead to both violence and nonviolence. With respect to the former, he discusses the pathways of "reality" and "confusion." With respect to the latter, he identifies four pathways. Each of these pathways—The Way of Acceptance, The Way of Peacemaker, The Way of Creativity, and The Way to Understand— entails 10 steps: acceptance involves 10 steps to personal power, peacemaker involves 10 steps to family peace, creativity involves 10 steps to community involvement, and understand(ing) involves 10 steps through the consciousness of culture. Critical to the loci of nonviolence are the steps involved in family peacemaking. Note that when the first letters in each of the steps are put together, they spell out "peacemaker."

- Practice positive discipline
- Expand emotional fluency
- Approach conflict with a win-win attitude
- Create connections
- Emphasize essential values
- Minimize media exposure

- Avoid victimization
- Keep celebrating diversity
- Engage in "bullyproofing"
- Reinforce resilience

Resilience in particular is of crucial importance for both perpetrators and victims of violence. It refers to a capacity in both the old and the young but is of special importance to the developing person: He or she must be able to rebound from misfortune, illness, or pain. Resilience also refers to psychological mindsets that build hardiness and engagement rather than separation and alienation. Psychological hardiness requires the learning and teaching of commitment, self-control, and change. It sees self-improvement and development as a gift of hardship and adversity. The net affect of psychological hardiness is a reversal of feelings of powerlessness and helplessness, as well as the acquisition of "protective factors," or safeguards, against risky behaviors that occur at the individual, family, school, and community levels (LaCerva, 1996).

In discussing the protective factors against risky behavior, including violence, LaCerva, a medical doctor, talks about the foundations of resilience as focusing on strengths of the individual, family, school, and community. The resilience perspective "seeks to expand on the positive potential that already exists within our children, that is part and parcel of who they really are. We reinforce the potential each time we create structure for them and give them our support and encouragement, each time we walk the way of the peacemaker" (LaCerva, 1996, p. 149). In characterizing the four foundations of resilience construction for children, LaCerva articulates ingredients or characteristics of each.

For example, the individual protective factors include "a sense of humor and the ability to have fun; a healthy sense of detachment" from parents, "and the presence of at least one healthy significant adult, not necessarily a parent, who provide a strong sense of bonding, nurturing, and a mirror reflecting other realities" (LaCerva, 1996, p. 146). Family protective factors include "good enough" parents who offer love and support, expect the best from their children, and involve them in family life. School protective factors include a caring and supportive environment, high expectations, and numerous opportunities for participation. Finally, community protective factors include fair witnesses who are able to provide psychic life rafts to which neglected and abused children may cling in hard times. By communicating to mistreated children that "what is happening to them is not right, not fair, not customary, not their fault, and not the way their lives will always be," these fair witnesses help children begin to realize that "they are not crazy and come to understand that they are living in a difficult family system that they will someday leave" (LaCerva, 1996, p. 147).

At the same time, a thematic stream that runs throughout LaCerva's nonviolence is the understanding of the need to develop what he refers to as "arcs of peace" within communities before entire communities of peace can be developed. Arcs of peace require the cooperation of all institutions in society, far beyond local communities, encompassing nation-states. LaCerva argues further that in these arcs of peace, abuse will be transformed into honor. Finally, in terms of youth development in particular, all types of partnerships within communities are required if young adolescents are to be brought into a mutually protective embrace.

LaCerva provides numerous ministeps connected to the larger 40 steps, all of which are too detailed to be identified here. One example will have to suffice. In his discussion on the family, he notes that parents who more than half the time practice what he calls "the Seven Ls of Childrearing" furnish their children with a healthy environment. These practices include the following:

- Love your children unconditionally. You may not like what they do, but always love them and let them know it. Express affection often, both physically and verbally.
- Listen to them. They will tell you when they are not getting their needs met, when they are carrying a secret, and what the best and worst parts of their day have been like. Listening with respect to their ideas and problems is a way of inviting their active participation in family life.
- Limit them. Boundaries are for "bouncing up against" in the process of discovering who they are. Proceed by first setting limits in your own life.
- Laugh with them, not at them.
- Let them live. Let go of inappropriate expectations, remembering that 2-year-olds act like 2-year-olds, not 5-year-olds.
- Learn from your mistakes. Feedback is the breakfast of champions, and mistakes are friendly invitations to try again. Provide a mirror to reality so that your children will know they are growing and learning.
- Lead them to increasing independence. A parent's job is to give over a little power every year and to show how to take on the responsibility that comes with it.
- Expect the best. (LaCerva, 1996, p. 147)

SUMMARY

Within the context of the "dueling" paradigms of adversarialism and mutualism, Chapter 9 has provided a framework for understanding the reciprocal (give-and-take) relationships between the pathways to violence and the pathways to nonviolence. Moreover, this chapter has presented the shared assumptions, ideas, attitudes, beliefs, emotions, rationales, actions, and outlooks of four models of nonviolence: mutuality, altruistic humanism, positive peacemaking, and resilience. What each of these models of

nonviolent social interaction emphasizes is the means for developing and expanding love, empathy, cooperation, and connection between humans. These and other models of nonviolence represent overlapping strands of social consciousness ("pathways") that allow people and nations to travel ways in which they can be more at peace with themselves and each other.

In tension with, if not in opposition to, those means that reinforce separation, division, hierarchy, inequality, social distance, and the demonization characteristic of pathways to violence, nonviolence pathways are indicative of a transformative agenda grounded within the fundamental needs and social ecology of all species and nature to *be* rather than to *have*. In addition, these informal and formal practices of nonviolence not only nurture the pathways to positive peace and social justice; in the process, they act to resist our interpersonal, institutional, and structural reliance on adversarial, competitive, and other violence-promoting enactments and interactions. In terms of the logic of the pathways to nonviolence, these modes and their various applications represent the linkages or connections between the kinds of recovery from violence articulated in Chapter 8 and the policies of nonviolence to be imparted in Chapter 10.

Finally, each of the emotional strands or pathways to nonviolence acts in reciprocity with the other strands and pathways. Like the strands and pathways to violence, those of nonviolence have their own cumulative effects as they interact across the interpersonal, institutional, and structural spheres. As the brief history of the sociopolitical struggles of nonviolence revealed, during the 20th century, contradictory pathways of nonviolence and violence both existed as means to conflict resolution. Comparatively, the pathways of nonviolence are less traveled, and often seem to pale next to the more dominant pathways of violence. Certainly, within contemporary adversarial modes of interaction, whether at the family, community, or nation-state level, there remains an urgent need for the mutualistically subordinate modes of existence and practice to blossom, both locally and globally, into a fully integrative pattern of social living and organization.

REFERENCES

Ackerman, P., & Duvall, J. (2000). *A force more powerful: A century of nonviolent conflict.* New York: Palgrave.

Barak, G. (Ed.). (2000). *Crime and crime control: A global view.* Westport, CT: Greenwood.

Barash, D. P. (1991). *Introduction to peace studies.* Belmont, CA: Wadsworth.

Beck, A. T. (1999). *Prisoners of hate: The cognitive basis of anger, hostility, and violence.* New York: Perennial.

Brunk, C. G. (2000). Shaping a vision: The nature of peace studies. In L. Fisk & J. Schellenberg (Eds.), *Patterns of conflict: Paths to peace* (pp. 11-33). Petersborough, ON, Canada: Broadview.

Chancer, L. S. (2000). Fromm, sadomasochism, and contemporary American crime. In K. Anderson & R. Quinney (Eds.), *Erich Fromm and critical criminology: Beyond the punitive society* (pp. 31-42). Chicago: University of Illinois Press.

Cohen, S. (2001). *States of denial: Knowing about strocities and suffering.* Cambridge, UK: Polity.

Cotton, A. (1984, February 6). This was some kind of jam session. *Sports Illustrated,* p. 26.

Erikson, E. H. (1964). *Insight and responsibility.* New York: Norton.

Fellman, G. (1998). *Rambo and the Dalai Lama: The compulsion to win and its threat to human survival.* Albany: SUNY Press.

Fornari, F. (1974). *The psychoanalysis of war.* Garden City, NY: Anchor.

Fromm, E. (Ed.). (1965). *Socialist humanism.* Garden City, NY: Doubleday.

Fromm, E. (1976). *To have or to be.* New York: Harper and Row.

Fromm, E. (1989). *The art of loving.* New York: Harper and Row.

Gandhi, M. K. (1957). *An autobiography: The story of my experiment with truth* (M. Desai, Trans). Boston: Beacon.

Global Alliance for Transforming Education. (1993, Winter/Spring). Education 2000. *Gateway: A Publication of the Global Alliance for Transforming Education,* p. 3. Retrieved November 17, 2002, from http://www. ties-edu.org/GATE/Education2000.html

Gorbachev, M. (1987). *Perestroika.* London: Collins.

Hahn, T. N. (1988). *The heart of understanding.* Berkeley, CA: Paralax.

Hollin, C. R. (1993). Cognitive-behavior interventions. In A. P. Goldstein & C. R. Huff (Eds.), *The gang intervention handbook* (pp. 55-85). Champaign, IL: Research Press.

Kohn, A. (1992). *No contest: The case against competition.* Boston, MA: Houghton Mifflin.

Kundera, M. (1984). *The unbearable lightness of being.* New York: Harper and Row.

LaCerva, V. (1996). *Pathways to peace: Forty steps to a less violent America.* Tesuque, NM: Heartsongs.

Moses, R. (1985). Empathy and dis-empathy in political conflict. *Political Psychology,* 6(1), 135-139.

Muste, A. J. (1942). *The world task of pacificism.* Wallingford, PA: Pendale Hill.

Oliner, S. P., & Oliner, P. M. (1988). *The altruistic personality: Rescuers of Jews in Nazi Europe.* New York: Free Press.

Pepinsky, H. E. (1991). Peacemaking in criminology and criminal justice. In H. E. Pepinsky & R. Quinney (Eds.), *Criminology as peacemaking* (pp. 299-327). Bloomington: Indiana University Press.

Quinney, R. (2000). Socialist humanism and the problem of crime: Thinking about Erich Fromm in the development of critical/peacemaking criminology. In Kevin Anderson and Richard Quinney (Eds.), *Erich Fromm and critical criminology: Beyond the punitive society* (pp. 21-30).

Chicago: University of Illinois Press.

Scholz, S. (2002, February 28). [Letter to Buddhist Peace Fellowship members]. Berkeley, CA: Buddhist Peace Fellowship.

Sharp, G. (1980). *Social power and political freedom.* Boston, MA: Porter Sargent.

Slater, P. (1991). *A dream deferred: America's discontent and the search for a new democratic ideal.* Boston, MA: Beacon.

Spretnak, C. (1991). *States of grace.* San Francisco: HarperCollins.

Thoreau, H. D. (1986). *Walden and civil disobedience.* New York: Penguin. (Original work published 1848)

Vellacott, J. (2000). Nonviolence: A road less traveled. In L. Fisk & J. Schellenberg (Eds.), *Patterns of conflict: Paths to peace* (pp. 103-142). Petersborough, ON, Canada: Broadview.

Wines, J. (1993, Summer). Architecture in the age of ecology. *Amicus Journal, 15*(2), 22-23.

REVIEW QUESTIONS

1. Describe the paradigms of adversarialism and mutualism, including their respective assumptions and arguments.

2. In the context of ritualizing adversarialism and mutualism, discuss the differences between the "rituals of coercion" and the "rituals of resistance." Provide examples.

3. In terms of nonviolent struggles for social change, which tactics do you think are best? Why?

4. Rank in terms of strengths and weaknesses the four models of nonviolence (or streams of nonviolent consciousness and action): mutuality, altruistic humanism, positive peacemaking, and resilience.

5. Aaron Beck's cognitive theory of behavior speaks in terms of the "brighter side of human nature." What does he mean by that phrase? How is it related to turning empathy on and off when responding to violent offenders?

NOTE

1. All quotes in Chapter 9 From Fellman are reprinted with permission.
   Fellman, G. (1998). *Rambo and the Dali Lama: The compulsion to win and its threat to human survival.* Albany, NY: SUNY Press.

CHAPTER 10

Policies of Nonviolence

Throughout this book, the pathways to violence and nonviolence have been linked, associated, or grounded in the customs, ideologies, and practices of adversarialism and mutualism, the two fundamental ways of organizing societies. In the case of the pathways to violence, I have contended that these are connected to values that support, reinforce, and reproduce compulsive or extreme forms of individualism, a lack of genuine empathy for other people, and a heightened or exaggerated fear of the "other." In the case of the pathways to nonviolence, I have contended that these are connected to values that support, reinforce, and reproduce patterns of caring, altruism, and resiliency as these envelop diversities of community. Similarly, I have maintained that the political and economic arrangements that attach to these opposing ways of organizing society are also reflected in the types of social interactions and in the levels of violence and nonviolence that occur.

Following the lead of Fellman (1998), I have regarded the two alternative ways of interacting with the material world as reciprocally inclusive of each other. Even though there is ample proof that systems of both competition and cooperation have existed side by side throughout human history, one should nevertheless acknowledge that, as a way of life, adversarialism is more socially,

politically, and economically developed than mutualism. This is not so only in the United States but in most of the developed nation-states of the world, with the relative exceptions of some of the Scandinavian countries and a few others like Denmark or Japan. In fact, some would argue that truly mutualistic social formations are virtually nonexistent except by way of inference and conjecture, or that the existing political and economic expressions necessitate the transformation of the dominant social structures before mutualism can become a reality (Morris, 2000).

Either way, any attempt to transform societies and the world from systems based on adversarialism to ones based on mutualism will be a difficult pursuit, with not a few obstacles and challenges to overcome. In part, this kind of transformation rests on a faith in the doctrine of universalism and the shared belief that humanity, despite all the evidence to the contrary, will ultimately get along. Of course, such an outlook and its philosophical dreams have always been central both to Marxism and to most of the world's religions. In other words, it is the communal desire and hope of many that some day all of the peoples of the world will actually get along. The pathways to this kind of harmony and security depend on the development of cultures of cooperation and peace rather than of cultures of conflict and war (Epps, 2002; Pepinsky, 1999; Schwebel, 1995). It is safe to say that we are a long way from this kind of transformation.

Among the most serious obstacles to such social change is a capitalistic advertising industry that stimulates an intensifying desire of extreme individualism and materialism as a means of satisfying the problem of consumption (see the section "Mass Media: Production, Distortion, and Consumption" in Chapter 6). The stories that are told by this industry about society and the pathways to happiness are grounded in individualism, and they tap into selfishness and greed, rather than narratives that speak of social or collective pathways to happiness and tap into altruism and empathy. As many have argued, the present individual and adversarial routes are certainly on collision courses with the depletion of the earth's natural resources and in danger of setting off a "war of all against all" in an artificially created new age of scarcity and barbarism. Such a reality is in opposition to mutualism and represents the antithesis of collectivism.

For a collective utopian vision in which the prevailing political and economic arrangements are conducive to nonviolence to become a global reality, it is necessary not only that the academic community reviews and assesses the present state of knowledge about both violence and nonviolence, but more fundamentally, American society at large must step back, reflect, and reassess its preoccupation with the consumption of violent dystopias (Haggerty, 2002). As Sasha Abramsky (2002), a freelance writer and author of *Hard Time Blues*, has put it:

> We have come to accept as normal incarceration rates that would have seemed the unlikely progeny of a dystopian fantasy a mere generation ago. And we have come to regard arrest, prosecution, and imprisonment as fundamental props of our mass culture, thus elevating one of the more unpleasant duties and obligations of the civil society—the prosecution and punishment of those who flout its laws—into a cultural commodity that may, ultimately, come to define what kind of nation, what kind of people, we become. (p. B12)

Even though the social and behavioral sciences have paid little attention to the institutional and structural forms of violence and nonviolence, the various disciplines that examine such phenomena are not without the data to understand the ways of reducing violence and of enhancing nonviolence, especially as these bodies of information pertain to interpersonal violence. In other words, there is no shortage of relevant research and evaluative study about what does and does not work regarding the inhibition of interpersonal violence, especially of a criminal or antisocial nature (Fishbein, 2000c; Goldstein & Huff, 1993; Riedel & Welsh, 2002).

At the same time, in relation to averting violence and stimulating nonviolence at the institutional and structural levels, the current state of affairs is underdeveloped because (a) the prerequisite questions have rarely been posed, and when they have been, they were not entertained as serious political questions; and (b) the necessary evaluations for obtaining a responsible knowledge base of what could or could not work in relation to the larger social and psychological conditions of violence and nonviolence have not been conducted (Mayor, 1995). So although there is an outstanding need to conduct additional research on the institutional and structural forms of violence in general and as these are connected with interpersonal violence in particular, there is no dearth of knowledge concerning the effectiveness (or lack of same) of the various responses of the criminal justice system to, for example, "crimes in the street." This contemporary knowledge, however, represents only part of what is required to grapple with the social relations of violence and nonviolence production.

Unfortunately, in the United States as well as in most other developed civilizations, the dominant policies of "crime control" are not driven by or related to the expanding bases of criminological knowledge. Moreover, even if the prevailing responses to individual or aggregate violations of criminal law in general or to criminal violence in particular were based on the available scientific knowledge, these responses would still constitute mostly reactive rather than proactive stances. That is to say, the current efforts to reduce interpersonal forms of violence by criminal punishment or treatment are directed almost exclusively at specific violators "after the fact." Instead, what are called for are public policy efforts or strategies directed at reducing the social and psychological conditions of violence "before the fact," especially those associated with youth who are most at risk for feeling and experiencing the effects of interpersonal, institutional, and structural violence.

Before turning to those policies of nonviolence that I believe represent the necessary "macro" pathways toward achieving a more peaceful America, both at home and abroad, I will present an abridged version of the major findings on the various forms of interpersonal violence, including an overview of those individuals and groups who have not only experienced the highest levels of victimization in the United States but who are also subject to the greatest risks and exposure to those factors most associated with interpersonal, institutional, and structural violence. Then, as a means of establishing a recognition of the need to move away from the adversarial and repressive war of violence and toward the mutualistic and therapeutic peace of nonviolence, I will provide an overview and critique of the limitations of the traditionally based, interpersonal approaches to violence reduction. Finally, as a way of ending this examination and analysis of the pathways to violence and nonviolence, I will finish the chapter by introducing the reader to the local and global emergence of institutionally and structurally based alternative approaches to the production and reproduction of nonviolence.

A SUMMARY REVIEW OF VICTIMIZATION AND THE PATHWAYS TO VIOLENCE

> In spite of perceptions by many that violence in the United States is out of control and beyond control, careful examination indicates that violence is more prevalent among some groups than others, occurs more in some places than others, and involves certain types of situations and participants more often then others. (Reidel & Welsh, 2002, p. 372)

The trends, patterns, and differential relationships of virtually all forms of victimization and violence have been influenced by or associated with the variables of class, race, and gender, as was shown in Chapters 1 through 4. Whether these acts or states of violence and victimization involve intimates or strangers, take place in the public or private spheres, and occur at the interpersonal, institutional, or structural levels of social interaction, they are most concentrated in and experienced by those persons who occupy relatively marginalized and powerless status in society (Barak, Flavin, & Leighton, 2001; Berger, Free, & Searles, 2001; Riedel & Welsh, 2002). What follows are the highlights of both the official ("counted"), or visible, and the unofficial ("uncounted"), or invisible, harms experienced by the most vulnerable socioeconomic groupings in the United States.

Officially, violent crime victims are disproportionately from the lower economic classes, although both age and gender affect these relationships, as described below. In 1998, for example, people at the lower end

Table 10.1 Estimated Rate (per 1,000 persons age 12 and older) of Personal Victimization By Type of Crime and Annual Household Income of Victim, United States, 1998

Type of Crime	Annual Household Income						
	Less than $7,500	*$7,500 to $14,999*	*$15,000 to $24,999*	*$25,000 to $34,999*	*$35,000 to $49,999*	*$50,000 to $74,999*	*$75,000 or more*
All personal crimes	65.5	51.1	40.7	43.1	33.3	33.1	34.1
Crimes of violence	63.8	49.3	39.4	42.0	31.7	32.0	33.1
Completed violence	23.7	18.5	12.4	14.0	8.9	7.3	8.7
Attempted/threatened violence	40.1	30.8	26.9	28.1	22.8	24.7	24.4
Rape/sexual assault	3.2	2.4	2.3	2.4	0.5[a]	0.7[a]	1.2
Rape/attempted rape	2.7	1.3	1.5	1.2	0.3[a]	0.5[a]	0.8[a]
Rape	2.2[a]	0.8[a]	0.7[a]	0.4[a]	0.3[a]	0.1[a]	0.6[a]
Attempted rape[b]	0.6[a]	0.6[a]	0.9[a]	0.7[a]	0.0[a]	0.3[a]	0.2[a]
Sexual assault[c]	0.4[a]	1.1[a]	0.7[a]	1.3	0.1[a]	0.2[a]	0.4[a]
Robbery	6.5	5.8	3.6	6.9	3.1	2.8	2.9
Completed/property taken	3.3	3.9	2.7	5.6	2.1	1.3	1.6
With injury	1.6[a]	0.9[a]	0.8[a]	1.1	0.6[a]	0.7[a]	0.4[a]
Without injury	1.7[a]	3.0	2.0	4.6	1.5	0.5[a]	1.2
Attempted to take property	3.3	1.9	0.8[a]	1.2	1.0	1.5	1.3
With injury	0.7[a]	0.6[a]	0.2[a]	0.4[a]	0.2[a]	0.3[a]	0.3[a]
Without injury	2.6	1.3[a]	0.7[a]	0.8[a]	0.8	1.2	0.9[a]
Assault	54.2	41.0	33.5	32.8	28.1	28.5	29.0
Aggravated	19.6	11.8	7.9	6.3	6.2	6.2	6.2
With injury	7.7	3.9	2.4	13	2.3	1.5	2.0
Threatened with weapon	12.0	7.9	5.4	5.0	3.8	4.8	4.2
Simple	34.5	29.3	25.7	26.5	21.9	22.3	22.8
With minor injury	10.2	9.1	8.0	5.3	4.1	4.2	4.0
Without injury	24.3	20.1	19.7	21.2	17.9	18.1	18.7
Purse snatching/pocket picking	1.7[a]	1.8	1.3	1.1	1.8	1.1	1.0
Population age 12 and older	11,724,160	21,132,940	29,783,090	28,314,520	34,039,640	33,179,460	29,414,500

NOTE: Table excludes data on persons whose family income level was not ascertained. Individual numbers may not add to total shown because of rounding.
a Estimate is based on about 10 or fewer sample cases.
b Includes verbal threats of rape.
c Includes threats.
Source: Bureau of Justice Statistics (2000).

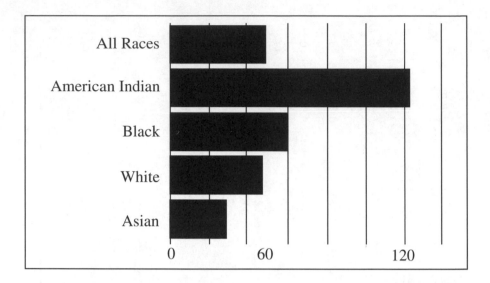

Figure 10.1 Violent Victimizations: Average Annual Rate, 1992-1996 (Number per 100,000 persons age 12 or older)

Source: Bureau of Justice Statistics (1999). *Sourcebook of criminal justice statistics, 1999* (NCJ 183727). Washington, DC: Author.

of the income distribution were more than twice as likely to be a victim of a violent crime than those at the upper range of the income distribution (see Table 10.1). This pattern held for all types of interpersonal violent crimes, including rape, robbery, and assault. Similarly, for 1992 through 1996, as well as for 1998, racial and ethnic minority groups (who were disproportionately poor) experienced higher rates of violent victimization (see Figure 10.1 and Table 10.2). During 1992 to 1996, these patterns of racial marginality held for victimization rates in general and for homicide rates in particular (see Figures 10.2 and 10.3). Among women, victimization was more likely for blacks than for whites or other racial minorities. For men, victimization rates, with the exception of homicide, were similar across racial categories (Craven, 1997). The only exception to these patterns of gendered and racial-ethnic relations of victimization is in the area of

Table 10.2 Rates of Victimization by Ethnicity (rates per 1,000 persons age 12 and older)

	Hispanic	Non-Hispanic
Violent victimizations	43.0	38.3
Rape and sexual assault	1.5	1.4
Aggravated assault	10.4	8.3
Simple assault	24.0	24.7

Source: Bureau of Justice Statistics (1998, p. 177).

rape and sexual assault, where it is estimated that some 2% of all men, as compared to 15% of all women, will be victimized in their lifetime (Greenfeld, 1997).

Victimization rates were generally highest, for both males and females, among those 12 to 19 years old who lived in the lowest-income households within urban areas. More specifically, the rates of aggravated assault

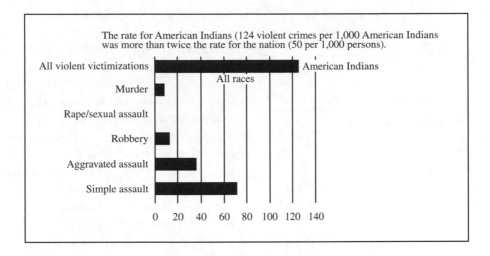

Figure 10.2   Average Annual Number of Violent Victimizations per 1,000 Persons Age 12 or Older, 1992-1996

Note: The annual average murder rate is per 100,000 residents of all ages.

Source: Bureau of Justice Statistics (1999).

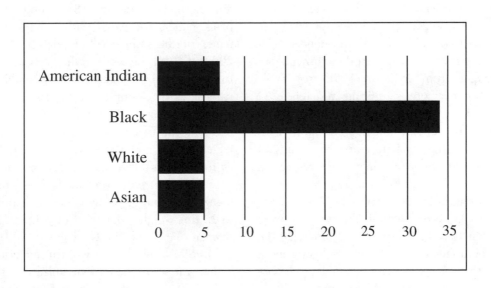

Figure 10.3   Murder, Average Annual Rate, 1992-1996 (Number per 100,000 persons)

Source: Bureau of Justice Statistics (1999).

Table 10.3 Rates of Aggravated Assault Victimization by Gender, Race, and Ethnicity (1998)

Victim	Characteristic	Aggravated Assault Rates per 1,000
Gender	Male	10.5
	Female	4.7
Age	12-15	12.2
	16-19	19.0
	20-24	16.0
	25-34	8.4
	35-49	6.8
	50-64	3.3
	65+	0.5
Race	White	7.0
	Black	11.9
	Other	6.6
Hispanic Origin	Hispanic	6.1
	Non-Hispanic	7.6

Source: Rennison (1999).

broken down by gender, age, race, and ethnicity for 1998 (see Table 10.3), the percentages of murder victims and offenders broken down by age, gender, and race for 1999 (see Table 10.4), and the victim-offender relationships for murder and non-negligent homicide from 1976 to 1996 (see Table 10.5) underscore significant differences in relationship to these three variables. With respect to gender, males were more than twice as likely as females to be victims of assault. At the same time, with respect to more than 960,000 incidents of violence against an intimate between 1976 and 1996, about 85% percent of the victims were women (Barak, Flavin, & Leighton, 2001). As for homicides, males were slightly more than three times as likely as females to be victims and slightly less than nine times as likely as females to be offenders.

Considering the victim-offender relationship, perhaps the most striking differences between men and women is that the majority (63%) of men's nonfatal violent victimizations are committed by a stranger, but the majority of women's nonfatal violent victimizations are committed by someone whom the woman knows (Craven, 1997). Similarly, with respect to homicide victims, one third of women are murdered by an intimate such as a spouse, ex-spouse, or boyfriend/girlfriend, compared to a rate of about 5% for men who are murdered. As for age, the highest concentrations of murders were found in the age group 16 to 24 years, with a rate of 17.5 per 1000 persons. Comparatively, the rates were 12.2 and 6.2 for those between the ages of 12 and 15 years and 25 and 64 years, respectively. Homicides among those under 12 and over 65 years old were statistically insignificant.

Similarly, death is a rare outcome of violent crime, occurring once for every 5.7 nonfatal gunshot injuries (Cook, 1991). Once again, factors of age and race are important, as "the risk of death is highly elevated for young people (age 15-34), particularly black males. Among teenagers age 15 to 19, the gun homicide rate was 83.4/100,000 for black males, compared with 7.5 for white males of the same age" (Reidel & Welsh, 2002, p. 298). However, when official rates for homicide are broken down by combining variables (for example, race and sex), black women die as a result of murder or justifiable homicide at twice the rate of white men, which is only about one quarter to one fifth as frequent as black males. Yet the rate of young black female homicide is 5 to 8 times higher than that of young white men, and 16 to 22 times higher than that of young White women (Barak, Flavin, & Leighton, 2001, p. 211). Similarly, black women experience higher rates of violent victimization than Asian men, rates almost as high as those of white men. Native American women experience the highest victimization rates—higher than Asian males, black males, and white males (see Table 10.6).

Table 10.4   Percent of Murder Victims and Offenders by Age, Gender, and Race (1999)

Characteristic		Victims (n = 12,658)	Offenders (n = 14,112)
Age	Under 18	11.5	6.7
	18 and over	86.9	59.0
	Unknown	1.7	34.3
Gender	Males	75.5	64.8
	Females	24.4	7.4
	Unknown	0.1	27.8
Race	White	49.8	33.2
	Black	46.3	35.7
	Other	2.9	2.2
	Unknown	1.0	28.9

Source: Federal Bureau of Investigation (1999).

Table 10.5   All Victims of Murder and Nonnegligent Manslaughter, 1976-1996 (in percentages)

Victim-Offender Relationship	Male Victims (n = 340,687)	Female Victims (n = 105,175)
Spouse	3.7	18.9
Exspouse	0.2	1.4
Girlfriend/ boyfriend or other intimate	2.0	9.4
Other relative, friend, or acquaintance, or stranger to victim	49.6	42.5
Unknown to police	34.4	27.8

Source: Greenfeld et al. (1998).

The variety of harms that are not counted or that remain unofficial, invisible, and hidden include those actions and conditions associated with the institutional and structural relations of violence that expose the poor and marginal to an assortment of risks and violations that are part of the so-called natural order of things. For example, whether a youth is subject to gangs or not is predominantly determined by whether he or she is a member of an urban underclass. In the United States,

gangs "consist overwhelmingly of poor youths, mostly minorities, with some recent immigrants thrown into the mix. These are the dispossessed members of our society" (Huff, 1993, pp. 464-465). Moreover, inferior education, impoverishment, structural underemployment, lack of health services, differential opportunities (e.g., crime), exposure to toxic waste areas, inflated incarceration rates, and so on and so forth, provide the conditions necessary for the production of depression, anger, low self-esteem, violence, and more.

Who is collecting the data on the pain and suffering experienced by some 45 million Americans who have no health insurance or immediate access to medical care? Who is talking about the higher infant mortality rates and the lower longevity rates among underprivileged minorities? What are the physical, emotional, and financial costs involved in these institutional and structural relations of violence?

In a slightly different context, it is the same marginal and minority groups who experience the higher rates of interpersonal offending and victimization (traditional criminal violence) that also experience the accumulation and intensification of the institutional and structural violations of

Table 10.6   Annual Average Violent Victimization Rates (per 1,000) for Persons 12 or Older, by Sex and Race, 1992-1996

	Woman	*Men*	*Men: Women Ratio*
American Indian	98	153	1.6:1
Asian	21	37	1.8:1
Black	56	68	1.2:1
White	40	59	1.5:1
All races	42	60	1.4:1

Source: Greenfeld and Smith (1999).

"environmental racism" or of a "criminogenic market structure" (Berger, Free, & Searles, 2001). With respect to the interpersonal violations, most violent victimizations are intraracial, and the patterns of offense are directly consistent with strong patterns of racial segregation (Massey & Denton, 1993). One subset of violent activity involving different races and interracial violence is that of *hate crimes*. Hate crimes are defined by law as criminal actions or motivations based on a bias against race, religion, disability, sexual orientation, or ethnicity and national origin. In 1997, race and ethnicity together accounted for 70% of bias crime incidents, with religion and sexual orientation contributing 15% each (Federal Bureau of Investigation, 1997, pp. 60-61). Hate crime statistics should be interpreted with caution because they are especially affected by police bias (Barak, Flavin, & Leighton, 2001). They also, as many feminists point out, exclude gender and, therefore, a lot of violence against women such as rape and other sexual assaults that can be attributed to sexist bias.

With respect to the institutional or structural violations, workplace hazards, occupational diseases, unnecessary surgery, and adverse reactions to prescriptions result in a conservatively estimated total of 50,000 deaths per year (Reiman, 1998). These hidden white-collar and corporate victimizations (murders) are disproportionately located in the lower-income groups. The injuries often involve more women than men and more minority women than Whites. Similarly, as we saw in the breakdown of the official victimization rates by race and sex, some groups of men were less likely to be victimized than some groups of women, and these were generally poor and minority women. Just as these women have trouble availing themselves of services for and protections from domestic violence, so do they for institutional and structural violations.

A REVIEW AND CRITIQUE OF THE ADVERSARIAL WAR ON VIOLENCE

The adversarial war aimed at reducing only interpersonal violence has traditionally emphasized "deterrence," "rehabilitation," or "incapacitation" as its policy goals. Since the 1980s, however, with the approval of flat, tough sentencing laws, there has also been a conflation or blurring of these three models of penal intervention. As part of the formal "criminal justice approach" to violence control, the roles of law enforcement, the courts, and corrections are employed as the primary agencies of social intervention. Research has shown for more than three decades that the criminal justice system is, at best, quite limited in its ability to reduce violence and, at worst, a repressive and discriminatory system of social intervention that disproportionately affects lower socioeconomic-status minority groups (Barak, Flavin, & Leighton, 2001; Blumstein, Cohen, & Nagin, 1978; Greenwood, 1982; Packer, 1968; Reidel & Welsh, 2002; Reiman, 1998; Reiss & Roth, 1993).

From the beginning, law enforcement's ability to identify and apprehend violent offenders has been highly inefficient. For example, clearance rates (the percentage of arrests made for crimes reported) for violent crimes hover around 50%: for murder, 66%; aggravated assault, 59%; forcible rape, 51%; and robbery, 26% (Reidel & Welsh, 2002, p. 357). At the prosecution and court-processing stages, cases are continually dropped, dismissed, and filtered out of the system. Of those arrested, only about 50% are convicted, and fewer than half of that 50% are sentenced to state prison (Greenwood, 1982). Postconfinement programs to reduce recidivism for violent and nonviolent offenders have had mixed results, succeeding with some inmates and failing with others. More important, prison is often a very repressive and violent place to live and a difficult place from which to emerge and be expected to make an easy transition back to the "free world."

Overall, the research and evidence on deterrence has found that it does not strongly support the existence of disincentive effects. Where effects do exist, research has found that the certainty of arrest and incarceration was more important than the lengthening of the sentence or the severity of punishment. The verdict is out on rehabilitation for a number of reasons. There are few programs and fewer evaluations of these programs going on, so nobody knows what works or does not work. This is not to deny that many former inmates have not only desisted from lives of crime after their return to society but successfully improved or altered their ways of interacting with people. In fact, according to the recidivism patterns of former prisoners 3 years after their release dates in 1994,

97.5% of rapists and 98.8% of murderers had not been rearrested for the same crimes (Bureau of Justice Statistics, 2002).

Estimates of nonrecidivism vary, but even conservative estimates put it between 1:3 and 1:2, or 33% to 50%. Some inmates refuse "treatment"; others are denied access to programs because of a lack of resources. Incapacitation (the idea that for as long as offenders are incarcerated they cannot commit crimes outside of prison) through longer and career-sentencing schemes such as the "three strikes" law has proven to be unreliable and expensive. With respect to *selective incapacitation* and the diagnosis of the "career criminal," there has been a huge false-positive problem: "A large percentage of those who are predicted to re-offend (based upon various models) indeed do not" (Reidel & Welsh, 2002, p. 350). As for *general incapacitation,* the indiscriminate longer sentences for all offenders have proven to be an inefficient, destructive, and costly enterprise for most state governments to endure. Budget growth expenditures for incarceration services have had a negative impact on public expenditures for education, health care, and other social services—a case of punishment overwhelming or subverting prevention.

The death penalty, which is still popular with the American people (~70% for and 30% opposed for the past 30 years), has generally proven to be more of a retributive and moral weapon than a deterrent to murder and other serious crimes. It has also been more expensive than lifetime incarceration. Finally, it has been shown to be racially discriminatory in many places and subject to numerous possibilities of error and manipulation (Bohm, 1999). Similarly, the effects of "three strikes" laws studied in both California and the federal system found that African Americans received discriminatory sentencing, especially in connection with drug violations. Moreover, these three strikes laws, allegedly designed to reduce danger and violence in society, have been applied in only some 15% of the total number of cases, the other 85% having involved nonviolent crimes (Greenwood et al., 1994).

Even if the inefficiency and inefficacy of the criminal justice approach to violence reduction could be reformed, which is not likely in the future if the recent or distant past is any indication, the outcome of a "new" and "better" criminal justice system could at best be a more efficient and humanistic processing of offenders. Current reactions to violent offenders, however, remain after the fact: *reactions* rather than *proactions*, defensive and responsive interventions rather than offensive and pre-emptive interventions. The strategies of criminal justice administration have become trapped and mired in the punitive and repressive hysteria of "crime control" that engages in an adversarial, retributive, and unforgiving approach to violence and victimization.

In contrast, the strategies of mutualism, restorative justice, and peacemaking criminology move away from punitive responses after the fact and toward preventive actions before the fact. Typically, multimodal, interdisciplinary, or community health approaches to preventing violence understand that it is, indeed, "possible to prevent all or almost all of the most serious forms of violence, even in the most violent environments and among the most violent people in our society" (Gilligan, 2001, p. 17). The approach to violence as a public health problem advocated by Gilligan and many others, including the U.S. Center for Disease Control, recognizes that punishment does not prevent violence, it causes violence: "*punishment is the most powerful stimulus to violent behavior that we have yet discovered*" (Gilligan, 2001, p. 18; italics in original). Ultimately, of course, if significant progress is to be made, the proactive, preventive, public health approach to violence reduction must intersect with the prevailing

political and economic arrangements of capitalism. In turn, these relations of public health and political economy may work in tandem with the criminal justice system in what some have referred to as a balanced approach of punishment and treatment and others as penal- or correctional-industrial complexes.

As a venue for resisting violence and establishing nonviolence, a more macro, global, and holistic approach to vulnerability and victimization seeks out those sources ("causes") of violence, places ("hot spots") of violence, and conditions ("environmental milieus") of violence. These sites of violence and nonviolence are located where the interpersonal, institutional, and structural spheres intersect. Almost two decades ago, Elliot Currie (1985) wrote similarly about the United States' relationship with violence and social organization and how these interpersonal and structural relations of violence are inseparable:

> If we wanted to sketch a hypothetical portrait of an especially violent society, it would surely contain these elements: It would separate large numbers of people, especially the young, from the kind of work that could include them securely in community life. It would encourage policies of economic development and income distribution that sharply increased inequalities between sectors of the population. It would rapidly shift vast amounts of capital from place to place without regard for the impact on local communities, causing massive movements of population away from family and neighborhood supports in search of livelihood. It would avoid providing new mechanisms of care and support for those uprooted. . . . It would promote a culture of intense interpersonal competition and spur its citizens to a level of material consumption many could not lawfully sustain. (p. 278)

Ronald Huff (1993) also argues that in terms of gang-related and non–gang-related interventions to reduce violence, the United

States must begin by rebuilding its human infrastructure. Furthermore, that the public-private sectors should come up with a national youth policy statement, or what Huff refers to as a "Domestic Marshall Plan." He states that if it is in our national interest to intervene, at great expense, in the Persian Gulf when Iraq invades Kuwait, then it is in our national interest to intervene in our urban cities, where far more people die each year in gang-related violence than died in the Persian Gulf War. This kind of intervention recognizes the underlying problems of inequality and social injustice as it addresses the problems posed by youth gangs from a macro-level perspective that sees violence of all kinds as deeply intertwined with other social and economic problems threatening society:

> We can keep the incentives that are the best part of capitalism and still broaden the opportunities for our less fortunate citizens. An affluent nation need not retain in its socioeconomic system the vestiges of Social Darwinism to which we cling. In the final analysis, global competition and the aging of our own population put all of us in the United States at risk, at least in economic terms. We will need the productive labor of all of our citizens to meet these challenges. (Huff, 1993, p. 474)

Finally, we will have to change our social and cultural discourses. As was pointed out in Chapters 6 and 7 (on media and sexuality, respectively), both the narratives and the social realities of masculinity in the West generally and in the United States specifically have reconstructed and reinforced in many forms a violence that has been installed within the machinery of the modern self—meaning, among other things, that masculine subjectivity is more about an aggressive posturing than about the "essence" of male violence and that the masculine sense of self is composed of the fiction of an unambivalent

male self-possession. The translation of this violence mythos across society has supported two related cultural assumptions about violence in the Western collective unconscious: "first, that violence is central to human nature, and its expression is inevitable; and second, that it is necessary to apply legal and cultural sanctions to prevent or curb violent individual behaviors" (Hatty, 2000, pp. 206-207).

When we move from an adversarial set of organized social relations to a mutualistic set of organized social relations, both of these cultural assumptions and the accompanying discourses about violence and nonviolence in the adversarial paradigm may give way to the emerging discourses of the mutualistic paradigm that favor constructs of interdependence and interconnectedness. Under these new social formations of violence and nonviolence, practices and policies would be contextualized within a framework in which attachment, rather than hierarchy, would become the hallmark of social relations. "The emergence of this mythos of interdependence would finally show that 'the hero has no armor, only skin, and the perpetrator no shadow, only face, and the victim no violence, only a need to live'" (Whitmer, quoted in Hatty, 2000, p. 207). Furthermore, the collective self and the interconnectedness of empathetic people would also move individuals not only to attempt to make sense of the concepts of justice, caring, and responsibility at the levels of both community and civil society, but to structure human relations in ways that would systematically encourage nonviolence.

At a more basic level, we need to create policies of nonviolence that ensure that all those traditionally excluded from civil society are accorded social position and status. This means opening up the narrow and individual-istically defined nature of *harm* to those harms embedded in the structures and every-day practices of governments, corporations, and associations (West, 1997). It also means challenging the limited versions of moral and legal discourse that help to separate the offender, the victim, and the society from their mutually informed civil bodies. In other words, stressing the otherness of the offender and erecting barriers between him and the rest of us portrays the violent person as fundamentally different than the nonviolent person, reducing the chances of developing his or our empathy. Of course, changing the public discourse or story of violence by moving beyond dualistic hierarchies of mind-body splits and the privileging of the control of self (especially emotions and desires) and the control of others (especially those deemed likely to provoke unsettling or disturbing emotions and desires) is necessary to transform the dominant narrative about gender and violence in the West (Whitmer, 1997).

The alternative approach to justice and responsibility turns on the development of a morality of caring and collectivity embodied in the ethic of social mutualism. Such a sensitivity in political approach recognizes the need to abandon the current preoccupation with the violent offender as a particular type of legal person, such as the "serial killer"—something *other*, something monstrous, to be treated as some kind of aberrant individual. The consumption of this belief excuses us from examining the ways in which the present arrangements of the political economy systematically encourage violence in the first place. The alternative discourse of social justice and collective action inspires and invokes the virtues of nurturance, compassion, and commitment rather than ones of retribution and retaliation.

Similarly, an alternative response to "recovery" in the areas of sexual violence or sexualized victimization would focus its attention less on the reassertion of women's responsibility for policing men's behavior and the familiarly dysfunctional reconstruction of the content of individual interactions. In contrast, an alternative response would not only concentrate more on self-defense and security responses for women and girls (i.e., escape, avoidance, accommodation) and on the treatment of their medical and psychological injuries after the event, but on the impact and consequences of sexualized violence with respect to both victims and perpetrators. This mutual emphasis on the private and public effects of violence recognizes that the meanings of victimization for women and girls are mediated by the possibilities of organized support, institutional responses, political change, and cultural socialization (Kelly & Radford, 1998). In addition, mutualism identifies the need for the further scientific elaboration of how different political and economic arrangements or contexts encourage or discourage sexual aggression and on how the social and cultural relations of power, sex, violence, and pleasure interact.

MUTUALISM AND THE STRUGGLE FOR NONVIOLENCE

Mutualism strives to "love your enemy," not "defeat your adversary" (Hopkins, 2001). Mutualism further believes that one must not only struggle against the social tendencies to defeat or to vanquish one's enemies, but find the resilience or inner strength to connect with one's adversaries. To do otherwise, mutualism argues, is to reproduce and perpetuate cycles of violence. Thus, terrorism cannot be defeated exclusively by counterterrorism; nor, for that matter, can any form of violence be overcome merely by resorting to other or counter forms of violence and repression. These truisms do not deny that some perpetrators of violence, as well as some forms of violence, require the use of the "stick" rather than the use of the "carrot" as a means (perhaps the only means) to resist or temporarily halt the various expressions of violence. At the same time, violent responses to violence have never been a foundation for alleviating violence for any extended period of time. To alleviate violence from the world and, more pragmatically, to reduce violence in and between societies, it is necessary to adopt preventive policies of nonviolence that indirectly and directly address the sources and conditions of violence rather than merely the symptoms or expressions of individual and nation-state violence alike.

Before turning to the policies of nonviolence, let me briefly recapitulate some of the major findings and conclusions of this study of the pathways to violence. First, violence and violent behaviors—interpersonal, institutional, and structural—represent social, psychological, economic, and cultural phenomena. In other words, violent perpetrators—illegitimate and legitimate—are expressions of underlying personal and social problems. Whether the issue is intimate violence, gang violence, corporate violence, war or genocide, each of these forms of violence is subject to, and the object of, policies of intervention and nonintervention, just as if violence were an outbreak of smallpox, homelessness, or drug addiction (Gilligan, 2001).

Second, most people, in the best as well as in the worst of circumstances, are able to control their feelings of anger and even rage without resorting to violence. Similarly, most people who are humiliated or shamed, or who are overwhelmed by emotions of inadequacy, dependency, or low self-esteem, rarely engage in acts of violence. Most people find less destructive ways to vent their feelings of indignity, lack of respect, and extreme embarrassment. Those who are not able to find alternative releases or nonviolent relief resort to making constrained choices, often feeling trapped and unable to do otherwise. These choices often result in the indifferent and nonempathetic consequences of lethal and less than lethal violence (Gilligan, 1996; Totten, 2000).

Third, whether the object of control, reduction, or prevention is gun violence, violence against intimates, school violence, or youthful homicide, trends both past and present reveal that the perpetrators of these acts are, more often than not, victims themselves, with a history of an assortment of sources for or pathways to violence, including child abuse and neglect, exposure to parental violence, and/or parents who were addicted, mentally ill, or involved in crime. Often suffering learning disabilities, limited school success, and the effects of fetal alcohol syndrome and brain injuries, and subject to bullying and harassment, these individuals frequently find themselves isolated and segregated as antisocial and deviant children. In addition, family breakdown due to divorce and parental abandonment, as well as negative social environments involving wide-scale poverty, community-based violence and disorganization, and exposure to alcohol, drugs, and crime, all contribute to experiences that can wear down even the resilience of those children who have developed the ability to overcome their adverse circumstances (Kelly & Totten, 2002).

Fourth, these vulnerable people resort to transgressions against the law, property, and other persons often because of inadequately developed egos, superegos, and social consciences. More important, these offenders have in common that they are fighting against their feelings of low self-esteem, lack of control and power, shame, and humiliation. Their actions stem from a sense of dependence and weakness, and their abusive and violent acts are directed at those persons whom they substitute for their own charged projections of negativity. Once these feelings are displaced on to the "other," the real or imagined enemies of these persons, they are then able to defend themselves from that which they fear by striking out at some "deserving" scapegoat (Beck, 1999; Gilligan, 1996; Levin & McDevitt, 1993).

Fifth, these vulnerable people are in need of the same things of which those who do not engage in violence are in need. Those at risk are without the means—psychological, social, or economic—to satisfy their needs for peace, love, and identity. They then compound the problem by striking out at others, acting in ways antithetical to their own vested interests. Thus, if societies are to reduce, curtail, or end their common forms of pathological violence, as well as the related and unrelated forms of adversarial violence, they need policies of nonviolence that (a) prevent the reproduction of antisocial behavioral pathways to violence; (b) stimulate cultures of reconciliation and peacemaking; and (c) transform the relations of distributive injustice into relations of social, political, and economic justice.

NONVIOLENT POLICIES THAT PREVENT ANTISOCIAL PATHWAYS TO VIOLENCE

The variety of underlying antisocial conditions and pathways to interpersonal violence calls for a comprehensive approach to assessment, treatment, and prevention. Ultimately, policies of nonviolence that address antisocial outcomes need to incorporate the perspectives of social workers, psychologists, physicians, teachers, urban planners, economists, community advocates, and other relevant specialists. Moreover, an all-inclusive approach to interpersonal violence prevention must focus not only on individual motivation but on the interaction between the interpersonal and the larger units of social organization such as communities, regions, and nation-states. This kind of multilevel risk approach attempts to account for the full range and integration of biological (e.g., neurobehavioral), psychosocial, microsocial, and macrosocial elements of violence.

Conceptually, vulnerability to violence may be influenced by interactions that occur primarily in (a) the brain, involving chemical, electrical, and hormonal reactions; (b) the mind, involving personalities, learned rewards, and emotional states; (c) the community, involving families, situational factors, and organizational and institutional processes; and (d) the organization of society itself, involving its political, economic, and cultural arrangements.

Ordinarily, prevention of antisocial behavior tends to be individualistically oriented, emphasizing primarily mental and health-care interventions involving the brain and mind, and often influenced by pharmacological intervention (Fishbein, 2000a, 2000b). Occasionally, these public health approaches to violence prevention venture into the areas of family and community practice. However, in the context of youth at risk, for example, these approaches have sought to "make young people, families, and communities more responsible for the prudent management of a diverse range of *institutionally generated* risks. Here risk management emerges as an increasingly individualized rather than a social responsibility" (Kelly, 2001, p. 97, emphasis added). Often not seen as a problem or addressed by these "community" health models are the macrosocial and organizational dynamics involved in the political, economic, and cultural arrangements of violence reduction. What are called for are policies of nonviolence to regulate those environments at risk, as well as policies of intervention for those vulnerable populations who are living in at-risk environments.

In short, preventing antisocial behavioral pathways to violence assumes that the world consists of nature-nurture interactions that operate at primary (i.e., keeping violence from arising in the first place, directed at the entire community), secondary (i.e., identifying and "treating" vulnerable or at-risk youths for violence), and tertiary (i.e., reducing the repetition of violent acts by violent offenders) levels of organization. In total, these interactions require an inventory of all the relevant factors that contribute to both violence and nonviolence. In turn, these factors require social policies aimed at structuring environments that will minimize the variety of risks for violent behavior. This, of course, also means seeing and understanding the relationships and making the connections between the three spheres or domains of violence and nonviolence. Unless policies engage the primary, secondary, and tertiary relations of violence and nonviolence, as well as the interdependent reactions of interpersonal, institutional, and structural violence and nonviolence, they will lack the comprehensiveness necessary for antiviolence measures. Moreover, when policies fail to address the domestic and global forces of capitalist production and consumption that help to generate the pathways to violence or nonviolence vis-à-vis the reproduction of inequalities and privileges, they are merely dealing with the interpersonal rather than with the institutional and structural relations.

In addition to addressing the interpersonal, institutional, and structural levels of violence, a viable approach to the prevention of violence must be both general and specific. With violence, as we have seen throughout this book, there are commonalities and differences between the various kinds of violence and violent behavior. These variations in types or expressions of "violence experiences" require diverse prevention, intervention, and follow-up strategies. And as if this diversity and complexity were not enough, mixed interventions directed at, for example, battering husbands enter contexts of contradictory messages and responses that may serve to assist or impede the aim of reducing or eliminating violence. "In turn, the responses themselves not only serve as enforcers or deterrents but also form a part of the expanding body of messages received by violent men, the women they abuse, and the society at large" (Dobash & Dobash, 1998, p. 164).

As the fundamental relationships between stratification and violence made clear earlier in the chapter, different ethnic and racial groups, different socioeconomic levels and classes, and different genders and sexualities experience different levels and rates of violence. Once these varieties of social reality have been acknowledged, then "we must cast a sufficiently wide net that incorporates certain principles that are not always closely linked to violence prevention" (Bell, 2002, p. 68). With respect to those vulnerable populations living in urban America, Carl Bell has identified seven basic principles of violence avoidance:

- Rebuilding the village
- Providing access to health care
- Improving bonding, attachment, and connectedness dynamics
- Improving self-esteem
- Increasing social skills
- Reestablishing the adult protective shield
- Minimizing the residual effects of trauma

These strategies of violence reduction are broad in gauge. They specifically tackle the environments at risk for violence by building public and private bridges between families, communities, and nation-states that are consciously striving to transform both the personal and the political. What makes these interventions especially preventive is the general targeting of, first, the vulnerable communities and second, the constituent members of these communities, as early as possible in their life cycles. Actual programs and evaluative research on the efficacy of these kinds of interventions, a number of them in the Chicago area, have proven themselves worthy of emulation (Bell, 2002). A few brief comments are in order for each of these nonviolent policy dimensions.

Rebuilding the village addresses issues of social disorganization and networking in a context of the development of protective infrastructures and community partnerships. These goals have come to fruition especially when there has been emphasis on "the interdependency among diverse elements in a community, encouraging affiliation among these elements, promoting development of 'system' thinking, and providing leadership to community organizations—religious, business, service, health, education, civic, and social—to enable them to *synergize* their efforts to promote healthy development of youth" (Bell, 2002, pp. 69-70, emphasis in the original).

Providing access to health care incorporates an appreciation for the necessary intervention into a range of epidemiological foundations and environments that may have a predisposition for violence or that may create physiologic responses that influence behavior. For example, research supports the hypothesis that "neuropsychiatric disorders among adolescents and children may predispose individuals to violence; specifically, neurophysiological brain impairments acquired since birth [not genetic] can lead to difficulty in bonding/attachment, poor social skills, and lack of impulse control" (Bell, 2002, p. 71). Similarly, environmental research has indicated that children with high levels of exposure to lead may be more vulnerable to violence. Furthermore, among preadolescent and youthful conduct disorders, as many as one third are related to some kind of impaired mental disorder, such as bipolar depressive disorder, attention-deficit hyperactivity disorder (ADHD), or post-traumatic stress disorder (PTSD). As the sophistication of neuropsychiatry develops and its diagnosis and treatment of some causes of violent behavior become more specific, however, it won't matter unless those communities with the greatest need for violence prevention programs also have an infrastructure in place for the delivery of that kind of service.

Bell (2002) captures the spirit of *improving bonding, attachment, and connectedness dynamics* when he notes that

> Low levels of parental warmth, acceptance, and affection; low levels of family cohesion; and high levels of family conflict and hostility have been associated with delinquent and violent behavior among juveniles. By paying attention to the attributes of the family—its beliefs and values, emotional warmth, support, and organization—communication strategies can be developed [to ensure mutualism in other institutions as well]. Providing early intervention programs for infants, toddlers, and preschoolers and their parents can teach both parents and their children the skills to enhance their sense of personal mastery and encourages strong intra-family attachments [that can be translated outside of family and into larger community-social relations]. Such attachments have been shown to reduce the risk of serious antisocial behavior and violence. Helping parents bond with their infants may seem a far cry from violence prevention, but enabling infants to grow up with basic trust and security provides the groundwork for future stable relationships that may be necessary to prevent violence. (p. 72)

Similarly, *improving self-esteem* is related to resilience and the ability to minimize the personal hurts, shames, and humiliations that are so frequently a basis for violence. Marginal elementary and middle school–age students are especially vulnerable to damaged self-esteems. These children and any others with low self-esteem or minimal social skills are in need of both ego strengthening and *increasing social skills*. Ego strengthening is obtained through experiences that provide a sense of power related to feeling competent to make decisions and solve problems, a sense of uniqueness that comes from acknowledging and respecting the qualities and characteristics about oneself that are special and different, role models that one can use to make sense of the world; and a sense of belonging that derives from being connected to people, places, and things (Bean, 1992). The ability for adolescents to increase their social skills can be developed through a diversity of projects that are aimed at improving parental training and monitoring techniques as well as humanizing their disciplinary efforts. Increased social skills may also be obtained when adolescents are provided with opportunities to serve their communities, help resolve disputes peacefully, and acquire leadership skills they can use to promote mutualistic alternatives to violence. If the self-esteem and social skills "things" are in place, then a community probably has various kinds of Big Brother/Big Sister programs in which adults can serve as positive role models and help to fill in the gaps, thereby *reestablishing the adult protective shield* in the community.

Finally, preventing antisocial pathways to violence means developing nonviolent policies for *minimizing the residual effects of trauma*. It must be remembered that a background filled with abuse, neglect, and violation of one kind or another is the source of the violence in many youths and adults. Much of the anger of violent people stems from their own experiences of hurt and victimization and the fear of being injured or harmed again. For example, it becomes incumbent upon service providers and others to identify those children suffering from trauma so that they may receive crisis intervention to reduce their stress and the long-term effects that very likely can turn into violence later on. To be most effective, however, these nonviolent policies of interpersonal violence reduction must be connected to and in sync with other policies of nonviolence that are addressing in tandem the sources of institutional and structural violence. These policies of nonviolence are interdependent with the building of pathways to positive peace, human rights, and social justice.

NONVIOLENT POLICIES THAT BUILD PATHWAYS TO POSITIVE PEACE, HUMAN RIGHTS, AND SOCIAL JUSTICE

The building of pathways to nonviolence and positive peace refers to diverse attempts to reproduce social conditions in which exploitation is minimized or eliminated, and in which there is neither overt violence nor the more subtle phenomenon of underlying structural violence (Galtung, 1985). Unlike the building of "negative peace" (absence of war, interstate, and/or domestic violence) primarily through the diplomatic efforts of peacekeeping or conflict resolution, the building of positive peace stems from a number of very different and older traditions—Greek, English, Arabic, Hebrew, Sanskrit, Chinese, Russian—that have valued an integrated harmony and justice that flows throughout societies and within and without individuals. For example, the

> ancient Greek concept of *eireinei* (English *irenic*) denotes harmony and justice as well as peace. Similarly, the Arabic *salaam* and the Hebrew *shalom* connote not only the absence of violence but also the present of well-being, wholeness and harmony within oneself, a community, and among all nations and peoples. The Sanskrit word *shantyi* refers not only to peace but also to spiritual tranquility, an integration of outward and inward modes of being, just as the Chinese noun *ping* denotes harmony and the achievement of unity from diversity. In Russian, the word *mir* means peace, a village community, and the entire world. (Barash & Webel, 2002, p. 8)

The pathways to nonviolence, in other words, are not about peacekeeping or the restoration of peace when war and conflict have already broken out. They are not focused on maintaining the status quo or in "keeping things the way they were." This does not mean that policies of peace and nonviolence ignore or deny conflict and violence. On the contrary, it simply means that although these policies recognize that the prevention of war may be a necessary condition for the establishment of peace, it is not sufficient alone for bringing about sustainable peace. Moreover, positive peacemaking is about favoring as well as opposing things: Rather than merely being against poverty, inequality, repression, war, imperialism, sexism, and other forms of exploitation, peacemaking stands for something positive and affirmative. It is not simply antiviolence and the negative of violence; it is also proenvironment, prohuman, prosocial justice, and propeace. Unabashedly, then, the goals of positive peace are aimed at the establishment of nonexploitative social structures and the creation of social orders that do not currently exist (Barash & Webel, 2002; Mayor, 1995; Schwebel, 1995).

Moving from cultures of conflict and warmaking to cultures of cooperation and peacemaking shifts the foci from violence and repression to nonviolence and emancipation. It also shifts the values and mindsets of people from actions that suppress people through killing or separating them from the social fabric in which they live to actions that encourage the weaving and reweaving of ourselves and the "other" in a social fabric of mutual love, respect, and concern (Pepinsky, 1999). Of equal emphasis, policies of peacemaking recognize the necessity of building peace not only at the intra- and interpersonal levels of microinteraction, but also at the institutional and structural levels of macrointeraction. These policies of nonviolence stress the reciprocal relationships between the personal and the political and between the social and the cultural. In different words, building policies of nonviolence and policies of positive peace depends on the joint pursuit of the inclusive development of both "human rights" and "social justice" in the context of collective and ecological well-being.

When it comes to peacemaking and nonviolent policy considerations, there have been national and international efforts to mobilize people in the struggle for human rights and social justice. Historically, these social movements have been global as well as domestic. Internationally, there have been the United Nations, regional organizations such as the Organization of African Unity (OAU) or the Organization of American States (OAS), intergovernmental organizations (IGOs), nongovernmental organizations (NGOs), transnational organizations (TNOs), and multinational corporations (MNCs). The activities of these diverse kinds of organizations have been restricted in their actual peacemaking effects or collective security worldwide. Nevertheless, in their limited capacities, these organizations have furthered efforts in peacekeeping, third-party mediation, global debating, regionalism, international law, and more, all of which contributes to an expanding and universalizing discourse of human rights and social justice. At the beginning of the 21st century, these kinds of international peacemaking efforts are seriously taking up the challenges of mutualism and adversarialism:

> Although their record has not been perfect, there is much to applaud in the activities of international organizations. Some of these—notably the United Nations—promote human and planetary betterment in numerous ways, including but not limited to the keeping of *negative peace,* that is, the prevention or termination of war. They also represent a partial step in the progression from individualism through nationalism to globalism, a transition that may well be essential if we are ever to give peace a realistic chance. As such, international organizations can be seen as possible halfway houses toward the establishment and solidification of international law, and perhaps even world government. (Barash & Webel, 2002, p. 371)

Domestically, peacemaking alternatives to the wars on crime, drugs, violence, sex, and youth, to the silences on white-collar and environmental violence, and to the actuarial and repressive policies on contracting law and order welfare states involve a number of deescalating and recovery efforts aimed at the prevention of further violence through the developing practices of mutualism, humanism, and social justice. Two obvious cases of domestic peacemaking include deescalating the war on drugs and regulating the worlds of while-collar violence. Policies of nonviolence with respect to these two problems focus their attention on the consequences of the "users" and "enforcers" in the area of illicit drugs and of the "abusers" and "nonenforcers" in the area of corporate violations.

With respect to deescalating the war on drugs, the 2001 California law requiring mandatory treatment rather than incarceration for first-time drug-using convictions was an effort in positive peacemaking. Having taken into account not only the psychological, physical, and economic costs involved in the punitive and retributive law enforcement approach but also the auxiliary costs related to the violence and theft associated with illegal drug use, as well as the additional expenses of militarization and reliance on aggressive police tactics, these social policies are reflective of those who have started to seriously rethink the repressive approach to drug enforcement. Given the ineffective and destructive nature of the war on drugs to date (Gray, 1998), many reformers call for an end to the war. Some critics of the law enforcement approach advocate decriminalization, others call for legalization, and there are also those who argue that the legal status should be determined on a case-by-case basis, as they argue that drugs and drug violence are not unitary social problems (Zimring & Hawkins, 1992).

More generally the "war on violence," from the selling of guns and other weapons to the numerous deaths resulting from unnecessary surgeries and unsafe working conditions to the exploitation and pollution of the environment, has involved a high degree of "regulatory omissions" rather than overly zealous enforcement. Such omissions, associated with these corporate acts of violence, as well as other kinds of deregulated white-collar practices, are legendary. Addressing these types of institutional and structural harms requires far more than simply raising public consciousness and establishing ethical codes of behavior. Without more regulation and prosecution of corporate and white-collar violations of legal and human rights, this abusive, neglectful, and violent behavior is not likely to stop. Nonviolent policies of control and regulation that have moved beyond publicizing the wrongdoing include corporate probation and management, public monitoring and supervision, suspensions from government contracts, and social capital formation and community development (Barak, 1998; Benson & Cullen, 1998; Friedrichs, 1996).

More broadly speaking, human rights, at least since the modern state system was established in the mid-17th century, have always taken a back seat to national sovereignty and the rights of other governments to treat their own citizens as they like. Within their own boundaries today, however, the supremacy of nation-states to do as they virtually wish has been contravened by the growing spirit of universal humanism. As Barash and Webel (2002) assess, "a great many human beings are denied some of the most basic human rights," and it seems that these rights "are more honored in the breach than the reality. Nonetheless, concern with such rights has, if anything, been growing in recent years" (p. 431). Real progress, in other words, has been made in the area of these rights, and more is anticipated in the future.

Today's political philosophy of human rights and humanism has moved beyond the adversarial tenets of "inalienable rights" and "natural law" liberalism characteristic of laissez-faire capitalism. In addition to the emphases on equal civil and political rights, contemporary human rights activists and policies of nonviolence promote a fundamental appreciation for mutual rights to national self-determination and economic development. The "collectivist" orientation that embraces this view of social justice (i.e., emphasizing socioeconomic rights and economic equity) is grounded in a new substantive way of thinking about the relationship of governments and their citizens that is intended to enhance the dignity of human beings rather than exploit them. Although the legal status of human rights has made some progress since World War II, it has begun to take off during the post–Cold War period, yet much more needs to be done.

The U.N.-sponsored Universal Declaration of Human Rights (UDHR) was passed in 1948. It consisted of 30 articles, of which the first 21 "are primarily civil/political, prohibiting torture and arbitrary arrest, guaranteeing freedom of assembly, religion, speech, emigration, and even the right to vote by secret ballot. The remaining articles are concerned with socioeconomic and cultural rights, including the right to work, to an 'adequate' standard of living, to education, to some form of social security, and even specifying the right to vacations with pay" (Barash & Webel, 2002, p. 444). The UDHR has the primacy of nation-state rather than international (i.e., global) sovereignty and a lack of transnational enforcement, as do an array of covenants, conventions, treaties, and declarations of diverse legal meaning. The UDHR thus remains only a recommendation and is not technically binding. Without international laws and tribunals (courts) and, ultimately, a world government, human rights aspirants will have their work cut out for them.

Finally, the theories and practices of nonviolence, social justice, human rights, and peacemaking employ strategies of social change, including policies of ecological (e.g., "sustainable" growth) and economic (e.g., "full" employment) well-being that are mutually reinforcing. That is to say, for example, that the denial of human rights is itself a denial of real peace. Moreover, the denial of human rights can provoke breaches of the peace, especially when other states become involved. Similarly, "a world in which there is no armed conflict but in which fundamental human rights are thwarted could not in any meaningful sense be considered peaceful" (Barash & Webel, 2002, p. 453). In other words, human rights are not only compatible with peace and security for individuals and governments alike, but these rights are absolutely necessary for the achievement of peace and security. There tends to be a reciprocal relation in the way that governments treat their own populations and the way they treat those of other nation-states. Stated differently, a nation's foreign policy is often reflective of its own domestic inclinations. Of course, claims of humanitarian intervention have often been used as excuses for aggression and warmaking.

In sum, these policies of nonviolence are "not limited to tactics of defending a given people; rather, [they are] directed toward overthrowing an entire system of relationships that is fundamentally based on violence, oppression, and the unfair dominance of some by others" (Barash & Webel, 2002, p. 532). These policies go beyond simply trying to prevent war or restore peace. They are about establishing and developing social justice, environmental protection, and the defense of human rights. These policies do "not aim at merely achieving a more effective national defense, but rather a defense of all humanity and of the planet against destructiveness and violence, by seeking to change the terms with which individuals and groups interact" (Barash & Webel, 2002, pp. 532-533).

TRANSFORMATIVE JUSTICE AND PATHWAYS TO VIOLENCE AND NONVIOLENCE

Within the context of developing political economies, the reduction of violence and the production of nonviolence are facilitated or impeded by the two contending ways of institutionalizing social interaction and social organization: adversarialism and mutualism. Throughout this book, it has been argued that the pathways individuals or nation-states travel to violence and nonviolence are manifestations of certain values and structures and that these are exemplified by one of two competing paradigms, each of which struggles with the vagaries of consumption and the distribution of justice. It has also been implied that changing and transforming individuals or societies at the interpersonal, institutional, or structural levels will work best when the transformation of all three is pursued simultaneously. Accordingly, reciprocal transformations or processes of humanistic and systemic change that embody the values of mutualism over adversarialism in the context of the political and economic arrangements as these are dispersed throughout the institutions of justice, media, education, religion, family, politics, economics, and culture are required so that the prevailing relations of the "geometry of violence" can be reconstituted by the alternative relations of the "geometry of nonviolence" (Pepinsky, 1991).

As part of the complex processes of "healing," "recovering," and "forgiving," Ruth Morris (2000) and others have argued that *transformative justice* is about dealing with both the injustice of being victimized and with the injustice of distributive justice. Transformative justice departs from the adversarialism of repressive, retributive, vengeful, and even restorative justice on the grounds that these forms of justice serve to perpetuate and reproduce the marginal and disempowering conditions of the victimized and the enraged. Instead, policies of nonviolence are called for that seek to transform the dominant practices of our penal-justice systems and of the larger systems of distributive injustice throughout society. At the same time, transformative justice seeks to move victims from vengeance to forgiveness, from defensive hatred and alienation to altruistic empathy and protectiveness, as it seeks to respond to the needs of the most vulnerable and harmed in our society who require at a minimum four things: (a) answers to why they were victimized, (b) recognition of the wrongs they incurred, (c) restitution for the injuries they received, and (d) the restoration or establishment of peace and security lost or never obtained.

Transformative justice is part of an ongoing historical process that has for more than two centuries sought consciously to transform distributive injustice. The real world, past and present, has always been challenged by and riddled with inequality, domination, oppression, and greed. In essentially every culture and throughout the modern and postmodern periods, privileged people (although initially only a minority of them) have renounced their "egocentric interests" derived from the inequities of class, ethnic, or gender relations so they could make the transition to a higher order of democracy, social justice, and human rights. If this had not been the case, then in the United States there would still be a system of slavery, and women would still not have the right to vote. Accordingly, the question is not whether transformative justice is or is not on the political and economic agendas of particular regimes or nation-states, but rather where we choose to locate our lives in the ongoing struggle for social change and constructive mutualism (Rossi, 2001).

In trying to transform destructive adversarialism and distributive injustice, Morris (2000) has identified seven pathways to nonviolence that are worth pursuing:

- Tuning Up Our Individual Lifestyles
- Using Our Consumer Power
- Disseminating Our Awareness Everywhere
- Transforming Our Sources of Information
- Changing Our Political Systems to Achieve Democracy
- Regaining Control of Corporations
- Building International Networks for Compassion (pp. 227-228)

The first two of these pathways articulate ways in which individuals can change their lives, families, and environments for the collective good and social responsibility of all. The next two pathways reveal ways in which popular ideas can be communicated in the context of a corporate-controlled media of disinformation. The last three pathways incorporate political actions to address international and global concerns of a safe and sustainable planet.

In the milieu of local and global change and in the context of an alternative vision of the human condition, the substitute narrative or the "story of mutualism" is grounded in empathy, altruism, social responsibility, and collective love. By presenting a more encompassing reality of community life and values, the alternative discourses challenge—at the interpersonal, institutional, and structural levels of social interaction—the adversarial messages of mass advertising and runaway consumption that communicate the fact that "corporate media are not open to carrying community messages, and they are committed to selling us on the idea that buying something, buying anything, will assuage the terrible emptiness that a consumer culture of materialism and winner-takes-all leaves in our souls" (Morris, 2000, p. 232).

More specifically, the mutualistic and collective pathways to happiness counter those pathways to happiness associated with extreme individualism and with hierarchy, inequality, and social injury. These mutualistic discourses and visions also counter the kinds of mainstream narratives and consciousness building that are almost exclusively derived from the powers and desires of egotism, narcissism, and self-aggrandizement. These alternative narratives, for example, expose how conspicuously unfocused the adversarial paradigm is on the burning social and environmental issues of our times. Naturally, getting out alternative messages involves finding a medium other than the corporate-controlled media for the purposes of disseminating information and of networking and organizing for change. Spreading the news about and marketing alternative perspectives, points of view, and plans of action is, obviously, necessary to transform distributive injustice at home and abroad. However, the usual difficulties in such an endeavor are joined by the equally necessary struggle to make the connection in the minds of the people that the personal and the global obstacles to obtaining human rights and social justice for all must be overcome together.

At the most personal level, *tuning up our individual lifestyles* means doing the collective rather than the individual thing whenever we can. It's about where we invest our dollars and purchase our goods and services. It's about environmental responsibility and about dropping our personal consumption of endangered sustainable resources—for example, by reducing our dependency on the car as well as driving smaller automobiles rather than gas-guzzling SUVs. Tuning up one's individual lifestyle and consciousness means getting in touch with oneself as a member of several communities, local and global. It also means finding ways to market the message of mutualism. Instead of wearing clothes with logos that read *Old Navy, Coca Cola,* or *The Gap* and becoming part of an advertising campaign for a fill-in-the-blank corporate megagiant, people can use their bodies, clothing, and other objects of desire to promote messages other than those of consumption. Some of these alternative logos, for example, have read *Save the Earth,*

No More Prisons, Domestic Violence Is a Crime, and *Living in a Global Village*.

How one lives one's life—"you are what you eat"—on the personal level also relates to *using our consumer power* in collective terms to enrich a world consumer movement for cooperative communities, balanced growth, and sustainable production. In today's world, consumer power is an important and yet surprisingly downplayed public resource. Boycotting, for example, can be a means of both spreading consciousness and changing public policy. By "outing" those multinational corporations that hide behind a combination of exploitative labor practices, ruthless destruction and pollution of the environment, and a world market dominated by laissez-faire, the mutualistic issues raised and discussed may have the effect of forcing the policies and practices of transnational corporations to bend and even to change. Perhaps one of the best examples was the successful worldwide boycotting of South African goods that eventually brought down the apartheid institutions and structures of that previously very violent society. All in all, today's alternative global message to conspicuous or greedy consumption is an environmental, "green" message of sorts where "less is more" and "small is beautiful."

Today's messages are also about *disseminating our awareness everywhere* and *transforming our sources of information*. In the context of violence, for example, these two pathways are working to engage the public in a different kind of discourse and in a portrayal of the violent offender as other than some kind of marginal and evil outsider. In related venues, there are the development of policies not only to resist the forces of alienation, joblessness, and insecurity, but to support prosocial welfare programs aimed at the most marginal and at-risk youth and families for violence. Alienation and insecurity affect not only the powerless and the marginal, but the "nonviolent" middle and upper classes, many of whom have lost their sense of footing or direction and are in need of a more satisfying and fulfilling American Dream than "making a lot of money." In addition to trying to find venues for disseminating "new" information and electronic action networking with an alternative message, collective consumer power can rate and censor the community friendliness of different media, promoting the best and resisting the worst. Consumer power can also help to rethink our dominant positions on social and economic issues by discounting "corporate media in our personal reading, quoting, thinking, advertising, and buying" and instead turning to alternative media sources for our everyday needs (Morris, 2000, p. 234).

The last three directions or pathways to nonviolence—changing our political systems to achieve democracy, regaining control of corporations, and building international networks for compassion—are not only connected to each other; they turn back to the sources of dissemination and information and the corporate-dominated media. The argument is that under the United States' present political system, corporations have become too powerful controlling both candidate selection and substantive content (e.g., party platform) because of the might of their campaign contributions, advertising revenue, and threat of pulling out of the economy. In a nutshell, corporate lobbyists and Corporate Party A or B and elected officials "get more perks for corporations in tax dodges, immunities, and rights to endanger our lives and health than would be possible if we had a true democracy in operation" (Morris, 2000, p. 238). Even though the political electorate has widened significantly over the past century, the corporate oligopoly has nevertheless been able to narrow the political process and the choices available to those who still bother to vote.

As an alternative to the "greed agenda" and as a way of organizing poor and middle class people to resist corporate-inspired interests, opting instead for their own working and collective class interests, it is recommended that the United States give serious consideration to "proportional representation" as an electoral tool. As many countries around the world have discovered, proportional representation, usually requiring a minimum of 5% of the votes cast, almost certainly guarantees minority representation in government and always guarantees that the opinions, even of relatively small minorities, will be heard. It is no coincidence that transnational corporations oppose politics of proportional representation because they know that it threatens their powerful monopolies and "monologues" regarding so-called public debates. During the summer of 2002, for example, Senator Joseph Biden and the Foreign Intelligence Subcommittee entertained 2 days of discussions on "how"—not on "whether or not"—the United States should make war on Saddam Hussein and Iraq.

As a means of controlling runaway transnational corporations with their adversarial agendas, it is necessary to empower both local and international governments so that they may have as much control as they need to rein in corporations. This and other, interdependent goals can be realized with less difficulty if they are nurtured and developed simultaneously or synergistically. In other words, "balanced and sustainable growth" should become the developmental watchwords in both the public and private sectors. If transnational corporations are ever to become socially responsible and accountable, then there are at a minimum four necessary

steps to be taken to reduce their domination in domestic and international affairs:

- Abolish Their Status as Persons
- Set Standards of Social Responsibility for Them, with Strong Measures, and Revoke Corporate Charters When Necessary
- Deny Them the Right to Move Businesses to the Country of Lowest Standards
- Curb International Speculation. (Morris, 2000)

Working toward these objectives can be facilitated through the building of grass-roots networking by way of the Internet. As a means of resisting the moneyed interests and by negotiating with the wider interests of the World Trade Organization, for example, public protests, discussions, and actions have moved the world closer to the development of caring, forgiving, and loving communities.

In the end, as Morris (2000) contends, transformative justice is a risk because it dares to risk community: "But without taking that risk, we plod robot-like toward a more and more divided world in which the powers of greed breed violence and unrest and anger, while destroying the environmental inheritance essential to the survival of all" (p. 256). In stark contrast, transformative justice pursues nonviolence and positive peace as a commitment to love and life rather than to antipathy and death. Finally, in the affairs of everyday survival, transformative justice pursues the expansion of human rights and social justice as key components in the struggle for nonviolence and recognizes that the fundamental challenge of market economies is to devise mechanisms of balance that channel the pursuit of profits in socially productive directions (McMillan, 2002).

REFERENCES

Abramsky, S. (2002, November 15). Crime as America's pop culture. *Chronicle of Higher Education,* pp. B11-B12.

Barak, G. (1998). *Integrating criminologies.* Boston, MA: Allyn and Bacon.

Barak, G., Flavin, J., & Leighton, P. (2001). *Class, race, gender, and crime: Social realities of justice in America.* Los Angeles: Roxbury.

Barash, D. P., & Webel, C. P. (2002). *Peace and conflict studies.* Thousand Oaks, CA: Sage.

Bean, R. (1992). *The four conditions of self-esteem: A new approach for elementary and middle schools* (2nd ed.). Santa Cruz, CA: ETR Associates.

Beck, A. T. (1999). *Prisoners of hate: The cognitive basis of anger, hostility, and violence.* New York: HarperCollins.

Bell, C. C. (2002, March). Violence prevention 101: Implications for policy development. In National Institute of Justice (Ed.), *Perspectives on Crime and Justice: 2000–2001 Lecture Series* (NCJ 187100). Retrieved November 23, 2002, from http://www.ncjrs.org/txtfiles1/nij/187100.txt

Benson, M., & Cullen, F. (1998). *Combating corporate crime: Local prosecutors at work.* Boston, MA: Northeastern University Press.

Berger, R. J., Free, M. D., & Searles, P. (2001). *Crime, justice, and society: Criminology and the sociological imagination.* Boston, MA: McGraw-Hill.

Blumstein, A., Cohen, J., & Nagin, D. (Eds.). (1978). *Deterrence and incapacitation: Estimating the effects of criminal sanctions on crime rates.* Washington, DC: National Academy of Sciences.

Bohm, R. M. (1999). *Deathquest: An introduction to the theory and practice of capital punishment in the United States.* Cincinnati, OH: Anderson.

Bureau of Justice Statistics. (1998). *Sourcebook of criminal justice statistics, 1999* (NCJ 176356). Washington, DC: Author.

Bureau of Justice Statistics. (1999). *Sourcebook of criminal justice statistics, 1999* (NCJ 183727). Washington, DC: Author.

Bureau of Justice Statistics. (2000, May). *Criminal victimization in United States: 1998 statistical tables* (NCJ 181585). Retrieved November 29, 2002, from http://www.ojp.usdoj.gov/bjs/pub/pdf/cvus98.pdf

Bureau of Justice Statistics. (2002, June). *Recidivism of prisoners released in 1994* (NCJ 193427). Retrieved November 23, 2002, from http://www.ojp.usdogj.gove/bjs/abstract/rpr94.htm.

Cook, P. J. (1991). The technology of personal violence. In M. Tonry (Ed.), *Crime and justice: A review of research* (Vol. 14, pp. 1-72). Chicago: University of Chicago Press.

Craven, D. (1997). *Sex differences in violent victimization, 1994.* Washington, DC: U.S. Department of Justice.

Currie, E. (1985). *Confronting crime: An American challenge.* New York: Pantheon.

Dobash, R. E., & Dobash, R. P. (1998). Violent men and violent contexts. In R. E. Dobash & R. P. Dobash (Eds.), *Rethinking violence against women* (pp. 142-168). Thousand Oaks, CA: Sage.

Epps, G. (2002, June). Civilization and its discontents: A video game makes you ponder the nature of history. *American Prospect, 13*(10), 33-34.

Federal Bureau of Investigation. (1997). *Uniform crime reports: Crime in the United States—1997.* Washington, DC: Author. Retrieved November 23, 2002, from http://www.fbi.gov/ucr/97cius.htm

Federal Bureau of Investigation. (1999). *Uniform crime reports: Crime in the United States—1999.* Washington, DC: Author. Retrieved November 29, 2002, from http://www.fbi.gov/ucr/99cius.htm

Fellman, G. (1998). *Rambo and the Dalai Lama: The compulsion to win and its threat to human survival.* Albany, NY: State University of New York Press.

Fishbein, D. H. (2000a). How can neurobiological research inform prevention strategies? In D. H. Fishbein (Ed.), *The science, treatment, and prevention of antisocial behaviors: Application to the criminal justice system* (pp. 25-1–25-30). Kingston, NJ: Civic Research Institute.

Fishbein, D. H. (2000b). Prospects for a public health model to prevent and treat antisocial behaviors. In D. H. Fishbein (Ed.), *The* science, treatment, and prevention of antisocial behaviors: Application to the criminal justice system (pp. 26-1–26-8). Kingston, NJ: Civic Research Institute.

Fishbein, D. H. (Ed.). (2000c). *The science, treatment, and prevention of antisocial behaviors: Application to the criminal justice system.* Kingston, NJ: Civic Research Institute.

Friedrichs, D. (1996). *Trusted criminals: White collar crime in contemporary society.* Belmont, CA: Wadsworth.

Galtung, J. (1985). Twenty-five years of peace research: Ten challenges and responses. *Journal of Peace Studies, 22,* 414-431.

Gilligan, J. (1996). *Violence: Our deadly epidemic and its causes.* New York: Grosset/ Putnam.

Gilligan, J. (2001). *Preventing violence.* New York: Thames & Hudson.

Goldstein, A. P., & Huff, C. R. (Eds.). (1993). *The gang intervention handbook.* Champaign, IL: Research Press.

Gray, M. (1998). *Drug crazy: How we got into this mess and how we can get out.* New York: Random House.

Greenfeld, L. (1997). *Sex offenses and offenders.* Washington, DC: U.S. Department of Justice.

Greenfeld, L. A., Rand, M. R., Craven, D., Klaus, P. A., Perkins, C. A., Ringel, C., Warchol, G., Maston, C., & Fox, J. A. (1998, March). *Violence by intimates: Analysis of data on crimes by current or former spouses, boyfriends, and girlfriends* (NCJ 167237). Retrieved December 1, 2002, from http://www.ojp. usdoj.gov/bjs/pub/pdf/vi. pdf

Greenfeld, L. A., & Smith, S. K. (1999, February). American Indians and crime (NCJ 173386). Retrieved December 1, 2002, from http://www.ojp.usdoj.gov/bj s/pub/pdf/aic.pdf

Greenwood, P. W. (1982). The violent offender in the criminal justice system. In M. E. Wolfgang & N. A. Weiner (Eds.), *Criminal violence* (pp. 320-346). Beverly Hills, CA: Sage.

Greenwood, P. W., Rydell, C. P., Abrahamse, A. F., Caulkins, J. P., Chiesa, J., Model, K. E., & Klein, S. P. (1994). *Three strikes and you're out: Estimated benefits and costs of California's new mandatory-sentencing law.* Santa Monica, CA: RAND.

Haggerty, K. D. (2002, November). *Competing dystopia: Kafka and Orwell on contemporary criminal justice.* Paper presented at the Annual Meetings of the American Society of Criminology, Chicago.

Hatty, S. (2000). *Masculinities, violence, and culture.* Thousand Oaks, CA: Sage.

Hopkins, J. (2001). *Cultivating compassion.* New York: Broadway Books.

Huff, C. R. (1993). Gangs and public policy: Macrolevel interventions. In: A. P. Goldstein & C. R. Huff (Eds.), *The gang intervention handbook* (pp. 463-476). Champaign, IL: Research Press.

Kelly, K. D., & Totten, M. (2002). *When children kill: A social-psychological study of youth homicide.* Petersborough, ON, Canada: Broadview.

Kelly, L., & Radford, J. (1998). Sexual violence against women and girls: An approach to an international overview. In R. E. Dobash & R. P. Dobash (Eds.), *Rethinking violence against women* (pp. 53-76). Thousand Oaks, CA: Sage.

Kelly, P. (2001). The post-welfare state and the government of youth at-risk. *Social justice: A Journal of Crime, Conflict and World Order, 28*(4), 96-113.

Levin, J., & McDevitt, J. (1993). *Hate crimes: The rising tide of bigotry and bloodshed.* New York: Plenum.

Massey, D., & Denton, N. (1993). *American apartheid: segregation and the making of the underclass.* Cambridge, MA: Harvard University Press.

Mayor, F. (1995). How psychology can contribute to a culture of peace. *Peace and Conflict: Journal of Peace Psychology, 1*(1), 3-10.

McMillan, J. (2002). *Reinventing the bazaar: A natural history of markets.* New York: W. W. Norton.

Morris, R. (2000). *Stories of transformative justice.* Toronto, ON: Canadian Scholars' Press.

Packer, H. L. (1968). *The limits of the criminal sanction.* Stanford, CA: Stanford University Press.

Pepinsky, H. (1991). *The geometry of violence and democracy.* Bloomington: University of Indiana Press.

Pepinsky, H. (1999). Peacemaking primer. In B. Arrigo (Ed.), *Social justice/criminal justice: On the maturation of critical theory in law, crime, and deviance* (pp. 52-70). Belmont, CA: Wadsworth.

Reidel, M., & Welsh, W. (2002). *Criminal violence: Patterns, causes, and prevention.* Los Angeles: Roxbury.

Reiman, J. (1998). *The rich get richer and the poor get prison: Ideology, class, and criminal justice* (7th ed.). Boston, MA: Allyn and Bacon.

Reiss, A. J., & Roth, J. A. (Eds.). (1993). *Understand and preventing violence* (Vol. 1). Washington, DC: National Academy.

Rennison, C. M. (1999, July). *Criminal victimization, 1998: Changes 1997-98 with trends 1993-98* (NCJ 176353). Retrieved November 29, 2002, from http://www.ojp.usdoj.gov/bjs/pub/pdf/cv98.pdf

Rossi, A. S. (Ed.). (2001). *Caring and doing for others: Social responsibility in the domains of family, work, and community.* Chicago: University of Chicago Press.

Schwebel, M. (1995). Introduction: Peace and conflict. *Peace and Conflict: Journal of Peace Psychology, 1*(1), 1-2.

Totten, M. (2000). *Guys, gangs, and girlfriend abuse.* Petersborough, ON, Canada: Broadview.

West, R. (1997). *Caring for justice.* New York: New York University Press.

Whitmer, B. (1997). *The violence mythos.* Albany, NY: State University of New York Press.

Zimring, F., & Hawkins, G. (1992). *The search for rational drug control.* Cambridge, UK: Cambridge University Press.

REVIEW QUESTIONS

1. From the contents of this book, what can we ultimately conclude about the pathways to violence and nonviolence as these are related to the paradigms of adversarialism and mutualism?

2. When all is said and done, what do we know about the relationships between stratification, victimization, and the pathways to violence?

3. What's wrong with the adversarial war on violence?

4. Discuss some of the nonviolent policies that prevent antisocial pathways to violence and build pathways to positive peace, human rights, and social justice.

5. Discuss transformative justice as it relates to the pathways to violence and nonviolence?

Index

About the Author

Gregg Barak is Professor of Criminology and Criminal Justice and former Department Head of Sociology, Anthropology, and Criminology at Eastern Michigan University. Barak is the editor and/or author of 11 books, including the award-winning *Gimme Shelter: A Social History of Contemporary Homelessness in America, In Defense of Whom? A Critique of Criminal Justice Reform, Integrating Criminologies,* and the recently published *Class, Race, Gender, and Crime: Social Realities of Justice in America* (coauthored with J. Flavin and P. Leighton). Among Barak's edited readings are *Crime and Crime Control: A Global View* and *Representing O.J.: Murder, Criminal Justice, and Mass Culture.* Barak has served as Chair of the Critical Division of the American Society of Criminology, was the Critical Criminologist of the Year in 1999, and has served on more than a dozen editorial boards. In 2003, Barak's outstanding contributions to the fields of crime and justice were recognized as he was made a Fellow of the Academy of Criminal Justice Sciences.